Mind-Matter Interaction

Mind–Matter Interaction

A Review of Historical Reports, Theory and Research

Pamela Rae Heath

McFarland & Company, Inc., Publishers
Jefferson, North Carolina, and London

LIBRARY OF CONGRESS CATALOGUING-IN-PUBLICATION DATA

Heath, Pamela Rae.
Mind-matter interaction : a review of historical reports,
theory and research / Pamela Rae Heath.

p.   cm.
Includes bibliographical references and index.

ISBN 978-0-7864-4971-2
softcover : 50# alkaline paper ∞

1. Parapsychology.   2. Psychokinesis.   I. Title.
BF1371.H43   2011   130—dc22   2010039979

BRITISH LIBRARY CATALOGUING DATA ARE AVAILABLE

On the cover: (left) CT brain scans; (center, left to right)
depictions of a mystic saint, seance, double-slit experiment,
spoon bending, PET brain scan and levitation

Manufactured in the United States of America

*McFarland & Company, Inc., Publishers
Box 611, Jefferson, North Carolina 28640
www.mcfarlandpub.com*

This book is dedicated in three parts, one section each to the three great women pioneers in the field of parapsychology.

Part I is dedicated to Louisa Rhine, known for her work collecting and analyzing spontaneous cases.

Part II is dedicated to Gertrude Schmeidler, a foremost experimental researcher with great insight into the human aspect of psi.

Part III is dedicated to Rhea White, who broke new ground with her phenomenological studies on exceptional human experiences and psi. This book could not exist without their insightful work.

Acknowledgments

This book could not have been done without the help of many. I would like to thank my parents for their love and support; Warren Hoover for the wonderful physical séances in Casadaga; the psi experimenters who have performed all the years of research (often as a real labor of love) that I try to summarize here; parapsychologists Jean Burns, Alexander MacRae, Roger Nelson, Dean Radin, Bill Roll, Marilyn Schlitz, James Spottiswoode, and Annalisa Ventola for their proofing assistance and insights into some of the material; and Chris Soth (skeptic though he is) for greatly improving my writing style. I'd also like to once again acknowledge my deep appreciation for the eight individuals who so kindly and generously donated their time to share their personal PK experiences with me, seven of whom are quoted here. Thank you, one and all.

Table of Contents

PART III: THE MMI MATRIX: EXPERIENTIAL RESEARCH 163

Abbreviations

ASC(s) Altered State(s) of Consciousness
ASPR American Society for Psychical Research
ATP Adenosinetriphosphate
BCE Before the Common Era (previously known as B.C.)
CE The Common Era (previously known as A.D.)
CNS Central Nervous System
CRV Controlled Remote Viewing
DCBD Deliberately Caused Bodily Damage
DMILS Direct Mental Interactions with Living Systems
EDA Electrodermal Activity
EEG Electroencephalogram
EHE(s) Exceptional Human Experience(s)
ELF Extra Low Frequency [a form of electromagnetic wave]
EMF Electromagnetic Field
ERV Extended Remote Viewing
ESP Extrasensory Perception
EVP Electronic Voice Phenomena
GCP Global Consciousness Project
GESP General Extrasensory Perception
GMF(s) Geomagnetic Field(s)
ITC Instrumental Transcommunication
LST Local Sidereal Time
MMI Mind-Matter Interaction
MOBIA The Mental or Behavioral Influence of an Agent
MPI Model of Pragmatic Information
NDE(s) Near Death Experience(s)
NLP Neurolinguistic Programming
OBE(s) Out-of-body Experience(s)
PEAR Princeton Engineering Anomalies Research
PK Psychokinesis
PKMB Psychokinetic Metal-Bending
PMIR Psi Mediated Instrumental Response
REG(s) Random Event Generator(s)
RNG(s) Random Number Generator(s)
RSMMI Recurrent Spontaneous Mind-Matter Interaction
RSPK Recurrent Spontaneous Psychokinesis
SHC Spontaneous Human Combustion
SPR Society for Psychical Research

Preface

What the debunkers state doesn't matter. What someone can do or cannot do is absolutely not proportional in any way to anyone else's belief or disbelief.... *Just go back through your history books and you'll discover that just about everything you take for granted today in your daily lives was absolutely impossible not so many years ago.*
— Martin Caidin[1]

I often hear the comment that psychic phenomena don't exist, and anyone who believes in them is delusional. When I ask those people whether they've bothered to read any journals or see what science says, they respond that they don't need to because no scientific journal of repute would waste its time on something so bogus. At this point, I could start listing journals, but I realize that there is no point. The real problem comes from a difference in opinion about what science is. How can that be, you ask? Surely science is the same for everyone? It is facts, right? Wrong.

The problem is one that Thomas Kuhn elegantly described in his book *The Structure of Scientific Revolutions*. What he demonstrated, using examples from chemistry and other fields, is that science is no more infallible than people are. Science is limited because it is based on fundamental beliefs. These beliefs form such an intrinsic part of our normal, everyday worldview that we never even realize we made any assumptions. But we have. And they are part of the underlying principles that make up a "paradigm."

A paradigm is an infrastructure of beliefs that underlies science and determines how we see the world around us. It acts as a model to help us make sense of things. More importantly, it not only determines what is true, but how truth can be determined. As such, it is both a help and a hindrance. Paradigms help us make sense of what is going on around us, but also limit our perception of the world and what knowledge we can attain.

Periodically, as science advances, an old paradigm has to make way for a new one. There comes a time when scientists wake up to the idea that their way of looking at the world leaves too many questions unanswered. Then it is time to experiment and see whether there is a better framework for understanding reality.

Anyone who has read about Copernicus or Galileo understands that the periods when paradigms fight for dominance can be rough on any scientists caught in the fray. What makes these paradigm shifts so bloody is that the paradigm itself determines what is "proof." Scientists from competing paradigms have trouble agreeing on almost anything, because in effect they speak two completely different languages and have no one to translate between them. What is "proof" in one paradigm is "worthless" in another. There can be no agreement. Typically, the new paradigm only wins out when the scientists who believed in the old one die off, and younger scientists see the advantages of the new. Eventually, the new paradigm becomes the new "normal science."

We are now in the middle of a paradigm shift. The classical paradigm, which we have held since Descartes, is based on the underlying assumption that the observer is separate from the observed. In essence, duality. It says there is a subject-object or mind-body split. This presupposes that there are objective ways to define and measure the fixed external world, which proponents of this paradigm would say is the only world that matters. Experimental design is the favored research methodology within the classical paradigm, as it presumes to measure the world in an objective way.

The emergence of quantum theory started a shift to a new paradigm, as people suddenly realized that there is always some indeterminacy in our measurements, and the act of measurement itself can define and change that which is being measured. In other words, the experimenter is always part of the experiment, and all our "objective" facts are, in fact, potentially flawed.

The scientists leading the way are not parapsychologists, but physicists. They are calling for a paradigm based on nonlocality, where the universe is a single whole, within which every part is intimately connected to every other part. Thus, the so-called objectivity of the classical paradigm is the true illusion, because an "observer effect" is inevitable in any observation. This new paradigm does not, in itself, "prove" psi exists. Nonetheless, it is highly compatible with the possible existence of psi, and would seem to make greater sense of the phenomena.

This an updated and expanded version of an earlier work called *The PK Zone*. Those who read the first version will note a number of changes. Some are stylistic, others relate to new or expanded content. Many of the quotes are gone.

There is some change in style between the three parts. In Part I, there is much use of terms such as "purported," "alleged," and "said to have." This is because I have no way of knowing how true these stories are. These phrases drop out in Part II of the book, since the research is documented. Where I had doubts about the integrity of the experimenters (as was true in the case of one known to have perpetrated fraud), I left the material out. Finally, in Part III, I return to subjective, personal accounts. In these cases, since I know all of the mind-matter performers, and trust their basic credibility, I speak of their events as fact. However, where I draw inferences from what they have told me, I will use words such as "appears" and "seems." This is because I cannot assume that I always interpret things correctly. I hope you enjoy the book, and that it gives you a greater understanding of, and appreciation for, this remarkable thing that we call MMI.

Introduction

Mind-matter interaction (MMI) is the ability of the mind to influence external objects and processes without the use of any known physical method, energy, or force.[2] Older, and less accurate, terms for these phenomena include psychokinesis (PK) and telekinesis. Stories have been told of individuals possessing these wondrous powers since the dawn of time, and one only has to look at the shelves of a bookstore, or turn on the television, to see that MMI is still a subject of intense fascination today. No one place or era has a monopoly on these tales. Reports of intentional and spontaneous MMI come to us from all parts of the globe. The fact that these occur in similar patterns regardless of culture or time suggests that something universal underlies these accounts — although what that something is remains obscure.

Considering the basic curiosity of humankind, and how long stories have been told of individuals possessing apparently extraordinary abilities, it should be no surprise that we are not the first to ponder their meaning. In fact, the veracity and significance of these purported phenomena have been questioned for thousands of years.[3] One can find dedicated debunkers thousands of years ago in ancient China.[4]

In the beginning, investigating meant critically listening to people's stories and/or carefully observing possible events — both of which are still fundamental methods of evaluation used today. The earliest recorded investigations were mostly archival research or case histories of saints, "demons," poltergeist phenomena, trance mediums, and healers. The vast majority of these were written by individuals who were either associated with the Church or were wealthy enough to have an education and be able to indulge in a hobby of collecting psychical stories.[5]

A number of factors helped to change this, including the advent of the printing press, greater access to education, and improved travel and communication. Spiritualism also played an important role in vitalizing interest in the field by making purported phenomena available for study. The high incidence of fraud and trickery in the séance parlor only increased the fervor of investigators to uncover the truth. However, only so much could be done in the uncontrolled setting of the real world.

At the turn of the century, psi research began to move out of the séance parlor and into the laboratory under the auspices of eminent scientists, such as Sir William Crookes and Charles Richet.[6] These men were well-grounded in the scientific method of the day and did their best to design careful experiments. Unfortunately, their task was made more difficult by the tremendous motivation for fraud, as mediums sought endorsements to promote their careers.

In the 1930s, J. B. Rhine took experimental proof research a step further by not only limiting his work to the controlled laboratory setting, but also avoiding "star" subjects.[7] He demonstrated that ordinary individuals could influence matter in small, but statistically significant, manners. In many ways, this changed our whole understanding of psi. Although a weak talent for most, it was clear that rather than being limited to a few select individuals, psi was a universal ability.

Since then, proof experiments have been performed by researchers in laboratories around the world with a great many participants. The same results occur repeatedly. The mental intention of ordinary individuals can influence a wide range of targets, including dice, spheres, and computer outputs, to name just a few. The effects may be small, but they are statistically significant. As parapsychologist Dean Radin noted, it is time to put the question of "Does psi exist?" behind us.[8] Better questions at this point are "What is it?" and "How does it work?"

Gertrude Schmeidler was one of the first to point out that parapsychology has long held the unspoken tenet that psi is a psychological function.[9] The idea that MMI could be a general (if often latent) human ability would seem to be supported by the widespread occurrence of similar forms of activity in virtually all cultures and times. In addition, the experimental literature shows that psi responds in similar ways to other human abilities.[10] It appears to be influenced by psychological variables, such as mood, emotion, motivation, and belief. The decline effect, sheep-goat effect, experimenter effect, and goal-oriented nature of MMI in psi studies also seem to suggest that MMI has psychological attributes.[11] Perhaps more importantly, the average college student or person off the street can often successfully perform psi. Together, these facts support the notion that MMI is a normal human ability.

Despite over 125 years of formal research, we still have much to learn about the nature of MMI and how it works. In the past, psi was considered to take one of two forms.[12] The first, ESP, was deemed to be "passive," with the receiver simply allowing in, or accepting, information. MMI, on the other hand, was thought of as "expressive," since it acted upon the external world. MMI was also considered to occur along a spectrum from large-scale phenomena (macro-MMI or macro-PK) to small-scale phenomena (micro-MMI or micro-PK).

Macro-MMI is typically defined as those effects that are large enough, or strong enough, to be apparent to the physical senses, and do not need statistics for their demonstration. This includes all of the MMI noted with mediums and poltergeists in the pre–J. B. Rhine era. Levitation, bilocation, object movement, raps, teleportation, metal-bending (PKMB), deliberately caused bodily damage (DCBD), fire-immunity, materialization, and thoughtography would all be considered forms of "macro" MMI using this description.

Micro-MMI, on the other hand, is traditionally defined as MMI effects that either (1) are slight or weak in magnitude and require statistics for their demonstration, or (2) involve atomic or subatomic processes. The Random Event Generators (REGs), which were developed by Schmidt to emit a "1" or a "0" on the basis of radioactive decay is a clear-cut example of micro-MMI.[13] The target system is, in essence, an atomic-level process, and statistics are required to demonstrate any effect that deviates it away from what would be expected by random decay.

Unfortunately, if we use these definitions, many MMI targets, such as dice, can be considered both macro and micro depending on the magnitude of the results. Even if the item one is trying to influence is large enough to be seen by the naked eye (which would suggest it is a "macro" target), if the results are weakly positive and require statistics for their proof, then "micro"-MMI was performed. Other targets, such as biological systems, which may involve atomic or sub-atomic processes, but create visible results, are equally problematic.

Yet another problem with the field is that although a variety of theories and models have been proposed, none of them are fully accepted.[14] This may be due in part to the relative dearth of process-oriented research. For a long time parapsychologists felt the need to "prove" to skeptics that psi exists.[15] Proof-oriented research thus became a priority, despite the fact that some disbelievers, particularly those who have an economic interest in their opinion, will never be willing to look at the facts with an open mind. Nonetheless, the long push for evidence that psi exists has served a purpose. Those who bother to read the formal research — comprising thousands of controlled experiments from laboratories around the world — have to admit that something anomalous is occurring.

Long shrouded in myth and mystery, MMI tantalizes us with our own potential. This book is an attempt to put together all the pieces — anecdotal, experimental, and experiential — that we currently have on this topic. Part I focuses on the historical and cross-cultural perspectives of MMI. It tells intentional and spontaneous stories of MMI from around the globe. These stories show recurrent themes across both cultures and times, which give us clues about the nature of MMI and how it can manifest. Part II covers the highlights of MMI research and theory. For a more exhaustive review of the literature prior to 1976, the reader is encouraged to read the *Handbook of Parapsychology*, edited by B. Wolman. Finally, Part III is a phenomenological examination of the lived experience of performing MMI — what it is like for the people who do it. The result is a fascinating look at the complex, interwoven nature of mind-matter manipulation.

One might ask why we should care about MMI. Even though the average person's ability to do it is small, it exists, and cannot be explained by known factors.[16] There are those who say that psi can be ignored because it is a minor effect. However, they are missing the point. These phenomena indicate there are gaps in our way of conceptualizing the world, which have to be explained. As such, MMI represents a clue that may bring us closer not only to a more complete understanding of ourselves, but also of reality itself.

People have these strange experiences. You can throw out the ones that might occur by chance, the subjective mistakes, but there is always a residue left over. What do you do about those? Scientists and skeptics would ignore them. That doesn't mean they go away. These phenomena suggest that there are gaps in the way we know the world.

— Dean Radin[17]

PART I

A Historical Cross-Cultural Review of Anecdotal Material Through the Ages: Religious and Spiritual

The following pages include the stories of a wide range of MMI performers — religious figures, physical mediums, healers, martial artists, athletes, poltergeist agents, and others. These individuals are not restricted to any one country, culture, or era. Nor do they seem to be limited in scope to merely one or a few types of MMI. Instead, it appears that if someone can do one kind of MMI, they are likely to perform others, as well. For example, a priest who can levitate may also be able to teleport, bilocate, multiply food, move objects, and have fire-immunity. MMI usually first manifests as a spontaneous ability and unexpected events often continue long after performers have become adept at intentional MMI.

It is important when discussing anecdotal material to add a word of warning. Medieval accounts of miracles tend to mirror the needs and social beliefs of the age.[1] In Europe, this meant earlier stories emphasized supernatural acts of protection and vengeance, while later miracles were more apt to depict mercy and cures. Accounts of apparitions also varied over time, reflecting the changing needs of the eras in which they were recorded.[2] These stories may thus reflect cultural bias, rather than an accurate depiction of MMI or fraud.

There are a number of ways that cultural bias can enter anecdotal material. Culture influences the frequency with which events are reported, their content, and how things were perceived. Shaping also occurs during the translation and transcription of older accounts. Finally, narratives are not preserved unless their content meets a certain level of social need (even if only for entertainment). Thus, these tales may not fully represent what truly happened. It is vital to keep this fact in mind as we proceed.

Religion appears to provide fertile ground for spontaneous and intentional MMI. Every great religious tract of mankind includes stories of people with the ability to heal and to multiply food, such as the Bible says about Jesus.[3] Other traditions have their own accounts, such as Moses parting the Red Sea, the multiplication of oil so that a one-day supply lasted for eight, and Muhammad being said to heal the sick.[4]

Purported miracles are not limited to the founders of various religions, but have also been reported in a variety of saints and mystics in recent years.[5] The Catholic Church in particular seems to have its share of miracle workers. However, they are by no means unique in this. As James McClenon pointed out, miracle-working is good for acquiring religious converts.[6] It is

7

to a religion's advantage to have members who can perform miracles and, perhaps more importantly, spread stories about them. This was just as true in Asia as it was in Europe, although the kinds of wonders the individuals performed varied somewhat over time.

McClenon proposed that it was the apparent ability of Fo-t'u-teng (one of the earliest Buddhists to enter North China) to perform miraculous feats that allowed Buddhism to gain a foothold in that country.[7] The biography of Fo-t'u-teng was written between 519 and 554 CE, about a century and a half after his death. It tells of his displays of magic, including using spirits as messengers, producing a lotus out of a bowl of water, drawing water from dried-up wells with toothpicks, divining the future, having clairvoyant visions of distant events, and being able to make rain. Indeed, his reputed ability to control the weather was a key feature of Fo-t'u-teng's popularity and success — not surprising considering the appeal it would have for an agrarian culture struggling with a hostile environment. Miracle-working monks were very popular in China. Between the fifth and tenth centuries, the Buddhists became especially renowned for their miraculous healing abilities.

The Islamic world has its share of miracle-workers, beginning with its founder.[8] Muhammad (c. 570 or 571–632 CE) and many Islamic saints were said to be able to pass through solid bodies, revive the dead, converse with angels, fly through the air, walk on water, heal, bilocate, teleport, make animals and trees speak, stop time, assume different shapes, be immune from fire, and transform one form of matter into another, such as water into honey. Like other saints, anomalous phenomena were associated with trance and ecstasy, whether invoked through prayer, rhythmic music, song, and movements, or purging.[9]

Grunebaum suggested that one of the key factors that kept the door to the supernatural open in Islam is that they did not develop the idea of an autonomous nature or any natural laws.[10] He felt this was because it would have offended divine omnipotence and removed God from the continued effective government of His world. Regardless of the cause, there are stories of a wide range of abilities. The purported transmutation of dirt, water, or other material into jewels or gold appears to be more common in Islamic lore than some of their religious counterparts.[11] Another thing that distinguishes Islamic saints from those of many other religions is that they are as quick to harm as to help.[12]

The dervishes are an outcast Sufi branch in which masters are said to instruct their followers to perform paranormal feats — such as DCBD — to demonstrate the spiritual powers of the master, and ultimately of the Prophet, who is the source of their abilities.[13] Thus, the dervish is considered a means for manifesting the spiritual powers, rather than a source of them per se. In this they are in agreement with Catholic saints, who have similarly said their powers come from God and not from within.[14] Idries Shah noted that dervishes have been reported to walk on water, appear in different locations at the same time, and have wounds heal or stop bleeding with remarkable speed, and often leaving little or no scar behind.[15]

The founder of Hasidic Judaism, Israel ben Eliezer, also known as Baal Shem Tov (which means "Master of the Good Name") was considered a preeminent miracle worker.[16] He lived in Poland from 1700 to 1760, and was said to be able to foretell the future, reveal secrets, and heal variously through prayers, "magical means," and homeopathic remedies. Other stories speak of rabbis who used the holy name to revive the dead, travel at great speeds, exorcise demons, know the thoughts of others, protect from harm, and punish or kill the wicked.[17]

The Catholic religion has its share of saints who could heal, as well as those able to multiply food, including St. Teresa of Avila, St. Rose of Lima, St. Clare of Assisi, St. Pius V, St. John Bosco, St. Jean Baptiste Vianney, and Ven. Angiolo Paoli.[18] Herbert Thurston, the well-known English priest who studied miracles, noted that Catholic records of mysticism contain an abundance of marvelous events.[19] The reason it is such a rich source of material is at least partly due to the fact that the Catholic Church has kept meticulous and detailed records of purported miracles for centuries.

One of the commoner forms of MMI reported in Catholic literature involves the transference of the Host through the air from the altar or the hands of the priest to the mouth of a waiting communicant.[20] Although one must always consider fraud and delusion, there appear to have been at least a few witnessed cases suggestive of true MMI. Herbert Thurston described several such incidents, including of St. Jean Baptiste Vianney (the Curé of Ars) and separately of the sixteenth-century Italian Ven. Domenica dal Paradiso and her confessor, Onesti di Castiglione. If one considers the extreme eagerness with which some spiritual figures have been reported to await their wafer, then the motivation for this event seems clear — they really want that wafer. Stories of levitation, bilocation, teleportation, and fire-immunity also abound in Christian literature and will be discussed in chapters devoted to those topics.

India is a rich source of reports of apparent MMI demonstrations by fakirs, or holy men. There are numerous accounts of practitioners, such as Sai Baba, performing miracles of materializing and dematerializing objects, multiplying food, healing, and appearing to move faster than possible by normal means.[21] In addition, Muslim fakirs have been said to make coins and other objects move on command, in one case reportedly making a rupee jump into someone's hands from ten feet away.[22]

Tibetan yogis rely to a greater degree on geometrical diagrams and chants, but also claim to have remarkable psi abilities.[23] These individuals are not considered to have been born "psychic."[24] Instead, they are thought to have acquired their powers either through a past life, or through meditation and spiritual development in their current life. Thus, there is the assumption that all human beings have the capacity (even if currently dormant) to perform psi.

Although there are many tales of enlightened Buddhist and Hindu masters who have the ability to perform miraculous feats, it is difficult to find proof of the matter, since they are generally unwilling to perform on command or be studied in the laboratory. This is said to be because Buddhist and Hindu yogis regard occult powers as a natural, but unwanted, by-product of spiritual development.[25] Psychic abilities therefore represent an obstacle to true enlightenment by creating temptation for worldly gain and glory. It is believed that the person who displays these *siddhis*, or psychic abilities for either good or ill, instead of renouncing them, so they can utilize their force towards enlightenment, will fall from the path lower than the ordinary person who has never done yoga.

Shamanic religions are not without their share of stories. Brian Inglis wrote that North American medicine men held séances in their teepees wherein there were unexplained noises and shaking suggestive of macro–MMI.[26] He described a number of such events, including one which was witnessed by Sir Cecil Denny, a member of the Canadian Mounted Police.[27] The officer heard an invisible bell ringing above his head. He then saw the heavy teepee rock, and then lift a foot or more off the ground behind him. Denny checked outside the tent but found no one in sight who might have caused the movement. And later, he reported even seeing the teepee's sides lift high enough that he could see no one was outside. During the whole event, the medicine man is said to have never moved.

Inglis noted that it was a shame that shamans were often the first casualties of colonialism, stating, "it was the magician who was the first victim, because whether or not he could work magic, his tribe believed he could, and that made him a threat in the eyes of the colonial officials."[28] As it was, their abilities were never systematically investigated.

The following nine chapters will look in more detail at some of the better documented reports of levitation, stigmata, inedia, teleportation, bilocation, fire-immunity, luminosity, the materialization/transformation of matter, hemography, DCBD, and weather MMI. These are frequently (but not always) associated with religious and spiritual figures. The line between spontaneous and intentional events is often blurred. However, many individuals seem to be able to perform phenomena on demand — albeit they frequently refuse to take credit for the events, instead attributing them to a supernatural source.

Levitation

Levitation is the paranormal mid-air suspension of objects or the human body. It is usually described as being spontaneous, and is primarily associated with religious and spiritual figures. As Herbert Thurston dryly noted, levitation should be easy to investigate since with good enough lighting, anyone, no matter what his level of education, should be able to check for illusion and tell whether a person is standing on the ground or up in the air.[29]

Skeptics believe that levitation has never happened, and attribute reported incidences to trickery or exceptional gymnastic ability.[30] They are not without cause for doing so. Indian fakirs have been caught in fraud, pretending to levitate when, in fact, they are supported by normal means such as hidden platforms, or were photographed while falling. Nonetheless, if we believe Church Inquiry records, at least some of these feats are beyond what could be explained in ordinary ways. Gymnastics could not account for an individual remaining suspended in mid-air for six or seven minutes or flying over the heads of a crowd of fifty people, as St. Joseph of Cupertino is said to have done.[31]

Whatever the truth or fiction of these accounts, reports of levitation appear across a wide swath of cultures, religions, and eras. Judaism, Christianity, Buddhism, Islam, Hinduism, Voodoo, and shamanic traditions from around the globe all have stories of individuals who were said to levitate.[32] Brian Inglis stated that levitation was considered to be common among northern Native American tribes and said to have been witnessed in the Zulu. Magician Harry Kellar (whom one would presume was well-versed in methods of trickery and deceit) was said to have been baffled when faced with a Zulu witchdoctor levitating an unconscious warrior three feet off the ground.[33]

Levitation is one of the most commonly mentioned miracles in the lore of Catholic, Tibetan Buddhist, and yogic literature.[34] Jesus is said to have walked on water.[35] After his illumination, Buddha is reputed to have risen into the air and cut off parts of his body, which on falling to the ground were then reunited.[36] A clearer reference to flight appears in stories of Milarepa (1052–1135 CE), a Tibetan Buddhist holy man.[37] According to his biographers, he was equally at home in the air and on the ground, and was said to be able to fly over vast distances.

"Magical flights" also crop up in Islamic literature. Muhammad is said to have ascended and "magically" flown.[38] The Iranian dervish, Haydar, who lived in the twelfth century, was noted for his sudden flights to treetops and the roofs of houses.[39] It is said that Sufi "Ahmade-e Khazruya had a thousand disciples, every one of whom walked on water and flew in the air."[40] The ninth century Muslim saint Abu Yazid al-Bestami was witnessed soaring into the air after a funeral in Tabarestan, as well as walking on water and being able to travel at incredible speeds. In fact, walking on water is frequently mentioned in the lives of Muslim saints, such as Sahl ibn Abd Allah al-Tostari, Habib al-Ajami, and Beshr (767–841 CE).

One story relates how Habib found his imam, Hasan, waiting for a boat that was late.[41] Habib was surprised that his old teacher was waiting. He reminded Hasan of spiritual values before departing across the Tigris River. Attar also wrote that Beshr was twice observed walking across the Tigris River.[42] As with many Catholic saints, Beshr asked his witness not to tell anyone what had happened. The tale was only passed on after his death.

The levitation of objects is also described in the Islamic literature. A story is told of a trunk containing a Muslim prisoner flying to Islamic territory, with its Christian guard sitting on top of it. Abu Ja'far was with the saint Dho 'l-Nun (796–861 CE) and his group of followers when a sofa was made to move around a house before returning to where it had started.[43]

Judaic literature hints at levitation, although the stories are often vague. Rabbi Ishmael, the Jewish High Priest in the time of the Roman emperor Hadrian, and author of a text describing "heavenly ascents," is said to have pronounced the sacred four-letter name of God and "ascended" to find out if the Jewish persecution was by divine decree.[44] Unfortunately, it is difficult to judge whether these and other "flights" and "ascents" were out-of-body experiences (OBEs), visions, or levitation.

Yogic teachings suggest that mastery of breathing and the use of oxygen can induce levitation, and various Indian yogis over the centuries have been said to levitate themselves or various objects.[45] In one case, a yogi is said to have levitated a table while two investigating professors were sitting on top of it.[46]

Reports of levitation have continued to occur in recent years. Douchan Gersi described seeing individuals rise upward in the air and stay there in India, Zaire, and Haiti.[47] Perhaps the most remarkable of these levitations occurred in Voodoo ceremonies. Let us consider these stories in more detail as they come to us from the Catholic Church and Voodoo.

CATHOLIC LEVITATORS

Catholic figures who purportedly levitated in recent centuries include St. Francis of Assisi, St. John Joseph of the Cross, St. Ignatius Loyola, St. James of Illyricum, St. Dominic, St. Dunstan, St. Philip Benite, St. Cajetan, St. Albert of Sicily, St. Bernard Ptolomaei, St. Edmund, St. Seraphim de Serov, St. Teresa of Avila, St. Joseph of Cupertino, Bl. Mary of Jesus Crucified, St. Gemma Galgani, and St. Pio of Pietrelcina.[48] Many of these levitations were reported by witnesses as occurring during prayer or communion, seemingly as by-products of the ecstatic state.

Herbert Thurston observed that it was unfortunate that many of these cases were not better documented and/or had processes of canonization no longer available for study.[49] However, Scott Rogo pointed out that, because of their humility and fear of publicity, most Catholic saints viewed levitation as an embarrassing power, and made an effort not to be caught in the act.[50] This limited the number of eyewitnesses.

Nonetheless, there are a few accounts written by apparently intelligent observers and the saints themselves. Rogo argued that, considering the painful honesty many of the saints displayed, it is likely that the latter can be taken as accounts of something truly experienced — although whether they were actually levitating or simply experiencing themselves as having levitated may be two different things.[51] In order to distinguish between those who imagine themselves as levitating and those who perform the feat, one must have outside observers.

St. Bernardino Realino (1515–1616), a seventeenth-century mystic, was a saint caught levitating by Tobias da Ponte.[52] Tobias was a prominent citizen of a nearby town who had gone to the monastery for advice. He was waiting by Realino's room when he saw bright light streaming out from the sides of the door. Concerned that a fire might have broken out, Tobias looked into the room. He found Bernardino floating in a kneeling position about two and a half feet off the ground, radiating light. As with other cases, the account was given in testimony to a Church inquiry. Although a single witness does not make for a strong case, Thurston pointed out that there was confirmation in other ways, including the cross-corroboration of Father Anthony Beatillo, and the reports of a number of witnesses who had seen a brilliant light radiate from the saint's face while in prayer.[53]

The Spanish priest, Father Francisco Suarez (1548–1617), was observed three feet off the floor in a kneeling position on a level with the table upon which a crucifix radiated a light of dazzling brightness.[54] Like many others, Father Suarez made the witness (Father Jerome da Silva) promise not to tell of what he had seen.[55] The story might never have gotten out save that at the order of his confessor, Father Silva wrote of two occasions when he had found Father Suarez in ecstasy. This document was sealed in an envelope with the proviso that it only be opened after Father Suarez died. The matter later came out during a Church inquiry.[56]

St. Alphonsus Liguori, founder of the Redemptorist Order, was said to levitate in 1750.[57] Three canons and members of the congregation testified that when he was preaching a sermon he rose off of the ground. Furthermore, members of his Order described seeing Liguori floating in his cell when rapt with prayer. Liguori apparently retained his ability to rise into the air during his later years, despite becoming a wheelchair-bound cripple — which casts serious doubt on the likelihood of gymnastics being involved.

Although most of these reports involve the levitation of self, Father Oscar Gonzalez-Quevado is said to have levitated others in broad daylight in Brazil.[58] His feats were performed outdoors in the presence of witnesses who were able to pass hoops over the levitated bodies to make sure there was no solid means of support.

Let us turn our attention to three Catholic religious figures whose levitations were particularly well documented: St. Teresa of Avila, Bl. Mary of Jesus Crucified, and St. Joseph of Cupertino.

St. Teresa of Avila St. Teresa of Avila was born at, or near, Avila in Castile in 1515.[59] Her mother died when she was fourteen. At the age of fifteen, she was placed in a convent, where many women of rank were educated. However, she fell seriously ill after a year and a half (possibly with malaria) and returned home for a time. St. Teresa decided to become a nun and, after her father died, applied herself vigorously to prayer. It was then that she began receiving internal visions and communications, sometimes rising into the air during her raptures.

St. Teresa was reportedly embarrassed that she was unable to stay on the ground during her prayers, and tried to hide what was occurring.[60] Despite this, she is among the few who wrote a first-hand account of her experiences.[61] St. Teresa described herself as powerless over the events and unable to resist. She felt as if a force beneath her was lifting her up. Though admitting to some fear about her levitations, she also reported rapture. St. Teresa still felt buoyant after the events, nearly weightless, and could hardly tell if her feet touched the ground. This combination of feeling actively lifted up and, at the same time, relatively weightless brings up the possibility that levitation could involve more than one process.

St. Teresa founded seventeen convents and monasteries before her death in 1582.[62] She was canonized in 1622. Witnesses who testified under oath during the process leading to St. Teresa of Avila's canonization corroborated her story.[63] One sister described St. Teresa in prayer half a yard from the ground. The nun said she was able to put her hands under the saint's feet for something like half an hour. Nine others reported witnessing feats of levitation despite the saint's attempts to ground her body by holding onto other objects. This inquiry began thirteen years after her death — thirty years after she wrote about her life — and provided evidence by individuals who would have taken their oaths very seriously.[64]

Bl. Mary of Jesus Crucified, "The Flying Nun" Bl. Mary of Jesus Crucified, a Christian Arab from Galilee, was another well-known levitator.[65] What makes her case unusual is that she could apparently rise from the ground at will in order to care for a lemon tree on the convent grounds.[66] These levitations were sometimes watched by her fellow nuns, as in the case in 1868 when she was seen several hand spans off her bed.[67] Groups of witnesses also reputedly saw Mary of Jesus Crucified levitate seven times between June and August 1873, and once on July 5, 1874. During the episodes she was said to glide up the outer edges of tree, or hop like a bird from branch to branch, before balancing at the top on a small branch, often singing in ecstasy. Unlike many levitators, Mary of Jesus Crucified could descend from the tree with equal ease at will when so commanded by a superior.

Some have voiced concern that Mary of Jesus Crucified sustained her levitations by touching small branches as she floated upward.[68] This raises the question whether she was simply adept at climbing trees. Two pieces of testimony make this unlikely. First, witnesses said that the nun did not grip the branches. Second, that the branches were said not to bend when she touched them. This suggests that they support little, if any, of her weight.

St. Joseph of Cupertino, the "Flying Friar" Although many saints and religious figures have been alleged to levitate upon occasion, it is St. Joseph of Cupertino (1603–1663) who is undoubtedly the best known for it.[69] It is with good reason that he was named the patron saint of aviators and astronauts. The "flying friar" is responsible for some of the most incredible, yet well substantiated, feats of levitation ever reported — some brief, others continuing for an hour.[70] The heights of these flights ranged from a few inches to several feet above the ground. Indeed, the wife of the High Admiral of Castile is said to have fainted when she and her husband saw the saint fly twelve paces over their heads![71] St. Joseph's flights were remarkably well documented — perhaps in part because he polarized his contemporaries, and a good number of them were eager to prove him false. The outcome of that furor was a good one for historians — there are numerous detailed accounts of events that were seen under good conditions by apparently unbiased witnesses.

St. Joseph was born Giuseppe Desa, to an extremely poor family.[72] He was interested in religion even as a child, and experienced his first state of rapture at the age of eight. St. Joseph was not by any stretch of the imagination a psychologically healthy individual, practicing flagellation, long fasts, and other austerities to extreme.[73] He was initially apprenticed to a shoemaker. This did not go well. At age seventeen, he applied to join a religious order. However, he was not readily accepted.[74] St. Joseph was completely turned down by one group and kicked out after eight months by another. Nonetheless, he persevered. Eventually he was allowed to work as a servant for the Franciscan friars at Grottella. In 1625, St. Joseph was permitted to begin his novitiate. He received his priesthood three years later.

It was shortly after this, in 1628, that St. Joseph had to stand before a Church commission in Naples on the charge of heresy.[75] The charges were eventually dropped against him and he was allowed to say Mass.[76] His first "flight" was said to have occurred while praying immediately after this Mass. According to witnesses, St. Joseph suddenly rose up from a corner of the church, flew across the chapel to the church altar, and alighted in the middle of the flowers and burning candles.[77] Then, with another cry, Joseph flew back to the other end of the building in a kneeling position and landed.[78] This scene was watched by the nuns of St. Ligorio and St. Joseph's traveling companion, Fr. Lodovico, who was said to have become used to such sights. In this case, the saint seemed to display fire-immunity, as well, since neither he nor his clothing was burned. Indeed, St. Joseph was said to have been seen in numerous such flights into altars where he displayed fire-immunity.

This was the beginning of many events that were observed by large numbers of individuals. Unlike St. Teresa of Avila, St. Joseph had no inhibitions about flying around in public.[79] He was said to have levitated in Rome, when he knelt to kiss the feet of Pope Urban VIII. He did it again in Assisi, at the sight of a painting of the Virgin Mary, apparently floating some fifteen feet over an entire group of worshipers so that he could kiss it. Dozens of onlookers were witnesses to these events.

St. Joseph's levitations generally followed a pattern.[80] They began with a cry, sob, or shriek, which was followed by his taking off into the air. St. Joseph would not upset the objects crowded around him on the altar in a church. Furthermore, he neither extinguished the candles nor caught fire when flying amongst them. His robes were said to remain dry in the rain, and his clothing was not disturbed by his movement through the air. Joseph's flights could be provoked by anything that aroused his religious awe. One imagines that it became quite a nuisance for his companions.

St. Joseph's flights were not limited to indoors.[81] In one case, on hearing a fellow priest comment on the beauty of the heavens, St. Joseph is said to have flown into the top of an olive tree and remained there in a kneeling position for half an hour. The branch St. Joseph alighted on was said to only shake a little, as if a bird had landed. This sounds similar to the descriptions of Bl. Mary of Jesus Crucified's flights into trees. However, unlike the flying nun, when the saint came to his senses, a ladder had to be fetched to get him down. St. Joseph was not unique in this — Douchan Gersi noted that the Voodoo worshipers also sometimes find themselves stuck high up in trees when their ecstasy ends, and have trouble getting back down.[82]

Another interesting feature of these levitations was that, similar to St. Teresa of Avila, St. Joseph could not always be held down. Onlookers who tried to restrain the saint were hoisted into the air along with him.[83] In one case, he was witnessed lifting a fearful companion into the air with him at a Church festival, while on another occasion he is said to have cured a man of lunacy by taking him on a flight.[84] After a while, riding on his back during flights became more of a game among his fellow friars.[85] One supposes that familiarity led to comfort with the phenomena.

In addition to levitating his companions, St. Joseph was also said to be able to levitate objects. The most famous example of this occurred when the friars were building a Calvary.[86] The middle cross of the group was 36 feet high, too heavy for even 10 men to lift it. St. Joseph is said to have flown 70 yards to the cross, picked it up in his arms as if it were a straw, and lifted it into the air to put it in its place. Perhaps it should not be surprising that St. Joseph is said to have remained perched on top of the cross for several hours afterward.[87]

During the 17 years St. Joseph remained in Grottella, he is reported to have levitated over 70 times — and this does not include those flights which were performed elsewhere.[88] Unlike many religious figures, his feats were not only viewed by clerics, but by many outside observers, as well.[89] Noted intellectuals of the day, skeptics, and even non–Catholics all — if sometimes reluctantly — testified to the genuineness of these events. An example of this was when Johann Friedrich (the Duke of Brunswick) and two traveling companions hid to watch St. Joseph. He gave a characteristic cry, rose up into the air, levitated several feet backward, floated toward the altar, and then returned to the ground. The next day Friedrich again observed St. Joseph in levitation, this time for 15 minutes. It must have been impressive, because not only is it said to have deeply disconcerted Friedrich's companions, but also it caused the Duke to convert to Catholicism.

The upper ranks of the Catholic Church found St. Joseph's flights, and his ability to attract large crowds, disturbing.[90] He was denounced by the Vicar General and again investigated by the Inquisitors of Naples, but, as they could find nothing to censure, St. Joseph was sent to his Minister General in Rome. It was there that, in ecstasy at the sight of Pope Urban VIII, St. Joseph again took flight, thus obtaining the Pope himself as a witness to his abilities. Nonetheless, a great many were made uncomfortable by the saint — which may have been as much due to his festering wounds as to his purported powers.

In 1653, the Inquisition placed St Joseph in isolated seclusion.[91] He was unable to leave the convent, send or receive letters, or speak to anyone besides his fellow friars. He spent the rest of his life in this way until his death in 1663. However, St. Joseph is said to have continued to have "supernatural manifestations" until the end. He was canonized in 1767.

St. Joseph of Cupertino provides some of the most durable and well-documented evidence of levitation from any era.[92] Over the years a large number of notables, including the physicians and surgeons who attended the saint as he was dying, witnessed, and later testified, as to the reality of his ability to rise into the air and fly, whether indoors or outside. St. Joseph was also credited with a number of other miracles, including multiplying food, miraculous healings, clairvoyance, and mind reading.[93] Nonetheless, he is best known simply as the "flying friar."

VOODOO PRACTITIONERS

Voodoo is a syncretic religion, which incorpates aspects of West African religions, Catholicism, beliefs of the Arawak Indians, and French and Indo-European magic.[94] Voodoo's presence in Haiti may date back to 1724, when it was seen as a snake cult that worshipped many spirits. Today, it has millions of followers and combines strong elements of mysticism and ritual magic. During his explorations in Haiti, Douchan Gersi reported witnessing men and women levitate numerous times in Haiti.[95] These events always seemed to occur when the individual was meditating, in trance, or in a state of "possession." The first time he saw levitation was in a sanctuary, when a woman sitting on a bench suddenly jumped in the air and, passing over his head, floated to twelve feet in front of him. The woman is said to have remained suspended five feet off the floor for at least ten seconds before she moved off to the left and finally hit the ground about twenty feet away.

These levitations occurred both day and night, inside and outside buildings.[96] The worshipers often initiated their trance states through dancing. Sometimes after rising vertically into the air, levitators were said to slowly turn upside down before hurtling into a tree and landing in the branches. The clothing of the individuals who turned over apparently did not hang downward as one would expect. It is interesting to remember that St. Joseph's clothes also did not show the normal effect of movement during his flights.

Gersi was unable to find any evidence for fraud or trickery, such as hidden ropes.[97] Although one might wonder whether he was duped, other observations that he made suggest that true MMI may, in fact, have been occurring. Perhaps first and foremost of these, was that Gersi consistently found that multiple sets of batteries would die simultaneously even when brand new. This happened more than 20 times when he tried to photograph levitations. Furthermore, even high-speed photo film came out totally black, or blurred and out of focus. Gersi speculated that the energy used in levitation somehow short-circuits batteries.

Gersi's difficulty recording MMI events are not surprising. MMI-machine interactions (using computers and other equipment as targets) have been shown to occur in the laboratory. Many psychics also report tape recorders malfunctions during particularly intense readings.[98] In addition, haunting investigators have often noted camera malfunctions and problems with new batteries abruptly appearing "dead" — only to read full again when away from the paranormal activity.

ARGUMENTS AGAINST LEVITATION

Now that we have looked at some stories of levitation, it is time to turn our attention to the other side of the coin — the arguments against its existence. The main ones are (1) gravity says it can't happen; (2) many of the levitations were unseen by the public or large groups; (3) the witnesses could have been biased observers; (4) reports could have been exaggerated by witnesses who simply observed good gymnastic abilities; (5) original documents from the canonization inquiries are not available for scrutiny; (6) many formal reports of these events were made a long time after their supposed occurrence; (7) some of the accounts of witnesses have differed; (8) the witnesses could have been experiencing collective hypnosis; and (9) it is possible for magicians to create the illusion of levitation.[99] Let us look at each of these possibilities in turn.

The first argument is that levitation can't exist because it contradicts science as we currently know it. There are two issues here. First of all, science itself is based on accepting data as it exists — falsifying data because it doesn't fit the results we want is fraud of the worst sort. It is inappropriate to ignore reports of levitation simply because we do not want to have to consider how they fit into our current model of the world. Furthermore, as physicist Max Planck noted, "We have no right to assume that any physical laws exist, or if they have existed up to now, that they will continue to exist in a similar manner in the future."[100] Science involves working models, not fixed principles, which are based on underlying paradigms. Because science is constrained by the paradigm it grows out of, it is imperative that we maintain an open and flexible attitude. Science changes and evolves as new facts emerge. The contention that levitation can't exist because gravity says so is completely specious.

In addition to the fact that known science can (and regularly does) change to keep up with new findings, our current level of science already includes a factor that could be responsible for changes in gravitational force — time. Many people forget that gravity is measured in Newtons, which is a force *dependent on time*. The usual formula to calculate out the gravitational force acting on an object is:

$$\text{Gravitational Force} = \frac{(\text{Gravitational Constant})(\text{Mass A})(\text{Mass B})}{(\text{Distant between A and B})^2}$$

The gravitational constant (*see* below) used in these calculations is itself dependent on time:

$$\text{Gravitational Constant} = \frac{(\text{meters})^3}{\text{kilograms}(\text{seconds})^2}$$

Thus, if time changes speed, it influences the gravitational pull. As the seconds get longer (i.e. time seems to slow for the experiencer compared to those around them), the gravitational pull would decrease. Objects of the same mass and distance from the Earth could change in weight (which is determined by both mass and the gravitational pull).

This creates the interesting question of whether levitation could be a result of alterations in time. In the third section of this book, we will see that many MMI performers described an altered sense of time associated with their experiences. If this is not a subjective artifact of their state of consciousness, then it is possible that at least some MMI could be a direct, localized effect on time, rather than matter. This would make levitation fully compatible with science as we know it.

The second argument is that many of the levitations were not witnessed by crowds, or "outsiders." This is true in many cases. However, it does not explain away the flights of St. Joseph of Cupertino, who was witnessed levitating by large numbers of people, including many skeptical outsiders.[101] Levitation need only have occurred once for it to be said to exist.

The third argument is that the witnesses were biased. If anything, witnesses were prejudiced *against* St. Joseph of Cupertino.[102] The Church had no wish to risk looking foolish or like they had made a mistake. Their normal conservatism was heightened by the fact that Joseph was a public relations nightmare. The Church would have far rather have swept him under the rug than appear to sanction or approve his extreme asceticism and odd behavior. St. Joseph's lifestyle and demeanor led many to doubt his sanity; his behavior was odd, and his physical condition repulsive. The Church was reluctant indeed to appear to endorse Joseph through canonization, and deliberated long and hard over it. In fact, Prosper Lambertini, who later became

Pope Benedict XIV, was one of the presenters at the Congregation of Rites who opposed Joseph's canonization as an affront to his religious aesthetics.[103] Lambertini was a critically minded man, considered the supreme Catholic authority on evidence of miracles, and well versed on both fraud and "ordinary" paranormal behavior. However, even Lambertini eventually had to yield to the evidence.

The fourth argument is that the stories of levitation were exaggerated and nothing more was going on than good gymnastics. Again, many witnesses were not disposed to look favorably on St. Joseph. If anything, they wanted to minimize his feats. Nonetheless, even critical observers reluctantly, sometimes irritably, admitted that they had seen him in flight.[104] They even confirmed the fact that he was not supported, but hovering, by passing their hands beneath the saint. Furthermore, for a person to fly 40 feet in a kneeling position over the heads of 50 people, as St. Joseph did, seems beyond an Olympic gymnast's abilities, let alone a priest who was rarely in good physical health due to his flagellation, chronic sores, and fasting. Nor was he alone in performing feats beyond what one would expect of a man in his physical condition. St. Liguori levitated when he was wheelchair bound. It seems clear that gymnastics cannot explain away all of the reported cases.

The fifth argument is that we are not able to review the original documents relating to levitating saints. In many cases this is true as a result of Papal policy.[105] However, it is relevant only if we doubt the sincerity of the Congregation of Rites. Certainly in the case of St. Joseph, the Church was not predisposed in his favor, and scrutinized the case closely.[106] Lambertini — who wrote the book on how to investigate miracles and eliminate claims due to fraud, trickery, and "normal" psychic powers — was the individual assigned to find flaws in the testimony. Furthermore, even if not all of the evidence is currently accessible for review, a lot of it *is* still available. The documented evidence we have for St Joseph strongly indicates that he levitated.

The sixth argument is that many of the reports of these events were written a long time after the events were said to have occurred. In some cases, the individuals testifying had been sworn to secrecy by the saints said to have levitated, and only came forward because they were under Church oath.[107] There are two issues here — memory and honesty. Both deserve attention.

Memory is an interesting topic. Psychology has long recognized the limits of accurate human observation, and the frequent degradation and change of memories over time.[108] Although this can be true of memory in general, for events that were interesting and impressive, memories may remain accurate and clear. Walter F. Prince tested his wife's ability to remember a psychic dream he had told her in 1902, which she had immediately recorded.[109] Eight years later, she rewrote it from memory. The two accounts were virtually identical. Rosalind Heywood tested her ability to remember a psychic experience ten years after originally documenting it, and again found no material differences between the accounts. Thus, the time factor may not be crucial when the event that occurs is dramatic, as many of the saints' flights must have been.

In a few cases, there are reports that were written soon after the events were witnessed. An example of this is the diary of a nun who watched St. Teresa of Avila levitating.[110] Other accounts, such as those of St. Joseph's flights, were deposed only two years after the saint's death.[111] However, the Church had admittedly little or no contemporary documentation in most of the cases it investigated.[112] They instead relied on cross-corroborating data, comparing the verbal reports from as many witnesses as possible. This technique is used in police investigations today, and is generally considered acceptable evidence even when performed years after an event.

The second part of this argument (which is implied by saying that witnesses exaggerated their accounts) is the question of how much we can trust the person who is telling the tale. Many of the individuals testifying were devout believers who were sworn before God to tell the truth.[113] This is not something that they would take lightly. Indeed, many probably believed that the ultimate disposition of their souls depended on their strict honesty. As one who read the original documents for somewhere between twenty to forty such cases, Herbert Thurston had little doubt as to their utter sincerity, observing that he "found very little trace on the part of witnesses or commissioners of a desire to manufacture evidence of marvels."[114]

The seventh argument is that some of the witnesses' accounts have differed. This is a problem with nearly any form of human testimony. People tend to remember what impressed them. Since they are observing from different physical and psychological perspectives, it is unsurprising that accounts can differ. However, rather than throw out all the data, it is better to look for how the reports agree, and use that information.

The eighth argument is that the witnesses experienced mass hypnosis. If the levitation was a hallucination, then it is hard to understand how that hallucination could land an individual in the top of a tree, where they need physical assistance getting back down to the ground.[115] Indeed, as Rogo noted, there is no basis or proof for the existence of mass hypnosis, let alone mass *psychic* hypnosis. The original mass hypnosis explanation of the Indian rope trick was a story fabricated by a newspaper reporter. Nonetheless, the theory of "group hypnosis" has persisted and is often cited by skeptics.

The last argument, that today's magicians, working with practice, preparation, experience, and accoutrements are able to imitate these feats, is immaterial to the question of whether levitation is possible. Just because something could have been fraudulently produced does not make it so.[116] Even an expert magician would be hard pressed to duplicate some of St. Joseph's feats, which were outside, in good lighting, on the spur of the moment, and without any preparation or visible assistance.[117] Moreover, it takes years of practice to perform magic well. The saints said to have levitated were not recorded as ever having an interest in, or knowledge about, magic. In addition, many of the current magicians' implements and knowledge of illusion only have been developed in the last century.[118] They were not available for use at the time of the majority of purported levitations. To suggest that if something could be duplicated by trickery or illusion means it has always been faked would be to say almost nothing exists, as magicians are capable of creating nearly any effect, whether scientific or miraculous. Whether something could have been duplicated through trickery is irrelevant to whether it could occur.

CONCLUSION

The seemingly universal claims of levitation by religions around the globe — including a few well documented cases in good lighting, outdoors, and with many witnesses — makes it probable that the phenomenon exists. That this feat can be duplicated through trickery is also clearly true.

If we cannot fully dismiss levitation, then we have to wonder how it works. One possible explanation is temporary weightlessness.[119] There have been many reports of levitating religious figures, such as the Spanish nuns Maria Coronel de Agreda and Sister Beatrice Mary of Jesus, who appeared to float freely in space, and swayed like a feather when others blew air in their direction or created a slight draft by moving past them.[120] Likewise, those individuals who landed in trees, such as St. Joseph and Bl. Mary of Jesus Crucified, never seemed to bend the branches on which they were sitting.

We will see in Part II of this book that psychics have been able to change the weight of objects placed on scales. However, the weightlessness theory does not explain why some saints appear to be rigidly fixed in space such that they could not be pulled down, as was the case with the physicians who were treating St. Joseph as he was dying.[121] It is possible that more than one process is involved, with weightlessness occurring in some cases, while an invisible source of support is used in others.

Two findings stand out. First an altered state of consciousness (ASC) seems to be a helpful — and perhaps necessary — condition. Many reports comment on levitation occurring when the individual is "entranced," or in the midst of prayer, a form of meditation that can involve an ASC — frequently that of ecstasy.[122] Second many of the individuals who developed this ability did so only after suffering a severe, and often life-threatening, illness.[123] It is unclear what role the latter plays in triggering levitation. It is possible that a brush with death triggers a greater spiritual fervor or causes a physical or mental change in the individual. Regardless, we will see more on this theme in the following chapters, as we continue to look at other forms of spiritual and religious MMI.

Stigmata

Stigmata are the apparent paranormal or miraculous production of marks on the body that correspond to the wounds of a religious figure. Although a few stories of stigmata appear in Hindu and Muslim lore — with the wounds mimicking the battle wounds of Muhammad in the case of Muslims — stigmata are predominantly seen in Christian devotees.[124] What makes them interesting is that they suggest the mind can recreate any image that is passionately embraced.[125] In Christian devotees, this has taken the form of bleeding wounds on the hands and the feet, punctures on the forehead simulating the crown of thorns, apparent lance wounds in the abdomen, bruises on the shoulders, and chafing of the wrists and ankles.

Stigmatic wounds are usually historically inaccurate.[126] Skeletal remains dating from the time of Christ bear out the fact that the Romans inserted the nails in the wrists (not the hands), which were more capable of sustaining the body's weight for crucifixion.[127] Thus, stigmata are a stylized representation of the Passion wounds, rather than a genuine impression. The wounds that manifest typically reflect those seen in paintings or on crucifixes in the churches.[128] Their variation in shape, size, and location implies that they are an auto-suggestive effect, perhaps not surprising given their common association with hysteria and central nervous system (CNS) disorders.[129]

St. Francis of Assisi is considered to be one of the first Catholics to exhibit these signs.[130] They began when he was on Mount Alverna in 1224, two years before his death. St. Francis was praying outside a cave when he had a vision of Christ on the cross. Wounds simultaneously opened on his hands, feet, and side, which then remained with him, neither healing nor becoming inflamed, until he died. The stigmata detail was remarkable, and even included blackened protuberances resembling nail heads in the middle of the wounds, which seemed composed of hardened flesh.

Since St. Francis, hundreds of individuals have seemed to bear the marks of crucifixion.[131] Most first manifest stigmata in youth or middle age.[132] However, the form and position of these wounds has varied considerably over the centuries.[133] For example, in the mid–thirteenth century, Elizabeth of Herkenrode was the first to bleed from the forehead while reliving the Passion and Crucifixion of Christ in a trance state.[134] Since then, stigmatic manifestations have shown other variations, including periodic bleeding, internal stigmata with emblems impressed on the heart, and bruising and physical depression of the shoulder where the cross was supposedly supported by Christ on his walk to Calvary.

As mentioned before, stigmata appear to be influenced by the imagination or surroundings of the individual bearing the marks.[135] An example of this is the Y-shaped cross borne by Anne Catherine Emmerich (1774–1824), which resembled the Y-shaped cross of the church in which she prayed. Emmerich's other stigma included wounds in her hands, feet, and right side, a double cross on her breastbone, and a circlet on her head that is said to have looked like the mark of a crown of thorns.[136]

Emmerich lived in Westphalia, during the time of Napoleon, under the direct rule of Joseph Bonaparte.[137] Her first wound was said to have appeared in 1812, and discharges from her hands and feet were reportedly regular until 1818.[138] The rationalistic atmosphere of the French revolution was violently opposed to anything smacking of the supernatural. Indeed, it may be no surprise that Emmerich and those connected to her were denounced as conspirators engaged in public deception.[139] Those who investigated her were not particularly credulous, nor were they prone to accept the phenomena as real.

Nine or ten physicians (including two local ones) were brought in to examine Emmerich, who, in addition to her stigmata, was said to be able to survive without the intake of food (a condition known as inedia).[140] A local priest, Dean Rensing, summarized some of the facts they determined as follows. First, that one wound (a double cross on her breast) bled every Wednesday, while the other bled on Fridays.[141] A circlet around her head was said to bleed even more frequently during the week. Second, that some of the wounds appeared in previously normal-looking skin, the blood exuding through it like perspiration. Also, it was painful when the blood ran in streams. Third, that the wounds remained unchanged — becoming neither better nor worse — even when bandaged and covered in plaster. Fourth, that Emmerich had imbibed nothing but water and the occasional bit of juice for around four to five months, and that her stomach would reject the juice. Fifth, that she experienced ecstasies that lasted for hours, during which time she lay rigid as a board. Sixth, that she sometimes appeared to be precognitive. Finally, that she was watched day and night for ten days in a row, during which time Emmerich was never caught eating, excreting substances, or doing anything to affect her wounds.

There are two particularly interesting features to Rensing's testimony. First, the lack of urination and defecation seems to support the idea that Emmerich had little, if any, oral intake. Her inedia has been seen in others, who will be discussed in the next section. Second, considering that it was an age without antibiotics, it is amazing that anyone could bear such wounds for years and not have them become infected. Nor, apparently, was this due to a naturally effective immune system. In 1815, a physician noted that skin on other parts of her body appeared to be prone to inflammation.[142]

Despite this long, detailed report, the civil authorities remained unconvinced.[143] The imputations made against her confessor and certain members of the clergy were so serious that the authorities decided to intervene. In 1819, Emmerich was taken to a house for observation under confinement away from any possible friends or accomplices for three weeks. She was cross-examined by a secular commission that was biased against her, and attended by a nurse appointed by them. Probably to their surprise, the nurse was said to have been satisfied as to the spontaneity of the phenomenon.[144] Although the commission was unable to find evidence of fraud, they remained divided in their opinion. Emmerich died five years later, in 1824.

Although not well documented, there was talk that Emmerich was associated with other forms of MMI, including (1) money teleporting or materializing, (2) levitation from her bed, (3) knockings, (4) lights appearing, and (5) the making of her bed by invisible hands.[145] Furthermore, Thurston stated that, as in the case of many other saints and mystics, her body did not exhibit the expected *rigor mortis* during the three days she awaited burial. Furthermore, when her body was exhumed six weeks later, it was found to be "free from corruption."[146]

It is possible that the cross on Emmerich's chest could be a similar process to the apparent ring-shaped modification of flesh said to sometimes form around a nun's finger, as a symbol of her betrothal to Christ.[147] These are known as "tokens of espousal."[148] Célestine Fenouil bore one of the better-known rings of flesh. Born in 1849, she developed stigmata at the age of seventeen. Then in 1874, she further developed a bright red line around her finger, with tiny crosses at intervals. Her token of espousal was purportedly more obvious on Sundays, when it was said to shine brightly. This was not simply callous formation or a scar because witnesses stated Fenouil's ring would disappear, only to reappear again at the same day and time. Unfortunately, the examining physician did not see the mark in the process of appearing and disappearing, which means it could have been due to fraud.

The life of Maria Domenica Lazzari (1815–1848) illustrates many of the common features of stigmatics.[149] Lazzari was pious as a child. After the death of her father when she was thirteen, Lazzari fasted and wept for four days and nights. After this, she became ill and, over time, increasingly unstable. She suffered a seizure at the age of eighteen after spending the night alone in a mill. From that point on, Lazzari remained bedridden and developed anorexia nervosa and hyperesthesia. Lazzari often showered herself with blows in a manner reminiscent of Elizabeth of Herkenrode. She purportedly developed a token of espousal and became inedic — giving up eating in 1834. She lived as an invalid with her sister until her death in 1848. However, Lazzari differed from many stigmatics in that she never experienced ecstasy or trance. Nor were her visitors particularly impressed by her holiness.

Lazzari was first impressed with stigmata in July 1837.[150] What made her weekly Friday bleedings particularly interesting is that some claimed that, rather than flowing in the normal direction down the side of her foot, the blood flowed upwards and over the toes, as it would do if she were suspended on a cross. This was witnessed by a number of travelers, as well as by physicians. However, in discussing these events, Herbert Thurston observed that gravity alone may have been responsible for this, since the bottom of Lazzari's foot would be nearly horizontal with her legs during this time, making the instep wound higher than her toes.[151] Thus, there may have been nothing paranormal about how her blood flowed from the wound.

Marie de Moerl (1812–1868) was a stigmatic from Kaltern, Tyrol.[152] She apparently began experiencing ecstasies at the age of twenty, remaining in that state of consciousness for the majority of her remaining 35 years, apparently emerging from it only when so ordered by the Franciscan who directed her. She developed stigmata two years into this period, which were said to shed blood only on Thursday evenings and Fridays. The blood was described as being very clear, making one wonder about it. According to the Catholic Church website at www.catholic.org, microscopic analysis of the red liquid from stigmata has often shown it is not blood but something else that may, like sweat, exude through the pores of the skin.

Marie-Julie Jahenny (1850–1941) was a French peasant girl who first developed stigmata in 1873, at the age of twenty-three.[153] She showed an amazing variety of wounds. They included not only the classic five wounds, but also (1) a crown of thorns; (2) an imprint on her left shoulder; (3) marks on her wrists; (4) an emblematic pattern in front of her heart; (5) stripes on her arms, legs, and side; (6) a stigmatic ring on the fourth finger of her right hand; (7) various inscriptions on the breast; and (8) in 1875, the words "O Crux ave" with a cross and a flower. Furthermore, it was said that while in a state of trance, those around her reported that she exuded an "incomparable fragrance" from her body.[154]

Jahenny is said to have exhibited her token of espousal for over 20 years.[155] Unlike Fenouil's case, multiple witnesses observed the process of Jahenny's stigmatic ring formation.[156] However, Jahenny showed a keen interest in impressing her witnesses, as well as a lack of the modesty and humility typically exhibited by stigmatics. As Herbert Thurston dryly noted, there are elements to her story that do not inspire confidence in her genuineness.[157] Certainly, a desire for attention provides powerful unconscious motivation for human MMI.

Gemma Galgani (1878–1903) was a saint said to have the gift of prophecy and suffer from stigmata.[158] Born the daughter of a pharmacist in a small Italian town — and never in good health — she came down with meningitis at the age of 20. Galgani managed to recover, but it was after that illness, at the age of 21, that she apparently began manifesting stigmata. Her life proved to be a short one. Galgani developed tuberculosis in 1903 and died a short time later. In 1940, she was elevated to sainthood.

During the years Galgani had stigmata, weekly bleeding from her hands and feet would start at 8 P.M. Thursday and end at 3 P.M. Friday.[159] Her confessor and biographer, Father Germanus, only observed their process of formation and closure first-hand a few times, but he chronicled those experiences in considerable detail. The stigmata began as red marks on the backs and palms of her hands. Then, an opening would appear on either side of her hands, as an oblong on the backs of her hands and irregularly round in her palms. This opening gradually grew in size until it was five-eighths of an inch long by one-eighth wide in the back of the hand, and about half an inch in diameter in the palm. The depths of her wounds could vary from shallow to deep, but at times Father Germanus stated that Galgani's wounds appeared to go all the way through her hands and were full of partly congealed blood. Furthermore, when the blood stopped flowing, the wounds were said to immediately close. Father Germanus never saw stigmata on her feet, and noted that there were times when blood appeared to seep through the skin, without signs of an opening or laceration for it to come through. On rare occasions, Galgani also had stigmata that looked like nail heads made of flesh.

This is a particularly interesting case both because of the care with which the events were documented in detail and because Galgani's stigmata developed in slow and consistent stages that could be observed. One cannot ascribe the protuberances resembling nail-heads to permanent callus or scarring when they appear on such a sporadic basis. Perhaps even more remarkable was the way in which the stigmata disappeared between events.[160] In others, such as Domenica Lazzari, the wounds were always perceptible in the form of a scar between bleedings. However, after her weekly Friday bleeding during ecstasy, Galgani's wounds would heal within a day or two. By Sunday, the deep holes in her hand would be completely gone, the skin looking the same as that around it save only for a whitish mark to show anything had ever happened.

Such a remarkable rate and quality of healing brings up the question of whether fraud could have occurred and wasn't uncovered, or whether the observers were inadequately scientific. However, this phenomenon is no relic of the past but continues to occur, and modern-day physicians have had no better luck at finding ordinary explanations for stigmata. Relatively recent individuals said to have bleeding wounds include Therese Neumann, Elena Ajello, St. Pio of Pietrelcina (better known as Padre Pio), Clorette Robinson, John Snide, and a woman known as Anna Maria T.[161] We will look at each of these cases in turn, beginning with Therese Neumann.

Therese Neumann (1898–1962) was a peasant woman born in Konnenberg, Bavaria, who suffered a string of illnesses and injuries in 1918, which led to her becoming a blind, bedridden epileptic.[162] At one point the bedsores on her left foot were so infected that it was thought she might require an amputation. However, these physical disabilities were then "miraculously" cured one by one after a vision of St. Thérèse of Lisieux and she was walking again within a month. Neumann's stigmata, in the form of the five classic wounds of the Passion, appeared soon afterward, during Lent in 1926. Eventually she was reported to shed tears of blood. By 1930, her stigmata had begun to imitate those of St. Francis of Assisi. Protuberances resembling nail heads slowly appeared within the wounds on her hands and feet. These protrusions were closely examined by physicians and appeared to be formed from hardened skin.

One of the more interesting, if brief, accounts of Neumann's ecstasies comes to us from the Hindu Guru Yogananda, who visited her when she was still alive in 1935.[163] When he met her, Yogananda observed what appeared to be freshly healed wounds on her hands. Later, he visited her room during one of her ecstasies while himself in a trance state, so as to share her vision. Yogananda reported seeing blood flowing in a continuous inch-wide stream from her lower eyelids. A cloth around Neumann's head was soaked with blood, and there were splotches of blood on her clothing from other stigmatic wounds. She was speaking to beings not visible in the flesh, in a language unknown to Yogananda, her eyes turned upward. He then claimed to have seen what she was looking at — a vision of Jesus carrying the Cross, a jeering crowd, and him falling.

In addition to her stigmata, Neumann was said to have a number of unusual abilities, including having clairvoyance while entranced, the gift of healing, bilocation, and inedia.[164] Also, according to Herbert Thurston, she displayed at least three different personalities — one in her ecstasies and two while awake. Neumann was reputedly ridiculed by Nazis during the Third Reich, but never physically harmed.[165] She suffered from angina for years, and eventually died of a heart attack on September 18, 1962. Proceedings were opened for her possible beatification in 2005.

Elena Ajello (1895–1961) was another contemporary stigmatic, who came from a highly religious family in a small town in Italy.[166] Her stigmata first appeared in March 1923. She was examined by a physician, Dr. Turano, who reported that the blood did not come from a wound, but instead appeared to periodically exude through the skin.[167] Nor was this a slow ooze. During her ecstasies (which appeared to be painful) blood was said to gush from her forehead. These stigmata reoccurred on every Friday until Good Friday and, on the last occasion that year, involved tears of blood instead of blood from the forehead. The phenomena then reoccurred in 1924 from Lent until Easter.

When the stigmata started up again in 1925, Ajello was thoroughly investigated by a number of scientists, including Dr. Vincenzo Bianchi, a professor of Pathology at the University of Naples.[168] In 1926, surrounded by journalists and medical men, things seemed to wind down. No blood came from her forehead, and only she shed tears of blood twice. Although one might speculate whether this drop in activity could have been because she was faking events, it is also possible that, as in poltergeist investigations, the presence of outsiders changed the family dynamics driving the MMI. Regardless, Thurston commented that even laymen could tell that Ajello was suffering from the symptoms of hysteria. Nonetheless, this is an interesting case because of the apparent ability of blood to be exuded through unbroken skin under the direct observation of a physician — a phenomenon that has been documented in other recent cases.

Francesco Forgione (1887–1968), perhaps best known as Padre Pio and canonized as St. Pio of Pietrelcina, is one of the few male stigmatics.[169] Said to also have had the powers of bilocation, healing, prophecy, telepathy, weather control, and the perfumed odor of sanctity, St. Pio practiced severe austerities, including long fasts, starting from a young age. Some believe that he began suffering invisible stigmata in 1915.[170] However, it was not until September 1918 that wounds opened during an ecstasy after saying Mass. St. Pio tried to conceal the stigmata by wearing gloves, but monastery officials nonetheless soon summoned physicians to examine the wounds. They extended completely through his hands, and the head of the monastery testified that he could sometimes see straight through St. Pio's hand by staring into the wounds when they had stopped bleeding. When probed with the fingers there was said to be "a sensation of empty space."[171] Oddly, the area around the wounds exhibited no swelling or inflammation. Although the stigmata occasionally scabbed over, they never healed. It was said that he lost the equivalent of a cup of blood a day, yet St. Pio never showed signs of anemia.[172] The stigmata continued until his death in 1968. He was beatified by Pope John Paul II in 1999, who later canonized him as St. Pio of Pietrelcina on June 16, 2002.

St. Pio's path to sainthood was not without its bumps. In 1923, the Church investigated him and declared that the stigmata were not supernatural in origin.[173] An agnostic examining pathologist, Professor Bignami of the Roman University considered the symmetrically arranged areas of skin necrosis to be due to unconscious suggestion, and felt that everything he saw could be accounted for by natural causes. However, for a man who believes in only the physical world and scientism, nothing can *ever* be considered other than by natural causes, if currently unknown ones.

One of the most fascinating and well-documented cases of stigmata occurred in a ten-year-old black Baptist girl, Clorette Robinson, from Oakland, California.[174] She developed bleeding on September 13, 1971, when studying the Crucifixion. She was examined by physicians at the Kaiser Permanente hospital in Oakland. Blood flowed through the skin of her hands, feet, side, and forehead. Physicians could neither stop the bleeding nor find its source. Furthermore, psychiatric examination showed Clorette had a normal personality. The bleeding ended on March 31 (a week after the story broke in the news media) and apparently never resumed.

This is an important case because not only was it recent, but in an industrialized country with a litigious medico-legal climate, which meant the wounds were documented promptly and thoroughly. Clorette was also examined by a number of presumably competent physicians — including emergency room physicians, a pediatrician, and a psychiatrist — rather than potentially biased religious officials. The fact that something unusual and inexplicable — blood seeping through unbroken skin — was occurring appears to be documented beyond doubt.

John Snide was a home health aide living in Massachusetts when his stigmata began in March 1998.[175] Like many poltergeist agents, his childhood was not a happy one. His parents were physically abusive, alcoholic drug addicts who eventually gave him up for adoption. Snide is reputedly unable to remember five years of his life during that time. He converted to his wife's religion of Catholicism in 1993. Blood initially appeared on the front and back of his left hand, before progressing to involve both hands, his wrists, his chest near the heart, and one foot. Eventually scratches appeared on his back, and his eyes began to bleed. These phenomena were purportedly associated with prayer.

Snide is also said to have manifested a number of poltergeist-type effects. Paranormal investigators who followed the case for two and a half years noted a wide variety of activity, including statues, beads and crosses weeping oil, blood appearing on some of the statues and pictures, materialization and of a variety of types of Host (religious wafers), and movement (often rotation) of some of the statues.[176] Glitter also sometimes showed up in the oil or on people. In one case, there was a popping sound (a characteristic of apports) followed by a Host appearing — all of which was caught on film. Analysis of samples found the blood was human, the oils were castor, and the glitter was all of the same type, a kind used in cosmetics. John Berkenbush, who helped investigate, noted that although some events appeared to be real, others may have been fictitious — a not uncommon finding in poltergeist cases. Snide enjoyed being the center of attention and was caught in some lies and faking an event. He has since dropped from sight.

Finally, we come to Anna Maria T., who was born in Milan in 1925.[177] Although not as dramatic a case as others, it is interesting because of the care with which it was studied. Anna Maria was not a typical stigmatic. Unlike most, she exhibited good health for the majority of her long life and was not particularly religious. She was widowed in 1987, but continued to work, running a general food store. In 1990, while in prayer, Anna Maria is said to have felt the sudden onset of forehead pain, after which she had a vision of Jesus wherein he approached her and touched her hands. The next morning, painful, round red marks appeared on her hands. These disappeared after two or three days, only to reoccur on a regular basis, showing up the first Friday of every month that followed.

Marco Margnelli studied Anna Maria's stigmata for over three years, using color photographs, infrared film, fingerprints, electrodermal measurements, plethysmography, and psychological testing. He found that the morphology of Anna Maria's stigmata varied from one month to the next.[178] Sometimes they only appeared as two bright red spots, 15 mm in diameter, while other times there was a fluid-filled oval blister, which would then break and dry up, forming a crust. Although the wounds were painful, they never bled. Margnelli noted that her Minnesota Multiphasic Personality Inventory (MMPI) showed no traces of hysteria or desire for suffering. He felt the stigmata looked most like burns. Her hands did show some sympathetic hyperactivity, but only within the reddened areas. Infrared photographs showed the area of skin where the stigmata existed were warmer than the areas around them, suggesting dilation of the capillaries. The skin temperature of the same zones returned to normal when the stigmata were absent. Finally, there was no change in sympathetic tone whether the stigma were present or not, and stigmatic zones were the same as the areas around them.

The case stories reviewed above suggest a number of common themes for full-blown stigmatics. These include (1) a major illness or life-changing event (2) religious fervor and (3) a frequent association with an ASC, such as prayer or ecstasy. The shapes, sizes, degrees, and recurrence rates may vary not only between individuals, but also for a given individual over time. In more than one case, the phenomena started in a limited fashion, and then progressed. The wounds themselves often appear to be genuine, but do not behave in a normal fashion — there are no reports of stigmata ever becoming infected and they often heal at remarkable rates. Even more surprising, many stigmatics exude some form of red liquid (which may relate to blood) through fully intact skin. Finally, at least some stigmatics clearly receive secondary gain — whether monetary or in terms of attention and prestige — from the situation. There is clear motivation for trickery, and, as with poltergeist cases, both outright fraud and fraud mixed with the paranormal may occur.

Let us consider possible ordinary explanations for stigmata. It became apparent during the seventeenth and eighteenth centuries that many stigmatics shared a personality type, which Charcot would have called hysteria.[179] The majority of stigmatics have histories of extreme religiosity, a severe illness, and the presence of hysterical symptoms prior to the appearance of their wounds. Furthermore, there is a relatively low incidence of stigmata in men. In 2002, Matthew Albright noted there were only 41 male stigmatics, as compared with 241 female ones.[180] Some suggest this may be correlated to the fact that hysteria occurs in men much less often than women.[181] Also, there may be a few cases of stigmata which involve neither religion nor an ASC.[182] William Needles wrote of a girl taking on the wounds of a brother she watched run a gauntlet for punishment, and a bystander developing the same bleeding wounds as a French soldier he watched in battle.

Two pieces of evidence suggest stigmata are more than hysteria alone. First, that some stigmatics, such as Clorette and Anna Maria, have apparently normal personalities on psychiatric exam.[183] One can argue that her lack of hysterical tendencies is why Clorette only exhibited stigmata for a few months. However, this does not explain why Anna Maria exhibited stigmata for over five years of monitoring. Second, if stigmata are psychosomatic, it should be possible to reproduce them with hypnosis. This may be possible to a limited degree.[184] Needles cited reports of nosebleeds, redness, blisters, and drops of blood triggered on command through hypnosis. However, hypnosis has not been shown to reproduce many of the other reported facets of stigmata, such as open wounds that bleed freely, a sweet scent to the blood, blood seeping through skin, and abnormal coagulation.[185]

Another ordinary explanation for stigmata is that the wounds are self-inflicted.[186] After all, many stigmatics appear to be involved in self-punishment and mutilation. However, even if this were true it would not explain why stigmata never become infected, let alone how they can mend so well. These wounds are found to be half an inch or more in depth on close examination. Yet when they heal, it is often without a scar, only to open up again later. In many ways, the development and healing of stigmata are reminiscent of the reports of psychic surgery.

The skeptics' typical response is to suggest that these wounds were merely painted on in the first place. This is a plausible idea, and it would not be at all surprising if, in fact, this has sometimes been the case. However, it does not explain away St. Pio's wounds, which were closely examined by skeptical physicians and found to be quite deep.

The question of fraud is a difficult one. Over the centuries, some have been caught cheating, while others, such as the Spanish nun Maria de la Visitacion in 1546, confessed to it.[187] Yet the truth may not be so simple. Herbert Thurston noted that Maria de la Visitacion's wounds could not be washed off. He felt that, given her states of ecstasy and the fact that witnesses reported watching the stigmata develop, the phenomena may have been genuine. She may have lied for good cause. At least some of the fraud that stigmatics admitted to during the time of the Inquisition was likely motivated by a desire to avoid being condemned as having made a pact with the devil, which was a far more serious offence than imposture or trickery. As it was, Maria's confession probably saved her from the stake.

If stigmata are real, we are still left with the question of whether they represent human MMI or are of divine origin. A devout Catholic himself, Herbert Thurston listed seven reasons why he did not believe stigmata were miraculous:[188] (1) stigmata were never seen before St. Francis, and the explosion of cases since at that time, suggesting a copycat situation; (2) stigmata vary in size, shape, and location between individuals, and often bear a striking resemblance to those seen on paintings or crosses at their local church; (3) there are so many more female stigmatics than male ones, along with the fact that physically vigorous saints — no matter their level of devotion — seldom exhibit stigmata; (4) stigmata often begin after a major illness involving the CNS (indeed, had fits and seizures, in addition to an array of hysterical symptoms, such as contortions, spasms, fugues, and paralysis); (5) he did not believe God would chose the bizarre behaviors exhibited by stigmatics as "a setting for a miracle to manifest His glory"; (6) the visions reported by stigmatics tend to be nothing more than standard reenactments of traditional Passion stories, often inaccurate in terms of historical fact, and inconsistent with each other, whereas one would expect a divine revelation (or even good ESP) to reveal new and accurate information; and (7) some stigmatics show signs of dissociative identity disorder (commonly known as multiple personality disorder), suggesting that psychopathology is involved, rather than divinity.[189]

These are telling points. One would expect miracles, if they exist, to be dependent upon the sanctity of the individual, rather than the time period. It is also hard to imagine why, if of universal origin, the stigmata (and visions of the Passion) are inconsistent and historically inaccurate, corresponding with whatever local images the stigmatic may have seen. Thurston's arguments make a strong case for the notion that stigmata are not bestowed by an outside agent, whether divine or demonic, but instead produced by auto-suggestion. If human MMI is indeed the cause, the frequent association between the ASC of prayer or ecstasy and stigmata becomes explained. So, too, is the fact that not all who bear these wounds come across to bystanders as being very spiritual — at least some appear motivated by greed or ego gratification. Unconscious needs and wishes can represent a powerful fuel for MMI.

If we eliminate those individuals who have created their wounds through trickery and self-injury, and accept Thurston's arguments that stigmata are not of divine origin, then there would appear to be at least a few individuals whose stigmata indicate the capability of the mind to change the body's matter. Perhaps, more than anything else, stigmata demonstrate the kind of feats the mind is capable of when backed by the energy of religious faith, with the full force of belief and emotion.[190]

Inedia

Inedia is the apparent paranormal ability of the body to survive without food, and sometimes without drink. It is often associated with stigmata and, although by no means limited to Catholic figures, is commonly attributed to them.[191] However, it is not considered "eating" in Catholicism when one partakes of wafers, known as Hosts, during Holy Communion. Religious figures reputed to be inedic include St. Lydwina (said not to eat for 28 years), Ven. Domenica dal Paradiso (said not to eat for 20 years), St. Nicholas von Flüe (said not to eat for 19 years); Blessed Elizabeth von Reute (said not to eat for 15 years), Maria Domenica Lazzari (ate only the Host for 12 years) and Louise Lateau (ate only the Host for 12 years).[192] Prosper Lambertini laid down the rule that long fasts could not be considered to be miraculous if they began as a result of illness or were associated with a drop in level of physical activity. Needless to say, this eliminated quite a few candidates.

Fraud is, and always has been, the simplest explanation for apparent inedia.[193] It is easy to do — especially with accomplices — and requires little knowledge or skill. Malobservation, and a desire for onlookers to believe the phenomenon is real, facilitate cheating. Formal investigations into inedia have, in fact, found deceit on several occasions. Alfonsina Cottini is a classic example of a fake inedic. She claimed to live without food for years but was caught by Church investigators slipping out of her bed at night to eat and drink.

Nonetheless, there are some cases that cannot be so easily dismissed. Louise Lateau, as mentioned before, was a French stigmatic who could not swallow a spoonful of water without vomiting.[194] She was examined by physicians, who were unable to find any evidence to contradict the contention that she hadn't eaten from 1871 until their published report in 1876. Nor did that change during the six years that followed. She went without food until her death in 1883.[195] Even medical men who were hostile witnesses had to admit they were unable to prove her false. She was never caught cheating, even during her active years of hard manual labor. Given the length of time Lateau was studied, one would think that if any trickery were involved that it would have been uncovered. Her ability to remain active is particularly impressive and sets Lateau apart from many of the other Catholic stigmatics who purportedly fasted for years but (unlike Lambertini's requirement) lived as invalids.

Therese Neumann (who was also stigmatic) was a Bavarian woman who stopped consuming solids after the Christmas of 1922.[196] In January 1927, Neumann had a vision in which she was told that she would no longer need food. From that point on, she supposedly neither ate nor drank anything except for the Eucharist and a little water. Later that year she apparently even stopped drinking water. Despite this lack of intake, she is said to have maintained her health and remained a sturdy woman capable of hard work.

In 1927, Neumann was watched by pairs of nurses under the supervision of a physician around the clock for a fortnight.[197] The nurses were responsible for making sure that she did not sneak any food or water, as well as measuring and recording Neumann's weight, temperature, pulse, and various forms of excretion, which included blood from the stigmata and excreta, which were submitted for analysis. During this time, she lost several pounds of weight during the Friday ecstasies, which was then regained during the following two to three days. Her total intake during the fifteen days was three Eucharist wafers and three spoonfuls of water.[198] Despite this fact, she showed no signs of dehydration, and was exactly the same weight of 121 pounds at the end of the study as at its beginning.[199] However, there were two curious findings.

Twice during that period Neumann urinated about 500 ml, and on two Fridays there was also a small amount of vomiting. Although the latter could have been due in part to swallowing blood from her eyes or forehead, the former elimination of half a liter is disturbing, and raises concerns that she was getting fluids from somewhere.

Some have believed that Neumann's refusal to undergo further surveillance, along with accusations of manipulations under the bed sheets, suggest that trickery was involved in both the supposed inedia, and the stigmata.[200] It is unfortunate that, because of a breach of faith on the physician's part (who publicly published his data after promising not to do so) Neumann's father refused to ever again allow her to participate in a study that might have put these concerns to rest.

Inedia has also been reported in Sufi and Hindu Saints.[201] A tale of one such Hindu was published in the *Civil and Military Gazette* on April 23, 1895.[202] The story goes that the man stayed under a banyan tree for three years. Initially, he ate a plantain or two or drank some milk two or three times a week. Then he extended the periods between meals, until after three or four months it was said he took nothing at all, spending his time huddled up by a fire and speaking to no one. He died shortly before the story was printed.

Yogananda described the fasting St. Giri Bala.[203] He was told she used a yogic technique to live without eating and that a neighbor claimed to have watched her, and never caught her cheating. Perhaps more significantly, the Maharaja of Burdwan performed an investigation, during which time she was locked away for two months in his home without eating. She returned twice after that — once for a stay of 20 days and another for 15 — after which time the Maharaja became convinced the inedia was real. This account sounds as if at least some attempt was made to place Bala in a controlled situation, where access to food could be restricted and she could be closely observed.

When Yogananda finally met the Hindu saint, she was 68 years old and in good health, despite having purportedly lived without food or drink for over 50 years.[204] Bala explained that her inedia began at the age of twelve, after her mother-in-law ridiculed her for her gluttony. She said that a guru was sent to her by God as an answer to her fervent prayer. The guru supposedly told her, "From today you shall live by the astral light; your bodily atoms shall be recharged by the infinite current."[205] Yogananda reported that she then told him she used a mantra and breathing exercises (said to be more difficult than most could perform) to free herself from the need for food. Furthermore, Bala noted that she had never been sick, was without children, and had no bodily excretions.

As in Anne Catherine Emmerich's case, a lack of intake was associated with the expected lack of output. However, unlike Emmerich, Bala was not a bed-ridden invalid, but continued to perform her domestic duties in the normal manner.[206] The fact that she never bore children likewise of interest. Anorexics and women who fast often cease to menstruate and are infertile. This seems to support the notion that Bala was indeed not eating. Unfortunately, one cannot come to a definite conclusion based on what is, in essence, hearsay, especially since we do not know many of the details of her stay with the Maharaja, such as the controls he put in place to ensure that Bala had no way of acquiring food or drink, and whether she lost weight during this time.

This concludes our brief review of the topic of inedia. Often associated with stigmata, inedia is a rare phenomenon. Although fraud is a frequent explanation for the apparent ability to survive without eating, there appear to be a few cases that are not so easily dismissed. Our next subject is a harder ability to fake — teleportation.

Teleportation

Teleportation is the paranormal movement of people or things over a distance and/ or through objects (such as into, or out of, a locked container). The transfer of a saint, while praying in one place, to a distant city, such as Mecca or Medina, in a flash is frequently mentioned in Islamic and Jewish legends.[207] For whatever reason, it is said that this sort of transfer is easier at night than during the day. Spontaneous teleportation appears to be rare and has been reported most often in secular individuals, especially children.[208] In many cases, it begins as spontaneous, uncontrolled events. Later, it may come under intentional control.

At the turn of the century, Charles Fort cited several cases of people apparently instantaneously disappearing from their homes or public sidewalks, only to reappear miles away with no memory of how they had gotten there.[209] Episodes of supposed teleportation have also been reported this century. For example, a baby was said to have repeatedly teleported from her crib into various rooms in a 1929 poltergeist case in Germany. There are also amusing tales of how St. Pio sometimes used teleportation to avoid unwanted visitors lurking outside his rooms.

For some unknown reason, teleportation is often associated with metal-bending (also known as PKMB). Uri Geller — known for starting the spoon-bending fad — is said to have transported himself quite unexpectedly from New York to the suburb of Ossining, where he fell through the roof of a sun-lounge.[210] In their book *Miracles and Other Realities*, Lee Pulos and Gary Richman noted that Geller "experienced a feeling of 'running backwards a couple steps ... then being sucked upward.' A few seconds later ... he crashed through a screen eight feet above the ground, injuring his shoulder as he landed."[211] The incident is even more amusing (and credible) given that he landed in the home of parapsychologist Dr. Puharich.

John Hasted reported that some of the metal-bending children he worked with could teleport.[212] It is not entirely clear whether these events were intentional or spontaneous. For example, Nicholas was said to be able to teleport in and out of locked rooms, while another child was said to teleport himself into odd locations and different rooms for several months.

This phenomenon has occasionally been interpreted (or misinterpreted) as a sign of demonic infestation.[213] One well-publicized case, which began in 1901 in Italy, started with typical poltergeist activity, such as pictures falling off the walls, furniture sliding across the floor, and knickknacks flying off shelves. Several days later, seven-year-old Alfredo Pansini began having spontaneous trances and bouts of catalepsy. The boy also claimed to have clairvoyant visions and "angels" speaking through his mouth. During this period, Alfredo began disappearing from the house, only to be found later, usually in a dazed condition, on the other side of town or in neighboring cities.

After Alfredo had been teleporting for three years, his younger brother, Paolo, began to do it, too.[214] They could disappear within minutes from their room even when all the doors and windows were sealed. One morning, while the boys were at home, they suddenly vanished from the house. They were found half an hour later on the grounds of a convent, 30 miles away. Their most spectacular double teleportation occurred later, when first Paolo, and 30 minutes later Alfredo, vanished from home to both appear aboard a small fishing boat several miles out at sea. These teleportation attacks ended in 1904 when Alfredo reached puberty.

A similar case of teleportation occurred in Manila with an adolescent boy named Cornelio Closa Jr.[215] Closa claimed that if he touched the apparition of a teenage girl dressed in white, he would "disappear" from wherever he happened to be. Closa would then reappear hours later, sometimes miles away from his home. Locking the boy into his room did not stop the disappearances. The apparent teleportations finally stopped sometime after Closa was exorcised by an American missionary.

The incident of the Pansini brothers disappearing from their home and reappearing on a boat that was out to sea seems particularly strong evidence that there is more going on to these changes of locale than simple trickery. The fact that the involved individuals were often found dazed suggests that they were probably spontaneous, uncontrolled events.

The Flying Men of Haiti (which is a separate sect from Voodoo) claims its members can teleport at will in a controlled and repeatable fashion.[216] Douchan Gersi witnessed some of these events. While dancing in a deep trance, these individuals sometimes disappeared before his very eyes. They were said to be able to carry objects with them when they traveled, which could serve as proof of their ability to near-instantly move to and from distant locations. However, as with levitation, it was said to be easier to get somewhere than to return, and people — especially beginners — could reportedly get stuck in far-off spots.

One of the more dramatic episodes Gersi described involved watching the head of the Flying Men, known as the Emperor, vanish in the blink of an eye just before hitting a hotel room wall.[217] The man reappeared again next to the bed exactly 32 minutes later, holding a notebook that had been left in a house one hundred miles away. On both his dematerialization and rematerialization, Gersi noticed heat coming from the spot. Perhaps more to the point, there appeared to be no normal way the man could have traveled to the house and back again in that length of time.

According to the Flying Men, in order to be able to dematerialize in one place and rematerialize in another, a believer must reach a state of trance and wait to be possessed by a female loa worshiped as the goddess of love and sex.[218] Gersi stated that the Flying Men in Haiti gave an impression of something like feathers behind them as they disappeared. These events always occurred at night, and every time he tried to film one, his batteries quit working.

The Cassowary Men sorcerers of New Guinea also appear to be capable of deliberate teleportation.[219] Again, these individuals are said to only "fly" at night. On one disappearance Gersi witnessed, the event was accompanied by a noise and Gersi again had an impression of feathers. He felt this event was similar to the teleportations of the Flying Men in Haiti.

There are also reports of individuals covering vast distances in very short periods of time, which may, or may not, represent teleportation. These include such things as Australian Aborigines walking through dreamtime, the movement of Tibetan Monks through mountain ranges, and the apparent ability of Sai Baba to cross rocky uphill terrain with incredible speed.[220]

Teleportation is an interesting, if rare, phenomenon that has not been well studied. Nonetheless, the anecdotal material suggests that an ASC is involved. The association of metal-bending with teleportation is a curious finding. It is unclear whether this is meaningful or merely a reporting artifact.

Bilocation

Bilocation is the purported ability to be in more than one place at the same time. It has been reported to occur as part of a host of MMI phenomena in spiritual figures.[221] Most of the time it seems to be a spontaneous event — although this is not to say that it may not serve a purpose. Natuzza Evolo was said to have had no control over her journeys — which occasionally involved trilocation — when she was seen in two places at the same time apart from where her body was situated.[222]

It is important to distinguish bilocation from the more common experience of feeling out-of-body. In out-of-body experiences (OBEs) people feel their center of consciousness as in a spatial location separate from their physical bodies.[223] The experience often includes an awareness of "leaving the body," traveling to a distant destination, being able to voluntarily control one's perspective, and returning again to the body.[224] OBEs are usually brief in duration and considered a form of ESP.

Bilocation, which is considered to be MMI, differs from an OBE in several ways. First, bilocations usually last longer.[225] Second, the person bilocating can converse, interact, carry objects, and perform physical acts at the distant location. Third, witnesses feel they are interacting with a real person. Finally, bilocators usually find themselves instantly transported to their destination without any awareness of leaving the body. Several Catholic religious figures have been reported to have this ability, including St. Clement I (died 97 CE), St. Ambrose (340–397 CE), St. Severus of Milan (died 420 CE), St. Anthony of Padua (1195–1231), St. Martin de Porres (1579–1639), Ven. Maria Coronel de Agreda (1602–1665), St. Liguori (1696–1787), and St. Pio of Pietrelcina (1887–1968).[226] Many of these individuals were seen in their cells or at prayer while simultaneously appearing at funerals or deathbeds miles away.

St. Liguori represents a typical case.[227] In 1774, while preparing to celebrate mass, Liguori suddenly went into trance. Two hours later, he came out of his ASC and said that he had been at Pope Clement XIV's deathbed in Rome. Sister Agatha Viscardi was tempted to laugh at this statement. However, she later learned from those who had been in attendance at the bedside of the dying Pope, that they had not only seen, but also talked to Liguori, who had led them in prayers for the dying. Thus, Liguori's body appears to have been observed in two locations at the same time by multiple sober, reliable witnesses.

Ven. Maria Coronel de Agreda (1602–1665) was yet another who bilocated in addition to visions, telepathy, and levitation.[228] She was a Franciscan abbess, said to have suffered a host of illnesses allegedly brought on by demonic attack, who practiced rigid austerities such as fasting, self-flagellation, and sleep deprivation. Her bilocations purportedly occurred both in the day and at night more than 500 times, and often involved appearing in Mexico and Spain at the same time.[229] During these travels, Agreda believed she instructed the natives in the Christian faith, distributed rosaries, and told them to travel to a distant settlement where they could receive baptism. It is said that on her advice, they went to the mission where, on being shown the picture of another Franciscan nun, the new converts recognized the habit as being the same as that of their visitor. Agreda was silent about her experiences at first, afraid that they were nothing more than hallucinations — despite the fact that the rosaries she saw herself distributing had disappeared from her cell.[230] What makes the story particularly intriguing is that it appeared to have been independently confirmed by Father Alonza de Benvides, who returned to Europe from New Mexico in 1630.[231] He said a Mexican Indian tribe had told him the tale of a strange woman who had told them to become baptized.

This tale of transcontinental bilocation is by no means unique. Others, such as St. Martin and Teresa Higginson, have been said to do the same.[232] Higginson's story is similar to de Agreda's, in that the schoolteacher from Bootle felt she visited natives in Africa on many occasions, during which time she both instructed and baptized them.[233]

In more recent years, St. Pio was said to have frequently bilocated at the bequest of his parishioners, either to heal the sick or to comfort the dying.[234] He referred to these visits as being an extension of his personality. His fellow priests noted that he often seemed to become distracted at these times, almost in a trance state. At times, St. Pio also appeared to be giving the last rites or hearing a confession. He was even thought to have left physical traces behind of his bilocation on some occasions. Perhaps the most dramatic of these was when he purportedly left five bloodstains from his hand on some bed linen. It is a shame that DNA testing was not available at the time, as it might have definitely answered the question of whether it was truly St. Pio's blood.

Christian ascetics are not the only ones who claim the ability to bilocate. In some dervish groups, such as the Persian Chakras, multilocation is said to have occurred — their founder having presented himself simultaneously in the form of 47 men.[235] The phenomenon is also reported in Hindu, Buddhist, and Tantrum literature, not to mention in contemporary individuals such as Alex Tanous, Dada, and Sathya Sai Baba.[236] Douchan Gersi said that the Flying Men of Haiti are also capable of this feat, but did not have the opportunity to witness such an event.[237]

Skeptics insist that bilocation does not exist. Instead, they postulate that these stories are perpetuated because the sick and the dying "hallucinate" the comforting presence, or remember an "astral" visit.[238] However, if this were the case it would not explain an incident when St. Martin de Porres suddenly appeared, laden with wine, cake, and fruit at his sister's house, summarized an argument that had just taken place, suggested an amicable solution, and stayed the night before leaving for Lima the next day.[239] When his sister later spoke to some of the monastery friars about her brother's timely appearance, they were astounded, as at that same time he had been working in the monastery infirmary.

One would expect that his family and fellow priests would know St. Martin de Porres well enough that an imposter would not be able to pass for him. Furthermore, none of the involved witnesses were either sick or dying, and it does not seem possible that either a hallucination or an astral traveler could have carried in all the wine, cake, and fruit—unless able to levitate multiple items simultaneously, which would still be MMI.

Another instance that is difficult to explain away was performed by Alex Tanous, who bilocated to Canada while his body was seen by witnesses, slumped in a chair in New York.[240] At the time of the event, Tanous was waiting to head out to a late lecture. His agent and at least one other person were with him when he sat down to rest. After Tanous closed his eyes in New York, his body apparently showed up on a friend's doorstep in Canada. Tanous drank tea and chatted for awhile before leaving. When the friend did not hear a car start, he looked out, worried that Tanous was stranded. However, he saw neither a car nor tracks in the snow. Confirmation came from his wife, who was upstairs at the time, and heard the conversation between Tanous and her husband. Also, the dog barked when Tanous first came to the door and reacted to his presence in the house. When Tanous straightened in his chair in New York, he told the people there that he had been to Canada and what had happened—all of which was later confirmed by the man and his wife in Canada.

Once again, the skeptic's arguments that purported bilocations are simply a hallucination by the dying or an "astral" visit do not hold up. The consumption of tea suggests that Tanous was not just an astral form. Hallucination seems unlikely since nobody was ill, the witnesses were in separate parts of the house, and the dog reacted to him.

In his book, *Miracles: A Parascientific Inquiry Into Wondrous Phenomena*, Scott Rogo pointed out that no one theory can explain all the facts of bilocation.[241] Occultists submit that the body possesses a double, or "soul body," which can take on various shades of density and travel. This suggests that OBEs could occur along a spectrum of soul densities. At one extreme would be the typical incorporeal astral traveler, while at the other there could be complete duplication of the body. Unfortunately, it is unclear how many elements are shared by OBEs and bilocation. Perhaps the biggest problems with this theory are that it (1) makes the assumption that the mind has the power to create a material form of itself during the experience; and (2) does not explain cases where the individual appears in three or more locations simultaneously.

The religious explanation for bilocation is that a divine superintelligence masterminds the physical duplication of the body. Little can be said about this, other than that if we define this process as "mind over matter," then it is still MMI whether that mind is a human one or of divine superintelligence.

A third possibility is that this is simultaneously an objective and immaterial phenomenon, where a witness perceives the spiritual presence of the bilocator.[242] Hence, the visual appearance may be more illusory than real. However, this would require that the bilocators be able to levitate, materialize, and teleport objects to explain the physical presence of food, and does not explain how they could eat and drink, unless it is by dematerialization of the consumables. Bilocation seems to require some form of MMI, regardless of whether or not the physical body is replicated.

Fire-Immunity

Fire-immunity is the alleged ability of a person to be able to come into direct contact with extreme heat without being burned. The control of fire has been associated with faith by many religious traditions. It is easy to see why. Fire has an almost unparalleled power of fascination for mankind. As mentalist Ron Martin noted:

> I am of the opinion that fire *is* magick [*sic*], at least in its effects on the minds of people. Imagine how we humans have sat in the dark, staring into fires, since our beginning.... Fire is a powerful, aggressive agent of change. It is life saving, and it is life taking. We love it, yet we fear it. We need it to survive, yet it's extremely dangerous.[243]

It is not surprising, then, that the ability to control fire would be a compelling symbol of power. This manifestation of MMI seems to be more common in religious figures than secular ones — although fire-walking was popular at motivational events for a time. Fire-immunity may take one of two forms. The first type is where the individual appears to be impervious to external fire, while the second is the apparent ability to withstand unusually high internal temperatures, such as occurs in *incendium amoris*.

EXTERNAL FIRE-IMMUNITY

Fire ceremonies have been used by cultures around the globe for millennia. Priestesses in early Greece walked barefoot on hot charcoal in honor of the goddess Artemis.[244] Similarly, devotees of the goddess Feronia in Italy walked on the embers of a pinewood fire. The old testament of the Bible also contains stories of fire-immunity.[245] Inglis wrote:

> There seemed hardly any limit to what a prophet could do when the hand of the Lord was on him. He could perform superhuman feats of strength or endurance of the kind for which Samson became renowned. Or he could become incombustible.[246]

One of the more dramatic stories is how Shadrach, Mesach, and Abednego were placed inside Nebuchadnezzar's burning furnace, yet remained completely unharmed by the fire.[247] Multiple witnesses reported that the three men had not a hair singed or thread of clothing harmed. Indeed, it is said that they did not even smell of fire.

In another tale, St. Polycarp of Smyrna is said to have been condemned to death at the stake in 155 or 156 CE.[248] He is said to have exhibited complete fire immunity while still alive. The pile of wood burned fiercely after lit, but the flames purportedly arced away from him, and although they encircled his body, they did no harm. His persecutors then dispatched him with a spear, after which all but his bones were reduced to ashes.

Ordeal by fire as a method of demonstrating faith has been used recurrently over the centuries, but was particularly common as a method of adjudication during the Middle Ages.[249] For example, in 1062 CE, a series of riots were sparked by a candidate using bribery to win the position of the deceased Bishop Gerard of Florence.[250] Peace was restored when the Abbot directed one of his monks, Peter Aldobrandini (later St. Peter Igneus), to perform a fire ordeal. The monk first spoke Mass, then took off his chasuble (retaining his other sacred vestments), and slowly walked along a narrow path ten feet long between two blazing piles of wood. Not a hair of his head was harmed. The crowd then considered God's will to have been made manifest, and the false bishop was deposed.

Islam has its share of reports of fire immunity as an act of faith. For example, Gurdjieff is said to have had Sufi *shaikh* perform a number of acts of faith, including licking a white-hot poker.[251]

Fire-Immunity was by no means limited to tests of faith, but has also been used in more practical ways.[252] Eight witnesses testified at the canonization hearing of St. Francis of Paolo (1416–1507) that they had seen him walk into the roaring flames of a burning furnace to examine its inner damage, and come out again completely unharmed, clothes and all. Not only was he habitually immune from fire, but he could also (as with D. D. Home centuries later) transfer this ability to others.

The stories about St. Francis of Paolo's fire-immunity seem to be nearly endless. One time, he was working with some charcoal burners.[253] They had done a poor job of building their stack, and flames were coming through gaps in the dirt that had been thrown on top. St. Francis of Paolo stepped over each of the gaps in turn with his bare feet to keep the fire in until the workers could close them with fresh soil. Another time, he was said to have picked up burning embers in the monastery kitchen, wrapped them in his tunic, and brought them to the church in order to ignite an incense burner.[254] Neither his hands, nor his clothing, were burned. The sheer quantity of stories about St. Francis of Paolo's immunity from fire is impressive. Both secular and spiritual individuals came forward to attest under oath to St. Francis of Paolo's feats. Although most of the tales were told 30–50 years after the events occurred, the witnesses probably found them quite memorable.

St. Catherine of Siena was also reputedly immune from fire.[255] She was born in Italy to a large family, being the twenty-fifth child of a wool dyer.[256] By the age of six, she was purportedly having mystical experiences and seeing people's guardian angels. At sixteen, she joined the Dominican order. One story of fire-immunity was when she was working in the kitchen. St. Catherine was turning a spit when she went into a state of ecstasy.[257] She fell forward into the fire. Another woman returned to find her body lying on the burning coals. She pulled the Saint out, fearing the worst. To her surprise, St. Catherine was completely unharmed—even her clothing was untouched. It seems likely that both the fall into the flames, and the protection from them, were due to her ecstatic state. It is perhaps unsurprising that St. Catherine entered an ASC, given the repetitive motion of turning a spit. In this case, her immunity was only one of a host of manifestations. She was also reputed to levitate, exhibit luminosity, be inedic, and suffer stigmata, including a token of espousal.

Other religious figures have also been said to exhibit fire-immunity. When in ecstasy, the seeress of Lourdes, St. Bernadette, was said to be able to hold her hands in flames for minutes at a time.[258] Another remarkable tale is of Claris, the Camisard leader during the rise of the Huguenots against Louis XIV of France. Claris was said, while in a state of religious fervor, to have climbed on top of a pyre in front of 600 men. He continued to speak as the flames rose above his head—making one wonder whether he had a paranormal ability to do without oxygen, as well. He did not stop until the wood was consumed. Not only was Claris unhurt, but also his attire was said to be unmarked by the fire. As we have seen, this is not an uncommon detail. Fire-immunity often (but not always) extends to shoes, socks, and clothing.

Although we have spoken primarily of Greece and Europe, fire-walking and fire ordeals are not unique to those cultures. They have also been performed as a sign of faith and divine protection in Africa, Fiji, Haiti, Hawaii, India, Japan, Malaya, North America, the Philippines, Tahiti, Thailand, Trinidad, Romania, and the West Indies.[259] In his review of the subject, Brian Inglis pointed out that magic practitioners were not the only ones thought to exhibit fire immunity.[260] Many cultures relied upon a trial by ordeal to prove the innocence or guilt of the average man. In some cases, this involved placing a hand in boiling water or holding a bar of iron that had been heated for a period of time. If the person was burned, they were pronounced guilty, whereas those who were unmarked were presumed innocent.

It is impossible to say how much spirituality and intentionality play a part in successful fire-immunity. Many such ceremonies involve a stage of mental preparation, and it is said that if participants lose their confidence or become distracted, they get severely burned.[261] However, numerous cultures consider this something every member of the community can potentially perform — although in some cases by proxy, with the power conferred upon them by another. For example, Native Americans in Canada, near Quebec, held a ceremony in 1637, during which medicine men reached into a fire, separated the burning brands with their hands, and pulled out stones that were red with heat.[262] Putting their hands behind their backs, the medicine men then put the rocks between their teeth and carried them over to their patients, remaining for some time without letting go. French bystanders were astonished to watch as the Native Americans rubbed their bodies with glowing cinders. In no case was anyone — whether a medicine man or a patient — said to have been burned.

A similar incident of fire-immunity conferred onto others was witnessed by the Catholic Bishop of Mysore in 1921 or 1922.[263] In this case, a Muslim man from northern India was working with a large number of individuals of different creeds. The Bishop wrote that 200 people crossed over the coals, half of whom walked through the middle of the flames. However, what makes this story different is what happened afterward. When the Maharajah stood up, indicating the end of things, the Mohammedan was said to have fallen down onto the ground, moving around as if in great pain. The Bishop was told that this was because he had taken onto himself the burning of the fire.

One can, of course, wonder whether the Muslim gentleman might have simply acted out a pretence of pain in order to justify a high fee for his service. However, it is also possible his beliefs played a role in this. If the man truly thought he should suffer, then he might have experienced his agony as a form of self-fulfilling prophecy. Most fire-walking ceremonies do not describe anyone taking on the pain of the participants.

Another question — of whether the fire was truly hot to begin with — was answered by what happened a fortnight later. In this case, after a number of fire-walkers had crossed unharmed, three people pushed their way in, despite having been told by the Muslim man not to try it. All three were badly burned and had to go to the hospital for treatment.[264] The Bishop who watched the event insisted that he had not hallucinated, but was in full possession of his senses during the entire ceremony. In addition, his account was essentially confirmed by four other witnesses.

Islamic Saints have also been reported to have fire-immunity.[265] For example, Al-shelbi was said to have thrown himself into a fire and remained unaffected.[266] Hasan of Basra (642–728 CE) was a Muslim of absolute piety who was said to have displayed a number of abilities (which he said came from God), including fire-immunity. In one case, he converted a fire-worshipper to Islam by holding his hand in a fire and remaining completely unharmed.[267] Even today, dervishes are reported to apply flaming torches to their face, arms, and legs for five to fifteen seconds at a time, as well as bite on, or hold in their bare hands, red-hot iron plates.[268]

Other cultures have their own ceremonies. The Navajo have one where men dance around a huge fire, and apply flaming wands to themselves and their comrades in front of them.[269] In Haiti, Voodoo rites are said to sometimes involve similar demonstrations where individuals place their hands or feet into fire yet remain unmarked. At other times, while in trance, the worshipers are said to be able to dance on the embers of a fire, and hold sizzling iron rods with their bare hands and be unharmed. In the fire ordeal of Guiana, male participants revel in the fire — bathing in flames as high as their waists, dancing in it, pressing blazing fragments of wood to their bodies, and chewing the red-hot embers. In this case, the virgin priestess in charge of the ceremony is felt to confer the fire-immunity on the participants. It is said that if she emerges from trance the dancers are no longer protected from the pain and burning. These priestesses are not taught, nor are their powers considered hereditary. Instead, the girl children are selected based on reports that their parents have seen them walking on, or playing with, embers on the cooking hearth.

Fire-Immunity has also been reported in Free Pentecostal Holiness Church members.[270] They are said to put flames to their chests, or slowly move the sides of their hands and little fingers to the midpoint tip of an acetylene flame for more than a few seconds, and to hold flaming coals in their hands for over a minute without harming their clothing or bodies.

In addition, there are cases of groups performing fire-walking for secular reasons with a fervor that is reminiscent of religion. Fire-walking was popular for awhile in the United States as a grand finale to motivational events.[271] It was generally done at the end of workshops or seminars on motivation or self-esteem, as a sign of the power that the mind has over the body.

A number of skeptics have been able to fire-walk successfully — which makes one wonder whether their skepticism might not itself be a form of religious fervor.[272] Immediately after the fire-walk these individuals have feet that are sometimes cool, and their leg hairs are typically unsinged.[273] Vincent Gaddis proposed that psychic energy creates a protective sheath around the body that insulates it from the heat. The limits of its protection might therefore be defined by the individual's belief system — which in some cases includes clothing.

Fire-Immunity sometimes appears spontaneously as an isolated ability that may, or may not, be associated with religiosity or an ASC. Nathan Coker was a blacksmith in the late 1800s who was said to be able to place a white-hot shovel on the soles of his feet until it had cooled to black again without being burned.[274] Coker could likewise hold glowing coals in his hands, and swill molten lead shot around in his mouth until it solidified. When asked about this, Coker said he from the time he was a young boy, he had held no fear of fire, and frequently took red-hot irons out of his forge using his hands without becoming burned.[275]

A New York physician described another case of isolated spontaneous fire-immunity in 1927.[276] The doctor was on a hunting trip in Tennessee when he came across a shy twelve-year-old boy who could hold burning brands taken from a fireplace without injury. The boy apparently discovered his ability by accident when he picked up a red-hot horseshoe in his uncle's blacksmith shop.

A similar immunity to fire seems to have existed for Lily White of Antigua, West Indies, in the early twentieth century. Her experiences almost sound the opposite of spontaneous human combustion (SHC). Lily's clothes would burst into flames while she was at home or in the streets, yet she was never harmed by the fires that burned around her.[277]

These last cases are interesting because this protection from fire seems to be a natural gift that spontaneously manifests, and does not involve any form of trance, such as is often described in the fire-immunity seen in physical mediums and religious figures. One has to wonder how much fire-immunity depends upon an ASC versus a person's system of beliefs, or other factors.

INCENDIUM AMORIS: INTERNAL FIRE-IMMUNITY

Incendium amoris is the reputed ability of individuals to generate and endure high body temperatures. The phenomenon appears to be primarily associated with religious individuals. It may be a form of fire-immunity, in that the body is apparently not only able to produce tremendous temperatures, but is also able to withstand them without permanent injury or brain damage. A number of Catholic figures, such as St. Catherine of Genoa (1447–1510), St. Stanislaus Kostka (1550–1568), St. Philip Neri (1515–1595), and Mary Magdalene de Pazzi (1566–1607), have been reputed to suffer from such "warmth of their love of God" that even in winter they asked for cold compresses.[278] In the last year of St. Catherine of Genoa's life, it is said that she lost a tremendous amount of blood that was extremely hot.[279] Not only was it said to have heated the vessels in which it was caught, but the blood also scalded her flesh wherever it touched it. If true, this sounds like far more than an ordinary fever.

In the eighteenth century, nuns are said to have watched as a ball of fire descended upon the prioress of the Carmelite convent, Ven. Rosa Maria Serio.[280] When they undressed Serio, they found her undergarments had a burn in the shape of a heart near her breast. If the fireball was a natural phenomenon — such as a plasma ball — then it is puzzling why the shape of the burn was not a simple circle or oval. The same burning, without the descent of a visible ball of fire, allegedly reoccurred six other years.

Ven. Orsola Benincasa, who founded an order of nuns, reputedly became very hot when in a state of spiritual emotion.[281] Some of those who had known her for 40 years later reported even when she placed her hands in the coldest water available, that sometimes steam would rise up, and the basin become uncomfortably hot. Although one might wonder whether Benincasa was simply suffering from severe hyperthyroidism, with an increased metabolic rate, it would not explain why she was also said to often gasp for breath while white smoke came out of her throat. Physicians do not see people breathe out smoke even with the highest of fevers, let alone those who merely have thyroid disease.

A number of those who have experienced incendium amoris have also been stigmatic.[282] Palma Matarrelli (1825–1888) was one such individual.[283] Dr. Inbert-Gourbeyre wrote an account of two episodes he had witnessed in 1871. His examination showed her skin had suffered the kind of injury that comes from contact with a boiling liquid (typically considered second-degree burns). Furthermore, he noted that linen placed on her chest over her heart during the events became marked with unusual patterns. Other witnesses also reported that cloths pressed to her breast were burnt away so as to leave clearly defined shapes, representing hearts, flames, and other pious symbols.

There are two potential problems with this evidence. First is the question whether Matarrelli could have secretly burned herself and then revealed the self-inflicted wounds later, after pretending to be on fire. Because of the modesty of the era, we have no reports of a continuous progression from unblemished skin to the appearance of burns appear without being touched by anything external. However, such trickery would not explain how Matarrelli could burn cloths placed on top of her body while under the watchful eye of observers. For that to be fraud, one would have to assume Matarrelli (or a co-conspirator) had prepared pre-marked linens that could be swapped out with those on her chest — which would rely on a fair bit of preparation, knowing what kind, size, and shape of cloth would be placed on her, *and* being able to both hide the pre-prepared object and distract her observers so as to make the switch. While not an impossible task, it does seem unlikely. Her colleagues of the time may have wanted to believe in her, but they were by no means fools.

The second question we must ask is whether the shapes created on fabric placed over her chest were truly meaningful, or simply the self-generated result of an early Rorschach test. The mind has long been known to have a tendency to create patterns where none exist. As we will later see with hemography, there is no easy way to know the answer to this question.

In addition to stigmata, teleportation, bilocation, and levitation, St. Pio was also said to occasionally run a fever with a temperature so high as to break a thermometer reaching 112°F.[284] This is remarkable. Although children can easily run fevers of 104°F, it is extremely rare to see an adult over 102°F, and over 106°F physicians become seriously concerned about the possibility of permanent brain damage.

Catholicism is not the only religion associated with incendium amoris. There are reports that the Muslim St. Sahl ibn Abd Allah al-Tostari (815–896 CE) went into states of ecstasy lasting for as long as five days, during which time he not only went without food, but also had sweat pour off of him, drenching his shirt even in winter.[285]

The question has to come up of whether the creation of a hypermetabolic rate, known as Tumo or Tum-mo (a Tibetan word for "inner fire"), might be related to incendium amoris.[286] Milarepa was said to have done this, in addition to his many other abilities. The technique allows yogis in India and Tibet to live practically naked in zero-degree temperatures. These individuals radiate so much heat that the snow melts around them. Its development is said to depend upon a combination of visualizing fire and using special breathing exercises while at high altitudes. Novices are trained by sitting naked under sheets soaked in ice water.[287]

There have only been a few published reports of investigations into Tumo. It is said that monks in the Himalayas can raise the temperatures of their fingers and toes by 17°F.[288] In February 1981, with the assistance of the Dalai Lama, Benson et al. studied three monks with a minimum of six years of daily Tumo practice.[289] They took readings for air temperature (which ranged from 16°C–23°C), humidity, heart rate, external skin temperature at multiple sites, and internal temperature using a rectal probe inserted 10 cm. As an aside, one would have to wonder whether the latter might not have been more than a little distracting for the monk when trying to concentrate. Nonetheless, their heart rates changed by only a few beats and their rectal temperatures were unchanged, while their fingers and toes increased in an average of 8.3°C. However, the lack of change in core body temperature suggests that this is a different process from incendium amoris.

This concludes our brief look at internal and external fire-immunity. External fire-immunity has been reported in a wide range of cultures, religions, and times. Emotions, beliefs, and ASC may all play some role in the phenomena. Although religious fervor is frequently associated with fire-immunity, it does not appear to be necessary to the experience. Even ordinary individuals, given a certain amount of fervor, can fire-walk. We will see more on this topic in Part II of this book, in the chapter on biological system research.

Luminosity

There are a great many tales of luminosity in religious figures, particularly in association with prayer or states of ecstasy. Whether as the cause or result, Patricia Treece noted, "In religious traditions of every type, light is intimately associated with the divinity, God or divine messengers often appearing as light alone."[290] Bodily luminosity has been reported across a wide swath of religions, sometimes as a halo of light, other times as light streaming from the face or body. Religions have different names for this phenomenon. For example, Treece observed that the Hindu term for luminosity related to spirituality is "Brahmic Splendor," while its equivalent in Judaism is "Meor Panim," which translates literally to "lighted face."[291] Regardless, all religions consider luminosity as being caused by, or a reflection of, an individual's purity of heart.[292]

Let us look at some such accounts. Christ was described as exhibiting luminosity in the Gospel of Matthew (17:1):

> Jesus chose Peter, James and his brother John to accompany him high up on the hill-
> side where they were quite alone. There his whole appearance changed before their
> eyes, his face shining like the sun and his clothes as white as light.

Since then, many others have been said to emit light when preaching, praying, or providing communion.[293] Catholic luminous figures have included St. Francis of Assisi, St. Phillip Neri, St. Charles Borromeo, St. Ignatius of Loyola, St. Francis de Sales, St. Bernardo Realino, St. Lydwina of Schiedam, St. Louis Bertrand, Blessed Leopold of Gaiche, St. Thomas of Cori, Blessed Giles of Assisi, Blessed Aleidis of Scarbeke, Ven. Vincent Morelli (Archbishop of Otranto),

Father Francisco Suarez, and John Tornerius. Muslim saints and mystics said to radiate light include Yusof-e Hossain and Najmoddin Kobra,[294] while Hindu ones include Sathya Sai Baba, Ramana Maharshi, and Lahiri Mahasaya (1828–1895).[295]

Many of better cases involved private situations, where individuals were discovered deep in prayer in their rooms, or while they thought themselves alone in a chapel. As mentioned earlier, St. Bernardino Realino (1515–1616) was caught by Tobias da Ponte levitating in his cell.[296] Tobias had gone to the monastery for advice and was waiting by Realino's room, when he saw a bright light streaming out from the edges of the door. Concerned, Tobias peeked inside. He found Bernardino floating in a kneeling position, deep in prayer, radiating light. Other witnesses also claimed to have seen the Saint's face radiant in other times of prayer.

St. Lydwina of Schiedam (1380–1433) was born in Holland, the only daughter among nine children.[297] A fall on the ice led to her becoming an eventual invalid, with nearly complete paralysis for 17 years. St. Lydwina was said to suffer from invisible stigmata, have a sweet fragrance, and be inedic. Moreover, it was noted that although she always lay in darkness, her cell would often appear to be flooded by light.[298] At times she was surrounded by such brightness that her companions were said to have been afraid to come near her.[299] In fact, it was said that her cell was frequently illuminated to such a degree at night that it looked as if it was full of lamps and fires. Although the Saint was reportedly unable to tolerate natural light—finding it unbearable to her eyes—she showed no discomfort from this spiritual radiance. St. Lydwina was unusual in that her luminance was a regular occurrence, witnessed by a number of individuals, and recorded in some detail by one of her contemporaries, Thomas à Kempis.

A more detailed, first-hand account of the phenomenon comes from a Franciscan who observed Blessed Leopold of Gaiche (1732–1815) in prayer.[300] The monk hid in a church confessional to watch after being told by a lay brother of the radiance seen around Leopold during prayer at night. An hour after arriving, he watched in secrecy as Leopold entered the church and knelt down to pray. Another hour passed before, arms outstretched and absorbed in prayer, Gaiche became radiant with a light that filled the entire church. The luminance was described to be like that of a full moon. The monk was certain this light could not have come from the normal source in the Sanctuary, which was already present and not nearly as bright. The glow lasted for about thirty minutes, during which Gaiche was overheard to say, "Heaven, heaven, how beautiful you are" two or three times.[301] The light then faded away.

St. Frances Cabrini (1850–1917) was born premature, the youngest of thirteen children.[302] She is known for founding the first missionary order for women. However, before St. Cabrini's travels took her to the United States, Sister Cairo was, for a short while, her roommate.[303] The nun woke from sleep in the middle of the night to discover the saint in prayer and their chamber (which had no lamps) filled with light. When she asked St. Cabrini about it in awe, Sister Cairo was told it was nothing and to go back to sleep. However, from then on the saint always slept alone.

The Muslim religion has its luminous saints. Islamic saint Rabe'a al-Adawiya was said to have performed a number of miracles.[304] In one incident, he was visited at night by Hasan and two or three friends who wished for light. The saint blew on his finger, which then was said to have glowed as brightly as a lantern until dawn.

Abu'-Hosaine-e-Nuri (also called Nuri) is a Sufi even better known for his luminosity.[305] There are three stories of how he got his nickname as the "Man of Light." Some say it was because he "declared inmost secrets by the light of intuition."[306] However, others claimed that if it was a dark night, that when Nuri spoke, light could be seen coming from his mouth. Yet a third contingent point to times when he would worship all night at a desert retreat. People who went out to see him reported that they observed a light coming from his cell, which shone through the night.

Although there are numerous tales of body luminosity, it has not been well studied. This is a shame, since, as Patricia Treece pointed out, this kind of visual effect (which is not as uncommon as some we have discussed) seems like the perfect subject to capture on camera.[307] Unfortunately, it often involves enraptured saints and mystics in the midst of private prayer. Such events seldom take place where there are many — if any — to witness them. Furthermore, given the ease with which video and images can be altered today, it would never be considered proof.

Treece stated that she witnessed luminosity when, at a lecture by Father Ralph Tichenor (1907–1983), she saw him "suffused by a yellowish-white light which streamed out."[308] This experience made it easier for her to accept this phenomenon as genuine. The author of this book has to agree, having once been quite startled to see a Franciscan priest standing in a darkened hallway, surrounded by a radiant light so bright that it was hard to look at him. The light lasted for several seconds before it disappeared. It was unclear whether he had been pulled from prayer to answer the door. However, it would not be surprising if that was so.

Luminosity may not be limited to religious figures. Rogo stated that D. D. Home was often said to "glow" during his levitations.[309] One of the modern cases involved Signora Anna Monaro, an Italian woman who caught the attention of the press in 1934.[310] She was an asthmatic hospitalized after fasting for Lent. Several times a night, while she slept, a flickering bluish glow was said to emanate from her breasts, which remained visible for several seconds. According to news reports, her breathing and heartbeat increased to a rapid rate during these periods, and she perspired heavily, suggesting the possibility of an increased metabolic rate and cardiovascular strain. One of the things that made this investigation remarkable was that film was used to document the events. The phenomenon continued for weeks, and was observed by a number of physicians, scientists, and government officials before it stopped.

There was a lot of theorizing about electrical and magnetic organisms and radiation from chemical compounds — even the idea that excess sulfides were produced by the fasting (since sulfides become luminous when excited by ultra-violet radiation) — but no one really knew why the glow occurred or what created the effect.[311] Vincent Gaddis felt her bluish glow was not a hallucination because the radiant power of her blood was found to be three times the normal amount. However, it is curious that the light from her chest was said not to cast a shadow.[312]

Over the years, there have been a number of explanations proposed for why some individuals might appear to be luminous, none of which appear to be fully satisfactory. For example, Gaddis put forth that bioluminescence might be due to the natural body chemical of ATP (adenosine 5'-triphosphate).[313] This is a co-enzyme that acts as an important energy compound in metabolism. Gaddis based his hypothesis on two facts. First, ATP is normally used by the muscles in the body during contraction. Second, Firefly ATP converts chemical energy into light. However, it is difficult to see how this could possibly explain the luminance seen in Monaro, since in women the breasts do not have significant muscle and consist primarily of adipose tissue (fat).

If luminosity was purely a physical effect, one would think that most, if not all, of the bystanders would be able to see the phenomena. However, this does not appear to be the case. If there is a group of witnesses, some will see the light while others will not.[314] Nor may this be entirely due to cognitive dissonance — the literal inability of people to see that which does not fit their worldview. Treece stated that there is no correlation between the sighting and whether or not the onlooker is spiritual or believes in the phenomenon.

Skeptic Joe Nickell had a different take.[315] He speculated that some people may be confusing radiance with seeing an aura. However, Nickell added that since auras have been shown not to exist, neither does luminosity. This is an interestingly circular argument. It is unclear whether

Nickell is implying witnesses are imagining the event, actively hallucinating, or are using ESP to "see" something that has no real physical existence.

At present, the origin of body luminosity remains one of life's mysteries. However, it is possible that the recent advances in technology, which now allow us to measure what appears to be a bio-energy field around the body, may yet led to an understanding of the phenomenon.

Materialization/Transformation of Matter

Materialization is a difficult topic. There no way to judge from anecdotal stories or field research precisely what is occurring. Is it the transformation of energy/matter from one type to another? Or truly something coming from nothing? Or a shift in dimensions or time? We do not know. Because of this, materialization and transformation will be discussed together, even though they may be different phenomena.

The multiplication of food is probably the most frequent feat of materialization/matter transformation spoken of in the religious and spiritual literature. Every great religion has its stories of this. Nor is this feat an isolated one, but rather seems to be associated with a host of other abilities. Catholics said to have multiplied food include St. Teresa of Avila, St. Rose of Lima, St. Clare of Assisi, St. Pius V, St. Bosco, St. Vianney, and Ven. Angiolo Paoli.[316] Let us look at some examples.

TRANSFORMATION OF MATTER

In some instances, the process is clearly one of the transformation of one form of matter to another. For example, while attending a wedding at a town in Galilee, Jesus is said to have somewhat reluctantly transformed six large stone jars of water into wine (John 2:1–11).

St. Bruno (1030–1101), who founded the Carthusian Order, is said to have transformed poultry into tortoises.[317] The situation arose because monks were forbidden to eat fowl on Fridays. One such Friday, the saint arrived at a monastery to find the monks sitting, unable to eat, before plates of poultry. St. Bruno sat down, made the sign of the cross over the food, and transformed the meals into that of tortoises, which they then consumed.

Sathya Sai Baba is said to transform matter, such as sand, into statues or jewelry.[318] According to Erlendur Haraldsson, this is the most common paranormal feat attributed to Baba. He stated, "They happened many times each day, frequently arising spontaneously out of a particular situation."[319] Baba has people pile up sand in front of him until it is a foot high. Then, he levels the top off with his hand and draws on the sand. When he has finished his design, he reaches into the pile and pulls out an object. In one case, this item was an eighteen-inch-high, polished gold statue.

There are likewise tales told in India of fakirs able to transmute copper into silver, or bronze into gold.[320] However, many of these so-called miracle workers later proved to be false.

MULTIPLICATION OF MATTER

The multiplication of one type of matter, whether it be food, oil, or wine, is a commonly attributed feat in the religious literature. One of the earlier recorded stories of this appears in the fourth Book of Kings of the Old Testament of the Bible. It tells of a poor widow who came to Elisha for help.[321] She had no money to pay her debts, and a creditor was threatening to take her two sons as bondmen.[322] Taking pity on her, Elisha asked what she had in the house, and was told only a pot of oil. He then instructed her to gather as many containers as she could from her neighbors, and to pour her oil out into them. To her surprise, not only was she able to fill all of the vessels, but her pot remained full. She returned to Elisha to let him know what had happened, and he told her to sell the oil. It gave her enough to settle her debts and have money left over on which she could live.

The miraculous multiplication of one night's oil supply into eight in 165 BCE is the basis for the Jewish holiday of Hanukkah.[323] A force led by Judah Maccabee managed to take back the Jewish Temple in battle from the Greeks. However, because it had been defiled, they needed to rededicate it. Unfortunately this required a specially prepared oil for the Menorah used in the Temple service. They only found one small jar of oil with the seal of the High Priest. It was enough for one single night — not the eight required. According to the Babylonian Talmud Tractate Shabbath (folio 21b), "yet a miracle was wrought therein and they lit [the lamp] therewith for eight days."[324]

Four gospels of the New Testament — Matthew (14:15–21), Mark (6:38–44), Luke (9:13–17) and John (6:1–14) — tell the story of Jesus multiplying five small loaves of barley and two fish to feed a tired and hungry crowd of 5,000 — and that is of men, not counting women and children. Jesus is said to have given thanks to God, then broken the bread into pieces and given them to his disciples to hand out to the crowd. After everyone had eaten and was satisfied, it was said they were able to collect twelve baskets full of leftovers.

Ven. Angiolo Paoli (1642–1720) was said to have multiplied food on several occasions, once satisfying fifty to sixty beggars with scraps of bread said to have been barely enough for seven or eight people.[325] This feat was witnessed by a number of individuals, including Father Maggini, who swore that Paoli never stopped to get more scraps. Other times, Ven. Paoli was said to have multiplied wine, such that no matter how many people drank from it, a half flask always remained. There are still further stories of him dividing some delicacy or fruit into portions that were then given out to three or four times as many people, every one of whom received a full serving.

St. Jean Baptiste Vianney (1786–1859), who was the Curé of Ars, was another said to multiply food.[326] Born the son of a shepherd in France, he spent time in the army before turning to the priesthood. One day, at the site of the orphanage he had founded, it was discovered that there was not enough wheat to make bread. St. Vianney went to the granary, and placed a religious relic with the small amount of grain that remained. He then prayed. The next day, it is said that they found the granary completely full, to the point that some feared the weight would be too much for its old wooden floor. Although one might wonder whether an unknown benefactor deposited the wheat during the night, there is another incident where the Saint was again associated with the multiplication of food. In this case, there was only enough flour for baking three loaves of bread, when ten were needed. St. Vianney instructed the cook to pray, then go ahead and bake the bread. To the woman's astonishment, she came out with ten large loaves of bread, each said to weigh 20 to 22 pounds.

In 1860, St. John Bosco supposedly multiplied the 15 or 20 rolls that were in his basket to feed 300 boys.[327] A witness to the event claimed that the same quantity remained in the basket from the first of the distribution to the end, although no other rolls had been brought and the basket had not been changed.

There is also the story of a Muslim man, Hasan Khan, who lived in the Calcutta region of India around the 1870s. Khan was said to have been gifted with special powers — including the ability to manifest or teleport food and bottles of wine — by a Hindu saint.[328] He did not perform in public, but was said to have sometimes demonstrated his talent in front of small groups of witnesses, including some who were European. Khan would accept requests for specific things, which, after reaching behind a door or under a table to retrieve the item, he then presented to the supplicant. He never took any payment for these performances. Simple trickery is the easiest explanation for this, given that Khan usually reached out of sight to acquire the article. However, in one instance, the Muslim was not the person to retrieve the object. John Campbell Oman relates an instance where a friend of his was traveling by train with Khan and asked him to manifest something for them to drink.

The saint told him to reach out the window, at which point, he said "a bottle of excellent wine thrust into the outstretched hand."[329] This story is even more interesting because not only was the item received by someone other than Khan, but because it was in response to a spontaneous request while the train was moving.

In the early 1930s, a dentist, Phillip S. Haley, who was then the president of the California Psychical Research Society in San Francisco, decided to perform an investigation on the multiplication of food.[330] Haley, who had a history of being able to perform psychic feats, used himself as a research subject. He found that he was able to multiply food on a consistent, repeatable basis. Moreover, these séances were not private affairs but witnessed by anywhere from 75 to 100 people. In his analysis of this series of studies, Scott Rogo noted that Haley appeared to be sincere. He never gave lectures on the topic or made money off of his research.[331] Even though Haley did not publish his research in the parapsychological literature, the meticulous care with which he performed and recorded his studies make it deserving of consideration as formal research in Part II of this book.

Hemography

Hemography is the paranormal patterning of bloodstains on cloth.[332] It appears to be a rare phenomenon, which is sometimes associated with stigmata. The aforementioned Palma Matarrelli, who also suffered from stigmata and incendium amoris, was said to have this ability. In 1872 a witness wrote to the Abbé Curicque that on his first two visits to Matarrelli, her forehead was clear.[333] Later, he watched four slow streams of blood, each the width of a little finger, ooze from puncture wounds in the middle of her forehead. This blood wet her face and hands. When she took a cloth to wipe it off, stains were created that looked like the clear outlines of hearts, nails, and swords.

One of the problems with hemography is that it is possible that the beholder is simply imagining patterns where they do not truly exist — somewhat like a Rorschach test. However, there may be more to this than simply a projected interpretation of an abstract design. Hebert Thurston, who comes across as being far from credulous, witnessed this phenomenon first-hand.[334] Although he had the opportunity to know four stigmatics, it was Matarrelli who impressed him most. In 1871, he was able to observe her for a few days. During this time, he held a handkerchief under the blood that trickled down her forehead's stigmatic puncture wounds, and watched as it formed patterns. His written description sounds as if the patterns were created *after* the blood had been absorbed by the cloth. Matarrelli was not without her detractors. There were some who felt her patronizing tone and thinly veiled desire to display her abilities indicated that she was not a sanctified person, and may have been performing fraud and/or MMI that did not come from God.

Natuzza Evolo is a more recent example of an individual said to perform hemography.[335] Born in 1924, she was said to have a number of unusual powers, including the ability to bilocate, see spirits of the dead, and diagnose illnesses. Evolo was a devoted Catholic with stigmata that appeared as cross-shaped indentations on her wrists and feet. According to Marinelli, a professor of Engineering at the University of Calabria, if Evolo's wounds were wiped with a cloth, the bloodstains would rearrange themselves into patterns, forming religious emblems, letters, and figures. The fact she was illiterate makes the intelligent formation of words and letters in blood even more surprising. In nine of her purported bilocations, Evolo was purported to have left bloodstains at the scene, and in at least one of these incidents, her figure was seen by a priest to whom she passed on a message.

Although hemography has been documented most often in Christian devotees (perhaps in part because a large portion of Muslim lore has not been translated out of Arabic and Farsi), it is possible that this phenomenon may have occurred in the earlier mentioned Sufi, Abu'-Hosaine-e-Nuri.[336] Attar wrote that during a mystic state, "The reeds pierced his feet and sides, and the blood gushed forth. Every drop that fell, the words, 'God, God' appeared."[337] Similarly, during the execution of Al-Hallaj it was said that, "every drop of blood as it trickled formed the word Allah."[338]

There are a number of unanswered questions about this phenomena. Assuming that fraud is not involved, there remains the issue of whether the so-called blood patterns result from passive diffusion, or whether the blood actively moves on its own after being absorbed by the cloth. Certainly Herbert Thurston's description suggests that the latter may be true. However, an even greater question is whether the patterns traced out in hemography are meaningful or not. This is the same problem that arose earlier, in talking about shapes burned onto cloth during incendium amoris. The mind is very good at finding patterns and seeing meaning where none exists. Indeed, that is why the ink blots in a Rorschach test work. One has to wonder whether the emblems said to be formed in hemography are random stains, their meaningfulness falsely attributed, existing only in the eye of the beholder.

Perhaps the only way to solve this question would be to do an experiment with a randomly chosen target shape, picked from a list of various designs that are not likely to naturally occur. The stigmatic could be asked to create the pattern selected on a clean, unmarked piece of cloth. An independent, blind panel of judges could then be asked to determine which pattern, if any, had been formed. Such a study, especially if combined with raw video footage of the phenomenon from start to finish, could provide valuable insight into this phenomenon. Unfortunately, these individuals would probably refuse, saying they have no control over the images, which, at least in their minds, come from God.

Deliberately Caused Bodily Damage Phenomenon

Deliberately Caused Bodily Damage (DCBD) phenomenon is a form of intentional MMI, where deliberate harm is caused to the body, often involving piercing or swallowing of sharp objects.[339] It is usually seen in association with religious fervor. DCBD may involve lack of pain, as well as control over bleeding, infection, and wound healing. In fact, the lack of a normal response to the damage, such as bleeding, and sometimes near-instantaneous healing when skewers are removed, means that the paranormal aspect of the feat may be the wounding itself.

What makes DCBD different from self-mutilation is that its purpose is not to damage the body but to demonstrate the celebrant's capacity to resist damage.[340] These feats have been reported in a variety of religious settings, from the Sun Dance of some North American Indian tribes, to the self-beating with swords in India, to the body piercing by Hindu devotees in Malaysia, to the rituals of dervishes by followers of Sufism in the Islamic world. Sometimes the phenomenon is associated with chanting, drumbeats, and dancing, which might induce an ASC, but this does not always appear to be necessary.[341]

In some cases of DCBD there appears to be accelerated, or even instantaneous, healing.[342] Idries Shah wrote:

> Professor Seligman was surprised to find that incisions made by certain dervishes in the flesh stopped bleeding with inexplicable rapidity. Other observers have noted that Rifai dervishes could cause wounds which seemed to heal without any scar, and with absurd rapidity. Until Dr. Hunt in 1931 showed a film of Indian Rifais performing these practices, the ordinary reaction had been to discount the whole thing, or else to attribute it to hypnotism.[343]

Larry Dossey noted that reports of DCBD in the Eastern world have circulated for centuries.[344] Even today, there are a variety of Sufi groups that perform these feats. Some of the better studied practitioners come from the Middle Eastern Sufi Tariga school.[345] This school is known as Casnazaniyyah, which translates from Arabic-Kurdish to "the way of the secret that is known to no one." According to the Casnazaniyyah, these abilities are not limited to a select few who have spent years training for it, but can be performed by anyone. However, the ability to heal rapidly in DCBD is said to be based on the spiritual link between the school's leader (known as the Shaikh) and the individual self-inflicting the wound. Furthermore, the abilities of the Shaikh are said to stem from his access to the "hidden powers" of the prophet Muhammad. The Shaikh must give his permission for the DCBD demonstration to occur.

The initiation ritual for devotees about to perform DCBD may vary anywhere from two minutes in the Califas dervish group to a month in some Thaipusam festivals.[346] Moreover, it may not be the healing that is paranormal, but the deliberateness in inflicting the injury. Dervishes who are wounded in a sudden accident go through the normal sequence of pain, bleeding, infection risk, and speed of healing.

As mentioned earlier, this phenomenon is by no means limited to Islam. The Dutchman Arnold Gerrit Johannes Henskes (1912–1948), who was sometimes called "Mirin Dajo," was also known for his self-piercings.[347] He believed himself to be a gifted clairvoyant and an anomalous healer who could not be killed by instruments in his body, which later turned out to be untrue. Henskes had his assistant, Johann de Groot, drive round stainless steel instruments slowly through his arms, legs, and chest until they emerged on the other side of his body. Sometimes these items were hollow, allowing water to be poured through them.

Henskes gave public demonstrations and was said to have also eagerly participated in formal investigations.[348] His DCDB performances came to an end, however, after he swallowed a stiletto, which had to be removed by surgery. He died two weeks later from complications resulting from having perforated his esophagus. On autopsy, there were many scars on his skin, liver, kidneys, diaphragm, and spleen, along with a single scar at the tip of his heart, but apparently no signs of prior injury to his stomach, intestines, or head. Peter Mulacz did not feel anything paranormal need have been involved. He wrote off Henskes' absence of pain during these events as due to the variability of pain thresholds from one person to the next, and the fact that internal organs tend to have limited sensitivity to piercing. Mulacz attributed the apparent lack of severe bleeding (internal or external) and infection as the natural result a slow rate of insertion, which he felt would "dilate" tissue or push it aside instead of perforating it — which would also explain the lack of scars to Henskes' gastrointestinal tract. However, it is surprising that Henskes never developed cardiac tamponade or mediastinitis after inserting instruments into his chest, especially as his heart had a scar on it, proving that at some point it had been pierced.

Jamal Hussein has witnessed hundreds of demonstrations of DCBD and performed the phenomenon himself in front of critical observers, making the reality of this phenomenon beyond question to him.[349] That these wounds heal without infection is even more remarkable given that Hussein noted:

> One such bizarre finding is that no matter how polluted are the instruments used in DCBD, the dervish would by no means be in danger of getting contaminated, even though the instrument he would make use of was deliberately polluted with HIV positive blood.[350]

Many researchers assume an ASC is involved that allows DCBD practitioners to self-heal, perhaps through autohypnosis. However, as Hussein and others who have researched this phenomenon have noted, both ASCs and hypnosis are poorly understood, and would not seem to account for the magnitude of the effect noted. It is also difficult to differentiate whether DCBD involves self-healing, or other-healing by the "experts" who perform the piercing.

DCBD is a repeatable, reproducible, and frequently reported event among Sufi schools in the

Middle East.[351] Unlike luminosity, which tends to occur in private prayer, DCBD is performed fairly openly in group situations. Because of this, there are numerous color photographs and video footage available of the phenomenon. It is therefore somewhat curious that DCBD it has not been better studied. Hussein and others proposed some years ago that this may be at least partly due to a cultural bias against self-mutilation. Furthermore, this bias may have entered into various interpretations of the phenomenon, limiting interest in its research. Fortunately, recent years have seen an increased number of investigators turn their attention on this interesting phenomenon. Their research will be covered under the DCBD subsection in "Biological System Research" in Part II of this book.

Weather MMI

Weather control is the purported paranormal ability to change the weather, usually rain and/or wind. A number of saints and religious figures have been said to do this.[352] For example, Jesus was said to have stilled a tempest on the Sea of Galilee, Moses to part the Red Sea, St. Joan of Arc (1412–1431) to change the direction of the wind through prayer so her troops could obtain provisions, and St. Pio to control a local rainstorm. Scott Rogo observed that although many saints have been apparently endowed with the ability to change the weather, it is seldom mentioned by writers or biographers. It is unclear as to why this gets omitted.

Weather control is not limited to any one religion. The story is told of an eighth-century Muslim Saint, Ebrahim ibn Adham, who was on a ship when the sky grew dark and the wind began to blow.[353] Another man, named Raja, cried out that he feared the ship would sink. However, a voice which was said to have come from the air reassured Raja that all would be well because Ebrahim was there. Immediately afterward, the wind died down and sky grew light again.

Buddhism has its share of stories about being able to influence the elements. Milarepa was said to have used his abilities (before enlightenment) for harm as well as good, wielding hailstorms as a weapon.[354] The monks Fo-t'u-teng and Srimitra were popular for their apparent abilities to produce rain in medieval China.[355] Even in contemporary times, an elderly lama was called upon to clear away a storm from an area of a celebratory gathering.[356] Dr. Barker noted that for the six hours of the ceremony there was rain and hail all around the field, but the storm never interfered with the site of the ceremony itself.

Weather control is also an important part of many religious rituals around the world.[357] African shamans, known as *tengsobadamba* (*Tengsoba* is a Mossi word that means master of the earth), are believed to be capable of controlling rain and lightning. It is thought that they teleport these phenomena, or the growing crops themselves, from one region to another.

Native Americans have their own ceremonies for rain. Diana Robinson reported that a group of Indians in Colorado was hired to perform a snow dance, and got four inches of snow afterward.[358] The Hopi also have a rain dance, which involves a group ritual on top of a mesa. This ceremony includes the use of sympathetic magic, where rattlesnakes, as representatives of thunder, are carried by mouth and herded in a circle by sticks held by costumed dancers.[359] The dance itself is performed in a large clearing in the center of the town in front of the entire community — many of whom watch from the tops of their adobe homes. Thus, it may tap into the group MMI of the bystanders.

Ted Owens (1920–1987) purportedly had considerable ability at manipulating weather. It was said he was particularly adept at controlling where lightning struck, producing violent and atypical weather and creating power blackouts.[360] His MMI demonstrations typically included a 90-day range for when events would occur, and his descriptions of what to expect were sometimes vague, making it difficult to assess the meaningfulness of his results. Owens was also said to be able to produce UFO appearances and believed that what happened was the work of "Space Intelligences."

Parapsychologist Jeffrey Mishlove reported that Owens' gift began in childhood with spontaneous levitation.[361] He worked for awhile at the Duke parapsychology laboratory with J.B. Rhine, but although it was noted odd things happened around Owens, he did not have his abilities documented. Mishlove attempted a variety of uncontrolled experiments with Owens, requesting that unusual events occur within a given time period at a given locations. Mishlove felt that unusual events occurred more often than could be explained by chance — although whether it was always weather MMI or a combination of MMI and surprisingly accurate premonitions is impossible to judge. Mishlove noted that Owen had about an 80 percent accuracy rate.

Although some may wonder at the effectiveness of weather MMI, the author was fortunate enough to attend a Hopi rain dance in 1979, before they become closed to outsiders. Clouds gradually appeared in the clear blue sky during the event. It rained just as the ceremony ended, making for an impressive finish.

Physical Mediums

Mediumship is the purported ability to receive communications from the spirit realm.[362] Mediums fall into one of two categories, either as physical mediums, who are said to produce paranormal events, or as mental mediums or "channels," who merely obtain information. Channeling differs from telepathy in that the medium is said to receive information from a mental source that is not from an incarnate person or his own conscious/unconscious mind. Because channeling is an ESP phenomenon, it will not be discussed further here. For detailed information on the subject, the reader is encouraged to turn to Jon Klimo's book, *Channeling: Investigations on Receiving Information from Paranormal Sources.*

Physical mediumship came into popular vogue in the 1850s with the birth of Spiritualism.[363] For a time it was widespread in the United States and Europe. There is a great deal of overlap between Spiritualism and religious and spiritual MMI. Indeed, the spiritualist movement started as a quasi-religion. However, because physical mediumship became a profession, it cannot be considered purely religious.

This chapter will look at the history of mediumship, including some of the more prominent Spiritualist mediums, with a focus on those events that seem to involve the use of MMI on the part of the medium, the sitters, and/or channeled entities. The experimental research performed with physical mediums will be covered separately, in Part II of this book.

HISTORY OF MEDIUMSHIP

Historical accounts of mediumship often start with the Fox sisters. However, this ignores the fact that mediumship existed since the dawn of time, often under the guise of divination or as an integral part of religious observances.[364] Indeed, it has been an uninterrupted part of the popular culture in many parts of the world, including Asia, India, and Tibet, for thousands of years.

The historical course of mediumship in Asia was different than that of Western Europe, because the latter did not integrate mediumship into its mainstream culture in the same way as Asia did. In pre–Buddhist Japan, the mediums were usually women.[365] Violent dancing was sometimes used to help them enter a trance state. Once in an ASC, their personalities would be displaced to allow a spiritual being to "possess" them and speak through their mouths. After Buddhism was introduced in Japan, the monks took on the role of summoning the deity by spells, questioning it, and dispatching it afterwards, while the medium (usually female) played a passive role as the vehicle. This oracle tradition has survived into contemporary times, and still relies on banging drums and chanting for the induction of trance. It is sometimes seen at Japanese village festivals and on a particular holy mountain where certain deities are thought to live.

Mediumship initially flourished in Greece.[366] Dodona was one of the earlier prophetic centers. Excavations show that it dates back to the eighth century. Oaks were felt to belong to Zeus. The tree itself, often mediated through interpreters known as *hupophetai*, was regarded as being able to answer questions. Likewise, a piece of the oak from Dodona was built into the stem-post of the Argo and said to "speak." Writers are vague about how the "talking trees" at the Oracle of Dodona in Greece gave their messages. There are several possibilities. Messages could have been spoken by interpreters, mediumistic voice phenomena (*see* Glossary), bird sounds, the noises of pieces of metal hung from trees, the rustling of leaves, or something else. One hint as to what may have been occurring comes to us from Aeschylus, who refers to the "unbelievable miracle, talking oaks, by which clearly and with no riddles you were addressed."[367] This sounds rather as if it could have been either trickery or a direct voice phenomenon.

The Greek oracle of Delphi was also famous for divination and divine utterance.[368] They used trained priestesses past childbearing age, known as Pythia. Depending on the fee paid, the Pythia would either enter a trance and channel a message, or pick either a black or a white bean from a dish for "yes" or "no." The Greeks and Romans of the late fourth century were convinced that the priestess' possession was due to vapors rising from a fissure in the rock. However, geologists have stated that the limestone there could not have produced such gases, nor has such a cleft been found.

Private magical rites became forbidden after Christianity gained supremacy in Europe, with only public augury permitted.[369] In 500 CE, all sorcerers were driven from Rome as pagans — an offence punishable by death. This probably related to the Church's desire for an undisputed power base. Supernatural events were considered to have only one of two possible causes — either from God or the Devil. Most reports of these events appear in either testimonies for sainthood or the trials of sorcerers. It is no wonder, then, that mediums hid their talent. Mediumship went underground.

Meanwhile, medieval Asia abounded with reports of apparitions, precognitive dreams, OBEs, contacts with the dead, poltergeist-type raps and object movement, and reincarnation memories, all revealing elements identical to those of modern experiences.[370] There are 40–60 accounts of the extraordinary from the Six Dynasties and the T'ang eras alone. Biographies of *fang-shih* (Chinese magicians) during the later Han Dynasty, indicated that they could vanish into thin air or ascend into the heavens, summon ghosts, divine the future, perform miraculous healing, pull objects from empty basins, guess the names of hidden objects, and supply wine to hundreds from a single cup. The Japanese likewise had stories during this period of apparitions, precognitive dreams, miracle cures, visions during meditation, near death experiences (NDEs), and contacts with the dead. Nor should it be assumed that these stories were accepted without scrutiny. As McClenon dryly pointed out, "All complex societies have individuals who, like the hunter, cannot resist shooting, either figuratively or literally, at apparitional images and the beliefs associated with them."[371]

The Asian concept of the occult was that atypical effects were produced by ancestors, ghosts, and other spiritual forces — if sometimes through sorcery.[372] These phenomena were felt to be part of the natural order, which differed from the medieval European belief that ghosts may exist, but God is responsible for any miraculous events that reward the faithful or punish the faithless. In this way, the Asians were closer to the Spiritualist belief system that the spirits were entirely responsible for paranormal events.

In 1233, the suppression of anything that looked like a supernatural ability reached new heights in Europe with the institution of the Inquisition by Pope Gregory IX.[373] The Inquisitors' initial mandate was to suppress heresy, but they were given the power to confiscate the lands and wealth of all who were convicted. In 1320, Pope John XXII expanded the role of the Inquisition by instructing the Inquisitors to also deal with witchcraft if it was connected with heresy.

By 1375, the Holy Office of the Inquisition had been so successful that they all but worked themselves out of a job.[374] Most of the true heretics were eliminated, and the fountain of confiscated lands and goods was drying up. The Inquisitors solved this problem by transferring their attention to sorcery. They claimed that all witchcraft was heretical because it involved associating with the Devil. The result was to effectively limit mediumship in Europe to a small, sanctioned group of individuals whose lives were clearly dedicated to, and controlled by, the Church.[375] However, even they were closely scrutinized for any taint of heresy.

Witchcraft hysteria has been linked to a number of factors including socially unsettled times and the outbreaks of plagues, such as the Black Death, which broke out in the Gobi Desert in the 1320s, and hit Asia hard before decimating much of fourteenth-century England.[376] Regardless of the socioeconomic factors that fed the fear and hatred of witches, there were undoubtedly many people who suffered — whether talented with psi or otherwise.

Witch hunting reached a peak in the sixteenth and seventeenth centuries.[377] Feeding the flames of witch hunts in both Europe and the United States at this time was the fact that the Protestants had recognized the benefits of using accusations of witchcraft to eliminate rivals and confiscate goods. Nothing makes this more clear than the fact that when an Imperial edict in Germany forbade confiscating the property of condemned witches, the accusations dropped from an average of one hundred a year to zero.

Meanwhile, Asia remained relatively immune. Divination and mediumship were an accepted part of the culture and psi experiences continued to be reported without interruption.[378] A Korean collection of ghost stories, NDEs, ESP experiences, visions, and performances by psychic practitioners was gathered in the 1600s, while their counterparts in Europe were mostly limited to tales of poltergeists and apparitions.

Physical mediumship got a fresh start in Europe and the United States, with the advent of the Fox sisters' rappings in New York in 1848.[379] In an era when there was little entertainment available, America was ripe for the excitement of the séance circles and the fun of talking to the departed.[380] Before long, the vogue spread to Europe.

John Beloff noted that Spiritualism was important for two reasons.[381] First, it revived the question of whether life exists after death in an empirically testable form. Second, it was the source of a steady stream of puzzling phenomena, much of it of a physical nature, which cried out for investigation. Indeed, as Fraser Nicol pointed out, this popularization of psychic activities, along with the ready availability for mediums to study, is what gave impetus to the birth of parapsychological research.[382]

The phenomena that were reported in the séance parlors covered a wide range of spontaneous and intentional MMI activity. Spiritualism was more of a movement than a religion, and was based on evidence (even if questionable) rather than on revelation or faith.[383] Like their counterparts in Asia, Spiritualist mediums attributed any physical phenomena to discarnate spirits, rather than recognizing that they might be the ones responsible.[384] Indeed, physical mediums often claimed to have "control" personalities with whom they worked.[385] These were thought to be the spirits of deceased individuals who operated through the medium's body.

Spiritualist mediums were said to be able to perform a host of feats: pass on messages from the dead; levitate people and objects; teleport and/or materialize objects, bodies, or body parts; create raps; manifest lights; change the weights of objects play musical instruments without touching them; elongate their bodies; and demonstrate fire-immunity.[386] Mediums were also sometimes able to apport objects, where a target object, could appear to be transported through matter by paranormal means out of a closed space, such as a locked box or safe.[387]

"Direct voice" was another phenomenon sometimes reported with physical mediums. This was where no form materialized, but an unknown voice was heard, which was felt to derive from the condensing or focusing of the entity's energies.[388] Spiritualists sometimes used a metal trumpet as a physical aid for this, which, according to Klimo, would "often float about the darkened room with the voice emanating from it."[389] For this to be MMI, one would have to rule out both fraud and telepathy.

In some cases physical mediums appeared to be able to pass on their abilities, such as fire-immunity, to others.[390] In 1917, entranced medium Annie Hunter was said to lift a red-hot log out of the fireplace and carry it about the room while talking excitedly in a foreign language. A reporter who was present backed away after his hair was scorched. However, the medium gave the log to Mrs. Crespigny, who held it across her arms for some seconds without harm. Mrs. Hunter explained later that she had been under the control of a Persian fire-worshipper. This transference of fire-immunity was also reported with D. D. Home and previously mentioned St. Francis of Paolo.

Many of the classic phenomena supposedly produced by mediums are remarkably similar to poltergeist activity — such as raps, object movements, apports, whistles, voice phenomena, and things levitating.[391] It is perhaps not surprising, then, that several of the famous trance mediums appeared to have been poltergeist agents as adolescents (or later), including Stanislawa Tomczyk, Stella Cranshaw Deacon, and D. D. Home.[392]

There is one way physical mediums of the past differed dramatically from those of today — they were purportedly able to produce something known as "ectoplasm."[393] This was a mysterious substance, thought to be semi-physical, which could be extruded through the medium's body orifices — and not just the mouth.[394] When visible, it was said to have had a misty, whitish appearance.[395] In addition, it was said to be easily damaged by light and, on occasion, was described as luminous. Sometimes forms would extrude out of the medium's body, and, if disturbed, would shoot elastically back.

Ectoplasm was thought to be capable of moving objects or being molded into shapes.[396] Photographs of the materializations purportedly formed by ectoplasm often had a flat, two-dimensional appearance that only added to the controversy of whether these materializations were formed from an unknown substance or merely a product of fraud. Frame by frame photographs of Stanislawa Tomczyk appear to show ectoplasm first extruding from her mouth and then reentering it, despite the fact her head was covered by a gauze garment to prevent the passage of physical matter.

Parapsychologist Scott Rogo felt that the most convincing evidence of materialization came from the hand mold experiments done with Franek Kluski in Warsaw.[397] These involved having the "forms" Kluski materialized dip into a bowl of hot paraffin, which left a cast behind. Splashing would be heard and, after the completion of the sitting, detailed molds representing human-looking hands would be found. Some of these molds had interlacing hands, or large hands with very small wrist openings, and were paper-thin. Rogo noted that no normal way to produce these unusual shapes has ever been found, and suggested that whatever formed them dissolved within the mold.

One eyewitness noted that it only took from 30–45 seconds for the spirits to create a mold.[398] When he tried to replicate the feat, it took several minutes for the wax to cool enough that he could try to remove it from his hand. He added, " Even then I found it impossible to strip the glove from my hand without breaking it; in fact I was unable to accomplish this with the coating of a single finger which I had dipped into the paraffine as far as the second joint."[399]

The rapid rise, and the equally rapid fall, of Spiritualism may be attributed at least in part to the commercialization of physical mediumship, which increased both the number of mediums available to perform and the charlatans eager to masquerade as such.[400] Opportunists found it all too easy to fool the public using sleight-of-hand. The rampant fraud in turn spawned the creation of professional psychic debunkers. Furthermore, in the United States, the Civil War, which began in 1861, diverted attention, disrupted homes, and destroyed small organizations like the budding Spiritualist church in the United States.[401] This mix of the genuine and the fake, with self-proclaimed talents everywhere, created a powerful impetus for the development of psychical research.[402]

In 1882—30 years after Spiritualism first spread to Great Britain — a group of intellectuals and scientists founded the Society for Psychical Research (SPR).[403] Their goal was to carefully and impartially investigate psychic phenomena. Three years later, an American branch (the ASPR) was formed, and the two groups carried out most of the important and scholarly parapsychological work throughout the world until J. B. Rhine stole the limelight in the 1930s with his experimental work at Duke University. Although many mediums were found to be using trickery to obtain at least some of their results, parapsychology still owes a debt to Spiritualism for initiating the modern movement for the study of physical phenomena.[404]

MARGARETTA AND CATHERINE FOX

It is difficult to speak about mediumship without at least a brief mention of the birth of Spiritualism in 1848 in a house in Hydesville, New York.[405] It started when the adolescent daughters of a Methodist farmer, Margaretta (or Maggie, age fifteen) and Catherine (or Kate, age twelve) Fox heard apparently intelligent rapping sounds in their bedroom.[406] Their mother asked the rapper to make two raps if it was a spirit, and two raps replied. With this, Spiritualism was born — a peculiar mix of fad, sincere belief, pseudo-religion, and after-dinner entertainment.[407]

Shortly after the initial spate of rapping, the sisters were separated and sent to live in other homes.[408] Rapping immediately broke out at both of these new locations, and, in fact, seemed to be contagious. Persons coming in contact with the Fox sisters soon developed their own abilities to produce sounds. One wonders whether this was fraud or an induction effect (*see* Glossary), similar to the way watching a spoon-bending performance may precipitate viewers having their own silverware bend, not all of which may occur by normal means.

Leah, an older married daughter of the Foxes, realized that her sisters could be exploited for commercial gain and encouraged them to tour.[409] By 1849, Kate was producing a wider range of phenomena at séances, including object movements, the playing of a guitar, and touches from spirit hands.[410] By 1850, the sisters were performing in front of large crowds on tour, becoming the first professional Spiritualist mediums and attracting the attention of P. T. Barnum. Although they never worked for him, the connection fueled controversy over whether the raps were produced by a combination of the girls cracking their knee and toe joints, the aid of hidden accomplices, and possible devices built into the medium cabinets, which were popularly used.[411]

Kate was the most notable performer; however, the sisters' success was short lived.[412] They were soon sunk in poverty and alcoholism. In 1888, Kate and Maggie publicly "confessed" to a history of fraud, only for the latter to recant it a month later.[413] The original confession may well have been motivated by the large (and much needed) bounty the destitute sisters were paid, as well as by a desire to discredit their older sister, Leah, who was still going on with the demonstrations after a serious family argument had alienated her from Kate and Maggie. Unfortunately, the truth of the matter will probably never be known as the sisters died a few years later.[414]

DANIEL DUNGLAS HOME (1833–1886)

There are several famous physical mediums from the 1800s, but the most eminent of these was Daniel Dunglas Home.[415] Born near Edinburgh in 1833, Home was adopted at an early age by his mother's sister. When he was nine years old, the family moved to America, where Home lived with his aunt and her husband until 1850. The aunt became alarmed when raps began to be heard and furniture moved about the room.[416] When exorcism didn't resolve the problem, she threw her nephew out of the house.[417] For the next five years Home stayed in various homes and gave séances in return for his board and some education.[418]

In 1855, Home was given money to go to Europe, both for his health and as a missionary of Spiritualism.[419] Once again, he began the circuit of staying as a guest in various homes, giving séances in return for his hosts' hospitality. It is said that never at this, or any other time, did he accept money for his services. Nonetheless, Frank Podmore noted that Home got to live among men and women of rank, wealth, and fashion, and received numerous expensive gifts, jewelry, subscriptions, as well as lavish hospitality that provided for all his needs. Home married twice, both times to Russian heiresses. He died of pneumonia in June 1886, after a long illness.

There are three curious features in Home's career.[420] First, when Home first came to England, he apparently changed how his name was spelled from Hume to Home. Second, in February 1856, after a warning from his spirit guides, Home's mediumistic powers left him. He was received into the Church of Rome, had an audience with the Pope, and even considered joining a monastic order. However, he changed his mind and resumed giving sittings in February of 1857, apparently having regained his powers. Finally, Home was twice attacked by a midnight assassin with a dagger — once in December 1855, and again thirteen years later — but the perpetrator was never discovered.

Home is said to have been a slight, fair man, with a joyous, child-like nature, who enjoyed the easy life, and was full of vanity.[421] An accomplished pianist, Home inspired people with his apparent frankness and sincerity, perhaps in part because of his tendency to deliver religious discourses while in trance. Thus, he was something of a bridge between the more secular physical mediums and religious figures with MMI abilities.

Perhaps because of these religious tendencies, Home demonstrated levitation and fire-immunity under better conditions than one might expect of someone playing tricks on the public. Home was said to be able to levitate both himself and other objects in full light during séances.[422] Even more significantly, he was observed in mid-air outside.[423] One time, when Home had just finished visiting a London church accompanied by one of his patrons, Lord Adare, and Adare's father, Home was noted to go into trance, float over a ruined wall (which was about two feet high) and continue floating mid-air for a distance of ten or twelve feet before returning to the ground.

Home's first-hand account of what it was like to levitate was quite different from that of St. Teresa of Avila. He described it as a kind of "electrical fullness about the feet."[424] He also spoke of being unafraid even though it felt like nothing was supporting him. Home's arms became stiff and rose above his head on a number of occasions while levitating, although he was sometimes able to relax them enough to write on the ceiling with a pencil. Home usually went up perpendicularly. However, after reaching the ceiling there were times when his feet would continue to go up until they were the same height as his face. Home noted that his levitations often lasted for four to five minutes.

In addition to his powers of levitation and mediumship, Home was also said to have an impressive degree of fire-immunity.[425] He could not only hold red-hot coals in his bare hands without harm, but also confer that ability onto others who believed in him.[426] Home's fire-immunity was observed at least 20 times by witnesses of the highest standing.

There are many stories of how, during his trances, Home would handle burning embers or coals, put his face in the embers, or stir the flames with his hand, and neither he nor his clothes would be harmed.[427] He was also said to be able to place a hot coal on the white muslin dress of his hostess without harming it, hold flowers from a vase in the fire without them being damaged, and apply red-hot coals to the heads or hands of people without them feeling pain or being scorched.[428] Home was furthermore alleged to sometimes make jets of flame up to nine inches in length emerge from his head and knees.

Thurston made the interesting observation that, "what I would more especially insist upon is the audacity of all this playing about with fire. There seems to have been very little of the dare-devil, either physically or morally, in the normal Home when not entranced."[429] Had any lady been burned or set on fire, it would have meant social ruin. Yet, he often was able to place red-hot coals on the hands, heads, and highly flammable muslin dresses of women without causing harm.

Home often appeared to be in a trance or semi-trance state when exhibiting fire-immunity, and there is some suggestion that an element of religious fervor was involved, as well.[430] One time, the distinguished scientist and member of the SPR, Sir William Crookes reported that Home took out a red-hot coal, almost the size of an orange, which he placed in his right hand. Home then covered the coal with his left hand, blew onto it until the lump was nearly white hot and had a lambent flame licking around his fingers, and yet, despite this, was unharmed. At the time, Home is said to have looked up in a reverent manner and said, "Is not God good? Are not his laws wonderful?"[431] Crookes is said to have remarked that, although certain chemicals can make the skin somewhat heat-resistant, there were none that he knew of that could fireproof the flesh.

Home performed his séances in somewhat better lighting than his contemporaries while demonstrating the usual array of raps, table and chair movement, bells, accordion and guitar playing under the table, spirit voices speaking through him, manifestation of spirit hands, and self-levitation that his colleagues did.[432] However, unlike most physical mediums, Home was never publicly exposed as an imposter, and although there were occasional rumors of fraud, there was no evidence that he engaged in trickery. Podmore felt that the fact he was in the role of guest at these sittings may have protected Home from accusations of fraud, but it is also possible that he was genuinely capable of MMI.

EUSAPIA PALLADINO (1854–1918)

Eusapia Palladino, in contrast to D. D. Home, probably qualifies as the most infamous physical medium of the nineteenth century. Born in Italy in 1854, Palladino, like Home, lived with an adoptive family.[433] Various forms of spontaneous MMI, including raps, were observed in her presence even as a child, and she was soon taken up by Spiritualists, and giving private séances in Naples.[434]

Eusapia was, by all accounts, a vulgar, earthy woman who liked "low company" and seemed to have a knack for "dematerializing" purses and other valuables during séances.[435] Palladino's preference for dark rooms, and her admitted penchant for cheating every chance she got, made it difficult to evaluate her purported ability to levitate tables, break crockery, materialize lights and hands, play musical instruments, move objects, and create raps and loud noises.

Palladino spent most of her time operating around Naples, but came to the attention of Richet, and eventually the SPR, as well.[436] Controversy raged over whether any of the phenomena she produced were genuine, and if fraud could ever be adequately controlled for in the dark rooms that she preferred. Gauld stated that it was a shame her reputation for trickery kept the SPR from paying attention to reports from their colleagues on the continent until she was nearly at the end of her career. Palladino's powers, such as they were, appeared to fade after a disastrous visit to the United States around 1910, and she died in 1918.

Many individuals brand Palladino a complete fraud and toss out all of the work that was ever done with her. However, a few things are difficult to explain away as simple trickery. These include (1) the curious protuberances that seemed to grow out of Palladino's body, (2) her dramatic weight loss (on the order of twenty pounds) at the end of a sitting, and (3) the clear movement of objects that were not attached to strings.[437] Sometimes, Palladino was said to have levitated in her chair to the top of the séance table, and lifted the table and other objects without touching them, in good light.[438]

We will later see that fraud is often intertwined with genuine MMI. Surprisingly, there may be good reason for this. Parapsychologist Kenneth Batcheldor even encouraged cheating as a method of "priming the pump," for group MMI.[439] Because of this, it is critical that any investigator not only distinguish fakery from the paranormal, but also recognize that just because fraud is occasionally employed does not mean that it is always involved.

WILLI AND RUDI SCHNEIDER

Willi and Rudi Schneider were Austrians who came to the attention of the well-known entrepreneur and psychic researcher Harry Price in the 1920s.[440] Both Rudi and Willi demonstrated MMI abilities as adolescents and gave family séances. Baron von Schrenck-Notzing performed a long series of controlled sittings with Willi and tested his ability to move objects when separated from them by a black gauze cage.[441] Not only did the objects move around, but there were also a variety of materializations that John Beloff described as having "flowing, changing and fantastic shapes."[442] These forms developed in such a way that von Schrenck-Notzing was convinced that they could not have been fraudulently produced. Willi grew bored with the repetitions demanded of him, and soon lost interest in mediumship, but Rudi volunteered to be a participant in Price's experiments.

Rudi's first séance with Price was in 1926.[443] The young medium was able to produce cool breezes, materialized hands, raps, and object movement. Like many others of his era, Rudi attributed these events to a "control personality," named "Olga," who was also said to have been his older brother Willi's spirit-control.[444] "Olga" would manifest in the trance state to direct the phenomena, and was said to have imperiously insisted that the sitters engage in a constant flow of singing and chatter.

When von Schrenck-Notzing died in 1929, there was no one else in Germany to continue the work with Rudi.[445] Harry Price quickly took advantage of the situation and signed Rudi up for a series of séances in London. Although Rudi had some impressive results in England, he left Price to work with Dr. Eugene Osty in France.[446] In 1932, Rudi returned to work with Price again. Unfortunately, it soon became clear that Price was jealous of Osty's work, which was generating more interest than his own. Months later, Price claimed that he had caught Rudi cheating, and produced a photograph allegedly showing Rudi freeing an arm to produce the manifestations. Rudi angrily denied the charge, but his mediumship came into doubt.

Forty years later, the photographic plate showing the alleged fraud was discovered among Price's archives.[447] Some believe that analysis of the plate shows it could have been a cleverly contrived composite, and speculate that Price created it to get revenge for Rudi choosing to work with Osty and other researchers. However, others believe Price is the one falsely maligned, and refute the notion that he faked the image.[448] At this point, the truth will probably never be known as to whether or not Rudi was innocent, as he claimed.

STELLA CRANSHAW DEACON

Stella Cranshaw (who later married Leslie Deacon) was a young British nurse with MMI abilities who was "discovered" by Harry Price in 1923.[449] They met by chance on a train trip. Casual conversation brought up the fact that she had a history of spontaneous MMI experiences, and Price promptly recruited her for a series of experiments.

Stella was able to produce full table levitations and object movements under good lighting and fully controlled conditions. In addition to these phenomena, lights would appear, raps occurred, toy musical instruments would play, and the room temperature often dropped, sometimes over ten degrees.[450] Once Stella even seemed to teleport (or materialize) a large sprig of lilac, sixteen and a half inches long and in full bloom, into the locked séance room.

It is unfortunate that Stella withdrew from psychical research after only fifteen sittings.[451]

Nonetheless, the great care that went into planning those experiments so as to preclude fraud has given her a place as one of the mediums who succeeded at MMI tasks which were impossible to fake.

SUMMARY

Physical mediumship has been around for millennia. Ancient Greece, China, Tibet, and Japan all have stories of individuals associated with divination and possible MMI events.[452] Mediumship virtually disappeared in Europe with the advent of the Inquisition during the Middle Ages, but continued to flourish unhindered in Asia as an integral part of the culture.

Physical mediumship underwent a major revival in the United States and Europe with the advent of Spiritualism in the 1800s.[453] Many physical mediums started out as poltergeist agents, with uncontrolled, spontaneous recurrent MMI.[454] Like their Asian counterparts, Spiritualist mediums attributed the MMI effects that occurred around them to the spirits of the dead (though not always their own ancestors), rather than to their own abilities.[455] They appeared to be capable of a wide variety of phenomena, including fire-immunity, levitation, teleportation, materializing and dematerializing objects or body parts, object movement, the production of voices, noises, and lights, and other miscellaneous activity.

The lucrative nature of a successful performance encouraged many mediums to resort to trickery.[456] Indeed, Palladino frankly admitted that it was easier to use fraud than it was to do the real thing. However, there does seem to be evidence that at least a portion of the phenomena produced by physical mediums was MMI. Some of the more convincing data comes from individuals such as D. D. Home, Rudi Schneider, and Stella Cranshaw Deacon.

Physical mediumship is similar to religiously associated MMI in four ways: (1) both groups include a wide variety of activity; (2) there can be a fuzzy boundary between spontaneous and intentional phenomena; (3) the results are generally attributed to a discarnate source, whether God, demons, or a deceased individual; and (4) trance states are often noted at the time of successful MMI performance.[457] Researchers are fortunate that, unlike most religious and spiritual MMI performers, physical mediums allowed their abilities to be formally investigated. The results of these studies will be discussed in Part II of the book under "Early Research with Physical Mediums."

Anomalous Healers

Parapsychologist Jerry Solfvin defined anomalous healing as "the practice of treating illness without a known physical curative agent." [458] It is inclusive of a wide range of methods, which have variously been called mental healing, psychic healing, shamanic work, prayer healing, miracle healing, angel healing, laying on of hands, therapeutic touch, paranormal healing, non-medical work, and magnetic healing. It is also possible that some cases of spontaneous remission may also fall into this group.

One of the advantages of using the term anomalous healing, rather than the others mentioned above, is that it accurately reflects our lack of knowledge about what underlying mechanisms are involved. As with religious MMI and mediumship, anomalous healing has a long anecdotal history. Stories of magical or anomalous healing abound in one form or another in nearly every culture around the globe from the earliest hunter-gatherer times onward.[459] In addition, many religious figures were known for healing in addition to their other powers.

There are a variety of ways to classify anomalous healers. Perhaps the simplest of these is whether the healer works in person or from a distance. When done in person, the process is often referred to as manual healing. In this case, a healer appears to influence the healing process by placing his or her hands over the afflicted area.[460] There are many variations to manual healing. Some healers specialize in bone fractures or other ailments and healing styles can differ: some healers touch the skin, while others pass their hands over the body without contact; some pray silently while touching the head, while others pray out loud; and some only manipulate the feet or appear to work on pressure points on the human body, not unlike acupuncture-point topography. Examples of manual healers include Oskar Estebany, who made gastric ulcers disappear within 24 hours as verified by X-ray, and Ambrose Worrall, who was said to be able to place his hands over tumors, which were visible under the skin, and have them vanish within a few hours.[461]

Distant healing involves a healer attempting to exert his or her influence while physically separated by space (and sometimes time) from the patient.[462] Distant healing is a common practice in England, South America, and by healing prayer groups in many different churches around the globe. What makes distant healing particularly appealing from a research standpoint is that it is one of the few practices that, if the patient does not know that any treatment is being administered, allows experimental parapsychologists to distinguish MMI effects from those of ordinary suggestion.[463]

Another method of classification is to divide anomalous healers by style. For example, some may use rituals, and others spiritual intermediaries, ASC, prayers, etc. Healer styles tend to vary depending on their society's level of technology.[464] Thus, they may be more reflective of a culture's needs than what is truly effective, per se. Krippner and Welch created a category system of five styles—shamans, shamanic healers, shamanistic healers, priests and priestesses, and mediums or spiritists.

On one end of this spectrum is the shaman.[465] This is a ritual practitioner who communicates personally with supernatural beings, frequently performs healing rites for one or more patients, and often discovers their abilities after a "divine stroke" or illness.[466] Shamans abound in hunting and gathering tribes. An interesting point is that even those shamans who admit their abilities are bogus often believe that other shamans have real powers.[467]

The next category is the shamanic healer.[468] These practitioners appear in sedentary, agricultural societies. Shamanic healers may still use disciplined alterations of consciousness to aid them in accessing the spirit world, but their social status is lower than that of the shaman, and they tend to work part-time. They are also less likely to communicate with spirits and more likely to rely on sleight-of-hand to obtain their results. Modern day Native American healers typically fall into this group.

Krippner and Welch's third category is the shamanistic healer.[469] They noted that many contemporary alternative health care practitioners fall into this category. These healers hold spiritual beliefs, and engage in procedures, which are based on assumptions about the human spirit. Shamanistic healing may involve rituals, but usually without a change in the state of consciousness. It tends to emerge in social groups where mediums, sorcerers, and other practitioners have preempted the use of ASC from shamans and shamanic healers. Radionics, homeopathy, and subtle energy healing would all fall into this category.

Priests and priestesses emerge in societies after the establishment of agriculture.[470] The priest or priestess acquires his or her role quite differently than the shaman, who must demonstrate unique abilities. Instead, they often inherit their positions or derive them from a body of codified ritual knowledge that has been handed down.[471] Furthermore, priests and priestesses are experienced at conducting rituals, which often occur for the benefit of the community and occur cyclically on specific calendar dates. As a general rule, they do not use procedures to induce an ASC—the power is thought to be in the ritual, rather than the individual.[472] However, like the shaman, they often enjoy a high socioeconomic status. Religiously associated healing, whether by a spiritual figure or a holy place, falls into this group.

The final category of healer is the medium or spiritist.[473] The only thing they have in common with the shaman is the use of an ASC. Unlike shamans, mediums are frequently not socially sanctioned, believe themselves controlled by their spirits (rather than controlling them), and work for individuals instead of the good of a group. Voodoo practitioners in Haiti and psychic healers in Puerto Rico, the Philippines, and Brazil fall into this faction.

When successful, all anomalous healing methods accelerate the normal healing process — although one can argue how much of a role placebo and psychosomatic processes play in this. Despite the advances of science, anomalous healing remains popular today. "Magical" healing is still practiced in the countryside of Italy, by cultists in Brazil, throughout South and Southeast Asia, in the Philippines, and in the former Soviet Union.[474] Sybo Schouten observed that anomalous healing practitioners offer their patients little in the way of explanation for how the process works and often have questionable results.[475] Yet despite both this and the excellent success rates of conventional medicine, anomalous healing still attracts a great many clients. We must ask why.

Needless to say, culture plays a major role in who uses these healers. In Lucania, Italy, anxiety is an undercurrent of life that is generated by superstition, so the healer is often sought out in preference to the doctor.[476] Likewise, in small Hindu villages, illness and bad luck are usually thought to be due to witchcraft, and must be cured by magic.[477] Considering that emotional, psychological, and unconscious factors are at work in most illnesses, it should not be surprising that magical cures are often effective.[478]

One of the key differences between anomalous healing and alternative therapies is that most of the latter involve some form of physical intervention. Anomalous healing, as Schouten pointed out, does not appear to involve any real kind of physical intervention.[479] Thus, we are left wondering how it works. The mechanisms underlying the mind-body link are still a mystery, and we do not yet know the limits of mental influence.[480]

This is a difficult area of investigation due, in part, to the complexity of the healing process itself. The placebo effect also complicates the situation. The word itself is Latin for "I will please."[481] A placebo can be any inactive substance, preparation, or procedure that is administered to satisfy a patient's symbolic need for drug therapy. Although long accepted by the medical community as an important factor in healing, it is not well understood. Placebos can cause remarkable cures, and in some cases can even have negative side effects.[482] Because of this, a placebo-treated group is always included in controlled studies to try to separate self-healing factors from those of the experimental treatment. It is only in this way that the true efficacy of the medicinal substance can be determined.

Harvey Irwin came to a number of conclusions after reviewing contemporary healer experiences.[483] He noted that many different rituals are used, especially when one looks across cultures. However, despite this variability, healer experiences appear to be consistent in many other ways. Healers often go into a state of trance or an effortless, highly focused state before they begin. This can involve either extreme of arousal — high or low. For low arousal, practitioners may use meditation, prayer, and relaxation techniques to enter a state where their muscles relax and there is a drop in their heart and breathing rates. Other practitioners will use dance or other methods to create a state of high arousal. Entering the correct state of consciousness need not take long. Some practitioners slide into an ASC very quickly, while others may simply reside in that state most of the time.

Irwin also discussed features of the experience from the viewpoint of the healers.[484] One of the first steps was a breakdown of separation between the healer and his or her patient, leading to feelings of merger and oneness. Healers often believed some kind of energy was involved, which came from either their own bodies or the universe. In addition, there was some suggestion that fantasy proneness may be a common trait of individuals who believe they can heal others. We will see in the final part of this book, that the anomalous healer experiences Irwin described are by no means unique. The use of an ASC, feelings of connection, and a sense of energy are all common features of an MMI experience, regardless of whether a spontaneous event or a result of intention.

HISTORICAL HEALERS IN EUROPE

Two European anomalous healers stand out in a review of the historical data — Valentine Greatrakes and Anton Mesmer. We will briefly discuss each of them, before turning our attention to anecdotal material from Asia, the Philippines, and Brazil.

Valentine Greatrakes Valentine Greatrakes was an anomalous healer who lived in seventeenth-century England.[485] Born in 1629, in 1662 he is said to have suddenly had the impulse to heal. Greatrakes felt he could cure scrofula (tuberculosis of the cervical lymph nodes), which was sometimes known as the "King's Evil" because it could supposedly be made well by royal touch. During the following three years, Greatrakes purportedly cured people with a variety of troubles. He was eventually invited by the king to London where the healer treated many thousands, including royalty and scientists.

Greatrakes would often respond to the sick in spontaneous, dramatic ways — stroking or massaging patients, lancing boils with a knife, offering his urine to drink or rub on their wounds, and spitting in the eyes of his patients.[486] His patients often had convulsive crises, exhibited temporary anesthesias, and could be cured by relics that were associated with him. Greatrakes always insisted that he was merely God's instrument, but it is interesting how similar the phenomena induced by his stroking were to Mesmer's almost a century later.

Franz Anton Mesmer Franz Anton Mesmer is probably the most famous of all historical European anomalous healers. Born in Switzerland in 1733, he was a Viennese physician.[487] Mesmer felt there was a fundamental type of energy in the universe, which was distributed in the body as "animal magnetism."[488] He further believed that this energy governed each individual's health. In many ways, his ideas were not unlike the Chinese *chi* theories and the Hindu concept of "prana."

In 1779, Mesmer published a paper in which he laid out his theory for how his method of healing worked.[489] According to him, everything — the heavens, the planet, and all the life on Earth — is interconnected by a subtle fluid, which is subject to laws we do not yet understand. As with magnetism, Inglis noted that Mesmer felt this fluid could be "tapped, concentrated, stored and communicated at a distance."[490] Mesmer speculated that the better understanding of this fluid might explain many of the mysteries of the past, including not only the laying on of hands, but also telepathy, MMI, divination, visions, and animal migration.

Mesmer initially used magnets, but soon found that he could get the same results by making passes with his hand or by stroking the patients.[491] The trance states induced by mesmerism appeared to cause a variety of psychic byproducts, such as participants being able to "read" minds or "see" events that were inaccessible to the ordinary senses.[492]

Inglis commented that Mesmer was "too successful, and too tactless, for his own good."[493] In 1778, Mesmer was hounded out of Vienna by his more orthodox (and possibly less prosperous) colleagues.[494] He settled in Paris, and set up a fashionable and lucrative practice, which soon aroused the ire of the French medical profession. However, Mesmer managed to attract the interest and support of both Charles D'Eslon, physician to the brother of King Louis XVI, and Marie Antoinette.

In 1784, the king set up a Royal Commission of Inquiry into mesmerism, which was composed of members of the Academy of Sciences, including several preeminent scientists, such as Jean-Sylvain Bailly, Dr. Joseph Ignace Guillotin, Laurent de Jussieu, and Antoine Levoisier.[495] Benjamin Franklin — who was there as the United States ambassador to France — was nominally in charge of the group. The resulting investigation left the team in no doubt that D'Eslon got results. His patients went into convulsions, which were almost contagious to those around them. Unfortunately, although the patients may have shown some benefit, the convulsions themselves were not without risk. Furthermore, tests showed that mesmerism had nothing to do with either magnetism or electricity. Having no proof of any so-called "magnetic fluid," the committee decided that, being nonexistent, it could not have any positive effects. They concluded that any results D'Eslon had obtained must have been due to the patients' imagination.

D'Eslon did not disagree with their conclusion that his treatments might be acting in large part as a placebo.[496] Instead, he replied to the committee that he understood that imagination might indeed be at the heart of mesmerism's effect, but added of the power of the imagination was "as extensive as it is little known."[497]

Not all of the investigators were convinced mesmerism was bogus.[498] Jussieu noted that patients sometimes reacted to an unseen rod, or a finger, which was pointed at them from six feet away, or from behind their back. Unfortunately, Jussieu's plea for further investigation was rejected and the practice of animal magnetism was banned.

Although the Academies were able to prevent healers from practicing mesmerism in Paris, they had far less control over what happened in the provinces.[499] Thus, it was possible for a few individuals, such as the Marquis de Puységur, to continue to explore its use, both for healing and for evoking paranormal abilities. The final blow to magnetism came from the French revolution in 1789. Both its adherents and its opponents were scattered, imprisoned, or killed. Puységur was jailed, but managed to escape the guillotine. Mesmer returned to Switzerland, where he lived out his remaining years in semi-retirement.

Beloff noted, "Almost certainly mesmerism, as originally practiced by Mesmer himself, and before it became inextricably confused with hypnotism, was little more than a new-fangled version of this age-old laying on of hands."[500] The only difference was that mesmerism made the healing practice more palatable by introducing the quasi-scientific concept of animal magnetism.

The nineteenth century saw a resurgence of interest in animal magnetism, and in 1826, the French Academies of Science and Medicine again appointed a commission to study it.[501] This time there was sufficient evidence for them to conclude that it was, while still far from proven, at least worthy of further study. Inglis noted that the reaction of the French Academy members to their committee's recommendation was "hostile," and their acceptance slow.[502] Nonetheless, mesmerism's legacy of hypnotism, wherein people are put into an ASC associated with increased suggestibility, is an extremely effective tool still used by medicine and psychotherapy today.[503]

HEALING TRADITIONS IN ASIA: *QIGONG* AND *KI* ENERGY

The opening up of relations between the People's Republic of China and the West has unveiled a long and rich history of anomalous healing. Leping Zha and Tron McConnell observed that Chinese texts have references to psychic phenomena that date as far back as two millennia.[504] China still maintains a tradition of healing that was developed as early as 500 BCE. It uses breath and movement exercises to focus thought and control the body's life force. The belief in a life energy is a widespread concept, which goes by the name of "qi" or *chi* in China, *ki* in Japan, and "prana" in India.[505]

The word *qigong* itself (which translates as "qi ability") is a relatively new term, coined by Liu Guizhen in 1955.[506] It was originally presented as a means of improving health through the practice of certain meditative exercises. However, in the late 1970s, Liu announced that this energy could be projected out of the body and into others. The communist takeover in China forced traditional healing underground for a period; however, it was allowed to emerge again after the Cultural Revolution in the 1970s, and gained official approval at the end of 1985.[507] During this time, qigong masters were studied extensively, and some such as Yan Xin, were said to be able to instantly heal bone fractures, as proven by X-ray.

China's leaders began cracking down on qigong masters again in 1989, as they became concerned over the healers' potential political power.[508] One method reportedly used was to diagnose "qigong deviation," and forcibly admit individuals to mental institutions. Although the official explanation was that these patients were being treated for symptoms such as speaking in tongues, hallucinations, channeling the messages of deceased political figures, paranoia, and self-absorbed and repetitive body motions, many patients protested that they were being punished for saying things that were politically incorrect. The fact that their "treatment" resembled the deprogramming of cult members, or the imprisonment of "deviants" in the former Soviet Union, lent some credence to their complaints. Fortunately, the combination of pride in their cultural tradition, and the fact that many of the ruling Communist leaders have received treatment from personal qigong physicians, tempered the magnitude of the Chinese crackdown on qigong as a social movement.

The Japanese have been actively interested in the use of ki for both its purported retardation of aging and other uses.[509] Sony Corporation had an investigative team that performed research on ki, Japan's Ministry of International Trade and Industry formed a committee to look into the practical uses of ki, and over ten companies were said to be paying for ki studies at Tokyo's University of Electro-Communications. It is a shame that the competitive nature of the corporate world markedly limits, and in many cases prevents, the dissemination of their findings. In addition, there was some decrease in the study of psi in Japan, as a backlash against the Aum Shinrikyo religious sect (the purportedly psychic group that unleashed the sarin nerve gas in the Tokyo subway system).

Psychic Surgery

Anomalous healers are sometimes said to perform "psychic surgery" on patients, seeming to insert their hands or knives into the body of their patients before revealing blood and body organs, and seeming to pull things out.[510] In addition, the wounds are said to close without a visible trace, or with a scar that heals rapidly, and remarkable cures are said to have taken place. Brazil and the Philippines are the two countries where one hears the most about psychic surgeons.[511] Because they have vastly different reputations, these groups will be addressed separately.

The Philippines Psychic surgery in the Philippines is practiced mainly by the Union Espirista Cristiana de Filipinas, concentrated in Pangasinan Province, north of Manila.[512] Many observers are convinced that some of these surgeries are genuine, stating that they inserted their hands into the incision before seeing it magically close.[513] However, Filipino psychic surgeons have frequently been caught using trickery, and James McClenon—who watched over a thousand of these procedures— believed that the majority of them were sleight-of-hand. Nor did he find it surprising that such hoaxes would be perpetrated, given the poverty-stricken nature of the country and the huge sums of money tourists were willing to pay for psychic surgery.

McClenon described Alex Orbito as a typical psychic practitioner in the Philippines.[514] Orbito was a high school dropout who had dreams of healing people. Supposedly, a wise, old hermit spirit guide gave Orbito a key to be able to enter a trance state almost at will. His healing career started when a neighbor, whose mother was paralyzed for ten years, asked Orbito to visit her. After his visit, she was allegedly healed, and Orbito's fame soon spread. He is said to have avoided his call as a healer for some time, but became seriously ill, and kept hearing voices ordering him to begin his mission. When he finally returned home and followed the directives of the voices, his sickness abated. Thus, his story follows the shamanic theme, of spirit guides, the "calling," spiritual sickness, and healing.

Orbito had weekend public healings.[515] These started with assistants preaching sermons—which strongly emphasized the importance of people healing themselves by faith—and offering prayers. Orbito then asked the patient for a diagnosis and explained his own interpretation of the problem. Each operation only lasted a few minutes. Orbito would quickly grope about with both hands, creating a slight popping sound as blood gushed forth. He would extract pieces of organic material and wipe the area clean, at which point the supposed incision "disappeared." Orbito washed his hands after each operation and wiped them with a fresh cloth, which gave him an opportunity to load his hands with new packets of liquid "blood" and animal parts to extract for the next patient. Orbito was careful to prevent viewers from seeing some aspects of his performance, and on one occasion the operations were delayed, only to be started after a man delivered a plate of meat scraps to the back of Orbito's house.

Brazil Brazilian psychic surgeries differ from those in the Philippines in that the healers use unconcealed instruments, rather than simply their hands.[516] Knives, razor blades, needles, and scissors are used to make deep incisions without either anesthesia or antisepsis, and many Brazilian healers close the wounds with stitches. The wounds bleed, but may heal rapidly, with little scarring and no infection. A variety of physicians and others have attested to the fact that this is more than sleight-of-hand, having not only witnessed these operations, but also participated in them, either as an assistant or a patient.[517] Most of these healers go into an ASC or channel while they are working.

Arigó (1918–1971) is one of the better-known Brazilian psychic surgeons.[518] He was a poorly educated man in Brazil who, between the ages of 30 and 32, suffered from depression, nightmares, sleepwalking, and sleep talking. He was told by a local spiritualist named Oliveira that it was due to a spirit trying to speak and act through him.

In 1950, Arigó entered the room of a state senator, named Bittencourt, after 2 A.M., produced a straight razor, and proceeded to operate on the politician's chest.[519] Arigó removed a tumor, then left. Bittencourt had been previously diagnosed as having inoperable lung cancer, yet after this incident the tumor appeared to have disappeared. Circumstantial evidence of the procedure included Bittencourt's torn and bloodstained pajamas, blood on his body, and an orange-sized piece of tissue found in his room. However, there was no scar.

Arigó continued to work as a healer for 20 years.[520] During this time, he was studied by a number of physicians and researchers. Perhaps the most amazing part of this is that, like most psychic surgeons, Arigó violated every principle of modern surgery. He worked in a dirty combination office and waiting room. Preparation and examination of the patient took under a minute. Arigó worked with any available knife, performed no antisepsis on the skin or the instruments, used no anesthesia, did not bother with hemostasis, employed neither gloves nor draping, performed no suturing, and provided no post-operative care. Yet, despite this, Arigó's patients never got post-operative infections. Puharich described his own filmed experience under the healer's knife, when a superficial lipoma (benign fat tumor) was painlessly excised with a dirty knife through skin that had not been cleaned. Despite this, the wound healed in half the normal time without any sign of infection.

Arigó had two methods of diagnosis.[521] The first was to simply look at the patient for a few seconds before making a diagnosis in sophisticated medical terminology—which in a few cases was checked and found to be accurate. The other way was for him to receive the information clairaudiently, as a voice in his right ear. Arigó said that this voice belonged to a deceased German medical student, named Adolphus Fritz, who never finished school.

A variety of Brazilian healers, including Edson Cavalante de Queiroz and Mauricio Magalhães, have also said they channeled Fritz, while others have claimed saints or other spirits as their sources of information and reason for being able to heal the sick.[522] Although the Spiritist Church frowns on any money changing hands for these services, many healers receive the popularity and acclaim of rock stars—at least until they run afoul of the authorities for practicing medicine without a license.

Sidney Greenfield observed the work of several Brazilian psychic surgeons in the field.[523] He noted that patient orientation sessions involving long, repetitive prayers and invocations, along with listening to the testimonials of others (enhancing their belief and suggestibility). This may induce a hypnotic trance state, which could be responsible for their freedom from pain. In addition, hypnosis can accelerate self-healing through its influence on the unconscious mind. This effect is not limited to blood flow or the immune system, but can involve genetic and cellular processes.

McClenon also believed that psychic surgeries can be best viewed as psychosomatic treatments.[524] Many practitioners not only take advantage of dramatic scenes of blood and gore to trigger therapeutic effects in the patient, but also give special attention to the attitudes and orientations of their clients' families. McClenon noted that the coupling of trance with fraud is a common feature of shamanic healing in general. He further suggested that the psychic surgeons may block out those perceptions or activities that contradict their beliefs. Thus, it is possible that entranced practitioners think real operations are occurring, and they and their patients simultaneously share the same apparitional image of an incision. Certainly all of the Filipino psychic surgeons McClenon interviewed denied engaging in deception. We will see more on this topic in Part II of this book, in the chapter on biological system research.

COMMON FEATURES

Krippner and Welch believed that any attempt at healing, whether orthodox or otherwise, involved four dimensions: (1) the environment, (2) the practitioner, (3) the patient, and (4) treatment procedures.[525] They stated that one or more of these dimensions need to be activated in order to have successful healing. Needless to say, sharing a worldview can be very helpful to this process.

Psychiatrist Jan Ehrenwald suggested that unorthodox healing was a mixture of magico-mythical, spiritual, and religious hopes and expectations, aided by suggestion or autosuggestion, placebo effects, and a hypothetical psi factor.[526] He felt there were three key features, which cut across all forms of anomalous healing, from shaman to physician. These were (1) the healer's faith in the efficacy of his or her treatment, (2) the patient's trust in the healer and his or her desire to be cured, and (3) the patient's friends and relations as participant observers, sharing both the anguish and the hopes of the patient. Successful anomalous healing enlists the power of the mind, not only of patients, but also their friends and family, to create an emotional environment favorable for healing.

Several authors have emphasized the advantages of a shared worldview in naming or identifying of the source of the problem.[527] Naming an illness and its cure has tremendous power in itself. Not only does it validate the patient's suffering, but it also says that the patient will not suffer alone, and that an optimistic prognosis is possible. The healer's personal qualities or charisma, the patient's mental attitude, and the effectiveness of the treatment itself are additional factors that may aid recovery.

In this chapter, we have seen that a tremendous range of activities all fall under the category of anomalous healing. These can vary by culture and personal style. Despite the advances of medicine, anomalous healing remains a surprisingly popular alternative (or adjunct) method of treatment today. Although McClenon believed the vast majority of psychic healing performed in the Philippines was a sham, it is possible that, rather like the Spiritualist physical mediums, psychic surgeons mix trickery with genuine paranormal healing. There appear to be at least a few healers who are capable of remarkable feats. We are still far from understanding how anomalous healing works, but it is likely that psychology and placebo both play important roles. We will see much more on this topic in "Biological System Research" in Part II of this book.

Martial Artists and Athletes

Martial artists and athletes have been said to able to perform amazing feats of MMI. In the case of athletic teams, this can involve a group effect, where a united goal appears to elevate them to a new level of skill, and permits objects (such as a ball) to behave in intriguingly nonordinary ways. Repetitive practice is a key aspect to all sports. However, martial artists often stress a spiritual side to their training, which goes beyond this. It is possible, given what we will later learn about the MMI experience, that this is why their reputed (and sometimes documented) abilities appear to go beyond that of a typical sport. Because of this we will look at the two groups separately.

MARTIAL ARTISTS

Martial artists often speak not only of kicks and punches, but also the use of *chi* or *ki* for combat. In some ways, this is the flip side of *qigong* healing. No one knows when the Oriental fighting systems originated, but estimates range anywhere from 4000 to 6000 BCE.[528] Martial artists claim to be able to knock people down without physically touching them by using "empty force"—called *jing* (force) by the Chinese—that is directed from the hand.[529] Like yoga, the martial arts teach methods of concentration and mind/body unification that allow practitioners to tap into this life force energy and perform extraordinary feats.[530]

Michael Murphy and Rhea White described the methods for developing *chi* (or *ki*) as involving five key elements: (1) relaxation and letting go, (2) concentration, (3) breathing exercises, (4) emptying the mind of thought, and (5) rhythmic activity.[531] It is felt that there is a certain rhythm, or harmony, which can be acquired to allow one to be in tune with the universe, and to move effortlessly. In many ways the martial artist combines a state of stimulation with a concentrated focus of energy and attention during their training—a combination that parapsychologist Kathy Dalton noted may be very psi conducive.[532]

There are, in fact, many stories of martial artists who appear to be capable of performing extraordinary physical deeds.[533] The Japanese have stories of the kiai-shout being used to heal, or harm, in ways that appear to be beyond normal explanation, while Tibetans are said to be able to disintegrate objects with a keynote of the right vibration. There are also tales of martial artists climbing up vertical walls, jumping over cars or across a 15-foot-wide stream, knocking someone unconscious with a shout, dropping 30 feet and landing without making a sound, becoming invisible, causing birds to drop unconscious from trees with a kiai-shout, using chi to push a man off balance from a distance, and knocking a person back 30 feet using only expelled breath.

Although it is difficult to evaluate the truthfulness of these accounts, there are martial arts masters, such as Guy Savelli, who have had some of their abilities tested in the laboratory.[534] Savelli has said he can paralyze people without touching them (which he calls "the mind stops"), put out a candle by looking at it, and perform the dim mak, or death touch, which is said to disrupt the victim's energy flow such that they die within 24 hours.[535] Kung-fu artist Kah Wah Lee is likewise alleged to be able to perform this feat, using what he said was his intrinsic energy, or chi, converted to a vibrating energy that enters the body and disrupts the blood flow and lung structure, causing a delayed death.[536]

At least one martial arts feat—the ability of a master to move unseen—was recorded on film.[537] The founder of aikido, Morihei Uyeshiba, was able to repeatedly shift from one position to another in a fraction of a second, seeming to disappear for an instant, and then reappear, sometimes moving as much as two feet, and facing another direction between one frame and the next.

Koichi Tohei, who did aikido demonstrations in the United States, believed that ki—a term which can mean intrinsic energy, momentum, intention, or breath force—flowed from the fingertips.[538] According to Master Masutatsu Oyama, the most important thing in breaking techniques was a confident belief that you could do it.[539] Indeed, the importance of belief is frequently touted as an important factor in all forms of human performance.

Glen Barclay stated that the use of intrinsic energy for attack or defense is mastered progressively over time, and that its mastery with age allows the martial artist to dispense with simple physical strength. The Asian belief seems to be that all martial artists are capable of acquiring occult abilities if they are willing to work hard enough and long enough, and that there is a standard procedure for acquiring these abilities. In this sense, they are in agreement with the Muslim and Hindu yogis, who state that everyone has the potential to control matter with their minds, that it is a universal human ability, which can be improved with training.[540]

OTHER ATHLETES

If we turn our attention away from the martial arts, we find that athletes are generally reluctant to talk about the possibility of MMI occurrences outside the locker room.[541] Nonetheless, there have been numerous individuals who believed they could "will" things to happen, such as golfers Jack Nicklaus, Bobby Nichols, and Arnold Palmer, who felt they could make their balls go into holes on command. There have also been reports from football players of balls that suddenly jumped over an interceptor's hands, or hung in mid-air so that they could be caught. It is also possible that group MMI — performed by the spectators — could be the underlying cause of the well-known phenomenon of "home court advantage."

Michael Murphy and Rhea White noted that some athletes seem to have the ability to levitate, or at least hang in mid-air beyond what would be expected by physics.[542] Basketball star Michael Jordan described his ability as a gift, rather than a case of physical performance. Ballet dancer Mikhail Baryshnikov has likewise seemed to float up, stop in mid-air, and sit in space. The legendary Russian ballet dancer Nijinsky appeared to use a combination of trance, breathing, and muscular control to pause in mid-air after a leap. Furthermore, he is said to have felt like the air supported him and that he could control the speed of his descent. Mountain climbers and runners have also spoken of their bodies seeming to lose weight or becoming weightless while in action. One wonders whether these athletes could be, on some level, using MMI to meet their performance needs.

One thing that sports consistently demonstrate is how the mind imposes barriers on the body.[543] Once one athlete has broken through that barrier, others soon follow. For example, after Roger Bannister broke the four-minute barrier for the mile in 1954, by 1990, 554 men had run the mile in under four minutes, and during 1990 alone 62 men accomplished the feat.[544] This is true for other skills, as well. Michael Murphy pointed out that when you look back at star athletes from the past, you soon see that their feats — once considered so remarkable — would today be considered common or average at best, and have been far surpassed by many around the world.[545]

Thus, as with the martial artists, the belief that you can do something appears to be crucial — at least when in a normal state of consciousness. Previous standards of excellence are continually being surpassed.[546] At least part of this may depend on the individual believing that something is possible because someone has done it. Sports psychologists use a variety of methods to enhance performance — including hypnosis, motivational techniques, biofeedback, meditative practice, and rehearsing an event mentally until the imagery is vivid — to help athletes excel.[547] These techniques can impact not only the athlete's belief that something is possible, but also the belief that he or she can perform the feat.

Parapsychologist Robin Taylor commented that athletes and psychics have a surprising number of features in common.[548] Both groups use imagery to prepare for, and perform, their feats and have to perform in front of, and be critiqued by, a sometimes hostile audience and judges. Perhaps most importantly, when athletes and psychics are performing well, they have highly comparable subjective experiences. Taylor observed, "They both describe feeling very powerful; awareness of the passage of time is distorted, total awareness of the complete environment and ineffableness."[549]

Taylor noted that this peak state, or "flow," experience is thought of by psychics as being in a mystical state.[550] This "flow" is described in Zen Archery as one of existing in the present without any awareness of the self, often involving calm detachment, being focused in a relaxed way, and merger with the target and/or process.[551] Murphy and White refer to this ASC as "the zone." The ability of athletes to enter the so-called "zone" may be a significant factor in extraordinary sports performances. In the "zone," it is harder to fail than it is to succeed.

The athletic "zone" has many features in common with the ASC noted by others thought to have MMI abilities.[552] Descriptions of it by athletes show the "zone" involves focused concentration, withdrawal of attention from distractions, in-the-moment beingness, effortless absorption, a sense of unity, and a feeling of moving in harmony with the universe. All of these could equally be applied to descriptions of the state of consciousness of yogis and extremely adept martial artists. Nor is the similarity missed by performers. Mountain climber Rob Schultheis compared extreme sports to shamanistic training rituals, which allow the athlete (at least temporarily) to feel a sense of power and ecstasy. Physical exercise is likewise used by Sufi mystics in their dervish dances, and by many tribal shamans, both ancient and contemporary.[553] Thus, it is possible that there could be an overlapping mental state — whether it be called the "flow," a "peak state," or the "zone" — which permits, or augments, MMI performance.

The correlation between ASC and extraordinary performances is intriguing.[554] Yogis, athletes, and martial artists all appear to describe a similar "zone" where remarkable things become possible. The essential features of this state appear to be focused concentration, withdrawal of attention from distractions, in-the-moment beingness, effortless absorption, a sense of unity, and a feeling of moving in harmony with the universe. We will see in Part III of this book that these characteristics also occur in MMI experiences.

Poltergeists

> *Poltergeist phenomena may not represent odd exceptions to the laws of nature but lawful processes which have so far escaped attention. Our findings suggest that poltergeist occurrences have nothing to do with spirits, demons, or ghosts, but that they represent natural physical and neuropsychological processes.*
>
> — William G. Roll[555]

Poltergeists are a form of recurrent spontaneous MMI (RSMMI) with a long, complex, and diverse history.[556] The term first appeared in the writings of Martin Luther (1483–1546) during the Reformation in Germany.[557] The word itself basically translates to mean a "noisy ghost" or "racketing type of demon."[558] This activity was initially attributed strictly to the devil. It was not until the early nineteenth century that Catherine Crowe recognized that poltergeist activity was a particular type of disturbance, which was different from hauntings or other psi phenomena. However, even these early investigators — well into the 1900s — believed that poltergeists were actual spirits with an impish personality.[559] That changed as modern parapsychologists realized that this activity is usually the result of RSMMI (better known as Recurrent Spontaneous Psychokinesis or RSPK) — although some would argue that this term inappropriately limits how we think of poltergeist activity, and implies we understand it better than we do.[560]

Regardless of what it is called, this kind of activity appears to be universal, not only in terms of time — with no century since the ninth having been without it — but also in terms of culture, country, type of habitation, and social status.[561] Unexplained noises and rock throwing are extremely common manifestations, which have been relatively unchanged since loud raps and showers of stones were reported in 355 CE.[562]

Poltergeist phenomena were originally thought to be signs of demonic possession, or the behavior of "evil spirits."[563] Parapsychologists Alan Gauld and Tony Cornell pointed out that of the 18 types of demon described by Martin Del Rio in Book II, Question 27, Section 2 of the *Disquisitionum Magicarum* (1599), one sounds suspiciously like a poltergeist.[564] It is described as haunting certain homes or locations, and not causing physical harm so much as a general upset and commotion. Del Rio gives as examples of this "demon" the cases of William of Paris (who was woken from sleep by thrown stones and the banging of pots, then had his mattress pulled away) and the so-called "fiend of Torquemada" (which indiscriminately hit people with large stones but didn't hurt them). This type of "demon," appears to still be with us today.

Most parapsychologists believe that poltergeists are seldom (if ever) discarnate entities at all, but rather human beings performing a mix of unconscious MMI and fraud, whether conscious or unconscious. This activity is felt to result from projected aggression, which has built up over time, repressed in the unconscious mind, only to be released as an explosion of MMI activity.[565] However, Scott Rogo thought that true demonic possession could account for a few of these incidents.[566] Furthermore, he pointed out that human RSMMI may not always be due to repression, but can have different psychological root causes. For example, in Brazil, where the working class is afraid of black magic, poltergeist cases may break out after someone in the family had been recently "cursed" by a neighbor. He added, "We are therefore faced with the curious paradox that, at least in some cultures, fear of the poltergeist is a common way of conjuring one into existence!"[567]

There have been a great many eyewitness accounts from reputable, intelligent, well educated, and skeptical individuals documented over the centuries, which show consistent patterns of raps and object throwing. The cross-cultural nature of their existence is demonstrated by the fact that poltergeists have been reported in Austria, Belgium, Canada, China, Finland, France, Germany, Greece, Holland, India, Indonesia, Java, Russia, Scandinavia, Spain, Sumatra, Switzerland, the United Kingdom, and the United States. [568]

It is controversial what constitutes the earliest known case of poltergeist phenomena. Some have speculated that poltergeist activity, rather than meteorites, was the basis of the "showers of stones" described by Livy.[569] This event was said to have been among the omens that frightened the Romans during the Second Punic War (218 BCE to 201 BCE). Another candidate for early poltergeist activity, which was written about by Flavius Josephus in 94 CE, is the overturning of a distant bowl of water as a sign of successful exorcism by Eleazar, or similarly of Apollonius of Tyana in the first century. A third likely case was documented in 355 CE, as mentioned earlier.[570] It involved loud raps and unexplained showers of stones.

It should probably not be surprising that there is a scarcity of detailed accounts from the time period between the fall of the Roman Empire and the sixteenth century.[571] Church records indicate a few cases of what sound like poltergeist activity, which, as one might expect, are attributed to the devil, but there is little other written historical data in Western Europe to draw upon during this time. One of the few such accounts is an Icelandic saga, called *Eyrbyggia* (890–1031 CE), which tells of poltergeist manifestations, including fish being torn apart by invisible hands.[572]

Poltergeist-like activity has also been reported in religious and spiritual settings over the centuries. The previously mentioned Curé of Ars, St. Jean Baptiste Vianney, was beset by a poltergeist for 35 years, during which he suffered a combination of loud knocks, the sound of a galloping horse below his room, and "a storm of blows on his furniture," in addition, once, as "he lay in bed, the devil pushed him about the room all night!"[573]

St. Godric is another example of a saint beset by these attacks. Born in Norfolk, St. Godric (1070s–1170) was a poet who spent sixteen years as a seaman before retiring to become a hermit at Finchale around 1110 CE.[574] He remained alone for twenty years, before being joined by his sister for the remaining forty years of his life. Although responsible for writing some of the earliest Middle English religious lyrics with music to survive today, he was also said to have suffered from a variety of "demonic" attacks.[575] Price cited an article by Herbert Thurston which said:

> His hermitage was bombarded with showers of stones and the "Poltergeist" threw at
> him the box in which he kept his altar-beads; took the horn which contained the wine
> he needed for Mass and poured it over his head; and ended by pelting him with almost
> every movable object that his poor cell contained.[576]

From a modern perspective, it would be fascinating to know whether the activity began before or after the saint was joined in the hermitage by his sister and the nature of their relationship.

Poltergeist cases have also occurred in stigmatics.[577] The Blessed Christina of Stommeln (1242–1312) reportedly had her body and other objects thrown about, hot nails and stones pressed into her, her clothes and shoes cut to pieces, and excrement spattered — all of which was, of course, attributed to the devil's malice towards people of sanctity. St. Paul of the Cross (1694–1775) was similarly said to have been assailed by explosions like pieces of artillery being discharged, visions of grotesque animals, the opening and shutting of the warming pan in his room, and being struck and bruised. If we look at this from the perspective of the modern psychologist, it gives one pause to consider what led these individuals to have such a strong need to be tormented.

There are also cases of religiously associated poltergeist activity directed towards others, making one wonder whether the individuals involved were forced into monastic life against their will. Gauld and Cornell described a case in Italy of a young man named Carlo Maria Vulcano.[578] The phenomena started rather simply on May 4, 1696, with stones thrown in the monastery corridors. After this relatively innocuous beginning, the destructiveness and array of activity rapidly accelerated. Phenomena included the "demon" speaking full sentences; the throwing of clothes, furniture, bedding, chamber pots, and dishes; loud noises; the supposed appearance of a figure dressed in white with a face the color of fire; the opening of a window; the breaking of a basin and pitcher full of water without a drop falling to the ground; the locking and unlocking of doors; clothing torn apart or sewn together; the print of a hand on a cassock; the shaking of rooms like an earthquake (causing structural damage, and, in one case, the ceiling to fall in); the replacement of the soft part of bread with horse dung; the binding of people's legs to their balusters; spontaneous fires; the teleportation of money (in some cases into fruit) and a book; a robe and a sheet that seemed to come alive; and the reported appearance of a double of Carlo who beat Carlo's brother, and vexed his mother, while he himself was at Mass. The phenomena ended on March 30, 1697, when it was decided that Carlo should not return to the monastery. One can only marvel at the stamina and determination of the monks to have withstood the onslaught for so long.

Numerous cases of secular and religiously associated poltergeist activity have been documented since the 1500s.[579] The phenomena tend to have a consistent pattern, frequently starting with raps and object throwing, which often escalates in intensity, until tapering off after weeks or months. Unlike hauntings, which are place-oriented, poltergeist phenomena are people-oriented and will tend to follow the focal individuals or families around, wherever they go. Exorcism has had variable success in ending the phenomena, and frequently seems to aggravate the situation, rather than to resolve it.

Scott Rogo noted that although many phenomena are universally reported — such as noises and object throwing — there are some manifestations that appear to reflect idiosyncratic cultural beliefs.[580] Thus, there may be an element of local social expectations shaping events. For example, poltergeist agents have vomited pins and manifested "animal familiars" in cultures where witchcraft traditions exist, while in other cultures the agent created apparent demonic manifestations in conformance with their local customs and beliefs. If this is true, it makes an interesting comment on how we feel about technology, given recent poltergeist activity with telephones and electrical appliances going haywire.

These stories give us a sense of the widespread cross-cultural and cross-temporal nature of spontaneous MMI. In poltergeist activity, psi seems to allow agents to act out and express their inner thoughts, feelings, and beliefs as a kind of living metaphor. As such, they tell us as much about human nature and personality as they do the capacity of the mind to affect the world around it. These cases have been a subject of considerable archival research and field investigation. For the sake of simplicity, the theories and explanations for poltergeist phenomena will therefore be reviewed in Part II of the book under "Poltergeist Research."

The Wild Card: Spontaneous Nonrecurrent MMI

Spontaneous MMI cases can be considered those unexpected and unbidden incidents that crop up in everyday life and cannot be explained through normal means.[581] They are important not only because they allow us to learn about the range of what is possible, but also because, as John Beloff noted, "it is the persistence of such spontaneous phenomena that has kept alive interest in the field among the broad public."[582] Spontaneous cases may appear as isolated events or recurrent ones.

Nonrecurrent spontaneous MMI is impossible to study in the laboratory since it is, by definition, a solitary, uncontrolled event. Thus, it can only be speculated about in anecdotal and case study literature. However, it is difficult to say whether single event MMI truly occurs, or whether it occurs frequently (or even constantly) in life in subtle, unrecognized ways.

There has been a variety of potential (but unproven) nonrecurrent spontaneous psi events anecdotally reported. First, it is possible that some of the incidents we hear of mothers lifting automobiles off their children, and other such extraordinary but unrepeated events, could represent this kind of phenomena.[583] Because the situations that precipitate these events are (fortunately) extremely rare, the events themselves could be nonrecurrent. Unfortunately, none of these cases has been well studied or documented in the literature, so it is impossible to truly discuss them.

Douglas Stokes suggested that the reports of MMI events that occur at the time of a person's death — such as clocks that stop, or portraits that fall off the wall, or objects breaking — may be examples of nonrecurrent spontaneous psi.[584] Louisa Rhine and others have described a variety of these incidents in detail, and even obtained corroborating statements to verify whether these events were more than just one individual's hallucination. Some phone calls from the dead may also fall into this category, as they typically only happen once, before the individual receiving the call knows the person on the other end of the line is deceased.[585]

Human-machine interactions are relatively common spontaneous events — although one suspects it is more often recurrent than recognized. Everything from telephones to cars to computers has been affected. Computer technicians appear to be aware of the impact emotion can have on operating systems and often ask users to consider stepping away from their computers for a bit to calm down. One of the more dramatic computer-related incidents was described by Lyn Buchanan in his book *The Seventh Sense*.[586] In 1984, he shut down major portions of the entire NATO intelligence network as well as the computer systems of many of the then Communist Bloc countries in a fit of rage. It was after that incident that he was recruited for the Stargate military remote viewing program.

Spontaneous human combustion (SHC) is another phenomenon that may represent spontaneous (but seldom-repeated) MMI. This is the rare event where a living human body purportedly ignites and consumes itself with its own heat.[587] In some ways, SHC could be considered the opposite of fire-immunity. It is an interesting, if highly controversial, phenomenon, rarely mentioned in the parapsychological literature, which may represent MMI or some other process.

Three things support the notion that SHC could be related to spontaneous MMI. First, there seems to be a correlation between SHC and the mood of the victims, suggesting that there may be a mind-matter connection.[588] Second is the apparent ability of poltergeist agents to set fires without using normal combustibles, sometimes producing extraordinary forms of incineration. Third is the fact that both religious and nonreligious individuals seem capable of demonstrating fire-immunity, which suggests that the opposite could also be true. Because of these three points and the fact that at least some informal research has been done on it, SHC will be reviewed here as a possible form of nonrecurrent MMI, even though this may not be the case.

About 200 to 300 purported cases of this phenomenon have been reported.[589] The destruction usually begins in the torso, often leaving the limbs and any surrounding items intact. Eric Frank Russell is said to have used the words "ultra-rapid holocaust" to describe this phenomena, and it seems an apt descriptive phrase.[590]

Despite the fact that stories of SHC have been around for over 300 years, little is known about the phenomenon.[591] It is said to have occurred in England, France, India, and the United States. Larry Arnold felt that the knight, Polonus Vorstius, may have been one of the earliest documented cases of SHC.[592] Around 1458–1476, Vorstius drank two ladles of strong wine and vomited a flame. He was said to have been totally consumed.

Another possible case was discussed in the *Acta Medica et Philosophica Hafniensia* by the Danish anatomist Thomas Bartholin in 1663.[593] In it, Bartholin described the case of a woman in Paris, who had long enjoyed her brandy. One night she went up in smoke as she slept, yet did little damage to the straw mattress of her bed and other surroundings.

Although most reported cases of spontaneous SHC involve a single individual, Arnold speculated that the Biblical story of the Assyrian invasion of Judah around 701 BCE might have been a case of mass SHC.[594] Arnold based his theory on material that comes from Egyptian and Hebrew sources, which described a "night of fire" for Sennacherib's army of 185,000, and stated that "their souls were burnt, though their garments remained intact."[595]

That their clothing was unharmed — a characteristic peculiar to SHC — would seem to lend some weight to this possibility.[596]

Archival research in medical jurisprudence texts can provide a valuable source of information, because suspicion of foul play encourages thorough investigation and documentation.[597] For example, in 1725, the wife of a Frenchman, Millet of Rheims, was found reduced to a pile of ashes. The presence of a pretty servant girl fueled concerns he was guilty, and Millet was charged with murder. However, at the inquiry, the incident was acknowledged as a case of SHC, and Millet was released.

Mary Reeser was one of the better known recent cases of SHC.[598] She was a mildly depressed elderly woman who died on the night of July 1, 1951. Her remains were found in a blackened circle on the floor, with a few coiled springs, a charred liver, a fragment of backbone, a skull the size of a fist, and, on the edge of the scorched patch where her armchair once stood, and a black satin slipper enclosing a left foot burnt off at the ankle. The case was investigated by firemen, arson experts, insurance agents, and pathologists, but no cause for the fire could be found. The gas heater was turned off both inside the house and outside at the tank; the stove and other electrical appliances were off except for the running refrigerator; and no fuses were blown. Nor was there the odor of burning flesh — often a problem with crematorium smoke — and no one had heard anything unusual.

The FBI was unable to find evidence of chemicals that would have accelerated the fire, and there were no indications of a storm or lightning strike that night.[599] At the inquest, it was said that even the crematorium fires of 2,500°F, which are maintained for four hours to incinerate a body, would not be sufficient to cause the degree of disintegration in which Mrs. Reeser's body was found.[600] Furthermore, a pile of newspapers less than a foot away was not burned. In addition, her skull was shrunk by the heat, which, according to pathologist Dr. Wilton Krogman, would normally have the opposite effect.

Most victims of SHC are reported to be elderly persons living alone, or people who are depressed.[601] There also seems to be a high correlation with alcoholism, as well as with being overweight and sedentary.[602] Although Vincent Gaddis stated that the preponderance of victims are women, Arnold disputed this, saying, "Parascience International's database indicates gender is inconsequential to classic SHC, with females statistically just *slightly* more predisposed to SHC."[603] The phenomenon has been reported in young people, but only rarely in children.[604] Arnold felt the youngest victim of SHC was six weeks, while the oldest was 114.[605] It may have a seasonal pattern, in that the phenomenon is almost exclusively reported during winter.[606] Arnold summed up the predisposition of invalids, widows/widowers, and chronically depressed individuals with the comment that, "being physically *and* psychologically moribund is a red flag for internal fire."[607]

The setting of SHC is usually in the victim's house (often a bedroom) although reports have occurred with individuals who were in boats, cars, and city streets.[608] Most of the time investigators can find no external source of a flame.[609] What makes SHC particularly remarkable is that the fire mainly consumes living flesh.[610] Although the body may be reduced to greasy ashes, the fire seems to be confined to a small area, often leaving the victim's clothes and nearby items virtually untouched. Another notable feature of SHC is that the people involved make no outcry. It is unknown whether this is because of the speed of the process, the presence of an ASC, some form of paralysis, or another factor.

There have been a few accounts of victims found in the process of being consumed with flames. For example, there is one reported case of a woman dying in public.[611] It was said that she had been out dancing all night, when on the dance floor she suddenly glowed with blue flames and was reduced to ashes. Unfortunately, this and other such reported cases have shed little light on the phenomenon.

Traveling salesman Jack Angel was one of the few survivors of apparent SHC.[612] He went to sleep at night in his camper at a Ramada Inn in Georgia on November 12, 1974, and awoke to find that his right hand was burned black, and other burns dotted his legs from groin to ankle. Remarkably, he was in no pain at this time. He showered and dressed before going to the hotel. There, he was shocked to discover the date was November 16th. Angel collapsed unconscious and was rushed to a nearby hospital where doctors examined him and found that the burn appeared to be from the inside out.

Angel's leg injuries healed, but his hand had to be amputated.[613] Electrical burns have been known to cause more internal damage than external damage; however, they would still have entry and exit wounds on the surface. The initial lack of pain could be true for a variety of possible reasons, including the total destruction of the nerve endings that could transmit pain, an ASC, shock, or drug usage. The fact that Angel awoke the second time (in the hospital) in excruciating pain suggests that the nerve endings had not been completely destroyed. Investigation into the cause of the fire revealed that no freak storms or lightning had occurred that night, the camper electrical system was normal, Angel was not smoking that night, and had not been scalded by boiling water. Angel's case is typical in the sense that those who are found alive usually have no idea why the fire began.

Unlike normal burns from fire (which are excruciating), SHC appears to be a painless process, even when the victims are awake and free from the influence of drugs or alcohol.[614] For example, in 1788, a man entered a room where a young English chambermaid was scrubbing the floor, oblivious to the fact that a fire was blazing on her back. It was only when he shouted and she turned to look that she became aware of the flames. Another such episode apparently occurred in 1916, when Thomas W. Morphey found his housekeeper, Lillian Green, burned and dying, with the floor under her body only slightly scorched and nothing else in the room showing signs of the fire or how it started. In the hospital, Green was able to speak, but could not explain what had happened. A third such case was that of Madge Knight, who woke the household with her screams on November 19, 1943, and was found lying in her bed with her back badly burned, but with no trace of scorching on the sheets or on her bedclothes. When asked how it had happened, Knight said she did not know.

In 1808, The French scholar Pierre-Aime Lair summarized many of the features noted in these cases in the *Journal de Physique*.[615] He noted that the victims had eight characteristics: (1) they had a long history of heavy alcohol intake; (2) they were women; (3) they were elderly; (4) the feet and hands were generally spared; (5) water sometimes increased the flames; (6) combustible objects in contact with them while they were burning were often spared; (7) their bodies left a residue of fat, fetid ashes, and a sticking, penetrating soot; (8) they did not take fire spontaneously but were burnt by accident. Although later purported cases have indicated that men can also be the victims of SHC, Lair's original description is still generally true.

Lair never offered a suggestion for what triggered this "accidental" fire, which makes one wonder if he simply could not accept the idea that combustion could be spontaneous. If so, he would not be alone. Most people have trouble accepting the existence of SHC. The problem it presents is an obvious one — there does not seem to be a normal way in which a body could produce the degree of heat needed for near total self-disintegration. On the other hand, if that high a temperature occurred outside the body, then it is inexplicable why the effects would be limited to the body, while leaving nearby, flammable objects completely unharmed.

In 1763, a respected physician named Jonas Dupont published *De Incendis Corporis Humani Spontaneis*, in which he proposed that the friction caused by particles in the bloodstream created animal heat.[616] He speculated that when the body temperature was raised past a certain threshold, it could touch off the alcohol to ignite a conflagration. That Dupont should have come up with this theory is, perhaps, not surprising considering that of the 23 examples of apparent SHC reported by the year 1800, 19 of them involved alcohol. In the centuries since then, a history of alcohol abuse has continued to be a frequent (but not universal) finding in SHC. However, if alcohol alone were the primary factor in SHC, one would wonder why more alcoholics do not go up in smoke.

In recent years, some have suggested that victims simply fell asleep while smoking — which would be more credible if all of the victims smoked.[617] Another theory is that there is a build-up of phosphagen (a naturally occurring substance in muscle), which is similar to nitroglycerin and might make the body combustible.[618] This does not explain why the phosphagen would build up or how the fire starts. Still other theories involve the "explosive" properties of human emotion, the presence of an undetected "pyrotron" particle, or being an obscure result of the fluctuating geomagnetic field of the Earth. None of these explanations seem very adequate or plausible.

Arnold proposed that SHC is related to Kundalini (*see* Glossary) energy.[619] He based his notion on the fact that Swami Rama is said to have once said that it was possible (if rarely done) to get rid of the body by meditating on the solar plexus until the "internal flame of fire burns the body in a fraction of a second ... and everything is reduced to ashes."[620] This self-incineration therefore a result of consciousness and energy. According to Rama, SHC is simply taking the same effect that can be used to warm yourself (a kind of body heat production known as "tumo") to extreme.[621] However, this does not seem to fit with the fact that most SHC victims are depressed, sedentary alcoholics, who do not appear to be particularly evolved spiritually.

Maxwell Cade and Delphine Davis argue that there is nothing "spontaneous" about the human combustion at all, because the real culprit is ball lightning, which may cook a body from the inside out by emitting micro-waves, or by a direct explosion.[622] Ball lightning is an unusual phenomenon with almost ghostly qualities.[623] Thought to be a form of electromagnetic plasma, it is capable of floating gently along, squeezing through keyholes and chinks in window frames, or down fireplace chimneys, can suddenly and dramatically change directions and rotate in the air, may bounce off surfaces, and been said to sometimes materialize inside rooms or airplane cabins. Furthermore, this natural phenomenon can be as small as a pea, or as large as a house, and may be violet, red, blue, or yellow, and may even change colors during its brief life. It may wreck a room, or silently fade away. Eyewitness accounts have described cases in which the plasma balls have caused burns, or exploded in a flash of fire to cause tremendous damage.

Not all would agree with Cade and Davis. David Turner observed that little heat is usually sensed and they do not cause any damage.[624] In addition, they tend to be brief phenomena, often lasting under a minute. In addition, William Corliss noted that ball lightning has seldom been known to harm people, and may even seem to follow them about.[625] However, Cade and Davis cited a case in April 1961, where a man responded to cries from the living room to find his wife lying on a rug on the floor, burning fiercely, and a blazing lightning ball hovering over her. The man was badly burned trying to extinguish the flames, and the woman did not survive. As with SHC, the rug on which she lay was not burned, nor was the rest of the room damaged in any way.[626] Cade and Davis also reported other cases where witnesses came upon individuals, still alive, who were actively burning. One would have to assume that these individuals might have been hit by a lesser version of ball lightning than that which would have reduced the body to ashes.

Ball lightning is an appealing theory for the causation of SHC and perhaps even some fires attributed to poltergeists, which would seem to fit many of the facts. The variability of the plasma balls themselves — both in terms of appearance and behavior — further adds to the plausibility that a rare variation of ball lightning might be able to cremate a body. However, there are three problems with this theory. First, that ball lightning usually explodes with a loud bang, or report like that of a cannon, while, in many cases of SHC, no one hears anything unusual, whether the victim crying out or a loud noise.[627] Second, it is unclear why a natural phenomenon, like ball lightning, would single out depressed, elderly individuals.[628] Third, there is the issue of why ball lightning would target human bodies, while leaving clothes, sheets, and nearby combustibles unharmed.

The seasonal association of SHC is a curious finding. It is possible that winter is what statisticians call a third variable, which is not directly related to SHC, but indirectly correlated to it. Thus, it could be that during that time of year meteorological variables are more conducive for creating a particular type of ball lightning, or the season has an effect on key human factors in the process, such as by increasing levels of depression. Norman Rosenthal noted that in recent years, science has begun to understand the importance of the changing seasons on human moods and behavior.[629] He reported that, "for as many as one in four persons, these changes are a problem.... [T]here are those for whom seasonal transitions trigger extreme changes in mood and energy, and produce sadness and despair."[630]

Seasonal Affective Disorder is a winter-triggered depression, which is now well recognized in the literature.[631] Depression is more common in women, with a lifetime risk of 20–36 percent, as opposed to men, who have an 8–12 percent lifetime risk.[632] However, although 80 percent of people committing suicide are depressed, a recent study of suicides in Finland shows that there is a decrease in suicide rate in the winter months.[633] This may be, in part, because when a person is severely depressed they do not have enough energy to kill themselves. Psychologists often worry far more about suicidal tendencies when patients are starting to recover from their feelings of depression.

Vincent Gaddis felt that, as most of these deaths show no signs of an external cause, the source of the fires must be from within.[634] He based this in part on the ability of poltergeist agents to sometimes burn objects from the inside out, and to instantly, and uniformly, destroy items with fire.[635] Should MMI be involved, then it might explain why a psychological state (in this case, depression) could be a factor. In addition, an ASC could be explain the lack of pain. A number of apparent cases of SHC have occurred in individuals who were in the process of (or perhaps focused on) committing suicide. It is unclear whether the mind can indeed destroy the body per se as a direct effect or an indirect one, perhaps by attracting or materializing ball lighting or through some other means.

SHC is an intriguing, if poorly understood, phenomenon that appears to have been around for centuries, if not millennia. There are a number of psychological variables that correlate with its occurrence, which suggests that something more than a physical agent may cause the phenomenon. It is unclear whether SHC is related to MMI. However, the fact that poltergeist agents can cause rapid and unusual fires would seem to raise the possibility of a connection.

Summary

Stories of MMI cut across all religions, cultures, and eras. Performers range from everyday individuals to poltergeist agents, African witchdoctors, Native American shamans, Haitian Voodoo priests, Hindu fakirs, Jewish rabbis, Catholic saints, nuns, and priests, Buddhist monks, and Islamic holy men. Similar types of events — including levitation, fire-immunity, stigmata, inedia, poltergeist activity, luminosity, incendium amoris, hemography, food multiplication, miraculous healing, teleportation, and bilocation — have been reported in most religions, although the kinds of miracles performed (and recorded) have sometimes varied depending on the culture's needs and interests.[636] The same individuals commonly exhibit several such abilities, which can change in character over time, depending, one suspects, on their needs (if only on an unconscious level).

A skeptic would point out that these similarities could also be because it is easy to perpetrate certain kinds of trickery. There is truth to this. Wherever there is potential gain — whether in terms of money, prestige, or winning converts to one's viewpoint or religion — there will always be impetus for fraud. However, many of those who studied or wrote about these events were no more credulous than we are today. Indeed, skeptics appear to have been around for as long as the phenomena themselves. James McClenon cited the presence of debunkers in early Asia, and Michael Loewe and Carmen Blacker noted a lot of cynicism regarding divination in early Rome as well.[637] Furthermore, the Catholic Church has always been cautious about accepting miracles and careful in its documentation, not wanting to look foolish. If the things that have been recorded — and in some cases witnessed by contemporary observers — are true, then at least some events appear to be beyond what fraud could explain.

Physical mediumship and MMI took a different historical course in the West than the East. For centuries, these abilities were only sanctioned in a few Catholic religious figures in Europe, whereas in Asia, the traditions of training and practice in healing and martial-arts psi continued virtually unchanged for thousands of years.[638] The advent of Spiritualism with the rappings of the Fox sisters ushered in a new era of interest in physical mediumship in Europe and the United States.[639] The resulting increase in numbers of apparent MMI performers provided researchers with participants for their experiments, and fueled popular interest in the field. This ultimately led to the formation of scientific societies dedicated to the study and understanding of psi phenomena.

The opening up of lines of communication between the East and the West deepened our understanding of the breadth and nature of MMI.[640] Two important pieces of information came to us from the Yogis and Masters of India, China, and Tibet. First, that these abilities can be used either positively or negatively, for healing or harm, defense or attack, depending on the intent of the practitioner and second, that every human being has the potential to develop psi abilities with sufficient time, dedication, and practice. Whether spiritual or secular MMI, these abilities have long been associated with ASC, frequently those of meditation, prayer, and ecstasy.[641]

There is a correlation between extraordinary sports performances and an ASC — often referred to by athletes as "the zone."[642] The athletic "zone" appears to be similar to an ASC used by Yogis and martial artists. A phenomenological study of the athletic "zone" described its essence as a state of focused concentration, withdrawal of attention from distractions, in-the-moment beingness, effortless absorption, a sense of unity, and a feeling of moving in harmony with the universe. Murphy and White speculated that psychic abilities may be an important factor in these performances. This may well be true, as we will later see that MMI experiential research reveals a similar (if not identical) ASC is employed.

Isolated spontaneous events may include clocks stopping at the time someone dies, mothers lifting cars off their babies unaided, and SHC. However, the bulk of spontaneous MMI is recurrent, and falls into one of two categories, either as poltergeist phenomena or as spiritually associated MMI, with some overlap between the two groups. In Part III of this book, we will see that there may be good reason for the frequent association of MMI with spirituality. Many of the features of fervent religious prayer — such as openness to the experience, feelings of connection to God and/or the universe, intense focus, lack of ego, suspension of the intellect, trust in a higher power, and an ASC, often one of ecstatic trance or meditation — are all constituents of the MMI experience. Whether one considers man or God to be the source of these abilities, they appear to represent the power of spirit, or the mind, over matter.

Although there are a few cultural variations, poltergeist cases typically have consistent patterns of activity across cultures and times, and involve such things as loud noises and object movements that occur around a single person or family.[643] These sometimes dramatic and robust phenomena frequently seem to occur in response to powerful needs and desires that cannot be met in other, more ordinary ways.[644]

Although case reports may have little evidential value, as Douglas Stokes noted, their quick dismissal by many is a mistake.[645] The observation of people, places, and events in their natural environment is a key aspect of most branches of science. These stories give us a sense of the scope and variety of phenomena. They show us the importance of ASC, the universality of MMI, its goal-oriented nature, and the fact that the unconscious mind can use MMI to meet its needs — with or without the knowledge of its conscious counterpart. With that said, it is time to consider the formal experimental research.

PART II

MMI Research and Theory

Research typically falls into one of three broad categories: (1) experimental research, 2) quasi-experimental research, and (3) nonexperimental research. Since each of these types of study has advantages and limitations, it is helpful to understand the differences between them.

True experimental research manipulates one variable (called the independent variable) while trying to control some (or all) of the other variables. The study participants (called subjects in the case of animals) are randomly assigned to different levels (groups) of the independent variable. Experimental research frequently uses control groups and/or single-or double-blind procedures in an effort to separate out those results due to the independent variable from those of other factors, such as third variables, experimenter bias, and expectancy effects. Changes in a dependent variable are often measured quantitatively, and the results may suggest or indicate causality — in other words, it can establish "proof."

Quasi-experimental research differs from experimental research in that the participants are not randomly assigned to the levels (groups) of the independent variable. A great deal of research involving human beings is technically "quasi-experimental," since one cannot randomly assign participants such things as gender, age, personality traits, or talent. Instead, the participants are assigned to their naturally occurring groups (such as male/female).

Non-experimental research includes archival research, case histories, surveys, and field investigations. This kind of work makes no attempt to control variables. Because of this, non-experimental research cannot provide "proof" or make cause and effect statements. However, what it can do is give a sense of the range and types of activity. It has good ecological validity in that it looks at a subject as it exists in the real world and is also useful in studying phenomena where other forms of research might be impossible or unethical. Furthermore, nonexperimental research is valuable in documenting the richness and variety of spontaneous psi, as well as giving us a general sense of the factors and themes associated with it.

The methods most often used to study spontaneous psi phenomena include (1) door-to-door, mail, or telephone surveys; (2) appeals for case reports made through the media; (3) analysis of unsolicited cases sent to parapsychological centers; and (4) diaries.[1] In his review of spontaneous psi phenomena, Douglas Stokes pointed out that the type of incidents one gets will depend in part on the way in which they are collected, as well as the criteria used as to what is, or is not, evidence of psi. Together, these factors can have a major impact on the final makeup of cases in a collection.

75

Each of the methods used to collect spontaneous case reports has its limitations.[2] Chief among these are obtaining a representative sample of the population, and having the person who is writing the questions or collecting the data do so in such a way that he or she doesn't bias the results. Experimenter bias can also creep into how questions are asked and the answers interpreted. Physical effects are reported much less frequently than ESP, but it is impossible to say whether this is because they are rarer, or simply noticed and/or reported less often. Performers who are questioned often start by saying they had only one or two MMI experiences, but then, as they start to think about it realize that they have had a great many more experiences than first thought.

Field investigation is an active and valuable area of nonexperimental research, which allows us to study psi phenomena in their natural settings.[3] Poltergeist research and haunting investigations rely on this method of study, since the events tend to stop when the family dynamics are changed, and ghosts seldom volunteer to go into the laboratory for testing. Although the data from spontaneous case reports and field investigations is not evidential in itself, it *can* shed valuable light on when, why, and how MMI operates. The following chapters will take a detailed look at a variety of kinds of MMI, and what we have learned about them using these various research methods.

Spontaneous Case Collections

Systematic scholarly research on psychic phenomena (often referred to as psi or Ψ) did not begin until the formation of the SPR in 1882 in London. The SPR was composed of a remarkable group of leading citizens and eminent scientists.[4] The latter group included Sir William Barrett (a professor of physics at the Royal College of Science in Dublin) who initiated the formation of the SPR; Sir Oliver Lodge; Alfred Wallace, a man of impeccable integrity; Sir William Crookes, discoverer of the element thallium; Nobel prize winner Lord Raleigh, head of the Cavendish Laboratory at Cambridge, and discoverer of the gas argon; and Nobel laureate J. J. Thompson, discoverer of the electron. Notable individuals included Henry Sidgwick, a Cambridge moral philosopher whose reputation for caution and skepticism made him a excellent choice as the SPR's first president; Sidgwick's Cambridge disciples Frederic Myers, Edmund Gurney, and Richard Hodgson; Sidgwick's wife, Eleanor Balfour, a pioneer of women's education and the first principal of Newnham College, Cambridge; and brothers-in-law Arthur Balfour, a philosopher and the Prime Minister of England from 1902–1905, and Gerald Balfour, a classicist and politician. Oxford graduate Frank Podmore was yet another key member, who became the SPR's leading historian. This core group, in addition to the occasional celebrities who joined them — such as Charles Dodgson (Lewis Carroll), William Gladstone, Alfred Lord Tennyson, John Ruskin, and the painter G. F. Watts — were a highly respected and intelligent group of individuals, whose standing in society, and the scientific community, meant that their findings carried significant weight.

Although motivated by a desire to establish survival of bodily death (with a large portion of their funding coming from Spiritualists), the society formed six committees. Each of these was responsible for the study of one topic: (1) thought-transference; (2) mesmerism; (3) Reichenbach's (*see* Glossary) and other phenomena involving the purported luminous emanations seen by certain "sensitives" as coming from the poles of magnets, crystals, and human bodies; (4) physical phenomena; (5) haunted houses; and (6) the literature.[5]

One of the early products of their research — which some would say was their crowning opus — was a set of spontaneous case reports called *Phantasms of the Living*. This two-volume work was published in 1886 by Edmund Gurney, Frederic W. H. Myers, and Frank Podmore.[6] This book focused on ESP, but also described a variety of apparent MMI events, such as clocks stopping at the exact moment of someone's death, and bilocation. It went beyond simple archival research by painstakingly combining case histories, anecdotal material, and archival research, cross-referencing every account where possible with those of other witnesses and sources of information.

Little was done with case reports again until 1948, when Louisa Rhine decided to evaluate the spontaneous cases that had accumulated at the Duke Parapsychology Laboratory.[7] Instead of trying to validate the individual reports, Louisa Rhine chose to accept at face value all of the accounts that appeared to be written in good faith wherein information was received without the senses and/or effects were produced without the muscles. She categorized the incidents by their basic features to get a sense of the types of phenomena reported and their relative rates of occurrence.

Most of the experiences collected by Louisa Rhine fell into the ESP category.[8] However, by 1963, she had collected 178 cases of apparent spontaneous MMI. These included 65 incidents of objects falling off walls or shelves; 49 incidents of clocks or watches showing erratic movements or stopping; 21 cases of objects breaking or exploding where they stood; 17 of lights turning on or off; 14 of openings, closings, locking, or unlocking of doors; and 12 cases in which objects moved or rocked.

Louisa Rhine recorded a number of these incidents in detail, and, when possible, obtained corroborating statements to verify whether these events were more than one individual's hallucination.[9] One such story of a nonrecurrent spontaneous MMI event that was sent to Louisa Rhine came from a Nevada woman, whose older brother, Frank, had given their mother a cut-glass dish, which her mother adored and kept out on the sideboard.[10] Two days after Frank left on a trip, the glass dish suddenly broke in two with a popping sound. Her mother cried out that she knew Frank had just died. It proved to be true. They later learned he was shot at the same time as the dish had broken.

There were a number of similarly detailed cases, wherein physical effects involving timepieces or other objects occurred at the time of a death. Louisa Rhine found that of the 68 episodes that involved vocal sound, only 28 percent were heard by a second person, whereas mechanical sounds, such as raps, were heard by 93 percent.[11] A similar study performed later by Leca Virtanen also found about 35 percent of sounds such as bumps, thuds, and rattles were heard by multiple witnesses, but had no cases in which clear words were perceived by more than one person.

Louisa Rhine made the important observation that spontaneous nonrecurrent MMI events were frequently linked with a crisis, and that many of the involved objects were personally meaningful.[12] She also recognized that two people were generally involved — one as witness to it and another undergoing a crisis, often at a distance.[13] In addition, the process appeared to be unconscious, with neither of the involved individuals knowingly "willing" the MMI to happen.

Louisa Rhine was aware that case reports could only suggest what was occurring, and never prove.[14] However, as with the stories in Part I of this book, they reflect the importance of meaning in MMI, and strongly suggest that the conscious mind need not be involved for events to occur. In his review of her case studies, Irwin observed that all of these reports had one feature in common — that of personal meaning.[15] This personal significance is a factor that, although sometimes overlooked by experimentalists, appears to be key to the manifestation of spontaneous MMI, whether an isolated episode, or, as we shall see in the next section, as recurrent events.

Poltergeist Research

Poltergeist activity is, by its very nature, difficult to bring into the laboratory. Also known as RSMMI (or more often RSPK), the majority of investigations have therefore relied upon archival research, surveys, and field investigations. This chapter will look at those studies, discuss the types and patterns of activity reported, and review possible theories and explanations for the phenomena.

Archival Research and Surveys

Although there have been a few surveys performed on metal-bending, the vast bulk of MMI archival research has focused on poltergeist activity and anomalous healing. Poltergeist activity has a number of advantages over other forms of MMI, in that it is dramatic (which allows the phenomena to come to the attention of the investigator), widespread (making it accessible), and tends to occur over a period that lasts from months to years (allowing it to be observed).

Curiosity about the truth of these reports is by no means limited to recent times. Attempts to ascertain whether something anomalous is going on, and, if so, what is involved, have been made for hundreds of years, using a variety of approaches. Early researchers collected poltergeist accounts as "ghost" stories, while later investigators worked to corroborate the data.[16]

Seventeenth-century Europe was fascinated by witchcraft. It was in this environment in the 1600s that Henry More, Joseph Glanvill, and other British intellectuals started meeting regularly to discuss paranormal topics.[17] They expressed many of the same concerns as parapsychologists do today. For example, Henry More wrote about the need to eliminate cases of fraud and hallucination in studying apparitions and poltergeist phenomena.[18] Glanvill, on the other hand, was more interested in the quality of the testimony. He developed a questionnaire for case histories, which was designed to document those events that were recent enough to permit reliable statements. These forms were sent out not only to learn the details of the case, but also the quality of the witnesses. Glanvill wanted to do more than just create an interesting collection of stories — he wanted to verify them. Because of this, many consider Glanvill to be the forerunner of psychical research. He eventually wrote a substantial book of psychical cases in 1700, some of which he had personally investigated.[19]

The Catholic Church was likewise interested in separating authentic "miracles" from various human cases, whether misperceived events, fraud, or MMI by the living. In the 1730s, they authorized Prospero Lambertini (who later became Pope Benedict XIV) to investigate case reports of psychic phenomena.[20] His dissertation, *De Canonizatione*, is still considered the official Church authority on miracles and a guide for papal authorities to determine which miraculous deeds of saintly individuals are divine in origin and which are "merely" a paranormal effect of the mind.

Despite having been put forth nearly three hundred years ago, Lambertini's findings are remarkably similar to our current thinking about psi phenomena.[21] He stated that (1) psychic experiences can occur to anyone and need not be divine miracles; (2) apparitions have little to do with sanctity or demonic beings; (3) prophecy occurs more often in sleep than in the awake state; (4) it is difficult for prophets to distinguish between their own thoughts and ESP messages; and (5) predictions often take symbolic forms. The fact that these conclusions have stood the test of centuries of observations suggests that a consistent process, rather than a cultural one, is involved.

Examples of contemporary spontaneous psi archival research include *Poltergeists: An Annotated Bibliography of Works in English, Circa 1880–1975* by Michael Goss, the compilations of cases included in *Can We Explain the Poltergeist?* by A. R. G. Owen, and *Poltergeists* by Alan Gauld and A. D. Cornell. Goss' book is, as the title describes, a summary and listing in alphabetical order by the authors of all the available references and articles to poltergeist activity published in the English language between the years of 1880 and 1975. It is an extremely thorough list, but gives little detail about what happened. Owen's book documents different types of poltergeist cases, spurious and otherwise, and interprets the data. However, the best read is Gauld and Cornell's book, which is a well-written and interesting compilation of poltergeist case histories listed in chronological order. They used a variety of sources for their material, including diaries, published treatises, pamphlets, letters, and court records.

Litigation over a leased house becoming uninhabitable, or some person being suspected of producing phenomena by natural or occult means, represents the majority of the cases suggestive of MMI in court records. Surviving official court records of trials that sound like they involve poltergeists are rare before the nineteenth century, and only a handful exist for the eighteenth century or earlier.[22] However, accusations of witchcraft were common in the seventeenth century. Sometimes fueled by the injudicious comments of the suspected perpetrator, things could go ill indeed for the alleged witch. Legal action seems to have been especially common in Germany, and torture or imprisonment sometimes followed.

The pattern of early poltergeist cases is similar to those of later decades. Gauld and Cornell described a number of these cases in detail.[23] One of the earliest occurred around 1525–1526, at the Abbey of St. Pierre in France. It involved raps and the apparent levitation of an eighteen-year-old nun who seemed to be the focal agent, but was successfully resolved through ecclesiastical ceremonies.

A second, and more dramatic, case involved a peasant farmer's family with their two sons, one sixteen and the other nine years old, in Germany on February 28, 1581.[24] The activity kicked off with raps and thrown clods of dirt, but then escalated to the throwing of rocks, plates, spoons, dishes, shoes, jars, and all kinds of household objects. Visits from priests caused only temporary respites, and the attacks grew more vicious.[25] Eventually the father and elder son were seized, partly strangled, and driven from the house under the pelting of axes, hatchets, oven-forks, and excrement. Half of the people in the village are said to have witnessed objects hurling out of the house. Repeated Masses were performed, and the phenomenon finally seemed to die out around April 28 — although whether of its own accord or due to the dramatic intervention of the Bishop casting himself face down on the living room floor to pray for the family, it is impossible to say.

Yet another sixteenth-century case involved the George Lee family in England.[26] It began with stone throwing through the roof of the house on November 29, 1591. No holes could be found that the rocks could have passed through — a not uncommon finding in poltergeist cases. As in some other cases, there seemed to be an intelligence involved and the "poltergeist" sometimes responded to requests to drop a given size or kind of stone. The family finally abandoned the house and moved in with the vicar.

Eventually, Edward Lee (the father of the man who owned the place) moved into it.[27] This time there was the sound of footsteps and other household objects were thrown in addition to the stones. Lee marked some of the landing spots for bolsters with chalk, but the chalk was wiped out despite the involved room being locked with no one in it. This activity continued until January 6, 1592. However, the break proved to be a short one. It started up again in a different form on February 15, 1592. This time, drops of what looked like blood appeared on the walls, the house lit up as if by a fire, apparitions of strange or grotesque animals (possibly dogs) appeared, and the stones fell more violently and followed George around. A variety of gentlemen investigated the case, including the sheriff. The phenomena only stopped with George Lee's death in May 1592.

These cases demonstrate the same basic patterns of poltergeist behavior as are seen today, despite the fact that they occurred over 400 years ago. Levitation and movement of objects — sometimes including heavy furniture, or tables with people sitting on them — is still frequently reported, in addition to the nearly universal raps, knocks, and scratching sounds.[28]

There are several reasons why these poltergeist stories should be considered carefully. First, these cases were witnessed by a large number of spectators.[29] Second, their reports appeared to be written by educated men who considered, and rejected, alternative explanations. Third, there was no financial gain involved — indeed the destructiveness of the activity often caused significant loss. Fourth, although fraud is always a concern, in these cases it would have required a large conspiracy of individuals. And finally, there are at least some incidents, such as the 1772 Stockwell case, which seem beyond that which could be performed by trickery. Price, an authority on conjuring, is said to have stated that the greatest living conjurer could not have produced the effects that occurred in a well-lit room while surrounded by people watching for trickery. In this instance, a young maid of twenty appears to have been the focal person. Liquids boiled over from their containers and there was tremendous destruction of pottery, glass, and china, some of which appeared to break spontaneously.

The majority of early poltergeist investigators were wise enough to look for normal explanations for the phenomena and motivation for fraud. In many cases, they were unable to find them, and as much of what has been written about these cases sounds as if it comes from prudent and educated men, consideration has to be made that at least some of this data is something more than the product of hysteria and misperception.

Field Investigations

Fieldwork was one of the earliest methods used by parapsychological researchers and remains one of the few ways that spontaneous MMI can be investigated. Case studies of poltergeists have been conducted since Robert Boyle first published a detailed treatise on the Perrault account of noises and object movements in the home of a Protestant minister in 1642 in France.[30] Many reports have followed in the centuries since then.[31] Harvey Irwin noted that although these cases may be categorized in terms of their predominant type of activity, their most common feature was object movement.[32] For a chart of the characteristics of 500 poltergeist cases from various periods and locales, as well as a listing of apparent cases in historical order, the interested reader should turn to pages 224–240 and 363–398 of Gauld and Cornell's book *Poltergeists*.

After successfully re-activating Tina Resch's poltergeist activity using hypnosis, Roll and Baumann brought her into the laboratory for some controlled MMI experiments.[33] The results of the tests were promising albeit inconclusive, but the experimenters observed that spontaneous MMI occurred during breaks in the test routine. They therefore set up a table of targets, which Tina was not allowed near, thus bringing a field investigation into the laboratory. A foot-long socket wrench was the heaviest item to move, and went 18 feet without catching the attention of either experimenter, both of whom stood between Tina and the starting position of the wrench. They recorded a total of 21 movements (8 from the target table) and observed a decrease in activity with distance.

Podmore was one of the first investigators to observe that in every involved home there was a prepubescent or teenage child.[34] He misinterpreted this to mean that all of the activity could be explained away as fraudulent. Although fraud often accompanies poltergeist phenomena, it does not appear to be the sum total of the experience.[35] One of the reasons that trickery has often been suspected is that the phenomena frequently go on hiatus when field investigators appear on the scene.[36] However, an alternate explanation is that the presence of strangers changes the family dynamics and alters the situation. This means that observers may need to stay until they are no longer noticed or else settle for working with the accounts of what happened before they arrived. Recent years have seen an explosion of interest by the general public in field investigations of hauntings and poltergeists. Unfortunately, few of these investigations are published in journals.

TYPES AND PATTERNS OF ACTIVITY REPORTED

Poltergeist cases can involve a wide range of macro–MMI effects, including biting, the movement of objects, percussive sounds, flickering or steady lights, apparitions, the appearance of water, spontaneous fires, the production of human voices, teleportation, and electrical disturbances.[37] One of the more curious kinds of phenomena is when objects arrange themselves into patterns or tableaus inside empty rooms or houses.[38] On the surface, these would seem to be wildly diverse alleged happenings. The reason that they are lumped together in one category is because they (1) are frequently localized around a person, instead of a place (as in a haunting); (2) are for the most part physical; (3) do not have an immediately obvious and normal explanation; and (4) seem to be associated not only with each other, but with percussive sounds and object movements.[39]

Fire poltergeists can be highly destructive, not only causing repeated small fires, but sometimes even burning down a house.[40] The quality of these fires can also be amazing at times, such as in the case of a book that, when taken from a desk drawer, was found to be burning inside, even though its cover was in perfect condition. Nor does there need to be any electricity or fire in the house for blazes to start.

The Douglas MacDonald family is an example of a fire poltergeist.[41] The family consisted of Mr. and Mrs. MacDonald and their three adopted daughters, the youngest of whom was 21. The incidents began on April 16, 1963, in Nova Scotia with a fire on the second floor of the house. The damage was extensive. Since the origin of the blaze was unknown, it was decided to cut off the electrical current to the house. Two days later, Mrs. MacDonald was cleaning up debris when an insurance investigator arrived. They began to smell smoke while they were talking. On investigating, they discovered a new fire on the second floor, which was easily extinguished. However, a few hours later, another fire broke out on the second floor, which spread rapidly and had to be extinguished by firemen working through the windows.

The MacDonalds decided to have the house rewired, despite the lack of power at the time of these fires.[42] On May 16, when Mrs. MacDonald and her adopted daughter Betty stopped by to check on the work, they noticed smoke and called the firemen. This time the fire was in a first floor bathroom, inside an enclosed recess in papers sitting in a cardboard box. The firemen put out the flames and left. By this time they should have known better, because they were back again less than 30 minutes later for a bedroom closet fire. After the flames were extinguished, the firefighters sought a cause, but could find no explanation and left again.

Two hours later, the firemen returned, this time to put out a fire inside a wall cupboard that seemed to have no source for the blaze, such as oily rags or chemicals.[43] They departed, only to be called back half an hour later for a small fire on the back porch. Apparently, the firemen finally learned their lesson, because after the blaze was out, the fire chief called the police chief, who in turn assigned an officer to remain at the house. Shortly afterward, a visitor noticed a section of wallboard was smoking. A neighbor pried it loose and stamped the fire out. The policeman examined the wallboard, but could find no smoke or sign of fire in the space behind the wall. Fortunately, this was the last fire.

Fire poltergeist agents are little different from their non-incendiary brethren in terms of often being adopted children or unhappy employees.[44] Although extremely destructive, the phenomena tend to be (fortunately) short-lived. These fires may be large or small, and often start while an object is being observed, which tends to rule out the more ordinary causes such as someone setting the fire with matches. It is also common for multiple small fires to be set off before larger ones occur.

Fire poltergeist cases differ from SHC in that people are seldom directly harmed.[45] Instead, it is the combustible belongings, or domiciles, which are attacked. Fire poltergeists appear to be motivated by conscious or unconscious grudges against the people they are living or working with, whereas many of the victims of SHC are isolated, solitary individuals who do not seem to have any particular enemies who might wish them harm. If SHC was a kind of poltergeist effect, it would seem more likely to be a case of a suicidal, self-directed fire than to be from an outside agent. However, if the victims of SHC are fire poltergeist agents, one must wonder why we don't hear of fires occurring prior to the fatal event.

It is currently unknown how poltergeists start fires.[46] Investigations by firemen and insurance agents find no obvious causative agents or chemical additives to explain the blazes. Gaddis theorized that at least some of these fires may be electrical in origin. Alternatively, Cade and Davis proposed that ball lightning could be the causative agent.[47] They felt that this could account for some of the explosions, object movements, and fires. However, this would still not answer the question of whether that ball lightning was a natural phenomena or an induced one.

Gaddis believed that poltergeist activity can best be described as "the projection and dramatization of subconscious, repressed tensions and conflicts."[48] Many would agree. And while it may at first seem to be playful and benign, these phenomena can take on a darker, more malicious turn. The emotions vented can be savage ones, including deep hatred directed against the self and others.

Poltergeist disturbances may be violent, but they are usually self-limited to a matter of weeks or months, and generally center around one person.[49] Many of the involved objects are personally meaningful, just as Louisa Rhine observed in her review of spontaneous MMI reports. In order to understand the underlying dynamics of what is going on, it is useful to ask five questions:

1. Who is being attacked or having their property damaged?
2. What is being damaged?
3. In what forms are the phenomena manifesting?
4. When is the activity occurring?
5. Where is the activity taking place?

These events are metaphors, much like occur during dreams. They express unconscious thoughts and feelings. It is likely that this why investigators often note a "focusing effect," where the same object repeatedly serves as the MMI target, sometimes being thrown repeatedly until it has broken.

THEORIES AND EXPLANATIONS

There are four common ways that skeptics try to explain away poltergeist incidents as ordinary. These are (1) saying that the events are due to fraud, whether by the poltergeist agent, the investigators, others, or a combination thereof; (2) blaming geophysical factors; (3) stating there was simply misperception and malobservation; and (4) suggesting that the memory of the people reporting or recording the events was faulty.[50] All of these possibilities exist whenever human beings are involved, and need to be considered when trying to evaluate the likelihood of what occurred and why.

Fraud Gauld and Cornell believed that fraud existed in approximately 8 percent of the cases they reviewed.[51] However, they felt that trickery simply could not account for all of the phenomena that are witnessed. Gauld and Cornell noted that most of the fraud was of a simple sort, even if it sometimes skillfully executed. Although conjurers might be able to duplicate some or even many of these effects with preparation, assistance, practice, and special props, few of the involved individuals showed an interest in, or skill at, performing sleight-of-hand. In fact, many poltergeist agents are young children with little or no knowledge of magic, and it is difficult to imagine how a child could move some of the heavy pieces of furniture that have been witnessed walking away from a wall.

Even though fraud could (and frequently does) account for some of the sounds and object movements, there are at least a few events — such as objects appearing mid-air and falling in a zigzag path, making mid-air 90-degree turns, and traveling at irregular speeds, and lamps exploding despite a stable current — that appear impossible to duplicate in normal ways.[52] Furthermore, in addition to their abnormal trajectories, apported and materialized objects are often found to be quite warm to the touch. Nor would ordinary methods seem to account for the apparent teleportation of children, such as was said to have occurred in the Poona case in India in 1928, and the Sandfeldt case in Germany in 1722.

Geophysical Theories A second method of trying to explain away poltergeist phenomena is to suggest that earthquakes and underground streams are responsible for the sounds and object movements. Certainly, paranormal investigator Loyd Auerbach received many calls from people thinking they had a poltergeist because of object movement during the aftershocks following the 1989 California earthquake.[53] However, the idea of a localized seismic activity that would only affect one house or one room seems extremely unlikely. Further doubt seems cast upon the geophysical theory by the fact that there is not a higher number of poltergeist cases in earthquake zones or associated with seismic activity.[54]

The idea that an underground stream might account for some noises is plausible, although it would not explain why poltergeist auditory phenomena have occurred when there is no subterranean water present.[55] Object movements are even more problematic. Experiments undertaken to see how much force would be required for the water pressure to jolt a house enough to move objects inside have shown that ordinary houses could not withstand that much force. House shaking experiments performed July 8, 1961, using maximal vibrator intensities for both horizontal and vertical vibrations were able to produce palpable jolts, some noise, and structural damage, but little in the way of object movement. In the view of an engineer, Mr. Turner, who was an expert on vibrations, the activity described in poltergeist would be more apt to occur with horizontal vibrations than vertical ones, but that a house would be apt to fall down before succeeding. Furthermore, jolting simply cannot account for many of the object movements associated with poltergeist activity. For example, an earthquake or underground stream could not explain the sponge which rose, floated slowly at shoulder height out of the kitchen, past a surprised British matron, into the living room, and then dropped six to eight feet into the lounge in front of her husband, who also saw it in flight. If one believes the reports, there are a great many other such incidents that cannot be explained by geophysical factors.

The science fiction author Eric Frank Russell proposed that perhaps a kind of temporary weightlessness occurs due to an as yet unknown physical cause.[56] However, although this might be vaguely plausible for some forms of levitation and object movements, it is hard to imagine how it could possibly account for the various raps and noises associated with poltergeist phenomena, let alone the appearance of water and spontaneous fires.

Experiments on levitation suggest that a certain amount of weight loss may be possible. However, one would think if localized weightlessness was a spontaneous phenomenon, it would have been noted and studied by physicists by now. Likewise, one would expect a natural geophysical phenomenon to center around a physical location, rather than occurring, as poltergeist activity does, in the vicinity of certain individuals or groups.

Misperception A third popular tactic for explaining away poltergeist activity is to say the witnesses simply misperceived, or hallucinated, the events. Clearly, there are cases where misperception is a factor. Furthermore, once people believe that something paranormal has happened, it is human nature for them to attribute any coincidental noises, previously unobserved sights or sounds, problems with equipment, and falling of breakables, to the poltergeist.[57]

Gauld and Cornell felt that misperception was far more frequent than fraud.[58] Some common animals in Britain (particularly owls and hedgehogs) can make an astonishing array of groans, screeches, snorts, snufflings, and sounds of heavy breathing. Likewise houses can settle, branches may tap on windows, pipes may create odd sounds, doors may be poorly hung, and electrical appliances can be incorrectly manufactured such that they behave oddly. Seeing what we want, or expect, to see can also lead to misperceptions and malobservation. However, at least some poltergeist events have been recorded on tape or film, giving strength to the notion that genuine phenomena do take place.

MMI Although an investigator must always consider, and rule out, human errors of observation, memory, and exaggeration, and ordinary causes — including geophysical, fraud, or magic within the capability of the agents — there still remain some occurrences that cannot be explained.[59] It is this residue of extraordinary incidents that interest us. As Gauld and Cornell put it:

> There are no 'ordinary causes' of objects rising slowly upwards and then shooting off sideways, or of their suddenly appearing inside closed spaces, or of their moving slowly and erratically through the air; nor are there any 'ordinary causes' of rappings responding intelligently to questions or following a particular person around the hours. If one wants to make 'ordinary causes' explanations cover all the phenomena, house has again to assume that the phenomena cannot in fact have been as they are reported to have been.[60]

It is evident from poltergeist accounts that most events are the same now as they were in the earliest-known reports — with the exception that modern plumbing seems to have saved us from one of the poltergeist's favorite early tricks, of throwing excrement and emptying chamber pots.[61] Most poltergeist cases center around the presence of particular individuals — often adolescent children — and in some cases an emotional shock triggers the events. These facts suggest that poltergeist phenomena represent an innate ability that humans (and possibly animals) have to affect matter.

If MMI is a natural potential within all of us, then it would seem logical to look for correlations with things, such as brain function, which might modulate it. William Roll suggested, based on a small number of study participants, that poltergeist phenomena may be related to epilepsy.[62] However, Martínez-Taboas pointed out that we should be cautious of assuming a connection between CNS dysfunction and poltergeist activity, given the small sample size, the fact that not all poltergeist agents have abnormal EEGs, and that an abnormal EEG itself does not signify epilepsy.[63] Indeed, 15–25 percent of normal children are said to have paroxysmal abnormalities and positive spikes at some time during an EEG.

The onset of poltergeist phenomena often seems to correlate with the raging hormones of puberty.[64] Nevertheless, there appears to be more involved than a simple overflow of "sex-energy." Owen pointed out that if it was merely a matter of energy, then we would expect poltergeist activity to correlate with both a person's overall vitality and with puberty in animals, not just humans. As he put it, "No one has ever found cause to recognize an animal as a poltergeist focus. The explanation would seem to be that it is a fact that poltergeist manifestations are essentially a purely human function."[65]

Lay analyst Nandor Fodor was the first to note back in the 1930s that the poltergeist is a "bundle of projected repressions."[66] Furthermore, Fodor recognized that the phenomena produced by those with psychic abilities could sometimes serve a beneficial purpose, and that "mediumistic activity may represent a form of self-therapy."[67] To say that his ideas were not well accepted at the time is an understatement. Yet, the years have tended to vindicate his observations. Poltergeist agents are often psychologically stressed, and their performance of MMI acts as a valuable relief valve.

Rogo observed that many poltergeist agents are adolescents who come from strongly religious families.[68] He speculated that their internal sexual conflict exacerbates their sense of guilt and strengthens the denial of these feelings. If true, this might also explain why poltergeist activity seems to be a uniquely human phenomenon, since (assuming psi abilities are not limited to people) animals don't repress their sexuality. Rogo also pointed out that the current increase in cultural freedom girls have to express their sexuality might explain why the ratio of girls to boys as poltergeist agents has changed from predominantly girls to an equal ratio of girls to boys.

Although researchers disagree on the degree of psychopathology or CNS dysfunction involved, they do agree on three points.[69] First, that poltergeist agents have strong internalized inhibitions against expressing aggression. Second, that they do not have outlets for the expression of hostility. Third, that there is psychological conflict between the expression and inhibition of aggression. Personality tests of Julio Vasquez, the Miami poltergeist agent, for example, showed high moral standards, feelings of unworthiness, guilt and rejection, passive personality traits, inner feelings of detachment and unhappiness, and dissociative tendencies, especially in regard to expressing aggression.[70]

Rogo noted that poltergeist cases are sometimes better approached as total family dysfunction, and need not always concentrate around a central agent.[71] In these cases, the family may possess personality attributes that, as a gestalt, represent the typical poltergeist personality.

Walter von Lucadou and Frauke Zahradnik theorized based on the Model of Pragmatic Information (*see* Glossary) that poltergeist phenomena represent a hierarchically nested system of complementary autonomy-reliability and novelty-confirmation pairs.[72] They postulated that there are four phases: (1) surprise, (2) displacement, (3) decline, and (4) suppression. Thus, things start off strongly when it is unknown who the agent is. Then, phenomena may change in an unpredictable way. Next, when the underlying message is understood and the activity is expected, the phenomena disappear. Finally, society reacts.

SUMMARY

Poltergeist cases remain one of the few areas of active field investigation in parapsychology today. Case studies, fieldwork, and archival research are valuable because they give us a sense of the scope and breadth of MMI phenomena as it naturally occurs. The widespread and ongoing nature of these phenomena suggests that MMI is a universal, if seldom visibly exercised, or recognized, human ability. The drawback, of course, of this kind of research is that it is difficult to control for confounding variables, misperception, and fraud. For this, we need to move into the laboratory.

Although ordinary causes — such as trickery, malobservation, and faulty memories — may account for many apparent poltergeist events, it cannot account for them all. The high incidence of certain personality types in case studies, existence of person-centered foci, and meaningfulness of the activity in terms of what happens where, when, and to whom all suggest a human component. The unusual trajectories of objects, materializations and dematerializations, indicate that that human component is more than simple trickery, or even good conjuring. This leaves us with the strong possibility that in times of stress, or when normal channels of communication are barred, that people may seek non-ordinary means, such as MMI, to achieve their goals.

Early Research with Physical Mediums

Scientists began conducting research using experimental methodology in the séance room and the laboratory in the late 1800s.[73] They were exciting times. Electricity, wireless telegrams, and X-rays were all new, fascinating, and controversial fields of study.[74] Small wonder, then, that another invisible form of activity that appeared to be transmitted through the "ether" — psi — should arouse the scientific curiosity of the day. Parapsychologists might be comforted by the "spectacular assaults upon Marconi for his claims about wireless telegraphy" that attempted to debunk it.[75]

Early psychical work usually involved the investigators trying to immobilize mediums by holding their hands and feet.[76] It was often difficult for researchers to impose good controls because the rooms were generally dark and the mediums frequently used cabinets, said to allow them to build up sufficient "power" to materialize things. Investigators were seldom allowed to examine the inside of the cabinet during the séance and had to settle for tying the medium up. The only accounts of complete materializations appearing and disappearing in good light with the medium in full view the whole time were obtained by mediums Francis Monck and William Eglinton in the 1870s.

Founding SPR members Myers, Gurney, and the Sidgwicks carried out a number of investigations of mediums in the 1870s.[77] They became convinced that all, or almost all, of the physical effects that they had witnessed were fraudulently produced. It was this, more than anything else, which led to the use of ordinary participants in psi research.

SIR WILLIAM CROOKES (1832–1919)

SPR member Sir William Crookes was an eminent scientist who performed some of the foremost early research in the field.[78] Although he often used a single subject design, he worked hard to devise experiments that controlled a variety of factors and eliminated fraud. During the years 1870–1872, D. D. Home — then at the zenith of his abilities — performed a long series of sittings for him.[79] As John Beloff stated, "it was to prove the most important step in bringing spiritualism into the laboratory."[80]

Crookes reported on a number of Home's capabilities, including his apparent ability to activate an accordion in a special cage without touching it, and to influence a balance scale, even when standing three feet away from it.[81] Chronicles of his experiments reveal that, although not always fully controlled, Crookes studied Home's abilities in a careful and methodical way that excluded the more obvious trickery of the times — such as illusions created in dim light, sleight-of-hand, or colluding partners. However, many of Crookes' colleagues were skeptical of his findings, and branded him either an incompetent fool or a co-conspirator in fraud. It is unfortunate that most of the scientists who were invited to witness or participate in the design and execution of these experiments refused to do so.[82]

Crookes' career as a psychical investigator hit a turning point in December 1873, when he began working with Florence Cook.[83] The seventeen-year-old Cook was said to be able to produce full materializations of "Katie King," the dead daughter of John King, who claimed to have been the seventeenth-century buccaneer Henry Morgan. At the time, the young medium was already under a heavy cloud of suspicion, having been accused of fraud. Crookes sat in a number of séances that were held in his home with Cook. A fellow scientist, Cromwell Varley, devised an electrical chair that would tell Crookes if Florence left her spot and flash photography was used to try to capture images of the purportedly materialized form. Crookes also had "Katie" dip her hands in dye. When Florence's hands were checked they were found to be unstained.

In 1874, Crookes published that he was absolutely convinced that Katie King and Florence Cook were two separate bodies.[84] By so doing, he unleashed a firestorm of controversy and conjecture about whether he was deceived or had become a willing accomplice to fraud, perhaps for sexual favors. Cook's reputation for consorting with mediums who had been exposed as fakes in addition to later acts of foolishness and trickery did not help the situation. However, if Cook had insinuated a confederate to play the role, the woman had to be virtually her double. We may never know the truth of it, but the outcome was clear. Crookes was bombarded with criticism from all sides and became an object of ridicule. As Beloff put it, "If his report on Home had been met with disdainful silence, his account of Cook was treated with open derision and contempt."[85] Crookes responded by leaving the field, and working instead on the properties of highly rarefied gases, spectroscopy, and cathode rays. However, he never turned his back on psychical research or retracted any of the claims he had made for Florence Cook or D. D. Home.

"Controlled" Studies with
Eusapia Palladino (1854–1918)

The frequent unveiling of trickery — even among unpaid amateurs — combined with the clear unreliability of witnesses, caused the other SPR investigators to be disenchanted with the whole notion of working with physical mediums.[86] It is probable that their prior unhappy experiences, which gave them a general distaste for physical phenomena, combined with their concern for the public reputation of the SPR affected the way they handled their investigation of Eusapia Palladino.

Eusapia was well-known in advance as a cheat.[87] However, most of her trickery was of a simple and well-known kind, which did not seem to account for all of the phenomena witnessed in her presence. Various SPR members, as well as researchers such as Charles Richet from France, performed a series of séances with Eusapia beginning in 1894. Eusapia made the normal immobilization techniques hard to maintain. Any attempt to hold onto her hands and feet was limited by what Eusapia permitted (which depended on her mood) and hampered by poor lighting, as well as Eusapia's thrashing about. To say that true control of her was difficult is probably a vast understatement. However, the investigators did their best. They dictated detailed notes to a stenographer during the séances and attempted to record when they thought they had the medium in hand. Those attending the séances varied considerably from one sitting to the next as to whether they believed Eusapia was able to produce genuine phenomena or not. After going back and forth on the topic, the investigators finally concluded, on the basis of some obvious trickery, that none of the phenomena had been authentic.

Harry Price (1881–1948)

Born in London, the son of a traveling salesman, Harry Price (1881–1948) was a ghost-hunter, writer, and entrepreneur.[88] He did not get along well with the leaders of the SPR. They felt he was not a "gentleman," and he considered them biased and "stuffy." However, he was not without friends in the SPR, and had the advantages of being wealthy, a skilled conjurer, an able investigator, and an ingenious inventor — all of which he used to good effect in his pursuit of psychical research.

In 1923, Price decided to establish the National Laboratory for Psychical Research.[89] It was three years before it opened on January 1, 1926, at its headquarters in Queensbury Place, South Kensington.[90] Price undoubtedly benefited in this endeavor from his name recognition (having written a string of popular titles at the time) and expertise at self-promotion.[91] As it was, Price was one of the best known psychical researchers during the period between the first and second World Wars. Unfortunately, Price's personal character was less than stellar. Beloff stated that, "he was everything that a scientist ought *not* to be: he was possessive, deceitful, spiteful and self-seeking. At the same time, even his enemies had to admit that he was extraordinarily energetic and enterprising."[92]

Price was almost the sole investigator of physical mediumship in England in the 1920s.[93] As John Randall observed, "He undoubtedly put more time, effort and money into psychical research than any other Englishman since the days of the founding fathers of the SPR. His experimental and investigative work was extensive, his reports voluminous and detailed."[94] Some of Price's best known (and most highly respected) work involved a series of thirteen controlled séances with Stella Cranshaw, which occurred between March and October 1923, and his investigations involving Rudi Schneider (*see* next section).[95] He did not use statistical methods, but instead relied on gifted participants and the best controls he could devise from modern technology.[96] In addition, Price was deeply involved in investigating ghost and poltergeist cases, and bringing the paranormal to the public via radio and television shows.[97]

In 1931, Price attempted a merger between the SPR and his National Laboratory for Psychical Research.[98] Enmity may have deepened at this time, as the SPR council felt that he had acted improperly in trying to bypass them by circulating copies of his letter, along with voting papers, to its members in advance of their meeting. They rejected his bid. However, one has to wonder how much this may have played a role in the so-called "dirty tricks" that Randall feels the SPR was guilty of perpetrating against Price in 1931 and 1932.[99] A longtime heavy smoker who suffered poor health for years, he died at his home in Pulborough, West Sussex, in 1948.[100] Although Price remains a somewhat controversial figure today, it cannot be denied that he significantly contributed to the field of parapsychology.

Experimental Research with Rudi Schneider (1908–1957)

Harry Price began working with Rudi Schneider in 1926.[101] Rudi's phenomena were sufficiently impressive during these séances that some suggested Price had not adequately controlled for fraud. In response to this, he developed a clever system, which used specialized gloves and metal inductors for all of the sitters as a form of mechanical control against trickery. Price then had all of the sitters, including Rudi, slip into the gloves while their feet were on metal inductors so that their movements could be displayed on a circuit board. This electrical signaling device was a step up from the old method of trying to control the medium by hand.[102] Rudi was still able to perform all his usual feats: moving objects and curtains, overturning the table, and materializing ectoplasic masses.[103]

Rudi then went to Paris to work with Dr. Eugène Osty, Director of the Institut Métapsychique, and his engineer son Marcel.[104] Osty felt that it was neither humane nor elegant to physically restrain a person. Rather than worrying about whether the medium was adequately immobilized, Osty set up a burglar alarm style of monitoring around the target objects using infrared beams, which would set off alarms and trigger cameras to take photographs whenever they were interrupted. This complex system avoided one of the pitfalls of previous methods of control, in that it excluded trickery by not only the medium, but by other participants as well. Furthermore, it could not be distracted as could a human observer trying to watch the medium or electronic control panel.

When the device was first put into effect, signals were obtained, suggesting that security had been breached and that something tangible had penetrated the infrared network.[105] However, the target objects were undisturbed, and the monitoring cameras, using magnesium flashes, showed no sign of an intruder to explain the cause of the beam disruptions, and Rudi was safe in his chair, with investigators holding his hands. Osty initially thought that his apparatus was malfunctioning. However, he then noticed that these alarm activations always correlated with attempts by the medium's spirit-control to move the targets. Osty concluded that a force invisible to the eye was leaving Rudi's body to move objects, and that it had enough substance to absorb about 30 percent of the beam, thus breaking it enough to set off the cameras.

In his next series of experiments, Osty discovered that Rudi hyperventilated during the sittings, and that the oscillations of the infrared beam were always exactly double that of Rudi's respiration rate.[106] Osty felt that this showed there was a connection between the MMI and the medium's body, and represented evidence that discarnate spirits were not responsible for the effects observed. This proved to be landmark research in demonstrating that the living person was, in fact, the one performing the MMI.

SUMMARY

In this section, we have seen some of the work of Sir William Crookes, Harry Price, and Dr. Eugène Osty, who performed important research on amateur and professional physical mediums under partially controlled conditions. The problems with this kind of research are obvious. There is a shortage of top-grade talent to test, it is difficult to impose effective controls, and those tested have incentive for trickery. Palladino was quite frank that it was much easier for her to perform fraud than real MMI. Add in rivalry and personality clashes between experimenters and their participants, and it is easy to understand why parapsychologists desperately wanted to find a better way to study psi. Nonetheless, this early research provided some valuable insights. Perhaps foremost among these was the eventual recognition that human beings, not spirits, were often the source of MMI. This notion was a critical one, because it paved the way for paranormal research to move in a new direction — formal, controlled studies with ordinary individuals for participants.

Dice and Sphere Experiments

The constant allegations, suspicions, and evidence of fraud soured many parapsychologists on the idea of working with physical mediums in the séance room, including a then young J.B. Rhine.[107] He solved the problem by moving psi research into the laboratory, switching to everyday people for his participants, and compensating for the smaller effect size through the use of statistics.[108] This had two major advantages. It gave Rhine greater control over experimental variables, and allowed him to avoid dealing with temperamental "stars" who sometimes had strong motivations for fraud.

J.B. Rhine began researching MMI after he was approached by a gambler who claimed to be able to influence the fall of dice.[109] Over the next decade, he studied the consequences of intention on die faces and placement, comparing the results to what would be expected by random chance. Although J.B. Rhine's initial studies were poorly controlled, with potential existing for biased dice, recording errors, and unstandardized procedures, he responded to the criticism of the times by improving his research design. Later studies controlled for physical contact as well as for biased dice, and used a wide variety of participants.

Eventually, Rhine expanded these experiments to look at the influence of a variety of factors, including the size, weight, and number of dice used.[110] The results of these studies were small, but statistically significant, and supported the MMI hypothesis. Better still, other experimenters were able to replicate J. B. Rhine's findings, using not only dice, but also coins, balls, and disks.[111] A large body of data was eventually compiled, which supported two conclusions — that people seem to be able to have some influence on how objects fall and this kind of testing shows a fairly consistent decline effect (*see* Glossary).

W. E. Cox in the United States and Haakon Forwald in Sweden developed a new approach to MMI research in the early 1950s, which came to be known as the placement method.[112] This consisted of participants trying to influence one or more objects, such as dice or balls, to move in a particular direction such that at the end of their fall (or in some cases, roll down an incline) they come to rest in one position or place rather than another.[113] Since the objects were subjected to randomizing influences upon their movement and target-side alternation was used to eliminate place bias, the results could be statistically evaluated using probability theory.

It is crucial to note that *any* deviation from chance, whether above or below, is evidence of psi if it occurs consistently enough over a series of trials. Psi-hitting occurs when psi is used so that the target at which the participant is aiming is hit significantly more often than would be expected by chance.[114] Psi-missing, on the other hand, occurs when psi is used so that the target at which the participant is aiming is missed significantly more often than would be expected by chance. However, both represent psi, if with different intentions.

Being an engineer, Forwald realized that measuring not only how many objects stopped their movement in the proper position, but also the *extent* of the movement involved, would allow him to compute the energy involved.[115] He also looked at the possible influence of physical conditions, such as surface texture of the cubes, the weight of the cubes, the material coating the cubes, and their thickness. Unfortunately, Forwald used himself almost exclusively as his only subject. His concept of a "PK force" was never consistently borne out in his work or in that of others.

The gradual accumulation of a series of published dice experiments eventually made it possible to use a statistical method known as "meta-analysis." This is a technique wherein the outcomes of individual studies on a topic are treated like data points in a much larger study, with a great many more participants. Needless to say this is not without a certain amount of risk — one has to be careful not to be lumping experiments together inappropriately. However, when done correctly, meta-analyses can greatly increase statistical power to uncover small but significant effects and answer a variety of interesting questions.

In 1989, Dean Radin and Diane Ferrari undertook a detailed meta-analysis of all the dice experiments that were in the literature.[116] They gathered 73 studies from 52 different investigators, and found an overall hit rate of 51.2 percent, which has odds of over a billion to one. Radin and Ferrari were aware of pitfalls that could skew the data, and attempted to address them.[117] One of these — which is commonly leveled against successful research — was whether the outcome could have been falsely significant or inflated due to selective reporting; i.e., that nonsignificant studies never made it into the meta-analysis because they remained unpublished — the so-called "file drawer" effect. Ignoring the fact that many of the parapsychological journals have a policy of accepting all well-designed studies, regardless of outcome, Radin and Ferrari calculated that 121 unpublished, unsuccessful studies would have had to have been performed for each of the successful ones to nullify the meta-analysis results. This means each of the 52 researchers would have had to perform at least one unpublished, nonsignificant experiment *every month* for 28 years.[118] Since this clearly could not have been the case, the results cannot be explained away as "selective reporting."

The possibility that a few wildly successful studies could have skewed the meta-analysis results is a valid concern. Radin and Ferrari therefore trimmed the study to delete outliers.[119] Despite this, they again found significant results at the odds of three million to one against chance. Radin and Ferrari then evaluated the possibility that only a few investigators were responsible for the majority of the results, compared the quality of the research designs with the hit rates, and checked for dice bias. Despite all this, they still found that the dice studies show a MMI effect that can be replicated across experimenters, participants, and time.

The Princeton Engineering Anomalies Research (PEAR) Lab performed a set of successful macro–MMI experiments using spheres, which duplicated the dice work's significant results.[120] This involved dropping 9,000 three-quarter inch polystyrene balls through a "quincunx" array of nylon pegs and dispersed into 19 compartments at the bottom. Participants were never in physical contact with the targets, but sat eight feet away, watching the device. The data was collected in sets of three — baseline, right, and left. When no one was trying to influence the spheres they fell into a normal Bell curve distribution. However, when participants were present, they could intentionally influence the shape of the distribution curve as measured by a computerized electronic counter.[121] Brenda Dunne, Roger Nelson, and Robert Jahn noted that their overall result from 87 series involving a total of 1131 formal sets (for a total of 3,393 runs) was highly significant. [122] The likelihood it could have been due to random chance was less than 1 in 10,000. In addition, 15 percent of the individual series were significant at the p<.05 level, and 63 percent met the intended direction (right versus left). This research is important because it used ordinary individuals and demonstrated the same key finding as had the die studies — that experimenters could obtain clear, repeatable, significant results that did not depend on "star" performers.

Unfortunately, studies using dice and spheres have two major limitations: first, that there is the potential for incorrectly recording the results and second, that both the sphere and dice experiments are only pseudo-random events that are being compared to true random chance. Because the results rely heavily upon statistics, even a small target bias can lead to a false conclusion. Some dice studies used counter-balanced design protocols to offset any possible biases, but this was clearly not an ideal solution. This set the stage for the next wave of research: the use of true random events for the target.

Random Generator Research

In 1969, German physicist Helmet Schmidt made the issue of target biases obsolete by creating a new device, called the REG.[123] This device used the truly random source of the β-emission radioactive decay of Strontium 90. The atomic process itself — the rate of decay — became the target. In essence, the REG, or its electronic counterpart, the Random Number Generator (RNG), generates either a 1 or a 0 (rather like heads or tails on a coin). Participant either aimed "high" (more 1s than statistically predicted by random chance), or "low" (more 0s than statistically predicted by random chance). As with the dice and sphere experiments, statistical analysis was required to determine the results. However, now a truly random target was being compared to random chance, and the computer, rather than a person, recorded the results.

The REG ushered in a new and exciting era of MMI research — that of micro–MMI target experimentation. It had many advantages over earlier targets. Not only could it produce a truly random target and eliminate recording error problems, but the REG could also rapidly perform large series of trials and easily control the target generation rate and other variables.[124] Perhaps best of all, it minimized the opportunities for non-mental manipulation.

Schmidt's early REGs used a circle of lights for feedback, which the participant was asked to move clockwise or counterclockwise. Eventually, interest in generating faster target rates than possible with a radioactive source (as well as health concerns over using radioactive material) led to the development of the purely electronic RNGs.[125] These devices could employ more engaging forms of feedback that could maintain participant interest, such electronic dice games, computerized horse races, and even a pulsating image of a Buddha that grows or shrinks in size.[126] Because of their versatility, REG devices represent the largest area of MMI research today.

In addition to their previously mentioned work, the PEAR lab performed nearly 30 years of RNG experiments.[127] They reported a small yet significant effect on the order of parts per thousand, with emotionally bonded pairs that worked together scoring higher. The lab also saw a temporary decline effect, which recovered. Roger Nelson noted two other general findings. First, that approximately 15 percent of randomly chosen participants obtained significant results. And second, that the size of effects seemed related to the length of time spent in intentional effort. Physical factors, such as the type of machine, distance, and speed of operation had little influence on outcomes. Because of this, Nelson felt psychological factors must far outweigh physical ones.

Parapsychologist Kathy Dalton investigated the ability of martial arts students to influence REGs.[128] She was surprised to find that those with two years or more in the martial arts had a *smaller* psi effect (in terms of psi-missing) than did novices with less than six months' training. However, some of her participants reported it had been difficult to sit and concentrate on a computer task immediately after a ten-minute workout. Dalton speculated that their change in tasks (from working out to sitting in front of the computer) could have disrupted their mental states. Unfortunately, there is no data regarding whether her participants believed in the existence of psi, which also could have influenced the results.

Although most studies have looked at how intention or concentration correlates with REG coherence, a few have investigated the influence of spontaneous emotion. Dr. Richard Blasband ran an REG in his therapy office during sessions with a nonrandom sample of eight female patients.[129] Videotapes of the women were analyzed by the psychiatrist and coded for emotionality. Blasband found that anger and sadness both caused an increase in order (although in opposite directions) from random chance. However, he acknowledged that this could have been due at least in part to the experimenter effect (*see* Glossary), or his consciousness in conjunction with the patients', since he, too, was in the room with them. In addition, it has to be noted that the non-blind situation created an obvious potential for bias.

James Lumsden-Cook performed a series of studies looking at emotion and REG coherence. In the first set of these, he looked at whether anger in animal rights activists could change REGs.[130] In his pilot study, he found that when participants read a section about animal cruelty, the high levels of anger were associated with REG anomalies. However, his followup experiment had null results. Lumsden-Cook speculated that this could have been due to the latter group having less emotional reaction due to familiarity with the trigger information. He then investigated the affect of mood shifts between anger and elation on RNGs using six participants. His findings were again nonsignificant.

Well over a thousand REG studies have been performed over the decades using either true random radioactive decay sources or pseudo-random computer noise.[131] In his chapter "Mind-Matter Interaction" in *The Conscious Universe,* Radin reviewed a meta-analysis that he performed with Roger Nelson in 1987.[132] They considered 832 studies performed by sixty-eight different investigators from 1959 to 1987. Radin and Nelson rated these studies for design caliber and checked whether the effect size correlated with the experimental quality (which it did not). They found a hit rate of 51 percent, with odds against chance of a trillion to one. This is very close to what the meta-analysis of the dice research found — which Radin believed meant they were the same kind of MMI.

Radin also discussed the additional 1,262 REG studies conducted since 1989.[133] Their outcomes closely replicated those of the previous decades. The results were not due to "star" performers, but instead demonstrated an accumulation of small effects from each participant.[134] It was further apparent that participants did not need to know whether they were performing a MMI test, or what they needed to do to accomplish their goal, in order to succeed.[135]

In a more recent review of RNG studies, Radin and Nelson added another 176 experiments to their database, 84 of which had been performed before 1987.[136] Radin and Nelson also collapsed all 258 studies — 20 years worth of PEAR lab RNG research — into a *single* data point, and performed a meta-analysis of 515 experimenters from 1959 to 2000. They again found that the mind had a small but statistically significant effect over matter which, in their words, "cannot be attributed to chance, selective reporting problems, or variations in design quality."[137] The average effect size was 0.7 percent, which may not sound like much until one realizes this is at an amazing probability of $p<10^{-50}$. Small or not, the MMI result itself is very real.

Finally, Radin and Nelson noted that computer generation rates have greatly increased since RNGs were first created, and compared the MMI effects with the various rates.[138] Normally, when dealing with cause and effect events where a participant's influence is exerted on an individual target event, one expects to see bigger effect sizes with larger samples. However, in this case, they noted that the effect size was *independent* of the number of bits in each experiment. As Radin and Nelson put it, this suggested that MMI "cannot be explained as simple, linear, force-like mechanisms."[139] In other words, something interesting was happening, and what that something was could be acausal — or at least not causal in the traditional time-forward way. We will later see that at least some MMI may operate in a retro-causal (future effect leading to an earlier cause) manner.

The meta-analysis data for dice, sphere, and REG/RNG experiments discussed in this chapter and the last would appear to be an impressive statement for MMI. However, it is not without controversy. There have been a number of attacks and heated debates on these meta-analyses in which skeptics argue that the results could be accounted for by publication bias or the results are unimportant because of their small effect size.[140] Counter-arguments point out that the Monte Carlo Method used to simulate how unpublished studies could reduce the results to insignificance is itself flawed, and that the fact an effect may be small does not mean it should be ignored.[141] The problem may well come down to one of paradigms, with no amount of proof ever being enough for some. Regardless, most parapsychologists today feel that their time is better spent focused on understanding the nature of MMI than arguing whether it exists.

GROUP MMI EFFECTS

Radin and Nelson reviewed group effects on REGs and postulated that the results were not so much a result of intention as they were an indicator of mental coherence.[142] In 1998,

Roger Nelson began the Global Consciousness Project (GCP).[143] This is an ongoing network of RNGs located around the world, which constantly collects data and sends it back for analysis via the internet. The idea was to see whether RNG output can be affected by a group of minds which are made more coherent by being focused on the same external person or event.

In 2002, Dean Radin and Roger Nelson published independent articles that looked at RNG coherence at the time of the September 11, 2001, terrorist attacks.[144] Intensive and widespread media coverage made it an event of unprecedented worldwide focus. A post hoc analysis of the correlations showed the international network of field REGs monitored from Princeton University had a major deviation in output.[145] Other significant worldwide events, such as Princess Diana's funeral, have shown similar patterns of activity. These effects are small (0.3 to 0.5 sigma) and typically last between one and two hours. In addition, the effect may not be completely nonlocal (as some have postulated for psi) but involve a kind of field effect. Nelson noted:

> The GCP effect we usually measure is most simply described as a small positive correlation between the widely dispersed RNG devices — where there should be no correlation at all. This correlation decreases as the separation between pairs of RNGs increases. This distance effect is important for theoretical considerations, since it is compatible with field-like models, and not with selection-type models.[146]

Those interested in this topic are encouraged visit the GCP website at http://noosphere.princeton.edu, which not only contains more information on this topic, but also allows viewers to watch real-time data displays from host sites around the world.

Although Nelson advised caution in interpreting his GCP data, one of the more curious features to emerge is the finding that anomalous changes sometimes appear to *precede* major events.[147] A number of laboratory studies have been done on presentiment (unconscious precognition), which seem to demonstrate that physiological parameters can begin changing *before* a randomly chosen stimulus is administered.[148] These studies have variously used a sound, light, or image (randomly erotic, violent, food-related, or calm) as the stimulus, and measured reactions in skin conductance, heart rate, EEG, fMRI, and pupil size. Although the effect seen in these studies is typically on the order of 1–5 seconds, Radin noted that this is almost certainly not an inherent limit of retrocausation, but due to the experimental design.[149] Of course, the fact that presentiment may exist in individuals does not mean this can also occur on a global scale.

The ability of groups to seemingly effect RNGs through "mental coherence" has also been tested in the laboratory. Radin and Atwater used binaural beat rhythms to entrain groups of 20–25 participants who attended one of 14 six-day workshops. RNG data collected between workshops was used as the control. They found a strong correlation (p=.008 level) between changes in RNG randomness and levels of group coherence, whereas control runs remained at random chance. However, the experimenters noted that they could not rule out retro-MMI or experimenter effect as possible alterative explanations for their findings.

RETROACTIVE MMI RESEARCH

Retroactive MMI refers to the ability of the mind to influence events that have already occurred, thus acting backward in time. Helmut Schmidt performed a series of experiments using REG and RNG targets that were pre-recorded (either on magnetic tape as a series of clicks or computer disk) before the participants were asked to try to influence them.[150] He found MMI could only act retroactively if no sentient observers had previously viewed the data.[151] Pre-observation of the target by humans blocked later participants from altering the REG data away from what was expected by mean chance.

This result would be compatible with the notion that an event is not determined until the moment it is observed.[152] Thus, there is no "reality" without an observer. Helmut Schmidt and Henry Stapp proposed that pre-observation makes the random decisions real, or determines the event, so that the participant's later mental effort would come too late to affect the results. Unfortunately, as Schmidt and Stapp noted, there is no way to rule out experimenter effect as an alternative explanation. Experimenters could create their findings through either precognition (telling them when to start their "runs") or through MMI (which can occur unconsciously) altering the REG output itself, the recording mechanism, or recorded data itself at a later time, while still unobserved.

That this is more than an experimenter effect would seem to be supported by a study Dean Radin performed, in which he created mathematical models to determine the causality of MMI in RNG.[153] He investigated three possibilities: (1) a passive retro-causal model, with the result obtained through precognition, as suggested with Decision Augmentation Theory; (2) a push forward through time in a cause-and-effect manner; or (3) a pull backwards as an active retro-causal method.[154] He found that the retro-causal model came closest to matching the experimental data. Thus a present intention creates a future outcome that then pulls us toward it. Radin noted that a growing body of research suggests that the traditional cause-and-effect chain may, in fact, be time-reversed with the effect leading to a prior cause. Such "backwards causation" is somewhat mind boggling even if it only applies to probabilistic events and not those that have already been witnessed in the past. Yet an examination of the formulas suggests that time should be symmetrical — we have only assumed it flowed in one direction (forward) because of our life experiences.

Eckhard Etzold looked for relationships between physical factors and retro–MMI results.[155] He used REG data pulled from more than a decade's worth of retro–MMI experiments conducted by Fourmilab over the internet. He found no effect from a full moon, tidal influences, solar wind, or GMF alone. However, he discovered a correlation occurred as an interaction between retro–MMI, a full moon, and two different indicators of solar activity: sunspot activity (significant at the p=.05 level) and the $F_{10.7}$ index (a measure of solar radio flux, significant at the p=.01 level). The lower the solar activity during a full moon, the greater the retro–MMI effect observed.

The magnetosphere of the Earth is blown by solar wind into a teardrop shape that extends 600,000 km out into space and away from the direction of the sun.[156] This means its trail reaches past lunar orbit. This magnetotrail changes constantly, particularly during times of high solar activity. Etzold speculated that that during the time of a full moon, the moon crossing through this magnetotrail somehow increases the generation of ultra-low frequency electromagnetic waves of 1–10 mH, which in turn enhances MMI performance. If true, it should be testable in the laboratory.

Animal MMI (Anpsi)

Anpsi is a term that refers quite simply to psi in animals. Most of the MMI experiments performed using animals (or in some cases insects) have involved the use of REG/RNG machines.[157] Typically these studies have placed their subjects in an uncomfortable environment — either in terms of temperature or mild periodic electric shocks — where the comfort level could be improved depending on the decisions made by the RNG. The experimental results have been weak and inconsistent. Researchers in South Africa looked at MMI in algae and chicks using two types of REGs, but had null results.[158] Schmidt performed a variety of experiments using animals as observers for retro–MMI, but had variable results.[159]

Anpsi research has been undermined by two factors. First, that a considerable body of research had to be thrown out after his colleagues caught a researcher fraudulently altering the data. Second, there is no way in which to separate out the effects of experimenter psi from those of their animal subjects. Until a solution to this problem can be found, it is impossible to interpret the meaning or significance of any anpsi investigative findings. This has discouraged many experimenters from pursuing the topic further.

SUMMARY

REG/RNG research is one of the commonest target systems used by parapsychologists today because of the ability to run large numbers of trials quickly, be able to easily analyze the data, make the tests fun, and use over the internet, thus permitting an enormous pool of participants. Unfortunately, there is a potential problem with the use of this data as MMI. It is unclear whether the REG data truly represent micro–MMI, or simply ESP precognition of the right moment to start gathering data, to allow it to appear (falsely) significant.[160] Of course, this would not account for macro–MMI events (such as sponges floating through the air from one room to another). However, precognition *would* explain why meta-analyses of dice and REG/RNG studies show similar effect sizes.[161]

We now have over four decades' worth of REG/RNG data available.[162] Meta-analysis of these studies makes it clear that whether this effect is small or not, it a genuine one, which cannot be explained away through chance, selective reporting, or poor research design. In addition, these effects may not be causal in a traditional time-forward cause-and-effect manner. Finally, as Nelson and others have observed, interesting things seem to happen when mass consciousness (or shared emotion) becomes focused upon a single person or event. REG/RNG data becomes less random, an effect that is sometimes seen even before the focusing event occurs. It is hoped that further research will clarify the meaning of this finding.

Biological System Research

The field of biological system research is a large and complex one. It includes a wide range of paranormal effects: protecting from harm, influencing physiological parameters, affecting how the body responds to wounding, changing the rate of healing, and curing disease. However, one factor they all have in common is that the target of this research is the human body. Thus, it includes not only anomalous healing research, but also that of Direct Mental Interactions with Living Systems (DMILS) and Deliberately Caused Bodily Damage (DCBD). Even fire-walking studies can be considered a form of biological system research, as the goal is to influence the body to become resistant to burning. Let us look at each of these in turn.

FIRE-WALKING FIELD INVESTIGATIONS

The ability of the mind to completely, if temporarily, protect itself from injury by fire is something that has been little studied despite the frequent incidence of fire-walking events and ceremonies around the world. Skeptics suggest that in some cases ash may insulate the body from the hot coals, such that it is protected from burns — because burns do occur. Aerospace engineer Jack Houck was one of the few to attempt field investigations on the topic. In his review of the hazards involved, Houck stated that "about 31 percent of the people who do the fire-walking seminars get small burn blisters and about 3 percent get badly burned."[163] It is unclear whether these individuals were burned because they did not have enough ash where they stepped, or for some other reason, such as insufficient MMI.

A key question is how hot are the coals being walked on? Houck tried to answer this by measuring the temperature two millimeters from the bottom of the foot.[164] He recorded data from 15 different fire-walks on a computer. Houck noted two major problems with his equipment — it was unable to go above 1400°F, and could not survive very long in the hostile environment it was attempting to record. Nonetheless, his data indicated that the probe maintained that maximum value of 1400°F during the first step, and tended to measure around 600–800°F during the second step. Thus, it seems clear that there is more than sufficient heat to burn the foot, even if the exposure time is brief. Unfortunately, as Houck concluded, "Current instrumentation is simply not good enough to help understand the mechanisms involved in protecting the body during these events."[165]

DIRECT MENTAL INTERACTIONS WITH LIVING SYSTEMS (DMILS) RESEARCH

Direct Mental Interactions with Living Systems or DMILS (previously known as staring studies) are when a distant individual isolated from all normal sensory cues tries to influence another living target system, whether isolated cells or an intact organism. It is a difficult area of research to categorize, since there is no way to determine whether the results come from MMI, ESP, or a mixture of both. Nonetheless, DMILS studies look at biological systems using experimental methodology and have potential implications for anomalous healing — which may not be pure MMI anyway, but also involve ESP.

Robert Morris noted years ago that physiological parameters were more apt to deviate with the onset of a target event than were verbal or behavioral changes.[166] As Morris put it, "There is fairly strong evidence, however, that psi expression does interact with detectable physiological events, some of which may serve as more direct indications of psi than our cognitively elaborated responses."[167] Thus, bypassing a participant's conscious mind allows experimenters to find greater evidence of psi. Early forms of DMILS experiments with human beings as targets investigated a variety of physiological parameters, including EEG, electrodermal activity (used in polygraph or lie detector testing), muscular tremor, unconscious muscular movements, blood pressure, respiratory rate, heart rate, and peripheral vasomotor activity.[168]

The typical DMILS study has two participants; one in the role of an "agent" and the other as a "receiver."[169] The agent tries to interact with some psychophysiological aspect or behavior of a living target system (often a person). This may involve the agent "willing" the receiver to change in some manner. During the experiment, the agent and receiver are kept in complete sensory isolation from each other, so that the only means of communication can be by ESP. There are usually a number of "sending" periods per session. A computer monitor will generally inform the agent which periods (determined by pseudo-randomization with counterbalancing) are to involve "calming" versus "activation." Active sending periods are typically followed by rest periods, during which time the agent does not try to interact with the receiver. Many DMILS studies also provide direct feedback to the agent of the receiver's physiological parameter being measured. The data is then analyzed through standard statistical methods, looking for the difference (if any) between measurements of the receiver's state of arousal during the calm and activation periods.

Currently, electrodermal activity (EDA) is the most frequent measurement taken in DMILS studies.[170] This is because EDA varies quickly and easily, is simple to obtain, and is relatively inexpensive. Since EDA measures arousal, the agent tries to either calm or activate the receiver's

EDA at various times during the session. Typical EDA-DMILS sessions include around 40 half-minute periods for a total of 20 minutes.

Telepathy could easily account for any and all DMILS results. Nonetheless, MMI — either in terms of direct effect on the receiver's body or on the recording/monitoring device itself— cannot be ruled out. However, the fact that a significant release-of-effort effect can sometimes be seen is suggestive of MMI involvement.[171] Unfortunately, as so often appears to be the case in parapsychology, an attempt to replicate this finding failed to reach significance, although the authors speculated that this could have been due to the way the study was set up. Delanoy et al. noted that, "the apparent DMILS effects were greater in the rest periods, than in the preceding 'intentionality' period."[172]

A number of factors have been investigated using agent-receiver pairs. Oddly enough, it is unclear whether emotional or biological closeness facilitates DMILS. Although earlier studies indicated a possible connection, Delanoy et al. were unable to find any significant improvement in scoring by participant pairs who were biologically related or who were emotionally close.[173] However, Delanoy later recalled that, "preliminary analyses ... suggested that the receiver's personality traits were more consistently related to session outcome than those of the agent."[174]

Many EDA-DMILS studies have assumed that an agent is needed. This may not be the case. Rainer Schneider, Markus Binder, and Harald Walach investigated this idea and found, "although a DMILS effect emerged when an agent was present, these DMILS scores were not significantly higher than the DMILS scores when there was no agent present."[175] This needs to be replicated before firm conclusions can be drawn. Nonetheless, it suggests that experimenter psi (either ESP or MMI) or receiver ESP/precognition could be the primary cause of the remote staring effect.

Local sidereal time (LST) may affect DMILS scoring in the same way as it does general ESP. Delanoy and Morris found in their initial look at the topic that DMILS results tended to mirror the same patterns as seen in ESP research, with a 400 percent increase in hit rate for those sessions performed within two hours of 13:30 LST, and a drop in hit rate for sessions within two hours of 18:30 LST.[176]

Stefan Schmidt and Harald Walach pointed out that the variability in most published reports on EDA-DMILS may be due to inconsistent technique.[177] They reviewed 39 studies and found that none of them included a description of state-of-the-art EDA methodology. Furthermore, they wondered why after more than 20 years of irregularities in the EDA data, the nature of those inconsistencies was never addressed. Irregular breathing was originally listed as a possible false influence on EDA. However, after investigating it further, Stefan Schmidt, Rainer Schneider, Markus Binder, David Bürkle, and Harald Walach concluded that both EDA changes and sudden, irregular breathing patterns may be part of the same remote intention effect from staring.[178]

The problem of researchers working with a technology they aren't intimately familiar with is clear when one reads Schmidt and Walach's long list of remaining artifacts that could make EDA falsely appear to be responsive or unresponsive, including drifts due to using the wrong kind of electrode gel or not enough of it; insufficient time between electrode attachment and recording the data; poor electrode attachment; hand movement; an inadequate process of filtering; inappropriate data recording (large effects may diminish or disappear if the sampling rate is below 10 Hz for the phasic component); and inappropriate methods of measurement or scoring.[179] Given so many potential pitfalls in technique, and the apparent lack of a set standard by which EDA-DMILS studies are performed, it is no wonder that there has been variability in the findings.

The experimenter effect has been reported in parapsychological research since the 1950s.[180] DMILS work is no exception and could be another reason, beyond that of technique, for inconsistent results. Investigators can determine whether their studies get significant results. Nothing made this more clear than a series of experiments performed by skeptic Richard Wiseman and psi-believer Marilyn Schlitz.[181] Wiseman had performed four remote staring DMILS studies, three of which had null results and one of which was thrown out because of inadequate randomization, whereas Schlitz had a long track record of success using the same protocol. Wiseman and Schlitz wondered whether their participant pools varied in talent.[182] The two decided to team up in order to figure out what was going on. Using the same protocol, Wiseman and Schlitz each acted as the experimenter, as well as the agent, in half of the sessions at the University of Hertfordshire, England (using Wiseman's laboratory and equipment), and half at the Institute for Noetic Sciences in Petaluma, California, with Schlitz's lab and equipment. Both experimenters were present for all of the sessions. The results were eye-opening. When Wiseman was the experimenter — whether in England or the USA — the participants had non-significant results, whereas when Schlitz was the experimenter — whether in England or the USA — significant outcomes were achieved.

A few years later, Schlitz and Wiseman performed a second joint study, this time just in the Institute of Noetic Science, in which trials were performed at the same time, with the same equipment, and the same participant pool.[183] It replicated the earlier study in that Wiseman's participants again showed no difference in EDA between stare and nonstare situations and the EDA of Schlitz's participants were significantly different — although in this case the EDA in non-stare situations was higher than when staring was occurring, the opposite effect of the first study. They noted there had not been quite as good of control for sensory leakage in this experiment as the first one because of space constraints and, unlike the first study, Schlitz had been forced to run some of her sessions without Wiseman present. However, there were no differences in scoring between trials whether only one of them was present or both. Schlitz and Wiseman again concluded that experimenters can influence whether they get significant or null results, most likely either because of using their own psi or by being better able to elicit it from their participants.

Finally, Schlitz and Wiseman decided to try to determine how much of their earlier two results were due to direct interaction with the participants when greeting them or explaining study, and how much might be a direct psi effect of the experimenter.[184] They employed better equipment, methodology, and statistical analysis. This time, they got nonsignificant results. Both experimenters noted a kind of emotional fatigue, in the sense of losing interest and motivation over the two years it took to complete. However, no correlation was noted between session order and its outcome. Schlitz et al. felt the inconsistent nature of this series meant that further research would be needed before any firm conclusions could be drawn.

In his review of the data, William Braud came to a number of conclusions.[185] Foremost among these is the fact that it appears possible for one person to influence another at a distance, even when shielded from all conventional forms of sensory, informational, and energetic impact. A number of different physical and mental activities have successfully been influenced. Moreover, these effects occur even when the agent and receiver are separated in *time*.

When distal mental influence is successful, it has three features worth noting.[186] These are that (1) people with a greater need to be influenced appear to be more susceptible; (2) it can happen without the target person's conventional knowledge or awareness that someone is attempting to influence him or her (which does not include ESP); and (3) there appears to be a correlation for some target systems between geomagnetic field (GMF) activity and receptiveness to distant mental influence. DMILS research has implications for anomalous healing, which is also said not to be limited by time or space, may occur without the patient's awareness, and in which healers claim those who most need healing and accept it will receive the greatest benefit.

DELIBERATELY CAUSED BODILY DAMAGE PHENOMENON RESEARCH

Deliberately Caused Bodily Damage (DCBD) phenomenon is where individuals cause (or allow others to cause) deliberate harm to their bodies, typically as a demonstration of religious faith. This can involve piercing the skin with sharp instruments, including spikes, daggers, or skewers, and swallowing sharp objects. What makes this different from self-mutilation or torture is that there is often no pain, little if any bleeding, and the wounds close with extraordinary rapidity. Recent years have seen some field investigations and formal studies into this phenomenon.

Field Investigations Most of the studies performed on DCBD have been field investigations, typically in Middle Eastern countries where such ceremonies are an accepted aspect of many Sufi groups. Peter Mulacz attended a large religious ceremony at Abu Bakr al-Hawaz in Syria.[187] Afterward, he watched a Shaikh insert a metal skewer into a male volunteer all the way through his abdomen, slowly but firmly (taking around five to ten seconds), until it exited out the man's back. The volunteer walked quickly counter-clockwise around the circle formed by his colleagues and bystanders before coming back to in front of the Shaikh, who then pulled the skewer out. Mulacz closely observed the procedure perhaps 100 times by different dervish groups, and in some cases took photographs. On at least one occasion when he had a particularly good view, Mulacz saw no bleeding from the hole where the skewer had been, and no blood on the skin surface or dripping outside, but there did appear to be a little internal bleeding into the adjacent tissue. Unfortunately, he was only able to watch the wound for perhaps 30 seconds after the skewer was removed before it was covered up by clothing.

Mulacz drew several conclusions based on his observations.[188] First, that given the number of old scars he witnessed on dervishes who had taken part in earlier DCDB ceremonies, it would appear that individuals not only survive the ritual, but are willing to repeat it. Second, that the individuals undergoing the piercing — although motivated and excited — were in a normal, or near-normal, state of consciousness during the ritual. Third, that those being pierced for the first time behaved no differently than those with prior experience. Of course, none of this would be surprising if it was the person doing the piercing who was the true agent involved for any paranormal wounding and/or healing. Mulacz did not feel what he witnessed was beyond the realm of what was naturally possible.

Controlled Experimental Research There are three limited reports of DCBD in the 1970s and 1980s, involving a total of four participants.[189] The first of these was an unpublished study from the Menninger Foundation in Topeka, Kansas. In it, Elmer and Alice Green observed a man place a knitting needle through his biceps. Apparently, a skeptical physician was unable to complete the feat until the participant took hold of the needle. In 1977, Peletier and Peper studied two participants, one who put bicycle spokes through his cheeks and the sides of his body, and another who skewered his forearm skin. In 1982, Larbig and others investigated a yogi who impaled his tongue, neck, and abdomen with unsterilized spikes. They suggested autohypnosis could be used to control the body's reaction to the piercing. However, other investigators feel no such ASC is involved.

Some of the best documented research came out of a collaboration between Western scientists and the Paramann Programme Laboratories in Amman, Jordan.[190] They investigated Casnazaniyyah practitioners. Before beginning their study, Howard Hall and Jamal Hussein (who is a Casnazaniyyah dervish as well as a parapsychologist) went to Baghdad where they watched spikes and skewers inserted into bodies, daggers hammered into the clavicle and skull, and glass and razor blades chewed and swallowed, all without any apparent injury to the body. In addition, practitioners appeared able to control or prevent pain, bleeding, and infection. Wounds that were visible tended to bleed for no more than 30 seconds.

The investigators then brought the Sufi Jamal Hussein to a radiology facility in Cleveland, Ohio.[191] There, they videotaped in front of witnesses as he inserted an unsterile metal skewer that was 25 cm long through one side of his face and out the other cheek. He reported no pain with this despite the fact that X-rays done after insertion clearly showed the presence of a skewer. One might think that this would have been followed up by other studies to better tease out the normal and/or paranormal processes involved. Unfortunately, this has not been the case. The heightened tensions between non–Muslim and Muslim countries in recent years, as well as cultural taboos against self-injury, seem to have (at least temporarily) blocked further research.

ANOMALOUS HEALING RESEARCH

The practice of anomalous healing dates back to the earliest human attempts at curing.[192] Evidence of it exists in virtually every society and epoch of human history. It includes a wide variety of practices and techniques, including passing hands over the patient, invoking the aid of spirit guides or deceased ancestors, prayer, administering magical medicines, using the "will" to make the disease disappear, visiting "power" spots or holy places, and radionics.[193] Early data was anecdotal, and case history reviews of claims of dramatic healings were often poorly documented, and did not control for placebo, suggestion, misdiagnosis, or inadequate reporting. Scientists have studied "unorthodox" medical treatments since at least 1784, when the French Royal Commission investigated Mesmer's animal magnetism treatment.[194] Similar investigations of anomalous healing — many with equally skeptical findings — have been performed during the centuries since that date.

Archival Research and Surveys Archival material has mainly been used to investigate patient outcomes for anomalous healing. Surveys lend themselves well to this topic, and allow us to better understand the types of people who go to anomalous healers, what kind of sensations are felt during healing, and how patients view their outcomes.

In 1899, Goddard reviewed the claims of mental healing as part of the Christian Science movement.[195] He cited case reports and cure rates, and included considerable background material to suggest the role of the mind in the cause and cure of disease. Goddard did not believe these cures involved an occult agency, but instead attributed them to the power of suggestion and the ability of any idea that strongly possesses the mind to materialize in the body.

In 1955, Rose looked at 95 of the "successful" healings performed by Harry Edwards — a famous twentieth-century British psychic who was said to have healed tens of thousands of people with the supposed aid of spirit doctors.[196] This study does not come across as being a balanced report, but more on the nature of an effort at debunking. After eliminating 58 cases for having insufficient data, Rose found 22 other cases to be so much at variance with the claims that he considered it useless to continue the investigation further.

Rose noted in his critique that two patients — one of a cataract and another of laryngeal cancer — improved after the healing treatment, while one hernia was completely cured.[197] He also felt seven cases showed improvement that either relapsed or was functional (no change in the organic condition), four cases improved but were also receiving traditional medical treatment (i.e., the change for the better could have been due to the allopathic care), and one case of a child with muscular dystrophy worsened. Rose did not believe that anomalous healing was responsible for either of the two improved patients. Instead, he suggested that the cataract patient could have spontaneously dislocated their clouded lens by coughing or straining (which is an unlikely event, but would have improved the vision had it occurred), while the patient with laryngeal cancer may have been lucky enough to have the diagnostic biopsy remove all of his cancer. Of course, the latter would be more believable if the pathologist had reported the biopsy margins free of tumor. However, no note is made as to whether this was in fact the case. Needless to say, Rose was not impressed that anything other than normal processes were occurring.

In *The Healing Intelligence,* Edwards discussed a number of his experiences, including cases of remarkable cures documented by physicians.[198] He wrote with some bitterness about the way the British medical profession had written off his healings, saying that every time he tried to offer them hard evidence of his abilities, it was rejected, with the doctors saying his results could have been due to a mistaken diagnosis, spontaneous remission, laboratory error, X-ray screwup, or insufficient time to see whether the healing worked or not. While each of these explanations is not, by itself, unreasonable, one has to wonder of the likelihood that they are true every time. It is no surprise that Edwards gave up trying to interest the medical profession in studying anomalous healing, saying, "One day, public opinion will succeed where I have failed in this task."[199] It is unfortunate that prospective double-blind controlled experiments were never performed with him. The results might have been interesting.

There have been numerous patient surveys in recent decades. Turner surveyed several hundred "absent healing" patients in 1969, and found that those who reported being "cured" also were more apt to report sensations of heat, cold, and tingling, while those who reported no sensations turned out to be mostly those suffering from various neuroses.[200] Another survey performed in the Netherlands in 1981 showed that patients reported relief after mental healing treatments just as often for organic disorders as for functional ones. Attevelt collected self-reports from over 3,000 patients who received anomalous healing, two-thirds of whom reported definite improvement — regardless of whether the presenting problem was organic or not, and independent of gender and the number of treatments performed.

In 1980, Haraldsson and Olafsson published findings they got by re-interviewing respondents to a random sample survey originally conducted in Iceland in 1976.[201] They found that two-thirds of respondents felt they had benefited from their anomalous healing treatment. Perhaps more importantly, this reported improvement did *not* correlate with prior belief as to the potential effectiveness of anomalous healing. One would think that if only placebo were involved (in essence, the patient creating a self-fulfilling prophecy) that the more they believed in the treatment, the greater effect it would have. However, this was not the case.

Sybo Schouten reviewed a number of surveys performed in Europe and the Netherlands on complementary medicine and psychic healer usage and apparent effectiveness.[202] Most of these looked at subjective feelings of well-being or improvement. Schouten felt they indicated a number of common trends, "with, on average, two thirds of the patients being female, most between the age of 40 and 60 and with chronic complaints."[203] He felt it was possible that this indicated, more than anything else, a group that was dissatisfied with traditional medicine.

Field Investigations Anomalous healing research has also been performed in the field. James McClenon monitored a number of psychic surgery treatments in Brazil and the Philippines.[204] He found that these operations produced no immediate effect beyond that of feeling excited and expectant. On follow-up, some individuals claimed to be "cured," while others believed that their medical conditions were worse. In general, clients evaluated their experiences as positive, even if their problem had not been helped. There were also a few instances in which the dramatic power of this experience — even if created in part (or fully) by sleight-of-hand — seemed to produce anomalous physical effects.

In 1997, Sidney Greenfield published a report on a Brazilian psychic surgeon, Mauricio Magalhães.[205] Magalhães is said to channel a spirit known as "Dr. Fritz," purportedly a deceased German medical student from World War I who was mentioned earlier in connection with Arigó. Greenfield went to Campo Grande for three weeks to observe Magalhães in action and interview patients who had undergone treatment during a time frame of 3 weeks to 6 months earlier. A total of 32 patients (10 male, 22 female) ranging in age from 1 to 66 years old were asked 18 questions including why they had sought out a spiritist healer, what kind of treatment they received, and whether it had helped them. In the case of the infant, the child's mother answered the questions.

Needless to say, this was not a random or representative sample, but one of convenience. Furthermore, not all the patients answered every question, making it difficult to know how much meaning to attribute to their responses.[206] Nonetheless, the results are interesting. Magalhães/Fritz inserted needles for 24 of the 35 complaints, which was sometimes followed by a surgical incision and the insertion of a hemostat or other blunt instrument four to six inches under the skin. However, only 4 of the 29 adults reported feeling pain. For the entire group, 88 percent felt the treatment had helped them, 64 percent believed themselves cured, and 95 percent stated they were more satisfied with the care they had received from Magalhães than they were with the conventional treatment they had received for their condition.

Norman Don and Gilda Moura traveled to Brazil for fieldwork on nine psychic surgeons.[207] They observed thousands of patients receiving treatment and videotaped several hundred cases. Using topological brain mapping, they found that the healers had an increase in brain activity (36–44 Hz) suggestive of hyperarousal while engaged in trance behavior. Despite the lack of anesthetic, those patients who were tested (there were only a few) had cortical quieting, suggestive of relaxation.

Controlled Experimental Research One of the first attempts at performing a prospective controlled study of anomalous healing occurred in the mid 1950s. The ground was primed for it in 1952, when Kurt Trampler (widely known in Germany and Switzerland for his anomalous healing) was tried and found guilty of violating the statutes governing the practice of medicine.[208] In 1954, Trampler asked parapsychologist Hans Bender at the Freiburg Institute to investigate his method of healing and its success rate. The result was a study that lasted from January until July 1955, during which Trampler was allowed on four successive days each month to treat a self-selected group of patients who presented themselves at the Institute.

The patients were asked to write a biographical sketch, describe their illness and its course, answer a detailed questionnaire, and (if they consented) take a battery of psychological tests.[209] The participants were also examined by physicians before meeting the healer. Trampler's sessions usually consisted of an hour talk on his methods, followed by purportedly sending energy with his hands to individuals within a group of 50–70 patients. After the treatment, the patients were asked for their sensations, general condition, and expectancy of a cure.

Of the 650 patients who were treated in this manner, 38 percent returned of their own volition for further treatments, and were questioned by the two doctors in the study [210] The physicians also summoned a chosen group of 160 patients for follow up clinical examinations— however, it is not stated on what basis they picked this group. Questionnaires were sent out to those patients who did not return. In some cases, these individuals were even called upon at their homes in order to follow-up on 538 of the original 650 patients.

This was not a blind study, and the attitudes and beliefs of the physicians involved were unstated, despite its obvious potential for bias. In addition, the results may have been confounded by the fact that 58 percent of the patients were simultaneously receiving medical treatment, and

75 percent of the patients were complaining of chronic disorders. It is of further concern that not only are we ignorant about what constitutes an effective healing session, but we also do not know how long it takes for results to manifest or how many sessions would be needed given the chronic nature of most of these illnesses.

Nonetheless, Inge Strauch concluded that of the 538 patients who were checked, 39 percent felt they had improved, 22 percent felt they had experienced temporary benefits, 29 percent reported no change, and 10 percent felt they had worsened.[211] The physicians who examined 247 of the patients, on the other hand, believed that 9 percent (22) showed improvement, 2 percent (4) had temporary benefits, 75 percent (187) were unchanged, and 14 percent (34) had worsened. Within the major disease groups, most of the objective improvements (15 percent) appeared in diseases of the digestive tract.

Strauch felt that this discrepancy between the physicians' findings and the patients' subjective results was due to the attitude of the patients, their expectations, and their readiness to respond.[212] One might wonder at her not feeling equal concern over the attitude of the doctors, their expectations, and readiness to accept that an alternative healing method could be effective. Not once does Strauch seem to consider the fact that the involved physicians might have had biases that could have made a difference in both the reporting, and the recording, of these illnesses. Her faith in the objectivity of the medical profession seems both touching and misplaced. Furthermore, Strauch attributed the decreased sensation reported by the unchanged patients to them not having as much expectation that they would be healed, rather than considering the possibility that they might have received less of a treatment from the healer.

Strauch concluded that the effectiveness of mental healing depended upon the faith and expectations of the patient (which is contrary to the survey mentioned earlier, performed by Haraldsson and Olafsson in 1980).[213] She then went on to state that the group that had improved with the treatment had a lower level of intelligence, less of a critical capacity, a more relaxed personality structure, and low self-confidence. However, Strauch admitted that, "in no case was his treatment objectively harmful."[214] The lack of a blind protocol makes it difficult to know how much weight (if any) to put on these findings.

Bernard Grad was one of the first researchers to take a systematic approach to anomalous healing in the laboratory.[215] He performed a series of studies with an increasing quality of control, using a Hungarian laying-on-of-hands healer, named Oskar Estebany.[216] These were longitudinal experimental research protocols with randomized subjects (in some cases mice and in others barley seeds) divided into treatment and control groups. Some of the studies did not adequately control for third variables — such as chemical or handling effects in the animal healing experiments, or seed weight in the early barley experiment — and a complete double blind was not always performed (if such can ever be done in a psi experiment). Nonetheless, the bulk of the evidence was very suggestive that the healers were able to affect both plant and animal recovery from injury. Unfortunately, although the reliability was impressive, these studies lack generalizability because one treatment and two people — Grad and Estebany — were involved every time. Thus, it is unclear what role each of these three elements — the experimenter, the healer, and the treatment — played in the results.

Dolores Krieger also worked with Estebany during the early 1970s.[217] She performed a series of non-blind studies, which seemed to indicate that hemoglobin values could be increased over a period of a few days in the participants whom he treated. Nor was Estebany the only self-proclaimed anomalous healer able to get laboratory results. Olga Worrall was also able to affect a wide range of test materials, and accelerate plant growth.[218] Delores Krieger later trained nurses to work with patients in a laying-on-of-hands method that she called "therapeutic touch."[219]

Graham and Anita Watkins studied the effect of participants who either claimed to be psychics or had performed well on psi tests in a series of experiments on resuscitating anesthetized mice.[220] Two mice were simultaneously rendered unconscious by identical etherizers and were taken to separate rooms. The healer for the trial would be in one of the rooms and attempt to exert his or her influence without contact. They found the experimental group required a significantly shorter time to come to their feet and take a step than the control group.

For the second experiment, Graham and Anita Watkins used the same room and table for both mice, with a screen separating the mice and the participant sealed at one end of the table such that they could only see the experimental mouse.[221] Once again, the experimental mice recovered significantly faster.

In a third experiment, Graham and Anita Watkins used the same room for the control and subject mice, but this time had the healer seated outside the room viewing them both through one-way glass.[222] For the first four runs of twenty-four trials each, the timers knew which mouse was being treated, and the results were the same as found previously. However, for the next seven runs, the timers were blind to which mouse the healer was trying to influence. At first, the side of the table that was being treated was randomized each trial, but the healers complained that they found it difficult to work like that. Therefore, for the final four runs a compromise was adopted. One side of the table was randomly designated the experimental side for the first half of the run, with the other side being used for the second half of the run, without the timers knowing which side was which. Unfortunately, as Watkins and Watkins admitted, some sensory leakage during these trials may have let the timers know which side of the table was being concentrated on by the healers. The results again showed advantages for the treatment group in the first and last runs, but no effect for the middle seven runs.

Seven more series were conducted using modifications of this theme, including substituting ordinary people for the healers, and varying the anesthetizers/timers.[223] In order to test for a possible treatment lag effect, the healers left the building after the first half of the healing time period, leaving the second half of the run to be conducted in exactly the same way, but without them. The results were as significant for the second half (no healer) as they had been for the first (healer present).

Overall, the experiments had two significant findings. First, in all of the experiments except for the one with non-talented participants, the treated mice recovered faster.[224] Second, there was a "linger effect," as the mice on the side of the table that the healers used continued to wake up faster for some period of time after the healers had left, when only control participants remained.[225]

Solfvin observed that the Watkins' series left room for bias because full blinds were not used, and the data were collected by hand-held stopwatches used with visual observation of the mice's awakenings.[226] Thus, there was potential for a variety of experimenter effects. In addition, Solfvin pointed out that the so-called linger effect could be more parsimoniously explained as an experimenter effect.

William Braud suggested that MMI factors might be just as important, if not more so, in self-healing than in healing others.[227] He tried to study this possibility by designing an experiment that looked at the rate of hemolysis of osmotically stressed human red blood cells in a test tube. Unfortunately, the large within- and between-group variability (perhaps in part due to their method of blood drawing, since vacuum tubes can be very damaging to red blood cells) and small sample size obscured any treatment effect. Braud re-evaluated the data, comparing each participant on an individual basis, and found nine significant scores among the 32 participants.

It is difficult to say much about the meaningfulness of this data, considering the high variability noted in the results, the post-hoc nature of the analysis, and the lack of sample randomization. John Palmer later investigated whether Braud's study results could have been generated through different starting times.[228] He performed 160 trials and found high rates of decline in absorption over time, demonstrating a high potential for artifact, and casting even greater doubt on Braud's initial findings.

Yount et al. performed a pilot study and two follow-up experiments on in-vitro cultures of human astrocytes (a type of brain cell) and qigong treatments administered over the series by 18 different practitioners.[229] The pilot study was performed in San Francisco and the formal experiments in Beijing. The researchers saw a trend toward increased cell proliferation in the pilot study (8 experiments) and a small follow-up (28 experiments) at the p=0.036 level. However, a larger study of 60 experiments with a sham control group did not show a difference between the treated and untreated groups. They noted an increasing amount of variability in every experiment for both for sham and qigong groups, which they felt could have been partly due to the less-than-ideal cell culture conditions in Beijing.

The reader will have noted by this point that healing studies are fraught with potential problems. It is generally difficult — if not impossible — with human patients to perform true experimental studies using randomized design. Nonetheless, three healing studies stand out in the literature as particularly convincing because of the quality of their research design, involving double- or triple-blind protocols and randomization.

The first of these studies was performed by Byrd in the 1980s.[230] He was interested in the effectiveness of prayer on patients who were admitted to a coronary care unit. This was a prospective study with a randomized protocol. Furthermore, the staff, patients, and experimenter were all blind as to who was assigned to which group. There were 393 patients, with the 192 patients in the experimental group receiving prayer from outside the hospital by members of local Protestant and Catholic churches. A comparison of medical indicators showed that the treatment and control groups were well matched at the start of the study. Byrd found that fewer patients in the prayer group required ventilatory support (p<.002), antibiotics (p<.005), or diuretics (p<.05), and that there was a lower incidence of congestive heart failure (p<.03), cardiac arrest (p<.02), and pneumonia (p<.03). Although the results did not show a large effect size — 85 percent of the prayer group had a "good" hospital course as opposed to 73 percent of the control group, and 14 percent of the prayer group had a "bad" hospital course as opposed to 22 percent of the control group — the relatively large number of participants, and the quality of the study's design, add weight to the findings.[231]

The second experiment of note was performed by Daniel Wirth.[232] He looked at the use of therapeutic touch on human participants after punch biopsy wounding. Not only did Wirth use a double-blind approach, with participants randomized into treatment and control groups, but he also attempted to eliminate placebo effects by using deception — he did not let the participants know that they were in a healing study. Unfortunately, time constraints prevented Wirth from also randomizing whether the treatment was administered in the morning or the afternoon (which may have inadvertently taken advantage of the linger effect). Nonetheless, he found that human healing was accelerated by therapeutic touch at eight days after wounding (p<.001), and that a greater number of experimental participants were completely healed at 16 days than control participants (p<.001), even though none of the participants were consciously aware that they were being treated. This is an important study because (although one might question Wirth's ethics) the findings seem to rule out the idea that therapeutic touch works only as placebo.

Wirth performed a replication of this study in 1993, along with Richardson, Eidelman, and O'Malley, using 24 participants whose wounds were photographed.[233] The photographs allowed the experimenters to have three independent physicians, who were blind to the study, independently rate the degree of healing on days five and ten. The results of this experiment also showed a significant difference between the treatment and control groups for day five, and a marginally significant difference at day ten.

Three later studies by Wirth on non-contact therapeutic touch yielded nonsignificant or reverse results.[234] Wirth and his colleagues offered a number of possible reasons for this; however, Schouten believed it was likely due to the small number of participants involved and the fact that anomalous healing can be influenced by a number of variables outside the experimenter's control.

A third impressive experiment, which was performed in San Francisco, examined the effectiveness of distant healing on AIDS patients.[235] The participants were pair-matched for important variables and assessed by blood and psychometric testing. The randomly assigned treatment group received anomalous healing for ten weeks in addition to regular medical care, while the control group received only routine medical management. The distant healing format permitted the use of a triple blind — the participants, their doctors, and the study personnel did not know to which group each patient was assigned.

Six months after the start of the study, a blind medical chart review revealed that the treatment group acquired significantly fewer new AIDS-defining illnesses ($p=0.04$), had lower illness severity ($p=0.03$), required fewer doctor visits ($p=0.01$), received fewer hospitalizations ($p=0.04$) and days of hospitalization ($p=0.04$), and showed improved mood ($p=0.02$). However, there was no significant difference between the two groups in the CD4 count (a common blood test used to follow the progression of AIDS). Although this study was a small one, its results were promising enough to warrant further research.

In recent years, investigators have tried looking at anomalous healers in new ways, beyond that of their influence on biological systems. Lumsden-Cook, Edwards, and Thwala examined at the effect of four Zulu healers (known as *isangoma*) on REG output.[236] They asked healers to focus their consciousnesses on the machine and send it healing for five minutes. Although an admittedly small sample size in this pilot study, they achieved significant results.

Schwartz and Boccuzzi noted that anomalous healers are always speaking of "high vibrational energy" and decided to look at the effect of consciousness on cosmic rays.[237] They created a sealed system with a low light CCD camera cooled to -77°C. Using 30-minute exposure times in a light-tight chamber, they performed runs imaging cosmic rays in total darkness against a white sheet of paper with three conditions: (1) blank runs, (2) runs where a spiritual healer was asked to meditate but not invite "universal energy" in, and (3) runs when the healer was asked to put energy inside the box. The control image was a random scattering of dots. However, when they asked a spiritual healer to put energy inside the system they saw a dense streak of dots down the center of the image, which was significant to the $p<.0000001$ level. Schwartz speculated that this may reflect a decrease in entropy.

Although the results of healing studies have been inconsistent, the data suggests that anomalous healing has at least some impact on health, with a greater subjective improvement reported by patients than that which is objectively measured.[238] Some studies suggest that it can be helpful for the patient to know that the treatment is being performed. However, this is not a necessary condition. Patients benefited even in the Byrd and Wirth experiments, when the healees were unaware they were receiving anomalous healing — assuming, of course, that true blind conditions are ever possible, given ESP. In addition, there have never been any real indications of patients getting worse with anomalous healing.

Possibilities for How Anomalous Healing Works Given the quality of at least some of the research, it appears that anomalous healing can improve patient outcome. How it works is unclear. We do not know whether energy is involved, or how the mind is able to influence a distant biological system. Although the effect appears stronger when the patient is aware that he or she is being treated anomalously, that knowledge does not seem to, in itself, be required for results to occur. This suggests that more than placebo, or self-healing, is involved. Nonetheless, placebo could be a factor in, or a result of, anomalous healing. Because of this, we will spend some time discussing the topic.

PLACEBO Placebo plays a critical role in all forms of healing research. Whether one is testing a medical treatment, a psychological one, or a psychic one, it is necessary to control (when possible) for the personal contact between the client and the healer.[239] This is because of the power of placebo, which involves patients knowing they are receiving a treatment, and their faith in the healer and the treatment. In addition, the placebo response is an intrinsic part of *every* healing situation, regardless of the type of treatment, whether conventional or alternative.[240]

The sugar pill form of placebo has been greatly studied in the medical literature.[241] It has been found capable of curing a number of organic diseases, as well as causing its share of negative side effects (known as nocebo). According to Schouten, studies show that placebo has 62 percent effectiveness at treating headaches, 55–60 percent the effectiveness of psychotropic drugs for depression and analgesics, 58 percent effectiveness treating seasickness and digestive problems, 17 percent effectiveness for hypertension, 7 percent for insomnia, and 5 percent for asthma. There are some medical conditions, such as epilepsy, for which placebo has no effectiveness at all.[242] However, in other cases, placebo response can be as high as 100 percent, suggesting that the mind may have far more control over the body than traditionally thought. Thus, the placebo response is a significant factor in a wide range of medical conditions — although the degree of effectiveness placebo has, and in what direction (whether positive or negative), may vary considerably.

The nocebo aspect — where an inert substance causes unwanted side effects — is an interesting phenomenon in itself. Does this mean a real effect is occurring, which has intrinsic negative consequences? Or that on an unconscious level people want these side effects? Or is something else going on? The answer is unclear. However, the nocebo phenomenon is not rare. Schouten reports that it shows up in 19 percent of 109 double-blind trials.[243]

There are a variety of therapeutic factors which help determine the effectiveness of a given treatment.[244] The administering physician (or other health practitioner) has a central role, in addition to a variety of situational variables, such as the color of the pill used as the placebo.[245] Nor do double-blind studies prevent the administering physicians' expectations and other nonspecific treatment effects from eliciting a healing response — particularly if the therapeutic agent has a weak or variable effect, making its intrinsic results less statistically robust.[246] In addition, there is some suggestion that treatment efficacy (whether placebo or otherwise) may correlate with the patient's discomfort, concern, and degree of stress.[247]

As Traut and Passarelli noted, placebo operates regardless of whether a treatment is "backed by the best physiological and pharmacological information" or "illogical, poorly conceived, or even dangerous."[248] It may be responsible for more subjective improvement than any single category of real drug, but placebo is a complex factor and difficult to control.[249] Healing studies that try to replicate results often fail because it is hard to create consistent expectancy, even when attempts are made to employ the same procedure on a similar patient group. Furthermore, although every human being appears to be capable of responding to placebo, the fact an individual has responded to it in the past does not indicate whether they will do so again in a different situation. This can make it something of a wild card in studies, unless they go for a long enough period for its impact to diminish. However, this may not be a short time. Although placebo is anecdotally felt to drop out after around six months, in some cases it has been shown to work for as long as 20 months.[250]

ENERGY Daniel Benor commented that although many healers claimed to feel colors, tingling, heat, or cold as they work, it is unknown whether this could be due to an energy transfer, or is a case of synesthesia (the crossing of sensory modalities).[251] However, there is some indication that a form of energy may be involved. Benor reported on studies that placed shielded photographic film either between the healer and healee or under the healee. The film showed exposure after psychic healing of a body part which needed it, but did not show exposure when the body part did not need healing. Furthermore, there was decreasing exposure with increasing distance from the healer. Of course, it is also possible, as Benor noted, that the effect could represent something emitted by the healee or a third variable, which is not directly related to healing. However, the early work by Schwartz and Boccuzzi on the ability of anomalous healers to change the pattern of cosmic rays photographed inside a sealed system suggests that healers may be able to influence energy.[252]

The study of anomalous healing energy is complicated by the fact that healers vary in the qualities and limitations that they attribute to it.[253] For example, some claim that their abilities are blocked by cardboard or paper, while others are unaffected. Thus, it is unclear how much of what we discover is due to anomalous healing factors, and how much is a product of healer and/or experimenter expectancy effects and belief systems.

A 1984 study by van Wijk, Schamhart, and van Wijk-Visser led parapsychologist Sybo Schouten to suggest that the sensations of heat reported by those being healed may be due to the healee's expectations, rather than the healing process itself.[254] Unfortunately, this study is problematic in that it used only one participant and one healer. Furthermore, it made the implicit assumption that the amount of time a distant healer sends energy is identical to the length of time the healee receives it, which may not be true. At present, it seems premature to draw any conclusions based on such a small and (probably) non-representative sample.

NORMAL FACTORS The complexity of the healing process makes it difficult to determine precisely how much, if any, anomalous healing success is due to a paranormal component. Normal variables can change in ways that give the process the false illusion of effectiveness. Schouten listed a number of such possible factors, including (1) patient exerted physical changes (2) improvement in the patient's ability to cope with his or her illness (3) natural variations in the patient's state of health (4) changes in the patient's lifestyle (5) self-healing as a result of removing the possible negative effects of conventional treatment or habitual drug use and (6) the "healing" of a faulty diagnosis (i.e., there was no illness to begin with).[255]

Yet another issue is that illnesses can undergo spontaneous remission. Nor is this rare. Data from the late 1900s suggests that spontaneous remission occurs in approximately 1:100,000 cases of cancer in the Netherlands.[256] Nor is it limited to cancer, but can happen in a wide range of illnesses, with over 3,000 reports appearing in over 800 medical journals. Spontaneous remission is a poorly understood phenomenon; however, studies suggest that changes in the patient's attitude and/or psychosocial situation are a factor. It is also likely that the placebo effect and other variables may overlap with, or be responsible for, spontaneous remission.

In his review of psychic healing and complementary medicine, Schouten generally discounted the significance of MMI and felt that, although it may make a slight contribution, it was minor compared to that of other factors.[257] Nonetheless, he pointed out that if we were to consider a patient's subjective feelings of health and well-being, then conventional and complementary medicine may not be all that different. Schouten concluded that "from a purely pragmatic point of view there seems nothing amiss with a treatment that makes people feel and function better and which in itself does not have negative side effects."[258]

EXPERIMENTER EFFECT The experimenter effect is yet another element that must be considered when looking at the anomalous healing research. Solfvin performed an ingenious study where he informed veterinary students that he had conducted a pilot series with a famous mental healer, which showed strong results that he now wanted to confirm.[259] Each student was given complete charge of one cage with twelve mice in it, six of which, the students were informed, had been given a full dosage of a malarial blood parasite, while the others had received a control dosage, and were not expected to manifest illness. The students were also told the mental healer would perform distant healing to half of each group, and that they were to care for the mice, weigh them every other day, and make behavioral observations.

Unbeknownst to them, the students were the real object of the study. [260] All of the mice had received the same dosage of the parasite and there was no healer. Despite this, the mice they were told had received a "control" dose showed statistically less blood infestation than those thought to have received the full dose. In addition, even though the students were blind to which mice were designated to be treated by the nonexistent distant healer, the supposedly "healed" mice showed a statistically significant advantage.

This study points out the difficulty in isolating the effects of mental healing treatments.[261] Experimenters are always worried about preventing normal sensory leakage, but extrasensory (or psi) leakage may be an even greater problem as it cannot be easily blocked — although Solfvin noted it might balance out somewhat if a mix of believers and disbelievers were used. Of further concern is the fact that the experimenter effect may be responsible for some of the results falsely attributed to various treatment protocols. Thus, the apparent effectiveness of anomalous healing in research studies may be due to a complex interaction of placebo, expectancy effects, unrecognized normal factors, the unintentional psi of participants and experimenters, in addition to any intrinsic therapeutic action(s).

SUMMARY

Healing is a matter of great complexity, with interwoven factors that make it difficult to tease out what is occurring. Research on the topic is hindered by the fact that we are not yet able to measure, let alone quantify, whatever external energy — if any — passes between healers and their patients. At this point in time, we do not know how anomalous healing works, or what its limits are, beyond the fact that placebo and expectancy undoubtedly play some role. Nonetheless, there are at least a few well-designed studies that strongly suggest anomalous healing taps into something, or some combination of things, which can influence both functional and organic illnesses. It is hoped that further research, along with the development of new technologies capable of better measuring the human bio-energy field and whatever subtle energy (if any) is used by healers, will eventually shed better light upon this topic.

Macro-MMI Research

Macro-MMI (more often called macro–PK) refers to effects that are large enough, or strong enough, to be detected by the naked eye. Thus, unlike its micro counterpart, it does not require statistics to be demonstrated. Examples of these large scale phenomena include levitation, teleportation, table tipping, and object movement. Although it has primarily been studied using individual "star" MMI performers, some research has also been performed with ordinary people working in groups.

Individual "Star" Performer Research

This section can only discuss a few of the better known star MMI participants from around the globe. Many, such as D. D. Home and Matthew Manning, began as poltergeist agents who later learned to control their abilities.[262] A few, such as Felicia Parise, taught themselves how to move objects by watching someone else do it.[263] It is worth examining the stories of these individuals to see what we can learn of how their skills developed, what they could do, and what they said about their experiences.

Individual macro–MMI research has been limited because of three factors: (1) the difficulty of working with stars (who often object to experimental controls); (2) increased concern over fraud by the participants; and (3) the limited quantity of individuals who can perform large-scale phenomena on command.[264] However, it should be recognized that — regardless of how difficult some of these individuals are to work with — they have greatly contributed to our knowledge of MMI. The fact that they could perform MMI on demand in controlled settings allowed experimenters to do research that not only provided some proof of psi, but also gave a cursory sense of its process. Perhaps even more importantly, these stars allow us a glimpse of what could be our own innate potential.

Nina Kulagina Nina Kulagina was one of the most renowned MMI performers ever studied. This Russian housewife seemed to be able to move lightweight objects, influence compasses, change the measured weights of objects, and have an effect on biological systems — such as slowing down a frog's heart, or causing people to feel heat on the surface of their skin.[265] She could also affect sealed photographic film, which would appear fogged when the negatives were developed.[266]

There are contradictory accounts of how she developed her MMI abilities, but it seems to have been accidental.[267] Kulagina's gift was discovered while she was working with L. L. Vasiliev in an experiment trying to distinguish colors by touch. She appeared to be able to move a variety of materials, including metals, plastics, fabrics, and organic materials. When working with new objects, they would always move away from her. She only attracted them after practice.

Performing MMI was frankly stressful for Kulagina. Her heart rate accelerated to 150–240 beats/minute, her blood pressure went up, her blood sugar rose, EEG amplitude over the occipital lobe increased by fifty times over her baseline relaxed state, her muscles ached, and she lost anywhere from 700–2000 grams of weight.[268] Even if we were to ignore the controlled conditions imposed by both Soviet and a few Western scientists (which limited possibilities for fraudulent object movement), the physiological changes by themselves are impressive.[269]

Kulagina's MMI appeared to demonstrate the "linger effect," in that objects sometimes continued moving even though she was no longer trying to influence them.[270] Factors that seemed to be important for Kulagina's ability to perform included her motivation, mood, and the degree of electricity in the air, as she disliked working in thunderstorms. She was often the focus of suspicion, but there was no serious evidence that Kulagina used trickery.[271] Her last public appearance, which was filmed, was in March 1977, and she died in 1990.

Chinese children with exceptional human functioning China has reported a number of children who were capable of what they call "reading with the ear"— a term they sometimes use for ESP.[272] Many of these children are said to also be able to perform MMI, such as opening flowers in vases, breaking sticks, teleporting objects, and even transporting surgically implanted colored stones out of a chicken. Most of these children have been pre-pubescent girls, and the Chinese believe that there may be a correlation between the onset of menstruation and a decline in the children's abilities. However, it is unclear how much this relates to cultural expectations, hormonal changes, and psychological changes, with, perhaps, a shift in priorities and interests.

Yan Xin Yan Xin was a qigong master from China who was said to be able to heal a complex fracture in twenty minutes.[273] He participated in a variety of research studies trying to understand chi energy. In some experiments, he reportedly altered radioactive decay rates — which is not surprising considering that a great many others have been able to also do this in REG research.[274] However, Yan also seemed to alter the refraction point of liquid crystal, changed hydrogen and carbon monoxide into carbon dioxide (a process that usually requires a catalyst, a pressure of 30 atm, and temperatures as high as 300°C), and affect a lithium fluoride heat-releasing light detector, which is usually used for measuring radiation dosage.

Yan sometimes emitted a sandalwood scent when sending energy.[275] This phenomenon was reportedly once noted by doctors traveling with him in a car on the way to see a sick patient. Chinese scientists measured a number of parameters on Yan. They found that when he was subjected to 200 volts of current, the resistance between his hands was several hundred times higher than the normal, and that if he used his psi abilities, Yan could increase his resistance to thousands of times higher.

Zhang Baosheng Zhang Baosheng is a qigong master who is the Asian equivalent of Kulagina.[276] He has been extensively studied by the Chinese. Zhang was born poor.[277] His original gift was primarily ESP, which he used on a job to catch thieves. His MMI gift apparently started (rather unfortunately for him) when he was in a shoe store admiring a pair he wanted for his girlfriend, but could not afford to buy. The shoes are said to have apported themselves into his bag and he was jailed for shoplifting.

Zhang is said to be a master of apporting objects, able to light fires, and capable of "walking through walls."[278] It is impossible to say whether the latter represents teleporting, or the use of a technique described by Savelli as "the mind stops" (where the observer's brain freezes, or ceases functioning, so he or she is unaware of normal movement that the eyes might be seeing). Zhang is also a prime example of why many researchers refuse to work with star participants. He is reputedly capricious, bad tempered, likes unpleasant practical jokes, and often threatens people.

Some of Zhang's more interesting purported feats include apporting living and inanimate matter through sealed containers and restoring torn cards or paper to a single piece.[279] Although many of the effects he is said to perform could probably be duplicated through sleight-of-hand or other tricks, there are at least a few bits of evidence that Zhang has genuine abilities.[280] One of the most remarkable of these is a film, taken by the Institute of Space Medico-Engineering (ISME) and recorded at 400 frames per second, which captures the passing of a marked medical pill through glass, including frames showing the penetration process.[281] Western researchers have had little or no access to Zhang, which has led some to wonder if he cheats, but tight controls are purportedly described in the Chinese investigators' formal reports.

Tomaz Coutinho Tomaz Coutinho was born in Brazil in 1947.[282] He apparently developed his psychic abilities after being struck by lightning on his twelfth birthday. Coutinho initially reported ESP experiences. However he later became a talented metal bender and was able to transform objects in his vicinity, such as a metal coin into a medallion, or aluminum foil into a bird sculpture. Coutinho sometimes attributed his phenomena (which could include flashes of light and the appearance of scents, such as jasmine) to extraterrestrials.

Coutinho was unusual in that he appeared to be able to create a field effect that allowed him to bend metal — not just silverware but heavier items like bowls and chairs — without touching it.[283] Furthermore, he could perform a wide range of other activity, including completely mending broken metal and torn paper, transmuting objects, levitating items, anomalous healing, teleporting, producing lights and spontaneous fires, changing the weather, and spinning compasses. A number of these feats were performed under laboratory conditions and documented by photographs.

Lee Pulos and Gary Richman noted that experiential factors associated with Coutinho's MMI success included (1) a deep sense of connection to the target item, (2) playfulness, and (3) feelings of energy building up or flowing through him.[284] Sometimes an ASC appeared to be involved during or after events. In addition, Coutinho was an extremely open individual, happy-go-lucky, and eager to experiment with his gifts. Although metal-bending seems to be effortless, when trying to affect a compass or reconstitute destroyed objects, Coutinho would hyperventilate and turn red, suggesting a certain amount of physical stress.

Like many mediums, Coutinho was accused of producing some of his phenomena through fraud.[285] In particular, William Roll is said to have filmed him bending silverware by force. Although some of his feats may well have been through trickery (whether conscious or unconscious), others seem inexplicable, and cannot be so easily explained away.

Matthew Manning Matthew Manning was eleven years old in 1967 when poltergeist phenomena broke out at his house.[286] An assortment of knocks, taps, "pinging," and object movements began to occur when he was studying for his exams. These events initially only happened when Manning was home from school. However, in 1971, four years after the initial onset of poltergeist activity at home, levitating beds, flying objects, overturned bookcases, and the appearance of pools of water, hot spots, and strange knives (which no one could say where they had come from) began happening at his boarding school, as well.

In May 1971, Manning began to perform automatic writing, which seemed to attenuate, and eventually abolish, the poltergeist manifestations.[287] He later went on to do automatic drawing in a variety of artistic styles, "see" apparitions, and bend metal. It is unfortunate that, like some other participants, Manning is said to have become bitter over his treatment at the hands of researchers.[288] Although he was involved in studies in a number of countries — including England, Canada, the United States, Germany, Sweden, and Holland, among others — Manning now devotes most of his time to writing and anomalous healing and has his own website at www.matthewmanning.com.[289]

Felicia Parise Felicia Parise was a medical technician at the Maimonides Medical Center with a history of some personal ESP experiences.[290] In 1968, she volunteered to participate in dream telepathy studies at their Parapsychology Laboratory and proved to have some talent. Her first known experience with MMI came after watching a film at a research meeting, which showed Nina Kulagina moving small objects without apparent contact. Parise was immediately convinced that the Russian star was genuine and was irritated at the skepticism of others at the meeting. Perhaps because of this, and as an escape from personal worries, Parise began trying to duplicate what she had seen.

One night, just after receiving a phone call that her grandmother was dying, she succeeded.[291] Parise then practiced for about a month to be sure that she could reliably move the small bottle she used as a target before telling Charles Honorton about her abilities. He found that she could indeed move small items for short distances without any physical contact. These sessions appeared to be difficult for Parise in that she often perspired, and developed a runny nose, runny eyes, and trembling. In the end, Parise decided that she did not want to continue with the effort that MMI seemed to require, and chose to go back to ESP research.

It is impossible to know how many of the similarities between Parise and Kulagina were due to Parise modeling her behavior after what she saw of the Russian on film. Both women were originally ESP participants, objects initially moved away from them, their MMI seemed to require tremendous effort, and there would sometimes be a linger effect.[292] Parise was said to have tried to develop "rapport" with the target objects, but felt that it took a lot of work for her to move things and that she had to practice continuously.

Parise's comments are interesting in light of the fact that, although some researchers have noted a correlation between the participants feeling of "resonance" with the target and success, experimental research also suggests that, in general, a tense, striving attitude inhibits MMI.[293] Parise's struggle may have been unnecessary. Honorton noted that one time Parise was able to effortlessly move a compass needle on saying "abracadabra" when she was in a hurry.[294] This seems to indicate that the only reason she required so much energy and straining to perform MMI was because Parise was emulating Kulagina.

Martin Caidin Martin Caidin was another self-taught MMI performer, who firmly believed that everyone could learn to perform MMI.[295] He frequently worked with a target called an "energy wheel." Originally developed by physicist G. Harry Stine, the energy wheel is a concentrically balanced object made from light material (like paper), and balanced horizontally on the sharp point of a needle held vertical by a suitable base.[296] These can be placed inside a glass jar (preferably sealed at the base with oil or Vaseline to discourage air drafts). A three inch square of paper (decorated to make it easier to spot movement) works well for this.

Being of scientific bent, Caidin set up an entire room in his house for MMI experimenta-tion.[297] This room was free from draft sources, having only a single door surrounded by rubber seals, and a glass partition to allow viewing of the targets. Caidin could repeatedly turn multi-ple targets from a distance of seven to twelve feet away, and was able to control both the specific target that was influenced (leaving others nearby unaffected), and the direction it spun.[298] Caidin noted that the target rarely turned when he struggled and strained, yet when he sat back and relaxed the targets would start spinning.[299] Because of this, he firmly believed that trying "too hard" inhibited MMI.

Caidin also observed two effects frequently discussed in the parapsychological literature. First, he described a linger effect, in that the targets would sometimes continue to spin for hours after he stopped trying to influence them.[300] Second, he reported a field effect, where neighbor-ing targets to the one he was working on would sometimes start spinning, even though he was not trying to make them turn.

Caidin held numerous workshops during which he taught other people how to move tar-gets.[301] He felt there were no gender differences in success at moving these wheels.[302] In addi-tion, Caidin believed that practice made a person stronger, and the only ones who failed at moving targets were those whose "minds were locked into a 'NO' mode."[303] He described the three keys to success as (1) merging with the target, (2) not trying too hard, and, most impor-tantly, (3) believing that one can do it.[304] It was a loss to the field when Caidin, a long-time smoker, died of cancer in 1997.

The problem of "not trying too hard," is an interesting one as it could be a factor in the so-called release-of-effort effect seen in many experiments, where MMI is only observed after participants stop trying to perform it.[305] Rex Stanford postulated that this effect may be related to striving having a blocking effect, whereas not trying so hard to produce MMI allows it to occur.

The issue of belief that Caidin discussed is often described as a crucial factor in success. Certainly, many individuals appear to be able to perform MMI after seeing someone else do it—whether that someone truly does MMI or simply fakes it.[306] The problem of self-created

Developed as a target by G. Harry Stine and popularized by Martin Caidin, energy wheels can be easily printed out as three-inch squares and balanced on a point. They are best used sealed under glass. Performers then try to make the wheel spin.

limitations in performance could confuse the situation should the participant be limited not only by the process itself, but also by his or her own beliefs. However, we will see later that this may be less of a problem when ASC or high levels of emotion are involved.

Alex Tanous Dr. Alex Tanous was a kind gentleman with several degrees, including an MA in philosophy and a doctorate in divinity.[307] He lived in Maine, and did much of his work quietly and without fanfare. He worked with Dr. Karlis Osis at the *American Society for Psychical Research* in New York City for over 16 years, and was involved in a number of experiments during that time.[308]

Among his other talents, Tanous was gifted at going out-of-body to examine or manipulate devices in other locations.[309] Whether he was using an astral body or MMI from a distance, the end result was that Tanous could influence mechanical strain gauges. He also had experiences with anomalous healing, bilocation (as previously mentioned in anecdotal intentional MMI), time slips, precognition, and other forms of ESP.

Although much of Tanous's work involved haunting investigations and aiding law enforcement, he also was sometimes "prescribed" as a treatment for terminally ill patients at a New York area hospital.[310] He had some success, both in terms of remissions, and, in a few cases, complete turnarounds. However, Tanous himself was uncertain how much of his results in healing were due to MMI and how much were from placebo effect. He died in 1990.

Ingo Swann New York artist Ingo Swann was said to have come into his powers because of past life work.[311] Swann may be best known for developing Controlled Remote Viewing (CRV) and working with the Stargate military research team.[312] CRV can be thought of as a way of obtaining psychic information at a distance. Although originally used for psychic spying, it also has widespread civilian and law enforcement applications.

Like Alex Tanous, Swann could go out-of-body at will, and was able to inspect and affect measurement devices at distant locations.[313] Swann reported being able to maintain a normal state of consciousness during OBEs.[314] His EEG during these times showed a decreased amplitude, and increased frequency of alpha waves. Experiments using target materials with perceptual characteristics that varied depending on the point in space from which they were viewed, seemed to indicate that he was not simply using ESP during OBEs, but appeared to have a kind of body or ability to perceive optical systems from a different experiential location of consciousness than that of his body.

In addition to his OBE ability, Swann was also able to perform a variety of MMI tasks, including to emit light from his hands and above his head when photographed in a dark room (which could represent either psychic photography or the actual emission of energy).[315] Swann has also been able to describe the insides of various pieces of equipment and affect their functioning — even with highly shielded magnetometers.[316] In yet another experiment, he altered the temperature of distant graphite thermisters.[317] An interesting finding in the latter study was that each time Swann influenced a specific sensor, the outlying thermisters in the same general area changed temperature in the opposite direction of the target item.[318] Rogo wondered whether Swann might have been redirecting, or reordering, random sources of physical or ambient energy.

Swann was involved in the submarine study that allowed researchers to evaluate, and disprove, the extra-low frequency (ELF) electromagnetic theory of psi.[319] In recent years, he has been ill and lived a secluded life. However, Swann's work both as a participant and as an experimenter has indubitably helped to advance the field of parapsychology.

Group Macro–PK Research

Kenneth Batcheldor was one of the first investigators to get success at eliciting physical phenomena in a séance type of group sitter experiment.[320] He theorized that there are three crucial factors that lead to the success or failure of MMI[321]:

1. Belief: Batcheldor felt that even the slightest doubt is unfavorable to success.

2. Ownership resistance: This is the reluctance of people to accept they are responsible for MMI.

3. Witness inhibition: This is the disturbance people feel on witnessing displays of MMI regardless of the source.

Batcheldor developed a sitter group method, which he felt minimized these three inhibiting factors.[322] It has three main features. The first of these was to have groups bypass the need for belief in the beginning by having one individual prime the pump by deliberately faking an event. Belief would then be gradually built up through repeating sittings. However, Julian Isaacs pointed out that the creation of suggestion may be more important than positive belief per se.[323]

The second feature of Batcheldor's sitter method was to use a group situation to diminish ownership resistance, since no one knew who among them might actually be responsible for the MMI.[324] The third feature of his technique was to use laughter, singing, and a light party-like atmosphere to minimize witness inhibition. The result was something of a cross between spontaneous and controlled activity, as requested phenomena often occurred.

The importance of ambiance was underscored by the results of a Toronto group, who tried unsuccessfully for over a year to get results using a sober, meditative atmosphere.[325] After one of their members read about the Batcheldor experiments, they tried creating a light, fun, atmosphere, and were soon rewarded with levitation, raps, and other phenomena. The success of Batcheldor's technique suggests that the unconscious knows how to do psi—it just needs to want the goal enough and find some way to keep the conscious mind from interfering with MMI production.[326]

SUMMARY

In this chapter, we have looked briefly at some of the large-scale MMI research that has occurred over the years. Much of it depended on star performers, extraordinarily gifted individuals from around the world. These people have contributed significantly to the field of parapsychology by showing what kinds of things may be possible to achieve. However, this form of research is seldom used today due to the rarity of such individuals, the occasional difficulty of dealing with their temperaments, and concern about fraud.

Kenneth Batcheldor did much of the original work on sitter groups, and found he could get good results using ordinary individuals, which allowed him to avoid some of the pitfalls of working with (or being unable to find) 'stars.' It was his contention that the three factors that hold most folks back from successful MMI are ownership resistance, witness inhibition, and a lack of confidence. Ironically, he encouraged initial fraud as a way to get around these issues and "prime the pump."

Metal-Bending Research

Metal-bending is an interesting form of psi that can occur on a micro and macro level. It is difficult to say whether this is a new phenomenon or has been occurring unnoticed for centuries — there are poltergeist cases that would suggest the latter.[327] However, it was not until the 1970s that Uri Gellar, an Israeli psychic entertainer, started the spoon-bending fad.

An induction effect, sometimes referred to as the "Geller effect," was soon noted.[328] Audience members in the studio and television viewers at home found that metal held gently in their hands — or even not held at all — would seem to bend during Geller's performances. Of course, if is likely that some pieces were bent before the broadcast, but only noticed after the show. It is also likely that a number of such bendings were done using brute force, either unconsciously or consciously. However, a few of the benders — particularly children — were able to repeat the phenomenon in the laboratory under controlled conditions.[329]

John Hasted investigated British child "stars" Nicholas Williams and Stephen North.[330]

They were able to bend metal, teleport objects in and out of sealed containers, and even create fantastic sculptures inside of glass balls that had openings only big enough for a straightened paperclip to be inserted.

The seeming link between metal-bending and teleportation is a curious one. It is unclear why this should be. However, Hasted noted that apparently transported objects were often unusually warm to the touch, and that a clicking sound or ping could accompany the event — observations that have also been reported in poltergeist cases when objects have purportedly been teleported.[331]

Survey Research

Two researchers have looked at surveys with metal-benders. Jack Houck gave his attendees a questionnaire to fill out at the end of his MMI parties. In them, he asked party-goers how much physical force they felt they used to bend their flatware.[332] Over the years, he collected 6,484 of these forms. In them, more than half of the people said that they felt they used less than half the force necessary to physically bend the flatware.

Cynthia Siegel did a mail survey of 750 spoon-bending party participants.[333] Of the 311 questionnaires she received back, 73 percent of respondents felt they had performed MMI, and 67 percent of them had done so at their first party. Of course, at least some of the metal-bending at these parties derives from the use of ordinary physical force. Thus, some or all of the respondents may have falsely thought that they were performing MMI when, in fact, they were not. Other interesting findings that came out of this survey included that (1) MMI belief increased after the parties, (2) 80 percent of those who bent at their first party could also bend at their second one, and (3) more people reported bending than not bending at the party. However, there was no difference between the number of benders and non-benders who made further attempts as MMI on their own after the party. In addition, many individuals who felt that they could perform MMI were not interested in doing it again. This response (or lack of it) to success is a bit surprising. It is a shame that we do not know more about the reason for the result.

It is unfortunate that, if Siegel received any data about the participant's subjective states at the time of the bending, this was not included in either the paper or appendices. The problems of a low return rate, the limited accuracy of self reports, incomplete answers, participant bias, and lack of verification whether physical force or MMI was used in the bending make it difficult to evaluate the significance of the findings.

Controlled Research

John Hasted performed extensive metal-bending research in children and adults.[334] He noted that the bent area does not need be touched by the performer for this to work. This finding led to the use of special equipment to measure the effect. By introducing a strain gauge into the equation, Hasted could identify minute amounts of bending, thereby opening up new possibilities for controlled research.[335] According to Beloff, this may have been Hasted's greatest contribution to the field. There was no longer any need for individuals to handle the target. Instead, effects could register when the MMI performer was simply "willing" it to bend.

In addition to determining the strain on the metal, Hasted also measured a variety of physiologic and psychological parameters.[336] Some participants, such as Jean-Pierre Girard, exhibited an almost exclusive alpha rhythm on EEG during the bending process, as well as heart rates of up to 160 beats per minute. Girard stated that bringing about MMI was similar to experiencing an orgasm — a comment reminiscent of what physical medium Eusapia Palladino said decades earlier.[337] Hasted made the important observation that the strength of a MMI effect

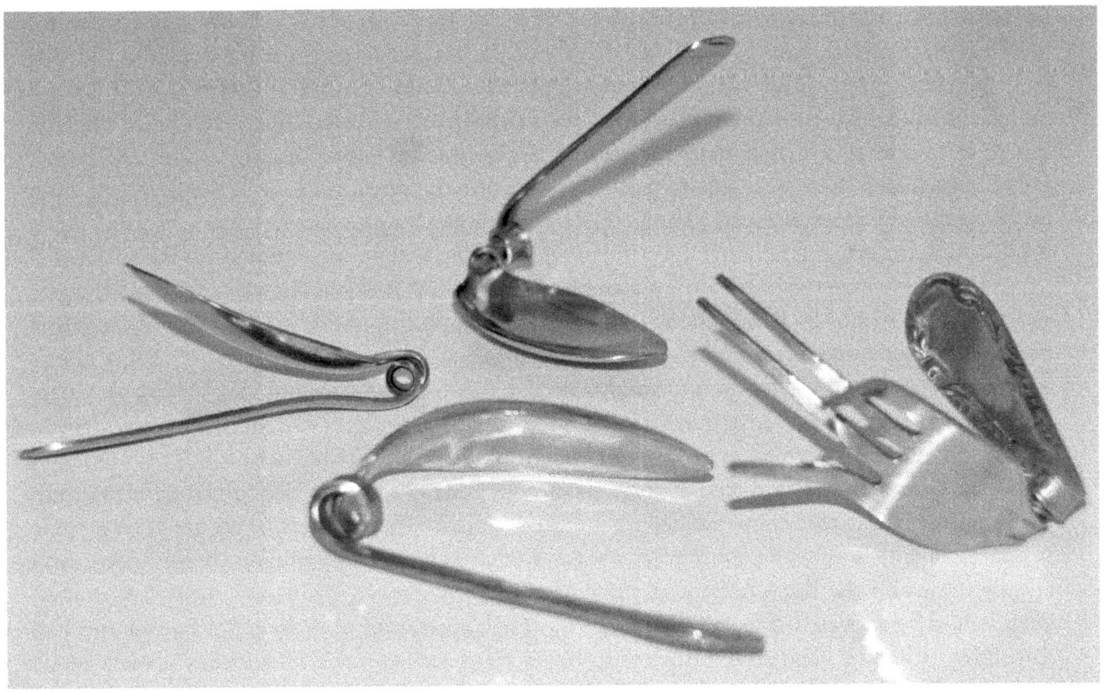

These are some spoons and forks bent by the author at an MMI party held by Jack Houck. The metal abruptly became soft enough to twist into the shapes shown for only a few seconds (perhaps 5–15) before becoming too hard to bend.

may not depend on the bender's physical distance from the target so much as his or her "perceptual distance" from it.

Hasted also extensively examined the target materials after they had apparently been bent by MMI.[338] He found (1) a decrease in yield strength (*see* Glossary), (2) a very slight magnetization of previously unmagnetized items, (3) no significant change in weight, and (4) effects as localized as 4mm and as strong as 80 Nm (Newton-meter of torque, *see* Glossary) of force, which is more than the 25 Nm which men can normally produce, or the 15 Nm that women can produce. Furthermore, Hasted noted that at the time of the bending the metal did not feel particularly warm. Instead, it seems to simply soften and become malleable or plastic. Because of this, Hasted suggested that temporary metal softening might be a more accurate term than metal "bending."

Sometimes metal is modified in ways other than bending.[339] Metal has been reported to undergo an alteration in the morphologic structural form and change in density, or hardness. Furthermore, some investigators have reported a "post-active" effect, similar to the linger effect seen in anomalous healing experiments, in that a target may continue to bend even after the MMI performer has ceased his or her efforts.[340] However, Hasted pointed out that this has not been well documented in the laboratory and could represent a release-of-effort effect.

In California, aerospace engineer Jack Houck started holding metal-bending parties, in which people came to have fun and many found that they, too, could bend metal, sometimes with little or no effort.[341] Houck preferred to limit these parties, which usually lasted about two hours, to 20–25 people, with a mix of 25 percent children or teenagers, 50 percent open-minded adults, and 25 percent people who are knowledgeable about psi.[342]

Houck's metal-bending parties had five stages: (1) the warm-up, (2) selection of the target (since he felt performers had to pick a piece of metal they "liked"), (3) bending instructions, (4) a bending period, and (5) the finale.[343] About 85 percent of attendees were said to be able to bend metal, often silverware. The actual process of bending often involves a 5–20 second period during which time the metal grows warm and pliable — sometimes even becoming too hot to hold — after which it hardens again.[344] Occasionally, loud popping sounds are heard. Houck postulated these were due to gas forming inside the metal because of the heat, and then breaking the object or its metal plating.[345] Rarely, the metal target can become very cold. Also, there is sometimes a color change near the bend, but this does not extend beyond the surface.[346]

Houck also experimented with placing brass strips in sealed glass bottles at the MMI party sites.[347] These would be bent and twisted by the next morning, and, if left at the site, continued to bend for three days. This would seem to argue against a simple release-of-effort effect. It is possible that a field effect was created at these parties, which continues for several days after people stop trying to bend, perhaps analogous to the linger effect. An alternative explanation is that it could have been an experimenter effect.

The detached ASC induced at these parties may allow some people to use more strength than they realize, so that they manually bend the spoons.[348] Nonetheless, there are at least some instances in which items have been bent beyond what is physically possible. In addition, metallurgy exams on the flatware bent at these parties often showed a different substructure than what would be expected if it had been bent by force, appearing as if the grain boundaries had somehow melted or vaporized, rather than being fractured or torn. This makes it seem likely that something more than force is involved.

Others have attempted experimental versions of metal-bending using aluminum strips, spoons, potassium dichromate crystals, and electronic sensors.[349] One of the more interesting series of experiments involved nitinol wire.[350] This is a nickel and titanium alloy that has the ability to "remember" the shape impressed upon it at high temperatures, usually around 500°C. Nitinol can be bent into different configurations while cool, but as soon as it is placed in hot water (approximately 80–100°C), it returns to its original shape. Experimenters have found that when this wire was bent by MMI, it does not return to its original form after re-heating and has an altered crystalline structure on analysis.[351]

Houck believed that confidence was important for success (repeating what others have said), and over-intellectualizing inhibited results.[352] Over half of those who were successful benders at his parties could later bend by themselves, while others needed the party environment to succeed. Houck also felt strongly that people had to have a target they "liked" to work on, such as nice shiny metal. In his words, "I have yet to see someone bend a rusty nail."[353] Other macro–MMI performers have also commented on having greater success with a target that they instinctively "liked."[354]

Houck believed that it helped to have the MMI party attendee first "ask" the metal target if it is "willing to bend."[355] If the attendee felt the target was "unwilling," then it should be replaced with something else. This could operate on several levels to enhance success. It could (1) serve to bypass ownership resistance by implying the target is doing the bending, not the attendee; (2) act to ensure there is no unconscious resistance to bending the target; and (3) give the unconscious minds of attendees the opportunity to decide whether they are willing to connect to the target and perform MMI.

John Hasted made observations about how to elicit metal-bending from participants, many of which parallel Houck's and Batcheldor's suggestions.[356] He thought that it was helpful to (1) have strain gauge sensitivity set so high that there is some artifact movement, which encourages the participant to believe paranormal activity is starting; (2) make the feedback fun, like a game; and (3) avoid over-concentration, since the strongest events often occur when the partic-

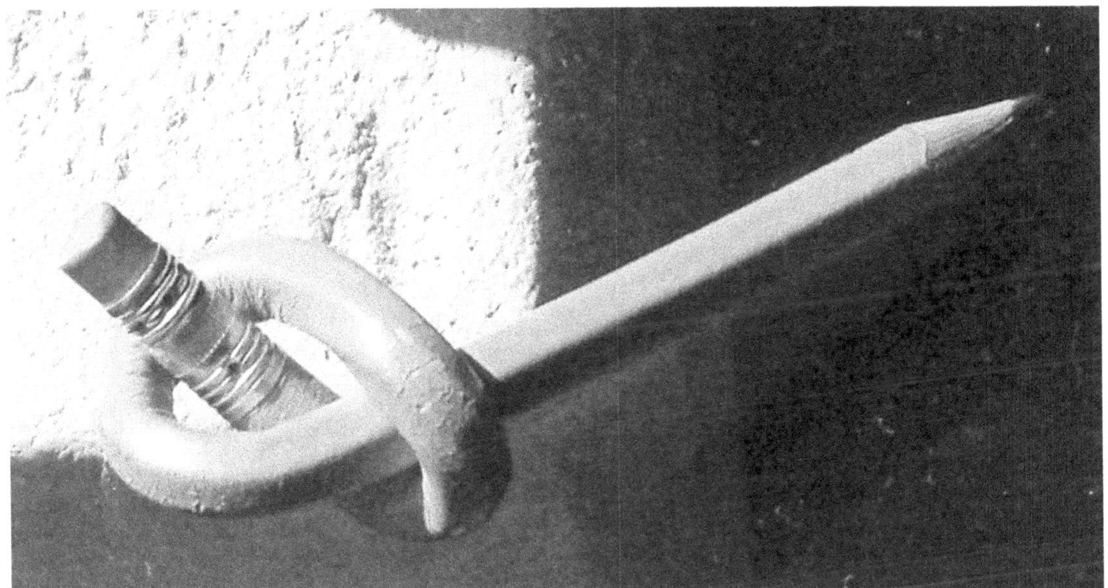

Ordinary wood pencil said to have been tied into a knot by the wife of a general directly in front of Lyn Buchanan. The fact that wood, and not just metal, can be bent, suggests there may be more to bending than a simple "melting" of layers.

ipant relaxes immediately after concentration. Hasted sometimes saw participants become fearful when they realized that they didn't need to touch the metal in order to bend it.

Like poltergeist phenomena and anomalous healing, MMI metal-bending appears to be a cross-cultural ability. It has been reported in Japan, Belgium, France, Denmark, Italy, Australia, Israel, Switzerland, Canada, the United States, and Great Britain. A few individuals, such as Silvio Mayer, also seem to be able to re-bond metal apparently broken by MMI. As with other forms of macro–MMI performance, a relaxed atmosphere, a target the performer feels comfortable with or "likes," and a belief that success is possible or probable all appear to be helpful. Fear, over-intellectualizing, and doubt, on the other hand, seem to deter success.

Instrumental Transcommunication Research

Instrumental transcommunication (ITC) is the purported communication by discarnate or otherworldly spirits (whether deceased human beings or other entities) through means of an assortment of electronic and related equipment, including (but not limited to) tape recorders, telephones, radios, televisions, and computers. These sounds and images are often not heard or seen at the time of original recording, and only appear later on playback. Many suspect that this process involves the mediumistic abilities of the incarnate human operators. This chapter will look at some of the more commonly reported forms of ITC, how they are used in field investigations, and the formal research in the field.

ELECTRONIC VOICE PHENOMENON (EVP)

Electronic voice phenomenon (EVP) is when sounds or voices said to come from the deceased, which were inaudible at the time of recording, are later heard on audio playback of a phonograph, tape, or digital media. Although one must always first rule out normal causes for apparently anomalous sounds (such as stray radio waves, cell phones, machine artifacts, etc.), there are a residue of cases left over that appear to be due to paranormal causes — although it can still be argued whether the material originates from a discarnate being or the still-living person doing the recording (as MMI).

A Brief History The first documented EVP may have occurred in 1901, when Waldemar Bogoras found spirit voices on a phonograph recording of a shamanic ritual in Siberia.[357] Other early methods of obtaining EVP included by telegraph and radio, but the vast majority were recorded using ordinary tape recorders.[358] As is still found today, some of the sounds that appeared were difficult to decipher, while others were very clear-cut and recognizably belonged to deceased individuals. For those interested in learning more about the history of EVP, the reader should to check out the review provided by Tom and Lisa Butler in their book, *There Is No Death and There Are No Dead.*

The first report on EVP in the parapsychological literature was made by Raymond Bayless in the *Journal of the American Society for Psychical Research.*[359] He wrote a letter of correspondence documenting a series of experiments that he had performed with von Szalay. These experiments were begun in 1956, and included an attempt at controlling variables so as to exclude fraud and normal causes of extraneous voices or sounds. They obtained a variety of whistles, repeated statements on command, rappings, and short phrases in male and female voices using a simple microphone setup. Von Szalay was not a professional psychic, but appeared to have considerable mediumistic ability, as described by Bayless in his book, *Experiences of a Psychical Researcher.*[360] It is surprising that this work did not stir up interest in the phenomena. There were no follow-up letters of correspondence or published attempts at replication of the study by other experimenters.

Tom and Lisa Butler noted that it was actually later that the artist and film producer Friedrich Jürgensen — who is often credited as the discoverer of the phenomena — announced his anomalous voice findings in Sweden.[361] Jürgenson began working in the field, when, by chance, he heard what he thought was his deceased mother's voice in the background of a tape he was making of birds singing in the woods. He later published a book, *Radio Contact with the Dead,* which inspired Latvian psychologist Konstantin Raudive to enter the field.

Raudive often obtained names and sentence fragments, which he documented at length in his book, *Breakthrough: An Amazing Experiment in Electronic Communication with the Dead.* EVPs are sometimes referred to as "Raudive Phenomena" in honor of the late Dr. Raudive, because of his extensive work in the field.

Raudive noted a number of characteristics to the kind of speech that he typically obtained on audiotape.[362] These voices are generally easy to distinguish from those of the living because they have a distinctive rhythm, have oddly constructed sentences, and demonstrate a uniform way of speaking or pronouncing words even when they incorporate words from several languages within the same sentence. These same EVP characteristics can make it remarkably difficult to determine the identity of the source trying to communicate and what they are saying.

Sarah Estep, who founded the American Association for Electronic Voice Phenomenon (AAEVP) in 1982, developed a grading system that divides EVPs into one of three categories, depending upon how clearly they may be understood.[363] "Class A" EVPs can be heard without headphones, may be as clear as a normal human voice, and people can generally agree on what it says.[364] With "class B" EVPs, a headphone is typically required to make out the message content, and not everyone will agree on what was said. Finally, with "class C" EVPs, not only are headphones a must, but the sound often needs amplification and filtering to make it out and even so may not be heard by others. This useful grading system has been widely adopted by investigators around the world.

Sarah Estep (who died in 2008) and the AAEVP deserve credit for raising public awareness of this form of ITC, and teaching people ways to record EVPs. Investigators have tried a variety of methods, including the use of different kinds of background noise, flame microphones, complex feedback systems, and other techniques. Unfortunately, what works well for one person does not always work well for another. Nonetheless, there does seem to be something going on that is beyond simply an audio Rorschach or the inadvertent recording of normal sound.

Characteristics Although some believe EVPs to be nothing more than auditory versions of a Rorschach test, this is untrue for class A EVPs.[365] As had Raudive before them, experimenters Tom and Lisa Butler and Alexander MacRae pointed out that EVP utterances have a number of unique characteristics that separate them from normal speech, even that transmitted by radios, cell phones or other sources, including[366]:

1. The cadence is often unusual, with words spoken faster or slower than normal and the intervals between segments or words can be short and standardized, making the speech sound faster without increasing pitch.

2. The frequency range may be higher than normal speech (often requiring an adjustment of plus or minus 10 percent).

3. Some of the normal frequencies of human speech may be absent.

4. The quality of sound may be mechanical, hollow, or monotone.

5. There may be precursor sounds, such as a popping or clicking noise, at the start of an EVP.

6. EVPs tend to occur in short bursts of complete words or phrases, with shorter utterances often louder than long ones as if there was an energy limit.

7. EVPs are usually in the same language as, or a language understood by, the experimenter (although it must be noted that this could at least partly be a reporting artifact).

8. That which is said is often appropriate to the circumstances, and may appear to be a direct answer to questions spoken by the person recording, or address the person recording by name.

9. Utterances sometimes appear to be precognitive in the sense they address something the researcher is about to say or do.

10. EVPs sometimes mimic a word or phrase just said by the researcher.

The click, pop, or bang often heard at the start of an EVP is particularly interesting from a parapsychological standpoint, since raps, pops, and bangs have often been associated with MMI events, including materializations. MacRae noted that the reference sound sometimes preceding captured utterances, "goes back in the history of EVP and has been likened to a mini sonic boom."[367] This suggests that a change in speed (hence in time) could sometimes be occurring. Such an event might well explain the variations in speed displayed by utterances, as one might expect the end result of a time/speed shift would seldom be an exact match for our own. EVP researcher Larry Flaxman observed, "I've experienced this for years, and truly believe it is significant. Some of the best class A utterances I have received have been immediately after this impulse 'pop.'"[368]

MacRae commented that oscilloscopes can show an abrupt acoustic impulse at the onset of EVPs. Senkowski also described precursor sounds, noting they can involve, "a remarkable reduction of the volume/noise coming from the radio receiver and starting with a sharp click like switching on. Afterwards, the receivers may be 'dead' for some time."[369]

In addition to the small "sonic booms," metallic sounds on tape are common, and many experience the voices as robotic or having a flat tonal quality.[370] Al Rauber postulated that the knocks that appear just before an EVP may be bursts of electrical energy coming through. Rauber has also occasionally gotten an electrical humming sound, which he felt was part of the necessary energy needed for success.

EVP Methods There seem to be nearly many ways of trying to record EVPs as there are those trying to do it. The technique that is preferred tends to depend upon the purpose of the investigator — whether to "prove" the continued existence of loved ones after their body is gone, as a way of learning information from the "other side," to understand the phenomenon itself, or for entertainment purposes. Basic methods for getting EVPs typically involve either asking questions, pausing for a few seconds, and immediately playing back the recording to listen for extra sounds, or asking a series of questions, pausing for a few minutes between each one, and then listening to the whole session at a later time in a quiet environment. Any type of recording equipment can be used, although digital is often preferred because of creating less background noise. Some have even used exotic microphones and speaker systems, such as those made of flame.[371]

Investigators vary in terms of what, if anything, they want as background sound/energy. Some like to tune a radio between stations to create static, which they feel can be used by the "other side" to create voices. Others use white noise, pink noise, or complex feedback loops. Still others (including the author), have had success with complete silence and no questions — simply a tape set on record. The fact that no one technique works equally well for all investigators suggests that the person recording the EVPs and/or the communicator(s) may be more important in determining success or failure.

The commonest initial EVP obtained by beginners is their first name.[372] David Fontana and Anabela Cardoso feel it improves success to set aside two or three regular times a week to record and continue this effort for several weeks or months.[373] This is not so different from what those who teach mediumship recommend to their students. Many researchers accept that MMI is involved and they are, at least in part, acting as a medium to help messages come through.

EVP as a Tool Although ITC involves all formats — including on telephones, faxes, computers, printers, VCRs, camcorders, and other equipment, it is audio EVPs (particularly on digital recorders) that have become a standard tool for investigating ghosts and hauntings. Al Rauber in the United States was one of the pioneers of this technique over three decades ago. He would compare what he got on EVP with what psychics and other instruments were obtaining at the same time in haunted locations.[374] His results were sometimes amazing, with different streams of information providing a level of cross-corroboration. The use of ITC as a simultaneous adjunct to other methods of investigation has since been widely adopted for use in ghost investigations by the media and paranormal enthusiasts — whether amateurs or professionals.

DIRECT VOICE PHENOMENA

ITC also includes "direct voice" phenomena. This is a bit different from the "direct voice" heard in the séance parlor, where the sound was attributed to an ectoplasmic creation of vocal cords (and was often due to fraud). Instead, with ITC direct voice the communication is heard real-time through a radio, telephone, or other device. DVP may not be as uncommon as one would think. Parapsychologists Scott Rogo and Raymond Bayless devoted an entire book to stories of phone calls that people said they had received from the dead.[375]

In the 1970s Americans George Meek and Bill O'Neil created an electronic system, called a Spiricom, through which they claimed to have good two-way radio conversations with the deceased.[376] Some investigators doubted the accuracy of this claim and wondered whether O'Neil might have been faking the communications as a way to get money from Meek. As evidence, they point out that O'Neil was very secretive about his discovery, not wanting others to examine the device too closely, and (perhaps far more damaging) that his gestures and body language always mimicked that of the messages supposedly coming from the spirit realm, as if O'Neil himself was the originator.

More recently, Frank Sumpton created the "Frank's Box." This is essentially is an AM radio with a broken tuner, which constantly scans up and down the frequency range. People have been said to get real-time answers to questions, including their own names (or those in a crowd) as well as a great deal of swearing and foul language. However, the constant radio chatter is bothersome and gives many investigators a headache. Given the fact that others have used the swept radio frequencies and moved on to more useful techniques, Frank's Boxes do not appear to have any particular advantages over other methods.[377]

Bill Chappell is a retired electronics engineer who invented the Ovilus. This device translates various environmental readings, such as temperature and EMF, and an element of random generation to generate phonemes or words. The Ovilus offers the options of 512 stored words, phonetic sounds, a combination thereof, or a yes or no mode. It has the advantage of being more understandable than many ITC, and, unlike Frank's Box, is silent between utterances. As with the Frank's Box, it is impossible to determine how much its results are simply human MMI and random chance.

In recent years, Anabella Cardoso of Portugal, Marcello Bacci of Italy, Mark Macy of the United States, and others have reported success at getting DVP radio transmissions from the dead. In 1998, Cardoso began a technique of turning on white noise generated by a radio, and listening for voices coming from the speakers.[378] She felt this process was guided and controlled by the other side, that she had no say over the timing of these communications, and that it was harder than EVP. However, in her opinion it also allowed for the transmission of longer utterances, which could convey more information.

ITC Images

Although EVP and DVP make up the largest proportion of ITC research, these phenomena are by no means limited to sound alone. Klaus Schreiber in Germany developed a way to apparently receive television reception of spirits, and captured the data on videotape.[379] Formal investigations of these techniques suggest that most if not all of the resulting images are either a kind of Rorschach — too fuzzy and vague to be meaningful — or fraudulent.[380]

Formal Research

The vast majority of ITC research has been published in books or newsletters, with a dearth in information appearing in parapsychological journals. This has the potential to be a problem, since, as Rick Berger, G. H. Hovelmann, and W. Von Lucadou noted, "The questionable quasi-scientific methods used in 'transcommunication' contain defense mechanisms and immunizing strategies that make critical examination and objections nearly impossible. At the same time, they guarantee that 'insiders' will not become aware of them."[381]

It is unfortunate that those well-grounded in parapsychological research findings and techniques have seldom shown an interest in the topic. Parapsychologist Charles Tart commented that "we particularly need some knowledge and rigor on the EVP/ITC stuff as I think most of us were repelled by the cultishness and sloppiness of it at the beginning and haven't followed it — for better or worse."[382]

Baruš also expressed concern over the lack of literature on EVPs in mainstream English-language science journals.[383] He pointed out that not only does it mean a lack of funding (a problem routinely faced by parapsychologists) but also that the investigators may be poorly trained and their protocols inconsistent — making it harder to evaluate the meaningfulness of any results. Indeed, Baruš noted, "those who have investigated the Raudive voices have found the probable influence of the imagination on the interpretation of unrecognized and ambiguous sounds that were being identified as messages from the dead."[384]

The popular wave of EVP (and anomalous photo) enthusiasm currently sweeping the globe is all too reminiscent of the advent of spiritualism, where a genuine desire to contact those departed led to widespread fraud. Indeed, a psi lit-base review shows only a handful of experimental studies — a shockingly small number considering this would appear to be a paranormal process of interest to parapsychologists.

After the published report in 1959 by Raymond Bayless in the *Journal of the American Society for Psychical Research*, there was a long silence in the formal literature.[385] In 1973, Peter Bander — a member of the Southern California Society for Psychical Research — reported some of his EVP research in the book *Voices from the Tapes: Recordings from the Other World*.[386] Among other findings, he mentioned having obtained voices twice when recording with a microphone in a Faraday cage, which he felt would block all radio waves. It is unfortunate that he does not mention the particular type of Faraday cage that was used, since these can, in fact, vary in terms of their effectiveness. Air vents or wire mesh construction (instead of steel plates) permit the penetration of some electromagnetic signals. That said, Bander had two other findings of note. In an attempt to investigate whether paranormal voices could appear if the tape had not been first placed in a recording device (as might be possible if EVPs are solely a result of MMI), he placed a sealed tape under his pillow at night. He did not obtain any EVPs. It is unclear whether this was a result of his own belief system that the recorder was required. However, Bander also found that in some cases paranormal voices appeared on fresh tape that *had not yet gone past the recording head*— suggesting that the device itself was not responsible for placing the sounds on the media.

Rick Berger, G. H. Hovelmann, and W. Von Lucadou published an ITC field investigation in 1992 in the *Journal of the Society for Psychical Research*.[387] They visited Martin Wenzel, who was said to get paranormal pictures on a television set with no antennae. Wenzel set up his equipment in front of the investigators and used new videotapes that had been sealed in their original wrappers. Berger and his colleagues noted that images formed and dissolved slowly and were poor in quality. They concluded "even the most impressive images that we witnessed in the course of the investigation could not be distinguished from images in a projective test, such as the Rorschach test."[388]

In 2001, Baruš published a study where he had two research assistants run 81 forty-five-minute recording sessions using white noise from radios and overhead fluorescent lights (with no mention whether either of them had experience with EVP work or mediumistic abilities).[389] He concluded that no successful EVPs were obtained despite a number of suggestive sounds, such as "Hello," "Gail" (the name of one of the experimenters), a kissing sound, a whistle, and the words "Tell Peter," which Baruš and one of his two assistants were able to independently identify that sounded like the voice of a dead woman the assistant knew, whose husband's name was Peter. Baruš admitted a number of problems with his study, including insufficient time or connection with those in the afterlife, inadequate equipment, and experimenters without sufficient psychic ability (if indeed this is needed). However, one might also wonder whether his criteria for requiring all three independent observers to identify the same words for a voice to be judged "paranormal" might also have been a problem, since people can vary on their responses even to ordinary human speech.

In 1981, Alexander MacRae acknowledged having little success with white-noise — popularly believed to be helpful for EVP production.[390] So, instead, he chose to investigate the common features of previously available material said to have been produced by paranormal means. MacRae used sounds obtained by Konstantin Raudive, Richard Sheargold, G. G. Bonner, and Peter Jones. Their main feature was one of being short — most being less than two seconds in duration. These short utterances were louder than long ones, and where a long sample was heard, it typically appeared to be constructed of normal-length utterances that were linked together by a pause.

Baruŝs experimented with a variety of pseudo-random letter, text, and yes/no generators, using the presence of a medium and had mixed results.[391] Only the yes/no produced anomalous results, with 9 of the 11 answers accurate ones. However, there was no way to rule out human psi as the source or, given the small sample size, random chance alone.

In recent years, Alexander MacRae published a series of controlled, well-designed experiments on EVP. One of these was performed in a sound-proofed Faraday cage (an 8- foot by 8-foot room) at the Institute of Noetic Sciences.[392] MacRae made sure that he had radio silence before proceeding. As in his earlier experiment, he used an alpha unit producing a signal around 1.2 MHz instead of a random noise generator. He obtained what sounded like a number of utterances, ten of which were then used, mixed in with decoy phrases, to check for consistency of interpretation.

MacRae's results showed that the anomalous voices he recorded were not auditory hallucinations, but genuine sounds.[393] He also performed spectrogram analysis on the EVPs, and found that the voices were dissimilar (they were not subvocalizations by the experimenter). Control sounds of random noise showed that respondents were unable to hear any words, again suggesting that true EVPs are not purely illusory patterns. This would at least seem to answer the question of whether EVP can be attributed entirely to stray radio signals or outside, ordinary sounds, and indicate that there is more to it than simply imagination.

MacRae took the question of what may be occurring in EVP further with his next series of experiments.[394] In them, he looked at what happens to the answers received with EVP if he asked the same set of questions over a long period of time. He intended to study whether the EVP recorded were (from time to time) responses to what the experimenter had asked or said. His initial results seemed to back up this assertion. However, this shifted over time. The speech segments became less correlated although more numerous and were often themed responses.

MacRae's observations required a new theory.[395] He realized he had to look at cognition (how we think). When we hear a response (whether an EVP utterance or normal speech), it takes us a moment to make sense of the sound. That period of unknowingness is one of intellectual tension as we seek through our experiences or cognitive database for a recognizable match. The more important it is to us to know the answer, the greater the tension during this data seeking. There is a sense of relief when we solve it by matching the sounds with a meaning. The unconscious mind does not like this tension, and will try to pre-supply probable answers. Because of this, expectation and perception play a role in EVP. It may not be (as some skeptics suggest) simply that you hear what you want to hear, but rather that you tend to hear what you *expect* to hear.

When listening for a response to a question (EVP or otherwise), we all have a mental library of possible or likely answers we expect to hear. We then compare the sound to our expectations and pick the closest match. The increase in themed responses may be due to a limited set of expected answers. Such expectation input (a feed-forward effect) would make sense from a survival viewpoint as it reduces our mental tension and speeds up our reaction times for making sense of things, which would not be limited to speech, but could include ambiguous sights and other perceptual input.

MacRae suggested that each of us has an idiosyncratic list of possible answers that influence what we think we have heard. This is beyond the effect of MMI (with us imprinting what we expect to hear on the tape/digital medium). It means we interpret EVP in a non-random way, based on a feed-forward expectancy effect. This is especially important given the common ambiguity of EVPs and explains why people may strongly disagree on what (if anything) was said. In the case of skeptics, it should not be surprising if they hear nonsense or static even with Grade A EVPs, since that matches their expectations. Preconceptions will also play a role in believers, who may make mental matches and hear words where others cannot.

Explanations for ITC

A number of possibilities have been put forth to explain ITC, including (1) discarnate spirits using MMI or otherworldly equipment; (2) human and discarnate MMI combined; (3) human MMI alone; (4) normal (if misinterpreted) TV, radio, or cell phone signals; (5) artifacts created by environmental or equipment noise; (6) subvocalizations by those around the recording equipment; (7) auditory or visual hallucinations with no basis in fact; and (8) fraud. Let us first look at each of the potential non-paranormal causes.

The inadvertent recording of normal broadcasts is a valid concern and has, in fact, been reported by some researchers.[396] However, should recorded utterances be from ordinary sources, one would expect them to contain normal speech frequencies; occur at normal speeds; never occur time-reversed; be the same language(s) as broadcast for that area; never be recorded in a shielded environment, such as a Faraday cage; and, by random chance, often appear to start and end in the middle of a sentence or idea. Since the aforementioned characteristics are frequently not the case, this would seem to be an unlikely possibility for explaining away all ITC.

Environmental and machine noise artifacts are another problem that complicates EVP and direct voice phenomena. This is especially concerning given (1) the often obscure quality of recorded utterances; (2) the general expectation or belief that some background noise or energy source is either required or at the very least facilitates the process of obtaining ITC; (3) the routine manipulation of the recorded material by sophisticated computer editing audio programs to "bring out" the voices; and (4) the limited control over conditions in which haunting investigations and many other ITC experiments are performed — especially when one may be picking up street noise or others who are on a different floor of the building. This kind of artifact probably represents a significant percentage of what ultimately becomes labeled as anomalous. Nonetheless, there appears to be a subset of class A EVPs, wherein without audio manipulation a voice that was not present at the time of the original recording is clearly heard on playback by all who listen and is meaningful to the situation. This suggests that some utterances cannot be ascribed to normal environment noise or machine artifact.

Subvocalizations would also seem an unlikely explanation for the bulk of the EVP material, given the variety and nature of many EVP results — such as the sheer number and variety of voices obtained during a single session by an individual experimenter (particularly with multiple voices speaking at the same time), the speed and quality of the speech itself (often at abnormal rates and lacking high frequencies), the occasional reversal of the speech in time (running backwards), the appearance of languages unknown to the persons present when they are recorded, and successful recording when no one is physically present.

The concern over auditory hallucinations is a valid one, especially given the reports by some (also experienced by the author) that EVPs can change over time, sometimes disappearing from material when they were previously clearly present. However, MacRae investigated this possibility and found at least some EVPs cannot be ascribed to hallucination.

Fraud must always be considered. In at least one case, MacRae and others have suspected that ITC fraud was perpetrated for financial gain (and possibly prestige).[397] The situation is made worse by the known fact that proprietary devices or equipment setups that work well for one experimenter may be worthless for another — making it hard to replicate findings.[398] Nonetheless, fraud appears to occur in a minority of EVP cases and does not explain controlled experimental results that have been replicated by independent researchers and laboratories.

Once the inadvertent recording of normal sound, artifact, hallucination, and fraud are ruled out, we are still left with a residue of utterances that cannot be explained away. Given the characteristics and nature of EVP, it seems likely that at least some anomalous sounds involve MMI, whether from living humans, discarnate entities, or both. It is also possible that (as some have suggested) other-dimensional equipment is responsible for at least some recordings — although this would probably not explain many of the sounds that have been picked up on haunting investigations.[399]

A number of factors suggest that human MMI is involved. These include that experimenters feel it is beneficial to feel energized or excited (known to be beneficial in MMI experiences), the pronounced experimenter effect, and the finding that EVP can be recorded when discarnate entities are not present.[400] The latter involves a finding by Loyd Auerbach and others that place memory (the apparent energetic imprint of information, produced by living beings and somehow stored by the environment) appears to be responsible for some EVPs.[401] An example of this is a case where the repetitive sounds of a slave rebellion and gunshots in the basement of a house — heard by a variety of percipients over the years — was successfully recorded. No discarnate entities appeared to be involved. This suggests that the information was either imprinted by human MMI or from energy in the environment — a notion supported by Roll and Williams who have suggested that MMI energy can be stored as place memory and later released.[402]

SUMMARY

ITC includes a variety of forms of purported communication by discarnate or other worldly spirits, whether deceased human beings or otherwise, through a variety of electronic equipment, including tape recorders, telephones, radios, televisions, and computers. Frequently these sounds and images are not heard or seen at the time of original recording, but only appear later on playback. The main exception to this is direct radio voice, although others have experimented with other types of equipment to get real-time answers.

EVP was one of the earliest forms of ITC and has been reported for well over a century. Recent decades have seen an explosion of interest fueled by TV shows demonstrating their use in haunting investigations. EVP can be a useful tool when combined with personal experiences and other forms of data.

EVPs have a number of characteristics that set them apart from normal human speech. The cadence is often unusual, with words spoken faster or slower than normal but normal pauses occurring in between them. The pitch and speed may differ from the norm, some normal frequencies of human speech may be missing altogether, the quality can sound mechanical, hollow, or monotone, and the sentences, which are usually short, may be constructed oddly and use words from different languages. There can also be a popping or clicking noise just before the EVP, and the responses can either mimic what was just said, or appear to be an answer to a spoken question or appropriate comment on what is occurring at the time of the recording. At times, answers may even seem to occur before a question is spoken out loud.

There is currently little agreement upon what is needed for true EVP production. Many recommend some source of noise or energy for acquiring anomalous voices — whether running water; white, pink, or brown noise; or a Tesla coil, radio, or TV. However, what works well for one researcher may be a complete flop for another, which Stefan Bion feels only bolsters the case for EVP not being either a purely perceptual-psychological phenomenon or an artifact of a given technique or type of equipment.[403]

Most researchers believe that human mediumship plays a role in successful ITC. However, it is possible that contact with the "other side" or "other realms" may not be a one-way effort, and that loved ones in spirit are actively trying to reach us. Some, such as Anabella Cardoso, have reportedly received messages stating that investigators need no mediumistic abilities, and the only thing that matters is the readiness of communicators in the afterlife to work with the human operator.[404] That said, regardless of whether on the part of the sender, the receiver, or both, there appears to be at least some aspect of MMI responsible for directly affecting the equipment used for communication.

These phenomena remain controversial. Some believe that the images and voices are illusory, nothing more than the false interpretation of static, or fragments of transmitted radio/cell phone chatter. However, this ignores the research where anomalous voices and sounds on playback are recorded inside sound-proofed and electromagnetically shielded rooms, and the apparent timely appropriateness of what may is obtained. It is probable that what gets labeled as ITC is, in fact, a mix of the real and the misinterpreted as is so often seen with parapsychological field investigations. Those who work with ITC need to understand that expectation and perception play a major role in how these signals get interpreted. People tend to hear what they expect to hear — whether static or meaningful words. Unfortunately, these phenomena cannot be considered proof of survival, since it is currently impossible to separate out human MMI from that of discarnate sources.

Anomalous Photography

Anomalous photography — also called psychic photography or thoughtography — is the apparent ability of the mind to influence photographs. It is a small branch of MMI research, which emerged shortly after the beginning of photography itself in 1849.[405] Many of the so-called "spirit" photographs seen in the 1800s could have been (and probably were) fraudulently created through double exposures, direct tampering with the photographic plate or negative, and the use of props or extras. In fact, the ease of such trickery made the existence of thoughtography questionable until the development of the Polaroid. These instant cameras (which are no longer made) limited double exposure and film negative tampering — although they still did not prevent the use of cutout overlays inserted into the cartridge, which was why most investigators of the time insisted on using their own, unopened, sealed film.

Jule Eisenbud and other researchers used the Polaroid camera extensively in their research with stars, like Ted Serios.[406] These individuals created a variety of effects on film, including:

1. All, or nearly all, white photographs, looking as if the picture had been overexposed,

even though in some cases no light had been permitted in the lens at all through normal means.

2. Mostly black photographs, looking as if the light had been excluded despite the fact light was known to have been introduced.

3. Images of a variety of locations and themes. Some of these were apparently places that Serios had been thinking about.

Serios preferred to work when he was drunk, and frequently insisted on holding a "gizmo" (a tube of some kind, often plastic) up to the lens.[407] Some people believe that Serios was able to somehow use this "gizmo" to fake results. However, Eisenbud reported that a number of different investigators, using a variety of controls — including no "gizmo," different cameras, and sometimes even no camera at all — still obtained anomalous results. Thus, something paranormal seemed to be occurring, whether Serios was affecting the film directly at a chemical level, creating images in front of the lens, creating bursts (or obstructions) of light inside the camera, or doing a mixture of these.

A few individuals have been said to be able to control whether their image will show up on a photograph. Van de Castle reported this as a feat the shaman Rolling Thunder could perform at will.[408] Erlendur Haraldsson said that Sai Baba could also choose whether he appeared in a picture or not.[409]

Recent years have seen an upsurge of interest in taking "ghost photos" during haunting investigations. We do not yet have a camera that can capture the true likenesses of ghosts, which means these pictures fall into the category of fraud, artifact, or MMI (whether on the part of the spirit, the photographer, or both). Many of these photos have been posted on the internet as "rods" (probably insects) and "orbs" (often CCD malfunctions and dust reflections, and referred to by Annalisa Ventola and Devin Terhune as "density spots").[410] The advent of cheap, widely available digital cameras (always at hand in cell phones) has only increased the number of these artifacts (often mistaken for something of interest) because their small lens apertures and placement of the flash close to the lens made them extremely sensitive to dust and tiny water droplets, in addition to the usual problems of reflections off of things in the environment, movement, exposure artifacts, and malfunctions with their sensor arrays. Add to that the ability to zoom in digitally, which can enhance pixels to the point that one can find nearly anything in them (the brain being good at seeing patterns, whether they exist or not) and it is no wonder who so many people get anomalous images — the vast majority of which are artifacts. Infrared cameras and various "night shot" views are also popular, but have their own normal (if unrecognized by nonprofessional photographers) set of common artifacts. However, some images cannot be easily explained away.

Devin Terhune, Annalisa Ventola, and James Houran measured a number of physical variables and took photos at a reputedly haunted house and a control house next door.[411] Unfortunately, the investigation had to be cut short because of aggressive behavior on the part of one of the residents of the haunted home, whom the authors suspected had been drinking alcohol. However, prior to that event, the investigators had collected 338 photos in a randomized fashion, which they later had rated by a group of eight professional photographers who were blind as to whether the photo came from the control house or the haunted one. These consultants rated 309 images as normal, which gave the experimenters a pool of 29 anomalous images. The prints taken at the active areas of the haunted house were rated significantly more anomalous than those taken in the inactive areas, and the overall anomaly ratings were higher for the haunted home than the control next door. In this case, the highest anomaly ratings came from the color film cameras.

A follow-up study by Ventola and Terhune used the same catalogue of photographs, but widened access to them by scanning and uploading them to a dedicated website.[412] Then 120 paranormal enthusiasts, professional photographers, and a "control" group (no haunting investigation or photography experience) logged in over the internet to rate the images for the type and degree of anomaly. What Ventola and Terhune found surprised them. With more consultants viewing the photographs, the digital and infrared images were rated as "more anomalous" when they had been taken in inactive areas of haunted locales than in active ones. They also reported that the kind of photographic anomalies related more to the type of film used (whether color, black and white, Polaroid, infrared, or digital) than the location (actively haunted or otherwise). Although all kinds of artifacts were seen with all types of recording media, density spots (AKA "orbs") were seen more often in digital and infrared pictures, light streaks in Polaroids and black and white film, shadowing in color film images, and fogging on infrared film. Anomalies were also more common in rooms with lower levels of light—which is no surprise, as it enhances risk of noise in the image, flash artifacts (if used), and movement artifacts, etc.

Many professional photographers remain skeptical of spirit photography, noting that most anomalous photographs can easily be recreated without involving anything paranormal. Sometimes it may involve quirks of an individual camera—including how clean it is, how a person angles the lens, or the quality of a particular flash mechanism—while simple lighting and flash artifacts, including lens flare and reflections, appear to be responsible for other images. Nonetheless, there are a few photographs that cannot be so easily explained away.

Although popular interest in anomalous images is high, anomalous photography remains a small area of research. However, the real problem with the field is that photographs can no longer be considered an acceptable form of evidence. Advances in computer-generated graphics have made faking photographs easy to do and difficult to identify. As a result, odd photographs can only be considered interesting, or, in a few cases, personal validation of an experience, but not proof of the survival of bodily death or (outside a research lab) even psi."

Other Areas of Research

This chapter looks at four miscellaneous types of MMI. Although each one is of interest, insufficient research has been done to say more than a few words about them at this time. We will review levitation, food multiplication, and double-slit experiments, which are areas of promising future research.

LEVITATION

The earliest levitation experiments were performed by Sir William Crookes, working with D. D. Home on decreasing the weight of objects on a balance scale.[413] The former Soviet Union is said to have also experimented with a method of inducing levitation, which they called "partial death."[414] This involved surrounding a recumbent participant with mirrors. Hasted attempted to verify these claims working with a Russian physicist, named Auguste Stern, and was able to document a weight loss of more than a kilogram for several seconds at a time. This suggests that levitation may indeed involve altering the body's weight, as has been subjectively experienced by some runners and mountain climbers.[415] These athletes sometimes said that, at least subjectively, their bodies seem to lose weight, or become weightless, while in action.

As mentioned in Part I in "Levitation," weight is determined not by mass, but by gravitational pull. Since gravitational force is measured in *Newtons*, it is dependent on time. Changes in the speed of time could therefore affect the gravitational pull. Objects of the same mass and distance from the Earth could therefore change in weight (which is determined by both mass and the gravitational pull). This creates the interesting question of whether levitation could result from alterations in time. It might be interesting to try to measure this in the laboratory.

MULTIPLICATION OF MATTER

Relatively little formal research has been done on the multiplication of matter. However, from the spring of 1933 until March 1934, Phillip S. Haley performed a series of experiments into the multiplication of food using himself as the primary subject.[416] The specific details varied from one experiment to the next, but were chronicled in detail with commendable care.

Haley noted that the participants often fasted before beginning, so as to create some sense of need.[417] Excess food was removed from the table. Haley and others would then count out a set number of pieces of fruit and/or bread on a plate which was placed before them on a table. The séances were performed in varied locations (usually someone's home), and were typically done in natural light, which varied in brightness but in some cases was excellent. The group would sit in silence, and then say a prayer, which was followed by asking for the food to multiply. Then, Haley and others would eat a few pieces in full view of all those present, one at a time, holding the piece up and calling out as they did so to the other to make sure they could keep count. All of the participants' hands remained in full sight. After everyone was finished eating their pieces, they would re-count the pieces remaining.

Out of 54 sessions (many with a number of outside witnesses), Haley reported 45 successes, 3 instances where there was a decrease in food, and 1 doubtful case.[418] He was able to multiply a variety of food types, including apples, pears, graham crackers, a variety of leavened and unleavened breads, oranges, raisins, pastries. He also performed less controlled experiments involving the successful multiplication of wood for his fireplace during the winter.

Haley noted that the created food had the same smell and flavor as its source, and was normally digested.[419] Furthermore, samples appeared to be normal in their histology. He also noted that the length of time required to multiply matter varied from minutes to days. To some extent, Haley felt this could represent changes in need — multiplication with prayer and visualization techniques tended to occur more readily when he had genuine need, whether due to hunger or cold.

There is always concern over fraud when sittings are done outside laboratory-controlled conditions. Indeed, Haley admitted that he could not always guarantee that trickery had never been perpetrated by those who attended the sittings, although he tried to take measures to discourage it. It would be interesting to see an attempt to replicate his findings in a more formal setting.

DOUBLE-SLIT EXPERIMENTS

Double-slit experiments are a classic target systems used by physicists. These often involve a laser, which shoots photons through a filter, before they pass through a double-slit. The resulting interference pattern reported by an optical detector will show whether the photon passed through the left slit, right slit, or both. Dean Radin, Paul Wendland, and Robert Rickenbach are doing a two-year series of ongoing experiments using a double-slit system as a target for MMI.[420] In an early part of this work, they asked random participants in a counter-balanced design to mentally "block" one of the two slits. Although this study is still in progress, preliminary findings suggest not only that consciousness can block a slit at will, but also that it can do so backwards in time, as retro–MMI. The authors acknowledged that they cannot yet determine whether this is occurring on a quantum level with consciousness causing a true collapse of the wave function, or as a direct effect on the laser, camera electronics, refractive index of area near the double slit, recorded data, etc. However, it would appear that something related to MMI is happening. This would seem to be a highly promising area of research.

Performance Factors

Now that we have reviewed the experimental literature for MMI research, it seems appropriate to step back and look at what has been learned from this wealth of information. This chapter will look at some physical and psychological factors that appear to correlate with psi performance, as well as how, if at all, the left and right hemispheres of the human brain may be involved in psi functioning.

TARGET AND ENVIRONMENTAL FACTORS

Parapsychologists have often longed for clear-cut physical factors that would correlate with MMI success or failure. There have only been a few variables found over the years that might qualify. These include the target type, electromagnetic (EMF) and geomagnetic fields (GMF), and local sidereal time (LST).

Target Type One of the earliest physical factors felt related to successful MMI performance was whether the experimental target was labile or static. It is often accepted that most participants get better results with labile or moving targets than static or inert ones.[421] Dynamic target systems are considered to be more labile, or readily capable of changing from one state to another. Thus, research is typically performed on objects in motion — such as pendulums driven by random noise vibration, or systems using random electrical impulses, molecules in random motion, or radioactive decay — instead of on systems resistant to change.

Nicola Holt and Chris Roe performed a series of experiments looking at an REG as a kind of virtual "receiver" in ganzfeld experiments, which allowed them to manipulate the degree of randomness in the system.[422] Early studies suggested that more random systems (such as an RNG as opposed to a random number table) might lead to better results. However, their attempt to replicate the finding did not succeed, and no significant psi was observed in any of the randomness situations. However, they then investigated whether there was an interaction effect between the target type and the participant's lability of personality.[423] Neither variable was significant by itself. Mood lability alone also did not interact with target type. However, participants with general personality indicators of lability (as measured on NEO Five Factor Inventory and three other psychological tests) performed better with static targets (p=.0009, one tailed), while stable participants performed better with labile targets (p=.04).

This is an intriguing finding. One has to wonder why it would occur. However, it might explain why poltergeists (who could be more labile) prefer static targets to moving ones while many laboratory participants perform better with labile targets. Poltergeist agents are usually in a state of high tension and emotional arousal at the times of their events, and unaware of their own responsibility for the phenomena (thus bypassing fear and belief issues). Participants in group sitter studies, REG research, and non-party metal-bending experiments, on the other hand, often report being relaxed when they are getting results.[424] It is unclear to what degree these findings relate to the personalities of participants interacting with target type, or other factors, such as participant/experimenter beliefs around what makes a target easy to influence and what is "liked."

EMF and GMF The naturally occurring (and fluctuating) electromagnetic field (EMF) of the earth is another factor that may be important. Some EMF/GMF variation is normal, depending on the position of the Moon and Sun, as well as the latitude (with the greatest intensity occurring at the North and South Pole, and the least between them at the Equator).[425] However, abrupt shifts in GMF may be associated with various events. For example, Marsha Adams reported seeing drops in GMF immediately preceding the appearance of anomalous luminous phenomena (sometimes called "spirit lights" or "earthlights").[426]

Wilkinson and Gauld performed a study that found "modest statistical associations between 'lows' in absolute levels of geomagnetic activity and the occurrence of spontaneous cases of ostensible telepathy/clairvoyance, and between geomagnetic 'highs' and the onset of cases of hauntings and poltergeists."[427] A number of others have also reported associations between high GMF activity and the magnitude of anomalous cognition, as well as the onset of MMI.[428] In addition, William Braud and S. P. Dennis performed a study that found a significant correlation between increased GMF activity the day before testing and apparent psi success at decreasing blood hemolysis rates.[429]

The question arises as to whether domestic or industrial-induced GMF — now common in developed countries — could also have an effect on MMI? Such artificial EMF fields could only have been a factor in poltergeist cases after the mid- to late-1800s, since Michael Faraday only invented the electric motor in 1821, with Edison creating the electric bulb in 1870 and Tesla demonstrating wireless energy transfer in 1803.[430] However, it is unclear whether spontaneous psi has changed in quality, frequency, or magnitude since then. Nor has there been much in the way of formal MMI research using man-made EMF/GMF. That which exists hints at a possible relationship between the these fields and result size.[431] However, as can be a problem any time you have pilot experiments and small sample sizes, these studies have had inconsistent results.

Nelson and Dunne looked at geomagnetic activity with both RNGs and a mechanical cascade.[432] They noted some correlation, but their results did not reach significance. Remy Chauvin and Benjamin Varjean put three years' worth of work into designing a study that performed 60 randomized trials with one subject (Chauvin).[433] They found that a low-level-induced EMF (via an applied electric current) appeared to enhance the MMI effect on a mechanical cascade.

Loftur Gissurarson did a retrospective analysis on 621 RNG studies.[434] He found no correlation between the overall RNG performance and geomagnetic activity as measured in three-hour windows called K-indices. However, he noted that the level of geomagnetic activity the day before the RNG runs correlated at the p=.078 level, with high scores preceded by high geomagnetic activity, and low scores correlated with low geomagnetic activity. Gissurarson also looked at participant gender and age, but the small sample size made it difficult to draw any conclusions.

Dave Schumacher, Cindy Heinen, and Chris Carter performed a small retrospective study that compared the geomagnetic activity to the number of recorded EVPs obtained using data from three sources.[435] It is unclear whether a blind judging panel was used to determine what was deemed to be an EVP or meaningless static. However, assuming consistency in this process, they found no correlation between the number of reported EVPs and the estimated GMF as measured in three-hour windows.

At this point, despite suggestive evidence that ESP is reported more often during low GMF activity, we do not know whether there is an inverse association between MMI and GMF, let alone whether that effect (if any) is a direct one or simply a third variable, since GMF correlates with a great many other factors that can influence biological functioning.[436] One problem with our current studies may be that the three-hour windows of geomagnetic activity are simply too long or too crude a measurement to pinpoint what is occurring. It is also possible that local artificial EMFs are drowning out any effect from the GMF or that complex interactions are involved, rather than a simple, direct effect. In the end, we are left with more questions than answers.

Local Sidereal Time Local sidereal time (LST) is a physical factor that correlates strongly with successful ESP performance, and may affect MMI performance as well.[437] Best known by astronomers, LST refers to the position of the Earth relative to the stars as it rotates around its axis. A solar day (which we use for clock time) is approximately four minutes longer than a sidereal day. This means that the LST only matches standard clock time one day of the year — on the vernal equinox, around September 22nd. Fortunately, free software that calculates the LST for a given latitude and longitude is widely available on the internet.

The correlations between certain windows of LST and psi hit rate are impressive.[438] These findings have cropped up consistently throughout two decades of experimental research by researchers from around the globe. Credit must be given to James Spottiswoode, who performed much of the original work on this topic. Spottiswoode gathered together 20 years' worth of data from laboratories around the world — approximately 1,500 trials — and analyzed their hit rates. Two main features stood out. First, there was a "hole" at around 18:00 LST when there is a hit rate of zero. Second, at 13:00 LST there was a 300 percent increase in hit rate, with a small increase at about 06:00 LST. Spottiswoode then opened up his database and asked others to see what they could find. The outside experimenters got similar results. This effect is consistent over massive amounts of data, regardless of the laboratory location or individual experimenter.

The experimenters then had to figure out why LST would correlate with psychic functioning. Spottiswoode speculated that it has to do with the Earth's rotational axis in comparison to the configuration of our galaxy. The galaxy is shaped like a thick plate with Earth off to one edge, far from the center. The galactic core is directly overhead (i.e., the bulk of the galactic star field is between us and deep space) at the time ESP vanishes to nil. On the other hand, when ESP is at its greatest, the Earth is pointed towards the depths of outer space with the least of the star field in the way. There is also relatively little star field between a person and deep space at the second-best time (06:00 LST) for ESP.

Ed May proposed that some form of radiation coming from the Milky Way Galaxy could interfere with ESP reception, either by decreasing the signal to noise ratio (through increased noise) or by acting directly on the brain[439]: At the time of the least success at ESP experimental tasks (somewhere around 18:00 to 19:00 LST) the participant might be getting maximum interference from stray radio waves or unknown other sources. However, Spottiswoode pointed out that the small amount of extra radio-wave interference from the galaxy, or alterations in GMF related to LST, is unlikely to make a difference in ESP functioning compared to the massively larger artificial fields observed in the environment today.[440] Furthermore, models he built to test for correlation did not produce good fits between radio flux from the galaxy and ESP data.[441]

This is an exciting discovery even if we do not yet understand why LST should correlate with psi. LST may be a valuable clue to how ESP (and possibly MMI) functions.[442] It is hoped that future research explores whether MMI performance is similarly associated with LST, and in what way. There also need to be investigations to learn whether other human abilities also vary with this factor. If so, it could mean that LST (or whatever it is correlated with) may act as a general modulator of human functioning, instead of a specific factor for psi performance.

Solar Activity Early findings suggest solar activity may be a promising area of future research. Alan Gauld and H. P. Wilkinson looked at how the sun correlated with psi reports and found most ESP cases occurred during times of the least solar activity.[443] However, they noted that this assumes psychic events are reported at a constant rate from one year to the next.

Eckhard Etzold compared retro–MMI results to a variety of physical factors.[444] Although there was no effect from a full moon, tidal influences, solar wind, or GMF alone, Etzold found an interaction between a full moon and two different indicators of solar activity: sunspot activity (significant at the p=.05 level) and the $F_{10.7}$ index (a measure of solar radio flux, significant at the p=.01 level). The lower the solar activity during a full moon, the greater the retro–MMI effect observed.

Psychological Factors

In recent years, experimenters have recognized the need for qualitative research if we are to advance in the field of parapsychology.[445] Looking back over the experimental research, we can discern certain key factors that have repeatedly surfaced across studies for a variety of targets, experimenters, and labs, which appear to be as significant for ESP as they are for MMI. This section will look those findings, which include personality and other psychological factors, as they may play out in the decline effect, the sheep-goat effect, experimenter effects, and the apparent goal-oriented nature of psi.

Personality Personality is a complex factor, which interacts with belief systems, emotions, perception, and other variables that impact MMI performance.[446] Gertrude Schmeidler observed:

> Over the years it has been hammered home to me that personality differences are
> so pervasive and powerful that they can affect responses to any conditions we want to
> study. This means that they will falsify any simple, precise generalization and that even
> learning or perception need families of sublaws to show how different individuals
> respond.[447]

We know little about how personality affects MMI performance. The majority of research has compared ESP test success with personality.[448] These studies suggest that extraversion and openness correlate with higher psi scores. Unfortunately, it is unclear whether these findings apply to MMI performance, or for that matter if they even apply to ESP, since they could be artifacts of the testing situation.

Schmeidler pointed out that gifted psychics fall all over the map in terms of social adjustment, from good to extremely poor. She also noted that research findings may differ because of the difficulty of accurately measuring these variables, as well as the way they interact. For example, she pointed out that "it is only when participants care about what they are doing that their tendency toward anxiety is likely to relate to their psi performance."[449] Because of this, she suggested that, among other things, researchers need to perform complete personality test batteries on their participants, rather than simply measuring isolated traits.

Finally, Schmeidler commented that unless confidence is taken to extremes, it correlates with MMI performance.[450] This has come up repeatedly in the research literature. Both participants and experimenters have stated that confidence is a key part of MMI success. However, we will later see that there may be some reasons why this need not be true of MMI when there is not a conscious need to perform on command.

Decline Effect One of the earliest trends noted by experimenters, beginning with the Rhine era, was that boring tasks — such as the early dice experiments — tended to show a decrease in positive scoring over time within a run, a session, or a longer period of testing.[451] This was particularly true for non-feedback conditions. Charles Tart suggested that this should not be surprising, considering the importance of motivation on human performance and the effect of boredom on the motivation to succeed.[452] Thus, the decline effect may not represent an inherent quality of psi performance so much as an artifact created by a poor learning situation.

Holger Bosch and Harald Walach have proposed that the decline effect could merely be a statistical artifact.[453] They reviewed a number of studies and discovered that when the data is looked at more closely, it shows the correlation of effect size and chronologic order is normally distributed. Bosch and Walach tested this hypothesis by sampling the data from two five-year periods of the *Journal of Parapsychology*. However, it is unclear whether third variables, such as the feedback quality, could have also varied along a normal distribution and caused the correlation.

Finally, there is a third possibility, which is that this decline is a real effect. Von Lucadou, Röemer, and Walach noted that their Model of Pragmatic Information (*see* Quantum Theories) would predict that continued research would naturally progress from significance toward the null hypothesis.[454]

Sheep-Goat Effect The sheep-goat effect is one of the most reliable and consistent experimental findings in psi research.[455] The terms "sheep" and "goat" were originally introduced by Gertrude Schmeidler.[456] She found that those participants who believed in the possibility that psi could exist ("sheep") performed better than skeptics who were convinced psi does not exist ("goats"). It is also consistent with the fact that most MMI performers, along with many researchers, such as Batcheldor and Hasted, have emphasized the importance of being open to the possibility of MMI for it to happen.

Experimenter Effects The "experimenter effect" is a third major and recurrent finding. This is not a case of carelessness, inexperience, or fraud on the part of the experimenter(s).[457] Instead, it refers to a variety of subtle (and possibly psychic) ways in which even the most careful experimenters can inadvertently influence their studies.

Experimenter effects have been known since at least the mid–1960s, when psychologist Robert Rosenthal wrote how researcher beliefs, attitudes, and feelings could affect participant performance.[458] Nor need this be blatant. Subtleties in how questions are asked, tone of voice, body language, etc., can effectively communicate an experimenter's expectations. As Schmeidler put it, this means "one of the variables to be controlled or measured is the internal state of the investigator."[459]

A wide range of things can fall under this umbrella.[460] Some are potentially universal — such as where there is an unconscious bias in designing, conducting, or interpreting studies (seen more often in believers and skeptics than either would care to admit). Others are individual attributes, such as an effect from the experimenter's age, gender, friendliness, confidence, and ability to motivate participants, in addition to unintentional expectancy effects. Additionally, there is the possibility of experimenters using their own psi to obtain whatever results they unconsciously desire — whether for or against significance.

Just as a psi-believer can unconsciously use their talent to get significant results, skeptics may use their abilities to block or counter-balance the psi of their participants. Perhaps the best set of studies on the experimenter effect were performed by Schlitz and Wiseman (*see* "Direct Mental Interactions with Living Subjects" under "Biological System Research").[461] They used the same research protocol, lab locations, equipment, participant pools, and blind statistical analysis. Despite this, Wiseman (a skeptic) and Schlitz (a psi-believer) got different results from each other in two of the three studies they performed together, with Wiseman having null results every time and Schlitz significance in two studies out of three. They seemed to have ruled out the likelihood of their contrasting results being due to different levels of talent between their pools of participants, sloppy technique, or fraud.

It is possible that (as suggested long ago by Schmeidler) that some experimenters are better at creating a psi-conducive environment than others, perhaps by being better at motivating their participants or putting them at greater ease.[462] Certainly, Schlitz is known for her warmth and friendliness with participants. However, it is also possible that the participants had nothing to do with the results and the two experimenters were responsible for any psi.

Schmeidler recommended using the terms "psi-permissive" and "psi-conducive" to differentiate between those experimenters who simply create a warm, friendly environment, and those who use their own MMI abilities in some manner (whether directly, or by augmenting the participants' own abilities).[463] She coined the phrase "psi-inhibitory" to denote those experimenters who can block MMI, and prevent successful results. Schmeidler suggested that the only data which can be trusted is that of psi-permissive experimenters. However, it might be that future skeptic-believer collaborations, such as pioneered by Wiseman and Schlitz, could prove to be of equal or greater value.

Goal Orientation Spontaneous case studies and experimental research suggest that MMI is goal-oriented and mediated through unconscious processes.[464] However, it is unknown how much the unconscious acts as a mediator for a gift that needs to be developed, and how much as a gatekeeper — blocking or permitting the psi that already occurs on an ongoing basis. If we assume, as Kenneth Batcheldor did, that psi is primarily an inherent gift, then it would seem prudent to focus on removing blocks or opening up the gates through conscious and unconscious techniques. On the other hand, if we imagine MMI to be an ability like any other, then learning theory becomes important and it should be possible to enhance MMI performance through training.

Tﬃ Brain

Participants and experimenters alike often speculate on the role of the right brain hemisphere in psi performance. This would seem to be anecdotally supported by the traditionally reported relative lack of left brain functions, such as sense of time, logic, and counting. Recent technical advances in the noninvasive imaging of brain functions have allowed us to better understand what may be occurring.

It is well accepted that the two hemispheres of the brain have different overall roles. Many studies have shown that the left hemisphere is better at language, task setting, and body movement, while the right frontal lobe dominates in musical and emotional aspects of language.[465] The right hemisphere has other functions, as well: It is important for maintaining global awareness, attention, error detection, and interpreting and expressing emotions.[466] The left hemisphere, on the other hand, is typically thought of as more rational, analytical, and detail-oriented. It oversees the functions of reading and writing.

Although these hemispheres have different strengths, they act in a coordinated way.[467] Both sides are need to work together for proper functioning of mood, emotion, and social behavior, not to mention be able to problem-solve, learn, talk, have coordinated movement, and access memories. Thus, although the left hemisphere is dominant in speech and language, the right hemisphere plays a role in the comprehension of language and verbal expression.[468] People who suffer injuries to the right frontal lobe have trouble formulating ideas, speaking concisely to the point, and understanding abstract concepts and metaphors. In addition, they tend to be wordy and tangential.

Despite the apparent clinical differences between the hemispheres in terms of speech, mathematics, logic, and emotion, when one measures "left" and "right" brain activity using PET and fMRI techniques, there is not a clear-cut shift when one changes activities. Although one side may appear more active than the other, *both* sides are involved.[469] Tasks once thought to completely reside on the left or right hemisphere instead involve corresponding regions on both sides. This duplication of function is particularly true for left-handed individuals.

Most brain operations are something of a balancing act, with the result depending upon both hemispheres.[470] Emotions are a case in point. Although the right hemisphere is dominant for the expression of emotions, the emotional state itself is a function of both. Left frontal lobe injuries tend to cause depression. Injure the right side, and you are more apt to see mania or inappropriate cheerfulness. Likewise, the blood flow to the left prefrontal brain increases in healthy individuals who are thinking sad thoughts. This situation can also be artificially induced, by transcranial magnetic stimulation (temporarily decreasing activity) of the left prefrontal region, which leads to reports of feeling less happy and more sad. This has led Daniel Geschwind and Marco Iacoboni to conclude that "the left frontal lobe is more specialized for positive emotions related to approach and exploratory mechanisms, and the right for negative, avoidance-related reactions."[471]

The fact that excited (or manic-type) states and sad ones appear to involve the activation of opposite hemispheres is significant because both positive and negative emotions are capable of triggering MMI.[472] According to the above data, the extreme sadness that appeared to cause object movement in one incident would have been associated with increased blood flow of the left frontal lobe. This would suggest that psi does not exclusively involve the right hemisphere as some have thought.

Another piece of evidence that would seem to indicate psi is not entirely a right-brain phenomenon is that detachment (which was noted strongly by Loyd Auerbach during his MMI) involves a decrease in right hemispheric activity.[473] According to Terri Edwards-Lee and Ronald Saul, damage to the right hemisphere can cause an "indifferent-euphoric reaction, characterized by minimization of symptoms, emotional placidity, joking, elation, or social disinhibition."[474]

Both detachment and euphoria can result from decreased right hemispheric function or increased left hemispheric activity. Thus, there may not be a simple shift in functioning from one hemisphere to another during psi performance so much as a complex interplay of activity between the two. However, some caution must be taken in trying to deduce hemispheric activity from emotion. Edwards-Lee and Saul pointed out that "the reported changes in mood, positive or negative, produced by right frontal lesions are inconsistent."[475] It is unclear how much of this is due to how investigators are defining each mood, versus variations in the size and specific location of affected brain matter.

The presence of focused attention is one of the most consistent phenomenological findings across all types of MMI experiences.[476] This is intriguing because it brings us back to the question of the role of the right side of the brain. Cheryl Grady stated, "Activations during attention tasks and motor or conditioning tasks are found only in the right hemisphere."[477] Attention is, in fact, one of the few functions unique to the right hemisphere.[478] Human fMRI research has also shown that shifts in attention can instantly change which regions of the brain light up.[479]

Attention is important for other reasons, as well. It has an organizing quality.[480] We typically think of the right side of the brain as being global intuitive. It takes in, and processes, many types of sensory, emotive, motor, and cognitive data. Sense has to be made of all this, which requires the ability to organize that information and focus on that which is important at the moment. Some have even speculated that the right side of the brain is interconnected with the "fight or flight" aspects of arousal and attention in the primitive brain. If so, then the ability of peak emotions to trigger MMI would make sense from an ecological standpoint. In life or death situations, the survival edge of being able to perform psi would be quite valuable.

A number of phenomenological characteristics of MMI performance — suspension of the intellect, emotion, and focused attention — are primarily (or in the case of focused attention exclusively) considered "right hemisphere" traits.[481] However, there is a vast duplication of function between the two hemispheres and the brain itself is far more plastic and adaptable than originally thought. In addition, some factors — such as that of emotion — are more complex than can be explained as a simple hemispheric shift in functioning.

Freedman et al. performed one of the few studies to look at the effect of frontal lobe damage on psi.[482] They noted that frontal lobe lesions were associated with patients having less self-awareness and compared six normal individuals with six who had frontal lobe damage (four with general damage, and one each with left or right frontal lobe damage) on REG. Only the patient with the left frontal lobe lesion had data that reached significance in the direction of intention. They therefore retested that individual for another 3000 runs, and again found he was able to influence the REG in the direction of his intention to a statistically significant degree. There are, unfortunately, a number of obvious problems with this study, not least of which are the small sample size, the possibility that other psi-related factors besides intention could have been affected by generalized frontal lobe damage, and the lack of mention of whether any of participants (some of whom were also experimenters) had history of psi performance or what their attitudes and beliefs were towards psi. Nonetheless, it is interesting that the only participant able to perform on the REG had a relative imbalance with greater right front lobe functioning than the left. Clearly a great deal more such research is needed.

Early understanding of the brain was based on what abilities were lost when certain areas were damaged.[483] Advances in neuroimaging have shown us that the two sides of the brain work together in complex and interactive ways. While some higher cortical processes show lateralization, very little of overall function is completely one-sided. For example, even moving the right hand (once considered a function of the left side of the brain) involves neuronal activity distributed throughout both cerebral hemispheres and the cerebellum. The primary senses of smell, taste, touch, hearing, and sight are all bilateral. Because of this, it may be unwise to speak of psychic functioning as a right-brain activity until the facts have been determined through neuroimaging. Until then, there is no way to know for sure what is occurring at a neuronal level.

MMI Facilitation and Training

Martin Caidin once announced, "There are three great secrets to successful writing.... And nobody knows what the hell they are."[484] The same might well be said for MMI. Current methods have had variable success at best.[485] Studies have typically fallen into one of two categories: facilitation or training. Facilitation refers to ways that make it easier for folks to succeed while training implies an organized method of instruction, which brings a complex skill to a proficient level of ability.[486] Moreover, training suggests repeat structured practice sessions with set goals. Although people can learn how to perform MMI on their own, and its performance can be facilitated or inhibited, it is unclear whether training is possible.

One might ask why parapsychologists would care about how to teach MMI. One purpose would be to convince people that MMI exists. As Martin Caidin once said, "Once you either see someone else do this, or you get some movement yourself, your skepticism starts to break down and lets your belief start to happen."[487] A second benefit would be that a successful training method would tell us something about the process of MMI.[488] A third motive would be to get more consistent MMI performances in the laboratory, while avoiding the pitfalls of working with stars.[489] After all, as Loftur Gissurarson has noted, it is hard to create and test good theories when you still lack a way of getting consistently measurable results.[490] One cannot study what cannot be found. Higher success rates could result in more robust data, allowing experimenters to better study the subtleties of the process.

Part of the problem with instructing individuals on how to do MMI is that we do not have a clear understanding of what factors are involved in the task. This makes it difficult to know precisely what to teach. However, if we presume (based on the ubiquitous nature of MMI reports) that it is a universal human ability, then we should be able to use the same kinds of techniques as are used by sports psychologists to train other forms of exceptional performance. This would suggest using hypnosis, motivational techniques, biofeedback, meditative practice, event rehearsal with vivid imagery, and finding a way for performers to reach the ASC, or "zone," where they are in a state of awareness that is conducive to successful MMI performance. To date, most psi studies have been oriented more toward psi facilitation, rather than training, per se.[491] The techniques studied fall into six general categories: (1) hypnosis, (2) feedback, (3) yoga and meditation, (4) relaxation, (5) negative reinforcement and punishment, and (6) visual imagery.

TECHNIQUES

Hypnosis has been used for psi enhancement since the late 1700s, when Mesmer discovered that some of his participants seemed to develop clairvoyance while in the trance state.[492] J. B. Rhine performed one of the earlier exploratory studies of MMI and hypnosis around 1946.[493] He used a dice-throwing machine with 96 dice thrown simultaneously, and found that positive hypnotic suggestions to have fun and be relaxed improved MMI performance, while telling them under hypnosis to concentrate hard worsened scoring in four of his five participants. He concluded that the unconscious mind has an impact on psi performance, and can be affected by hypnosis.

Hypnosis was frequently used in ESP studies in the 1960s, but was seldom explored in conjunction with MMI enhancement.[494] It lost popularity as a technique for enhancing ESP after the ganzfeld sensory deprivation approach was developed. This may have been partly because effective hypnosis relies upon the expertise of the hypnotist—which can vary considerably—whereas the ganzfeld technique requires no special skills and gets more consistent results.

A study by Breederveld and Jacobs in 1979 used a single participant to look at whether hypnosis combined with suggestions of high scoring would lead to a national selection of lotto numbers on TV which matched the target numbers.[495] Confusing the issue is the fact that this task could involve either ESP, in the sense of making an accurate prediction, or MMI, by influencing the lotto selection to match a desired outcome. They found a significant difference between success during the hypnotic and waking states at the p=.002 level. However, this was primarily due to psi-missing in the waking condition.

One of the most interesting uses of hypnosis was published in a study in 1986 by Jennie Stewart, William Roll, and Steve Baumann.[496] They showed that hypnosis could reactivate poltergeist activity in an agent, thus emphasizing the role of the unconscious mind in poltergeist cases.[497]

Schmeidler believed that hypnosis enhanced psi in the same way that meditation and other ASC work—by allowing us to dissociate from our normal worldview.[498] This in turn allows a suspension of disbelief, as was recommended by Kenneth Batcheldor. It can also make people feel more relaxed and comfortable, which might in turn foster a sense of openness. Other ways hypnosis could be effective include by: (1) empowering instructions to score well, (2) improving visualization, (3) enhancing unconscious intent, (4) boosting access to unconscious abilities, (5) bypassing conscious blocks, and (6) augmenting psi via the hypnotic link between hypnotists and their clients. Further research is clearly needed.

Feedback Motivational techniques have been nearly absent from the parapsychological arena other than indirectly as the experimenter effect. This may partly be due to the difficulty of providing good feedback (which is itself motivational) to MMI performers. Accurate, immediate feedback can be difficult to achieve with psi experiments since a certain number of "hits" are due to random chance alone — meaning that the performer can be falsely rewarded.[499] As the majority of MMI research is done using targets such as dice, spheres, and computers, which all have a statistical hit rate by random chance, this is a valid concern.

Julian Isaacs attempted to train metal-bending in five women.[500] He pre-screened his participants for MMI potential by a mass screening technique or their self-report of macro–MMI abilities. Isaacs used a quasi-experimental longitudinal design with repeated measures using a piezoelectric crystal as a target. Unfortunately, there were a number of problems with his study. The biggest of these were that there was no control group and the piezoelectric detection device that Isaacs used to measure the metal-bending was sensitive to ambient noise and vibration, leading to the possibility of artifact. He attempted to control for this by simultaneously recording ambient sound levels, but there was no control for vibration. Other concerns with the study include the unknown validity of Isaacs' screening test, and whether his device was measuring metal-bending or something else.

RNGs have been widely popular MMI targets because of their convenience and the speed with which data can be collected.[501] Experiments testing the value of RNG feedback on MMI training have had inconsistent results.[502] Some of this may be due the feedback being inaccurate and interaction with other variables, such as striving. Varvoglis and McCarthy performed a study which they felt showed that RNG feedback can improve task performance. However, confounding variables — such as participant-experimenter conflict in one of their experiments, and the possibility of experimenter psi — meant that these results must be considered tentative at best.

Chris Roe and Nicola Holt noted that feedback could be problematic if it acted as a distracter from the task.[503] They looked at this possibility in a study using RNGs and found that participants who used goal-directed intention as a strategy did better with ongoing, real-time feedback than when it was delayed (p=.02, one-tailed). However, when participants used absorption in the task as a strategy, there was no significant difference between the types of feedback — both had hit rates of about 30 percent.

Dobyns et al. looked at REG results where no sensory feedback was provided.[504] Participants had three choices of visual environment, a blank screen, a mandala design (the Sri Yantra) as an active image of changing colors, or the same mandala but static. Participants also had a choice of sound, whether single or double drum beats, their own music CD, or silence. A total of 61 participants contributed to the series of 1,017. The lack of feedback made no difference to experienced female participants, who obtained consistent statistical levels of result regardless of their visual and auditory environment, whereas male participants and females new to REG work were more sensitive to environmental factors, showing better results with a static image. Dobyns et al. also observed that "the aesthetic preference for a particular environment" was no guarantee that performers would get psi results.[505]

Loftur Gissurarson observed that a number of studies indicate that normal sensory feedback is unnecessary for successful MMI.[506] This may not mean that feedback itself is unnecessary, but rather that participants can obtain their own feedback through ESP. It is also possible that feedback interacts with the participants' belief system, initial level of talent, degree of interest, and motivation in a complex way. Furthermore, personality variables could alter the significance, and effectiveness, of feedback. Additional work is needed both to determine what kind of feedback, if any, augments MMI learning, and what kind of participant might benefit from it.

Yoga and Meditation Meditation increases ESP performance, and in most studies seems to enhance MMI abilities as well.[507] Unfortunately, it is impossible to say to what degree these results are due to the personality of someone drawn to practice meditation, a product of the experimenter effect, or a consequence of meditative practice.[508] Most assume that the key element here is a relaxed, open state combined with a narrowing of awareness.[509] Certainly, the use of an effortless approach together with focused attention is often reported in successful MMI experiences. However, other factors may be involved as well. While experience with the ASC of meditation could enhance a participant's ability to enter the correct state of consciousness for MMI performance, it is equally possible that it represents a third variable.

We are again left with more questions than answers for why yoga and meditation are associated with better MMI performance. It may be that there is not a simple relationship between MMI and meditation, but rather a complex interaction of multiple factors, which work both together and separately to enhance performance.

Relaxation and Emotional Factors Gertrude Schmeidler long ago noted the importance of emotion in human performance.[510] Primary traits and attitudes can only describe typical behavior—they cannot predict how a person will behave in a particular situation. This is because transient moods and feelings act as powerful moderators for behavior. Individual situations often evoke conflicting traits or opinions. Which one wins out can depend on how we feel at the time.

In the case of MMI research, emotional factors are important for both the experimenter and the participant.[511] Julian Isaacs believed these can influence (1) performance anxiety, (2) the participant's confidence of success, and (3) motivation. Too much stress in the private lives of either experimenters or their participants can have an inhibitory effect. The interpersonal relationships between the experimenter and his or her participants can also affect success.

Loftur Gissurarson reviewed a number of studies and found that anxiety generally inhibited successful MMI, whereas a certain amount of relaxation and imagery enhanced it.[512] However, this may be misleading. Anxiety and relaxation are fuzzy terms, which are measured in different, and not necessarily equivalent, ways.[513] Moreover, these factors interact with the participant's personality. Although relaxation may enhance ESP, the opposite may be true for MMI. Stories of gifted MMI participants often include comments and descriptions suggesting high autonomic arousal.

Furthermore, if we look at spontaneous poltergeist cases, it is clear that frustration is often associated with the greatest MMI activity.[514] Frustration may modulate, or be modulated by, interactions with basic personality traits, other emotions, historical tendencies, and a great many other factors. This could explain why correlations of elation, and other moods, with ESP performance have been inconsistent.[515] Mischo and Weis published a pilot study in 1973 that looked how mood interacted with MMI. They found that MMI scores were lower after frustration for those who were habitually depressed, neurotic, or inhibited. However, participants who tended to be calm and outgoing scored higher.

It is possible that this could be a reflection of the Yerkes-Dodson law of psychology, which says that performance tends to follow an inverted U curve.[516] People tend to do better at mid-levels of arousal than when they care too little or too much. Furthermore, each of us, based on our own experience, personality, and self-efficacy, may have different "best arousal" midpoints, which in turn can shift with the surrounding situation and our mood. This complex interplay makes it difficult to predict in what manner a given mood and experimental situation will affect MMI performance.

Margaret Obendorf noted an association between the Emotional Position questionnaire (said to measure the emotional state) and MMI success at computer tasks.[517] How much the MMI test was enjoyed by the participants also seemed to influence scoring, while actively "striving for success" correlated with psi-missing.[518] Thus, the best state may be a calm, detached mind. When Gissurarson reviewed what methods facilitate MMI in 1997, he was surprised to note that there had only been one report of three combined experiments by Honorton and Barksdale in 1972, which looked at the effect of relaxation on MMI — although it did not measure the depth of relaxation achieved.[519] The results suggested that mental relaxation promoted MMI.

The term "mental relaxation" is a fuzzy one, which could represent being nonanalytical, passive, not trying too hard, and being noncompetitive.[520] J. B. Rhine noted in a 1946 pilot study that MMI scores using dice for targets dropped to that of random chance when his participants were told to concentrate hard, but increased above chance when they were asked to be relaxed and have fun.[521]

Gissurarson has proposed that the "linger" and "release-of-effort" effects could be nothing more than relaxation.[522] John Palmer and Wim Kramer performed an RNG study that instructed participants to relax and merge with the target rather than try to force a change.[523] They did not find a "release of effort." This would seem support Gissurarson's notion that if there is no tension to begin with, a release of effort is unnecessary.

A number of experimenters have commented on the apparent importance of a person's mental state for successful MMI performance. John Hasted noted that for most of his participants it was a matter of (1) learning to believe in themselves and (2) acquiring the ability to be inattentive or alternate concentration with periods of relaxation.[524] He further stated that it helped to turn practice sessions into a game. This "fun" aspect that Hasted tried to engender might work in part by countering any performer fears that could arise.

Fear of success, either in the experimenter or the participant, appears to be markedly inhibitory whether one is talking about macro- or micro–MMI.[525] It may be that experimental participants need a relaxed and detached state of mind to block ownership resistance and fear, while poltergeist agents bypass their fear issues by blaming an unknown agency or cause for the disturbance. This would be consistent with the fact that the poltergeist events frequently stop when agents accept the fact that they were responsible for the phenomena.[526]

There are a number of ways that fear of success could be countered. As mentioned before, poltergeist agents and others have often blamed outside forces (often extraterrestrials, angels, demons, and spirits).[527] This may likewise factor into the induction effect. Those who perform spoon-bending after watching someone else do it frequently place the responsibility for their newfound success on the performer they had originally seen carry out the task — regardless of whether that person was actually using MMI or trickery.[528] John Hasted and Kenneth Batcheldor have also suggested a fun atmosphere mitigates fear issues.

Given that mood is a key factor for many human abilities, it is likely it influences psi performance as well. As Gertrude Schmeidler noted years ago, mood changes can affect even established skills.[529] It does not matter how much you may have practiced and trained for an event — whether as a musician, dancer, athlete, game show contestant, or anything else — your mood affects your performance. This becomes even more of a problem when an ability is weak or inconsistent — as in the case of psi for most people. The less established a talent, the more important a role mood will play in how well a person does.

Experimenters and performers alike have commented on the impact mood has on MMI. Unfortunately, moods are difficult to measure, and the fact mood interacts with personality traits can make the specific effect on performance difficult to quantify or predict. However, at least some factors — such as low anxiety/relaxation, motivation, and confidence — appear to enhance MMI performance in a wide range of settings.[530]

Punishment and Negative Reinforcement Punishment and negative reinforcement refer to different ways of using an aversive stimulus to modify behavior. With negative reinforcement, an aversive stimulus is removed when a desired response has occurred. A simple example of this would be if after touching something extremely hot we jerk away and the pain ends. This is an example of negative reinforcement. The behavior of moving away from an object causing pain is rewarded by the end of that discomfort. Punishment, on the other hand, involves applying an aversive stimulus when a desired response does not occur. Variations of negative reinforcement and punishment are frequently used in "conditioning" experiments, and also occur naturally in life as everyday behavior modifiers (with varied levels of success).

Only a few studies have looked at the effect of aversive stimuli on MMI performance.[531] In his review of the topic, Gissurarson pointed out that Camstra's study in 1973 could be considered a form of negative reinforcement. It "rewarded" participants every time a certain number was generated by an RNG by eliminating the white noise from pop music for ten seconds. This, of course, assumes that the participants liked the pop music and disliked the white noise. Those who were asked to concentrate on the task had null results. However, participants who were not asked to concentrate had significant results, especially those who were lied to and told it was an ESP test.

Unfortunately, it is difficult to draw conclusions from this given the potential confounding variables of relaxation, state of consciousness (which may have varied from one participant to the next depending on how they reacted to the music and white noise), and experimenter psi. A similar study, which removed a disturbing video program when the target number was generated, did not confirm the first one's findings.[532]

Richard Broughton, Brian Millar, and Martin Johnson used "strong" electric shock as a punishment for RNG psi-missing in a pilot study with three participants and a follow-up study of four.[533] Although these are usually small group sizes, it has to be recognized that it is not easy to get people to volunteer for anything involving electric shocks. The participants performed eight sessions of twenty-four runs each. There was no apparent improvement.

Although negative reinforcement may have some potential application, learning theory suggests that punishment is not, and never has been, an effective tool for any form of learning.[534] This is particularly true when one is trying to develop a new behavior. Consequently, it seems unlikely that this technique would hold much, if any, promise for enhancing MMI.

Imagery Training Popular books on psychic self-development have long advocated the use of imagery to improve psi performance.[535] This is not surprising, considering its apparent effectiveness at enhancing other skills. Visual imagery training is routinely used in sports to improve performance, reveal the mind's workings, remold physique, alleviate stress, and catalyze spontaneous powers.[536] Surveys show that top athletes use imagery more frequently than their less successful colleagues. Mental rehearsal may be of particular value in sports with a large cognitive component.

Early experimenters, such as Forwald (who used himself as a research subject in MMI studies in the 1960s), felt that visualizing the desired physical outcome improved his success rate.[537] As a result, a number of investigators have looked at this topic. Unfortunately, the effect of imagery techniques on MMI in the laboratory has not been clear cut.[538]

Given the apparently strong anecdotal support for imagery, and its effectiveness in other learning situations, one has to ask why the experimental literature has shown there to be little, if any, enhancement of psi from imagery training. Robin Taylor suggested that there could be a variety of reasons for this, including (1) insensitive experimental design, (2) inadequate imagery training, (3) a different aspect of imagery was used in the experiments than is utilized by psi, and (4) imagery is only of tangential value.[539] Nor are these the only possibilities. Gissurarson pointed out that concentrating too hard on the imagery could block MMI through "striving for success" (which is presumably the opposite of relaxation).[540]

One problem is that the effectiveness of visualization training is typically not well measured.[541] In most cases, the imagery was quantified by self-report or via tasks that were believed to require it — each of which has its own set of problems. One cannot expect improved imagery if participants receive confusing or inadequate instruction in its techniques. Needless to say, one cannot begin to measure visualization-related effects on MMI if there are no changes in skill at imagery.

Another possibility why imagery may fail could be that the participants tried to visualize the wrong thing. There is some indication that goal-directed imagery is more successful at enhancing MMI than is process-oriented imagery.[542] Loftur Gissurarson reviewed eight studies, which used goal-oriented imagery in the production of MMI.[543] He found that although seven of them trended in the expected direction, only three of them (all of which included immediate feedback) did so to a statistically significant degree. This brings up the question of whether it was truly the imagery, the feedback, or an interaction between the two that was important.

In his series of experiments on rifle shooters, jugglers, and gymnasts, Robin Taylor found to his surprise that the control group improved more than the group using mental rehearsal/imagery.[544] He postulated that this could have resulted from overloading the attentional capacity of the participants. Taylor further suggested that for the best short-term gain, a program should make the athlete believe he or she will perform well, and have little in the way of cognitive demand, while for the best long-term gain, the athlete should be trained in mental rehearsal probably a minimum of four times a week for 10 to 20 weeks.

There may be yet another reason why imagery training is not significantly improving participants' imagery skills, beyond there being an insufficient length of training, incorrect form of training, inherent limitations in a participant's imagery abilities, and rehearsing the process instead of a goal. It is possible that experimenters have not considered how their participants process information.

According to neurolinguistic programming (NLP), individuals tend to have one primary coding system (visual, auditory, or kinesthetic) that they use in preference to others, particularly in times of stress.[545] Thus, some people will naturally use visual imagery to code and process data; a few deal best with auditory forms of speech, while still others are prone to remembering, or relating to, body sensations or feelings. Examples of the kind of language exemplified by these systems would be, "I see what you mean" (visual), "I hear what you are saying" (auditory), and "I feel what you mean" (kinesthetic). Although most individuals mix these styles in everyday life, NLP points out that only one of these comes easiest, and it is this one that a person reverts to under pressure — which can make it difficult for them to comprehend anything that is said in the other two forms of language.

Allan Cooperstein is one of the few to describe the variation in types of imagery in anomalous healing.[546] He observed that while mental imagery may be of use, it is by no means required. Some healers do not use visualization at all, but instead sense things in their bodies, often as heat or cold. He also noted that the kind of imagery used is usually either realistic or quasi-realistic imagery.

The idea that imagery may be somatic, instead of visual, would fit with NLP theory and might explain why visual imagery training could be unhelpful. One could postulate, based on NLP theory, that imagery training might not enhance learning in a participant for whom visual coding is already dominant, and be difficult to master for someone who prefers auditory or kinesthetic coding.

Taylor reported that spontaneous case reviews show that the majority of events occur in a visual and/or auditory mode, rather than in an "intuitive" mode.[547] However, this association has not been well duplicated by research. There are a variety of reasons for why this could be — from reporting artifact to the cultural bias in virtually all anecdotal material (both of which could influence what mode is reported as used in spontaneous cases) to flawed experimental designs or techniques. It could be interesting to test individuals for their preferred coding systems to see whether they achieve different degrees of MMI improvement with effective imagery training.

In conclusion, imagery training would seem to hold promise as a potential, if inconsistent, method for enhancing MMI performance. It is hoped that further work may better delineate how, and when, this technique may best used to advantage.

QUALITATIVE REPORTS

At least some participants, such as martial artist Guy Savelli, could tell when they were in a mode to successfully perform MMI.[548] Because of this, it is valuable to pay attention to percipients' statements about what works for them. Let us look a bit closer at these comments.

Although Julian Isaacs' 1982 study was only suggestive that metal-bending can be learned, the qualitative reports of those who improved with training are intriguing.[549] They noted that an alert state, loss of awareness of their surroundings, passive concentration, and feelings of confidence aided success. Other investigators have also made informal observations that reiterate the helpfulness of alertness and a relaxed, detached state of mind.[550]

Matthew Manning said that he had two ways of doing MMI.[551] The first, which was more spontaneous and difficult to control, was related to physical exertions and/or psychological irritation or friction (i.e., stress). The second technique involved two steps. First, Manning would create a sense of calm and oneness with the universe, and then he mentally talked to the target that he was trying to influence. This is not a unique method. Participants in MMI studies have often reported a sense of merger with the object or person they were trying to affect.[552]

Manning noted that three principles applied to both of his methods.[553] He had to desire the event to occur, believe that it could take place, and expect it to occur. These statements echo Martin Caidin's comment that to succeed at MMI, you have to believe that you can do it.[554] Nor is this notion reflected only in Western thought. Paul Dong and Thomas Raffill stated that all qigong researchers know that "doubts or reservations about something will affect the ability to perform it."[555]

There is another interesting factor to this as well. Manning reflected that MMI phenomena often occurred when he was in a state between intense concentration and distraction.[556] This "release-of-effort" may in part be a way of "letting go" or not trying too hard. Effortfully willing the sensor to respond did not correlate with success in influencing piezoelectric detection devices in at least one metal-bending study.[557] Most PK performers feel that striving blocks their ability to succeed, with perhaps the notable exception of Felicia Parise, who learned how to do MMI using Nina Kulagina as a model.[558] Increasing levels of competition, or striving, might initially improve MMI performance up to a given point, and then level off as a plateau before finally declining. It is quite possible that the level at which a participant achieves his or her maximal performance could vary on an individual basis.

Finally, Manning observed that the experimenter had a major impact on the outcome.[559] He got his best results when working with experimenters who were relaxed, jovial, and sympathetic. Manning concluded, "I believe that the researcher contributes to the results of any parapsychological experiment at some level."[560] Although known for her trickery, physical medium Eusapia Palladino, too, was said to be able to produce impressive phenomena under tight controls when she was working with investigators whom she liked.[561] This may be a more important factor than many would care to admit.

Martin Caidin and Jack Houck both devoted a lot of time to teaching ordinary individuals how to perform MMI. Their recommendations were nearly the same. Caidin stated that it was helpful to have a target you like, while trying "too hard" inhibited MMI.[562] He also noted that the other two keys to success were merging with the target, and believing that you can succeed. Jack Houck stated that confidence was important for success, while over-intellectualizing (perhaps a form of "trying too hard") inhibited getting results.[563] Furthermore, Houck believed that people need to have targets they "like" working on, such as nice shiny metal. It is possible that "liking" targets makes it somehow easier to merge with it.

SUMMARY

MMI can be affected by a complex interplay of psychological factors involving not only the participant, but also the researcher, as well. Motivation, belief systems, mood, and rapport may be particularly important in normal states of consciousness. Although psi has continued to be somewhat elusive in the laboratory — probably because we do not yet understand all of the factors that must be controlled — the sheep-goat effect and experimenter effect partly determine the direction and magnitude of the results.

A number of methods have been tried to facilitate and/or train MMI performance. These have included ASC — such as hypnosis, yoga, and meditation — in addition to feedback, positive and negative reinforcement, punishment, relaxation and imagery techniques. Of these, relaxation, meditation, and goal-oriented imagery have been the most consistently promising.[564] Unfortunately, as Gissurarson pointed out, there appear to be no fast or easy ways to teach people how to perform MMI.

The participant's basic personality, in terms of being persistent and patient, in addition to his or her level of talent, motivation, interest, and belief system, may all impact the effectiveness of a training method.[565] In general, performers emphasize being self-confident, relaxed, and happy with their situation — both in terms of their experimenter and their target — as key elements to successful MMI. Other critical factors seem to involve not trying too hard, being able to merge with the target, and the ability to access a certain state of mind — although what that ASC is may vary from one participant to the next.

Michael Murphy suggested that psi research might benefit from considering what is required for obtaining successful experimental results in other areas of exceptional human functioning, such as sports.[566] He believed investigators should complement disciplined controls with persuasive confidence, sufficient practice time, and other procedural catalysts as needed. It is possible that the very neutrality cultivated by many experimenters may prevent them from getting results. Crucial components to MMI performance may involve a mixture of the helpful beliefs (in both the experimenter and the participant), the right kind and degree of motivation, accurate feedback, a detached, focused mental state, and an ability to visualize success. It seems likely that training/facilitation methods would be more successful if we could learn how to optimize these and other such factors.

What Learning Theories Suggest About MMI

Buddhist and Hindu traditions state that occult powers, or siddhis, can be acquired by any person with sufficient spiritual practice.[567] If we assume that MMI is a universal human ability, it should be possible to discover clues as to the nature of MMI and how to develop it by looking at what we already know about other human aptitudes. Since psychomotor skills are frequently a mixture of innate talent and learned behavior, it would seem useful to consider how such behavior is learned.

There are three basic types of learning: (1) classical conditioning; (2) instrumental learning, also known as operant conditioning; and (3) social learning. Classical conditioning is a form of associative learning in which an unconditioned stimulus is paired with a conditioned stimulus to create a conditioned response.[568] This kind of learning is limited to inborn, or previously conditioned, responses that are reflexive, rather than voluntary.[569] Since we are currently unaware of an unconditioned stimulus that elicits psi, this form of learning cannot be used, and will not be discussed. Instead, this chapter will look at what operant and social learning theories suggest about MMI training.

Operant Learning Theory

Operant conditioning is a form of learning in which the organism's voluntary behavior is instrumental in bringing about the occurrence of the conditioning stimulus in the form of a response from the environment.[570] To put it more simply, subjects perform or initiate an action and are rewarded as a result. Shaping is used to selectively reinforce those responses that can lead to an increasingly specific behavior or series of behaviors. It can also be used to train organisms to discriminate the precise stimulus they should respond to, while chaining allows the formation of very complex series of behaviors. In some cases, even autonomic functions, such as heart rate, can be controlled. This makes it likely that MMI could also be trained, whether it is under autonomic or voluntary control.

Traditionally there are three primary components to the reward or reinforcement conditions: (1) the number of reinforced responses; (2) the quantity and quality of reinforcement; and (3) the delay of reinforcement.[571] An immediate and continuous reinforcement schedule creates the fastest, if shortest lived, learning. However, the best long-term behavioral learning, which is highly resistant to extinction, occurs with a variable ratio schedule of intermittent positive reinforcement. This is best exemplified by slot machines. The number of times the machine lever must be pulled to get a jackpot varies. It might be once. It might be a thousand times. The gambler doesn't know, and cannot predict, when their behavior will be rewarded.

Several factors that have been shown to influence psychomotor skill development — such as practice, feedback, a task's complexity, and motivation — are also important in operant learning. Psychomotor skill practice increases a participant's opportunities for both reinforcement and feedback. Feedback itself acts as a reinforcer. Operant learning theory research indicates that (1) without feedback there is no acquisition of psychomotor skill; (2) progressive gains in proficiency occur in the presence of relevant feedback; (3) performance is disrupted when relevant feedback is withdrawn; (4) delayed feedback in continuous (but not discrete) tasks is detrimental; (5) augmented or supplementary feedback usually results in learning improvements; (6) the more frequent the reinforcing feedback the better the skill development; and (7) the more specific the feedback the better the performance.[572]

Charles Tart suggested that immediate feedback could diminish, or even eliminate, the decline effect.[573] However, REG experiments that have tried to evaluate the value of feedback have had variable results at best.[574] This could be because it is difficult, if not impossible, to either completely eliminate feedback through ESP or to give accurate sensory feedback in tasks where the randomness of the process means that a certain number of apparent "hits" will be due to chance alone, causing them to falsely reward performers at times when MMI played no role in the outcome.[575]

Operant learning theory tells us that task complexity can hinder skill development in three way: (1) affecting the inherent level(s) of task difficulty; (2) making it harder for a participant to discriminate between their response choices to react with the right one; and (3) changing the required length of behavior chaining needed for a successful response. It is difficult to say how much this factors into MMI (if at all), given that recent theories (*see* next chapter) tend to lean toward MMI being a simple task and possibly one that is not cause-and-effect in a traditional time forward way.

Finally, motivation is important, as it can influence the perceived quality of the reinforcer. Some participants are best motivated by getting a dollar for every hit, while others may put out their best effort for a piece of chocolate (especially if they are hungry) or the satisfaction of knowing they were successful in a task.

Punishment has not been shown to be an effective method for developing a new behavior or extinguishing an unwanted one in either animals or humans.[576] Positive reinforcement is far more apt to promote MMI than is the punishment of failure. In addition, Tart noted that the fear, anticipation, and generalized arousal that are evoked with aversive conditioning would tend to increase the "noise" level of irrelevant mental processes.[577] The ineffectiveness of punishment for MMI development has also been suggested by experimental literature.[578]

In conclusion, operant learning theory would be consistent with many of the findings of MMI research. It would suggest that accurate, immediate feedback and offering quality rewards to motivated participants would create the best learning atmosphere.

Social Learning Theory

Social learning theory states that people learn by observing and imitating the behavior of others.[579] This could explain the "Geller effect," where members of an audience are able to bend spoons after watching Uri Geller do so. Observational learning relies mainly on verbal and imaginal systems. People who code modeled activities into words, concise labels, or vivid imagery learn and retain behavior better than those who simply observe it. This would indicate that visualization techniques could be helpful *if* that is how participants code their thoughts.

Social learning theory also says that how well or quickly a person learns depends on a variety of factors. These include (1) the quality, or anticipated quality, of reinforcement; (2) the individual's inherent motivation; (3) the salience and complexity of the behavior to be learned; (4) the level of motor skill required; and (5) the presence and quality of performance feedback.[580] Motivation would seem to be of key importance. It increases how closely a person will observe a behavior, their likelihood of imitating it, the probability they will practice the behavior, and how well they will remember the desired response pattern. Thus, it impacts learning on a number of levels. Other forms of ability training, such as with biofeedback, have also shown the importance of adequate motivation if they are to succeed.[581]

Hasted noted the value of motivation in his investigations of metal-bending. [582] He tried to instill curiosity about the phenomena in participants and their families, or used their likelihood of feeling rewarded by the pleasure of seeing their finished articles, decorative or useful, in bent metal. However, he avoided using token economies as rewards because of concern that it might encourage fraud.

Explicit, challenging goals have been shown to enhance and sustain motivation.[583] Some MMI researchers have tried to address the issue of motivation by recruiting participants who were already interested in psi tasks, or creating inherently fun tasks set in festive atmospheres, such as Houck's spoon-bending parties, Batcheldor's sitter group séances, or computer psi games.[584]

Some RNG studies suggest that slower target generation may improve the hit-rate even when participants are unaware of the speed being used.[585] The reason for this is unclear. It could be a reflection of task complexity, due to experimenter effects, caused by the decreased psychological value and distinctiveness of the trials, or a result of some other factor.

Feedback is a key part of social learning.[586] It shapes and guides behavior, allowing successive approximations to the desired outcome. As mentioned before, this can be problematic with psi experiments, which often rely on target systems where a certain number of "hits" are due to random chance.[587] This makes it hard to know which subtle aspects that participants are "learning" are necessary to MMI performance or extraneous.

One solution is to have MMI tasks that do not have any possibility of "hits" by random chance. An example of this would be moving objects that are protected from electrostatic and magnetic effects, and sealed from air currents, such as energy wheels. Certainly, Martin Caidin had a lot of success at teaching himself and others to spin targets under a bell jar.[588] His training sessions with others may have taken advantage not only of modeling (as people watched him spin the targets), but also of participants being able to receive accurate and immediate feedback. From a social learning theory standpoint, Caidin's choice of target and method of instruction were well chosen.

SELF-EFFICACY

Self-efficacy refers to a person's beliefs in his or her capabilities to organize and execute the courses of action required to manage prospective situations.[589] It is not how well a person can handle a given situation, but how well they *think* they can handle it — thus getting back to the issue of belief. Albert Bandura noted that self-efficacy influences how people think, feel, motivate themselves, and act and is a significant and pervasive determinant of what an individual will achieve.

Bandura stated that people's beliefs concerning their efficacy can be developed in four ways.[590] The first, and most effective, is through what he called "mastery experiences." Achievements build robust belief in one's personal efficacy — as was noted by Caidin.[591] Bandura also pointed out that if people are only used to easy successes, they may not learn persist in the face of adversity. This ability to rebound from setbacks (which results from a resilient sense of efficacy) only comes from the experience of overcoming obstacles through perseverance. This would explain why people with certain personality traits, or "ego," might be more successful at doing a task that others say cannot be done — as in Caidin's ability to turn energy wheels.

A second way of creating and strengthening efficacy is through the vicarious experiences provided by social models.[592] How much impact modeling has depends on a number of factors, including the perceived similarity of the observer to the model. Of course, whether the modeled behavior is adopted depends on the anticipated satisfactions, the observed benefits, the experienced usefulness, the inferred risk, the self-evaluative derivatives, and economic constraints.[593]

One of the "belief" issues, which may need to be addressed with participants, is their anticipated outcome should they succeed at a psi task. There are very few current MMI stars who might serve as positive role models. Instead, such individuals are more likely to be viewed as "weird" or "crazy," or of taking a big risk of censure; provoking fear (which can have negative consequences); and providing a visible target for ongoing organized verbal and written attacks by psi disbelievers. Even if monetary reward could offset this negative anticipated outcome, the general social climate discourages MMI learning.

Bandura listed social persuasion as the third way of strengthening, or weakening, an individual's sense of self-efficacy.[594] He observed that it is far easier to undermine personal efficacy this way than it is to improve it. People who have been persuaded that they lack capabilities tend to avoid challenging situations or activities that could cultivate their potentialities and give up easily. Thus, it is easier for skeptics to convince individuals who do not have a high sense of self-efficacy that they cannot perform MMI than it is to convince would-be performers that they can do it.

The fourth, and final, factor in efficacy is how the individual feels, both physiologically and emotionally.[595] People tend to interpret stress reactions and tension as signs they may not perform well. Self-efficacy can be improved by (1) enhancing physical status, (2) reducing stress and negative emotional proclivities, and (3) correcting misinterpretations of bodily states. A positive mood tends to enhance perceived self-efficacy, while a despondent mood reduces it. It is possible that this plays a role in group metal-bending parties and table-tipping experiences, where performers have described needing to have an upbeat, playful atmosphere.[596]

It is critical to note that it is not the intensity of emotional and physical reactions that is important, but *how they are perceived*.[597] This might explain findings that, while many people perform better on MMI tasks in a relaxed (no stress) state, there are some individuals who do better with competition and tension.[598] Participants may vary according to whether they interpret their physiological state positively (as excitement) or negatively (as stress).

Efficacy plays a key role in motivation.[599] It not only determines what goals people set for themselves, but also how much effort they expend, how long they continue in the face of difficulties, and their resilience to failure. Strong perseverance contributes to accomplishment, while distress tends to impair it. This would again suggest the limited value of punishment in training psi.

Collective efficacy may be a factor in séance group macro–MMI. This form of efficacy refers to how the group perceives it is capable of working together to achieve its goals.[600] Although the self-efficacy of individual members of the group contribute to collective efficacy, there can be added factors of how much those in the group believe they can work together in a unified manner and their endurance should the group not get quick results. It is possible that the long periods of time that the Philip group spent working together aided their collective efficacy and allowed them to produce dramatic results which might not have been possible individually.[601]

MMI Models and Theories

Although it is quite possible that MMI and ESP are the same process called by two different names (an idea that we will consider later), the majority of MMI theories treat it as distinct from ESP. This chapter will look at various models and theories that have been proposed for MMI in chronological order, beginning with the idea of energy transfer.

ENERGY TRANSFER THEORIES

The earliest mind-matter theories proposed the involvement of an unknown form of energy or biological field.[602] Both Hatha Yoga and Chinese *qigong* theory fall into this category. With Hatha Yoga, proper diet, breathing exercises, and the practice of certain postures are said to improve the flow of vital energies through subtle channels in the body, known as *nadis*.[603] The *prana*, or breath and vital energy, is then manipulated to maximize health.

The Chinese energy theory believes that *qi* or *chi* can come from one of two sources.[604] The first is *yuan chi*, a primary "psycho-body" energy that is acquired at birth and is stored in the *dan tian* (below the navel by three finger widths). Unfortunately, *yuan chi* gradually disappears as one matures. However, it is possible to replenish *chi* by means of a second source — *qigong* practice.

Qigong is a system of exercises that allow a person to combine his or her *yuan chi* with *tian chi* (heaven *chi*), *di chi* (earth *chi*), and *ying chi* (*chi* derived from food and water) to form *zhen chi* (true *chi*), which controls all of life's energies.[605] The *zhen chi* is thought to be connected to everything, and can be guided by the mind to heal the sick or knock a person down.

The older European theories were very similar to Chinese thought.[606] They postulated that MMI was a biological semi-physical force, not necessarily linked to the mind, but stored in the physiology and activated by conscious or unconscious mental activity. Thus, the early French researchers spoke of a "psychic fluid," and even Mesmer referred to a universal energy that he called "magnetic fluid." This trend in thought continued in the early twentieth century. In 1909, Hereward Carrington proposed that MMI is a force of some sort stored or housed within the mind and body. He theorized that this energy served a normal purpose, such as homeostasis, within the organism.

In 1939, a neuropsychiatrist named Wilhelm Reich claimed to discover "orgone energy."[607] This was said to be a mass-free primordial energy that operated throughout the universe as the basic life energy. He went beyond the Chinese theory of *chi* by proposing that this cosmic energy governed the entire organism, and was expressed in the emotions and the biophysical movement of the organs. Reich believed that orgone energy was contained in the body fluids, rather like the magnetic fluid proposed by Mesmer in the eighteenth century.[608] However, unlike Mesmer, Reich felt that this energy could be freed up by mobilizing the patient's emotions. Orgone energy was also considered to be sexual energy — the basis of Freud's concept of libido.[609]

Reich believed that anxiety was sometimes expressed as muscle rigidity, or body armor, and could act to inhibit the orgone current.[610] Sexual excitation, on the other hand, was said to promote this energy flow. His goal in therapy was therefore to help his patients break through their armor and experience a potent orgasm — which Reich viewed as a surrender to the cosmos and natural release of orgone energy.

Reich was a prolific writer, and made many valuable discoveries on subjects such as the nature of human sexuality, character analysis, and cancer research.[611] He believed that he could store up this universal energy in accumulators that could then be discharged into the patient. Reich also played a key role in getting Bernard Grad to begin his now classic series of anomalous healing experiments with Estebany.[612] Unfortunately, his development of orgone-energy accumulators and treatment methods brought him in conflict with the United States Food and Drug Administration (FDA). In 1954, the FDA filed an injunction against Reich that subsequently led to his imprisonment and death.[613]

In 1947, J. B. Rhine revised Carrington's theory by suggesting that MMI is the intermediate force linking mind, brain, and body.[614] Rhine viewed MMI as an energy or force that somehow translated thought into action. Thus, he thought mental energy directed nervous energy, which commanded muscular energy, which in turn moved physical objects. In 1953, Eccles proposed a nearly identical theory, that MMI was the interface between the mind and brain. Both Rhine's and Eccles' theories postulated that MMI had a natural function as a normal bodily energy, and explained the apparent ability of animals to perform MMI — although the experimenter effect would also account for any anpsi results.

Doubt was soon cast on these theories. If Rhine's and Eccles' theories were true, some believed that projecting MMI would interrupt the mind-body homeostasis, which has not been borne out by the majority of experimental EEG research.[615] However, an alternative explanation could be that psi is constantly operating in our environment (and possibly within ourselves) in subtle, unrecognized ways. Thus the larger, more visible manifestations would not be so much a case of "projecting" the MMI as shifting its intent and direction of focus.

In the 1960s, William Roll proposed that RSMMI was caused by psychic energy fields.[616] He based this on the fact that certain intentional macro performers, such as Kulagina, showed a diminished ability to move objects the farther they were from the target. Assuming this was not a self-imposed limitation (which is common among MMI performers), the implication is that the energy level decreases as the distance from the focal agent increases.

Based on his analysis for the object movements in the Miami case he investigated, Roll postulated that the force used in poltergeist activity is a rotating beam.[617] He found that object movements that were close to the agent tended to be short, radial (inwards or outwards), clockwise, outward and to the right, whereas object movements that occurred farther from the agent were predominantly long, tangential, counter-clockwise, inward, and to his left. Roll found a similar distribution in the Olive Hill case.[618] To account for this, he theorized that objects are caught up in an expanding and contracting rotating beam of MMI energy that is asynchronously radiated from two different positions in the agent's body. If one presumes that the sources of the energy originate from the two halves of the brain, and that the rotating energy from the agent's head moves from his or her left to his or her right, then objects in front of the agent would tend to be carried clockwise, whereas objects behind the agent would move counter-clockwise.

Based on his theory that poltergeist phenomena were due to a diversion of neural impulses from the body to objects in the environment, Roll predicted that an obstruction in the brainstem made these impulses deflect from the body to the objects, thereby causing their movement.[619] Bauman, a neurologist at the University of North Carolina, tested Resch and found abnormally fast transmission electrical impulses from the pons area of her brainstem. Because the pons may be involved (along with other parts of the brain) in selective attention, Roll speculated the faster streams of electric pulses may have amplified her capacity to focus on objects, and added that the abnormality may have been caused by an injury at age twelve, when Resch was pushed off the school bus, hit her head, and lost consciousness.

Although this is an interesting theory, the object movements seen in poltergeist cases do not always follow the patterns that it would predict.[620] Another problem with the idea of agent-generated fields is that some poltergeist activity — such as the movement of a four-hundred-pound storage cabinet in the Rosenheim case — would require huge amounts of energy.[621] The electrical currents transmitted through the brainstem are minuscule by comparison, whether "deflected" or not. Furthermore, researchers who looked for this by putting a hidden REG next to their target system found no such evidence of a psi field.[622] Thus, there does not currently seem to be much support for a rotating energy beam.

ELECTROMAGNETIC THEORIES

There have been a number of electromagnetic psi theories, most of which spoke of these fields as mediators for ESP.[623] Perhaps one of the earliest of these was Mesmer's animal magnetism theory. Although electromagnetic theories were popular during the early part of the nineteenth century, they fell into disrepute when it became clear that psi is not blocked by Faraday cages or magnetic shielding.[624]

In 1974, Persinger proposed that extremely low-frequency (ELF) electromagnetic waves carried telepathic and clairvoyant information, but not precognitive data.[625] In 1986, Persinger and Cameron extended this to suggest that some poltergeist-type phenomena might not be paranormal at all, but a result of electromagnetic fields generated by geological stresses.[626] They felt that the ELF portions of these fields could be particularly problematic, capable of inducing visual, auditory, and olfactory hallucinations. In addition, current surges with transient EMF fields could also be responsible for anomalous telephone rings, light-bulb malfunctions, and other phenomena that get interpreted as paranormal.

Interest in this theory grew with the discovery that the earth's geomagnetic field (GMF) affects biology, as do ELF electromagnetic fields.[627] Studies have found correlations between changes in planetary GMFs and some forms of unusual and abnormal human behavior. There is also some evidence that psi improves as the GMF decreases. Since geomagnetic activity produces noise in ELF waves, it was postulated that ELF waves might be the carrier for psi information.[628] This would explain the apparent correlation of low levels of GMF with more reported cases of telepathy and clairvoyance. Adding to the plausibility of this hypothesis is the fact that ELF waves cycle at the same frequencies as the brain, and have little attenuation with distance.[629]

Since seawater is excellent at blocking ELF and higher-frequency signals, it was realized that this ESP theory could be tested using the ocean as a shield.[630] An experiment was designed with psychics Ingo Swann and Hella Hammid in a submerged submarine. The experimenters found that psychic functioning was unaffected, indicating that at least the remote viewing aspect of psi is not diminished by distance, high- or low-spectrum electromagnetic shielding, or even seasickness.

ACAUSAL THEORIES

Jung's theory of synchronicity was one of the first acausal models.[631] Jung believed that it was futile to look for causal connections between synchronistic events and that psi was mediated by the archetypes, which are dispositions of the collective unconscious and not available to the conscious mind other than as symbols and images. Of course, this assumes the unconscious is capable of absolute knowledge, and that the archetypes can exert their influence on and create events extending beyond the percipient. Rao pointed out that it is difficult to imagine the built-in biases of the participants mysteriously synchronizing with the assumed bias of the target sequence.

Another version of acausal theory was put forth in recent years. Originally referred to as Intuitive Data Sorting, it is now called Decision Augmentation Theory, or DAT.[632] DAT proposes that REG results — and possibly all MMI findings — could be a result of ESP, with individuals using ESP to know when to start runs so as to take advantage of locally deviant sections from a longer random sequence. Thus, REG study results might not measure MMI at all, but rather be tests of precognition, with ESP allowing the participant or experimenter to pick the right moment to start their runs or data collection to get whatever results they want.

Ed May, Jessica Utts, and James Spottiswoode suggested that in at least some studies using systems other than the RNG — such as healing research with rats — information-sorting could also be a factor in obtaining the right participant pool to obtain the experimenter's desired outcome (whether significant or null).[633] Although DAT is an appealing theory and may well account for a number of experimental results, it does not explain how the information transfer occurs, nor does it seem to account for large-scale phenomena, such as object movement or materialization.

Mind-Matter Interplay Theories

The best models for MMI may be those of constant mind-matter interplay.[634] There is more than one way in which mind-matter interplay can work. The first method involves conformance. Conformance theory suggests that the universe will change itself to match the desires of the mind. Observational theory, on the other hand, postulates that either (1) the mind is informed of the right time or place to get its desired response by collapsing a probability wave (quantum theory) or (2) that the mind and the universe are one (the holographic model). Other theories that have emerged rely on quantum events, including entanglement and the ordering of quantum fluctuations. Thus, we have a number of different takes on MMI.

Conformance Theory Rex Stanford proposed the conformance model as an extension of his theory of Psi Mediated Instrumental Response (PMIR).[635] PMIR itself submits that the organism uses psi to scan its environment — just as it does with its sensory organs — to look for objects and events relevant to the needs of the organism, and any information that is crucially linked to such objects and events.[636] Stanford listed his formal assumptions as follows:[637]

1. The response aspect of PMIR can be psychokinetic in nature, irrespective of whether the information thus responded to is obtained through sensory or extrasensory means, or both.
2. The application of MMI to the target is guided by extrasensory means (i.e., ESP).
3. The mental or behavioral influence of an agent (abbreviated MOBIA, *see* Glossary) on a target person is a form of MMI.
4. MMI as PMIR is facilitated when the goal event is not in the conscious focus of the MMI agent, but has definite motivational salience, particularly if the goal event has recently been in conscious focus, but has just left the focus of consciousness without having been realized.
5. The most frequent PMIR function of MMI is MOBIA.
6. MMI can occur as a response to extrasensory or sensory information, which has never been in the conscious focus of the MMI agent, and can act upon objects, events, or organisms to accomplish effects related to such information.

Key features of this model are that MMI (1) is goal-oriented, (2) uses ESP as part of its data gathering process, and (3) can occur on an entirely unconscious level of awareness. What makes this model different from the others is that it postulates that MMI is independent of both energetic aspects and factors related to information processing.[638] Furthermore, it suggests that there are two forms of telepathy — "percipient-active," with the percipient actively scanning and obtaining information, and "agent-active," with the percipient passively receiving the information impressed upon his or her mind.[639]

A number of experimental findings are compatible with this theory. Conformance model fits with the idea of an energy field that continues for a period of time after the MMI performer has quit trying to influence the target.[640] Hence, it could explain the so-called "linger effect" that has been reported in some healing and metal-bending experiments. Also, there does appear to be a goal-oriented quality to MMI, whether one looks in the laboratory or in the field, where the MMI of poltergeist agents seems to be used to express hostility or resolve conflict.[641] Likewise, task complexity has not been an important factor in MMI performance.[642] Furthermore, participants do not have to consciously know what the task is in order to be successful — they only need to try to "make it come out right."[643]

However, this brings up one of the intrinsic problems of MMI research — separating the experimenters' results from those of their participants. If MMI is goal-oriented, then it is difficult to say whether or not it can occur entirely on an unconscious level, or even whether MMI can be retroactive, since the experimenter (who is presumably capable of MMI) is always conscious of his or her purpose in doing the study and wants to get publishable results.

Similarly, the "newer First Look" theory proposed James Carpenter is similar to PMIR, in that it says all of us constantly use ESP to get a "first look" at everything, and that the purpose of the unconscious mind is not to acquire psychic information, but rather to block out all that which is irrelevant.[644] As such, psi helps us construct our perceptions and experiences. Carpenter noted MMI would be a natural extension of this. He wrote:

> In general, I think that psi is unitary, a condition of basic engagement in an extended universe, and the engagement is based on intention. With our intentions (mostly unconscious) we act upon our perceptual/cognitive processes and act to include distant ESP information all the time. With PK we act upon our own central nervous system and set it in motion in terms of our intentions, just as my intentions are guiding my typing at this moment.
>
> It is the mind-matter bridge in our own CNS. With our intentions we also act immediately upon the object of intended action (I think it may be the case that the pressure on my keyboard keys diminishes slightly just before I actually press upon them in an anticipatory way, just as ESP works in an anticipatory way — but that experiment hasn't been done yet to see if that is so).
>
> I expect that PK, like ESP, is bidirectional, as apt in everyday experience to run counter to explicit intention as with it, and that the same psychological considerations should lawfully select which direction is chosen at any given time. Situations in which neither direction of outcome is any more desirable than the other will not show directional trends, but if it something that arouses serious interest we will see large deviations that vary in direction. If the thing is clearly secondary in terms of interest deviations will be small as with ESP. This is why Roger Nelson finds large deviations in the global network at times of great concentrated interest. There is no overall excess of either 1s or 0s, since who cares 1s or 0s, we only care about the inauguration or whatever and so unconsciously act to make random events more coherent.[645]

What psychological research there is seems to show patterns that are quite similar, and meaningful in just the same ways, as those found with ESP. This means that MMI would simply be one of many methods by which organisms meet their needs.

Quantum Theories Quantum theories of psi are of relatively recent origin, emerging from the insights of modern physics.[646] To understand them, it is necessary to review a few key concepts from quantum physics. First and foremost, a quantum state, unlike a classical one, can be described in terms of a combination of differing states, with a probability specified for observing each state.[647] The selection of a definite state is only determined by measurement, and the process by which this definite state is selected is called "collapse of the wave function." In the view of proponents of Observational Theories, collapse of the wave function can only occur when a conscious observer is involved.

Secondly, systems can reside in different complementary states. Complementarity refers to a relationship between two apparently contradictory concepts, which at the same time both exclude and complement each other (like yin and yang).[648] Both are needed to create a complete sense of the phenomenon. Examples of complementary pairs include particles-waves, energy-time and mind-matter.

Third, if two parts of a quantum system are linked, measurement of one will instantaneously determine the result of measurement of the other, corresponding part.[649] This is true even if the two parts are so far away that a light signal could not travel from one to the other in the time allotted between measurements. This relationship between the two parts of a quantum system was named "entanglement" by Schrödinger.[650]

In addition, the vacuum state is not an empty void, but a state where fleeting particle-waves pop in and out of existence.[651] These "virtual particles," which are mainly photons, only exist for fleeting periods of time. However, during this time they interact with ordinary particles and produce random fluctuations in their coordinates. In this way, the virtual particles may be regarded as the source of quantum fluctuations in the coordinates of ordinary particles.

Finally, there is no reason, based on current understanding, that time should move in only one direction. As noted before, there has been an increasing amount of MMI research suggesting that retro-effects are possible with a variety of targets.[652] Such "backwards causation" is somewhat mind-boggling, even if it only applies to probabilistic events and not those that have already been witnessed in the past.

Although multiple psi theories have emerged from quantum theory, we will focus on the three that seem to do the best job of explaining MMI. These are (1) observational theory (including the Holographic Model), (2) quantum entanglement, and (3) the ordering of quantum fluctuations.

OBSERVATIONAL THEORIES Observational theories are based on the uncertainty inherent in measuring quantum events and the premise that events remain in a state of probabilistic uncertainty until observed by a conscious person. These psi theories incorporate the axiom that that a person observing an event with a "quantum mechanically uncertain outcome" can potentially impact what happens.[653] Evan Harris Walker may have been the first to suggest this theory in 1973. Two years later, Helmut Schmidt proposed that the probabilities of otherwise random events can be influenced by the observation of research participants. In 1977, Houtkooper came up with the term "observational theories" as a generic label.[654] One of the advantages of this theory is that it explains the consistent finding that observing data *after* it has been recorded *can retroactively influence the results*.[655] Houtkooper observed that observational theories could also explain ESP phenomena, as a disguised "retro" MMI effect.[656]

The Holographic Model David Bohm created his own twist on observational theory by suggesting that ESP is actually a form of MMI, and that MMI arises if the mental processes of one or more people are focused on meanings that are in harmony with those guiding the basic processes of the material systems being affected.[657] This theory is very similar to Beloff's and Madhyamika Buddhist thought, which says that the mind creates the illusion of the world.[658] Unfortunately this theory has the problem not only of being vague—in terms of what "meaning" is, how much "harmony" is needed, what are the "basic processes" which can be affected, etc.—but also of not being falsifiable. Furthermore, it does not explain why the linger effect or field effect occur, or why some individuals, such as Nina Kulagina and Felicia Parise, expend so much effort to perform MMI.

Collapsing the Probability Wave The first quantum theory proposed by Schmidt and Walker is that observers are able to bias the outcome of random events by collapsing the probability wave at the moment that an event is witnessed.[659] Walker argued that "will" causes changes not only in the brain, but also in the world outside, as the observer and the observed are not independent.[660] Thus, according to this theory, MMI would work by the will of the participant and/or experimenter determining the collapse of the state vector for a physical system at the quantum level with macroscopically diverse potential states.

This theory is compatible with a number of experimental findings, including the apparently goal-oriented nature of MMI, and its independence from the space and time of the target. However, quantum theory does not explain why MMI sometimes seems to take on the attributes of a physical energy, such as is seen with the linger effect, the field effect, and the decay with distance seen in some poltergeist and macro MMI events.[661] Although one could postulate that these effects are the result of the MMI performer's belief system, there is enough cross-cultural evidence of certain patterns of MMI activity to indicate otherwise. The apparent ability of physical mediums to produce ectoplasm and perform materialization could also suggest that MMI involves a biological force, as much as a mental one.

If MMI is a "force" that can manipulate and reorder normal forms of energy, directing it to carry out our wishes, then we are still at a loss to understand how the mind acts to collapse the state vector of any indeterminate process, and what is "will."[662] Another problem is that Observational Theory is not falsifiable — i.e., you cannot prove that it is "wrong," which means you also cannot prove that it is "right."[663] Supporting experiments for it can just as easily be explained by competing hypotheses, such as experimenter effects or as psi-mediated data sorting.

ENTANGLEMENT has led to a number of psi theories. Atmanspacher, Röemer, and Walach proposed "Weak Quantum Theory," which suggests that ESP occurs through the entanglement of minds in a collective unconscious.[664] However, this does not seem to provide for MMI.

Walter von Lucadou proposed the Model of Pragmatic Information (MPI), which essentially assumes that all complex systems are entangled complementary pairs of structure-function.[665] Entanglement in turn means nonlocal correlations occur (note: this is not the same as causality). This model has been used to explain synchronicity and all forms of psi (including poltergeist phenomena) through system entanglement correlations.[666] The intrinsic variability of a stochastic system would determine the potential magnitude of what could happen. However, there is no transfer of information — everything is correlational.

Lucadou, Röemer, and Walach noted that this MPI would explain some commonly reported effects in the literature.[667] The decline effect would simply be the natural return towards the null hypothesis. Psi's so-called elusiveness would simply be a result of the "displacement effect," which is the tendency for phenomena to disappear when sought and show up in an unexpected manner or location. Also, the larger the MMI event, the less easily it could be reproduced.

Dean Radin agreed that psi could be explained by minds entangled with everything in the universe, including other minds and matter that is distant in space-time.[668] If we assume that every particle has, at one time, if only during the Big Bang, had the opportunity to interact with every other particle in existence, these separate but co-mingled particles do not pass signals between each other, yet remain correlated. Psi would not need to involve information transfer if your unconscious is not so much as a way of acquiring information as one of filtering it out. In this case, the unconscious mind would always be aware of what was going on in distant, correlated locations, and could, when it was of interest, not only attend to it, but also pass awareness of that data on to the conscious mind. As we saw with Conformance Theory, this would fit with James Carpenter's First Sight Theory, of ESP, wherein psi is used all the time to get a "first look" at everything. Nor would entanglement be limited to explaining ESP. Nonlocal minds could, through entanglement, influence whatever matter exists in an indeterminate state on the quantum level — even if this is true for a nanosecond. Moreover, time would be irrelevant.

Mind could influence matter whether it is in the past, present, or future. This is an intriguing theory, but would appear difficult to prove or disprove. However, recent results from Roger Nelson's global consciousness project suggest that locality is, to at least some degree, a factor.[669]

THE ORDERING OF QUANTUM FLUCTUATIONS Jean Burns suggested that MMI takes place through the ordering of quantum fluctuations, or, equivalently, by the ordering of the vacuum radiation that produces them.[670] This ordering takes place within the limits of the Uncertainty Principle and is very small. However, Burns has shown that subsequent interactions of ordinary particles act to magnify these changes, and can thereby account for micro–MMI. In addition, Burns demonstrated that macro–MMI can occur for targets (such as a tumbling cube) sensitive to their starting conditions.[671] In these cases, a small influence early on can have a significant impact on the outcome.

SUMMARY

A number of MMI theories have been proposed over the years. Energy theories fell out of favor because there is little evidence that any type of MMI-mimicking cosmic energy exists in the universe.[672] Research on electromagnetic waves showed that blocking ELF waves (the only frequency that was a likely candidate as a psi carrier) did not interfere with psi function.[673] Quantum psi theories of collapsing the probability wave, entanglement, and ordering quantum fluctuations currently represent the most interesting — and difficult to grasp — theories of psi functioning.

To date, the anecdotal and experimental data have not been able to tell us which model or theory of MMI is correct. We need a new perspective, which can provide us with fresh clues. One such possibility is to examine the nature and meaning of MMI. No technique is better for this than phenomenology. This leads us to the final section of the book, which will be devoted to experiential research — understanding the lived experience of performing MMI.

PART III

The MMI Matrix: Experiential Research

Now that we have reviewed the anecdotal and experimental data, there remains only one aspect of MMI to cover — its experience. Phenomenology is a rigorous method specifically developed for this purpose. It allows investigators to scientifically examine experiences and boil them down to their fundamental essential features.

The bulk of the data discussed here comes from work conducted in 1999 examining the lived experiences of eight individuals who performed what appeared to be MMI. Participants were picked to provide the greatest diversity of experiences possible, so that the end result would be more likely to reflect the underlying process. Their events covered a wide range of spontaneous and intentional MMI, including poltergeist effects, religious and spiritual MMI, sports MMI, anomalous healing, metal-bending, and human-machine interactions.

Before the study was begun, a list of nonleading open-ended questions and requests for clarification were prepared for use. The interviews were almost all performed over the phone (the only exception being Loyd Auerbach) and took place during the spring of 1999. Each interview began with "Please describe for me an occasion of performing PK. Tell me exactly what happened the way you would tell a friend so they would know exactly what it was like for you." Other questions included "Could you say more about that?" or "Can you remember anything more?" The sessions, all recorded for later transcription, ranged from 90 to 120 minutes. In a few cases, participants either spontaneously emailed other comments or responded to a request for clarification on something they had said during the interview. The study was not concerned with either the magnitude, or the ultimate reality, of the event. It only focused upon the experience itself.

Perhaps because of the altered states involved, these experiences appeared to be more fluid than normal ones and had fewer boundaries. As the experience itself was not linear (where A leads to B, which in turn leads to C), neither could it be described as such. Instead, the MMI experience consisted of constituents that formed shifting patterns. The term "constituents" was used, rather than "essential features," to emphasize the interactive and co-dependent nature of what made up this experience.

Most of the results described here are the same as were originally cited.[1] However, there are a few differences. Whereas the original study listed seventeen constituents, continued review of the data led to a decrease in this number to fourteen. This is because it became clear that (1) an altered sense of time was either an aspect of the ASC or a result of the MMI rather than a constituent; (2) the "release-of-effort" effect — where a performer has to stop trying to do MMI for it to happen — could be a form of, or substitute for, trust in the process; and (3) it may not be appropriate to consider ESP as a separate constituent of the MMI experience because even though remote viewing, telepathy, and precognition can occur during these experiences, ESP and MMI may be the same thing by two names. Many performers speak of ESP and MMI as identical experiences, suggesting they could be one psi process. Because of this, descriptions of ESP were subsumed as an aspect of "knowing."

To appreciate the meaningfulness of the results, one must first have some understanding of phenomenological technique. The first section in this part of the book will review its history and methodology. The following sections will describe fourteen constituents of the MMI experience. These are (1) an altered state of consciousness (ASC), (2) connection, (3) dissociation from the individual ego identity, (4) suspension of the intellect, (5) playfulness and/or peak emotion, (6) a sense of energy, (7) physical sensations/effects, (8) focused awareness, (9) trust in the process, (10) investment, (11) openness to the experience, (12) "knowing," (13) guiding the process, and (14) impact. The constituents are *not* listed by order of importance. It is far better to think of them as the deeply intertwined components of an enmeshed system. The final chapters in this section will look at the possibility ESP and MMI overlap, possible MMI facilitation and inhibition, and a brief summary of what we have learned from the anecdotal, experimental, and experiential data.

Phenomenology

To understand why phenomenology was developed, one must first appreciate the concept of paradigms. A paradigm is an infrastructure of beliefs which underlies science and determines how we see the world around us.[2] It acts as a model to help us make sense of things. Furthermore, it determines not only what is true, but how truth can be determined. Thus, a paradigm is both an aid and a hindrance. It not only helps us make sense of what is going on around us, but also limits our perception of the world and what knowledge we can arrive at.

Every form of research relies on underlying (and often unexamined) assumptions which shape what is studied, how it is studied, and what conclusions are drawn from the results.[3] These assumptions are therefore critical. Assumptions intrinsic to paradigms define and limit what knowledge is possible and how the world can be understood.

The classical paradigm, which we have held since Descartes, is based on duality.[4] It says there is a subject-object or mind-body split that allows the fixed external world — which the proponents of this paradigm would say is the only world that matters — to be measured and defined in objective ways. The favored research methodology within the classical paradigm is experimental design, as it presumes to measure the world in an objective way. Science based on this paradigm is not interested in subjective phenomena.

The emergence of quantum theory started a paradigm shift.[5] Scientists suddenly realized that there is always some indeterminacy in our measurements, and the act of measurement itself can define and change that which is being measured. Physicist and parapsychologist Dean Radin describes the new metaphysics as one in which the universe is a single whole, with every part intimately connected to every other part. This ultimately limits objectivity, as an "observer effect" is inevitable when making an observation. Furthermore, it suggests reality can be contacted not only through the physical senses, but also through deep, inner, intuitive knowing.[6] Because the classical paradigm has no way of handling the material, a new technique was needed. What emerged was phenomenology.

Phenomenology is a rigorous qualitative and descriptive method that is used to capture the lived experience.[7] It was created by German philosopher Edmund Husserl (1859–1938), who believed that the meaning of things could only be grasped through the exploration of human consciousness.[8] Husserl felt that consciousness is intentional and that it is oriented toward a world of evolving meaning.[9] In his later work, Husserl developed his idea of the individual and his or her world as being an indissoluble unity. He saw the world not as the external environment, but rather the Lebenswelt, or life-world — the socially constituted meanings that we take for granted as common sense.[10]

Two influences enriched phenomenology.[11] The first was the existentialist movement — making it "existential phenomenology" — which brought the concept of the "lived-body" or "human-situated" experience. The second was Martin Heidegger's idea that the Cartesian subject-object split was a false distinction. He believed that people are intimately involved in a complex dynamic network of interdependent, ongoing relationships that demand response and participation. It is through this participation that our world comes into existence. Thus, Heidegger felt we are both the illuminator and the creator of our own world(s).

The existential-phenomenological approach is not without its own set of assumptions, in particular that identically named experiences refer to the same reality.[12] For example, the essence of the experience of loneliness is considered the same from one person to the next. An investigation can either focus on the general structure of a phenomenon (for example, loneliness itself), or on a process structure that describes the unfolding of the phenomenon in terms of sequential essential stages (for example, development and manifestation of loneliness). Afterward, anyone who reads the resulting description should be able to understand what that experience feels like.

The first step in performing a phenomenological investigation is to formulate a question, such as, "What is the experience of...?"[13] The investigator then gathers a number of naive descriptions from people who either are having, or have had, the experience being investigated.[14] There are three types of sources used to generate descriptions of an experience: (1) from the researcher's own personal experiences and self-reflections; (2) from the written material or words of study participants; and (3) from depictions of the experience in research, fictional literature, art, dance, poetry, etc.[15] The richer, more detailed, and more dramatic the experiential descriptions are, the better will be the researcher's chances of drawing meaningful conclusions.

The investigator (who is considered a participant observer) carefully follows a set of steps to analyze the descriptions to reveal the common elements (typically referred to as core constituents) that make up an experience. Investigators must set aside any presuppositions about what they will find.[16] This is done by laying out any preconceived thoughts and beliefs in as clear and complete a form as possible (called "bracketing"). Bracketing is not simply done before the interviews are begun, but occurs repeatedly throughout the data analysis.

The second method of preventing bias is the use of imaginative variation. This involves playing mental games with the material to see if they could have more than one possible meaning. Where a sentence is found that could have more than one meaning, the descriptions are checked to see whether other sentences can clarify it. If it still remains in doubt, the participant is asked to please explain what was meant, or "say more about that."

There are four stages to the data analysis.[17] First, the entire description is read from beginning to end as many times as are necessary to get a sense of the whole. Second, the same descriptions are read more slowly, noting each time that a transition in meaning is perceived. Reflection and imaginative variation are used to elucidate the psychological aspects that are involved. This leads to the delineation of a series of meaning units or constituents. Third, all of the units are reviewed for their underlying psychological insights. Finally, the previously achieved insights are synthesized and integrated into a consistent statement or description of the experience. In the final synthesis, individual themes can be clustered into general themes, while trying to ensure that no important aspects of the experience have been overlooked or left out.[18]

Phenomenology differs from many other forms of data analysis in that to be done well, the investigator must alternate back and forth between rigid analytic thinking and a global intuitive state. It can perhaps best be thought of as a kind of disciplined spontaneity.[19] Amedeo Giorgi noted that one must first find the meaning units and only after that, with continued analysis, figure out their full significance. As he put it, this is more about discovering what is than proving a preexisting hypothesis.

The end product of any phenomenological study should be a report that accurately describes the lived experience.[20] Thus, phenomenology is a form of content analysis that translates the everyday level of the life-text narrative language, through reflective analysis, into structural conceptual language that reveals the universally valid meaning of a given experience.

Phenomenology has been used to describe synchronicity, channeling, apparent ESP, NDEs, and exceptional human functioning in sports.[21] The work by Michael Murphy and Rhea White is particularly relevant. They used in-depth interviews to look at the qualitative state that an athlete experiences as the "zone" where he or she is capable of extraordinary feats, which sometimes sound suspiciously like MMI. Murphy and White noted that the zone often involved feelings of well-being, calm, peace, stillness, detachment, freedom, weightlessness, floating, ecstasy, power, control, being in the present, instinctive action, mystery, awe, immortality, and unity. Occasionally, athletes also spoke of time slowing down or stopping. Many of these descriptions — such as the calm, detachment, being in the present, an altered sense of time, and feelings of unity or connection — have also been described by MMI performers.[22] Furthermore, when we look at the constituents in MMI experiences — ASC, connection, dissociation, suspension of the intellect, playfulness and/or peak emotions, a sense of energy, the physical state, focused awareness, trust in the process, investment, openness to the experience, a sense of "knowing," guiding the process, and impact — we find that Murphy and White documented all but openness to the experience in their book on transcendent experience in sports.[23] Considering that athletes endure hours of training and painful ordeals in order to excel in their sports, it seems likely that they are open to the very experience that may result in their success. Thus, it would appear that MMI and transcendent experience in sports have a similar, if not identical, fundamental structure.

All of the following chapters that discuss key features of the MMI experience will follow the same format. First, there will be a short introduction to give the reader a general idea of what we are talking about. This will be followed by a brief review of what the literature has said about the topic. Then things get more interesting. We will hear from performers about their experiences in their own words. These quotes will help illustrate how the constituents have manifested in their experiences, including how each one overlaps with the others. It is hoped that reading these descriptions will help to bring home to the reader exactly what it is like to be there experiencing MMI. Finally, there will be a brief summary of the most important features of this aspect of the lived experience.

Altered State of Consciousness (ASC)

ASCs have long had the reputation of being helpful for all forms of psi experience. The word "altered" is not meant to imply a state that is abnormal or drug-induced. All of us experience a variety of "normal" ASCs on a regular basis, such as dreaming, road hypnosis, deep prayer/meditation, and the hypnagogic (on the edge of falling asleep) and hypnopompic (just starting to awaken) states.

The MMI performers interviewed frequently noted some degree of an ASC during their experiences. The ASC associated with MMI varied, but was often ineffable (hard to put into words) and involved an altered sense of time — most often of time being slowed down or stopped. Other constituents are often deeply enmeshed with the ASC, including feelings of being deeply connected to the universe and (rather than thinking or analyzing the situation) simply being and doing.

The MMI ASC was fluid, with amorphous boundaries. It was hard, if not sometimes impossible, to separate it from the other constituents. Furthermore, it flowed and changed as needed within an experience. Thus, the ASC changed in both quality and depth, ranging anywhere from a mild alteration in consciousness to a deep trance state.

The ASC appeared to be a key constituent. In some ways, it is easy to understand why. Its influence is complex and multifaceted. An ASC can enhance many of the other experiential constituents: it can make it easier to let go of the belief systems that make up our individual identities, helping us to suspend the intellect and connect more easily to the world around us. We will look first at what others have said about ASC and psi, before turning our attention to the specifics of what MMI performers said on the topic, and how their states of consciousness appeared to relate to the other constituents.

WHAT THE LITERATURE SAYS

ASCs seem to be integral to many psi experiences. As parapsychologist Carlos Alvarado noted, they have been associated with spontaneous and intentional psi from the times of ancient oracles on to the modern-day use of dreams, hypnotic states, and partial sensory deprivation.[24]

The dream state is probably one of the oldest known methods of psi-enhancement. Dreams have been used for divination (and in some cases for healing) for thousands of years by a variety of cultures, including in ancient Babylon, Egypt, Greece, Israel, and Japan.[25] Dreaming may also be used for other purposes. For example, Australian Aborigines have the Dream Time, an eternal Now, which is the source of everything and which appears to allow them access to paranormal information and abilities, such as of walking through solid stone.[26]

Early parapsychologists noted the association between the dream state and ESP in surveys of spontaneous cases. Mrs. Henry Sidgwick reviewed cases sent to the SPR in the late 1800s.[27] There were only a few that appeared to be precognitive, but all of those occurred during dreams. However, the relatively small percentage of psychic dreams meant that large numbers of reports were required for meaningful analysis. Fortunately, there have been several such studies over the years. J. C. M. Kruisinga of Holland analyzed 1,444 dreams, of which he felt 62 were precognitive.[28] Louisa Rhine compiled the informal reports of 3,290 ESP experiences from letters sent to the Parapsychology Laboratory at Duke University.[29] Approximately 40 percent of the cases were precognitive, while the rest were a mixture of telepathy and clairvoyance. She found that 68 percent of precognitive experiences and 35 percent of telepathic and clairvoyance ones occurred in dreams. The ESP experiences while awake may, or may not, have been during a completely normal state of consciousness, since there was no attempt to check for variations. The Institute for Border Areas of Psychology and Mental Hygiene at the University of Freiburg has also received over 1,000 reports of psychic experiences, half of which occurred during dreaming.[30]

The Maimonides lab performed a decade of formal research on dream telepathy.[31] Despite considerable variability between dreamers, it found that ESP seemed to occur. Van de Castle concluded that these studies provided "very encouraging evidence that telepathic incorporation of distant stimuli into dreams can be demonstrated under good experimental conditions."[32]

To date, there has been little in the way of research on MMI and the dream state. One of the few such studies was performed by McConnell in 1955.[33] Nine participants (including the experimenter) tried to program themselves before falling asleep to influence the fall of machine-thrown dice. However, only the experimenter had significant results — the other participants did not.

Hypnosis is another technique for psi enhancement with a long history, going back to the days of Mesmer. However, most studies have focused on its use in ESP. J. B. Rhine performed an exploratory study in 1946, and found that positive hypnotic suggestions improved MMI scoring.[34] More recently, Stewart, Roll, and Baumann showed that hypnosis could be used to reactivate poltergeist activity in an agent.[35] These successes may not be surprising given that many feel the unconscious mind is the gateway or conduit for psi. However, more data is required before firm conclusions can be drawn.[36]

Martial artists, Buddhists, and yogic masters have long reported that ASCs as associated with their ability to perform mind-over-matter feats.[37] Experimental research shows meditation appears to enhance MMI abilities.[38] Charles Honorton pointed out that if we think of psi as a signal-to-noise ratio problem, then reducing the "noise" would make it easier to pick up on a weak "signal."[39] This might also explain why situations involving mild sensory deprivation (as is used in the ganzfeld procedure) seem to enhance ESP success.[40] Meditators may learn to silence their thoughts and turn attention away from distractions in the outer world, while at the same time be alert and open and ready to receive subtle input.

Unfortunately, we still have limited experimental data on precisely how altered states affect MMI.[41] Julian Isaacs reviewed the self-reports of participants who were trying to learn metal-bending in an effort to uncover aspects of the MMI ASC.[42] He found that those who were more successful in his MMI experiments used an ASC that involved a loss of awareness of their body and their surroundings. Participants also variously described being alert with a passive, focused awareness, and in a calm, confident, relaxed state. At least one participant specifically tried to avoid becoming frustrated.

Irwin noted that before beginning treatment, anomalous healers often entered into an ASC, which he described as being one of strong, yet effortless, engrossment or absorption in their experience.[43] They employed a variety of methods to enter this state, including relaxation techniques, meditation, prayer, and ritualistic dance or other practice. At this point, they often described themselves as in an altered reality, where temporal-spatial, physical, and personal boundaries are no longer solid, but permeable.

Allan Cooperstein studied the reports of anomalous healers.[44] His findings reiterated those of Irwin. Once again, healers spoke of a change in consciousness that was sufficiently distinct, stable, and lasting to be an ASC. This ASC involves diminished effort, and absorption, whether on an object or inner processes. However, when attention was turned inward, there remained some continued awareness of the external world. Furthermore, Cooperstein noted that a key sign of this ASC was sometimes the distortion of time, often to the point of a feeling of timelessness.

Outside the laboratory, mediums often seem to produce dramatic, and genuine, physical phenomena while in a trance state.[45] However, there are also reports of them performing equally impressive events when their consciousness is in a normal or near-normal state. Moreover, Rex Stanford observed that ASC cannot be required for MMI, since much of the successful research done on the topic has been with participants in a "normal" awake state. The current experimental results, while tantalizing, do not allow us to draw a firm link between meditation and successful MMI performance.

Gertrude Schmeidler suggested the reason robust psi can occur in both "normal" and trance states may be due to a lack of appreciation for the full range of normal states and how they can shade into those that are altered.[46] These states are not discrete, black-and-white or clear-cut, but instead exist along a continuum that may constantly shift and adjust. A light trance can be hard to distinguish from a "normal" state (or may even be what a psychic would call their normal state of consciousness).

In addition, two highly psi-conducive elements can appear during in normal consciousness: intense focus and spontaneity. Intense focus blocks out stimuli that would otherwise be attended to and can be seen as a mild form of dissociation that occurs naturally when reading, thinking, or watching an engrossing show. Spontaneity represents moments of unexpected thoughts, movements, or ideas, which surprise us when they come. Both spontaneity and absorption may briefly pull individuals out of their normal reality-oriented state. Thus, it is possible that there are psi-conducive states of consciousness that occur in a natural way which are not recognized as "altered." When we look at successful methods of enhancing psi, most of them involve a long, leisurely introduction, positive suggestions that the technique will aid psi, and a period of relaxation while the participant waits for images or impressions to appear. It is possible that these characteristics more important than the ASC per se.

Michael Murphy and Rhea White studied the ASC known to athletes as the "zone," where exceptional performances can happen.[47] This is an ASC similar to what is described as the "flow" — the state in Zen archery of existing in the present without awareness of the self, where the archer is detached, calm, focused in a relaxed way, and at one with the target/process.[48] In the "zone," it is harder to fail than it is to succeed.

The description of the athletic "zone" has many features in common with the ASC noted by others thought to have MMI abilities, such as yogis and martial artists, during their nonordinary experiences.[49] Athletes described this state as one of focused concentration, withdrawal of attention from distractions, in-the-moment beingness, effortless absorption, a sense of unity, and a feeling of moving in harmony with the universe. These could equally be applied as descriptions of the ASC of yogis, and adept martial artists. Mountain climber Rob Schultheis compared extreme sports to shamanistic training rituals that allow the athlete to (at least temporarily) feel a sense of power and ecstasy.[50] Physical exercise is likewise used by Sufi mystics in dervish dances, and by many tribal shamans, both ancient and contemporary.[51] Thus, it is possible that there could be an overlapping mental state, whether it be called the "flow," a "peak state," or, more recently, the "zone," which can be tapped into for MMI performance.

Overall, the "zone" would seem to involve elements of connection, focused awareness, altered body awareness, and effortlessness, in addition to an altered sense of time.[52] Athletes may feel as if time is either moving faster, slower, or not at all. In some cases, they described a centered moment alone, with nothing before or after it. The moment-to-moment passage of time may be all that matters. In Murphy and White's chapter on altered perceptions, runner Steve Williams said he believed he could sometimes control time, such that others would appear to be in slow motion. Football player John Brodie also reported feeling as if others would go into slow motion, giving him all the time in the world to assess the game and act.

The issue of time seeming to change may be extremely significant. Retro-MMI experiments are beginning to alter our understanding of what time is, and how it may operate. If we think of time as energy, then there is no reason why it could not be an MMI target. At this point, it is unclear whether alterations in time are an aspect of the ASC seen in psi experiences, an effect produced through MMI, or both.

Aspects of the ASC

1. There may be a feeling of being in another dimension or alternate reality. Several MMI performers noted a sense that the normal rules no longer apply, or of standing between two realities. Winter Robinson said, "It's like you step into another dimension or something, just briefly." Stephan Schwartz described it as simultaneously having a sense that everything is both normal and extraordinary. He recalled:

> There's both mundaneness and extraordinariness to these things. All of the experiences I've had [are] like this. On the one hand, you're doing something that's mundane — I mean you're walking. But at another level, you're doing something that's quite extraordinary. And so you're standing at a threshold between two realities, which is a peculiar sort of synchronistic experience.

2. There may be a spiritual aspect to the ASC. Alan Vaughan felt that through accessing their own spirits, people could become aware of all dimensions across time and space (including discarnate entities). He stated, "I think they involve a spiritual level, and they also involve other dimensions. That the spirit is [connecting us] and that's why it can work because the spirit can go through the different dimensions of space and time." This may explain in part why Vaughan referred to connecting in the ASC as being like "a flash of divinity."

Robinson commented, "It's almost like ... I've moved into sacred space." Schwartz felt there was something special about the ASC that could be accessed with group intent. He said, "It's as if you've created a sacred space, only this isn't really a sacred space in that way, but it's definitely a ... transformational space."

Don Wigal reflected, "There's something spiritual connected with this." He added:

> Especially when I'm like with the birds or meditating on nature, flowers, or something to connect with nature or the elements, like a storm, whatever. It's wonderful to feel connected that way. And that becomes a spiritual, not necessarily religious, but a spiritual union.

In yet another place, Wigal said:

> And now these same experiences that I used to think were some strange biological/chemical kind of combination, now I know they might be more spiritual. And especially when I'm trying to meditate and these things happen ... it's become a spiritual experience for me.

3. Time may feel altered or nonexistent. An altered sense of time was often noted by participants. Time slowing down or stopping may be a function of the ASC or a product of MMI. In some cases, there was no sense that time even existed. Suspension of the intellect and an intense focus of awareness (with a relative blocking out of everything else) may also contribute to this. Vaughan said, "I would describe the state as beyond time and space," and "I lose sense of time."

Wigal similarly noted, "I probably lose sense of time.... I'm thinking of one time when that did happen. I let something burn on the stove." He also stated, "I've never said it this way before I guess, but this feeling I'm in when it happens is the way I think that the eternal Now is supposed to feel."

Annette Martin reported a complete lack of awareness of either past or future when healing — everything is now. She said, "There is no time ... and in fact I use that terminology a lot. There is no time."

Schwartz commented, "There is a kind of flip. I mean there are a number of these healing experiences and they're all the same. A kind of flip into this timelessness again."

On occasion, time was felt to exist, but have altered characteristics. Robinson recalled an anomalous healing experience where "it was almost like one of those things when things slow down," and "it was like a real shift in time." In addition to his timelessness experiences, Schwartz reported it as slowing down here:

> It was like many altered state experiences.... At the time you go through these things, time has a different quality.... You have plenty of time to go through things. Whenever you're in ... dangerous situations, where your life is threatened..... But in situations where your actions are controlling the outcome, there is a kind of timelessness that occurs.... Time stretches out.

4. There may be a sense of vast complexity. Vaughan felt that there can be a sense of vast complexity, which is difficult for the ordinary mind to understand. He explained:

> I can also sympathize with the physicists who try to describe, you know, ten, eleven dimensions, and they just say, well you can't picture this, so don't even try, you'll just get a headache. Our minds just aren't accustomed to dealing with that — certainly not American minds. Maybe Hindu minds could do it, because they talk about these other dimensions, and cosmic pulses of time over many thousands of years.

5. There may be a sense of "flow," "rightness," or being in the "zone." Angela Thompson Smith referred to the ASC used in REG experiments as "train of flow." For her, this is "a very flowing, relaxed state doing that." Schwartz commented, "You get into a kind of zone, and I was definitely in an altered state and had worked to get into that state."

6. There may be a sense that nothing is unconscious. Schwartz described the ASC in the following manner:

> It's expanded and narrowed. At the one hand, it's expanded because all of your senses are heightened. So, your data intake, or at least your data recognition — I think it's probably the latter — is greatly increased. And yet, at the same time you have the ability to switch between the senses you want to be focused on. Nothing is happening unconsciously. You are in the now. And so, nothing is unconscious.

7. The state may be similar to, or the same as, that of meditation. Vaughan stated, "Essentially I would go into a kind of self-healing meditation," and "I also do this in trance. In fact, it's usually stronger when I do it in trance." Wigal noted that his experiences occur during meditation. He recalled, "I would think the normal pattern of this is I am meditating."

8. The state may have an ineffable quality. Although the level or quality of the ASC may vary depending on the situation and the need, it always seemed to have a quality that could not be described with language. Smith, for example, commented, "It's hard to describe though. It was just a subtle shift, and it's very hard to put into words."

HOW THE ASC RELATES TO THE OTHER CONSTITUENTS

Connection: *1) Connection and the ASC may be inseparable.* ASC can involve the feeling of a merger of consciousness on a spiritual level and/or oneness with the universe. Smith said, "I can describe it as a state of immersion."

Vaughan likened it to "a feeling of being joined together on a spiritual level," and, "a joining of consciousness, a very deep one." He also noted, "I become connected to a greater reality."

Wigal reported the ASC as involving, "A spiritual, not necessarily religious, but a spiritual union.... That feeling I'm in when it happens is the way I think that the eternal Now is supposed to feel. It's a feeling of union, togetherness." He also said, "I feel very magnetically connected with things that are also alive, fish, or birds, or these appliances."

Similarly, Robinson noted that her ASC during spoon-bending was as follows:

> It's like ... and I almost want to say of oneness. Although I have been in that state of oneness and it's been somewhat different from what I'm describing here. But at the same time that's probably the best thing I can say. And I'm trying to see how to explain this..... It's like I am the spoon, I'm the person I'm talking to, there's no separation.

2) Focusing on the sense of connection may be used to access the ASC. Wigal often entered a psi-conducive ASC when meditating on his feelings of being connected to animals. He recalled, "One of the things I meditated on the most, I think, was harmony with nature." He later added that his experiences were particularly associated with "meditating on nature, flowers, or something to connect with nature or the elements like a storm, whatever, it's wonderful to feel connected, that way."

Dissociation: *1) Dissociation may be associated with the ASC.* Schwartz reported that in the ASC used for fire–walking, "you're definitely dissociated." Loyd Auerbach also noted a detachment that was suggestive of some degree of dissociation during MMI, particularly with sports events. He stated:

> There was a sense of detachment [that would] come over me every once in a while. It wasn't something I could bring on. It was first a sense of calm, and then it was like an ultra–calm in a sense at that point. And almost that I would watch, consciously watch, my body move on its own.

This also occurred during the ASC used during metal-bending. Auerbach said, "Being able to watch the, my hands just take this thing and tie it into a knot." The slip, of starting to say "the hands" instead of "my hands," is an indication of the dissociation that occurs during these detached states. Auerbach noted that other athletes could relate to the detachment in the ASC for sports MMI, and told the following story:

> The last time I went bowling was with Marty Caidin in Florida. And, even then, I remember that sense coming over me, by the time we got to the third game ....
>
> I had no way of knowing how to do it. When it happened with Marty, and his friend Ken, when we went bowling, and by the third game it was going on, and, like Marty and I were talking about that, because we talked about this whole detached sense. And he could relate to that. And he told me that other athletes he'd talked to related to that. And I have talked to athletes who have that same sense over the years, where they knew that they were going to hit that peak thing. And I remember saying to Marty, I'm going to get a strike right now. And he said, "How do you know?" And I said, because I FEEL it.... I walked up and threw the ball, and I turned around and came back. The first time I did it, he yells, "God damn it, that's PK!"

2) There may be sense of being in a dimension that transcends the ego. Vaughan observed that along with the ASC comes a sense of dissociation from the self. He said, "It's like I go into another world, sometimes, beyond my ego.... It's almost like I forget who I am."

Suspension of the Intellect: *1) The ASC may be associated with suspension of judgment.* Suspension of the intellect seemed to be associated with, or a product of, certain ASC. Schwartz noted suspension of the intellect in the ASC used in metal-bending here: "It takes you a moment to realize, wait a minute, you shouldn't be able to bend bars of metal like that! So while it's happening it's just, sort of, happening. But then, immediately afterwards you go, wait a minute!" With fire–walking, he said, "It slipped from the intellectual to the direct experiential."

2) There may be a complete suspension of thought associated with the ASC. Auerbach described suspension of thought for both sports MMI and metal-bending. During MMI parties, Auerbach stated there was "non-thinking about what was going on." He went into more detail about what this meant in the following passage:

> I feel I'm very easily able to just not be thinking. To just be absorbing, to just be observing. And, you know, it's one of those things that when your wife says what are

you thinking, you just say, "Nothing," at least Julie understands that that's possible. I've been around other women who like, how can you not? How can you be thinking nothing? Well I'm thinking nothing. My senses are observing, I mean there's information coming in, I'm just not internally commenting on anything.

Robinson remembered an incident where she had complete suspension of the intellect. She noted, "I don't remember what she said. In fact, it's almost like the two things I remember after that [are] I remember ... reaching behind the sofa and playing with these toy cars, and I remember saying goodbye to her." This suggests that there was no thought or memory of the time passing in between those moments.

Playfulness or Peak Emotion: *Emotions may be associated with the ASC.* Vaughan stated that with his MMI experiences:

> Well, I guess one thing that they all involve is for me to feel really good. It's just my technique. I know other people do it differently. But for me, that seems to be a key to opening up, to channeling higher energies.

Smith said of an event with a spinning bowl that It was a very light, playful, loving situation. Where we were discovering new things about each other. And a lot of talking. And, so ... it was not a normal state of consciousness."

The ASC (as well as the sense of MMI energy) may be inextricably meshed with euphoria or high excitement. Robinson noted sometimes having a feeling of being energized, not in the sense of a normal physical energy, but like the intense raw excitement of a manic or hypomanic state. She explained:

> It's like being in that state where you really need little or no sleep. You know, it's like you get on this ... high, because you're connected to a greater source, or a different dimension, or an altered state. And I know that, again, when I think of the times of what [it] would be like at Monroe, similar feelings, I would go for seven or eight days as I was training, feeling fine, not tired, sleeping very, very little.

Sense of Energy: *The ASC may enhance the sense of mental or physical energy.* Robinson felt mentally energized in this state, as described above. Vaughan noted more awareness of energy in the ASC, and stated.

> I become very aware of energy centers within my body, especially the solar plexus, becoming activated. And energy feelings running up my body through the spine. And sometimes down my spine, as well. I feel energy expanding around my head.

In talking about the energy, Schwartz commented, "In the altered state things are labile .... You can move them around, and mold them." He went into more detail about the relationship between the ASC and energy:

> For me it's about trying to get to the state where I can feel the energy coming in.... It's like a waterfall coming in, but it's like a garden hose going out from me. There's this huge inflow of energy and ... I know from experience that when I get to a certain feeling tone that it will work. And so, the game is to try to get into that feeling tone. And it's like trying to play a very pure note. Well tone, yes, but I don't mean tone as a musical tone. Although that sometimes happens. But it has a tonal quality. It's tone. It's nuance in a certain way. First of all, you have to become aware of energy in a certain way, and that takes a moment. You have to spend a little time doing that. You get IN to the state where you can recognize the energy. And then you have to FEEL the energy that is outside of you.

Physical State: *1) There may be a sense of being physically relaxed in the ASC.* Wigal said, "I stay very relaxed, it's a VERY deep relaxation." Smith described it as a "relaxed state." In another place she noted, "I would leave what I was doing at my desk, and once I closed the door in the experimental room, and set everything up, then there was a sense of being alone, relaxing, doing my own thing."

2) Relaxation may help maintain the ASC. Wigal recalled, "A couple of times when I was more relaxed, because there were no other deadlines or anything going on, I could sustain this. I could keep it going, like for a minute." Wigal also avoided things that might interrupt the state. He stated:

> I can move. I don't want to because I'm afraid that will cut it short if I move. I stay very, very relaxed.... So, I like for it to last as long as it can. And I think that I can prolong it by will. But not [long], only to a point.

3) The ASC may alter the body's sensory input. The ASC of fire–walking, in particular, may cause heightened or altered sense perception. Schwartz noted:

> All your senses are heightened. Although you have the capacity to be very selective about which one you focus on. In other words, you can hear the sounds, and know that the sounds are present, but if that isn't the point you have to focus on, you focus on the thing that matters.

Sensory input may also be altered from what would normally be expected. Schwartz reported:

> It was a very extraordinary experience ... because the subjective experience was like walking on popcorn. It went crunch, crunch, crunch. It gave way, but it went crunch underneath.... And so, it was a very odd sensation.

At times, the alteration in sense perception may be only partial, rather than complete. Schwartz reported of a fire–walk:

> On the third time I walked I got, not burned, but I felt heat just on the threshold of being uncomfortable, like you'd stepped on a coal. It was not general to the whole foot, which was very strange. I mean I remember thinking at the time it was very strange, because I'm walking on coals.... You ought to feel heat all over. But instead, I felt very localized heat between the first, the big toe and the second toe on my right foot, and on my left foot on the outside. It was very odd that you would feel that kind of localized, instead of generalized, heat.

Another way that the altered sensory input can manifest is as a decreased awareness of the body. The ASC frequently involved a narrowing of attention with a concomitant loss of awareness of the body and surroundings. Wigal noted that his awareness of distracting unpleasant internal stimuli diminished while in the ASC during energy flow. Wigal reflected on this in the following passage:

> You know I'm not sure that the pain leaves, I'm just completely unaware of it during those times.... I don't care about the pain, let's put it that way, so much when these things happen, but I also don't care about the tinnitus while these things happen. Whereas normally the tinnitus is very unnerving, and sometimes it's nerve wracking.

Focused Awareness: *There is often a narrowed focus of attention with a loss of awareness of surroundings associated with the ASC.* Martin simply stated, "I kind of feel like I'm in a void.... It's like a non space. It's so concentrated." She also noted that when she does MMI work there is "intense focus.... Nothing else is going on around me." Robinson observed, "To heal someone, bend a spoon, or whatever. It's almost as though I become, I get so ... focused." Similarly, with fire–walking Schwartz said:

> We went to a training program that ran in front of this, and it would probably identify the person who was teaching it, he was using the phrase cool moss, cool moss. You focused on that. So, it was a focusing technique to get down into the zone. And there is

any number of these techniques, but the point is to get you into a one-pointed state of consciousness where your attention is very clearly focused onto getting a particular task done.

Trust in the Process: *1) Trust in the process may facilitate the ASC.* This was a subtle finding. Nonetheless, having a trust in the process seemed to make it easier to access the ASC for performing MMI. Robinson described several instances in which there seemed to be a sudden shift in the state of consciousness at the moment of distraction. Since distraction is the commonest form of the release-of-effort effect (which may be a precursor or form of trust in the process), then we might consider these cases an example of trust affecting the ASC. One particularly dramatic shift in the ASC is described here:

> Where she says the turning point came was I'm talking to her, suddenly I look over
> behind the sofa, and there are these kid's toy cars. And I start playing with these toy
> cars. And, you know, I was distracted, I guess. I don't know. But what happened was I
> know that when I looked behind the sofa and saw these toy cars then my attention
> went from reading her, went to the toy cars, the energy shifted. And .... that night her
> epilepsy stopped.

Wigal noted of the MMI state and energy flow that "for it to be its most effective you have to just really let it happen." There is, thus, a sense of surrender to the experience, which suggests some degree of trust in the process.

Likewise, Auerbach became aware of the detached ASC because he learned that it meant success. He stated:

> I couldn't tell you when the first time that I had that experience was.... All I know is as
> I got older I took more note of it. I was more aware of having that detached experience.

Auerbach also reported doing things (or avoiding them) to try to maintain the state, suggesting that the state was an important (and trusted) part of the process. In one case of an ashtray being moved with MMI (which will be described in more detail later), he said, "I was watching it move, rather than jumping up and down and pointing at it. I knew I didn't want to do that, as I figured it would stop."

2) The ASC may be associated with both a "knowing" of success and a trust in the process. There is a strong sense in the following story that Auerbach trusted whatever happens during his ASC to do what is needed for him to get results. He remembered:

> I knew when I was going to get a strike. It had nothing to do with how I threw the
> ball, it had to do with a sense. I had this calm sense come over me as I was getting up
> to walk towards the alley, towards the foul line. And I just simply, literally, throw the
> ball and turn around.... And it was inevitably a strike when that happened.

Openness to the Experience: *1) There may be a sense of dropping barriers or making boundaries permeable to allow consciousness to expand.* Schwartz spoke of a deliberate opening up with anomalous healing here: "I'm trying to reach out, and trying to open my valve."

Vaughan also observed, "I would kind of open up my consciousness." He explained:

> Well, first of all, I'm aware of, like an armor around me, like a psychic armor, that's
> usually there, that I consider like an aura. And I just sort of let my defenses down. And
> I feel like I'm expanding my consciousness, it's growing. It stretches out farther from
> me, and it no longer prevents things from coming in, as it does ordinarily.

Martin indirectly referred to the fact that she is open during these experiences, by commenting that she closes down afterward. She said, "So we stopped, and I closed my hands and I do my white light thing and closing myself down. And had everybody else close themselves down."

2) The ASC may be associated with openness to the experience. Martin noted that in the ASC for psi there is "complete openness! And so it's that child-like behavior of trusting the world, of loving the world, loving everything, and not seeing negativity."

Fire–walking participants also indicated greater openness towards the experience during the ASC used than they feel after returning to normal consciousness. This seemed to be reflected when Schwartz noted, "I looked back at the coals after the last walk and thought, you know, conceptually, I mean ... logically, this is really crazy!"

3) There may be an openness to sensory information in the ASC associated with MMI. Schwartz described an opening up to sensory information. He said of the ASC that: "It's expanded and narrowed. At the one hand it's expanded because all of your senses are heightened. So your data intake, or at least your data recognition — I think it's probably the latter — is greatly increased."

"Knowing": *1) The ASC may enhance the sense of "knowing."* Robinson referred to the ASC as one of, "a place of being very open, and getting information .... like being in that space of knowing." Martin repeated Robinson's comment verbatim, and said it was, "like being in that space of knowing." Vaughan reported that he could receive psi information from other places, times, and dimensions when in his ASC. He recalled, "it's as if our ordinary reality ... is covered with a sponge, and this was kind of like seeing through the sponge."

2) The altered state may be associated with both a "knowing" of success and a trust in the process. The sense of "knowing" associated with this ASC (*see* above) and the ease of trusting in the process were again evident when Auerbach commented, "As soon as the ball let go there was no point, to me there was no point in watching the ball hit the pins, because I knew the outcome."

Guiding the Process: *The process may be guided by the ASC.* Controlling the energy flow may involve responding to a felt sense of being in the right ASC. Schwartz deliberately varied his ASC depending on what was needed for energy flow. He stated:

> For me it's about trying to get to the state where I can feel the energy coming in.... I know from experience, that when I get to a certain feeling tone, that it will work. And so the game is to try to get into that feeling tone.... You have to become aware of energy in a certain way, and that takes a moment. You have to spend a little time doing that. You get IN to the state where you can recognize the energy.

The ASC may affect the ability to focus awareness, and guide the energy, as noted in this passage where Vaughan recalled: "I also do this in trance. In fact, it's usually stronger when I do it in trance. In which my guide, Li Sung, takes over, and he seems to be able to focus and channel the energy, and focus it more and in a stronger way."

Summary

Experimental research and anecdotal material have long reported the association of ASC with psi. Although most studies have focused the value of using natural and induced states, such dreaming, trance, meditation, and partial sensory deprivation to enhance ESP, it is possible that the same facilitation occurs for MMI.

MMI performers described the ASC as deeply enmeshed with most of the other elements of the MMI matrix. In fact, investment and impact were the only two constituents that did not directly relate to the ASC. The most outstanding characteristics of the MMI ASC are an extremely narrowed focus of attention with a loss of sense of surroundings, feelings of connection/merger, and an altered sense of time. The ASC may also involve a sense of dissociation, suspension of the intellect, emotions of well-being or excitement, physical relaxation, enhanced awareness and control of energy, altered body sense perceptions, and a sense of "knowing." Furthermore, there may be a phase of opening up to the ASC and an implicit trust in the process. Various other aspects to the ASC may include feelings of being in an alternate reality, a spiritual aspect, a sense of vast complexity, feelings of "flow" or rightness, and a sense that nothing is unconscious. Some participants also reported the ASC for MMI as being the same as, or similar to, meditation.

The ASC appeared to be central to many of the experiences. It is easy to see why. ASC may enhance a sense of connecting to the universe or a transcendent realm, and allow performers to let go of their belief systems (which reflect their individual identities). This may explain why a person's normal beliefs and confidence (or lack thereof) may not always matter to MMI performance — they become irrelevant in a deeply altered state. Thus, it may be that beliefs are only important when the state of consciousness is normal or only mildly altered.

It is time to turn our attention to the other constituents. The following chapters will follow the same format as this one. In order to avoid repetition, there will be just a brief reminder of interactions that have already been covered in earlier chapters. Thus, illustrative quotes on how the ASC relates to connection will appear in the ASC chapter (which comes first), and only be summarized in the subsequent chapter on connection.

Connection

Connection is a term that can have many different meanings. For MMI experiencers, it was often more than just a physical or emotional link — although physical proximity to the target was sometimes helpful. There was often a transcendent level to what is occurring, whether spiritual or otherwise. In addition, emotional closeness to the target was far more important than any intrinsic quality of the target itself. Connection was closely intertwined with many other constituents and appeared to be a key component to successful MMI. Suspension of the intellect was the only constituent that did not appear to directly affect, or be affected by, connection.

Experimenters (especially those who teach MMI) frequently speak of the importance of some degree of merger with the target. Indeed, parapsychologists who have studied spontaneous experiences often emphasize the meaningful nature of MMI, and that in the real world it typically involves people and things where there is a strong emotional connection. Performers sometimes describe feeling deep levels of connectedness to their target or the cosmos, sometimes to the point of complete unity or oneness. In fact, being able to connect to the target — if only on an unconscious transcendent level — would seem a probable requirement for success.

WHAT THE LITERATURE SAYS

Many researchers have written on the importance of being able to connect to the MMI target on a nonphysical level, whether mental or emotional. It is not a new idea that the universe has a transcendent level of interconnectedness that would allow MMI performers to make that connection. Stanley Krippner noted, "Mystics from both Eastern and Western cultures have contended that we are linked to each other in subtle ways."[53] Lawrence LeShan pointed out the widespread nature of this belief, whether one speaks of physicists, mystics, or psychics.[54] He compiled quotes from all three groups which speak of a world in which everything is interconnected and inseparable. Furthermore, there are no clear-cut, fixed distinctions in time between past and future.

The idea of a transcendent level of interconnectedness may be an old one, but it is not incompatible with modern physics and has had growing acceptance. If we assume, then, that interconnectedness exists, the next question might be how the experimental literature suggests we can access it? One possibility, which comes from ESP research, is that emotional closeness is the key. Elizabeth Mintz and Gertrude Schmeidler observed that spontaneous cases of telepathy and precognition almost always involve individuals bound by love, friendship, family bonds, or a therapeutic relationship.[55] Laboratory tests tend to bear this out. For example, five-year-old children are more likely to perceive telepathic communication from their own, physically separated, mother than they are from the mother of a different five-year-old.

This agrees with what Louisa Rhine concluded from her collection of spontaneous cases years earlier.[56] There often is meaningfulness to the events associated with people in crisis. She reported that the spontaneous cases she looked at always seemed to involve close friends or relatives of whoever was dying.[57] The recipients were affected by these deaths, and the events themselves a sometimes poignant message.

This sense of closeness or emotional connection may be even clearer when a living person is facing death or disaster. As Louisa Rhine put it, "While one of them is affected primarily, the fact must not be missed that the observer is also very much concerned.... The common denominator one can be sure of, then, is not only a crisis, but a *crisis of the observer.*"[58]

The importance of an emotional connection has also been noted by experimenters who teach people how to do intentional MMI. Jack Houck, who is well known for his parties where participants try to bend metal through psi, said that the first step is to connect mentally with whatever you want to affect.[59] Connection does not need to happen on a conscious level — it is the unconscious mind's feeling of connection that is important. Houck felt the process could be assisted by picking up and holding a piece of flatware so participants would know exactly what they were trying to influence and where it was located. He also suggested asking the item if it is "willing" to bend.

One might find it puzzling why one would bother asking an inanimate object if it is willing to do something. The ability to connect is affected by how easy it is for the performer to relate to, or "like," the target. Asking the question "Will you do this?" gives the unconscious mind the chance to say "no," preventing a person from wasting time trying to do something unlikely to succeed. Macro-MMI performers have greater success with a target that they instinctively "like."[60]

The experimental literature also speaks of the importance of feeling a sense of connection to the target, although it is sometimes spoken of using other terms, such as having "rapport." Felicia Parise only started moving objects after watching the Russian star Nina Kulagina do it on film.[61] She spoke of developing "rapport" with the target through focused awareness.

At times, MMI performers speak of a level of connection that goes beyond rapport, to merger. For example, John Hasted and Julian Isaacs both stated that their metal-bending experimental participants often reported a sense of merging with the object or person that they were trying to affect.[62] Martin Caidin, who taught people how to turn energy wheels, also said, "You must become part of, merge with, what you're going to do."[63]

Anomalous healers often speak of merging with their patients. Harvey Irwin concluded that the step where there is a breakdown of interpersonal boundaries and merger between anomalous healers and their patients is a critical part of the process.[64] Furthermore, he described this state as a "sense of oneness" which is "characterized by an unconditional regard for and empathy with the healee and an unequivocal intention for that person's good."[65]

This result was replicated by Allan Cooperstein, who found anomalous healers experience feelings of interconnectedness to the world around them.[66] This merger involved setting aside personal identity, cultural beliefs, and values. Local consciousness became more global — sometimes even universal — allowing the performer to access non–local information and affect other people, places, and things. Cooperstein also felt that these feelings of unity were aided by performers becoming less aware of their own identities as they focused their attention elsewhere.

There are times when this merger or connection may be sensed as oneness with the target and/or the universe. Michael Murphy and Rhea White spoke of "unity" in their book on transcendent experience in sports.[67] This took a variety of forms, including mind-body merger, feelings of oneness with their equipment, the environment, others on their team, or even the entire cosmos. Separateness disappears.

Exceptional Human Experiences (EHEs) commonly involve an element of dissociating from a sense of individual ego identity and connecting to something transcendent or greater than the self. This may, in fact, be key to these experiences, and permit personal growth that would otherwise be impossible. Rhea White noted that experiencers felt a greater link to the cosmos and less association with their normal sense of ego identity.[68] This sometimes led to a long-term transformation, with feelings of connectedness to other beings, the planet, and beyond.

As mentioned before, poltergeist agent and MMI performer Matthew Manning said that he had two methods for producing MMI.[69] One of these, which he used for intentional events, involved a sense of calm and oneness with the universe, and mentally talking to the target he is trying to influence. Thus, connection and merger were an integral part of this method.

We have seen that connection has repeatedly appeared in the literature, both in the statements of participants and by experimenters. It has been described variously as rapport, merger, oneness, or unity. This constituent appears to be a crucial element for successful MMI. Although touching the target may be helpful, it was more important that there be an emotional-mental feeling of closeness to the target — or at least, not a conscious or unconscious aversion.

Aspects of Connection

1. There may be a spiritual aspect to the transcendent level of connection. Vaughan spoke of levels of connection involving a spiritual aspect. He reflected, "I think they involve a spiritual level, and they also involve other dimensions ... and that's why it can work because the spirit can go through the different dimensions of space and time." He also described deeper levels of connection as involving, "a feeling of being joined together on a spiritual level, a joining of spiritual energies." Vaughan further believed in interconnectedness through the transcendent level of spirit. He stated:

> I think the difference between a good and positive prayer and a spiritual prayer, is
> that the spiritual prayer actually involves spirit. And I think that's what's connecting
> people. And so, to me, talking about healing on a spiritual level is a very literal thing.

Wigal also reported being deeply and emotionally connected to a higher or spiritual source in the ASC where MMI is performed. There was sometimes a sense of loving connection to the target, as well. Wigal stated: "I think around that time during this experience, this is when I feel ... very magnetically connected with things that are also alive — fish, or birds, or these appliances. There's a certain life to electricity, I think."

2. The quality of the connection can vary. Vaughan implied that the level or quality of the connection could be affected by a level of investment in the process, possibly for both the recipient and the performer. He commented, "I know when the psychic connection works best is because the person has a genuine need."

3. Experiencers may not know to whom or what they are connecting. In one of Vaughan's distant healing experiences he admitted, "I didn't at the time connect it to her. It was only later, when she told me she'd heard me ... that I realized that I must have been there."

4. Target Type (inanimate or animate) does not seem to matter as much as emotional proximity. There is not a clear difference between inanimate and animate target experiences. Three (38 percent) participants out of the original eight in the study spoke of human (but not animal) patients as being able to determine whether or not anomalous healing was received and/or effective. What participants could connect to easily was more dependent on their belief systems and personalities than any intrinsic qualities of the target itself. Those that were "easy" to connect to were also "easy" to affect. But what was (or was not) "easy" varied from participant to participant. Wigal, for example, had no difficulty relating to, or influencing, inanimate objects, which he saw as valued partners. He reflected:

> There's something about electricity, or these certain electrical appliances that they seem to be alive. They seem to want to participate ... more it seems in our life than they do. And, we don't usually let them. But they're partners here, not as much as animals, but since they're man-made we seem to think that their energy is less noble, but I really do feel that ... they often really do want to be more a part of our lives than we allow them to.

5. There may be a sense of mutual understanding. Wigal stated:

> My birds get so respectful of this when it happens. They seem to know. They get very quiet, and like let's wait until this is over, and then they get back to their [chirping] ... and the appliances seem to do that, too. Now I know that really sounds crazy.

How Connection Relates to the Other Constituents:

Altered State of Consciousness: *1) Connection and the ASC may be inseparable.* ASC can involve the feeling of a merger of consciousness on a spiritual level and/or oneness with the universe.

2) Focusing on connecting may be used to access the ASC. Some participants seemed to use feelings of connection as a way of getting into an altered state.

Dissociation from the Individual Ego Identity: *Dissociation may occur in association with deep levels of connection.* Dissociation from the individual sense of identity often occurred with deep levels of connection. This could relate to having more permeable ego, or "self'" boundaries. In some cases, deep levels of connection made it easier to let go of the individual identity. Several participants spoke of merging with the target item or person, with a resulting loss of any sense of separate identity. For example, Vaughan stated, "There is a joining in with the person's energies. It's like you become one for a moment."

As previously mentioned, Robinson sometimes noted levels of connection that are so deep that they involve a complete loss of ego identity. She said, "I'm trying to see how to explain this.... It's like I am the spoon, I'm the person I'm talking to, there's no separation." Another time, Robinson stated that with the "target person it's like I become their body." Furthermore, she had a sense of being part of a joint body of information in doing psychic diagnosis (which sometimes involved anomalous healing). Robinson noted, in reference to her long-time professional partner, that when they "would start to work together, it was like one. We would be one body of information." This also seems evident in statements she made, such as "We have the body" instead of "I have the body."

Playfulness or Peak Emotion: *1) Connecting may lead to feeling certain emotions.* Sometimes there is an emotional, feeling component that occurred in conjunction with connecting to the target. Vaughan reported deep levels of connection as being like "spiritual love." He also noted that there could be a combined spiritual, emotional, energetic, and physical component at the moment of connection. Vaughan described this in the following passage:

Well, it was coming from my solar plexus, just like a flash of divinity. A thrill, a wonderful thrill. Well, like going down a roller coaster. You know, when you feel a thrill at first, not too much, just the beginning of it.... I mean the rush is just a descrip tion of the thrill. But it's an energetic feeling of the energy, maybe flowing out, or being connected to, someone else or something else.

2) Emotion may enhance connection. Emotions, such as love, may lead to greater feelings of connection. Although not directly addressed by the participants, Smith described a situation wherein emotion seems to be linked to a high degree of connection. She recalled:

I came here to Las Vegas about six and a half years ago, and met Dave, and when we were dating we were in a Mexican restaurant. This was something between us. We were very excited to be together, and really felt this lot of chemistry between us. And we sat in a booth, with our heads across the table, holding hands. You know, his hand holding my hand, with a chip bowl between us. One of those little aluminum bowls. And we were talking to each other, a lot of eye contact, and emotion, and the chip bowl started spinning and tilting [laughing]. And he said, did you touch that? No. Did YOU touch it? No.

Sense of Energy: *1) There may be an energetic quality to connection.* Some participants described connecting to the target as having energetic attributes. As mentioned earlier, Vaughan observed, "It's an energetic feeling of the energy, maybe flowing out, or being connected to, someone else or something else."

2) Connection may be felt as a shift in the energy. Schwartz noted that connection could be felt as a shift in energy in anomalous healing. He said:

It's a shift in energetics and you know that the connection's been made. You know. I mean you know it because energetically that's the way it feels. It's like two tones. You know when you have a radio and you have two tones together, kind of a wah-wah-wah-wah-wah [imitating discordance] sound? Or when airplane propellers, when you tune two airplane propellers, the engines, and they're in perfect sync and they sound together? But until that moment they're going wah-wah-wah? You know what I'm talking about? Right? That's what it's like. When you get it tuned, so that it's sort of in resonant frequency, do it where it stops going wah wah-wah, and it's so calm. Just calm. Then that's when the connection occurs.

3) There may be a sense of merged energy with connection. Vaughan described, "a joining of spiritual energies, and I'm visualizing or seeing this energy, you know, these energies coming from them and participating in them." There may also be a sense that connection enhances energy or leads to a kind of "group energy."

Physical State: *1) Connection may be felt in the body.* Vaughan experienced connection as an energetic feeling coming out of his solar plexus. In another place, he described his felt sense of connection in this way:

It's like you become one for a moment ... [first on] a visualization level, and then a feeling level. It's like I'm reaching out to embrace them. I'm always telling people that I'll send you a three-thousand-mile-long hug. And I really feel it.

2) Connection may be made through the voice. Martin said that she forms a conscious connection with her clients by speaking their names out loud (although this is not always required for a successful connection). She stated:

In all my work that I've done the first name of the birth name is the most important thing. That's all I need from somebody is their birth name. That's on their birth certificate.... So, if a relative or a friend is giving me the name, then there's a particular sound wave on the name, there's a vibration on the name.... It's like a direct connection, it's like a telephone connection.... I'm dialing right into the electromagnetic field of that person.

Martin does not like to use nicknames, last names, pet names or changed names. Instead, she uses their "true" first name, such as would appear on a birth certificate. Also, Martin noted that the way she says the name is different from the way you would do so in ordinary conversation. She explained: "There's a sound that comes out of my body at the same time that I'm saying the name. It's a very deep sound when I'm saying their name, and the breath has a very deep sound to it. It's very unusual."

Focused Awareness: *1) Deep levels of connection may be associated with a narrowed focus of attention.* Immersion is associated with a narrowed focus of attention. However, whether this is an indirect effect (mediated through the ASC), or a direct one on awareness is unclear. Smith described the ASC during macro–MMI event in this way: "It was ... not a normal state of consciousness, you know, awake, alert, aware of our surroundings. We were very immersed in each other."

Robinson described a discussion she was having with a priest during the time that a spoon melted. She noted being absorbed in the conversation with her friend, saying:

> We would just have wonderful conversations because he would talk to me about things, about how he thought the Bible was mistranslated, or stuff like that. We'd get into these really deep conversations.... And each time I would talk to him, we would find ourselves just totally engrossed in, you know, the what ifs of the world.

Robinson observed that it was during this conversation that:

> I was holding the spoon, and I was talking to Jim, and all I remember was at some point in that conversation, it's like when get you really get energized about what you're talking about, and, as I waved the spoon around, it just spun out. It was like it just melted.... The spoon, it just became liquid.

2) Focused awareness may lead to a sense of connection or merger with the target. Smith noted that in her computer RNG target work, she was often focused on the task and had a sense of being "immersed with the machine, not really noticing my surroundings, just paying attention to the task." This is stated again as "a sense of being focused on the machine and not worrying about my surroundings."

Wigal said that when he focused his awareness in meditation and triggered the MMI energy, it was associated with feelings of connection. He remarked:

> The normal pattern of this is I am meditating, and on some days, I think to myself that everything is right. This is the right harmony, the right time to bring on this other experience.... I think around that time during this experience, this is when I feel ... very magnetically connected with things that are also alive, fish, or birds, or these appliances.

Trust in the Process: *The belief in, or feeling of, a transcendent level of connection may make it easier to trust in the process.* It seems likely that the belief in the interconnectedness of the universe may make it easier to let go of the need for action and trust in the process. Participants often felt there was a transcendent level to the connection that they made with the MMI target. Sometimes this interconnectedness was also a part of a performer's belief system. Smith explained:

> My worldview is that we are all part of a greater universe anyway. So, that's my worldview. I love nature. I love animals, plants, and the rocks. When I was a little girl I loved to garden, you know, just used to love to plunge my hands into the earth. I've always felt at one with things, as well as people. So, there's always been, I suppose, a merging at some level with other things. I don't see myself as this tiny little discrete body that's me separate from everything else. I think that we are part of a much larger merging of the universe. Now that sounds very New Age, but I don't mean it in that respect. But I've always had this feeling, right from being a little girl.

Investment: *Investment by the performer and/or the target may enhance the quality of connection (see* next quote). Vaughan believed that investment — whether on the part of either the participant or the target person — could affect the quality of the connection.

Openness to the Experience: *1) Openness to the experience may enhance ability to connect effectively.* Vaughan noted differences in connection that seemed to relate to both investment and openness. He stated:

> I've found people it doesn't particularly work well for are, like, psychic vampires. They are forever grasping at other people's energy, and they'll start this story, "Oh I've been to 28 doctors," and so on, and so forth, and "Nothing's going to work." And you just feel this intense negative attitude. And that somehow they've karmicly arrived at this position for a good reason. And that you can't really interfere. There's not much you can do about it. But that's an extreme. Most people in the middle are, you know, generally open, and they're not demanding. They'll say, "Well I'm not terribly sure I believe in this, but I don't think it will hurt." Those, you know, are the people it generally seems to work with.

2) Feeling connected may make one feel more open. This was sometimes implied in the experiences, though never stated outright. This might explain some target preferences.

"Knowing": *Connection may enhance the sense of "knowing" or receiving information about the target or what needs to be done.* The "knowing" that occurs with connection may involve ESP. Martin, for example, views the patient clairvoyantly at the moment of connection:

> On the third breath when I send them the goop, of course I don't know what this person looks like, okay? But, what happens is I immediately get a picture of that person. And it's like they're a long ways away. I can see them, they're either standing, sitting, sometimes I've seen them in bed. I've described the whole room.... And what has been so extraordinary, especially in the class with a group, is that they will go right back and, you know, see that person, talk to them or find out what happened at that particular time. We always date everything and time it, the time it happened. And, that's where the person was, they were either in the bedroom, they were sitting on a chair, they were in the place. I mean I saw them where they were.

As Martin noted earlier, using the person's first name is "like a direct connection." Thus, her third breath is when connection occurs. The term "goop" came from a description her son gave Martin after receiving his first anomalous healing from her. She recalled:

> I was teaching a class in Los Altos.... I always had everyone sit in a circle and hold hands and send energy around the circle. And the energy, of course, was always white. And I would see it like, you know, those circular neon lights.... And everybody would just feel so wonderful.
>
> Well, this particular evening I was doing that, and I saw my son Scott's face.... And I thought ... that's really weird. And I didn't think anything [more] of it. Of course the white light was going all around, you know. So, we finish the class, and I go home. I walk in the front door to find my son laying on the couch with a blanket over him. And he goes, "Oh, Mom, I've been so sick since you've been gone." And he said, "Thank you so much for that white goopy stuff that you sent me." And I said, "What?" I said, "Say that again." He said, "Yeah, I was laying here," and he said, "and just suddenly I felt like I was covered in this white light, but it didn't look just like white light, it looked ... a little bit like cottage cheese and sour cream kind of all mixed up all together.... And after you sent it I felt so much better." He said, "I had a fever, and my fever went away."
>
> Well, I sat down. I said, "Okay, tell me more. Tell me what you felt, what it was like." I was trying to analyze the thing. He said it just suddenly came on him. He felt it come down from the top of his head, just like the white light, and go down his body. And he said it just felt so good.... And he was fine. The next week I told the class. Oh my Lord, they went crazy.... "Annette, do you think you could send that white stuff?" And I said, "Yes, let's just call it white goop."

Guiding the Process: *Levels of connection may be altered as a method of guiding the process.* Vaughan indicated that different levels of connection can be used, which suggests that this may be an aspect that is controlled depending on the need. When asked whether he could feel differences in level of connection, Vaughan said, "Absolutely." When asked what that difference was, he explained:

> I don't do this very often.... There has to be a good reason for it. Well, I think there's like a joining of the spiritual being, a joining of consciousness, a very deep one. Well, frankly I don't like to do that with the average person. But with this particular one person, she herself is very spiritual, so that was fine with me.

This passage implies that Vaughan can choose what level of connection he wants to use. This may, in turn, affect the process, allowing him to guide the outcome.

Summary

The importance of being able to connect to the target has often been reported by experimenters and experiencers alike. Those who teach MMI have emphasized "liking" the target and being able to merge with it. Performers described feelings of deep levels of connection, including complete unity, merger, and oneness.

Connection is deeply enmeshed other constituents of the experience. The ASC frequently has elements of transcendent interconnectedness. Deep levels of connection can lead to a lack of awareness of the self with dissociation and subtle energetic shifts. There are times when the body may aid in forming the connection (as with the voice), and, in a few cases, connection was physically felt. Focused awareness on the target seems to be important to (and affected by) connection. Investment and openness to the experience likewise appear to modify the quality of connection. One participant suggested that the quality of connection could be used to guide the process. Furthermore, there was sometimes a "knowing" that connection had occurred.

We have seen in this section that connection involving a transcendent level is a core constituent, intertwined with all but one of the others. In fact, suspension of the intellect was the only constituent that did not appear to overtly affect, or be affected by, connection. Conscious awareness of whom or what was being connected to was common, but did not always occur. Perhaps the two most important things to recognize are that (1) as with ESP, MMIs are meaningful events, which typically involve people, places, and things with which the performer feels an emotional connection; and (2) what it is easy to connect to may be idiosyncratic, with emotional closeness far more important than either physical distance or the intrinsic qualities of the target.

Dissociation from the Individual Ego Identity

In its purest sense, dissociation exists when people's behavior and experiences separate from their mainstream consciousness, stock behaviors, and/or self-identities.[70] Although dissociation can be used as a defense mechanism, it also serves a useful and socially adaptive role in everyday life. Thus, dissociation can be thought of as existing along a continuum with varying degrees of volitional control. The question in terms of psychological health may be "Do you control it, or does it control you?" In the case of the vast majority of psi practitioners, the dissociation appears to be both healthy and helpful.

The parapsychological literature has long noted the association of dissociation with all forms of psi phenomena. Dissociation from the individual ego identity is a common (but not universal) finding in MMI experiences. Performers often lose any sense of the separate self or awareness of themselves as they normally move through the world. Instead, they either exist without thoughts of the self, or feel merged with something that is beyond themselves. While dissociation is usually associated with suspension of the intellect, it sometimes occurs separately — hence, despite their similarities, the two are different constituents.

Finally, it is unclear how much dissociation comes first, as a primary element of MMI experiences, or shows up later as a byproduct of other factors. Dissociation can be the natural outcome of an ASC, merging with the target, suspending the intellect, and/or an extremely narrowed attention (which permits no thoughts of self). Some emotions can also make it easier to dissociate. In addition, where there is a strong sense of trust in the process, or a lack of awareness of responsibility (as in poltergeist phenomena or other spontaneous events), dissociation may be less important to the experience.

WHAT THE LITERATURE SAYS

One of the problems with the term "dissociation" is that it is associated in our culture with psychopathologies, such as dissociative identity disorder (formerly known as multiple personality disorder). However, Stanley Krippner pointed out that it can be a useful and adaptive skill.[71] Dissociation permits the control of pain, allows us to discover creative solutions through daydreaming, and permits us to "tune out" that which would otherwise be boring or offensive. In point of fact, all of us dissociate at times — it is a common process.

Dissociative trance states, such as hypnosis or automisms, have been associated with a dramatic improvement in psi performance.[72] There have also been reports that one of the sub–personalities in dissociative identity disorder can sometimes be highly psychic. Gertrude Schmeidler's speculated that disconnecting from one's normal reality-orientation makes it easier to stop analyzing and simply allow things to be what they are.[73] In essence, it permits that same kind of temporary suspension of disbelief as is seen in audiences during an engrossing movie.

Batcheldor believed there were three factors that determined whether table tipping was successful or not.[74] These were (1) belief (or its lack), (2) ownership resistance, and (3) witness inhibition. Ownership resistance could be diminished by a degree of dissociation.[75] Schmeidler also noted that being relaxed and comfortable (which could be considered a determinant of openness) may impact on our ability to dissociate and/or allow our state of consciousness to alter as needed for psi functioning.[76]

Michael Murphy and Rhea White described exceptional sports experiences in which dissociation was associated with merger with something, or someone, outside the self.[77] Athletes may not only become one with their fellow teammates, but also with their opponents. Martial artists, in particular, may focus on becoming one with whomever they are fighting. White noted that dissociation is a key feature of EHEs and stated that in many of these situations, "The experiencer becomes more dissociated from the ego-self and begins to associate more to the All-Self."[78]

Allan Cooperstein noted that anomalous healer experiences often include a sense of dissociation.[79] This can represent a shift from identification with the ordinary self to that of discarnate beings and energies.[80] Thus, as we saw in the last chapter, dissociation and an enhanced sense of connection to something, or someone, beyond the self can go hand in hand. Let us now turn our attention to what MMI performers have said.

HOW DISSOCIATION RELATES TO THE OTHER CONSTITUENTS

Altered State of Consciousness: *1) Dissociation may be associated with the ASC.* Several participants described a sense of detachment or dissociation from their individual ego identity during the ASC associated with MMI.

2) There may be sense of being in a dimension that is transcendent of, or beyond, the ego.

Connection: *Dissociation may occur in association with deep levels of connection.* Dissociation from the individual sense of identity was often associated with deep levels of connection. This could relate to having more permeable ego, or "self'" boundaries. In some cases, deep levels of connection can also make it easier to let go of the individual identity. Several participants spoke of merging with the target item or person, with a resulting loss of all sense of separate identity.

Suspension of the Intellect: *Dissociation is often associated with suspension of the intellect.* Dissociation and suspension of the intellect frequently occurred together. A subtle example is when Auerbach commented that his state was one of "Non-thinking about what was going on. Being able to watch the, my hands just take this thing and tie it into a knot." Non-thinking represents suspension of the intellect, whereas the slip of saying "the hands," rather than, "my hands," suggests dissociation was probably occurring as well. Since the intellect is the bastion of individual ego identity, it should come as no surprise that suspending the intellect and dissociation nearly always go hand in hand and only rarely occur separately.

Playfulness or Peak Emotion: *Peak emotions may trigger, or be associated with, dissociated states.* Auerbach, in particular, noted that he became detached during extreme boredom. He commented that this state is sometimes initially associated with a sense of feeling very calm, followed by an actual lack of emotion. It is hard to say how much this was a by-product of the ASC or related to the dissociation itself. Nonetheless, Auerbach acknowledged that being a detached observer is an important aspect of his experiences. He said: "I recall having a sense of boredom plus a sense of detachment. Watching it with kind of the Vulcan eye. The sense of that being extremely fascinating." This detachment seemed to be a prominent part of his sports MMI. Auerbach related the following story:

> A sense of detachment came over me every once in a while. It wasn't something I could bring on. It was first a sense of calm, and then it was like an ultra–calm, in a sense ... I would almost watch, consciously watch my body move on its own. So I would intellectually be aware — totally unemotional, totally removed from emotion — but intellectually be aware of everything my body was doing at that point .... And then I'd turn around and then it was sometimes gone. Sometimes it would last ... I'd get a couple, three strikes in a row, four strikes in a row. And, at that point, I do remember my friends if they were talking to me, I still had that very same sense of detachment. I was removed from the conversation a lot.

Auerbach also noticed detachment with metal-bending. He recalled:

> I remember getting that sense of calm and detachment before I'd do the first bend, and I was often, out of most — I don't even remember how many we did, but we did at least five parties, many parties, maybe more. And we did more with Julian Isaacs later after that. And [sigh] inevitably, I was the one. The first person to bend stuff. Also the first person to get called on it because people knew I was a magician. So, it was like, "Aw, he doesn't count because he's a magician." I remember Jack handed me a hacksaw blade and I tied it into a knot. I did that several times, or spirals, and hacksaw blades being brittle metal that wasn't really possible. Jack knew right away that I was not faking anything, couldn't be faking anything. I took a spoon, a bowl of a spoon, and pulled it over. I still have that spoon, in fact .... And actually I remember watching people, other people, when I was facilitating and not taking part, having this kind of blank look on their faces when they would bend things. And other times they were really excited and I could see them putting pressure on it. So, I really think that those other people also felt that sense of detachment.

Focused Awareness: *The shift in focus away from the individual ego identity may lead to dissociation.* As MMI performers narrow their focus of attention (often by concentrating on the target or energy flow), it seems to lead to a loss of awareness of other things, such as the self, resulting in dissociation. Schwartz stated, "You're definitely dissociated," and, "you're less focused on the self because you're trying to link in. And so, you have to become resonant in a way that you're not normally in your normal waking consciousness." Thus, there seems to be a combination of focusing on the needed ASC/connection/energy flow and a shift away from awareness of the self.

Trust in the Process: *Trust in the process may make it easier to dissociate from the individual ego identity.* Martin explained:

> All I do is focus on sending the white light. And it will do whatever it's supposed to do. And I have complete faith that it will. And so I think that that speaks so well about not having you in the middle of this. The ego cannot be any part of this. At all. And you, yourself, have to be confident enough to know that it's okay to do that.... It's not detachment. No, that word is not in my vocabulary.

Martin's faith in the process allowed her to let go of the self. She also felt that it was important to teach this to others, saying, "The ego cannot be there in any way, shape or form. And one of the things that I do in teaching my students is to make sure that their ego is out of the way." The fact that she never feels detachment, while other performers did routinely, is interesting. One wonders whether detachment might take the place of trust in the process for some individuals.

SUMMARY

It is unfortunate that the word "dissociation" has negative connotations in our culture, suggesting psychopathology. Dissociation never appeared to be negative or problematic in any of the MMI experiences described. Instead, there was a sense of normalcy to the temporary suspension of individual ego identity. It is impossible to say how much dissociation is a primary feature or merely a product of other factors — such as the ASC, merger with the target, suspension of the intellect, and a narrowed focus of attention. Certain emotions and a trust in the process may both make it easier to dissociate from the sense of self. Likewise, where there is a strong sense of trust in the process, or a lack of awareness of responsibility (as in poltergeist phenomena or other spontaneous events), dissociation may be of diminished importance in the experience.

Suspension of the Intellect

Suspension of the intellect refers to a lack of critical analysis and/or internal dialogue, which frequently takes place during MMI experiences. As we have seen with the other constituents, this is not an abnormal or unusual state. A temporary suspension of disbelief is a common occurrence while watching an engrossing movie or TV show. It may also happen naturally while meditating, dreaming, being exhausted, or feeling extremely emotional.

Most of the time, suspension of the intellect was closely associated with dissociation. However, it is listed here as a separate category for two reasons. First, dissociation seems to be a nonverbal sense of I-thou-it, which does not rely on the intellect. Second, some participants described suspension of the intellect occurring separately from dissociation. Some performers had a sense of "I" but no thought, while others had no sense of "I" but retained the ability to analyze what was happening.

It is possible that suspension of the intellect is a reflection of what happens when an individual moves from the analytical mode to direct experiential participation in the MMI process.

Alternatively, some participants felt it represented a shift towards global intuitive thinking. For that matter, this effect could be nothing more than a natural consequence (whether alone or in combination) of (1) the ASC, (2) extreme dissociation, (3) an intensely narrowed focus of attention, or (4) strong trust in the process. Regardless of how it comes about, a suspension of thought, which places one's belief systems temporarily in abeyance, appears to be a key factor for the success or failure of intentional MMI.

WHAT THE LITERATURE SAYS

The importance of suspending rational analysis has frequently appeared in the research literature, particularly among those who teach metal-bending and table tipping. For example, Jack Houck stated that over–intellectualizing blocked or inhibited MMI performance.[81] Kenneth Batcheldor similarly observed that the ideal sitter group atmosphere for table tipping was one where the participants were "alert but nonanalytical"[82]

The formal experimental research would seem to agree. At least three studies have compared how well participants perform MMI while engaged in nonanalytic versus analytic tasks. [83] The analytic tasks varied, but included verbal, math, logic, and analytic problems. Nonanalytic tasks involved things such as listening to music or sounds (not speech), solving spatial problems, perceiving depth, and imaging. When Rex Stanford pooled the results of all three studies together, he found that those in nonanalytic conditions greatly outperformed those trying engaged in analytic tasks, being successful at the p=.0014 level whereas their counterparts were unable to reach statistical significance, scoring at or near chance.

Murphy and White noted that the lack of conscious thought was often an element of EHE in sports.[84] There could be a spontaneous and instinctive aspect to athletes' performances where they may not even know how they did something. Instead, sports figures will use terms such as "unconscious," "in the zone," "without thought," or even "out of their mind." There was often action without prior thought — a case of being and doing without planning or analysis. The intellect was suspended.

Allan Cooperstein found that anomalous healers experienced a qualitative shift in intellect — although this did not always mean a decrease in or suspension of thought.[85] Sometimes thinking increased, while other times the mind is fell silent. However, when thinking did occur, it tended to be nonanalytical and non–critical. Cooperstein also noted that ambiguity was better accepted, which he felt suggested that a healer's worldview (and therefore beliefs) may diminish in importance.

ASPECTS OF SUSPENSION OF THE INTELLECT

1. There may be a sense of shifting to right-hemisphere-dominant functions. Vaughn commented, "I lose my ability to recall names of things and people." When asked to confirm whether there is a setting aside of the intellect (which was implied but not stated), Vaughan said:

> Very much so. And I know, for instance, in doing psychic readings I won't be able to get the simplest names, because they're over in my left hand, left side, I mean, but I'm over in my right side. And the same is true in PK. It's very much of a feeling, and visualizing, and energetic aspect, and the niceties of logic, names or dates, that sort of thing, just aren't there.

Similarly, Smith noted:

> I think the common thread that runs through them is that the cognitive left brain analyzing part of the mind is out of the picture for awhile, either through my getting

> very emotional, or deliberately occupying that part of my mind with something else. So
> I think getting that, you know, cognitive, verbal, the part that says oh, you can't do it,
> just disabling that, or putting it out of the way for awhile seems to help.

The intellect would re–engage after the event was over. Smith recalled, "Then there's a period of analysis, like what happened here, so I get back into a left brain mode, and then there's an acceptance. That it's okay. It happened."

2. Distractions may be used to keep the intellect out of the way. Smith felt the conscious mind does not need to attend to the task in MMI, and may, in fact, interfere with it. She attributed a failure to bend a spoon during a metal-bending party to "being the scientist. I wanted to see how much effort people were putting into bending their spoons." Because of this, Smith deliberately tried to get her intellect out of the way in intentional MMI through distraction. She recalled:

> When I was working with the REG, you know, the random number generator, it
> would be a relaxing, a physical relaxation, and a refocusing of my attention onto some-
> thing else, so becoming immersed in an article, or I'd take catalogs in often and just
> browse through catalogs, something fairly trivial I think to occupy the verbal part of
> the mind. You know, the part that steps in and says, oh, you can't do this, or ... over-
> riding that. And then letting whatever other part of consciousness needs to, needs to be
> awake, you know, to do that.

3. There may be an effortless complete lack of thought. Auerbach noted he often experienced effortless lack of thought during MMI. He said: "I feel I'm very easily able to just not be thinking. To just be absorbing, to just be observing.... I'm thinking nothing. My senses are observing — I mean there's information coming in — I'm just not internally commenting on anything."

How Suspension of the Intellect
Relates to the Other Constituents

Altered State of Consciousness: *1) The ASC may be associated with suspension of judgment.* Suspension of the intellect was associated with, or a product of, certain ASC.

2) There may be a complete suspension of thought associated with the ASC. Robinson and Auerbach both described a complete absence of thinking during some MMI experiences.

Dissociation from the Individual Ego Identity: *Dissociation is often associated with suspension of the intellect.* Dissociation and suspension of the intellect frequently occurred together. Since the intellect is the bastion of individual ego identity, it should come as no surprise that suspending the intellect and dissociation nearly always go hand in hand, and only rarely occurred separately.

Focused Awareness: *Highly focused awareness may prohibit thought and encourage suspension of the intellect.* Schwartz described a fire–walking experience in this way: "I'm in focus. I'm doing this. Oh, this is kind of interesting. I'm walking across this popcorn. This is really strange. This is a very strange experience, yet at the same time I am completely focused."

Wigal also spoke of this, and admitted that his focus on the energy flow can make it hard to use his intellect:

> I do pray, sometimes, when I'm in that same posture, but hardly ever when I'm in
> that emotion, when I'm in that rush. Because that demands all your attention! You have
> to, for it to be its most effective, you have to just really let it happen. And even prayer
> is distracting.

Trust in the Process: *1) Suspension of the intellect may make beliefs irrelevant and criticism nonexistent, thus removing blocks from trusting in the process.* Suspension of the intellect seemed to allow participants to shift to a state of being and experiencing, diminishing the importance of their belief systems. Judgment was not allowed to interfere with the process. There is a hint of this in the previously quoted passage, where Schwartz noted, "It slipped from the intellectual to the direct experiential."

Other participants referred to this more directly. Martin remarked, "I feel very child-like when I'm doing my work." When asked what was meant by the term "child-like," she replied, "In that children don't make judgments." She added:

> You have to just let it come, and you can't make any judgments. You have to let it just be there. Most important thing. And you have to trust that it is going to be there. And that's the hard part, you know, because we're so judgmental as human beings, and we're concerned, oh, am I going to fool myself, and this is not going to work.... What happens when I'm doing this is that's just gone. It's just erased. And it's like okay, here we are, we're just going to do this, and send the white goop, and it's just going to be there. And my trust and faith that it's just going to be there. And it will take whatever form it needs to take.

2) Trust in the process may make it easier to suspend the intellect. Those performers who implicitly "knew" and trusted the process to handle things for them seemed to find it easier to silence their thinking. Smith used distraction to get the intellect out of the way because she believed it was important to let "whatever other part of consciousness needs to, needs to be awake, you know, to do that." As with Martin's statement, this implies that she was okay with silencing her rational brain because she trusted the process to do what is needed.

SUMMARY

A number of researchers and performers have commented on the importance of suspending the intellect to have successful MMI. Suspension of the intellect was generally a subtle finding, but appeared to be quite important for successful intentional MMI. Perhaps part of why it was such a difficult constituent to tease out from the interviews was because when the intellect is suspended, there is no observer to remember (and record into memory) what is occurring.

Four major interactions were noted between this constituent and the others in the experience. First, suspension of the intellect almost always occurred in conjunction with dissociation from individual ego identity. Second, an ASC and a narrowed focus of attention seemed to make it easier to set aside the intellect. Finally, trust in the process appeared to be aided by the suspension of disbelief that occurs when the analyzing function of the mind is held in abeyance.

Playfulness or Peak Emotion

Playfulness is hard to categorize. Is it an emotion? A style of being in the world? A kind of openness? Or perhaps all that and more? It seems likely that playfulness is the latter. However, it comes closest to fitting in the category of being a type of emotion, whether as a milder form of hilarity or something else. In support of this is the fact that playfulness seems to have the same effect as peak emotions in facilitating MMI.

Parapsychologists have long recognized the association of high levels of emotion (whether repressed or openly displayed) with poltergeist phenomena and other forms of spontaneous MMI. Those who teach MMI have also commented on the helpfulness of a certain amount of playfulness when trying to get results. So, it is no surprise that emotion plays a valuable role in both spontaneous MMI experiences and early attempts at intentional MMI. Performers spoke of both high levels of emotion (or playfulness) and physical activation during in these situations. Trust in the process and ASC appear to fall by the wayside and are less needed — or at least less obvious. This trend changes as performers gain greater mastery over their abilities, after which they rely less on emotion and more on ASC and trust in the process.

One of the more curious and unexpected findings was that almost *any* emotion was capable of triggering spontaneous MMI — whether love, joy, anger, fear, sadness, ecstasy, boredom, excitement, hilarity, or playfulness. In fact, self-frustration was the only emotion that inhibited MMI. It is possible that this relates more to the impact of frustration on other constituents — such as creating difficulty suspending the intellect or dissociating.

This constituent appeared to interact with quite a few of the others. Some emotions, such as love, were closely linked to feelings of connection and enhanced openness to the experience. MMI performers often associated emotion with energy. Euphoria and feelings of well-being were particularly associated with MMI energy, which sometimes had almost a sexual quality to it. At times (especially with anomalous healing), the body reflected and contributed to the emotions felt by MMI performers. Narrowed awareness can block some emotions and it is equally likely that some emotions, such as anger and love, could enhance an individual's ability to focus.

WHAT THE LITERATURE SAYS

Peak emotions have long been associated with spontaneous MMI experiences, such as poltergeist activity.[86] Unfortunately, it is difficult to study spontaneous peak emotions in the laboratory. Nonetheless, there would seem to be anecdotal support for emotions playing a role in MMI activity. In addition, emotion is known to modify personality traits.[87] These traits in turn have the potential to influence a number of constituents to the MMI experience, such as whether the participant feels open to the experience or is able to connect with the target.

A variety of emotions have cropped up in phenomenological studies of EHEs and MMI. For example, Murphy and White reported that sports EHEs can involve feelings of mystery, immortality, control, power, ecstasy, and awe.[88] Cooperstein found anomalous healers spoke of feeling caring, love, joy, and harmony — sometimes to an intense degree.[89] Furthermore, some positive emotions — such as love, empathy, patience, hope, and determination — were deliberately cultivated by healers.

The usefulness of having a sense of playfulness in MMI has frequently been discussed (or implied) by parapsychologists. In 1940, J. B. Rhine and others published a book on the need for psi tests to be fun and challenging, like a game — at least to the extent it was possible while maintaining experimental controls.[90] Others agreed. Robert Thouless got his best results when competing with his son and other family members to see who could do the best MMI with dice.[91] He felt that a playful attitude fostered the right kind of investment. Thouless also recommended having an emotionally stimulating environment, saying, "The tense atmosphere of the hushed experimental room is likely, on the whole, to prove unfavourable [sic] for most."[92]

The importance of fun is not limited to dice experiments, but appears to be true for other forms of intentional MMI, as well. John Hasted, who before his death worked with metal-bending children in England, emphasized the importance of turning practice sessions into a game.[93] In addition, Kenneth Batcheldor wrote of the value of playfulness in minimizing ownership resistance for table tipping, explaining:

> The problem is to retain belief while avoiding the undesirable effects of resistance.
> In practice, one way — but I stress not the only way — of doing this is to encourage
> plenty of noise, laughter, singing, and trivial chatter. This can keep up belief by

preventing cognitive analysis while at the same time preserving a light-hearted tone. The sitters can laugh at their own fears.[94]

Creating fun and exciting situations with good controls that do not become boring long before the psi test is completed was difficult in the days before computers. Although many researchers tried, the resulting effect size of their efforts was distinctly underwhelming.[95]

The advent of RNGs and advanced computers — with their sophisticated graphics and ease of programming — has changed this. Recent years have seen an explosion of psi tests, particularly on the internet. These computer games have many of advantages for psi research — thousands of targets can be quickly generated, people can play them from anywhere in the world (creating an enormous potential subject pool), and they lend themselves well to statistical analysis. Furthermore, these tests can be challenging and fun, adding motivation to the task even as it can hide the testing aspect and any negative feelings that might arouse.[96]

Unfortunately, there is a problem with relying on games as our only source of data — ecological validity. If there is one thing that appears true about psi abilities, it is that they develop for a *reason*. They serve a purpose, even if that purpose is an unconscious one. This is particularly true of spontaneous MMI, where the events, when studied, are clearly meaningful. It seems likely that Broughton and Perlstrom's final statement still holds true, which is that although computer games may be well suited for psi testing, "the experimenter must be prepared to capture real-life psi, psi that is more subtle and more aimed at serving the needs of the participants than conforming to pre–set notions of success and failure."[97]

Finally, although playfulness and peak emotional states may facilitate psi, their presence is not required for success. A few participants reported feeling detached from their emotions when performing MMI. This detachment is also a common finding in sports EHEs.[98] Thus, there may be different ways of performing MMI. This would seem to be confirmed by Matthew Manning's account that he had two methods for producing MMI.[99] One involved an ASC, while the other, which is more spontaneous and difficult to control, is related to physical exertion and/or psychological irritation or friction. Thus, although emotion may facilitate MMI — particularly for spontaneous events and early attempts at intentional MMI — it does not appear to be a necessary component to the experience.

Aspects of Playfulness and Emotion

1. Strong emotions of almost any kind may facilitate MMI. Peak levels of emotion can facilitate MMI, especially for spontaneous events. This seemed to be true for a wide variety of strong emotions, including anger, frustration with others, sadness, excitement, and love. When it was reflected back to Smith towards the end of the interview that there didn't always seem to be an ASC in her experiences, she responded:

> Not always. It's ... an altered mood, as perhaps [when] Dave and I were holding hands. Definitely a different mood. I was very sad the time when things fell off the table after my remote viewing. So there are differences in mood.

Smith described her mood immediately prior to another event here:

> I was in a highly emotional state. I'd been in a disagreement with a colleague and didn't feel I'd got my point across. So [I] got very annoyed and frustrated, but ... it was in a professional setting so I couldn't vent my frustrations ... So I went to sit at the computer, to do some computer work, and as I sat there, fuming, there was a rock that was set there by the computer ... So, I thought that I was misunderstood, and I hadn't been able to explain fully what I meant in the situation. So I'm going, oh gosh, why couldn't he let me just explain what I meant!

Smith later admitted that there was, "perhaps some anger there, too." With another event she was feeling "sadness, extreme sadness," while with another there was "excitement." The only emotion that seemed to inhibit MMI, instead of promoting it, was self-frustration.

Auerbach described a number of cases where extreme boredom seemed to trigger both OBEs and MMI. He said of one event:

> I don't recall what the occasion was, but I distinctly remember being extremely bored .... So there was that crystal ashtray that weighed about a pound or two pounds, sitting on the dining room table. My cousin, Robin, was across the table from me, and my hands were kind of like planted on the table, just kind of resting above the elbow. The ashtray was maybe a foot or so away from that. It was closer to my one hand or the other — I can't honestly recall whether it was the right hand or left hand — but I do remember seeing what I thought was movement, and then watching as it very slowly moved across the table from one hand towards the other hand. The last bit of it my cousin said, "Did that move?" .... I think it stopped because my cousin noticed it moving. I think the moment was lost, the moment was gone. So, some sense of disappointment, but I was still bored by the dinner [laugh]. But the sense of detachment was gone.

Auerbach also reported MMI events that were triggered by anger or stress. The following story is an example of this:

> I zoomed home, raced inside the house, the apartment, put my key in, turned the lock, opened the door, slammed the door behind me, put my keys back in the pocket, started looking around my apartment, and I suddenly felt like something was moving inside my pocket. And pull out the keys and my apartment key was bent slightly and was still bending.

Robinson noted that high levels of excitement could trigger both metal-bending and human/machine interactions. She recalled:

> This was also at exactly the time when I was just getting back into all this, so it was a time that I bent the spoon and, you know, other things, fascinating things were happening. But it would consistently, like if I had ... been doing something that would create the energy, talking with people and getting all excited about something metaphysical or out–of–body, or what have you, I'd go out and the car wouldn't start. Would not start. And what I found was that if I went in and sat down and I got really calm, I could go start the car. It was just really strange. And it happened. You know we had it checked out. There was nothing wrong with the car. You know the little RX-7s they can plug into this thing, and they showed everything was fine. There was nothing wrong with the car. But it would be me.

2. The MMI experiences may have a playful, entertaining quality. Schwartz emphasized the importance of playfulness, saying, "Play is very important in these sorts of things.... It's entertainment at a certain level.... It has a thrilling quality." Smith believed that a light, playful, or joyous mood aided success during computer RNG runs — when in the zone, she felt a strong sense of relaxed pleasure and enjoyment. The playful aspect was indicated in her comment that "It was a game." Martin likewise noted a playful quality to her experiences, and said:

> I have to put this in, because this is important. It's like a child. And I feel very childlike when I'm doing my work. And you've experienced me that way when I do ghost work. Okay? It's very child-like. It's just wonderful fun. I just love it.

Smith reported strong positive feelings during and after her spoon-bending. She remembered:

> There was this feeling of exultation. Yes! And I was able to bend it. I'd seen others twisting it around, you know, making real twists in the handle, so I just twisted it and twisted it around, you know, the head of the bowl around and got it into a pretzel

shape. And then, of course, it goes hard. And I said whoa, I did it! So there was a feeling of achievement, and actually doing it.

How Emotion Relates to the Other Constituents

Altered State of Consciousness: *Emotions may be associated with the ASC.* The ASC can be inextricably meshed with a variety of feelings.

Connection: *1) Connecting may lead to feeling certain emotions.* Sometimes there was an emotional, feeling component that occurred in conjunction with connecting to the target.

2) Emotion may enhance connection. Emotions, such as love, seem likely to lead to greater feelings of connection. However, this is not directly addressed by the participants.

Dissociation from the Individual Ego Identity: *Peak emotions may trigger, or be associated with, dissociated states.* Auerbach, in particular, noted that he would become detached after extreme boredom. He commented this state is sometimes initially associated with a sense of feeling very calm, followed by an actual lack of emotion. It is impossible to say how much this was a byproduct of the ASC or related to the dissociation itself. Nonetheless, Auerbach believed that being a detached observer was a very important aspect of the experience for him.

Sense of Energy: *1) Strong emotions can increase (or in some cases diminish) the sense of energy.* Emotions may affect the sense of energy in both a positive and a negative manner. For example, excitement can be associated with feeling physically charged with energy. An upbeat, energized atmosphere, especially when combined with a bit of playfulness and joking around seems to be especially helpful for the production of macro–MMI and metal-bending. Vaughan noted:

> Now say with bending metal — and I've led groups doing this a number of times — again, it's a feeling of high hilarity. You make jokes, and ... just say outrageous things. They get them in a lighthearted mood. And again, now most the time I've done this, it's involved shouting at the top of my lungs like Jack Houck taught me.

Although, high emotional energy was helpful, it was not required for MMI. Vaughan remembered:

> [One time] my throat was kind of ticklish, and I didn't really want to shout, so I led the group in a chant, just a harmonious chant. And that worked just as well. And one person later told me, now when I could hear that chant going "bend," then the metal would become soft, at that moment, and it would be real easy just to bend with your fingers.

A sense of playfulness and joking around may enhance the sense of energy. Vaughan thought this was a large part of his success table tipping. He explained:

> Like table tilting with Russell Targ, it was a matter of becoming excited. And sort of a feeling of hilarity, or ... humorous, definitely humorous. They had tried with a number of sessions before, without any results.... I thought they were all, well they're overly solid, of course. And I led a group, you know, doing a lot of shouting, and making jokes. We were trying to conjure Maxwell's entity, whom I called Max, I figured that would be his name. Come on Max, you can do it! And so on. And quickly began to feel an energy flow around, around the group of us putting our hands on top of the table. And within a few minutes, I'd say within ten minutes, it began to feel like glue. Sort of a gluey energy that was flowing through. And then the table would begin to rise, or rock back and forth, and make cracking noises. And it would proceed to the point, where with only our fingertips on top of the table, the table would rise up. And this was a substantial weight. I mean this was a regular kitchen table, it wasn't a card

table, or anything like that. And I was intrigued one day — oh we did this for about five sessions — until the table reared up on one leg, and it broke.

Fear and hostility, either in the target person or bystanders, and/or defensiveness in the performer, may block MMI energy. Vaughan noted:

> When you have a group of people who are very positive, are open, and enthusiastic, then it works. Where if you have a group of skeptics standing around looking, sort of daring you to, saying this is unnatural or foolish ... then it doesn't work. There's no energy. It's just dead.

Auerbach recalled an event in the ASPR lab wherein his anger appeared to manifest as felt energy: He reported:

> Something rose up inside me and I could feel it going out, and it broke the infrared beam. It was like a wave of energy, of, you know, heat almost, coming across my body, going out through my hand. So, it was as if I was popping it up and putting it out.

When asked what this energy was associated with, Auerbach replied firmly, "Anger. It was definitely anger. There's no question about it."

Smith felt MMI involved an energy generated by intense emotion. She gave an example of this when describing a particularly intense remote viewing session:

> I did what is called an extended remote viewing, which is sitting or lying down in a relaxed state, and allowing the consciousness to access the information. And, so, saw the plane, saw the pilot, saw him come down, and I was able to cue myself to remember what I am perceiving. And, as he came down, I said I've to follow him to see where he goes.... And it was a very, very emotional scene, because he'd lost his glasses, his uniform was very wet. He knew he'd never see his family again. He went down on his knees by a river and I stayed with him through that experience, and, he died. It was a very, very emotional experience and I was crying. And, as I terminated the experience, a plant that was hanging over my bedside table started swinging, stuff fell on the floor, and my cat, who was on the bed with me, stood upright and with a very fixed stare was looking at the corner. Again, I think this was a psychokinetic event in which just the energy from the emotion caused that to happen.

2) The MMI energy may (along with the ASC) contribute to feelings of well-being and euphoria. Martin has feelings of well-being and exhilaration, which linger after she does anomalous healing. She said, "I feel wonderful. I don't feel tired. I'm never tired after my readings or sending the white goop. I'm exhilarated." Martin also stated that doing MMI is "a wonderful feeling. Euphoric."

Wigal also enjoyed the energy. He stated, "One of the reasons I did this so much is because that feels good.... It does kind of give a warmth right at that spot." Moreover, there were times when the sense of well-being associated with this energy reached the point of ecstasy: He struggled to describe what this was like below:

> It's something like the twilight after orgasm. It's that complete, relaxed, deep, satisfied, fulfilled emotion. I don't associate it with any of the emotions like fear or anger, or any of that.... You know what I once thought that it was like? When you've been out into the snow too long and you come in right as your body gets back to its normal temperature there's a moment there where you're in transition for ... a few seconds. And it's wonderful.

Wigal's reference to there being an almost sexual-release quality to the MMI energy has been reported before in the literature. In particular, Jean-Paul Girard (metal-bender), Eusapia Palladino (physical medium), and Wilhelm Reich (anomalous healer) all ascribed a similar quality to this energy.

Physical State: *1) The physical state may contribute to emotion.* This seemed to be particularly true for Wigal, who noted, "There's no pain, there's no distracting, irritating noise. It's a state of almost ecstasy. It's really wonderful." On the other hand, being physically drained can make it harder to feel positive or upbeat.

2) High levels of emotion may affect the physical state. High levels of emotion led to the body becoming energized. It is also possible that physical energy may contribute to or correlate with the energy that is produced by the emotions.

Focused Awareness: *1) Focused awareness can lead to the inhibition of, or detachment from, potentially distracting emotions during the MMI experience.* Schwartz that the extreme narrowing of attention during fire–walking permitted individuals to block out their emotions. He explained:

> You don't get frightened because you are so focused on what you're doing and what has to be done in order to get out of there without getting really hurt, that you don't have time. You get frightened afterwards. Or you think it's really weird, or it's really scary, or you're fearful of injury in the case of the fire–walk.

2) Strong emotions may enhance the intensity of focus on a person, object, or thought. Some strong emotions, such as anger or love, help to narrow awareness. This seemed to be the case in the incident of the spinning bowl that was described previously when there was "a lot of eye contact, and emotion." Smith later added, "We were very immersed in each other." This immersion suggests a combination of connection, dissociation from individual ego identity, and focused awareness.

3) There may be a playful quality to what is focused on. There can be a playfulness to the way in which attention is focused on a target or a distracter. Smith made a game out the way she handled her REG/RNG trials. She said: "If it was going in the right direction usually I just went okay, keep going, and I went back to my magazine. If it was going in the wrong direction, then I would pay some attention to it." However, "as soon as it started going in the direction that I wanted it to go in, then I would go back to my magazine. It was a game."

Trust in the Process: *Playfulness and a relaxed attitude may reflect a learned trust in the process.* A certain amount of playfulness (or a non–serious approach) may come about as performers learn to stop trying to think about things or force them to happen and just trust the process. Vaughan mentioned having fun, being open to the experience, suspending the intellect, and trusting the process all in the following story:

> That's the mistake a beginner always makes, is trying too hard. And with my software you can see it dramatically, with people scoring way below chance. Both in the ESP and the PK mode. And then once they begin to loosen up — and I went through this myself, it took me forever because I was being so super serious about this. And it took me a very long time to be able to do well with that. And I always think of Jack Houck's experience when he first started spoon-bending, that he was so fascinated by the first two, three times, the first couple times he tried this he couldn't bend anything because the intellect was really involved there. But then once he kind of loosened up and just said, well, I'll just try to enjoy myself, and then it happened.

It seems probable that a playful, relaxed attitude, rather like openness, also makes it easier to trust the process.

Investment: *A sense of playfulness may foster the right kind of investment.* As mentioned in the quote above, a relaxed, playful attitude fosters helpful investment.

Openness to the Experience: *1) Openness may contribute to the emotions that are felt during MMI.* Martin said that for her there was:

Complete openness! And so it's that child-like behavior of trusting the world, of loving the world, loving everything, and not seeing negativity.... And no fear whatsoever. I have no fear of anything negative coming whatsoever. I just won't let that. It's just not there.

2) A sense of playfulness may enhance openness to what is possible. A number of participants spoke of the value of playfulness, but Schwartz came the closest to explaining how it can lead to greater openness. He stated:

Play is very important in these sorts of things.... It's entertainment at a certain level.... When you are touching these aspects of yourself, which you don't normally interact with, very often there's a thrilling quality to it. Because you're doing it. Well, because you're experiencing an extension of what normal human functioning is supposed to be. And you know that it's genuine, because you're the one who's having the experience.... You know the authenticity of the experience. That's what I'm trying to say. But we'll go around and around about this. You know the authenticity. And so these things where you are having an extended awareness experience and you recognize that the limitations of reality that you have accepted are not the final limitations. That you can go beyond this.

Impact: *The experience may cause the performer to feel strong positive emotions.* A positive emotional impact was common for MMI experiencers. Schwartz confessed, "There's a thrilling quality to it." He also mentioned of another event that "it was a very impressive, very moving, experience, as well." Robinson acknowledged that her spoon-bending "was incredibly exciting!" Wigal described joy when interacting with a hardware store light display.

Martin explained, "The joy of being able to help someone is just unbelievable." She told a story illustrating the emotional impact that anomalous healing work has on her (and the person healed) here:

Someone came in and said a friend of a friend's child was in a car accident and he's in a coma at Stanford hospital and do you think you could help him? And I said, "Well my God, let's at least try, you know." So at the end of the class I did the whole thing, and sent the white goop to him and saw his face. Okay. Didn't hear anything back. About maybe a week later the person came back actually and she said, "I want you to know the boy came out of the coma, and he's fine." I said "Oh my gosh, that's great." End of story, okay?

About two months later there's a knock at my door at my home, and I open the door and there's this young man. And he goes, "You're Annette Martin." And I said, "Yes, can I help you?" And he goes, "I'm the young man who you brought out of the coma at Stanford Hospital. I saw you." Well, I thought I was going to faint on the floor.... I bring him into the house.... So he sits down, and I said, "Now tell me this again. Let me get this straight." He said, "I was in a coma. They thought I was going to die. They were going to pull the plug. And suddenly I saw your face, and your face was filled with light. It was light all around you." And he said, "I opened my eyes." Boy, I tell you we sat there and bawled our eyes out. I mean I just couldn't believe it.

Smith reported a wide range of positive emotions after MMI, including feelings of surprise, exultation, awed pleasure, amazement, validation, and pride. For example, during and after successful spoon-bending, she noted, "There was this feeling of exultation," and, "there was a feeling of achievement."

There are also times when the impact that MMI has on emotion can serve an immediate and useful purpose — by changing the mood from a negative state to a positive one. An example of this was when Smith made a rock jump. Beforehand, she felt, "very annoyed and frustrated" and "perhaps some anger there, too." This changed after the event to "kind of a feeling of awe. Of pride ... and that was basically it, just pride that it happened." Similarly, after metal-bending Smith commented that:

> My mood changed, the first part where I was observing other people, I was very
> quiet, watching other people, seeing what they were doing, occasionally focusing on my
> own spoon, is this thing going to bend? But after I bent the first spoon, my whole
> mood changed. There was a lighter feeling, more joyful ... more of a lighter mood.

SUMMARY

High levels of emotion, whether repressed or openly displayed, have long been associated with poltergeist phenomena and other forms of spontaneous MMI in the research literature. However, the role of emotion is not limited to spontaneous events. Participant experiences suggest that high levels of nearly any kind of emotion facilitate all forms of MMI, whether micro-, macro-, or RNG/REG work (whether it is ESP or MMI). In fact, self-frustration appeared to be the only emotion that could block or inhibit MMI.

The role emotion plays in MMI may vary depending on whether the experience is spontaneous or intentional. It is of obvious importance in spontaneous events, where peak emotions predominate, along with physical activation and a relatively normal state of consciousness. This changes with intentional MMI, particularly as performers gain control over their abilities. In these cases, an ASC often dominates over emotion and physical activation. Another distinguishing characteristic is that in spontaneous events, awareness is often focused on something *other* than the target — although it varies what that attention is on, whether a mood, thought, memory, another being, or even the emotion itself.

J. B. Rhine, Kenneth Batcheldor, John Hasted, Richard Broughton, and Jack Houck have all emphasized the value of incorporating fun and play into things if you want to have psi occur. Thus, it is no surprise that playfulness came up repeatedly in performer descriptions of their experiences, and often seemed to be able to substitute for peak emotions and ASC in facilitating psi. Although playfulness would seem to be an emotion — perhaps a mild form of hilarity — it also involves a state of mind with qualities of openness to the experience and a willingness to suspend disbelief. Therefore, playfulness may represent a MMI-conducive conglomerate.

Emotion/playfulness appears to influence or be enmeshed with many of the other constituents, including ASC, connection, dissociation, sense of energy, physical state, focused awareness, trust in the process, openness, and impact. There was a clear-cut association between emotion and energy in descriptions of MMI experiences. Love, in particular, may be closely linked to feelings of connection and enhance a sense of openness to the experience. MMI energy was associated with euphoria and feelings of well-being, and there could be something of a sexual aspect to this, reminiscent of what Girard, Palladino, and Reich have said in the past. The body sometimes reflected and contributed to the emotions felt by MMI performers. The focusing of awareness sometimes blocked emotion, and it is easy to imagine that emotions, such as anger or love, could equally well enhance the ability to focus.

Emotion is a ubiquitous and often complex aspect of human nature. Always changing and seldom pure or simple, it is a powerful modifier of personality traits and plays a role in all human behavior. In this, MMI is no exception.

Sense of Energy

MMI participants often commented on the involvement of some kind of energy in their experiences. They spoke of opening or closing to the energy, feeling it around them, sensing its flow, and actively manipulating it. The most detailed accounts of this energy showed up in descriptions of metal-bending and anomalous healing experiences, where the focus of awareness was often on the energy itself. Nearly the only time energy *wasn't* mentioned was during fire–walking. It is impossible to say whether this was due to the extremely narrowed focus of attention (with energy not being important at the moment) or indicated that MMI can be non–energetic.

Nonetheless, for the vast majority of MMI experiences there was at least some mention of energy, along with the implication that a transcendent level of connection was involved, which allowed that energy to be accessed. Furthermore, performers often referred to this energy as "subtle," involving a "higher vibration," and/or having an ineffable, transcendent quality which distinguished it from "ordinary" or "physical" energy. Some participants also felt that their physical bodies both contributed to and reflected MMI energy.

WHAT THE LITERATURE SAYS

Anomalous healers and martial artists have often reported some kind of energy in MMI.[100] Phenomenological reviews of anomalous healer experiences performed by both Harvey Irwin and Allan Cooperstein found that many practitioners believed a type of energy that was important to the process. [101] Some felt this energy came from their own bodies, while others experienced as coming from a transcendent, and sometimes cosmic, source, which was then channeled through them. Cooperstein noted anomalous healers were more apt to believe in unproven "quasi-realistic energies," which went under a variety of terms, including qi, prana, or an abstract kind of light or ray.

Athletes have also sometimes reported a sense of energy during EHEs.[102] In these cases, the energy could even involve a group quality or be a result of the group's focused awareness. John Brodie experienced this effect during some football games and described it as a unique feeling of power — like a rush of energy — that occurs when an entire team is completely focused on one goal. This concentrated awareness is said to make the whole team go up several notches and be capable of accomplishing amazing feats.

ASPECTS OF THE SENSE OF ENERGY

1. There may be a transcendent or spiritual aspect to the energy. Vaughan believed that the energy he used in MMI came from a higher source. He said, "I'm aware of, well let's call it channeling, channeling energy, from ... like the center of the universe, or cosmic, or a God-like energy." He also spoke of connection as involving "a joining of spiritual energies." Wigal noted a similar transcendent quality to the energy that he feels flowing through the spine, stating, "There's something spiritual connected with this."

2. There may be spiritual or transcendent limits to how the energy can be used. It is unclear whether this limitation is absolute or self-imposed. Vaughan told a story about the well-known anomalous healer, Gerard Croiset of Holland, who, "complained to me, though, that his mother died of cancer and there was nothing he could do about it. And so he felt there were strong limitations. That sometimes there's just nothing you can do."

Vaughan also believed there were some kind of spiritual or transcendent limitations to how MMI energy could be used. He thought it could explain what happened in the following story:

> I remember when Uri Geller first came to America in 1973, and I did tests with him. You know, I was fairly amazed. But then he went out to Las Vegas for a few days, and lost everything. He didn't win anything. And I had thought about that once. He sort of pooh-poohed it, you know, oh, well, it didn't mean anything. But I think it's fairly typical of people.... I would not describe Uri as particularly ethical or moral or you

> know. I think he is essentially, but it's not his prime motivation. His prime motivation
> was to become a millionaire, and that's what he's done. But he's still a compassionate
> person though.... His basic formula for the way he works is finding a win-win situa-
> tion. If he can help somebody find millions of dollars worth of gold, or oil, whatever,
> and then he gets a cut, then he feels that's the way to do it. In a way, I think it's sort of
> a spiritual obligation. It gets in the way winning at gambling, even with a small
> amount. But when it comes to tipping the scales, balance, it doesn't seem to work. So,
> there, there are definite restrictions on the use, or on the success of using, psychic ener-
> gies.

In addition to transcendent limitations to what can be accomplished, there are two other possibilities for what occurred in this story. If Geller had too much ego in the situation or the wrong
kind of investment it could have affected the other constituents and blocked MMI. If one cares
too much about the outcome, wants the gain too badly, this desire can leads to an active intellect, awareness of the self, too much effort, and make it hard to trust the process. However, it
is equally possible that this limitation on energy was self-imposed, because the performer unconsciously believed it was "wrong" to succeed in this manner.

3. There may be a warm-up period before the energy begins to flow. It sometimes took
a few minutes before energy was sensed as flowing. With anomalous healing, Vaughan stated,
"I'll put forward my hand next to their body, but not touching [it] and feel the energy…com-
ing through my hand. And it takes about one or two minutes to warm up to do that." This
brief delay (whether real or simply perceived as such) also seemed to happen in group situations. Vaughan recalled doing table tipping, where they "quickly began to feel an energy flow
around the group of us putting our hands on top of the table. And within a few minutes, I'd
say within ten minutes, it began to feel like glue."

4. The energy flow may not last for a long period. More than one anomalous healer
noted that energy may only need to be sent for a short period of time. Vaughan said that for
him, the energy flow may only last for a few minutes, specifying, "I probably wouldn't do it
more than seven minutes." Similarly, Martin recalled of one healing incident that "I did it for
about, probably five to eight minutes. I was afraid to do it any longer than that."

5. Accessing the energy can be effortless. Martin had an effortless sense of energy flow.
She stated, "I don't have to visualize it. It's just there. Okay? And it's always been there, ever
since I've been a child."

6. There may be a feeling of being completely surrounded by the energy. Martin
described feeling MMI energy all around her when working. This energy entered her through
the upper top of the head. She explained, "I'm bringing the white light through the frontal lobes,
or the crown chakra." Martin described the energy again here:

> I see this very large stream.... It's like a stream, a river, of white light coming down
> through the top of my head. It goes down and goes throughout my whole body. It goes
> out my feet and encircles my whole body. And so ... my whole auric field is encased in
> white light.

It is only after this energy was gathered up that she sent it on to the person she was trying to heal.

7. There may be a sense of group energy. It is possible that group energy (even when
only two or three comprise the group) may enhance MMI success — whether this is by effecting the energy itself, enhancing connection/dissociation, working through the belief system, or
by another process. Robinson noted, "It seems to me that, that my most ... profound PK experiences happen with other people involved somehow. So maybe it's a belief system of mine or
what have you. But ... there's always another person involved somehow."

Vaughan referred to a group kind of energy in table tilting, even when there is only one other person present:

> We were trying, just the two of us, and we put the lights on, you know, because ordinarily, we did this in the dark — I mean there was some light, but not very much. Well once after we put on the lights, Jeffrey and I could still feel the energy and we just put our hands lightly on top of the table, and it came zooming up, so ... there was kind of a collective glue, that kind of feeling.

Group energy, in the sense of two, may also have been involved in the spinning chip bowl, where Smith remembered, "We were very excited to be together, and really felt this lot of chemistry between us." She concluded, "I think perhaps it was the energy generated between us."

Schwartz also believed that being part of a group that has an intent to do MMI may enhance the energy — particularly when that group is upbeat and happy (*see also* "Aspects of Focused Awareness"). He talked about this here:

> And there were a whole bunch of people and so everybody was laughing, and again it was a group experience, where you get a lot of group energy. And you have that sense of being in group energy. And you also have a sense of altered awareness.... You're aware of the group energy. It's as if you've created a sacred space, only this isn't really a sacred space in that way, but it's definitely a ... transformational space. And there is the sense of a group doing it ..... I mean teams of athletes have that feeling sometimes where ... everyone just locks on together, and it's a resonance. That you're in a kind of resonance, one with another.

Martin suggested that group energy needs to be focused for it to be helpful. She recalled an experience involving a group of students, and said, "I felt that they were definitely contributing their energy, because they were very focused in their energy."

8. There may be awareness of an abrupt energy shift either just before the MMI occurs or at the moment of being distracted from the target. The energy may be felt to change qualitatively or quantitatively just before MMI success or at a moment when there is a shift of attention away from the target. This appeared to happen to Robinson in an anomalous healing experience. She said, "I know that when I looked behind the sofa and saw these toy cars then my attention went from reading her, went to the toy cars, the energy shifted." Similarly with metal-bending, she revealed, "That was probably one of the first times of ... feeling an energy shift, feeling something happen and then literally seeing it because ... the spoon, it just, like, became liquid." It may also have occurred in another incident involving a woman with epilepsy, although it is difficult to judge how much of the result was other-healing versus self-healing. Robinson recalled:

> I remember looking at the right hand .... It was interesting that the shift occurred again. This time the energy shift occurred because in my mind I saw, like, the Chinese that used to let their nails grow through their hands so they didn't have to work. I saw that. And so I told her that story .... And I remember she said, "Oh my God, I just had that dream" .... It was probably a week later when Al, the physician, called me and said did you hear what happened to so-and-so? .... He said every night, you know, she goes to bed she puts these splints on her hands, and she went off to Maine, and she forgot to put the splints on. She woke up in the morning and her hands were normal.

How the Sense of Energy Relates to the Other Constituents

Altered State of Consciousness: *The ASC may enhance the sense of mental or physical energy.*
Connection: *1) There may be an energetic quality to connection.* Some participants described connecting to the target as having energetic attributes.

2) Connection may be felt as a shift in the energy. A shift in energy sometimes seems to occur at the moment of connecting to the target.

3) There may be a sense of merged energy with connection. There may be a sense that connection enhances energy, or leads to a kind of "group energy."

Playfulness or Peak Emotion. *1) Strong emotions can increase (or in some cases diminish) the sense of energy.* Excitement was associated with feeling physically charged with energy. Indeed, high levels of emotion — of almost any kind — appeared to facilitate all forms of MMI, whether macro- or micro- (including RNG work). Likewise, an upbeat, energized atmosphere, playfulness, and joking around seemed to be especially helpful for the production of macro–MMI and metal-bending. On the other hand, fear and hostility, either in the target person or by-standers, and/or defensiveness in the performer, blocked MMI energy.

2) Playfulness can be an effective way of building up MMI energy. Vaughan spent time training with the anomalous healer, Gerard Croiset, in Holland and told how the man used jokes to enhance the energy levels:

> Right where Croiset was putting his hand I could feel this kind of tingling energy. And that seemed amazing to me. And, now he would [do it] for people, I don't know, maybe, five, seven minutes, and all the time he was joking.... the place was packed with people. And he's like a nightclub entertainer, telling jokes and carrying on, and building up the energy. And then, he'd take a break for twenty minutes, half an hour, and then go back to it. But he'd been doing this for many years. And for him, it was really essential, you know, to build up this energy.

3) The MMI energy may (along with the ASC) contribute to feelings of well-being and euphoria. Participants reported feelings of well-being, exhilaration, and even ecstasy during the experiences, which they sometimes associated with MMI energy. Furthermore, there was sometimes almost a sexual-release quality to the energy.

Physical State: *1) Energy may be felt in the body.* Energy could be felt in a variety of physical locations and manners. Auerbach described MMI energy once as "something rose up inside me and I could feel it going out, and it broke the infrared beam. It was like a wave of energy, of ... heat almost, coming across my body, going out through my hand."

Vaughan reported feeling MMI energy in the body in a number of ways. In one case, he noted, "I could feel this tremendous amount of energy flowing through me, really, really hot, and then for a long time." He likewise remembered feelings of physical/emotional well-being during the event, saying, "Yes, a feeling of well-being.... Which I associate with energy from my spiritual being." That the physical state was involved with this was clearer when Vaughan stated, "I can sense that there's a lot of energy that's been through me, and that I've used up a lot of energy, but I feel pretty good — usually better than when I started."

A number of participants experienced energy in their hands when performing anomalous healing. For example, Vaughan commented:

> Well, there's a feeling of the heat on the palm of the hand, but there's more than that. Sort of like a kind of a mild electricity, an actual energy, and usually the other person can feel it as well.

Martin not only felt heat in her hands, but also a sense of warmth and of activity in her frontal lobes with both ESP and MMI. At times the heat in her hands was intense. She stated that in one case, "My hands were so hot, they were just burning up." Martin added:

> I will [get] a modest sensation at my frontal lobes.... Like something moving in there. Activity. A lot of activity. When I'm doing police work, which is the most strenuous thing that I do, because I go on for hours, the top of my head will hurt when I finish. And it's because I'm bringing in the energy with information through there.

The energy effected Wigal's entire body. He described the feeing as being similar to Kundalini experiences in that his body had a tingly feeling of being charged with energy — rather like static electricity — yet, at the same time, pleasurable and relaxing. Wigal remembered "hair standing up on the back of my arms, on the back of my neck, like a balloon had just been rubbed on it, or something." He noted, "When this is at its, what I call the best, the whole body at the end tingles and feels like it's been charged.... The feeling like if someone touched me now they'd get shocked."

Nor was Wigal the only performer to report physical benefit from MMI energy. Martin noted she was energized by doing anomalous healing. She also stated (unlike some healers) that being in a state of ill health did not interfere with the process, but that she and her patient both benefited from the experience and she would feel better afterward.

Martin made one other interesting observation about the body after MMI. She said, "I do feel lighter in my body, too, when I finish doing this." She was uncertain whether this was a subjective weight loss or an objective one. However, one cannot help but wonder, given Palladino's massive recorded weight losses after séances, whether this could indeed be a genuine and measurable effect. If so, it brings up the intriguing question of how and why this is occurring, and whether the body could be transforming its own matter to generate energy for MMI.

2) The energy may have different qualities, which are reflected in the MMI performer's body sensations. The energy felt by the body can be experienced as having a variety of characteristics, including kinds of sensation, levels of intensity, and rates of flow. Vaughan said that with table tipping the physical sensations were "sort of a gluey energy that was flowing through." He also noted "that [energy] was very palpable. I mean it really felt like a psychic glue." At another point, Vaughan described the energy "almost as if you're holding a magnet, and you suddenly come across, or close to, a magnet of the opposite pole. It's that kind of pull. Like a magnetic pull." Vaughan stated he was aware of the rate or magnitude of energy flow, explaining, "I can tell by the intensity of the energy." With healing, however, Vaughan described the energy as a gentle flow of warmth or tingling in the hands.

For Schwartz, healing energy felt more like water. He stated, "I mean ... you just feel it flowing in. It has a liquid quality." Stephen also noted that in healing, energy "sort of pulses through — and it's definitely a pulse."

3) The MMI energy may cause the body to relax. Wigal experienced physical relaxation during MMI energy flow, along with increased mobility of his normally rigid spine and a loss of awareness of his chronic pain and tinnitus. He stated:

> I seem to elongate my spine and stretch out. Maybe, probably, that's part of the general relaxation.... I stretch the middle of the spine, and it's oh so relaxing to do that! Normally I can't, I don't get much flexibility there.... I think I probably breathe deeper and slower.

Sometimes Wigal's body became relaxed to the point of limpness. He noted that at times he had to limit the full experience because of this, and said:

> At the tropical fish store when the lights went out I stopped the process because in the public place it's a little awkward, because ... you get very limp, and I wasn't able to sit in a yoga posture in a fish store.

Wigal's experiences end abruptly just after the energy felt from above and below meet. He noted,

> It fades very fast and it tends to go all at once. Just in a flash it's all gone.... I think I'm more relaxed for awhile after it, and I think I can have more flexibility for awhile ... but I soon get stiff again.

4) The physical state may affect the quality and type of energy flow. Vaughan said, "I found that what seemed to work best was feeling very positive and energized." And again, in thinking about his MMI experiences, Vaughan stated, "I guess one thing that they all involve, though, is for me to feel really good. It's just my technique. I know other people do it differently. But for me, that seems to be a key to opening up, to channeling higher energies."

An empty stomach may likewise enhance the sense of energy, while a full one may be seen as "grounding." Wigal in particular noticed that an empty stomach affected the strength and quality of his experiences. He said:

> On times when I'm really relaxed and really thinking about it, and I haven't eaten for awhile — I just had supper a while ago so it's less likely to happen, but when I haven't eaten for awhile, then it starts at the bottom, too, and they kind of meet in the lower back.

5) The MMI energy may be triggered by a body posture. Wigal noted, "By getting in a yoga state, a yoga posture, I can cause my body to have that rush, that tingling all over." This position was not required for the experience, but did seem to lead to a greater result. He commented, "The fingernail-pressed-into-the-hand technique need not always be called on, or both hands need not be used, but when the full ritual is called on, I can usually expect a fuller effect."

6) The MMI energy may be experienced by the recipient as various body sensations. Martin experienced the energy as heat, but noted that those being healed may experience receiving it in a variety of ways, where some patients, "felt cold, they would get goose bumps, some would feel tremendous heat, some would feel a tingling sensation in the area where they had a problem."

Wigal was both as a performer and a recipient of anomalous healing. He noted that the energy felt very much the same for both kinds of experiences. He recalled:

> I had a Hindu nun speak one evening at my social club and after her speech I was preparing food in the kitchen and I cut my finger badly. It was bleeding, bleeding badly. She came out in the kitchen and put her hands around my finger and it healed. Well, as soon as the cut happened one of my moderators called the paramedics from Less Hill, which is not far away. By the time they arrived there was no bleeding and this thing had healed. And they billed me, and put on the form that this was a prankster that had called. Of course, there were many witnesses, as well as the blood on the floor, that showed that, indeed, I was cut! But they didn't believe it.... The reason I brought that up, is the same kind of feeling around the healing at that time by this nun, Bonnie, my massage therapist used to do. She's into Rolfing, also, so she can do both. She can do the very deep massage and then this kind of healing or whatever, by not touching me. It's the same kind of warmth that I get at the bottom of the spine at the end of this. I have mixed emotions when that heat comes because I know that's at the end of the experience.

Focused Awareness: *1) Awareness may be focused on the sense of energy.* This seems to be particularly true for anomalous healing experiences, where the MMI performer responds to how the patient's energy is "felt." For example, Schwartz was focused on the subtle energetic level when treating his daughter for a fever: "And began to pull this energy off of her. It felt like cotton wool. Sort of like pulling cotton off, but not quite. Softer than that. But more ... ethereal. It was like pulling heat out of her. It was a very strange experience."

2) Focused awareness may affect the sense of energy. The degree to which attention can be focused may influence the strength or magnitude of the MMI energy that results. For example, Vaughan said, "My guide Li Sung takes over, and he seems to be able to focus and channel the energy, and focus it more, and in a stronger way."

3) There may be a group energy associated with the focused awareness. Vaughan suggested that intent was itself a form of energy, and in the case of collective intent that "joint visions can carry a collective energy." Thus, groups may be able to have stronger MMI because of their communal intent. Schwartz also felt there could be group intent in fire–walking events. He explained:

> The way we did it ... we went to a training program that ran in front of this, and that would probably identify the person who was teaching it. He was using the phrase cool moss, cool moss. You focused on that. So it was a focusing technique to get down into the zone. And there are any number of these techniques, but the point is to get you into a one-pointed state of consciousness where your attention is very clearly focused onto getting a particular task done.... So we did that for a couple of hours before we did the fire–walk, maybe an hour and a half. It was good. It was very appropriate. So you went up, you're all standing in a line, and then walking across, and it took maybe — you know it must have been eighteen feet because it took me six steps.... And we were standing in line, and you sort of stepped up to it. Occasionally people wouldn't do it, they would lose focus. Some of them would go back to the end of the line. There was a lot of group energy about it. It was a kind of late-twentieth-century Western American version of a Brazilian shamanic ritual.

4) Energy may be required to focus. This was not stated, but would seem likely given that it takes energy to focus (as anyone who has ever been exhausted or ill can attest) and may be a factor in why low energy states make it harder to access ESP information.

Openness to the Experience: *There may be a deliberate opening up to the energy.* Vaughan noted a conscious dropping of barriers and opening up to access the energy and information needed to perform MMI. He described it in this way: "Well, first of all I'm aware of ... like a psychic armor, that's usually there, that I consider like an aura. And I just sort of let my defenses down." In another place, Vaughan stated simply that, "I would kind of open up my consciousness." Similarly, Schwartz commented that in MMI, "What you're doing is awakening yourself, opening yourself, aligning yourself."

Sometimes the openness needed seemed to go beyond what is required for ESP. Robinson said, "I'm in a place of being very open, and getting information that's even beyond what's even being 'intuitive' or just 'psychic.'"

This topic will come up again in the section on MMI Facilitation and Inhibition. It may be no surprise that where openness to the experience enhances feelings of energy and its flow, defensiveness appears to block access to, or awareness, of MMI energy.

"Knowing": *Energy may be sensed as a form of "knowing."* "Knowing" appears to play an important role in guiding the type and intensity of energy flow, as well as providing valuable feedback on how well the MMI energy is being received. Anomalous healers often reported a sense of "knowing" the healee's energy pattern, as well as the quality of healing energy being sent. For Martin, this energy was seen intuitively as entering the patient the same way (top down) as it entered the healer. She explained that she "watches" its entire delivery and distribution, and affirmed, "Yes, seeing it arrive, and when it arrives it goes again to the top of the head and then it kind of oozes down into them." Martin also described the experience of "knowing" whether the energy has been received as an intuitive vision where:

> Most of the time, I would say probably 85 to 90 percent of the time, the person will stand in front of me, or be right in front [of] me, their face. Okay? And I see the white goop going down them. Then I know that they have accepted it. But, sometimes that other 10 or 15 percent have turned away from me. When they turn away from me and they do not accept the white goop it means that they want to die.

Guiding the Process: (*1*) *The energy can be guided.* Vaughan was aware of guiding the energy. For him, it was simply a matter of "You put out the energy or direct it, direct higher energies to go there." Schwartz similarly stated that once focused, he can guide the energy wherever he wants it. He remarked, "It's very real.... It's hard to get focused like that again. But once you make the click, then you can, then you aim the energy down or towards someone, or some goal, some thing."

2) Guiding the process can be an interactive process, which is determined (at least in part) by how the energy is sensed. Performers may use their sense of energy (whether felt physically or through "knowing") to guide the process. This guidance in turn often takes the form of directing and controlling the energy. Thus, the sense of energy is critical to the feedback loop used in some forms of MMI, particularly anomalous healing. Schwartz described manipulating the energy based on how it "felt" in this passage:

> I was sending energy.... I was seeing light — well that's my visualization of energy — pouring through me, like water going down a waterfall.... And so I was doing that, but then, at the second phase of it, I was pulling stuff off that I experienced as toxic.

How the energy was handled was determined at least in part by how it was sensed. Schwartz allowed in what he felt to be "good," and pulled off energy he felt was "bad."

Robinson guided her psychic diagnosis/anomalous healing experiences through a combination of sensed energy and body movements. After opening to the energy, she sensed and adopted the patient's energy pattern. This was followed by deliberately erasing the energy pattern after the reading is finished. It is at this point that anomalous healing sometimes occurred. Robinson described her process in this way:

> I slide into their body. What happens is I relax, and then I always feel we have the body, and that helps me, and I say it.... Then I'll go through the body and just see what comes up, or what I notice, what information comes up to be passed onto the person. Then when I'm finished I always make sure I erase the body ... you know, the body that I'm reading. And I do that by, literally, I ... take my hand and just erase. It's like I'm erasing down my physical body. And what I found is that sometimes the person I'm reading, it's like I've erased it from their body.

SUMMARY

There is often a sense of energy associated with MMI experiences. Anomalous healers in particular often spoke of this constituent in detail, suggesting that they are focused on the energetic level when working. This does not seem to be the normal physical kind of energy (although that may impact it), but rather has more of a subtle or transcendent quality. In addition, there may be limits (whether universal or self-imposed) on how this energy can be used. Participants described opening up to this transcendent energy by dropping barriers and/or having a sense of expansion. Accessing MMI energy was typically effortless. However, delays were sometimes experienced before the energy began to flow — although it is unknown to what degree those waits were real or simply perceptual. Once started, the energy did not need to last long to be effective — anomalous healers spoke of it requiring eight minutes or less.

Experiencers reported a variety of impressions regarding characteristics of the sensed energy, as well as its intensity and rate of flow. Energy in the body was most often felt in the hands as warmth or tingling, although some noted it in other body parts or even the body as a whole. The sensed quality of the energy may shift suddenly just before MMI occurs or when attention is taken away from the target.

MMI performers also described a kind of "group energy," which occurred when more than one individual was working towards the same goal. It is unclear exactly how this works. Groups working together could conceivably facilitate MMI through a variety of means, including (1) having a direct effect on the level or quality of energy; (2) enhancing the quality, or type, of connection; (3) causing a loss of sense of self or individual ego identity through merger with the group; (4) increasing the effectiveness of focus through collective intent; (5) removing ownership resistance and witness inhibition; or (6) in some other unknown manner. Regardless of how groups accomplished their result, it is interesting to wonder whether group energy — and possibly group intent — could be partly responsible for a variety of effects, from "home court advantage" in sports to a kind of group experimenter/participant effect.

The Physical State

The constituent of the "physical state" refers to how the body felt or was used as part of the MMI process. Although many MMI performers have a narrowed focus of awareness with loss of awareness of the body as well as surroundings, the body may still contribute to, and reflect or modulate, the sense of energy. Furthermore, bodies (especially the hands) were sometimes actively used, whether for connection or (more frequently) to guide the process.

The literature mentions the physical state mostly with regard to anomalous healing. There is typically little awareness of the body during MMI experiences, perhaps in part because performers frequently have such a narrowed focus of attention. If that attention is on something other than the body itself, then the physical state is ignored. As it is, this constituent is mostly mentioned in fire–walking, anomalous healing, and Kundalini related experiences. Since Kundalini almost by definition involves feeling energy moving through the body, it is not surprising that the physical state would be prominent in descriptions of these kind of experiences. Awareness of the body does not mean that the sensations are always normal ones, but may be markedly altered.

In addition to beginning and actively guiding the process through the voice, use of postures, or hand gestures, the physical state may also be able to aid focus and connection through physical proximity (especially by standing near to the target or touching it), affect the quality of energy flow, and provide feedback regarding how the experience is progressing.

WHAT THE LITERATURE SAYS

Body sensations mostly show up in reports of anomalous healing experiences, both during diagnosis and treatment. Harvey Irwin noted that anomalous healers often reported feeling heat, cold, tingling, or prickles in their hands or other body parts.[103] Some practitioners diagnosed their patients' illnesses based on how their own body felt. This was sometimes an idiosyncratic code, whereby specific sensations represent particular illnesses, such as asthma or cancer.

Some healers reported being exhausted after their sessions, while others were energized by the experience. It is unclear why this should be. Two possibilities are that it could be due to (1) a self-fulfilling prophecy (i.e. they believe the work should tire them, so it does); or (2) there are differences between the ways energy is used or accessed, such as whether it is self-generated (coming from their own reserves) or channeled from an external source.

Allan Cooperstein found that although anomalous healers varied in their levels of arousal, most spoke of being relaxed, with lowered heart rates and slower, deeper respirations.[104] He also commented on the way healers used gestures to sense their patients' energetic states or send energy.

Michael Murphy and Rhea White's study on exceptional human performance in sports found feelings of freedom, as well as altered sense perceptions of weightlessness, floating, and well-being.[105] Of these, only well-being and, in one case, feeling lighter were reported by MMI experiencers.[106]

How the Physical State Relates to the Other Constituents

Altered State of Consciousness: *1) There may be a sense of being physically relaxed in the ASC.* Wigal and Smith both said they were very relaxed when in the ASC for MMI.

2) Relaxation may help maintain the ASC. Wigal felt relaxation allowed him to maintain the right ASC for MMI a longer period of time.

3) The ASC may alter the body's sensory input. ASC may cause heightened or altered sense perception, particularly in fire–walking. Sensory input can be completely or partially altered from what would normally be expected. Another way that the altered sensory input can manifest is as diminished awareness of the body.

Connection: *1) Connection may be felt in the body.* Vaughan felt his connection to patients as activity in his solar plexus.

2) Connection may be made through the voice. Martin reported that speaking the birth first name of a patient was her way of forming a conscious connection to a target person (although this was not required for a successful connection).

Playfulness or Peak Emotions: *1) The physical state may contribute to emotion.* Being physically drained made it harder for performers to feel positive or upbeat, while feeling physically good sometimes led to euphoria.

2) High levels of emotion may affect the physical state. High levels of emotion were associated with the body feeling energized. It was also possible that physical energy contributed to or correlated with the energy produced by the emotions.

Sense of Energy: *1) Energy may be felt in the body.* Energy was felt in the body as heat, tingling, something moving through the body, and activity in the head. Martin also reported feeling lighter after performing anomalous work, which made her wonder whether she weighed less then.

2) The energy may have different qualities, which are reflected in the MMI performer's body sensations. The energy felt by the body can be experienced as having a variety of characteristics, including kinds of sensation, levels of intensity, and rates of flow.

3) The MMI energy may cause the body to relax. Wigal observed that energy flowing through his spine led to relaxation, increased spine mobility, and a loss of awareness of distracting chronic internal stimuli, such as tinnitus and pain.

4) The physical state may affect the quality and type of energy flow. The condition of the body (in terms of its level of energy) seemed to influence how easy it was to access MMI energy. Some felt that an empty stomach enhanced the sense of energy, while a full one was "grounding."

5) The MMI energy may be triggered by body posture. Wigal stated that he triggered energy flow by using a yoga position.

6) The MMI energy may be experienced by the recipient as various body sensations. Patients may experience receiving MMI energy in a variety of ways, including as cold, heat, and tingling.

Focused Awareness: *1) There may be physical feelings that reflect focused awareness.* Schwartz said that he felt it in his forehead when he was intently focused.

2) The level of focused awareness may determine whether one is sensing the body. Awareness of the body may depend on what kind of MMI is being attempted. In comparing metal-bending to anomalous healing, Schwartz explained:

> Healing has a very ethereal quality. The PK things had a much more physical quality to them. They're dealing with the physical realm. Healing, you're dealing with the energetic realm by definition. And that's the entry point of the healer. So, that's where you're focused. Whereas [with] the PK thing you're focused on physical. You know you're feeling metal moving, so you have direct tactile sensation in a different way.

Wigal believed that his focusing on the experience led to a lack of perception of distracting internal stimuli, such as pain and tinnitus, even though they are normally difficult (or impossible) for him to ignore. He stated:

> You know I'm not sure that the pain leaves, I'm just completely unaware of it during those times.... I don't care about the pain, let's put it that way, so much when these things happen, but I also don't care about the tinnitus while these things happen. Whereas normally the tinnitus is very unnerving, and sometimes it's nerve-wracking.

"Knowing": *There may be a sense of receiving information or "knowing" as changes in the body.* Robinson reported feeling the patient's body as her own until she "erased" it. She said,

> I feel it on my body. I feel it. Just like I feel their pain. I feel it. And so, I let go of it because I don't want to carry it. I don't want whatever they've got. So, my erasing is my way of letting go of it.

This physical feeling was in the manner of a code that Robinson was able to translate into a medical diagnosis:

> I really feel it, it's something that's going on. I feel it and I have my own code for like MS [multiple sclerosis], to me, feels like somebody put me into a corset and pulled it really tight. I have my own language for certain diseases or things going on. My own physical code for it.

Guiding the Process: *1) The process may be guided or affected by physical proximity.* Spontaneous MMI targets were often physically near Smith. This pattern was shared by a number of others. Robinson was physically holding a piece of silverware when it bent. She recalled, "And so that day, just because I tend to be antsy I was picking it up and just waving it around."

Wigal believed that physical proximity to a target determined whether an effect would occur, and to what degree. He remarked:

> We do have, in the hallway, a round fluorescent tube.... And when I was able to walk a little better than I can now, I used to walk by that a lot. And once I stopped there and thought about this, and got into this state standing. And the light did seem to dim ... there did seem to be some effect on it ... the closeness, the proximity seems to have something to do with it.

Wigal had a similar experience in childhood where physical proximity clearly seemed to have an effect on a light display. He recalled:

> My mother worked in the National Hardware retail association in Indianapolis where they had a model hardware store. You couldn't buy anything there. It was just perfectly set up, like a perfect hardware store. And they had an electric light exhibit.... It was about [19]47. I was a freshman in high school. I remember going back to the exhibit and all these lights, and I felt very connected to these lights. And I remember dancing, kind of, like a kid would do, moving my body in front and back, and noticing that the lights would get brighter or darker depending on my moving around these lights. And

then later when I told my mom about that wonderful exhibit, she says, "Well, that's
not the way that exhibit [works]. They are just lights there. They're just on, that's all."
I said, you know, "No, no ... when you move they go on and off, and they get brighter
and darker." She said, "No, there's no exhibit [like that] there" .... [laughing] It was
wonderful! And I was dancing literally with joy in front of these lights, and they were
kind of reacting the way animals do almost, when you're around them.

Proximity was also an issue mentioned indirectly when Wigal remembered that "I removed
the loud smoke alarm from my ceiling because it went off several times when I called up this
event near it."

2) The event may be triggered by a body position. As mentioned before, Wigal noted that he
triggered MMI through a particular yoga posture. He said:

The normal pattern of this is I am meditating, and on some days I think to myself
that everything is right. This is the right harmony, the right time to bring on this other
experience. And then I can do it by triggering. By pressing my finger into my thumb,
my fingernail, I can start this sensation.

Wigal also stated:

Yes. I can cause it to happen. I can cause it to happen now.... I get in a yoga posture
and when I press my fingernails slightly into my thumb in both hands at once, and
think about it.... I can get this.... When I'm in that state, I seem to be able to do these
things with these electrical things, the fax machine, the fluorescent tubes, not regular
light bulbs, but fluorescent. Things with starters in them, [it] seems to me.

3) Changes in how the body feels may be used to guide the process. There may be a sense of
receiving information or "knowing" as changes in the body. Robinson reported feeling the
patient's body as her own until she "erased" it.

4) The body may be used to guide the energy. Vaughan stated, "Well if the person is with
me, you know, in my presence, I'll put forward my hand, next to their body, but not touching." Schwartz described using his hands in anomalous healing, too, and explained that he will
"move over the body with ... circular motions to close things and counterclockwise motions to
open things up."

Martin also involved her hands when healing in person. She noted:

I had her lay down on the floor and ... I put my hands over her, over the area.... And
within a split second, I could feel heat coming out of my hands.... So I did it for about,
probably five to eight minutes. I was afraid to do it any longer than that, you know. So
we stopped, and I closed my hands.

Martin also used her breathing and voice to both gather and guide the energy. She said:

I sit and I open my hands. First of all, I take in my three deep breaths, bringing the
white light to me.... I breathe in through my nose and I'm bringing the white light,
and I exhale through my mouth. And then I breathe in the second time and exhale
through my mouth. And the third breath I send the white goop and I say the person's
name ... as I'm exhaling.... It's all happening on the third breath.

Robinson controlled the energy (if only in her own body) through a mixture of focused
intent, the felt sense of the energy in her body, and the use of hand gestures. This was particularly true at the end of psychic diagnosis sessions, when she was careful to "erase" the energy
pattern, or "neutralize" it. She described this process here:

"And so my erasing is my way of letting go of it. I don't send it back to them. And
this wasn't something, a conscious thing that I know of, that I learned. I just know that
once I had done the reading I let go of it, and in my mind I'm just neutralizing all of
that into ... being neutral."

Robinson's MMI seemed to be related to the above-mentioned clearing of the patient's energy pattern. She observed:

> I'll go through the body and just see what comes up, or what I notice, what information comes up to be passed onto the person. Then when I'm finished I always make sure I erase the body — you know, the body that I'm reading. And what I found is that sometimes [with] the person I'm reading, it's like I've erased it from their body.

The fact that this seemed to have an effect on the physical state itself— and not just the subtle energy pattern — was seen in two instances when Robinson was unable to erase the pattern and suffered physically until it could be dealt with. She mused:

> There have only been two times when I could not erase.... One time was a young boy who'd been hit in the head with a bat, and I don't know why I couldn't. I just could not let go of that headache, which was strange. The other time was a woman who was allergic to her environment. And it made me feel extremely dizzy. And I couldn't let go of that.

SUMMARY

There is typically little awareness of the body during MMI experiences, perhaps in part because performers frequently have a narrowed focus of attention on something else, leading the physical state to be ignored. It all depends on what/where the mind is focused. As it is, this constituent was mostly mentioned in fire–walking, anomalous healing, and Kundalini-related experiences. However, awareness of the body does not mean that the sensations need be normal ones — fire–walking participants often have markedly altered sensory perceptions.

The research literature mentions the physical state mostly with regard to anomalous healing. Performers have reported a variety of feelings associated with healing energy, including heat, cold, tingling, and prickles in their hands or other body parts. Though the way energy is felt in the body can vary in quality and location, there similar sensations were reported by anomalous healers who described their experiences here. In addition, there can be feelings of relaxation and physical well-being during MMI experiences, often in association with emotional well-being.

The body may be useful to MMI experiences in a variety of ways. The physical state may affect an individual's state of consciousness, since being tired and sleepy is a psi-conducive state. It can also aid focusing on, and connecting to, the target through physical proximity, whether by standing near the target or by touching it. Events can be first triggered, and then manipulated, through use of the voice, postures, and hand gestures. Although many MMI performers have a narrowed focus of awareness with loss of awareness of the body as well as surroundings, the body may still contribute to and reflect or modulate energy flow. Perhaps even more importantly, body sensations may be used as a way of "knowing" information about the target, both in terms of a patient's illness and to provide valuable feedback regarding how the healing process is progressing.

Focused Awareness (Attention)

Focused awareness is a narrowed focus of attention. Of all the constituents noted in MMI experiences, it is by far the most consistent and universal. Every individual was focused on something or someone during their experiences, regardless of the type of MMI being performed. Spontaneous or intentional, small scale or large, religious or secular, all forms of MMI involved this element. The only difference that shows up between them is what the mind is being concentrated upon — whether the target, the performer's state of consciousness, a person (self or other), a goal, an emotion, a thought, the sense of energy, or even the process itself. And although that which is the center of attention may vary from one situation to the next, a performer's awareness is *always* focused.

So, what variations do we see in this constituent? Generally, in spontaneous MMI, attention is on a thought or an emotion, whereas in intentional MMI it is usually on either the intent or the target. Contrary to what some have suggested, concentrated intent was by no means necessary for successful intentional MMI. Events could occur without it.

Focused awareness is enmeshed with a number of the other constituents. It appears to be inextricably related to the state of consciousness and is often a big factor in connecting to a target. In some cases, it may lead to dissociation and allow one to silence (or ignore) the intellect. A narrowed attention on energy may also aid in accessing and manipulating it. In fact, it is possible that awareness is *itself* a form of energy, which can be directed and used by MMI performers. Finally, focused awareness appears to be an important method of guiding the process.

WHAT THE LITERATURE SAYS

Focused awareness has been reported in a variety of ways in the literature. In his review of subject reports, Loftur Gissurarson noted that participants typically spoke of "concentrating" on the target or "willing" things to occur.[107] This would seem to involve focused awareness, whether on the target or the intent. Gissurarson found that more than half of the successful trials were due to one of three strategies: (1) concentration (22 percent of the significant runs), (2) imagery (19 percent of the significant runs), and (3) "resonance" (13 percent of the significant runs).[108]

Michael Murphy and Rhea White reported a similar pattern in sports, where alertness combined with the ability to focus intently, tuning out internal and external distractions, is a critical component to success.[109] Both will and awareness are heightened in sports, even without the issue of an EHE or MMI. Murphy and White observed that, "athletic skill depends on one's ability to focus unbroken attention on the space, objects, and other people involved, and on one's own kinesthetic sense of the body.... The greatest athletes are legendary for their powers of concentration.[110]

Athletes are not alone in this ability. Allan Cooperstein commented that anomalous healers will, with deliberate effort and in a controlled manner, become focused on their inner experiences when working.[111] During this time they ignore extraneous streams of information, whether from the environment or their own body's sensory input, unless they are relevant to what is being done. There can sometimes be even an element of surrender to this state.

The role of attention in MMI performance is a curious one. Attention is often a part of connection, yet some (but not all) of the participants felt that disconnection is required at some point for MMI to take place. One possibility for this could be that it reflects that they have been trying too hard, or lack trust in the process, causing too much effort to be put into attention on the target. On the other hand, spontaneous events often stop when attention is placed on the target item(s). It is unclear whether this is due to distraction being a necessary element for spontaneous MMI, an integral part of the ASC, or a third variable. If the former is true then one might wonder whether this is related to fear of the responsibility MMI represents, or the ability to control unconscious needs (or get them met in another way) once they are recognized and made conscious. Likewise, one can also ask whether the apparent need for a release of attention is a result of a delay effect, a need to let go, trying too hard, or a combination of factors.

The fact that release-of-effort/attention is unnecessary for MMI when a strong sense of detachment is present suggests that at least part of the answer might be one of adequate immersion in the process. Immersion would seem to be the classic depiction of being "in the flow," as described by Eugen Herrigel in his classic book, *Zen and the Art of Archery.*[112] In it, individuals lose their sense of having a separate self and fully trust in the transcendent process in which they are engaged. When in the flow, mastery becomes effortless.

ASPECTS OF FOCUSED AWARENESS

1. The focus of intention is intensely narrowed. In considering what differentiates ESP experiences from MMI ones, Robinson mused:

> I'm sort of thinking of the experiences to see what is the difference.... It's not like I'm sitting there consciously running energy to do something. To heal someone, bend a spoon, or whatever. It's almost as though I become, I get so [pause] maybe focused.

Concentration tended to be on the target in intentional MMI, whereas awareness was more often focused on something other than the target item (such as a conversation or an idea) in spontaneous MMI. In healing, attention may be concentrated on the energy itself, or on the specific level of consciousness needed for the required energy flow. In metal-bending, there can be focused awareness on both the target and the intent.

Schwartz felt that being focused was crucial. He stated, "That's it. It's the one pointedness [that] is the key. Is that ... you get to the point of focused intention. That's the critical issue." The focus is of such an extreme degree that there is no room for thought or emotion (hence, detachment from emotions and suspension of the intellect). Schwartz also said that there can be a ritualistic quality to the development of this intense focus. He noted of a fire-walk that:

> You focused on that [phrase]. So it was a focusing technique to get down into the zone. And there are any number of these techniques, but the point is to get you into a one-pointed state of consciousness where your attention is very clearly focused onto getting a particular task done.... It was a kind of late-twentieth-century Western American version of a Brazilian shamanic ritual.

2. What the attention or awareness is focused on can vary. Participants were always focused on something during their MMI experiences, but what that something was varied considerably. Attention was concentrated on any of the following:

a) Awareness may be focused on the target. Vaughan explained, "it's a feeling of ... affecting whatever one wants. Whatever it's focused on." When asked what was involved in focusing, he replied, "Well, it's just very simple. It's just putting one's attention on that particular thing." Wigal often focused on a specific topic or focused on a target item, such as when he was, "contemplating at the fish tank, and contemplating especially on how I provide the light and the food for these fish." Martin described her focus in non-distant healing as being on a target area, for example, "With his elbow, I was completely focused on his elbow and I couldn't see anything else."

b) Awareness may be focused on the physical (or energetic) experience. Wigal noted that he focused his awareness on the sensations of the experience, admitting, "It's hard to do anything but sort of focus on that rush when it's happening."

c) Awareness may be focused on an emotion. Awareness was often focused on an emotion during spontaneous MMI events. Smith was variously focused on sadness, excitement, and anger during her spontaneous events.

d) Awareness may be focused on the intent. Intentional MMI was, perhaps not surprisingly, sometimes focused on that intent. Schwartz said, "You get to the point of focused intention."

e) Awareness may be focused as group intent. There can sometimes be an added dimension of group intent. Schwartz commented, "In the case of the spoon-bending you have shared intent. Again, it's the same issue. Focus and intent and [in] both of the stories I've described, a group activity as well. A linking in with group intention."

f) Awareness may be focused on a distracter. Smith focused on something other than the target item (or the intent) for both spontaneous and intentional MMI. For intentional MMI she described the process as first stating her intention, and then distracting herself from it through focused awareness on a magazine. Smith explained:

> [I] wrote it down. Sometimes I verbalized it, said come on computer, now you can go high ... as a way of objectifying it, getting it out of my consciousness, saying this was what I would like to happen. And then letting it go.

Smith added that she would "Put my attention away from it. Stating it and then turning my attention to another task." She referred to this as "diffuse attention," although her awareness was focused on something that could serve as a distraction. For example, Smith often concentrated on a magazine to (in her words) "immerse part of my consciousness in a story or article."

g) Awareness may be focused on the process. In some cases, the focus is not on the goal (which for anomalous healing would be the outcome) but on the intent to send healing energy (which could be considered the process). Martin stated, "There's no focus on the goal. If the goal is that the person has cancer in the stomach, okay? I don't focus on curing the cancer in the stomach.... There's no focus on the goal.... All I do is focus on sending the white light."

Similarly, Robinson noted that in those cases where anomalous healing occurred, her intent was simply to help, suggesting she was more focused on the process than the outcome. She declared, "The intention, and the intention of those I've worked with, has always been to help the person, and help the person get better, but not 'to heal' the person. It was just to help them."

3. Intense focus may lead to a loss of awareness of external surroundings. The performer may have a complete loss of awareness of his or her surroundings, which occurs as a natural result of intense concentration. Martin explained:

> It's a point of awareness of isolating the situation. And so, when I'm focused on a whole human being that's having a problem, I'm so totally focused on that person there's nothing else there. Everything else ... is not there. So, if I'm focused on a particular area, where with his elbow, I was completely focused on his elbow and I couldn't see anything else.

Wigal also reported an intense narrowing of focus of attention with a resulting loss of awareness of extraneous internal and external stimuli. He noted,

> I have had this experience that people will call and say, "I've been at your door knocking. I was worried. Are you all right?" And if they were at the door knocking and I was in this state, or whatever it is ... I just block all that out.

Similarly, Smith said:

> I felt pretty much focused on the experiment itself. I didn't hear things from outside the room or, you know, was just aware of what I was doing with the experiment. It's as if the outside world got shut off for awhile.

4. There may be a focused awareness on a group level. Some performers mentioned having a shared, focused group intent. This is referred to in a group MMI event that Schwartz witnessed. He remembered:

> I looked over, and ... for an instant, there was a kind of flicker, like a neon flicker, red neon flicker, and then it coalesced, and it was there as a ball of light. A kind of ... electric red, and dark, an electric wine red. And it was like a fog that hung in a ball, and it just was there for a couple of beats. And I was absolutely stopped in my tracks

that clearly these people had made this thing manifest in their shared intention. Again, focus. I just have never seen anything like it. I mean it just had a very powerful effect. And then it was gone. But I've never forgotten it as an example of shared intention. I think it was the first time I'd thought about it that way. Yeah that's actually, I think, in many ways, my most interesting psychokinetic experience because that really was something ... it had never occurred to me that these people lying there, having gone through this thirty minute build-up with music and pulsing, and all sorts of things, would achieve that, that threshold of power.

HOW FOCUSED AWARENESS RELATES
TO THE OTHER CONSTITUENTS

Altered State of Consciousness: *There is often a narrowed focus of attention with a loss of awareness of surroundings associated with the ASC.* The MMI ASC frequently involved intense concentration on a thought, feeling, person, or thing, which led to a natural loss of awareness of the environment.

Connection: *1) Deep levels of connection may be associated with a narrowed focus of attention.* Feeling deeply connected to the target was associated with having a narrowed focus of attention. However, it is unclear whether this is an indirect effect (mediated through the ASC) or a direct effect on awareness.

2) Focused awareness may lead to a sense of connection or merger with the target. Focused concentration on a target item was often associated with deep feelings of connection or even of union.

Dissociation: *The shift in focus away from the individual ego identity may lead to dissociation.* As performers narrowed their attention (often concentrating on the target or energy flow), it led to a loss of awareness of other things, such as the self, resulting in dissociation.

Suspension of the Intellect: *Highly focused awareness may prohibit thought and encourage suspension of the intellect.* Intense levels of concentration or narrowed attention appeared to help suspend the intellect.

Playfulness or Peak Emotions: *1) Focused awareness can lead to the inhibition of, or detachment from, potentially distracting emotions during the MMI experience.* In some cases intense concentration blocked emotions. This was particularly true of fire-walking experiences.

2) Strong emotions may enhance the intensity of focus on a person, object, or thought. Some strong emotions, such as anger or love, were able to help narrow attention or awareness.

3) There may be a playful quality to what is focused on. Participants sometimes described a playful quality to their focusing.

Sense of Energy: *1) Awareness may be focused on the sense of energy.* This was particularly true for anomalous healing experiences, where the MMI performer responded to how the patient's energy "felt."

2) Focused awareness may affect the sense of energy. The degree of focus may influence the strength or magnitude of the MMI that results.

3) There may be a group energy associated with the focused awareness.

4) Energy may be required to focus. This was not stated, but would seem likely.

Physical State: *1) There may be physical feelings that reflect focused awareness.* Participants noted that intense concentration could sometimes be felt in the head during anomalous healing.

2) The level of focused awareness may determine whether one is sensing the body. Awareness of the body depended on what was being done, and therefore what is being focused on.

"Knowing": *What the performer is aware of through "knowing" may be determined by what his or her mind is focused on.* This interaction was implied by Stephen when he stated that in "healing you're dealing with the energetic realm by definition. And that's the entry point of the healer. So that's where you're focused."

Guiding the Process: *The process may be guided through focused awareness.* Vaughan said, "It's a feeling of affecting whatever one wants. Whatever it's focused on." Although Wigal initiated energy flow through the use of a specific yoga posture and noted the effect may vary based on physical proximity, he directed the energy through intent or focused attention. Wigal explained:

> But, I thought, why does it just work with that fish tank, and nothing else? Well, I found out it does work with other things. It works with my fax machine. And I've done this with neighbors in the place, too. I can go to their place, too. I can go over and think about the fax machine, and get that rushing feeling, and it beeps like it's receiving paper, and I'm not touching it.

SUMMARY

Focused awareness was the most consistent and universal factor in all descriptions of MMI experiences. This was as true for spontaneous events as for intentional ones — although what they were focused upon at the time varied. Spontaneous events often involved an intense narrowing of awareness to something other than the target — whether a person, feeling, or thought — while with intentional MMI, attention was more apt to be concentrated on the target or an intent.

Focused awareness was enmeshed with several other constituents. It appeared inextricably related to the state of consciousness and could act as a factor in connecting to the target. It also sometimes led to dissociation and helped performers to silence (or ignore) the critical, thinking part of their minds. Consciousness researcher Charles Tart noted, "Attention/awareness constitutes the major energy of the mind, as we usually experience it."[113] It may well be that awareness is itself a kind of energy, which can be directed and used by MMI performers as narrowed attention often involved, and affected, the sense of energy. Focusing was used to access the energy (through fine-tuning the ASC), direct it, as well as to guide the process.

Trust in the Process

Trust in the process was sometimes implied, but seldom mentioned. Only Martin spoke of it outright. The other performers referred to it indirectly with comments, such as "lack of effort," "effortlessness," "not trying too hard," "surrendering to the experience," "letting go," and "not getting in the way of whatever needs to do the PK."

Regardless of the wording, these comments suggest that it is important not to act in order to accomplish the result, but to instead to allow the process itself to accomplish it for you. This letting go of control by the self may be associated with a sense of "rightness," as well as feelings of detachment and a lack of worry. However, more than anything else, it represented a willingness to relinquish an egocentric center of control, and trust something else — the process — to do whatever is needed for success. Thus, a single umbrella category of "trust in the process" was used for this constituent.

The release-of-effort or attention sometimes seen immediately prior to MMI success was a frequent, if inconsistent, finding in participant experiences. It varied in quality from being deliberate to natural and inadvertent, and most often occurred by distraction. Although referred to in the literature as a "release-of-effort," in point of fact there is little, if any, effort ever noted in successful experiences. Hence, the phrase "release of attention" is probably a more apt description for what is occurring.

The original phenomenological study of the MMI experience included release-of-effort or attention as a separate constituent.[114] However, two lines of evidence suggested that trust in the process was the true underlying variable. First, everything that influenced release-of-effort also had an effect on trust in the process (meaning it could be subsumed under it). Second, when there was trust in the process, release-of-effort/attention appeared to become unnecessary. Therefore, it seems likely that release-of-effort is a version of, or substitute for, trust in the process.

What the Literature Says

Trust in the process is an underlying psychological meaning which has typically been referred to as other terms in the literature, whether "effortlessness," "not trying too hard," or "nonstriving." For example, many of the researchers who have tried to train MMI performers have spoken about the importance of "not trying too hard." This included Martin Caidin (energy wheels), Loftur Gissurarson (anomalous healing and other MMI), John Hasted (metal-bending), Jack Houck (metal-bending), and Julian Isaacs (metal-bending).[115]

The release-of-effort effect refers to a phenomenon long noted by experimenters, which is where MMI is produced as soon as the performer stops trying to make it happen. This often occurs in conjunction with a sudden shift of attention away from the target. It is possible that the release-of-effort effect may also be a factor in creativity and general psi. Joseph Rush pointed out that "creative ideas or insights often emerge in consciousness during relaxation or distraction *after* intense concentration on a problem. Many incidental observations suggest that success in ESP or MMI tasks follows a similar pattern."[116]

Both anecdotal accounts and experimental studies appear to support the notion that this effect is very important to MMI.[117] Perhaps even more to the point is that this is a concept which can have practical applications. Jack Houck has incorporated the release-of-effort into how he ran his MMI parties, which seemed to have a very high rate of success.[118] In them, he emphasized the importance of distraction and "letting go," saying:

> The bending usually starts within seconds after I say "Release it," meaning the thought. From that point on it really does not take any concentration. In fact, the more distractions, the easier it is for people to "let go." I encourage people to scream and get very excited when their flatware is bending, because it helps the other people "let go" by distracting them.[119]

Unfortunately, like so many findings in psi research, the release-of-effort effect is not a consistent one in the literature. Loftur Gissurarson noted that formal studies vary considerably in terms of whether they have been able to document this result.[120] Some indicate it, while others do not. Gissurarson proposed that this could relate to whether or not there is an attempt to force the target system to change, causing "mental tension." In at least one case when there was no apparent release-of-effort effect, the participants were told simply to merge with the target.

The idea that a deep level of connection with the target (without a forcible attempt to influence the system) makes release-of-effort unnecessary would fit in with the findings of Murphy and White's study of exceptional performance in sports.[121] Release-of-effort or attention is unnecessary when there is a strong sense of detachment from emotions and trust in the process.

Trusting the process, rather than trying to control a situation, also appeared as a theme in Rex Stanford's excellent summary of the experimental MMI research leading up to the mid–1970s.[122] Stanford pointed out that most formal studies show that trying to make things happen in an egocentric way does not work. There is greater success when participants suspend their normal analytic, self-oriented "I" mode, and simply passively wish for the desired result. Stanford stated, "A real effort to succeed, Thouless felt, led directly to failure. He described the proper attitude as 'effortless intention to succeed,' one in which 'I want to succeed but I don't really care whether I do or not."[123]

In working with metal-benders, Isaacs also found that trying with effort to "will" metal-bending (as measured by a piezoelectric detection device) did not work.[124] This agreed with what others have noted.[125] Likewise, in their study comparing striving and nonstriving, Debes and Morris concluded that, "quiescent, nonstriving instructions appeared to facilitate psi-hitting for both high- and low-competitive subjects, and active, striving instructions appeared to facilitate psi-missing for both groups.[126] Striving would seem to imply an attempt to actively control what happens. If we consider its opposite to be "nonstriving," then this would be a form of trusting the process. However, not all MMI performers would agree that an unforced approach is best for MMI. Felicia Parise believed it took both effort and constant practice for her to move objects — although this may have been a self-fulfilling prophecy.

The issue of trying to accomplish a task without using effort is an interesting one. We saw a hint of this earlier, when speaking of an ASC sometimes referred to as being in the "zone." Gissurarson observed that some participants speak outright of using "effortless effort" to get results.[127] But is this simply the byproduct of an ASC alone? Perhaps not.

In his review of MMI training, Gissurarson noted how many of the descriptive terms used in the literature — such as, nonstriving, non-analytical, passive, and effortless — could all fit comfortably under the umbrella of a relaxed frame of mind.[128] If we set aside "non-analytical" as being already covered in the constituent "suspension of the intellect," then it would appear that the other factors discussed by experimenters — such as nonstriving, lack of effort, effortless effort, passive volition, and not trying too hard — would all appear to entail trust in the MMI process at a fundamental level of psychological meaning. It involves a lack of control, participating and responding rather than trying to act upon. While this seems dramatically different from how we are used to operating in the world, it is in complete conformance with the descriptions of successful intentional MMI performers.[129]

Murphy and White came the closest to directly discussing trust in the process with their emphasis on instinctive action and trust in a something that is greater than the conscious mind.[130] They refer to this as one of the great secrets of sports — that the athlete can reach a point of oneness, both in terms of inner harmony and between the self and the outer world. During these moments, acting by instinct is faster and more effective than waiting for the conscious mind. Rather like religion, there is a need for to be open and surrender to something beyond the self. And by doing so, the athlete can accomplish that which would otherwise be impossible — sometimes reaching remarkable levels of achievement. To open up in such a way and surrender the self, there must be trust that this is okay, that it will work out.

Perhaps one of the earliest descriptions of this comes from the well-known classic on strategy and tactics, *The Book of Five Rings*, which was originally written in 1643 by the peerless samurai swordsman Miyamoto Musashi.[131] In it, he wrote of what he calls the "Emptiness Scroll," which involved letting go (at least consciously) of all that one has learned. Musashi explained:

> The reason this scroll is entitled Emptiness is that once we speak of "emptiness," we can no longer define the inner depths in terms of the surface entryway. Having attained a principle, one detaches from the principle; thus one has spontaneous independence in the science of martial arts and naturally attains marvels: discerning the rhythm when the time comes, one strikes spontaneously and naturally scores.[132]

Thus, the key is trusting that if something is important, it will occur as it is needed — without thought, planning, or effort. This trust is a crucial part of the in-the-moment beingness of flow, long discussed by martial artists, and more recently by athletes.[133] To be in this ASC is to have success virtually guaranteed.

Of course, this state is not reached without a certain amount of learning, whether on a conscious or an unconscious level. However, at some point it becomes necessary to let go of the safety net of knowledge and control, and allow the transcendent process to take over. This may be the hardest lesson of all to learn, but once mastered, may allow us, like Musashi, to perform astounding feats.

ASPECTS OF TRUST IN THE PROCESS

1. There may be lack of effort. There can be a sense of effortlessness to the MMI itself, as well as the energy flow through the body. The experience can sometimes be harder to stop than it is to let it happen. Wigal admitted, "Once it's started there's no stopping. It's like it starts to have a life of its own." Robinson stated, "The only effort is in maintaining focus when we start. After that, it happens on its own."

2. Trust in the process seems to be something that develops, or is learned, over time. As noted in the above quote, Vaughan gradually recognized with practice that he had to not try so hard, and tried to teach that strategy to others. Auerbach also commented that over time he learned to trust whatever happened during his detached state. He said, "I couldn't tell you when the first time that I had that experience was.... All I know is as I got older I took more note of it."

3. There may be a letting go of the need to control things. Vaughan said it was crucial to "let go" of the need to actively cause a result. He added: "I found that I had to be careful not to try too hard.... And so, I'm feeling very positive, and gently encouraging, but not outright pushing, or trying too hard. That's what I will tell people to avoid, don't try so hard." Similarly, Smith noted that, in the case of spoon-bending, she had to let go of the need to succeed. She stated:

> I thought it would go almost right away.... So, there was an expectation it was going to happen. And the longer it didn't happen, the more frustrated I got.... And then, all of a sudden there was a shift.... I think it was a letting go of the expectation of having a bent spoon, and not worrying about it. I suppose it was not worrying about whether it would bend or not. It was letting go of the expectation that it was going to bend. And then it did, you know!

Smith's trust in process was also reflected by her lack of effort and willingness to allow the process to proceed unhindered when she worked with RNG targets. She noted, "I know there are some people who went in, and they would sit in front of the computer and go 'go high, go high,' and they would curse at the computer. But mine was more stating it and letting go ... and putting my attention to some other task."

4. There may be a lack of emphasis on, or concern about, the outcome. Robinson stated that her focus was only on helping her patients improve, not them being healed. She said of her psychic diagnostic work (which sometimes seemed to result in anomalous healing) that "the intention, and the intention of those I've worked with, has always been to help the person, and help the person get better, but not to 'heal' the person. It was just to help them." There is a subtle, but implicit, sense that good may come of this without the need to act.

Martin likewise reported a complete lack of concern over the outcome of her anomalous healing sessions, which was related to trust. She explained, "That's not what is important to me. What's important is focusing and sending it to them. Whether it's going to work or not seems to me immaterial." She added,

> There's no focus on the goal. If the goal is that the person has cancer in the stomach, I don't focus on curing the cancer in the stomach. I don't focus on that.... All I do is focus on sending the white light. And it will do whatever it's supposed to do.

5. There may be surrender to the experience. Wigal observed, "For it to be its most effective you have to just really let it happen." His surrender to the experience allowed the process to occur unimpeded. He reflected, "I get into a very cooperative state, like letting this happen, a very passive ... feeling" and, "I just let it happen."

Schwartz commented, "I try to lay my groundwork. But once I get to a point where ... I've done everything I can do on it, you have to just surrender. That's very important. And go for it." Surrender cannot occur without trust. It is a letting go of the need to act, and the willingness to allow things to unfold naturally.

6. The target may be ignored by the performer. Ignoring a target they wanted to influence indirectly demonstrates trust in the process. Smith felt that taking no notice of the target helped both intentional and spontaneous MMI. She stated, "My best results were when I was just ignoring the thing."

Many spontaneous events stop when attention is paid to them. This was noted in the earlier story Auerbach told of the moving ashtray. Similarly, Smith reported:

> I think with the micro–PK, with me, not paying attention to it helps. And with the chip bowl, you know, we weren't paying attention to it, we were paying attention to each other, and so ... we noticed it was spinning, and then we looked at it, and it stopped.

Vaughan also spoke of instances in which he was initially unaware he was causing MMI, which ended when he accepted responsibility for the events. Vaughan recalled of his telephone:

> It had no automatic features at all. But it kept on doing this [calling people on its own]. It was over a dozen times. And it would call people I knew for the most part.... And occasionally, it would talk to people's answering machines. And I called the phone company. I was getting upset about this ... I just couldn't figure it out. And they said it was impossible because it was dialing out of the area code. They said the only way it could be happening was with somebody with three way dialing who would know the numbers to call. And this didn't seem possible. I mean, how would somebody know what number I had just dialed, and then call again? Or call a friend? So and then the guy, the telephone guy, repairman gave me a number to call to check with him, and I called that number and it was Motown records. I mean that's the number I got. And somehow, after that, it stopped.... But when the phone man said it was impossible, with a hint of relief I said, "Oh good heavens, it's just psychokinesis."

7. There may be a release-of-effort. MMI experiences frequently include descriptions of some variation of release-of-effort/attention. Perhaps because little, if any, effort is reported during most experiences — often only what was needed to get into the right ASC and/or maintain a narrowed focus — this generally manifested as a release of attention, usually as a result of distraction. It is not always present in experiences. Release-of-effort/attention seemed not to be needed when there was a strong sense of detachment and trust in the outcome.

The shift of attention may or may not be a deliberate one. Vaughan noted that he sends healing energy "until I usually get distracted." Schwartz also reported metal-bending occurring at the exact moment that his awareness is diverted away from the target. He said:

> Just when my consciousness shifted away from the spoon, just in that fraction, that instant, all of a sudden the spoon felt like stiff plastic when it's just about to go gooey. When you heat plastic up, you know, and there's this stiff part, and stiff, and stiff, and you know it's right on the edge of being plastic? Labile? And that's what it felt like ... and it bent!

With RNG targets, Smith would objectify her intent by writing it down and/or verbalizing it, and then put it out of her conscious thoughts. She described this as a state of diffuse attention, with deliberate distraction from the target by focusing elsewhere to aid this letting go. Although this usually worked for RNG targets (it did not work for her in metal-bending), if things went badly, then she changed strategies by shifting attention back to the target and cajoling it.

For Martin, who connected through saying the patient's birth first name, the release-of-effort/attention is a natural byproduct of her breath ending. She believed the healing energy "stops after I let out the breath." However, she added that, "being a singer, when I let out the breath it goes on for quite a long time because my lung capacity is terrific."

How Trust in the Process Relates to the Other Constituents

Altered State of Consciousness: *1) Trust in the process may facilitate the ASC.* Having a trust in the process appeared to make it easier to access the ASC for performing MMI. Robinson described several instances in which there was a sudden shift in the state of consciousness at the moment of distraction. Since distraction is the commonest form of the release-of-effort effect (which may be a precursor or form of trust in the process), then we might consider these cases an example of trust affecting the ASC.

2) The ASC may be associated with both a "knowing" of success and a trust in the process. "Knowing" the outcome of a situation leads to a natural sense of trust, and ability to allow the process to unfold.

Connection*: The belief in, or feeling of, a transcendent level of connection or interconnectedness may make it easier to trust in the process.*

Dissociation from the Individual Ego Identity: *Trust in the process may make it easier to dissociate from the individual ego identity.* Martin said her faith in the process allowed her to let go of her sense of self. She also felt that it was important to teach would-be psi performers to do the same.

Suspension of the Intellect: *1) Suspension of the intellect may make beliefs irrelevant and criticism nonexistent, thus removing blocks from trusting in the process and allowing the participant to shift to a state of being and experiencing.* Several participants spoke of the importance of withholding judgment. There is often a stated or implicit trust that the process can do whatever is needed for success as long as it is unhindered by the intellect.

2) Trust in the process may make it easier to suspend the intellect. Those performers who implicitly "knew" and trusted the process to handle things for them seemed to find it easier to silence their thinking.

Playfulness or Peak Emotion: *Playfulness and a relaxed attitude may reflect a learned trust in the process.* A certain amount of playfulness, or a non-serious approach, may be associated with trusting the process.

Investment: *The wrong kind of investment, especially if it has a controlling quality, may adversely affect trust in the process.* Vaughan stated, "That's the mistake a beginner always makes, is trying too hard." Smith also described a situation where her desire to succeed appeared to be one of the things blocking her success. She recalled:

> I wanted to bend a spoon! I had tried many, many times on my own. And I had
> never been able to do it, and I was really hoping that I would at the workshop, and to
> know that time was closing, I kept looking at my watch and thought gosh we don't
> have much time left, am I going to bend a spoon or not?!

Other factors that may have contributed to Smith's eventual success include increased focused awareness, suspension of her intellect, and letting go of her frustration. However, there may have also been an element of letting go of this investment. Smith remembered, "I said well, if I'm going to be the only one left without a bent spoon, well so what! You know! There'll be other opportunities. I think it was a letting go of the expectation of having a bent spoon, and not worrying about it."

Martin reported experiences where tape recording was somehow blocked by caring too much. She stated:

> I've had pieces of the tape erased, where there'll be blanks. And the client will call me in tears, almost in tears, saying the part that I was really looking forward to hearing is gone.... It's very weird. Because ... it'll pick up, you know, in other places. That's very strange, too. It's just stopped. The tape is going on, but it's just cut out. In very poignant places.

Martin interpreted this to mean the person wasn't supposed to hear that section of the tape again. However, it is also possible that by wanting it recorded too much, they caused the reverse to happen.

Robinson also had several experiences with tape recorders, where caring too much seems to make the equipment malfunction. She commented:

> More times than not, it will not record even though I know everything is fine and set up. One of the most unusual sessions I ever had with a tape recorder there were two tape recorders — this is really far out! Again, I was in the ashram, and there were some people who wanted a reading with me, who claimed to talk to extraterrestrials, and they so wanted it, the session recorded, that they brought their own tape recorder, and I had mine.... I just know that mine was plugged in. And we would have checked everything because they definitely wanted the session recorded. And all I know is ... none of it recorded. Neither one [machine]. None of it recorded....
>
> And I have had, just over the years, times when tape will play and should have recorded but in fact it happened just this week I was doing a telephone reading for a man in Malibu, and he was real excited about talking to me. It was funny. He was just real excited. And it didn't record.

Robinson felt that excitement alone was not enough to make this happen. She explained:

> I've been in spaces where everything is real excited and had things record, so it's not that.... It's almost as though if someone really, really wants it recorded it's not going to. That's almost the way I feel about it. If somebody comes in and says I have to have this recorded, I think uh-oh, you know, because you can bet something's going to go wrong here.

"Knowing": *1) "Knowing" that there will be a successful outcome can make it easier to trust the process.* Auerbach said, "As soon as the ball let go there was no point, to me there was no point in watching the ball hit the pins, because I knew the outcome." He had complete trust in the process that he would get a strike regardless of how the ball was thrown in these situations. This "knowing" allowed Auerbach to happily walk away without watching to see what would happen to the ball.

2) Trust in the process may facilitate "knowing" what to do. This seemed implicit when Martin said, "I was told intuitively put them in a circle around you, and have her lay down and put your hands just above the ... gallbladder. And so, being the good girl that I am, I always listen. So I did just that."

Impact: *Successful MMI can enhance trust in the process.* Positive impact from prior experiences sometimes enhanced a performer's subsequent ability to trust in the process, which in turn made it easier to perform MMI again. For example, Auerbach looked forward to the detached ASC that denoted MMI because he knew from prior experiences in the "zone" that his success was guaranteed.

SUMMARY

Trust in the process is something that has come up in the experimental literature as "release-of-effort," "lack of effort," "effortlessness," "nonstriving," "effortless effort," "not trying too hard," "surrender to the experience," "letting go," "mental relaxation," and "not getting in the way of whatever needs to do the PK." It would seem likely that the release-of-effort effect is either a form of, or substitute for, this trust.

One of the keys of MMI experiences appears to be that instead of acting "in order to" accomplish things, performers allow the process to accomplish it for them. This letting go of control by the self may also be associated with a sense of "rightness," detachment, effortlessness, and lack of worry. However, more than anything else, it represents a willingness to let go of an egocentric center of control, and trust something else — the process — to do whatever is needed for success.

If we consider the MMI performer to be like the swimmer in the ocean, we can understand that the ocean cannot be "controlled," yet the direction of movement can be "guided." Furthermore, a focus on either the individual steps needed to be able to swim, or frequently stopping to look at the island one is swimming to, will only hinder the process of getting there. Once the swimmer knows where he or she wants to go, it is better for him or her to simply set off in the right direction and concentrate on swimming, without worrying about how long it will take to get there, or how hard it might be. The same analogy works for the MMI performer. Micromanagement and goal-directed intentional behavior only seem to get in the way.

Trust in the process appears to be one of the most crucial constituents to the intentional MMI experience, even if it was the subtlest. It also appeared to be the aspect that most correlated with increasing skill and control over MMI. In addition, it would be hard to over-emphasize the importance of this sense of participation in something transcendent, where the performer does not control the process, so much as provide a gentle, almost effortless, guidance of it.

Investment

The word "investment" refers to a commitment of time or support to an outcome. It appeared to be the only constituent that could both enhance and inhibit MMI. The key lies in why this word was chosen, instead of the term "motivation." By definition, to be motivated is to be moved to action. This does not seem to work well for MMI. There is a world of difference between whether one is motivated or impelled to force the world to change or is willing to become a part of a greater whole, which moves one towards a desired goal (investment).

Although motivation and goals have long been considered important factors in learning theory, they rarely came up in MMI performer interviews.[134] Indeed, motivation was mentioned by only two of the eight participants in the original study, only one of whom spoke about goals, and that was just to comment that they could be stacked successfully. This is not to say that these individuals were disinterested in whether or not they got results. Far from it. Judging by the degree of emotion that resulted from MMI success or failure, they were extremely invested in the outcome. However, for the most part, the focus seemed to be on the process needed to accomplish the MMI, rather than the goal itself.

Although a certain amount of investment seems to improve the ability for MMI performers to connect to their targets, if there was too much investment (or perhaps, more accurately, if there was a need to control the process and an inability to let go of the self) then it hindered MMI. It is possible that this is the root cause of the energy limitations to what can be done, which some performers believe exist. The optimal situation appears to be one of caring about what happens combined with trust that things will work out as they should. Thus, MMI seems to be about trust and participation in a process, responding to input, and acting reactively to remain in harmony with what is occurring, so that the desired outcome would result.

What the Literature Says

Investment involves interest in an outcome without the need to actively control events. Most of the prior research literature is oriented instead of towards motivation. Nonetheless, some studies have indicated that wanting to succeed at a task can both enhance, and inhibit MMI success. Robert Thouless was one of the earlier researchers to discuss this.[135] He performed dice experiments using himself as his own main subject. Although he admitted at least a little motivation was needed to succeed, he found that effort and being overly motivated always led to failure. Instead, he got his best results using what he called "effortless intention," or, in his words, "the attitude must be that expressed by the words: 'I want to succeed but I don't really care whether I do or not.'"[136]

The research literature would also seem to support an enmeshment of motivation with trust (or the lack thereof). Stanford noted that "while motivation is important for PK success, it can have self-defeating consequences when for any reason (e.g., fear of failure) it leads to a direct effort to 'make things happen.'"[137]

The problem of motivation both helping and hindering performance (depending on the level involved) shows up in sports.[138] If athletes are overly attached to a goal, such as winning, they are more apt to fail. Murphy and White suggested that when individuals cannot bear to lose, it is difficult, if not impossible, for them to let go of their sense of self and trust the transcendent process.

Aspects of Investment

1. Investment may be reflected in perseverance at the task. Prior to Robinson's success at metal-bending, she had made repeated efforts to bend a spoon. She recalled,

> I had gotten a thick one, and I would practice running the energy, you know, into my head and down my arm and into the spoon and then forget about it, and try to see if it would bend, and it wasn't.

2. Investment may be reflected indirectly in the emotional impact of MMI success or failure. Investment in the events was not addressed directly, but seemed evident in the magnitude of the emotional reaction to success or failure. Auerbach said after one event, "A part of me was jumping up and down inside."

Smith noted her emotions after attempting MMI varied based on her level of success: "It depended on the results. If it really went backward, terribly, if it went really low when I really wanted it to go higher I went, oh, blow, you know! And if it went high it was ecstatic. Like whoa, I got it, I got it!"

Martin also received great satisfaction from being able to perform MMI. She stated,

> The joy of being able to help someone is just unbelievable, for me. It's just unbeliev-able. And it's a gift, you know, that I always have to use, because that's why I'm here, I feel. And so, it just brings me great joy.

Robinson's intense excitement after finally succeeding at metal-bending likewise seems to reflect investment. She stated:

> I was talking to a friend who was a priest. And all I can remember is I was holding a

spoon in my hand.... It wasn't a lightweight metal spoon, it was pretty heavy. And I'd been thinking about some friends of mine who are quite good at spoon-bending, and I hadn't had any luck with it. So, I was holding the spoon, and I was talking to Jim, and all I remember was at some point in that conversation, it's like when you really get energized about what you're talking about, and, as I waved the spoon around, it just spun out. It was like it just melted ... it just became liquid.... And it literally just curled up.... It was incredibly exciting! It was absolutely ... incredible.

Schwartz implied investment in a number of his outcomes. This was the clearest when he speaks of how in fire-walking he is focused on, "what has to be done in order to get out of there without getting really hurt." In anomalous healing, his investment was implicit in dealing with his daughter's illness, which Schwartz described as involving "a scary fever."

3. There may be investment in the process, rather than in the outcome. Robinson noted that her goal in doing psi was to simply help the person (often by giving information through psychic diagnosis), rather than to perform MMI per se. Yet, in several of the cases described, there was no way she could have helped the person without resorting to MMI.

How Investment Relates to the Other Constituents

Connection: *Investment by the performer and/or the target may enhance the quality of connection.* Vaughan felt that the quality or amount of investment in the outcome of the participant or the target person (in anomalous healing) can influenced the quality of the connection that the healer establishes with the healee.

Playfulness or Peak Emotion: *A sense of playfulness may foster the right kind of investment.* This was implied, never stated.

Trust in the Process: *A controlling quality to the investment may prevent or limit trust in the process.* Too much investment or a need to control the situation may limit or inhibit the ability to trust in the process.

Summary

Investment is the commitment to a given outcome, a case of lending yourself to a greater process without trying to force a change through action. Thus, it is different from motivation, which involves goal-oriented activity in order to achieve an outcome — with the focus being on the "in order to," and involving the issue of control, the self acting on "other," in a linear cause and effect manner. Thus, investment and motivation represent very different approaches. MMI experiences appear to benefit from a non-controlling investment in the outcome, which permits trust and participation in the MMI process, rather than from a strong motivation to succeed.

Participants seldom spoke of either investment or motivation. Most of the time, investment was implied either by the emotional impact of success (or failure) or the effort put into performing a task. Investment only appeared to interact (at least in an obvious way) with a few of the constituents and was the only constituent that seemed to be able to both promote and inhibit MMI. This may reflect different qualities to the constituent. Playfulness seemed to foster a helpful type of investment, which was less controlling, and more apt to allow for trust in the process.

Openness to the Experience

Openness is considered one of the basic personality traits in psychological testing, and remains fairly stable over the course of a lifetime.[139] However, as a constituent it was spoken of as variously involving "opening up" to the energy, dropping barriers, and/or being curious about their experiences. All of the MMI performers, either implicitly or explicitly, came across as being open to their experiences and willing to play with possibilities.

In the case of MMI performance, this factor may go beyond simply that of a personality style. Openness may also mean a lack of rigid beliefs. A flexible worldview would not only allow performers to do MMI, but also to recognize and accept their experiences. Although it is possible that openness to the experience is a response artifact (as those who were willing to talk about their experiences by definition were open to this), certain things, such as the way a recipient's openness to anomalous healing enhanced the process, suggest that openness to the experience may indeed be important to success.

Belief systems seemed to play less of a role than the literature would suggest. Confidence — or a belief by either the target or the performer that the performer could do MMI — was neither necessary nor sufficient for success.[140] Six of the eight participants (75 percent) were able to perform MMI that they didn't believe they could. One participant commented that confidence was important for public performance of MMI. The need for confidence in the public arena may relate to the fact that two of the five participants who had been in large-group experiences noted that active hostility to MMI is inhibitory. It is possible that confidence, while not a constituent of the experience, could be a modifier, which aids psi functioning in stressful or inhibiting situations.

WHAT THE LITERATURE SAYS

Openness has been indirectly measured as sheep-goat scores, personality tests, and questionnaires looking at personality traits.[141] Gertrude Schmeidler noted that studies suggest extroversion and openness correlate with higher psi scores. However, it cannot be assumed that the personality traits as measured during the ordinary state of consciousness will necessarily be the same during the ASC accessed for psi. Mood and emotion can also have a powerful impact on altering these characteristics. Thus, while prior research suggests openness (by being "sheep," extroverts, or generally open) is related to successful psi performance, some of these personality factors (such as extroversion) may not be as important during the MMI experience as whatever openness exists during that particular state of consciousness and mood. Nonetheless, openness could be viewed as part of the suspension of disbelief that Schmeidler advocated to facilitate psi. She pointed out that being at ease with ourselves and our situations makes it easier for us to set aside our ordinary kind of critical alertness.

Parapsychologists Nancy Zingrone, Carlos Alvarado, and Kathy Dalton found that psi reports correlated with the openness factor on the NEO-PI-R psychological test.[142] Although Murphy and White did not describe openness to the experience in sports EHEs it would seem implicit in those situations — it is hard to imagine putting in so many hours of rigorous training and practice unless an athlete truly wanted to achieve the peak performance associated with being "in the zone."[143]

Murphy and White believed that confidence — athletes being utterly without doubt — was a key aspect of transcendent experience in sports.[144] It is possible that sports MMI, which often involves group spectators and potentially hostile bystanders (such as crowds rooting for the other team), may be a different situation than performing in a friendly, or solitary, setting.

The fact that belief or confidence is not enough to make MMI occur would conform with the results of ESP studies on patients in mental institutions who, despite sincerely believing they had psychic abilities, performed poorly on psi tests.[145] Psychiatrist John Nelson observed that although there are many stories of ESP in psychotics, the six formal experiments he was able to find on the subject indicated that schizophrenics were not any better at card guessing than others. However, two studies did suggest that the manic state was associated with above-chance ESP hits. Nelson speculated that this could relate to schizophrenics being overwhelmed by psychic input. As he put it, "The weakly bounded schizophrenic self is continually deluged by a torrent of telepathy.... Schizophrenics perform poorly on formal psi testing because they cannot select the targeted input out of a churning background sea of psi activity.[146] Thus, more than belief in one's abilities or access to information may required for psi success — there also has to be an ability to focus and discriminate.

Looking at the other end of the "belief" spectrum, we can see that many mothers and children, close family members, and therapist-patient dyads manifest psi despite not "believing" it exists, because of a sense of deep connection and focus.[147] However, these tend to occur in supportive (or at least familiar) environments. Confidence may be more of a factor in inhibiting situations, such as being around hostile bystanders or stressed by the need to perform in public.

One MMI performer suggested that belief determines what can, or cannot, be done — regardless of whether it is based on fact or not — but that these limits can be bypassed if we don't think about them.[148] This certainly could be part of what is happening in highly emotional states and ASC. Our beliefs become irrelevant. Beliefs and confidence represent part of our intellectual worldview and sense of reality, both of which are often suspended by performers during MMI.

ASPECTS OF OPENNESS TO THE EXPERIENCE

1. There may be an openness in personality style. Vaughan exhibited openness by dropping barriers and opening up to energy, the way that he experimented with targets and his willingness to change beliefs when experiences indicated that his old ones were incorrect. An example of the latter was when Vaughan first witnessed anomalous healing:

> Well, at that time ... I was a skeptic about the whole business, but he ... demonstrated to me, you know, that this was a palpable energy that I could feel. He had me put my hand between his hands and the arm of a boy he was treating.... I could feel this kind of tingling energy. And that seemed amazing to me.

There was also a sense of openness in how Schwartz approached life. He admitted, "I like adventure. I want to have a good time and ... I like explorations. Of all kinds. I like exploring. I've always liked exploring and I have a good time with it." Martin also had an open approach to MMI, which showed up when she said, "I said, sure, let's try it. Why not? I mean, you know, it was just like okay, let's see if this works."

2. There may be an openness in worldview. Smith was very open and accepting of these experiences (and really enjoyed them) because they were an integral part of her worldview. She stated:

> I think for me these experiences are part of my wider worldview. I accept them as something within the normal experience. They're unusual and uncommon, but they fall within the normal range — probably way out on the fringe, you know, if you have a bell curve they're way out — but they still part of our normal experience. But I feel that I accept them within my normal range of things that happen. They don't happen often, and they only happen under certain circumstances. But they're still within our normal range.

3. Openness to the experience does not guarantee success. Robinson gave an example of this with spoon-bending, where openness to the experience and an initial expectation of success were not fulfilled:

> I was told how to do it, and I had a good friend who she and her husband were the ones who taught the people in Washington to do it. And so I'd seen it, I knew it could be done, and I couldn't figure out what was getting in the way of me, why I couldn't do it..... I wasn't expecting it. I was just waving the spoon. I know I had had it on my desk because I'd been trying to bend it and I couldn't.

The MMI event finally occurred after Robinson no longer expected success, and other factors — such as excitement and being energized — came to the fore.

4. Openness may not be associated with confidence, or a belief that the individual will be successful at performing MMI. Confidence, or a conscious belief that you can do MMI, is unnecessary in either the performer or the target (in anomalous healing) for MMI to sometimes occur. This is less surprising if we remember how many poltergeist agents perform MMI without either knowing that they are doing it or believing that MMI is possible for them (or at all). This was seen in an anomalous healing experience when Vaughan admitted, "It never occurred to me I could do such a thing.... It just sort of happened. Like some other aspect of me, some subconscious part of me, did it."

Another example of this occurred with a previously mentioned telephone interaction that appeared to be a recurrent spontaneous event. Although Vaughan was open to psi, he did not believe beforehand that MMI could dial his phone and that of another person, and make both ring simultaneously. He stated:

> Well, I remember that, just being absolutely puzzled, and then amused, oh, that the damn phone is ringing. It's making calls again. And then, getting really angry at it. But not having any feeling of it being tied into me. Not until the phone guy told me it was impossible. Then I sighed in relief.... I said, "Oh good heavens, it's just psychokinesis."

Robinson actively disbelieved MMI would happen before her anomalous healing event, yet it still occurred. She recalled:

> I do know that in the instance of when I was working with someone else or the three of us, say, were in this session to help, what we thought was just to get information to help the person treat themselves, I probably would have vehemently said no change will take place, this is strictly information gathering, and, when in fact, the change did take place, and I can remember at one of the sessions arguing with one of the voices in my head that I didn't do healing. That I was just there to gather information.

The argument that Robinson mentioned above (which ended with her apparently at least temporarily healing the patient of epilepsy) was described in the following passage:

> I heard a voice saying, "Heal her." And so, I went back to the voice and I said, "I don't do healings." And the voice, or the thought, said, "Heal her." At this point I actually heard a voice in my head. And I said, "No, no, I don't DO healings. I do, you know, diagnosis." So, literally I was arguing with that higher self or some part of me and then ... I said, "Couldn't you give me someone easy? This is really hard!"

Martin also noted cases where anomalous healing occurred even though neither she, nor the recipient, were confident of success. She related the following story:

> I told her to close her eyes, and it wouldn't hurt, and ... if she felt anything to let me know because this was the very first time that I have ever done this. But I was being directed to put my hands over her body. And I said, "I want you to know I'm not a healer, I've never done this before." And so she knew, you know, the whole thing. And she said, "I don't care, Annette. Just do it...." And within, oh, a split second, I could feel heat coming out of my hands. I mean it was the most extraordinary experience because I had not ever experienced that before.
>
> She had her eyes closed, and suddenly she opens her eyes, and she goes [gasp], "Oh!" I said, "What?" She said, "I feel something cracking in there." I said, "You do?!" And

she said, "Keep it up, whatever you're doing!" [laugh] This is called the blind leading the blind, you know! And ... she said, "I can feel heat ... I feel something in there...."

And so I did it for about, probably five to eight minutes. I was afraid to do it any longer than that, you know.... Because it was so hot. My hands were so hot, they were just burning up. And not knowing what in God's name I was doing.... I just felt that that was enough. So she sits up and she says, "I feel wonderful." And I said, "Good. Well," I said, "we're not going to know anything I guess until you go back to the doctor." She said, "Well, I'm going back to the doctor tomorrow." And she said, "I'm supposed to go in for X-rays before the operation." I said, "Okay. Well, call me, and let me know."

All right. The next afternoon I get this phone call.... And it's this woman.... And she goes, "Are you ready for this?" And I said, "What? What happened?" She said, "Well, I went to the doctor and he took an X-ray, and he come storming out of the X-ray room and he sits me down and he says, "WHAT DID YOU DO WITH THEM?" And I said, 'What? What are you talking about?' And he goes, 'What did you do with those stones? They're gone!'" And ... she said, "I just sat there hysterically laughing."

However, there may be one time when confidence is indeed necessary for MMI to occur—and that is in front of a hostile audience. Vaughan stated, "Confidence is necessary for PK performances in public." We will see in the section on "MMI Facilitation and Inhibition" that there are a variety of ways in which antagonistic spectators could influence the constituents of the experience—which does not even get into the issue of whether they could actively (and unconsciously) use their own psi abilities to block performer psi.

How Openness to the Experience
Relates to the Other Constituents

Altered State of Consciousness: *1) There may be a sense of dropping barriers or making boundaries permeable to allow consciousness to expand.* Several participants spoke of opening up, or later closing down, as part of their psi experiences.

2) The ASC may be associated with openness to the experience. Fire-walking participants, in particular, indicated greater openness towards fire-walking during the ASC used than afterwards, when they returned to normal consciousness.

3) There may be an openness to sensory information in the ASC associated with MMI. There may be an opening up to sensory information during MMI experiences.

Connection: *1) Openness to the experience may enhance ability to connect effectively.* Vaughan felt there were differences in his degree of connection, which appears to relate to both his investment and to the openness of the person or animal that he is trying to heal. He commented that a lack of openness in the target person blocked anomalous healing.

2) Feeling connected may make one feel more open.

Playfulness or Peak Emotions*: 1) Openness may contribute to the emotions that are felt during MMI.* Martin seemed to suggest that her complete openness led to a lack of fear or negativity and engendered feelings of joy.

2) A sense of playfulness may enhance openness to what is possible. Although several participants talked about of the value of playfulness, only Schwartz suggested that it may work (at least in part) by enhancing openness to the experience.

Sense of Energy: *There may be a deliberate opening up to the energy.* Vaughan reported a conscious dropping of barriers and opening up to access the energy and information for MMI. The openness described by MMI performers sometimes seemed to go beyond that which was needed for ESP.

"Knowing": *1) "Knowing" that an outcome will be positive may make the participant more* *open to the experience.* An example of this was when "knowing" indicated that a desired outcome would occur, which then enhanced openness to having that experience. This was clearly true for Auerbach, who said, "It was inevitably a strike when that happened. Not that it happened that often! I wish it could have!" Thus, "knowing" he would be successful in the detached MMI state not only made it an ASC that he welcomed, but also made him wish he could initiate more often.

2) "Knowing" that others are not open to MMI healing may cause the performer to stop his or her efforts. A healer may quit if they get a sense that the energy is not being accepted. Vaughan explained, "On rare occasions, I'll feel it's not doing any good. This person is really resisting this. So, I'll just stop."

Impact: *Successful MMI can enhance openness to further such experiences.* Smith pointed out that successful MMI may increase a performer's sense of efficacy, which may in turn create more openness to the experience and facilitate subsequent events. She stated of her metal-bending experience that "before I knew it was possible for other people, I didn't think it was possible for me. When I did the first spoon, then my belief changed, and I believed that I could do it." Her immediate reaction was to bend a number of other spoons. She stated that the next ones were "a lot easier! I put that one aside because I wanted to take it home to show David, picked up another spoon, and within a matter of seconds that one went soft and ... I twisted up three or four." However, other factors, such as relaxation, trying less hard (or trusting the process), and a mood shift could also have been involved here.

Summary

Openness appeared to be crucial to MMI and showed up in a variety of ways. Performers often opened up by dropping barriers to allow information and energy flow in. However, they were also open to their experiences, perhaps in part as an result of their personality styles and worldviews. A belief that one can do MMI is unnecessary for spontaneous MMI and a fair bit of intentional MMI as well, as long as the performer is open to the experience on some level. Confidence may be helpful for overcoming inhibiting factors, such as performing in public or with hostile bystanders. However, it is not by itself either necessary or sufficient for MMI to occur.

Openness was enmeshed with a number of the other constituents. In a way, openness to an experience represents a willingness to suspend disbelief, and to see what can happen without the interference or criticism of the intellect. It also suggests a lack of attachment to a rigid worldview. Hence, it is possible that beliefs could act to modify MMI performance either through encouraging the performer to be open to the possibility of MMI, and/or willingness to open up to that state, as well as effect what can be connected and how deeply.

One MMI performer brought up the subject that having a model to work from was important, but astutely noted that whether or not that model was correct did not matter. Many of the other participants also mentioned having a model they liked to use, several of which differed in fundamental ways, yet appeared to be equally effective.

Having a model for MMI might assist performers on a number of levels. It could (1) create a structure of beliefs that make MMI acceptable, hence normalizing it; (2) generate (rightly or wrongly) a sense of control over the process and enhance the "comfort zone" of performers; (3) bypass ownership resistance by crediting the MMI to a discarnate source, ritual, or another entity; (4) get the conscious mind out of the way of whatever really needs to happen; (5) be correct and guide performers in MMI; (6) allow performers to let go of the need to analyze what is going on since they have a "reason" for what is occurring; and (7) enhance a sense of trust in the process. It was noted during the interview process that a worldview that supported the idea of MMI appeared to make it easier for performers to accept responsibility for their events. However, it was unclear whether this also had an effect on MMI performance per se.

"Knowing"

The word "to know" is a vague one in English, with diverse meanings. For the purposes of this book, "knowing" refers to knowledge where there is not a known explanation or obvious factual background for the origins of the data. This may involve a mixture of ESP, input from forgotten sources, subliminal information, and cues picked up by the unconscious mind that are too subtle for the conscious mind to recognize. It is often impossible to tease out just where this information comes from, whether paranormal or otherwise. Hence, they are lumped together as one constituent.

The potential for nonparanormal aspects to "knowing" are of critical importance. If it were not for subtle, subliminal, and forgotten information, it is possible that "knowing" would not exist as a constituent. This is because for decades the parapsychological literature has argued over whether ESP and MMI are truly different processes or really the same thing, which should be more accurately referred to as simply psi. If ESP *is* the same as MMI — as we will later see is not incompatible with the data — then the fact that ESP as "knowing" appears so commonly during these experiences is only to be expected. It would be like asking whether psi happens during psi experiences. How could it not? It does by definition. The real surprise might be for this constituent to be absent — although given the sometimes subtle qualities of "knowing," there would be no way to tell whether it was really missing or simply unrecognized.

A sense of "knowing" was very common during MMI events, and appeared to play a number of roles in the experience. It was deeply enmeshed with the ASC, connection, the sense of energy, focused awareness, openness, trust, and guiding the process. Also, in some cases the "knowing" involved the physical state. However, perhaps more than anything else, "knowing" was a necessary part of guiding the process. There was frequently an intuitive sense of what needed to be said or done and an awareness of completion when the work was finished. There could also be a "knowing" the outcome of the MMI attempt.

What the Literature Says

A sense of "knowing" may be an aspect of what Murphy and White referred to as instinctive action in sports.[149] Indeed, Murphy and White noted that many athletes had a sense of "inward knowing."[150] Given the hours and years of training often involved, it would seem likely that this is the result of more than just ESP — although Murphy and White described ESP as part of sports EHEs.

"Knowing" would also seem to be an aspect incorporated by advanced martial artists. As mentioned before, the Japanese sword master Miyamoto Musashi wrote of the importance of forgetting everything one as learned and acting by instinct.[151] As he put it, this allowed the fighter to strike spontaneously and beat his opponent.

Finally, "knowing" appeared to be an aspect of the "resonance" described by Loftur Gissurarson.[152] He pointed out that "resonance" seemed to be the most successful strategy for computer tasks. This "resonance" was portrayed as a mixture of MMI constituents, including "immersion in the process to the point of some loss of awareness" (which may be suspension of the intellect and/or dissociation from the ego identity), connection, and "knowing" what to do.[153]

Aspects of "Knowing"

1. There may be a "knowing" of the outcome. Robinson sometimes "knew" when she was going to succeed at a task or cause a tape recorder to malfunction. She stated, "Sometimes I know. That's the only thing I can say. Sometimes I know." She also said of an experience when she healed a patient's hand, "it's like this knowing, suddenly, just before it curled ... I had this knowing." With "zone" experiences, "knowing" was more apt to manifest as an awareness of what was going on with the patient, or whether the patient would be okay. Robinson noted, "I just remember the feeling of doing this reading in this very lovely room where I sat by myself and ... basically, I knew as I brought up the body, and I read it, I knew it was going to be fine."

Smith commented that her RNG flow experiences often involved a sense of "knowing." This manifested in one of two ways. In the first, it was as an intuitive feeling of confidence that she would be successful. She reported, "Sometimes, occasionally, I would know it was going to be a ... good run." In the second, she experienced a "knowing" of what she needed to do to succeed. Smith recalled that information sometimes came in chunks with the Psychic Reward program.[154] She reflected:

> I think when I first started it I would be more deliberate with which key I pressed. After a while, it was like, okay, it's T, R, and F. You know, one would come after the other. I wouldn't just go and press one key. I'd say okay, I know which sequence is going to come up, so I would press those. So, that happened a couple of times; they came in chunks.

It is also possible that precognition (as described in DAT theory), was what was really being used rather than MMI. Smith acknowledged:

> I went down with a spirit of inquiry ... and started doing some of the micro–PK experiments, and found that I was moderately successful.... I don't know if I was forcing it in the direction of intention or whether there was some other pattern, perhaps, in the device which I was recognizing.

2. There may be a "knowing" of responsibility for the MMI event. Auerbach declared:

> I knew it was PK. I mean, I knew internally that it was me causing it.... I just knew that it was me.... Just like I know when I pick up a piece of paper. It didn't feel any different to me internally, you know. Externally when you pick up something you feel it with your fingertips, and you feel the weight, but internally I'm picking something up. That's kind of what it felt like, I'm moving something. But I didn't feel the touch of it, or the weight of it.

The same sense of "knowing" was present for Auerbach with metal-bending as well. He noted,

> There was that same sense of knowing.... I mean, I bent some other spoons that, that night in a slightly altered state, because everybody was in that sense. I knew implicitly when I was bending it physically and when I wasn't.

With spontaneous MMI there was often no awareness that something would be affected until it happened. The MMI event itself may be abrupt and without warning—although Smith sometimes had a sense of "knowing" responsibility after the event, such as when a rock jumped next to her.

3. There may be a sense of knowing that it is time to stop sending MMI energy. Vaughan said, "You mean is there a switch that says okay, you've got it, that's enough? Well, sometimes there is."

How "Knowing" Relates to
the Other Constituents

Altered State of Consciousness: *1) The ASC may enhance the sense of "knowing."* Robinson and Martin both referred to their ASC as "being in that space of knowing." Vaughan stated that his ASC allowed him to receive psi information from other places, times, and dimensions.

2) The altered state may be associated with a "knowing" of success. Auerbach, in particular, noted that he has a specific detached ASC associated with "knowing" he will be successful.

Connection: *Connection may enhance the sense of "knowing" or receiving information about the target or what needs to be done.* The "knowing" that occurred with connecting to a target may involve ESP. Martin, for example, views the patient clairvoyantly at the moment of connection.

Sense of Energy: *Energy may be sensed as a form of "knowing."* "Knowing" played an important role in guiding the type of energy, its intensity, and flow, as well as providing valuable feedback on how well the MMI energy is being received. Anomalous healers often reported a sense of "knowing" the healee's energy pattern, as well as the quality of healing energy being sent.

Physical State: *There may be a sense of receiving information or "knowing" as changes in the body.* Robinson reported "knowing" what was wrong with a patient by how her own body feels. This physical feeling is in the manner of a code that she can interpret.

Focused Awareness: *What the performer is aware of through "knowing" may be determined by what his or her mind is focused on.* When healers were focused on the energetic level, it allowed them to sense specifics about what kind of work is needed, a patient's energy pattern, and various characteristics or qualities of the energy being used.

Trust in the Process: *1) "Knowing" that there will be a successful outcome can make it easier to trust the process.* As noted before, Auerbach "knew" it was okay to trust what would happen when he entered the detached ASC he associated with MMI.

2) Trust in the process may facilitate "knowing" what to do. Martin spoke of trusting the information or guidance that she received through "knowing."

Openness to the Experience: *1) "Knowing" that an outcome will be positive may make the participant more open to the experience.* This seemed to be true for Auerbach's MMI, where being in the detached state and "knowing" the outcome was something he welcomed (indeed, relished) and wished he could initiate more often.

2) "Knowing" that others are not open to MMI healing may cause the performer to stop his or her efforts.

Guiding the Process: *1) There may be a "knowing" of how to guide the process.* Participants often said that knowledge acquired as "knowing" told them what to do. Martin, for example, reported being told by spirit guides what to do. She stated, "I was being directed to put my hands over her body," and, "I was told intuitively put them in a circle around you, and have her lay down and put your hands just above the ... gallbladder."

Schwartz remarked that "knowing" was part of a feedback system, which helped him to guide anomalous healing energy. This was an interactive process, as he described below:

> You send it through and then ... it sort of comes, this kind of echo that comes back up and it's at that point that you start pulling off the ... things that are imbalanced. And you move over the body with ... circular motions to close things and counterclockwise motions to open things up. And you just do that the way it feels.

Schwartz also told of an incident where the "knowing" of what to do guided him in healing his daughter. He recalled:

> I just had this very strong knowing. I just put my hand down and just prayed for her and just sent healing to her.... I was asking to be a channel of energy for her. I was seeing light — well that's my visualization of energy — pouring through me, like water going down a waterfall.... And so, I was doing that, but then, at the second phase of it, I was pulling stuff off that I experienced as toxic.... Anyway, I did this with my daughter and I felt her fever break. It just broke.... The crisis passed. It happened in about, oh, I don't know, three or four minutes.... All of a sudden, I just felt this thing give way. And she was healed. Not only did the fever break, but ... whatever it was she had ... was over.

2) There may be a "knowing" that guides the performer as feedback. An example of this was when "knowing" recipients were not open to receiving MMI healing and guided performers to stop their efforts. As mentioned earlier, Vaughan commented that he stops sending energy if he has a sense of "knowing" that it is not being accepted. He explained, "Sometimes, every now and then, on rare occasions, I'll feel it's not doing any good. This person is really resisting this. So, I'll just stop.... Most people, or certainly animals, animals often go with it, they never fight you back."

Similarly, Martin said that she knows intuitively if a healing is not being well received. She stated, "When they turn away from me and they do not accept the white goop it means that they want to die."

SUMMARY

"Knowing" refers to knowledge without a known explanation or obvious factual background for the origins of that data. This can be a complex jumble of ESP, information from forgotten sources, subliminal input, and other, normal cues picked up by the unconscious mind that are not consciously recognized.

Performers often described a sense of "knowing" during their MMI experiences. This variously involved feelings of confidence in the outcome, a sense of responsibility for the event, remote viewing, or a "knowing" that the energy is not being received and the healer should stop. The constituents of an ASC, trust in the process, and a sense of "knowing" were often tightly interwoven. Furthermore, "knowing" appeared to be closely associated with or enhanced by feelings of connection. Energy was often sensed or understood in terms of "knowing," and the body itself was sometimes the instrument by which this type of knowledge was understood or interpreted. Openness to the experience could both enhance "knowing" and, in some cases, be enhanced by the feelings of impending success that "knowing" brought. More than anything else, "knowing" was used to guide the process, especially during anomalous healing experiences. Considering that ESP offers potential immediate feedback even for long-distance targets, it is not surprising that "knowing" would be such an integral and important constituent of the MMI experience.

Guiding the Process

The term "guiding the process" emphasizes that MMI performers were not *controlling* events so much as they were becoming a part of the process, enabling them to act (or react) in a cooperative manner. This guidance was gentle, almost effortless. This constituent only showed up in visible ways during intentional experiences. Although it is possible (even probable) that a certain amount of direction occurs on a subconscious level in spontaneous events, there is no way to determine this for sure. Spontaneous events were frequently of brief duration. However, the fact that spontaneous events often meet needs (even if just venting off steam) and are personally meaningful would seem to suggest that they are not completely random events.

Typically, the research literature speaks of using visualization or focused intent to make MMI occur. However, this may not be the best approach for would-be performers to take. Descriptions of successful intentional MMI suggested that guidance was an interactive, non-controlling process which involved a transcendent level. Such guidance could involve a combination of visualization and intent. Perhaps more importantly, this constituent was deeply enmeshed with the ASC, connection, sense of energy, physical state, focus awareness, and "knowing." The latter was particularly important, as MMI frequently involved ongoing intuitive feedback, which allowed performers to adjust their techniques as needed for a better outcome. This was especially true for anomalous healing experiences, where most participants spoke of "knowing" of what needed to be done and doing it.

WHAT THE LITERATURE SAYS

Most of the research literature has focused on how participants try to "control" events. For example, Loftur Gissurarson described the use of visualization and focused intent (sometimes involving use of the hands) in his review of methods used to control MMI.[155] Michael Murphy and Rhea White observed that similar techniques are used in sports EHEs.[156] Athletes frequently spoke of "willing" things to happen, such as to make a football or golf ball change direction mid-flight. At times, they created a mental picture of what they wished to have happen and believed they could make it occur through the power of their minds.

ASPECTS OF GUIDING THE PROCESS

1. The process may be guided by visualization. Many of the participants used visualization to guide MMI events. Vaughan gave the following example of how he typically performed anomalous healing:

> The model I use in the meditation, sort of, is to bring it down through the top of my head. To visualize like the universe, the center of bright light, coming down like a laser beam through the top of my head and through my body, and to flow through me and to where ever I direct. I do a fair amount of absent healing, too, where I visualize the person, and visualize light coming around them, and I also have a feeling of well-being that I try to project to them, see a smile on their face, and then have their, that they have their own connection with that source of energy.

Vaughan noted that he sometimes used a kind of image of his hands to guide the process and explained, "Even if they're at a distance. Every now and then, I'll sort of mentally put my hands around them." However, Vaughan felt visualization was ineffective unless energy was put into it. He stated, "Just picturing something in your mind is not enough. I mean you could be picturing a TV show you saw last night, so what? You have to energize. You have to supply that picture with energy."

2. The process may be guided by intent. As with athletes, MMI performers sometimes spoke of using intent, or "wishing" to make things change in the desired manner. Smith said, "There was a sense of perhaps my wishing or willing it could make it change."

How Guiding the Process Relates to the Other Constituents

Altered State of Consciousness: *The process may be guided by the ASC.* Controlling the energy flow may involve responding to a felt sense of being in the right ASC. The ASC may also affect the ability to focus awareness, and guide the energy.

Connection: *Levels of connection may be altered as a method of guiding the process.* Vaughan used different levels of connection in various situations, which suggested that this may be an aspect which is controlled, depending on the need.

Sense of Energy: *1) The energy can be guided.* Simply put, there was a sense that the energy could be directed wherever the MMI performer wished it.

2) Guiding the process can be an interactive process, which is determined (at least in part) by how the energy is sensed. Performers often used their sense of energy (whether felt physically or through "knowing") to guide the process. This guidance in turn frequently took the form of directing and controlling the energy. Thus, the sense of energy was critical to a feedback loop used in some forms of MMI, particularly anomalous healing.

Physical State: *1) The process may be guided or affected by physical proximity.* Smith reported that spontaneous MMI targets were often physically near her when she affected them. This pattern was shared by a number of MMI performers, sometimes even true for intentional targets.

2) The event may be triggered by a body position. Wigal triggered his experiences through the use of a yoga posture.

3) Changes in how the body feels may be used to guide the process. There may be a sense of receiving information or "knowing" through changes in how the body feels.

4) The body may be used to guide the energy. Participants used their hands, breath and voice to direct energy, especially during anomalous healing.

Focused Awareness: *The process may be guided through focused awareness.* MMI energy was sometimes directed by intent or focused attention.

"Knowing": *There may be a "knowing" of how to guide the process.* Participants often used knowledge acquired as "knowing" to tell them what to do. This had an interactive quality, whereby the process was guided by an intuitive sense of the qualities of the energy being sent, the energy state of the recipient, and what kind of effect the process was having.

Summary

Although most of the research literature has focused on how to "control" MMI, this may not be the best way to accomplish it. More often, successful intentional performers guided the process in a non-controlling, interactive, participatory manner. Some referred to this as involving "wishing," or a kind of effortless "intent." Visualization or imagery was commonly used, but may not be enough by itself. Instead, this image may have to be energized in some way in order for it to be effective.

Guidance of the process involved the use of other constituents, including a combination of the ASC, connection, a sense of energy, focused awareness or intent, use of the body (such as postures or hand gestures) and "knowing." Physical proximity was helpful in some cases — particularly in spontaneous events — but by no means necessary.

Almost by definition, one does not see a conscious or deliberate guidance of the process during spontaneous MMI. However, the meaningfulness of these events has to bring up the question of whether guidance might not still be occurring on an unconscious level.

Impact

MMI can have a definite impact on performers — and probably witnesses, as well.[157] This should not be surprising, given that the events often have intense personal meaning. As such, they can bring up strong emotions and cause major shifts in worldview — sometimes acting as pivotal life events. Except for a few cases involving MMI parties, impact was rarely a factor during the experiences themselves, more often occurring afterwards. Because of this, impact is better thought of as a long-term factor.

One often hears stories of teenagers playing with Ouija boards, triggering spontaneous MMI with objects flying all over the room, and terrifying the participants, sometimes leading to a deep-seated fear of psi. However, none of the experiences in the study were negative ones. It is possible that this is, at least to some extent, a reporting artifact. All the participants were volunteers who had a long history of MMI. They probably would not have had so many (often intentional) events or been willing to talk about them if they had not been comfortable with their experiences.

The greatest overall impact of MMI was on a performer's worldview and his or her openness to having future experiences. In some cases, there were also positive physical, emotional and psychological benefits, whether temporary — as in improving a bad mood or stiff back — or more permanent, as in long-term self-esteem, happiness, and spirituality.

Impact only appears to be associated with a few of the constituents of the immediate MMI experience. For the most part, successful MMI can affect mood and emotion (often for the better), make it easier to have more trust in the process, and create greater openness to future experiences.

WHAT THE LITERATURE SAYS

Little has been said in the literature about the impact of MMI on performers. Michael Murphy and Rhea White addressed it the best, describing a number of cases where transcendent experiences in sports have a positive impact.[158] At times, this was simply feeling good afterward. However, the effect could go much deeper, as with athletes and martial artists feeling more in touch with their true core essences, being uplifted, having new insights, and experiencing personal growth. In some cases, it even altered their entire worldviews and deepened their spirituality.

ASPECTS OF IMPACT

1. The experience can be empowering. Several performers said their experiences changed their beliefs about what they were capable of doing. Smith said, "Before I knew it was possible for other people. I didn't think it was possible for me. When I did the first spoon, then my belief changed, and I believed that I could do it." She also commented:

> I think it's a change of belief. That you feel you're not able to do something, you
> think everybody else can do it, but you can't. And it happens, and you do it, and
> you've been told that it's one of the things that's almost impossible to do, but you do it,
> and you go wow! I did it! So, it's a feeling of achievement.

Schwartz noted: "You recognize that the limitations of reality that you have accepted are not ... the final limitations. That you can go beyond this. And here's an example. You're doing it. So there is an empowering aspect to it."

2. The experiences may provide validation. Smith welcomed her MMI experiences because they validated her worldview. She reflected:

> I think there's a feeling, when the event happens — like the bowl spinning or the rock jumping — there's an immediate sense of surprise, making me jump, whoa! Then there's almost a feeling of pleasure that these things still happen, because ... these things fit ... into my wider worldview, and I still like to think that they happen.

For Auerbach, the impact was a sense of satisfaction. It also reinforced why he chose the low-paying field of parapsychology for his career. He recalled of a time he made a heavy ashtray move that "a part of me was jumping up and down inside, but part of it was saying this is why I'm in the field."

3. The experience can enhance spirituality. Although Wigal was more affected by the ASC associated with his MMI than from the events itself, he admitted that they gave him an enhanced sense of interconnectedness and spirituality, saying he felt "much more in union with the deity now."

4. The experience can change a person's worldview. MMI experiences can change the way individuals view reality. Schwartz said of a group MMI event that "I just I didn't anticipate it, I didn't think it was going to happen.... It really showed me that consciousness has the capacity to alter time-space."

Vaughan also commented that his psi experiences, including MMI, have affected his view of reality and how the world works. He explained:

> My feeling about it is that we have realms of responsibility, or realms of experience, the things, that we can recognize things about our own personal life.... But ... that this is part of a larger collective vision, and event. And so, people can realize that their joint visions can carry a collective energy. They can create that positive reality. And it starts with each person's participation.

5. The experience may be life-changing. Schwartz felt that MMI experiences are intrinsically deeply meaningful. He explained, "My whole life has been changed because at various times I have been privileged either to experience or witness the occurrence of things which tell you that the world is not put together quite so simply as you thought."

How Impact Relates to Constituents of the Immediate Experience

Emotion: *The experience may cause the performer to feel strong positive emotions.* Positive emotional impact was common after MMI and can include feelings of validation, pride, joy, excitement, surprise, exultation, awed pleasure, and amazement. Furthermore, it sometimes transformed a negative state (such as anger or frustration) into a positive one.

Trust in the Process: *Successful MMI can enhance trust in the process.* A past history of successful MMI made it easier for performers to trust that the process would work for them again.

Openness to the Experience: *Successful MMI can enhance openness to further such experiences.* Successful MMI increased performer feelings of self-efficacy, which in turn created more openness to the experience and facilitated subsequent events.

Summary

MMI experiences often had an impact on the people who performed them. This should not be surprising, given that these events often have intense personal meaningfulness. Nor is this impact necessarily a small or transient one. MMI can bring up strong emotions and cause major shifts in worldview — sometimes acting as a pivotal, life-changing event.

Impact is rarely a factor at the moment of experience itself, occurring more often between them. Because of this, impact is better thought of as a long-term factor, instead of an aspect of the individual experience as it is occurring.

There is relatively little in the literature about the impact of MMI. Murphy and White have noted how an EHE can have a positive effect on an athlete's worldview, sense of spirituality, and personal growth.[159] Certainly, all of the experiences reported by participants were positive ones — although it is possible that this was a reporting artifact, since all of them were volunteers who had a history of repeated MMI performance and were willing to talk about their experiences. However, the literature generally supports the notion that the majority of psi experiences have a positive impact.

The overall effect of impact is on a performer's worldview and his or her openness to having other experiences. In some cases, there were also positive emotional and psychological benefits, whether temporary — as in improving a bad mood — or more permanent, as in long-term feelings of empowerment, awe, and joy. Feeling better physically (as Wigal did after his experiences) tended to be more of a short-term benefit. There were some instances, such as at MMI parties, when performers felt that the positive impact of being successful at MMI made it easier for them to bend more metal. It is possible that this may be because of enhancing trust in the process. Regardless, MMI experiences generally seemed to have a positive impact and enhanced the lives of those who had them.

ESP and MMI Overlap

ESP was originally listed as a constituent of the MMI experience.[160] However, continued review of the data suggested that ESP experiences might be virtually identical to, if not the same as, those of MMI. This brought up the idea (long discussed in the parapsychological literature) that ESP and MMI could be the same thing by two names. Less than a year after the original study, this author was already leaning in that direction, noting that ESP and MMI may, in fact, have the same core experience, with the apparent differences more superficial than real.[161]

Although there have been some phenomenological studies on synchronicity, NDEs, and various specific subtype ESP experiences, there have been as yet no formal definitive phenomenological studies on ESP as a whole. This chapter considers the possible overlap between ESP and MMI experiences in the literature, as well as what MMI performers spontaneously mentioned.

WHAT THE LITERATURE SAYS

The literature has long noted the overlap between MMI and ESP and the possibility that they are, in fact, the same thing. There are three ways of looking at these phenomena as one: (1) MMI and ESP are a unitary process called psi, which has active and passive aspects; (2) there is only ESP, with MMI falsely appearing different; or (3) there is only MMI, with ESP actually a form of MMI. All three notions have been put forth at one time or another in the literature.

Gertrude Schmeidler discussed the idea that MMI and ESP are intrinsically the same process at length in her book, *Parapsychology and Psychology: Matches and Mismatches*. She cited a number of experiments in which ESP and MMI were intrinsically related. These included work with Ted Serios, Ingo Swann, and Alex Tanous, where successful ESP was associated with changes in physical instruments. Such changes were not seen when the participants were unsuccessful at ESP. Schmeidler concluded, "On balance, the theory of an intrinsic ESP-

MMI relation still seems worth considering, and recent research has given results in line with it."[162]

The idea that MMI might really be ESP is the basic premise behind the theory of Decision Augmentation Theory (DAT). Of course, this works better with RNG/REG computer targets than it does for watching a spoon flop over or an ashtray move on its own. However, the notion that participants and/or experimenters use precognition to chose when to start their trials, or what final outcome to shoot for, so as to get the results through random chance is likely to factor into at least some successful events.[163]

Parapsychologist Rex Stanford proposed a theory that ESP was a form of MMI.[164] The notion that telepathy results from the sender actively causing a change in the brain chemistry of the receiver is referred to as the Mental or Behavioral Influence of an Agent (MOBIA). Unfortunately, this is not currently verifiable — in other words, can be neither proven true nor false. Nonetheless, it would appear that the line between ESP and MMI may be a blurred one, difficult to determine.

Recent years have seen a resurgence of interest in the idea that all psi is one process. Lance Storm and Michael Thalbourne pointed out that "what appears as PK under one ontology appears as ESP under another ontology."[165] This leads to an impasse, which can best be broken by using a neutral term (the reason parapsychologists adopted the Greek letter of "psi" in the first place). Storm and Thalbourne proposed the theory of psychopraxia — which basically translates from Latin as the soul or self achieving goals.[166] It suggests that ESP and MMI emerge from the same underlying process, and vary in only minor ways, if at all. Although some have found the term awkward to use, it does a service in emphasizing the goal-directed nature of psi.

If MMI and ESP are the same, one would expect their core experiences to be identical. Phenomenological ESP reports have mentioned some of the same constituents as are listed by MMI experiencers. For example, Michael Murphy and Rhea White looked at anomalous experiences in sports and felt ESP and MMI experiences both appear to occur in the same ASC known as "the zone," although they acknowledge that some situations make it difficult, if not impossible, to separate out subtle sensory cues from extrasensory information.[167]

Dorothy Hanson and Jon Klimo investigated the experience of synchronicity, which they described as "coincidence that is acausal, wherein certain events do not seem to be connected by normal causal means, and that is also particularly meaningful to the experiencer."[168] They analyzed the descriptions of 28 participants. They found (1) 45 percent surrendered control (trust in the process); (2) 61 percent experienced inner, or intuitive, promptings (a sense of "knowing"); (3) 46 percent had a peak experience, spiritual experience, or transpersonal state of consciousness (ASC); and (4) 43 percent felt faith or trust.

Kathleen Barrett studied the experiences of nine mediums who felt they were receiving, or channeling, information from paranormal sources.[169] She looked at the experience from two viewpoints — that of the person receiving the information and that of his or her "source" (which is a valid experience whether that source is a discarnate entity or an aspect of the medium's unconscious mind). Barrett found a number of themes that will by now be familiar to the reader, including (1) the sense of a close relationship to the entity channeled (feelings of connection); (2) the reception of information, which was then expressed by the mediums ("knowing"); (3) mental and emotional detachment from the channeled information (dissociation); (4) physical sensations related to the transmission (physical state); and (5) positive feelings about their experiences (impact). She also noted that the mediums (1) perceived their sources of information as being separate nonphysical or nonhuman entities; (2) felt they were cooperating in a working partnership; and (3) had a sense of control over the over the transmission (which might be, on some level, an indication that they can guide — or at least initiate — the process). Furthermore, it was also possible, based on their statements that "channeling helped them to balance their logical, left-brain activity in a constructive way," that mediums had at least partial suspension of the intellect during these experiences.[170]

The sources, as interviewed through their channels, had similar experiences with the addition of four elements: (1) a sense of adjusting their vibrational frequency in order to communicate (possibly an awareness of energy); (2) monitoring and protecting the channel's body/mind ("knowing" and awareness of the medium's energy and physical state); (3) fulfilling a previous commitment (investment in the process); and (4) viewing channeling as a learning experience (impact). There would appear to be considerable overlap between Barrett's constituents and that of MMI experiences. One cannot help but wonder whether an ASC was not also a major aspect of these experiences, if unexpressed, as well as a certain degree of trust in the process.

Henry Reed looked at the experiences of ordinary individuals who felt they were in psychic contact with another person during workshops where they were paired up and asked to imagine being in contact with the other person.[171] He obtained descriptions of this experience from participants. Based on that material and his own experiences, he noted that there appeared to be three phases. First, a sense of "contact," which sometimes involved images of light, warmth (often in the hands), or energetic images suggestive of merger. Some participants felt a barrier disappeared during this phase (openness). Second, a period of mild dissociation, or a lapse of attention or consciousness (possibly suspension of the intellect). Descriptions of this phase suggest that shifts in consciousness are important for making a connection. Finally, participants experienced a narrative fantasy, or sense of merger (connection and, if accurate, "knowing"). Afterwards, these individuals had feelings of satisfaction and felt closer to their partners (impact). Focused awareness was intrinsic to the situation, since couples were told to imagine being in contact with each other.

Timothy West studied ten individuals with NDEs.[172] He found seven constituent themes, which included (1) leaving the body, traveling, and returning to the body (suggesting possibilities of dissociation as well as awareness of the physical state); (2) experiencing infinity with a surrender to and/or merger with a higher power (a combination of connection and trust); (3) experiencing divine refuge and/or homecoming with feelings of love, acceptance, peace, and joy (peak emotion); (4) experiencing absolute truth and divine knowledge (possible ASC); (5) recognizing the experience as ineffable (again, possibly indicative of an ASC and suspension of the intellect); (6) perceiving a personal message (which could be by "knowing"); (7) seeing the experience as transformative (impact). There was an intrinsic meaningfulness to the event, which related to it having a positive impact.

Harvey Irwin described OBEs as involving somatoform dissociation and psychological absorption.[173] He stated that this is where people are completely engrossed in their own thoughts, such that there is "'total' attention."[174] This suggests an element of focused awareness in addition to the altered perception of the body that is characteristic of the experience.

Joseph McMoneagle, one of the leading remote viewers today, believed an ASC, suspension of the intellect, focused awareness, and openness were important factors for successful clairvoyance.[175] When asked how to best learn remote viewing, he described it as similar to the mental and spiritual state of Zen, where the ASC focuses the viewer to the point that they have no other thought. McMoneagle also spoke of openness in two ways. First, that remote viewers must be open to the possibility of psi (which is not to say that they are sure it exists, but only that they are willing to consider the notion). And second they must be open to whatever works. McMoneagle added,

> In the land of remote viewing, anything is possible. It is usually the surprising information that proves to be correct. The more open someone is to any possibility and the least wedded they are to a fixed reality, the more likelihood of success.[176]

In his review of anomalous healers, Allan Cooperstein found that ESP often happens during healing experiences.[177] This most often appeared as telepathy or a clairvoyant sense of what was wrong with the patient. However, other forms of ESP also occurred, including precognition, retrocognition, and a visual or kinesthetic sense of the patient's energy field.

ASPECTS OF OVERLAP BETWEEN MMI AND ESP

1. ESP and MMI are both active, energetic processes. Vaughan felt that MMI and ESP were integrally related, with both using the same energy and being active, expressive processes. He commented:

> It is an extremely important point that there is an energy that enables one to bring through information from another person, or about another person, or whatever. And also healing. I mean my model of it is that one is putting forth thought-consciousness-energy to the target. I would call that ESP, but it's also part of healing, that you put out the energy, or direct it.

Vaughan was emphatic that mentally reaching out to tune in and connect to the unique code of a person or information is an active process. He explained:

> Well, consider that there are billions upon billions of humans, living and having lived in the past, and everybody's got their own code, everybody's different. And so it's like dialing that access code, to tune into that individual person. And so it's an art ... I feel like I'm putting out energy, kind of scanning to find that right person.

When asked if something Martin had said earlier in the interview meant ESP is an active process, she replied, "Definitely ... Very active. That's where the energy comes from. That's where I feel it comes in. And then ... it's just like I'm a television set, you know, I'm getting a picture ... and all kinds of stuff."

2. ESP and MMI are facilitated by the same ASC. Smith described an experience where the MMI event occurred towards the end of an extended remote viewing (ERV) session. Thus, the same ASC that she used for ESP also worked for MMI performance.

Robinson felt the state she used for MMI was similar to, but deeper than, that needed for ESP. She said, "I'm in a place of being very open, and getting information that's even beyond what's even being 'intuitive' or just 'psychic.'" Robinson was usually in an ESP task just prior to, or during, the time that MMI occurred, which were often toward the ends of her sessions.

Auerbach observed that the state he was in when he had OBEs was the same as he used for MMI. In talking about the time an ashtray moved, he reflected, "I distinctly remember being extremely bored. This was around the time when I also was having, had had a couple of out-of-body experiences. So, I was not unused to that. That also happened when I was bored, too."

Wigal also felt his ASC were essentially the identical for the two. He reported multiple experiences of ESP — such as knowing when the phone would ring, knowing where people are in buildings, and communicating with animals — that seemed to occur in the same relaxed meditative state that facilitated MMI.

3. ESP and MMI may occur simultaneously: *(a) Clairvoyance may occur during MMI.* Martin frequently clairvoyantly "saw" the patient at the moment of connection during MMI healing. She said, "It's like remote viewing.... It's the same process." Martin talked about this in the following excerpt:

> On the third breath when I send them the goop ... I immediately get a picture of that person. And it's like they're a long ways away. I can see them, they're either standing, sitting, sometimes I've seen them in bed. I've described the whole room.... And what has been so extraordinary, especially in the class with a group, is that they will go

right back and, you know, see that person, talk to them or find out what happened at that particular time.... And, that's where the person was, they were either in the bedroom, they were sitting on a chair, they were in the place. I mean I saw them where they were.

b) ESP frequently seems to guide the MMI process. This was especially true for anomalous healing. Schwartz noted how energy would be moved around, or the ASC adjusted, depending on how it "felt." This "feeling" sense seemed to be a combination of ESP and knowing. Other anomalous healers also spoke of this.

4. The physical sensations for MMI may be the same as for ESP. Martin noted that the same area of the frontal lobes that feel active during MMI will hurt after intense ESP sessions.

5. ESP and MMI may have a shared limit. Overuse of one form of psi appeared to disable the other. Vaughan remembered what happened after a particularly intense anomalous healing session, saying:

> I could feel this tremendous amount of energy flowing through me, really, really hot ... for about half an hour. And she felt great. But I felt then, later on, I felt like I had this hole in my stomach. And I couldn't do anything for two or three days because of it.

Vaughan also noted, "At the very extreme end, it feels like I've got a hole in my stomach. It feels kind of nervous, and, but essentially it prevents me from getting any accurate psychic impressions." It is possible that this may relate in part to the active energy needed to connect for ESP.

6. RNG/REG experiences (which may be ESP) were not different than macro–MMI experiences. There was only one participant who seemed to have a different experience for some (but not all) RNG targets than for other kinds of events. This seemed to suggest that micro–MMI in general, and RNG/REG targets specifically, did not represent different experiences but were, in fact, similar or the same.

MMI Constituents that Appear in ESP Experiences

Although participant interviews were focused on MMI, a number of performers spontaneously mentioned ESP experiences as well. Because these experiences were not pursued in depth during the interviews, the following comments can only be suggestive of what ESP constituents would come to light in a proper phenomenological study. It is possible that constituents that are not part of the MMI experience might emerge.

Altered State of Consciousness: *An ASC is frequently involved in ESP.* Auerbach and Wigal both noted that the state for MMI is the same as, or similar to, what facilitates ESP. Wigal reported multiple experiences of ESP, such as knowing when the phone would ring, where people are in buildings, and communication from animals, which all occurred during the same kind of relaxed meditative state as he used for MMI. He told the following story:

> A similar experience now that I think about this.... We had a dog in the building here, about a year ago, running around in the hallway. And I got to know him and I got to feel that I was having conversations with the dog. We really seemed to have a rapport. I had a very relaxed feeling when I was with the dog. And once in the hallway when I was in this state, the dog came out and was going up and down the hallway, and I felt that his name was Grass. I didn't really know the owners, but I asked the owners," What's the dog's name?" And they told me. I said, "Did you ever think of calling him Grass?" They started to laugh, and they said, "Well, that's what he loves — grass — but we're going to move soon to where we have a yard." Right at that moment I glanced at the dog, and I actually felt like he was saying, "See, that's what I was trying to tell you!"

> It was really a weird feeling. I felt a communication with him. And another time
> when I was pretty much in this state out in the hallway, the dog ran by and he seemed
> to say that he didn't like the cold. He liked the part of the hallway where there were
> rugs, but not where there's tile, linoleum-like tile. He seemed to say, "Can't I avoid this
> cold thing and just walk on the rug part?" But I did feel his name was Grass. They
> moved ... to a place that had lots of grass. But those two times with the dog were only
> when I was in this relaxed stage. I saw him at other times when he was just another
> dog.

Participants spoke of altering consciousness to "tune in" information, or being in a place of "knowing." Vaughan described the ASC as involving an awareness of other dimensions. In recalling his first ESP experience, he noted, "And then I felt psychic. I mean, that is to say I felt other dimensions around me for about two hours."

Smith said of the ASC, "I've developed a technique where I can go into an ASC, do remote viewing in the ERV state." She also remarked,

> I've never actually done any measurements of that state doing remote viewing, but I
> think I go into a theta state, that cusp between the alpha and theta. I think that's where
> I am when I do ERV. And I think coming back up, probably into low alpha.

Robinson implied an ASC when doing psychic diagnosis here:

> I remember the state I was in for doing the reading.... I just remember the feeling of
> doing this reading in this very lovely room where I sat by myself.... The illness was the
> person's choice.... I mean that, of course, sounds pretty simple but that's really what it
> felt like in that state.... I just remember I was in an incredibly peaceful, centered place
> when I did that reading.

Connection: *ESP involves a sense of being connected to the target person or body of information.* Wigal spoke of having ESP experiences (such as knowing where they were) with people or animals when he felt connected to them. Vaughan reported connecting to people to whom he gave ESP readings and said, "Well, essentially my way of doing a psychic reading is to merge consciousness with the other person, you know, whether they're in the same room with me, or on the telephone, or off in a jungle in Brazil." Vaughan felt this was an active process.

Smith commented on how often people who are emotionally close know each other's thoughts or needs. She remarked:

> Dave and I do things all the time, you know.... I'll be in the kitchen and I'll pick up
> something not thinking, and he'll come in the kitchen and I'll hand it to him. [Imitat-
> ing male voice] "Oh yes, that's what I wanted." It's what he was looking for. But I
> think a lot of couples do that. You know, you get into a sync.

Robinson described connecting to a partner when performing psychic diagnosis. She recalled, "Al and I would start to work together, it was like one. We would be one body of information.... We never met the people. And often we'd be working only with a name and location." Robinson said of her diagnostic targets that "I slide into their body."

Martin used a person's name to connect in her ESP work. She explained:

> In all my work that I've done, the first name of the birth name is the most important
> thing. That's all I need from somebody is their birth name ... not what they use every
> day. I've had people call me on the radio — and you know I've done a lot of radio — and
> give me this name, and I'll stop and I'll say, "That's not your real name, is it?" And
> after a dead silence, they'll go, "No, it isn't, how did you know that?" [laughter]
> "Remember, I'm the psychic."

When asked how she knew the name wasn't right, Martin noted,

It doesn't feel right. It's the sound. It's on a sound wave.... You have to remember now, I'm a former opera singer, so I'm very tuned to sound waves. So if a relative or a friend is giving me the name, then there's a particular sound wave on the name, there's a vibration on the name.

Dissociation: *There may be dissociation from the individual ego identity during ESP.* Robinson reported a loss of individual identity during her psychic diagnostic sessions. She said, "I always feel we have the body, and that helps me, and I say it, I say we have the body." The shift from "I" to "we" suggests a loss of individual identity. She also mentioned that at the end of her sessions, "my intent was to bring me back to me." This again suggests that in some manner she does not feel her ordinary, individual identity during her ESP readings.

Suspension of the Intellect: *There is a suspension of the intellect during ESP.* Vaughan mentioned that he shifted away from analytical functioning when doing ESP. He said:

> That's the mistake a beginner always makes, is trying too hard. And with my software you can see it dramatically, with people scoring way below chance. Both in the ESP and the PK mode. And then once they begin to loosen up.... And I went through this myself ... it took me forever. Because I was being so super serious about this. And it took me a very long time to be able to do well with that.... I know, for instance, in doing psychic readings I won't be able to get the simplest names, because they're over in my left hand, [laugh] left side, I mean, but I'm over in my right side.

Martin also remarked that she suspends judgment whether doing ESP or MMI work. She stated, "You've experienced me that way when I do ghost work. Okay? It's very child-like. It's just wonderful fun. I just love it." When asked what she meant by child-like, Martin said, "In that children don't make judgments." She also stated that the following paragraph applied to ESP as well as to MMI:

> The ego cannot be there in any way, shape or form. And one of the things that I do in teaching my students is to make sure that their ego is out of the way. You have to just let it come, and you can't make any judgments. You have to let it just be there. Most important thing. And you have to trust that it is going to be there. And that's the hard part, you know, because we're so judgmental as human beings, and we're concerned, oh am I going to fool myself, and this is not going to work, and blah blah, blah, and the conscious mind is blah, blah, blahing to you all the time. What happens when I'm doing this, is that's just gone. It's just erased.

Emotion: *1) Emotions may be reported with ESP experiences.* Vaughan reported that during his first ESP experience he had "this most incredible sense of well-being that I'd ever felt ... before or since." Martin said of both ESP and MMI that she felt joy during the experiences. She noted, "It just brings me great joy. What can I tell you? And I do more laughing when I'm doing my readings. I'm always laughing, my clients are laughing." Martin also experienced positive feelings when using ESP with plants. She said, "I feel like they're talking to me. And it's just a wonderful communication, I just get thrilled.... It's a very strong sense of love. I think that's the best word to use, I guess."

2) Emotions may be able to trigger ESP events. Auerbach noted, "I've had other psychic, like out-of-body, experiences happen to me when I'm bored as well."

Sense of Energy: *1) ESP may involve energy.* Martin and Vaughan both specifically spoke of ESP using energy. Martin said that when she used ESP, "The top of my head will hurt when I finish. And it's because I'm bringing in the energy with information through there." Vaughan commented, "I was on a boat in the Caribbean, trying to do a whole bunch of readings on the last day, and about 5:30 this woman from Brazil, and I could feel energy giving out." Vaughan saw energy as necessary for performing ESP, and felt negative energy could prevent it. He told the following story:

> I recall doing an ESP experiment in San Francisco at the offices of the Examiner. And the object, well, it was an experiment I had done successfully many times before detecting which of ten film cans had a hidden object in it. And a friend had come along with me and he'd arranged the cans while my head was turned, and I tried, and again, I could put my hand over the top and feel the energy. Again, it was like a magnetic energy, over the target can and, sure enough, I was right. And then Percy Daeconus tried it, and he's a mathematician, who's written in the *Journal of Science* scathing attacks on parapsychology, and when he was there absolutely nothing happened. There was no energy. Just as if it didn't exist.

2) ESP may give the performer information about what is occurring on an energetic level. Robinson noted during a psychic diagnostic session that "I'll see how the energy is running through the body." She also noted in one particular case:

> I could feel her turning her energy in on herself. It felt like ... energy came from her spine and moved around the sides of her body, and went into her heart. And it just rotated that way, was the feeling I had. And I remember talking to her about it needed to not do that. It needed to go outward. Which I later learned was the way that the epileptic brainwaves grow, and what I was describing was the way that she needed to turn her brainwaves out, but I didn't know that.

Physical Sensations: *1) Doing ESP may cause the body to feel different.* As noted before, Martin said of her ESP experiences that "When I'm doing police work — which is the most strenuous thing that I do because I go on for hours — the top of my head will hurt when I finish."

2) ESP information may be received as body sensations. Auerbach and Robinson both mentioned getting ESP information as body sensations. As we saw with psychic healing, for Robinson, the diagnosis that preceded it gave her information as body feelings. She explained,

> I feel it and I have my own code for like MS [multiple sclerosis] to me feels like somebody put me into a corset and pulled it really tight. I have my own language for certain diseases or things going on. My own physical code for it.

Focused Awareness: *Awareness may be focused on what one is trying to get information about.* As noted earlier, there appeared to be an active focusing on the person one is trying to get information about through "tuning them in." Robinson also noted the importance of concentration when she performs psychic diagnosis with her partner, saying, "The only effort is in maintaining focus when we start. After that, it happens on its own."

Trust in the Process: *Trust is involved in getting ESP information.* Martin said that trust is a part of ESP experiences, the same as it is for MMI. She stated, "It's that child-like behavior of trusting the world."

Openness to the Experience: *There may be a sense of opening up to the information to get ESP.* Robinson described openness both to intuitive information and anything she could learn about psi at the onset of her ESP experiences. She recalled:

> It's like someone dropped a rock on my head and suddenly out of, it seemed out of nowhere, I was beginning just to have information, and it seemed like for no logical reason. I didn't know why suddenly why the top of my head had opened up and I was getting all this information. So that in itself was exciting to me. It was like suddenly there was a world out there that, you know, I innately knew was there but had forgotten about. So, I had started on this journey of reading a lot of things, and talking to everyone I could, and, you know, just ... couldn't get enough information.... I was reading everything I could get my hands on.

Vaughan implied that he dropped barriers and opened up his consciousness whether performing ESP or MMI. Martin also described her ESP work as involving "complete openness."

"Knowing": *ESP may involve a sense of "knowing."* Robinson mentioned a sense of knowing when doing psychic diagnosic work. She said, "I brought up the body, and I read it. I knew it was going to be fine. I knew that." The knowing may also come as being told things clairaudiently. Robinson observed:

> My background is in forensic psychology. So before all this started happening to me I was the one who evaluated people for insanity ... but I never thought I was crazy when I heard the voice. It was a male voice, and it sounded like it was off at a distance. And when I first realized I was hearing it, it was a little scary. I thought I had one foot in the grave or something like that. Then I realized I didn't. It was just a voice that made a statement. Never with judgment. It would just make a statement. And what I found was that the statement would be accurate.

Guiding the Process: *There seems to be an element of guiding ESP when obtaining the information.* Vaughan and Martin both mentioned actively scanning for the right person or information for ESP. Vaughan said, "It's like dialing that access code." This implies that they are somehow guiding the process of obtaining that information. Smith stated, "I did what is called an extended remote viewing, which is sitting or lying down in a relaxed state and allowing the consciousness to access the information."

Impact: *1) ESP experiences can impact spirituality.* In Wigal's case, a NDE had more impact on him than his seventeen years as a monk (or the MMI experiences by themselves). Wigal commented:

> I went through a special three-year training with the Dominicans in Chicago, which people who teach in novitiates are expected to go through — its courses in mysticism, asceticism, and so forth. And you study the Spanish mystics, and study all the odd aspects of spirituality in three intense summers at the Dominican House of Study for the Spirit of Theology. And I was about the only non-priest there. I was a monk, I was what some orders would call a brother..... And we had to study exorcisms, and study odd, strange, phenomena connected with spirituality, and during all of that, I never really had a deep spiritual experience. It was all academic. I got the certifications, I got the degrees, got the Masters in Theology from Notre Dame, and taught theology then at a Catholic university, and never had a real deep what I would call spiritual experience. It was only after coming back to the real world, and especially after my mom died and the near-death [experience] ... now I think I have a better feeling of why we're here, and what we're about. Now, I had these [PK] experiences like we began to talk about before, but I didn't connect them to spirituality.

2) ESP experiences can be life-changing events. Vaughan described the following after an experience with a Ouija board:

> And then I felt psychic. I mean, that is to say I felt other dimensions around me, oh, for about two hours. It was the most remarkable feeling to me, because I'd never experienced anything like this. In fact I'd always thought it quite impossible.... I became aware of the future before it happens. And I remember taking a taxi and, oh God, telling the taxi driver what was in his mind, what was going to be happening, and so on. I became aware of entities — call them ghosts, or spirits, or apparitions — well, I could sense them, and then later on that night I could see them, as well, which was very disturbing as I didn't believe in such things.

Not only did Vaughan's worldview change, but his career as well. He became a professional psychic. He also pointed out that precognition has the potential to change one's life in significant ways, saying:

> Sometimes we can precognize things which we can prevent from happening. Negative things. There have been lots of stories of people having an image of being in a crash, auto crash, but then they see the situation start to develop, then they act and prevent it from happening.

SUMMARY

Parapsychologists have debated for years whether or not MMI and ESP should be considered separate or the same process. The current experiential data is compatible with ESP and MMI being one process that is active, energetic, facilitated by the same ASC, and able to evoke similar body sensations. Clear-cut ESP (particularly remote viewing) frequently occurs during MMI, and ESP and MMI may have a shared limit. The fact that overuse of one form of psi appears to disable the other would seem particularly significant. All of the MMI constituents were brought up when participants were incidentally describing ESP experiences. Thus, there would appear to be considerable overlap between the two experiences. This might explain why RNG/REG experiences — thought by some to represent ESP — were identical to macro–MMI ones.

Unfortunately, the lack of a definitive phenomenological study of ESP means that there could still be aspects of the experience unique to ESP. Also, bias may have been introduced by using stories from the same performers who were discussing their MMI experiences. Clearly, it would be better to perform a new phenomenological study devoted only to ESP, with different participants and bracketing all of the MMI constituents listed here to avoid bias. At this point, all that can be said is that there appear to be similarities between ESP and MMI experiences.

That said, it is entirely possible that we are better off speaking of phenomena simply as psi. If future work should determine that MMI and ESP are identical experiences, then it would suggest that they may be fundamentally the same process and should not be treated as distinct. Needless to say, this could have a profound impact on the field of parapsychology. It is hoped that future studies will resolve this issue.

MMI Facilitation and Inhibition

Although MMI can be learned, it is somewhat questionable whether training per se is possible. Instead, we may be better off talking about facilitation — providing the would-be performer general suggestions and a permissive environment. Many of the constituents of the MMI experience can be thought of as facilitators, just as their reverse tend to be inhibitors. In particular, an ASC, connection, suspension of the intellect, playfulness and/or peak emotion, focused awareness, openness to the experience, and trust in the process seemed to have a synergistic effect — more potent in combination than alone. Let us consider then the modifiers of success.

FACILITATORS

Openness to the experience appeared to be critical to MMI success, whereas (contrary to what many have said) belief and confidence were not required. This may be because dissociation from the ego identity during the experience meant there was no "I" to have beliefs. Suspension of the intellect means a lack of thought about one's beliefs and how they might relate to what is happening. The ASC also tended to make normal belief systems irrelevant. Granted, a confirmed disbeliever might be a lost cause, but for those at all open to the idea of psi — even if they don't think they can do it — beliefs may be irrelevant to success when in an ASC.

Investment seemed intrinsic to MMI experiences. However, some of the traditional elements of learning theory, such as motivation and goals, were surprisingly absent from performer descriptions. This could be due to participants being immersed in the process. Although invested in the outcome, most participants did not focus on acting in order to accomplish the goal, but rather whatever was intuitively sensed as helpful.

Despite the fact that people have long touted visualization for MMI "training," the experimental results have been inconsistent at best.[178] Focused awareness often utilized visualization as a means of guiding the process, but visualization did not appear to be a separate constituent of the experience. It is possible that training visualization could be a double-edged sword. On the plus side it might improve the ability to focus attention. However, focusing on visualization in order to control the process, rather than allowing visualization as a natural result of what intuitively feels needed, might block trust in the process, ignore "knowing" what is needed, and thus hinder MMI. Gissurarson noted that participants naturally use a variety of tactics to perform MMI, and that while 30 percent may use either goal or process-oriented visualization, this is by no means the only strategy.[179]

Feedback would seem to be intrinsically difficult to do well during the events, unless that feedback is in the form of ESP (which often seemed to be the case). If feedback changes the ASC, alters the connection to the target, activates the intellect, returns the performer to a sense of individual ego identity, or prevents focused awareness, then, whether that feedback is accurate (which is itself problematic) or not, it may inhibit or interrupt psi functioning.

All of the participants used at least some degree of ASC, and those who subjectively felt in control of their MMI also reported dissociation from their ego identities and suspension of the rational, analyzing part of their brains.

High levels of emotion and ASC seemed to interact and sometimes overlap in function. They share a number of potential ways of effecting MMI performance. Both may facilitate or enhance (1) ability to connect to the target; (2) narrowing or focusing of attention; (3) increasing or perhaps allowing the transformation of the energy level; (4) dissociation from the ego identity or awareness of self; and (5) shifting activity away from the rational left brain and suspending the intellect. Whether emotion might also function by providing energy, altering the state of consciousness (or intrinsically being an ASC), or through some other manner is unclear.

One of the more interesting facets of the experiences was how spontaneous MMI performers and intentional MMI beginners relied to a greater degree on high-emotion states for success with half of the participants reporting highly emotional states as being associated with spontaneous MMI. MMI experiences changed as participants became more adept. The ASC, guiding the process, and trust in the process all gained in prominence as practitioners became more accomplished at controlling their abilities. This progression towards greater emphasis on an ASC (and less on emotion) suggests a certain amount of "learning" occurs.

INHIBITORS

In many cases, those things that inhibit MMI are the opposite of what facilitates it. For example, some participants spoke of occasions when they felt their MMI abilities had been blocked. Because this was not the focus of this investigation, the findings cannot be considered a rigorous look at the experience of MMI inhibition. Nonetheless, the results were suggestive of a number of conclusions. We will look first at what the literature has suggested about MMI inhibitors, and then at what the participants themselves have said.

What the Literature Says Most researchers have focused on what leads to MMI success, implying that the opposite will lead to failure. However, some clues as to inhibitors can be found in the comments of participants. Robert Thouless noted he did poorly on ESP and dice experiments when tired, ill, or out of sorts.[180] In addition, he observed that a non-threatening atmosphere made a difference. As he put it,

> [P]ositive results tend to disappear if there is any hint of a hostile or suspicious attitude on the part of those present or if tension is increased by over-emphasis on experimental precautions.... If witnesses are present, their attitude should that of co-operative friendliness.[181]

Mathew Manning said that he always got his best MMI results, whether spontaneous or intentional, when working with experimenters who were sympathetic, friendly, and jovial.[182] Because of this, those running the experiments are factors in determining what kind of results are obtained.

Eusapia Palladino purportedly could produce impressive phenomena under tight controls when working with those she liked.[183] It is possible that a performer "liking" his or her experimenter(s) could impact a number of psychological variables, not least of which could be a sense of ease. J. B. Rhine's 1946 study that looked at the effect of hypnotic suggestion on MMI could also be considered supportive of this.[184] His hypnotic instructions to concentrate hard were met by scores dropping to chance levels. When told to be relaxed about the dice-throwing psi test, his participants returned to an above-chance hit rate.

Experimenters have stated that feeling confident and being in a relaxed, detached, alert state of mind are important to MMI success.[185] This suggests that making performers feel defensive or uncomfortable (thus undermining any confidence and preventing a relaxed state) would diminish MMI performance.

Kenneth Batcheldor wrote about macro–MMI inhibition.[186] As mentioned earlier, he theorized that there were three crucial factors which led to the success or failure of MMI: (1) belief, (2) ownership resistance, and (3) witness inhibition. He noted that fear of success — either in the experimenter or in the participant — had a markedly inhibitory effect on macro- and micro-MMI performance.[187] It may be that experimental MMI participants need a relaxed and detached state of mind to block ownership resistance and fear, while poltergeist agents bypass their fear issues by blaming some unknown agency or cause as the source of the disturbance. This would be consistent with the fact that the MMI frequently stops when agents accept the fact that they are causing the phenomena.[188]

Striving for success has also been said to inhibit MMI.[189] It is difficult to say how much this represents simply the opposite of relaxation, or the involvement of other factors. Martin Caidin and Jack Houck both devoted considerable time to teaching novices how to perform MMI and said that belief or confidence were important; it helped to "like" their targets, and trying "too hard" or over-intellectualizing inhibited MMI.[190]

What the Participants Say

1. There may be limitations to what can be achieved by MMI. Vaughan felt that there were limits on psychic energies. He suggested that win-win situations are the best strategy, mentioning that he thought that Uri Geller operated in this manner. Vaughan noted:

> I would not describe Uri as particularly ethical or moral or you know. I think he is essentially, but it's not his prime motivation. His prime motivation was to become a millionaire, and that's what he's done. But he's still a compassionate person, though. And ... my feeling is that ... his basic formula for the way he works is finding a win-win situation. If he can help somebody find millions of dollars worth of gold, or oil, what-

ever, and then he gets a cut, then he feels that's the way to do it. In a way, I think it's sort of a spiritual obligation. It gets in the way winning at gambling, even with a small amount. But when it comes to tipping the scales, balance, it doesn't seem to work. So there are definite restrictions on the use, or on the success of using, psychic energies.

2. There may be MMI-ESP energy limits. As mentioned earlier, Vaughan said that after overuse of psi, "It feels like I've got a hole in my stomach ... but essentially it prevents me from getting any accurate psychic impressions." He also believed that psi could cost the body both short-term, in terms of energy, and long-term, in terms of health.

> Well, let's put it this way. I know of people who brought themselves to an early death by trying to do too much of this work. And, and in England it's what the mediums call over-sitting, and so it can be very perilous to one's health. The mediums I knew they were forever getting sick.

Vaughn felt this problem could be minimized by consciously drawing in more energy while performing psychic work. Vaughan commented, "Now I will admit that over the years, I've learned how to channel more energy into me, especially for healing sessions."

How the Constituents Relate to MMI Inhibition

Connection: *The inability or lack of desire to connect may inhibit MMI.* Vaughan had difficulty connecting to perform MMI when he didn't care about the target person. He said:

> Well, I have to say this, that I know when the psychic connection works best is because the person has a genuine need, and is not just curious, or like skeptical and wanting to be convinced, that sort of thing.... So I find myself not caring one way or the other, don't bother me, go do it yourself, if you want to convince yourself.

Dissociation from the Individual Ego Identity: *A sense of ego may block MMI.* One participant spoke about the ego as blocking MMI performance. Martin stated: "The ego has to be out of it.... The ego cannot be there in any way, shape or form. And one of the things that I do in teaching my students is to make sure that their ego is out of the way."

Suspension of the Intellect: *Analytical thinking inhibits MMI.* Half of the participants mentioned that analytical thinking blocks MMI. Vaughan said (referring to someone else), "He couldn't bend anything because the intellect was really involved." Similarly Smith recalled, "I took part in one of his workshops and was one of the very last people to bend a spoon. Because I think I was being the scientist."

Playfulness or Peak Emotion: *Self-frustration may inhibit MMI.* Frustration with oneself was the only peak emotion that did not facilitate MMI activity. Instead, it blocked it. It is possible that self-frustration — as opposed to frustration with others, which *does* facilitate MMI — involves an increased sense of individual identity and activation of the intellect with negative self-talk, such as "Why can't I do this?" Smith described a situation where she was unable to bend a spoon at a metal-bending party, and said, "So there was an expectation it was going to happen. And the longer it didn't happen, the more frustrated I got." During this time, she reported negative self-talk, and said, "I'm thinking, gosh, I'm going to be the only one here who doesn't bend a spoon."

Sense of Energy: *A lack of energy may prevent MMI.* A lack of energy was mentioned in two situations: (1) being in a hostile environment and (2) as a result of doing too much psychic work. Vaughan stated that fear and hostility, either in the target person or bystanders, and/or defensiveness in the performer, may prevent MMI by blocking the energy. He reflected, "If you have a group of skeptics standing around looking, sort of daring you to, saying this is unnatu-

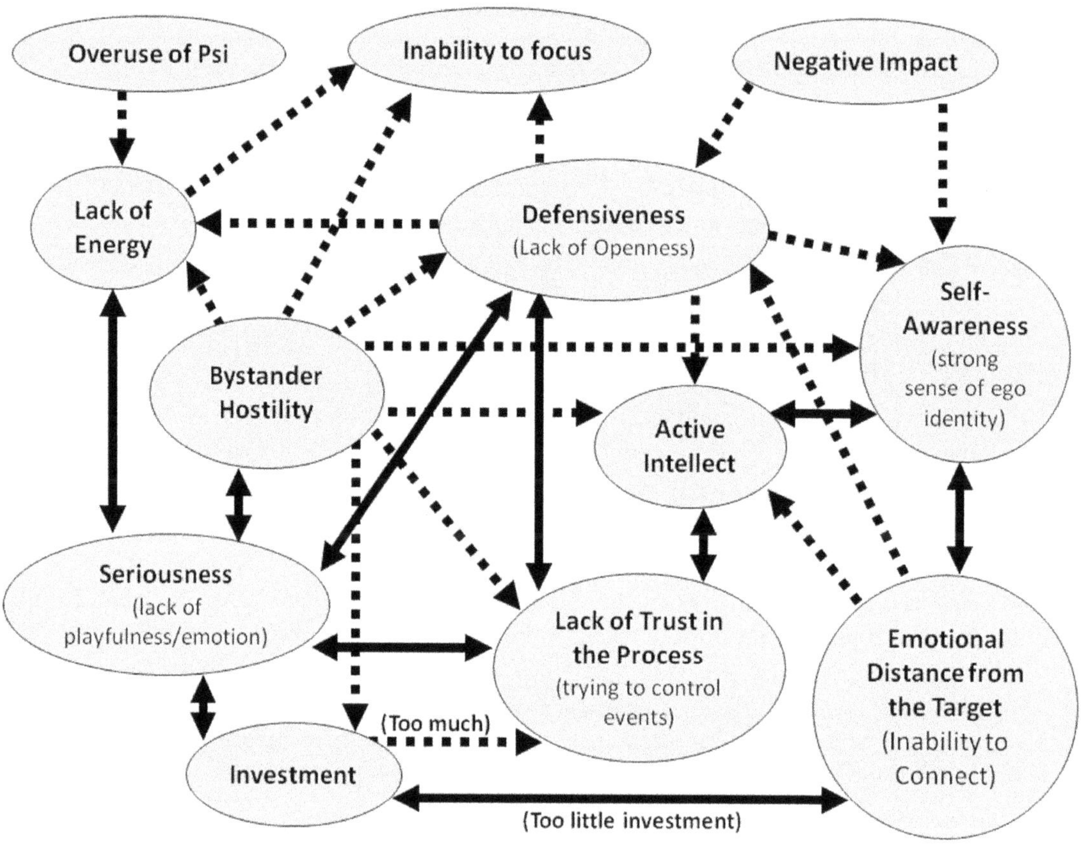

This diagram charts some of the interactions between constituents, which result in inhibition. Solid lines represent two-way interactions, whereas dotted lines are one-way. Investment was the only constituent that could result in inhibition if it was either "too much" or "too little."

ral ... then it doesn't work.... There's no energy. It's just dead." Vaughan felt that actively hostile beliefs in the target and/or bystander(s) could inhibit ESP as well as MMI. He recalled an incident where a previously successful psi task could not be performed with an ardent psi disbeliever present. Vaughan said, "When he was there absolutely nothing happened. There was no energy. Just as if it didn't exist."

Lack of energy was also reported as resulting from overuse of psi. Vaughan stated that an overuse of ESP can block further ESP or MMI functioning. He noted that after too much work, "At the very extreme end, it feels like I've got a hole in my stomach. It feels kind of nervous ... but essentially it prevents me from getting any accurate psychic impressions." Nor could he perform MMI.

Physical State: *The state of the body may limit MMI.* Wigal noted that a full stomach could limit or diminish the magnitude of his experiences. He observed, "When I'm really relaxed ... and I haven't eaten for awhile — I just had supper a while ago so it's less likely to happen."

Focused Awareness: *A lack of focus to awareness may block MMI.* Smith noted that MMI seemed to occur when there was an inward focusing and narrowing of attention, rather than a general awareness of what was going on at the spoon-bending party. She said that what worked for her "was a shift of attention ... into myself. I had been very focused on the group, in watching the group, then I seemed to focus more inside ... and at that point, the metal went soft." Thus, scattered attention may inhibit MMI performance.

Trust in the Process: *A lack of trust in the process, as evidenced by effort, may block MMI.* Two participants stated that effort blocked MMI. Vaughan said, "I found that I had to be careful not to try too hard." In fact, according to several participants, the only effort during MMI is whatever is needed to access the ASC and maintain the focused awareness. Robinson noted, "The only effort is in maintaining focus when we start."

There was also a sense in performers' stories that goal-oriented activity could hamper success. For example, the desire to bend a spoon may have prevented one participant from doing it, and it was the letting go of this need to act on the spoon, and an allowing of things to simply happen that finally worked. Robinson said:

> Usually what ... I've found, though, in my life, was ... once I started investigating things, like I would read about something or I would try and couldn't get it to work, then, when I was least expecting it, it would happen to me. So that almost went along with that. I wasn't expecting it. I was just waving the spoon. I know I had had it on my desk because I'd been trying to bend it and I couldn't.

Investment: *The wrong kind of investment may block MMI.* Investment was interesting in that it was the only constituent that showed up as both a promoter and inhibitor of MMI. On the one hand, too little of investment resulted in emotional distance from the target and diminished ability to connect. However, too much desire to succeed sometimes appeared to block MMI. It is possible that the true issue is one of the quality of investment, and whether it involves the need to control a situation and lack of trust.

Openness to the Experience: *1) A hostile environment may inhibit successful MMI.* Two of the five participants who had performed MMI in group settings (25 percent of the total eight, or 40 percent of those with group experiences) noted that active hostility to MMI was inhibitory. Vaughan stated that fear and hostility either in the target person or bystanders and/or defensiveness in the performer blocked MMI (as well as ESP).

Vaughan recalled an incident where a previously successful psi task could not be performed with an ardent psi disbeliever present, and noted, "The people around one can determine whether or not one will be successful. And I'm not the only one that's reported this. Many other people have, too."

It is possible that hostility could affect a number of the constituents, such as causing performer defensiveness, discouraging connection, inhibiting the ability to open up to the energy/state of consciousness, enhancing awareness of the individual ego identity, preventing suspension of the intellect, blocking the ability to trust, inhibiting investment in the outcome, or other methods. Hostility may also be a factor in the experimenter effect and could furthermore operate in manners additional to simply affecting constituents of the experience, such as by directing energy/intent towards MMI failure. Considering that openness seemed to be such a consistent constituent of the MMI experience, it is not surprising that defensiveness might prevent successful MMI performance.

2) Lack of openness in the recipient of anomalous healing may block MMI. Three (37.5 percent) of the eight original participants felt that human patients could block anomalous healing. Vaughan noted how the recipient can inhibit MMI in the following story:

> Sometimes, every now and then, on rare occasions, I'll feel it's not doing any good. The person is really resisting this. So, I'll just stop. Yes, I had one client I recall, only one, but she was the member of some cult, an Eastern cult, and she was terrified.... I don't know what on earth she'd been taught that interfered, but it obviously was not

working. And I told her, "I think you're going to have to get some counseling before I can help you with this...." But it's unusual to feel that kind of panic and obstruction.

Summary

Many of the factors that hindered or prevented successful MMI performance were the natural opposite of what facilitated it. These include emotional distance from the target (lack of connection), sense of individual ego identity or separateness (lack of dissociation), an active intellect (rather than suspension), seriousness (the opposite of playfulness/emotion), effort/lack of trust in the process, lack of focused awareness, defensiveness (the lack of openness), and the absence of energy, with a possible effect on the ability to either access, or accept feedback from, information acquired as a sense of "knowing." Self-frustration may inhibit MMI in part by activation of the intellect and ego identity. Overuse of ESP was also noted to block successful MMI and vice versa.

Bystander hostility might act by causing performer defensiveness, activating the intellect with its defense mechanisms, and somehow blocking access to, or awareness of, MMI energy. Additionally, feeling under attack could make it hard to enter an ASC, focus awareness, feel open, or trust.

It is possible that the ordinary state of consciousness may indirectly partially inhibit MMI through its tendency to maintain the intellect and ego identity. However, there were a few performers who were successful at MMI despite being in what was for them an "ordinary" state of consciousness. It is unclear whether this means that the state of consciousness is irrelevant if the individual has a supportive belief system or the other constituents are strongly facilitative (such as trust or detachment), or whether those particular individuals are always in what others would consider an ASC, and therefore don't recognize what is used for MMI as being "different."

Study participants did not report negative impacts from their experiences. However, they were also all individuals who were comfortable with their abilities. It is possible that anticipation of an imagined or real negative impact — such as heckling, ridicule, and being the target of skeptics and disbelievers — could potentially block MMI by interfering with a number of constituents, such as by activating the intellect, impairing a sense of playfulness, scattering the focus of attention, inhibiting trust in the process, and blocking openness to the experience. In this manner, negative impact could act in a similar way to bystander hostility.

Conclusions

In the first part of the book, we saw how MMI has, at least anecdotally, occurred in similar forms in cultures around the globe from the beginning of recorded time. We noted that these phenomena have common patterns of behavior, which seem to be far more than simple trickery. Next we reviewed over 125 years of MMI research. Together, they suggest that psi is a universal ability, which responds to normal psychological variables. Finally, we used phenomenology to try to better uncover the meaning and significance of the phenomena.

Despite the wide range of experiences, targets, and settings described by participants, the same constituents appeared repeatedly. For the most part, successful intentional MMI performers focus on being a part of the process, or in harmony with what is occurring, so their desired outcome occurs. Furthermore, the process is not so much controlled as it is guided through focused intent, which is adjusted on an ongoing basis, as needed, through various forms of feedback, including ESP. In fact, the only variation noted was that conscious guiding of the process is not seen in spontaneous events — although it is still possible that the unconscious mind provides direction. The fact that these spontaneous events often meet unconscious needs (even if just venting off steam) and can be personally meaningful would seem to suggest that this is indeed the case.

With greater practice and control, there is more emphasis on the ASC and less on requiring the physical and mental activation of peak emotions. This is not to say that skillful performers are necessarily detached — euphoria can often be present and is felt to be associated with the MMI energy or process and being connected to a greater source. Those who believe they have some control over MMI also report dissociation from the individual ego identity and suspension of the intellect. Trust in the process appeared to play a bigger role as the performer became more adept.

The fourteen constituents to the MMI experience are:

1. The presence of an ASC that often involves a narrowed focus of attention, loss of awareness of surroundings, and an altered sense of time.
2. Connection to the target on a transcendent level.
3. Feelings of dissociation or detachment from the individual ego identity.
4. Suspension of the intellect.
5. The presence of playfulness and/or peak levels of emotion.
6. A sense of energy, which may have a transcendent quality.

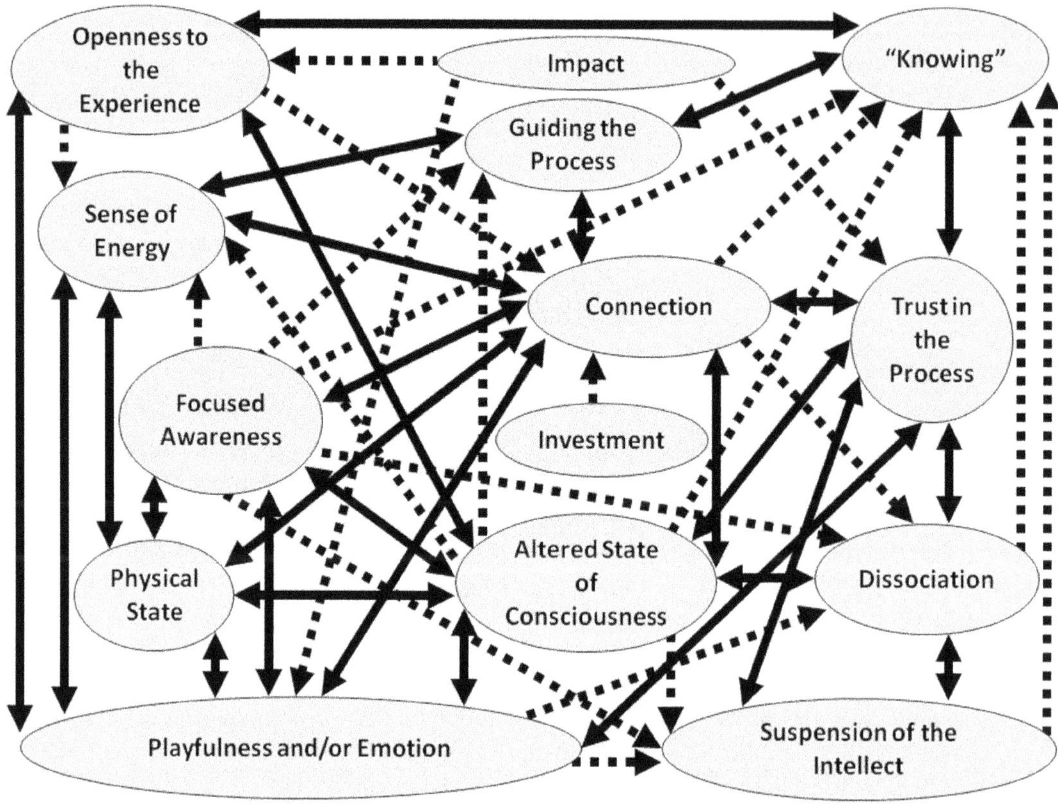

This diagram charts some of the interactions described between constituents for the MMI experience. Solid lines represent two-way interactions, whereas dotted lines are one-way. The end result is a complex matrix — especially when one realizes there may be more interactions than listed here. Because of this, it may be best to think of the constituents as deeply enmeshed.

7. A physical state that may contribute to and reflect MMI energy.

8. Awareness that is focused.

9. Trust in the process (sometimes seen as a release-of-effort, effortlessness, not trying too hard, and surrender to the experience).

10. Investment in the event.

11. A sense of openness to the experience.

12. A sense of "knowing" or intuitive knowledge.

13. Guidance of the process in an interactive (or reactive) manner (seen on a conscious level only with intentional MMI).

14. Impact (usually positive) on the performer, usually after the event is over.

These constituents are highly interactive and interrelated. As a result, the MMI experience is an extremely fluid one, without the static qualities of fixed boundaries, discrete elements, or a linear configuration as is associated with normal experience. To think about MMI we must think in terms of shifting configurations, somewhat like a kaleidoscope where the same elements may form a variety of patterns that give the illusion of greater differences than really exist. The overlap and interaction between the constituents represent a matrix that is a confusing web of interconnections, which interact in varying degrees, depending on the individual experience.

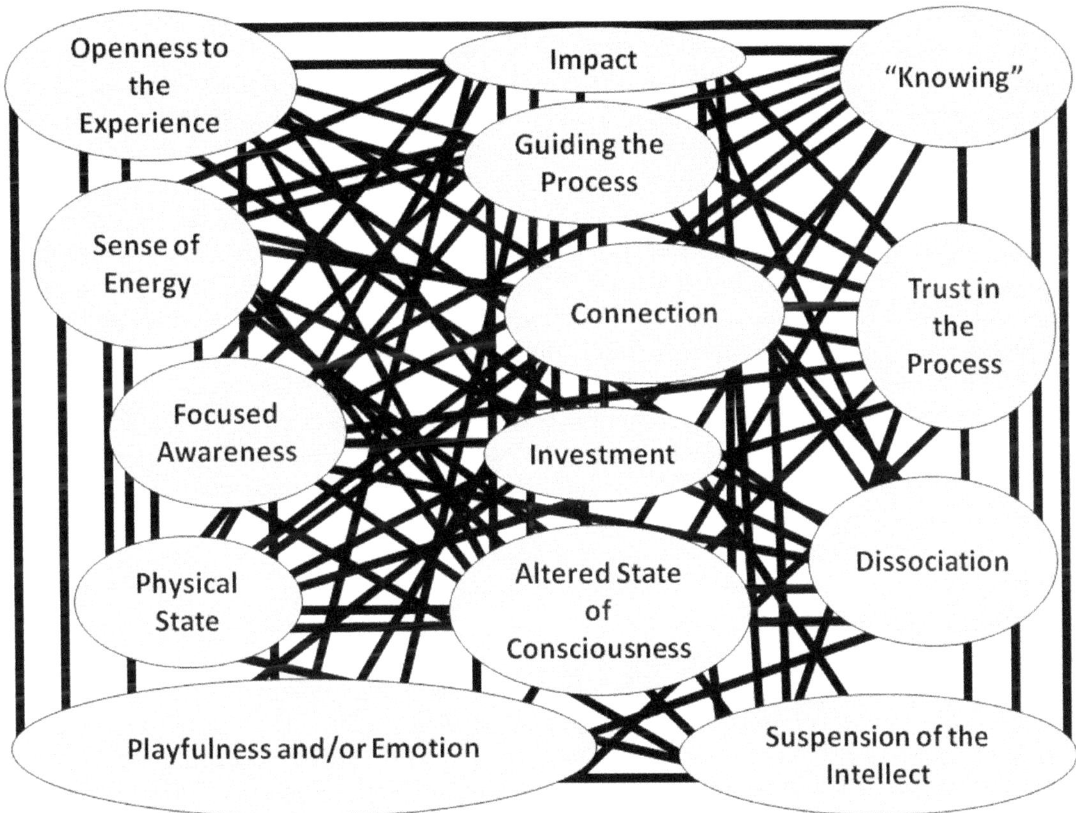

If we consider that not all of the existing interactions have been charted, it is likely that the MMI matrix is a deeply enmeshed system of interlinking constituents that need to be considered as a whole, rather than as discrete elements that sometimes influence each other.

More than anything else, MMI involves participating in an active process, and reacting to feedback (often through ESP) to stay in harmony with the experience. To affect something in this way, an individual must first become a part of a greater whole. This involves being open and able (or willing) to connect. Likewise, trust in the process appears to be a crucial constituent of this experience, and sometimes appears as release-of-effort/attention (although it seemed of less importance when there was detachment). More often it is seen as "not trying too hard," effortlessness, and/or surrender.

Dissociation from the individual ego identity and suspension of the intellect sometimes appear to be byproducts of an ASC that accesses a transcendent level of reality where everything is interconnected. Both the letting go of a sense of self and putting the analytical component of the mind on hold could have the effect of making it easier to trust the process — and may partly explain why belief and confidence did not appear to be important to the experience (except possibly for performing in front of a hostile audience). Belief limits can be bypassed if we don't think about them. Thus, highly emotional states (which inhibit rational thought) and ASC are both psi-facilitative. Beliefs become irrelevant when our intellectual worldview and sense of reality are disengaged.

Impact tends to be more of a long-term factor, visible primarily between experiences. However, the fact that these experiences are sometimes empowering and life-altering should not be surprising given the fact they represent exposure to phenomena that our physicalist upbringing tells us cannot occur.

MMI inhibition most often seems to occur when the natural opposites of the constituents were present — emotional distance from the target, awareness of individual ego identity, an active intellect, seriousness, lack of trust in the process, inability to focus awareness, and lack of openness. The effectiveness of bystander hostility in blocking MMI may relate to the way it triggers performer defensiveness and the activation of normal psychological defense mechanisms. This could potentially affect a number of the constituents, such as by making it difficult to access an ASC, sense the energy, focus awareness, feel open, suspend the intellect, or trust the process. Likewise, an anticipated (or real) negative impact — such as heckling, ridicule, and being the target of both skeptics and disbelievers — may also prevent MMI. Investment was the only constituent that appeared to be capable of both helping and hindering MMI. Too much investment (or, perhaps more accurately, the wrong kind of it) seemed to block trust in the process, while too little led to difficulty connecting with the target.

Another finding that emerges from the phenomenological data is the intriguing possibility that ESP and MMI may not be separate experiences, but are part of the same fluid, interactive matrix. Performers speak of ESP and MMI as being closely intertwined, using the same kind of active energy to reach out and tune in, and involving the same/similar ASC. It is possible that their superficial differences have blinded us to their similar core essence. However, this can only be definitively determined by further investigation.

This leads us to our final, and most important, conclusion. MMI involves taking part in a transcendent (and sometimes transformative) process. It requires the performer to let go of his or her individual sense of self and belief systems, and to trust and participate in something beyond our normal, everyday reality. Thus, MMI is totally unlike almost everything else we do. Ordinarily, we think of ourselves as having to act directly upon the environment to get a specific outcome. Intentional MMI appears to be quite different from that. Instead, performers lend themselves to a greater process, and, although invested in what happens, there is a letting go of control by the self, and a sense of allowing things to happen as they should. The results can be remarkable.

Glossary

Altered states of consciousness (ASCs). States other than ordinary waking consciousness, such as daydreaming; sleep dreaming; hypnotic or trance states; meditation, mystical, or drug-induced states; or half-sleeping (hypnagogic) or half-waking (hypnopompic) states.

Anomalous photography. The projection by allegedly paranormal means of mental images on film, digital media, or photographic plates. Also known as thoughtography or psychic photography.

Anpsi. Psi in animals.

Apport. An object alleged to arrive in a closed space by paranormal means, indicating the supposed passage of matter through matter. *See also* teleportation

Automatic writing. Handwriting or typewriting done without conscious control, the source of which is apparently not the self.

Bilocation. The apparent ability of the body to be in two locations at the same time. This "second self" in many cases is said to be able to eat, drink, and carry out any physical act the body is capable of performing.

Channel (verb). To receive and convey information or energy that is said to come from neither one's own self nor from other embodied minds, nor from physical reality (as defined by current physics and physiology).

Channeling. The process of receiving information from some level of reality other than the ordinary physical one and from beyond the self as we currently understand it. This includes messages from any mental source that falls outside of one's own ordinary conscious or unconscious mind, and is not from anyone else incarnate on the physical level of reality. Classically, channeling involved an identified or self-identified source said to be responsible for the information coming to or through the channel.

Clairaudience. A form of ESP in which the extrasensory data is perceived as sound.

Clairvoyance. Extrasensory awareness of objects or objective events, technically involving the sense of sight (a "vision"); however, it is more often used loosely as a term for ESP. It is distinguished from telepathy, which involves extrasensory awareness of thoughts.

Collective unconscious. Jung's term for the shared memory and accrued archetypal dispositions of the human species.

Decline effect. The tendency for positive scoring in psi tests to decrease, within a run, a session, or a longer period of testing.

Deliberately Caused Bodily Damage Phenomena (DCBD). This is where individuals cause (or allow others to do) deliberate harm to their bodies, typically as a demonstration of religious faith. This can involve piercing the skin with sharp instruments, including spikes, daggers, or skewers, and swallowing sharp objects. What makes this different from self-mutilation or torture is that there is usually no pain, little if any bleeding, and the extraordinarily rapid healing of wounds.

Direct Mental Interactions with Living Systems (DMILS). This is where a distant individual (isolated from all normal sensory cues) tries to use psi to influence another living target system, whether isolated cells or an intact organism.

Direct Voice. The paranormal production of voices from discarnate sources or no longer physically embodied human beings that are heard real-time, sometimes said to have been aided by the use of a trumpet in séances.

Direct Voice Phenomena (DVP). A form of instrumental transcommunication where the production of sound through paranormal means is heard real-time through electronic equipment, such as radios, telephones, televisions, telegraphs, and other devices.

Ectoplasm. A substance alleged to issue from the bodies of some physical mediums, out of which materializations were said to be formed. It was primarily noted during the Spiritualist era.

Electronic Voice Phenomena (EVP). A form of instrumental transcommunication where voices not heard at the time of recording later appear on playback. These voices often have a flat tonal quality and may be preceded by a metallic knock.

Exceptional Human Experience (EHE). These are experiences that involve (1) a spontaneous anomalous experience (which may include such things as psychic events, NDEs, mystical experiences, and encounters); (2) a sense of personal meaning; (3) inability to explain the experience away as normal; (4) a genuine or real experience; (5) feelings of separation from consensus reality; (6) becoming "tuned in" to what is experienced as a "different frequency"; and (7) dissociation from the ego-self and more association with the All-Self. This may lead to a transformation of personal identity and worldview.

Experimenter effect. A term used to refer to the finding that experimenters working under the same objective conditions and with subjects from the same population may get different or conflicting results, which conform to their own expectations.

Extrasensory perception (ESP). Knowledge of, or response to, an external event or influence not apprehended through known sensory channels. May involve clairvoyance (information that is seen), clairsentience (information that comes as "knowing" or feeling), or clairaudience (information that is heard).

Fire-Immunity. The alleged ability to come into direct contact with fire or extreme sources of heat without being burned.

Focusing effect. The general tendency for ESP or MMI success to be concentrated upon particular targets more than upon others; also a form of target preference.

General extrasensory perception (GESP). ESP that could be either telepathy or clairvoyance, or both.

Hemography. The paranormal patterning of bloodstains on cloth.

Hyperesthesia. The inability to be touched without suffering severe pain.

Incendium amoris. The reputed ability of individuals to generate and withstand high body temperatures, which were commonly ascribed to "the warmth of their love of God." This may be a form of fire-immunity.

Induction effect (Geller effect). This is where an individual may be able to perform MMI after watching someone else apparently be successful at it. It does not seem to matter whether the person being observed is using MMI or not, and seems to relate more to the percipient's mindset that MMI is possible and social learning by modeling an observed behavior.

Inedia. The apparently paranormal ability to live without nourishment, which is sometimes seen in association with stigmata.

Instrumental transcommunication (ITC). The purported communication by human spirits, said to have survived the death of their physical bodies and exist in an afterlife or astral realm, through means of an assortment of electronic and related equipment, including tape recorders, telephones, radios, televisions, and computers. Often these sounds and images are not heard or seen at the time of original recording, but only appear later. Sounds heard real-time are referred to as direct voice phenomena (DVP), while those only noted on playback are referred to as electronic voice phenomena (EVP) or Raudive phenomena.

Kundalini. In some Tantric forms of Yoga, this is the cosmic energy that is believed to lie within everyone, pictured as a coiled serpent lying at the base of the spine. Kundalini experiences are said to occur as part of spiritual awakening, when the energy rises up through the subtle energy channels of the body through chakras towards the crown. There can be a variety of physical, emotional, and psychic experiences associated with this, depending in part on whether the individual has been prepared for this by the resolution of emotional blocks and traumas and by the strengthening of the subtle energy channels and physical body. If personal growth work has not been done, great emotional disturbance can result. Furthermore, there can be alarming physical and energetic symptoms, especially in the heart and nervous system.

Levitation. The raising of objects or bodies in the air by supposedly paranormal means.

Linger effect. Also referred to as a "post-active effect." The apparent continuation of MMI at a location where it has recently been used after the MMI performer has appeared to cease his or her efforts. It has been noticed primarily in healing and macro–MMI experiments. Some have speculated that it could be a result of relaxation, while others have postulated that it may be an experimenter effect.

Macro-MMI (Macro-PK). Directly observable MMI. In other words, the effects are large enough, or strong enough, to be detected as such by the naked eye, and thus do not require statistics for their demonstration. Examples include levitation, materialization, metal-bending (PKMB), and object movement.

Medium (trance medium, physical medium). An individual who seems to be able to receive communications purported to come from the deceased and transmit them to the living, and who may be able to produce physical effects, alleged to be paranormal and sometimes attributed to a discarnate agency.

Mediumistic voice phenomena (*see* Instrumental Transcommunication)

Mental or behavioral influence of an agent (MOBIA). Term suggested by Stanford as a new term for "active-agent" telepathy; he proposed that the agent can play an active role in telepathy and that such telepathy is really a form of MMI. Stanford suggested that the telepathic sender creates an electrochemical change in the receiver's system, which allows the receiver to passively acquire the message.

Meta-analysis. A method of statistical analysis wherein the units of analysis are the results of independent studies, rather than the responses of individual subjects. It is an analysis of analyses, and the data points are the results of separate experiments, which are weighted according to factors such as the type of controls and number of subjects.

Micro-MMI (Micro-PK). MMI effects that are weak or slight in magnitude, which can rarely be identified as such by the naked eye and usually require the application of statistics for their demonstration. Examples include changing radioactive decay rates or affecting enzyme activity.

Mind-matter interaction (MMI). The influence of the mind on external objects or processes without the mediation of known physical energies or forces. Also known as psychokinesis or PK. May occur on a recurrent basis and be spontaneous or intentional.

Model of Pragmatic Information (MPI). This model was proposed by Walter von Lucadou and presumes that all complex systems are entangled complementary pairs of structure-function. This entanglement means that nonlocal correlations occur. The intrinsic variability of a stochastic system determines the magnitude or variety of outcomes.

Newton-meter (Nm). A unit of torque in the meter-kilogram-second system, equal to the torque produced by 1 Newton of force acting at a perpendicular distance of 1 meter from an axis of rotation.

Nocebo. A negative placebo — i.e., an inactive substance, which appears to have negative side effects, such as nausea, vomiting, headache, etc.

Ouija. A trademark for a board with letters of the alphabet and other symbols on it that is used with a planchette (or sometimes a glass) to purportedly spell out messages obtained telepathically from discarnate entities or ESP.

Out-of-body experience (OBE). An experience, either spontaneous or induced, in which one's center of consciousness seems to be in a spatial location separate from that of one's physical body. There is often an awareness of "leaving the body" and traveling to a destination. OBEs are typically of brief duration. They are generally considered a form of ESP.

Paranormal. A synonym for psychic or parapsychological; beyond what should occur if only the known laws of cause and effect are operating.

Percipient. A subject in an ESP test, or a person who has a spontaneous ESP or MMI experience.

Placebo. Latin for "I will please." It is an inactive substance or preparation given to satisfy the patient's symbolic need for drug therapy, and used in controlled studies to determine the efficacy of medicinal substances. Also, a procedure with no intrinsic therapeutic value, performed for such purposes.

Place memory This is where the energy of the living is recorded by or imprinted upon the inanimate physical world (including objects, buildings, and the environment) as information, which can be perceived by those sensitive to it as impressions of past events and feelings.

Poltergeist. A wide variety of recurrent spontaneous MMI activity, including noise, light, and object movement, which is typically centered around a living individual (known as the agent and frequently an adolescent) or group. The events are often a living metaphor for repressed thoughts and emotions.

Psi. A letter of the Greek alphabet (Ψ), which is used as a neutral general term to identify a person's extrasensorimotor communication with the environment. Psi includes ESP and MMI.

Psi-hitting. The use of psi so that the target at which the subject is aiming is hit significantly more often than would be expected by chance.

Psi-missing. The use of psi so that the target at which the subject is aiming is missed significantly more often than would be expected by chance. This tends to be noted in individuals who do not believe psi exists (*see also* sheep-goat effect) and therefore appear to unconsciously use their psi to miss the target.

Psychic photography. *see* Anomalous Photography.

Psychokinesis (PK). The influence of mind on external objects or processes without the mediation of known physical energies or forces. Also known as mind-matter interaction.

Radionics. A controversial approach to distant diagnosis and treatment of plants, animals, and humans using non-electronic devices and probably the psychic ability of the practitioner.

Recurrent spontaneous mind-matter interaction (RSMMI)/Recurrent spontaneous psychokinesis (RSPK). Spontaneous physical effects, inexplicable in terms of known physical energies, which occur repeatedly over a period of time, especially poltergeist disturbances.

Reichenbach's phenomenon. Named after the Baron Carl von Reichenbach, a Moravian industrialist, these phenomena are the luminous emanations said to be seen by certain "sensitives" in the somnambulistic state as coming from the poles of a magnet, crystals, and the human body.

Release-of-effort effect. The apparent sudden production of MMI as soon as the performer has ceased his or her efforts. Possibly related to striving, and the result of unblocking MMI by not trying so hard to produce it.

Self-efficacy. A person's beliefs in his or her capabilities to organize and execute the courses of action required to manage prospective situations.

Sheep-goat effect. Term coined by Schmeidler to indicate the relationship between acceptance of the possibility of ESP under the given experimental conditions and ESP scoring level, those accepting the possibility (sheep) tending to score above chance and those rejecting it (goats) at or below chance.

Siddhi. Sanskrit term for psychic power. In Yogic philosophy, siddhis may awaken in the course of one's spiritual development but should be ignored because they are a hindrance to attaining enlightenment.

Spiritualism (Spiritism). A religious-type movement inspired by the resurgence of channeling activity in upstate New York in the mid–nineteenth century, which reached international proportions (called Spiritism in Europe) and exists to this day. It holds that we survive our physical deaths as spirits who can communicate back to the living through channels (usually termed mediums) and that all spirits, whether incarnate or discarnate, are immortal, ever-learning, and evolving toward the one God of All That Is.

Spontaneous psi experience. Any unanticipated experience of ESP or MMI occurring in the course of daily living. Such experiences are characterized by the lack of planning and control characterizing laboratory experiments in which, however, spontaneous psi may play an important part.

Stigmata. The apparent paranormal or miraculous production of marks on the body, which in Christians correspond to the wounds that Christ received during the Passion and Crucifixion.

Telekinesis. An older term for a specific type of mind-matter interaction, where the mind is able to move objects.

Stochastic System. A nondeterministic system that contains one or more elements which vary randomly. Because of this, a given input will not always lead to the same outcome.

Teleportation. A form of MMI phenomena in which objects or people allegedly move over a distance and/or through other objects. (*See also* Apport.)

Third Variable. This is a term in statistics that refers to the possibility that a factor may not be directly related to the variable being studied, but instead is correlated to yet another variable, which truly is linked to what is being studied. Hence, if A has a direct effect on B, and C changes when A does, C may appear to influence B when it is, in fact, only a third variable.

Thoughtography. *see* Anomalous Photography.

Trance. A term used by some for any hypnotic-type ASC; characterized by conscious attention being turned away from the normal senses and the ordinary, day-to-day, physically oriented public reality shared by most people (consensus reality).

Voice Phenomena (*see* Instrumental Transcommunication)

Yield strength. The stress at which a material exhibits a specified deviation from proportionality of stress and strain. Stress is the force acting across a unit area in a solid material, such as metal, in resisting the separation, compacting, or sliding that tends to be induced by external forces. Strain is the change in length of an object in some direction per unit undistorted length in some direction, not necessarily the same.

Notes

Preface

1. Caidin, "Fiction This Ain't," 214–215.

Introduction

2. Dale and White, "Glossary," 931.
3. Gauld and Cornell, *Poltergeists*.
4. McClenon, *Wondrous Events*.
5. Ebon, "A History of Parapsychology"; Gauld and Cornell, *Poltergeists*.
6. Braude, *The Limits of Influence*; Rogo, *Mind over Matter*.
7. Stanford, "Experimental Psychokinesis."
8. Radin, *The Conscious Universe*.
9. Schmeidler, *Parapsychology and Psychology*, 6.
10. Schmeidler, *Parapsychology and Psychology*; Stanford, "Experimental Psychokinesis"; White, "The Influence of Experimenter Motivation, Attitudes, and Methods of Handling Subjects on Psi Test Results."
11. Palmer and Rush, "Experimental Methods in PK Research"; Schmeidler, *Parapsychology and Psychology*; Stanford, "Experimental Psychokinesis."
12. Eisenberg, *Inner Spaces*.
13. Schmeidler, "Psychokinesis"; Stanford, "Experimental Psychokinesis."
14. Varvoglis, "Goal-Directed and Observer-Dependent PK."
15. Radin, *The Conscious Universe*.
16. Ibid.
17. Brown, "They Laughed at Galileo Too."

PART 1: A HISTORICAL CROSS-CULTURAL REVIEW OF ANECDOTAL MATERIAL THROUGH THE AGES: RELIGIOUS AND SPIRITUAL

1. McClenon, Wondrous Events.
2. Finucane, *Ghosts*.
3. Neiman, *Miracles*; Robinson, *To Stretch a Plank*.
4. Robinson, *To Stretch a Plank*; Rogo, *Miracles*.
5. Grunebaum, "The Place of Parapsychological Phenomena in Islam"; Robinson, *To Stretch a Plank*; Rogo, *Miracles*.
6. McClenon, *Wondrous Events*.
7. Ibid.
8. Guiley, *Harper's Encyclopedia of Mystical and Paranormal Experience*.
9. Attar, *Muslim Saints and Mystics*; Grunebaum, "The Place of Parapsychological Phenomena in Islam."
10. Grunebaum, "The Place of Parapsychological Phenomena in Islam."
11. Attar, *Muslim Saints and Mystics*.
12. Grunebaum, "The Place of Parapsychological Phenomena in Islam."
13. Hussein et al., "Deliberately Caused Bodily Damage Phenomena."
14. Rogo, *Miracles*.
15. Shah, *The Sufis*, 372.
16. Noveck, *Great Jewish Personalities in Ancient and Medieval Times*.
17. Nigal, *Magic, Mysticism, and Hasidism*.
18. Robinson, *To Stretch a Plank*; Rogo, *Miracles*.
19. Thurston, *The Physical Phenomena of Mysticism*, 1.
20. Ibid.
21. Haraldsson, *Modern Miracles*.
22. Barclay, *Mind over Matter*.
23. Ibid.
24. Bharati, "The Ontological Status of Psychic Phenomena in Hinduism and Buddhism."
25. Barclay, *Mind over Matter*; Bharati, "The Ontological Status of Psychic Phenomena in Hinduism and Buddhism."
26. Inglis, *Natural and Supernatural*.
27. Ibid., 36.
28. Ibid., 29.

Levitation

29. Thurston, *The Physical Phenomena of Mysticism*, 2–3.
30. Nickell, *Looking for a Miracle*.
31. Robinson, *To Stretch a Plank*; Rogo, *Miracles*.
32. Dingwall, "The End of a Legend"; Gershom, *Beyond the Ashes*; Gersi, *Faces in the Smoke*; Inglis, *Natural and Supernatural*; Rogo, *Miracles*.
33. Inglis, *Natural and Supernatural*, 38.
34. Rogo, *Miracles*.
35. Neiman, *Miracles*.
36. Dingwall, "The End of a Legend."
37. Rogo, *Miracles*.
38. Grunebaum. "The Place of Parapsychological Phenomena in Islam."
39. Michell and Rickard, *Phenomena*.
40. Attar, *Muslim Saints and Mystics*, 173.
41. Ibid., 38.
42. Ibid., 83.
43. Ibid., 96–97.
44. Gershom, *Beyond the Ashes*.
45. Murphy and White, *In the Zone*; Rogo, *Miracles*.
46. Barclay, *Mind over Matter*.
47. Gersi, *Faces in the Smoke*.
48. Rogo, *Miracles*; Thurston, *The Physical Phenomena of Mysticism*.
49. Thurston, *The Physical Phenomena of Mysticism*.
50. Rogo, *Miracles*.
51. Ibid.
52. Rogo, *Miracles*; Thurston and Attwater, *Butler's Lives of the Saints*.
53. Thurston, *The Physical Phenomena of Mysticism*.
54. Rogo, *Miracles*.
55. Thurston, *The Physical Phenomena of Mysticism*.

56. Rogo, *Miracles.*
57. Neiman, *Miracles.*
58. Barclay, *Mind over Matter.*
59. Thurston and Attwater, *Butler's Lives of the Saints.*
60. Robinson, *To Stretch a Plank.*
61. Thurston, *The Physical Phenomena of Mysticism,* 9–11.
62. Thurston and Attwater, *Butler's Lives of the Saints.*
63. Rogo, *Miracles.*
64. Thurston, *The Physical Phenomena of Mysticism.*
65. Treece, *The Sanctified Body.*
66. Rogo, *Miracles.*
67. Treece, *The Sanctified Body.*
68. Rogo, *Miracles.*
69. Walsh, *Butler's Lives of Patron Saints.*
70. Rogo, *Miracles.*
71. Cavendish, *Man, Myth, and Magic.*
72. Braude, *The Limits of Influence.*
73. Braude, *The Limits of Influence;* Rogo, *Miracles.*
74. Walsh, *Butler's Lives of Patron Saints.*
75. Rogo, *Miracles.*
76. Braude, *The Limits of Influence.*
77. Rogo, *Miracles.*
78. Braude, *The Limits of Influence.*
79. Rogo, *Miracles.*
80. Braude, *The Limits of Influence.*
81. Rogo, *Miracles.*
82. Gersi, *Faces in the Smoke.*
83. Rogo, *Miracles.*
84. Braude, *The Limits of Influence.*
85. Kelly and Rogers, *Saints Preserve Us!*
86. Walsh, *Butler's Lives of Patron Saints.*
87. Kelly and Rogers, *Saints Preserve Us!*
88. Walsh, *Butler's Lives of Patron Saints.*
89. Rogo, *Miracles.*
90. Walsh, *Butler's Lives of Patron Saints.*
91. Ibid.
92. Rogo, *Miracles.*
93. Kelly and Rogers, *Saints Preserve Us!;* Rogo, *Miracles.*
94. Dakwar and Wissink, "Voodoo Therapy: History"; Gersi, *Faces in the Smoke;* Guiley, *Harpers Encyclopedia of Mystical Paranormal Experience,* 635.
95. Gersi, *Faces in the Smoke,* 635.
96. Ibid.
97. Ibid.
98. Heath, *Into the Psychokinetic Zone.*
99. Nickell, *Looking for a Miracle.*
100. Bartlett, *Familiar Quotations,* 686.
101. Rogo, *Miracles.*
102. Braude, *The Limits of Influence.*
103. Braude, *The Limits of Influence;* Thurston, *The Physical Phenomena of Mysticism.*
104. Braude, *The Limits of Influence.*
105. Rogo, *Miracles.*

106. Braude, *The Limits of Influence.*
107. Rogo, *Miracles.*
108. Gauld and Cornell, *Poltergeists.*
109. Rogo, *Miracles.*
110. Ibid.
111. Thurston, *The Physical Phenomena of Mysticism.*
112. Rogo, *Miracles.*
113. Ibid.
114. Thurston, *The Physical Phenomena of Mysticism,* 23–34.
115. Rogo, *Miracles.*
116. Auerbach, *Mind over Matter.*
117. Rogo, *Miracles.*
118. Auerbach, *Mind over Matter.*
119. Rogo, *Miracles.*
120. Rogo, *Miracles;* Thurston, *The Physical Phenomena of Mysticism.*
121. Rogo, *Miracles.*
122. Gersi, *Faces in the Smoke;* Rogo, *Miracles.*
123. Kelly and Rogers, *Saints Preserve Us!;* Robinson, *To Stretch a Plank.*

Stigmata

124. Rogo, *Miracles;* "The History of Miracles," 1993.
125. Murphy and White, *In the Zone.*
126. Auerbach, *Mind over Matter.*
127. Rogo, *Miracles.*
128. Auerbach, *Mind over Matter.*
129. Rogo, *Miracles.*
130. Brown, *The Little Flowers of St. Francis;* Rogo, *Miracles.*
131. Murphy and White, *In the Zone.*
132. Thurston, *The Physical Phenomena of Mysticism.*
133. Nickell, *Looking for a Miracle.*
134. Rogo, *Miracles.*
135. Murphy and White, *In the Zone.*
136. Thurston, *Surprising Mystics.*
137. Ibid.
138. Rogo, *Miracles;* Thurston, *Surprising Mystics.*
139. Thurston, *Surprising Mystics,* 39.
140. Ibid.
141. Ibid., 43–44.
142. Ibid., 47.
143. Ibid.
144. Ibid., 39.
145. Ibid.
146. Ibid., 55.
147. Murphy and White, *In the Zone.*
148. Thurston, *The Physical Phenomena of Mysticism,* 130–131.
149. Rogo, *Miracles;* Thurston, *The Physical Phenomena of Mysticism.*
150. Rogo, *Miracles.*
151. Thurston, *The Physical Phenomena of Mysticism,* 76.
152. *Mystical Stigmata,* http://www.catholic.org/saints/stigmata.php (April 13, 2007).
153. Thurston, *The Physical Phenomena of Mysticism.*

154. Ibid., 64.
155. Murphy and White, *In the Zone.*
156. Thurston, *The Physical Phenomena of Mysticism.*
157. Thurston, *Surprising Mystics,* 64.
158. Ball, *Modern Saints;* http://en.wikipedia.org/wiki/Gemma_Galgani (March 28, 2007).
159. Thurston, *The Physical Phenomena of Mysticism,* 53–54.
160. Ibid.
161. *Living Miracles,* http://www.livingmiracles.net/Snide.html (April 13, 2007); Nickell, *Looking for a Miracle;* Thurston, *Surprising Mystics.*
162. Albright, "The Stigmata"; Rogo, *Miracles.*
163. Yogananda, *Autobiography of a Yogi.*
164. Thurston, *The Physical Phenomena of Mysticism.*
165. Vogl, *Life and Death of Therese Neumann, Mystic and Stigmatist.*
166. Thurston, *The Physical Phenomena of Mysticism.*
167. Ibid., 189–190.
168. Ibid.
169. Neiman, *Miracles;* Rogo, *Miracles.*
170. Rogo, *Miracles;* Thurston, *The Physical Phenomena of Mysticism.*
171. Rogo, *Miracles,* 72.
172. Auerbach, *Mind over Matter;* Rogo, *Miracles.*
173. Thurston, *The Physical Phenomena of Mysticism,* 99.
174. Rogo, *Miracles,* 76.
175. "John Snide," 2005.
176. Berkenbush, Interview by Garrett Husveth, Haunted New Jersey Podcast 15, http://hauntednj.libsyn.com/index.php?post_year=2006&post_month=02 (April 13, 2007).
177. Margnelli, "An Unusual Case of Stigmatization."
178. Ibid.
179. Rogo, *Miracles.*
180. Albright, "The Stigmata," 333.
181. Cavendish, *Man, Myth, and Magic.*
182. Needles, "Stigmata Occurring in the Course of Psychoanalysis," 37.
183. Margnelli, "An Unusual Case of Stigmatization"; Rogo, *Miracles.*
184. Needles, "Stigmata Occurring in the Course of Psychoanalysis."
185. Margnelli, "An Unusual Case of Stigmatization"; Rogo, *Miracles.*
186. Nickell, *Looking for a Miracle.*
187. Thurston, *The Physical Phenomena of Mysticism.*
188. Ibid.
189. Ibid., 126.
190. Auerbach, *Mind over Matter.*

Inedia

191. Rogo, *Miracles;* Thurston, *The Physical Phenomena of Mysticism.*
192. Thurston, *The Physical Phenomena of Mysticism,* 341, 357–358.

193. Nickell, *Looking for a Miracle*.

194. Rogo, *Miracles*.

195. Thurston, *The Physical Phenomena of Mysticism*, 350.

196. Rogo, *Miracles*.

197. Thurston, *The Physical Phenomena of Mysticism*.

198. Treece, *The Sanctified Body*.

199. Thurston, *The Physical Phenomena of Mysticism*, 366.

200. Nickell, *Looking for a Miracle*.

201. Shah, *The Sufis*; Yogananda, *Autobiography of a Yogi*.

202. Oman, *Mystics, Ascetics and Saints of India*, 55–56.

203. Yogananda, *Autobiography of a Yogi*, 525–526.

204. Ibid.

205. Ibid., 536.

206. Ibid.

Teleportation

207. Grunebaum, "The Place of Parapsychological Phenomena in Islam."

208. Gersi, *Faces in the Smoke*; Hasted, *The Metal-benders*.

209. Rogo, *Miracles*.

210. Hasted, *The Metal-benders*.

211. Pulos and Richman, *Miracles and Other Realities*.

212. Hasted, *The Metal-benders*.

213. Rogo, *Miracles*.

214. Ibid.

215. Ibid.

216. Gersi, *Faces in the Smoke*.

217. Ibid.

218. Ibid.

219. Ibid.

220. Auerbach, *Mind over Matter*; Barclay, *Mind over Matter*; Haraldsson, *Modern Miracles*.

Bilocation

221. Thurston, *Surprising Mystics*.

222. Rogo, *Miracles*.

223. Ibid.

224. Hastings, "A Comparison of Recent Research in Brain Stimulation and Virtual Reality with Psychological and Parapsychological Research on Out-of-Body Experiences"; Rogo, *Miracles*.

225. Ibid.

226. Rogo, *Miracles*; Thurston, *Surprising Mystics*.

227. Neiman. *Miracles*.

228. Rogo, *Miracles*.

229. Rogo, *Miracles*; Thurston, *Surprising Mystics*.

230. Thurston, *Surprising Mystics*.

231. Ibid., 127.

232. Rogo, *Miracles*.

233. Thurston, *Surprising Mystics*.

234. Rogo, *Miracles*.

235. Grunebaum, "The Place of Parapsychological Phenomena in Islam."

236. Auerbach, *Mind over Matter*; Rogo, *Miracles*.

237. Gersi, *Faces in the Smoke*.

238. Nickell, *Looking for a Miracle*.

239. Rogo, *Miracles*.

240. Loyd Auerbach, personal communication to author, 1996.

241. Rogo, *Miracles*.

242. Ibid.

Fire-Immunity

243. Martin, *The Tarot Reader's Notebook*, 9.

244. Barclay, *Mind over Matter*.

245. Inglis, *Natural and Supernatural*.

246. Ibid., 49.

247. Ibid.

248. Thurston, *The Physical Phenomena of Mysticism*, 171.

249. Ibid.

250. Ibid., 172.

251. Dossey, "Deliberately Caused Bodily Damage," 16.

252. Rogo, *Miracles*; Thurston, *The Physical Phenomena of Mysticism*.

253. Thurston, *The Physical Phenomena of Mysticism*, 175.

254. Rogo, *Miracles*.

255. Ibid.

256. *Catholic Online*, www.catholic.org/saints/saint.php?saint_id=9 (April 13, 2007).

257. Thurston, *The Physical Phenomena of Mysticism*, 176.

258. Gaddis, *Mysterious Fires and Lights*.

259. Barclay, *Mind over Matter*; Gaddis, *Mysterious Fires and Lights*; Inglis, *Natural and Supernatural*; Rogo, *Miracles*.

260. Inglis, *Natural and Supernatural*, 25.

261. Ibid.

262. Ibid., 39.

263. Thurston, *The Physical Phenomena of Mysticism*, 188.

264. Ibid., 189.

265. Attar, *Muslim Saints and Mystics*.

266. Ibid., 280.

267. Ibid., 24.

268. Dossey, "Deliberately Caused Bodily Damage," 103.

269. Gaddis, *Mysterious Fires and Lights*.

270. Rogo, *Miracles*.

271. Auerbach, *Mind over Matter*.

272. Ibid.

273. Gaddis, *Mysterious Fires and Lights*.

274. Michell and Rickard, *Phenomena*.

275. Thurston, *The Physical Phenomena of Mysticism*, 180.

276. Gaddis, *Mysterious Fires and Lights*.

277. Michell and Rickard, *Phenomena*.

278. Cavendish, *Man, Myth, and Magic*, 2700.

279. Thurston, *The Physical Phenomena of Mysticism*.

280. Ibid., 221.

281. Ibid., 114.

282. Cavendish, *Man, Myth, and Magic*, 2700.

283. Ibid., 79.

284. Ibid.

285. Attar, *Muslim Saints and Mystics*, 157.

286. Gaddis, *Mysterious Fires and Lights*; Tummo, http://en.wikipedia.org/wiki/Tummo (October 19, 2009).

287. Benson et al., "Body Temperature Changes During the Practice of G Tum-mo Yoga."

288. Crommie, "Meditation Changes Temperatures."

289. Benson et al., "Body Temperature Changes During the Practice of G Tum-mo Yoga."

Luminosity

290. Treece, *The Sanctified Body*, 30.

291. Ibid., 35–36.

292. Attar, *Muslim Saints and Mystics*; Treece, *The Sanctified Body*.

293. Thurston, *The Physical Phenomena of Mysticism*; Treece, *The Sanctified Body*.

294. Attar, *Muslim Saints and Mystics*, Treece, *The Sanctified Body*.

295. Haraldsson, *Modern Miracles*; Murphy and White, *In the Zone*; Treece, *The Sanctified Body*.

296. Rogo, *Miracles*; Thurston and Attwater, *Butler's Lives of the Saints*.

297. *Catholic Information Resource*, http://www.infocatholic.com/viewSaint.aspx?SID=395 (April 9, 2007).

298. Murphy and White, *In the Zone*.

299. Thurston, *The Physical Phenomena of Mysticism*, 167.

300. Treece, *The Sanctified Body*, 60–61.

301. Ibid., 61.

302. Ball, *Modern Saints*.

303. Treece, *The Sanctified Body*, 32.

304. Attar, *Muslim Saints and Mystics*, 45–46.

305. Ibid., 222.

306. Ibid.

307. Treece, *The Sanctified Body*.

308. Ibid., 44.

309. Rogo, *Miracles*, 40.

310. Gaddis, *Mysterious Fires and Lights*; Thurston, *The Physical Phenomena of Mysticism*.

311. Ibid.

312. Price, *Fifty Years of Psychical Research*, 90–91.

313. Gaddis, *Mysterious Fires and Lights*, 163–165.

314. Treece, *The Sanctified Body*, 43.

315. Nickell, *Looking for a Miracle*.

Materialization/ Transformation of Matter

316. Rogo, *Miracles*.

317. Webster, *Miracles*, 12.

318. Haraldsson, *Modern Miracles*.

319. Ibid., 36.

320. Oman, *Mystics, Ascetics and Saints of India*, 59–61.
321. Webster, *Miracles*, 5.
322. 2 Kings 4:1–7; Webster, *Miracles*.
323. *Everything Jewish*, http://www.everythingjewish.com/Hanukah/origins.htm (April 13, 2007).
324. *Babylonian Talmud*, http://www.come-and-hear.com/shabbath/shabbath_21.html#PARTb (April 13, 2007).
325. Thurston, *The Physical Phenomena of Mysticism*, 393–394.
326. *Catholic Online*, http://www.catholic.org/saints/saint.php?saint_id=3946 (April 13, 2007); Webster, *Miracles*, 11–12.
327. Rogo, *Miracles*.
328. Oman, *Mystics, Ascetics and Saints of India*, 61–62.
329. Ibid., 62.
330. Haley, *Modern Loaves and Fishes and Other Studies in Psychic Phenomena*.
331. Rogo, *Miracles*, 303–305.

Hemography

332. Rogo, *Miracles*.
333. Thurston, *The Physical Phenomena of Mysticism*, 79.
334. Ibid., 78–79.
335. Rogo, *Miracles*.
336. Attar, *Muslim Saints and Mystics*.
337. Ibid., 230.
338. Ibid., 271.

Deliberately Caused Bodily Damage Phenomenon

339. Hussein et al., "Deliberately Caused Bodily Damage Phenomena."
340. Ibid.
341. Gersi, *Faces in the Smoke*; Hussein et al., "Deliberately Caused Bodily Damage Phenomena."
342. Hussein et al., "Deliberately Caused Bodily Damage Phenomena."
343. Shah, *The Sufis*, 372.
344. Dossey, "Deliberately Caused Bodily Damage."
345. Hall et al., "The Scientific Study of Unusual Rapid Wound Healing," 203.
346. Ibid.
347. Mulacz, "Deliberately Caused Bodily Damage (DCDB) Phenomenon."
348. Ibid.
349. Jamal Hussein, email to author, June 21, 2005.
350. Ibid.
351. Ibid.

Weather MMI

352. Neiman, *Miracles*; Rogo, *Miracles*.

353. Attar, *Muslim Saints and Mystics*, 77–78.
354. Lhalungpa, *The Life of Milarepa*.
355. McClenon, *Wondrous Events*.
356. Rogo, *Miracles*.
357. Skinner, "African Beliefs in the Psychic Manipulation of Material Phenomena."
358. Robinson, *To Stretch a Plank*.
359. Cavendish, *Man, Myth, and Magic*.
360. Mishlove, *The PK Man*.
361. Ibid.

Physical Mediums

362. Klimo, *Channeling*.
363. Beloff, *Parapsychology*.
364. Loewe and Blacker, *Oracles and Divination*.
365. Ibid.
366. Ibid.
367. Ibid., 96–97.
368. Ibid.
369. Cavendish, *Man, Myth, and Magic*.
370. McClenon, *Wondrous Events*.
371. Ibid., 162.
372. Lhalungpa, *The Life of Milarepa*; McClenon, *Wondrous Events*.
373. Cavendish, *Man, Myth, and Magic*.
374. Ibid.
375. Rogo, *Miracles*.
376. Cavendish, *Man, Myth, and Magic*; Knox, "History of Western Civilization."
377. Ibid.
378. Ibid.
379. Robinson, *To Stretch a Plank*.
380. Braude, *The Limits of Influence*.
381. Beloff, *Parapsychology*.
382. Nicol, "Historical Background."
383. Beloff, *Parapsychology*; Ebon, "A History of Parapsychology."
384. Rogo, *Mind over Matter*.
385. Beloff, *Parapsychology*.
386. Braude, *The Limits of Influence*; Robinson, *To Stretch a Plank*; Rogo, *Mind over Matter*.
387. Nicol, "Historical Background."
388. Klimo, *Channeling*.
389. Ibid., 232–233.
390. Gaddis, *Mysterious Fires and Lights*.
391. Gauld and Cornell, *Poltergeists*.
392. Ibid.; Robinson, *To Stretch a Plank*.
393. Gauld and Cornell, *Poltergeists*.
394. Rogo, *Parapsychology*.
395. Gauld and Cornell, *Poltergeists*.
396. Rogo, *Parapsychology*.
397. Ibid.
398. Greber, *Communication with the Spirit World of God: Personal Experiences of a Catholic Priest*, 227.
399. Ibid., 227.
400. Beloff, *Parapsychology*; Gauld, *The Founders of Psychical Research*.
401. Ebon, "A History of Parapsychology."

402. Rogo, *Mind over Matter*.
403. Ibid.
404. Nicol, "Historical Background."
405. Ebon, "A History of Parapsychology."
406. Nicol, "Historical Background."
407. Ebon, "A History of Parapsychology."
408. Podmore, *Mediums of the 19th Century*.
409. Irwin, *An Introduction to Parapsychology*.
410. Gauld, *The Founders of Psychical Research*.
411. Podmore, *Mediums of the 19th Century*.
412. Nicol, "Historical Background."
413. Rogo, *Parapsychology*.
414. Nicol, "Historical Background."
415. Podmore, *Mediums of the 19th Century*.
416. Nicol, "Historical Background."
417. Ibid.; Robinson, *To Stretch a Plank*.
418. Podmore, *Mediums of the 19th Century*.
419. Ibid.
420. Ibid.
421. Ibid.
422. Barclay, *Mind over Matter*.
423. Rogo, *Miracles*.
424. Home, *Incidents in my Life*, 66.
425. Rogo, *Mind over Matter*.
426. Thurston, *The Physical Phenomena of Mysticism*, 181.
427. Rogo, *Mind over Matter*.
428. Gaddis, *Mysterious Fires and Lights*.
429. Thurston, *The Physical Phenomena of Mysticism*, 183.
430. Gaddis, *Mysterious Fires and Lights*.
431. Ibid., 119.
432. Podmore, *Mediums of the 19th Century*.
433. Robinson, *To Stretch a Plank*.
434. Rogo, *Mind over Matter*.
435. Gauld, *The Founders of Psychical Research*.
436. Ibid.
437. Ibid.
438. Nicol, "Historical Background"; Rogo, *Miracles*.
439. Batcheldor, "Contributions to the Theory of PK Induction from Sitter-Group Work."
440. Rogo, *Mind over Matter*.
441. Beloff, "Historical Overview"; Dingwall, "A Report on a Series of Sittings with Mr. Willy Schneider."
442. Beloff, *Parapsychology*, 106.
443. Rogo, *Mind over Matter*.
444. Beloff, *Parapsychology*.
445. Ibid.
446. Rogo, *Mind over Matter*.
447. Ibid.
448. Randall, "Harry Price."
449. Ibid.
450. Ibid.
451. Ibid.
452. Loewe and Blacker, *Oracles*

and *Divination*; McClenon, *Wondrous Events*.

453. Robinson, *To Stretch a Plank*.
454. Nicol, "Historical Background"; Rogo, *Mind over Matter*.
455. Robinson, *To Stretch a Plank*; Rogo, *Mind over Matter*.
456. Gauld, *The Founders of Psychical Research*.
457. Rogo, *Miracles*; Rogo, *Mind over Matter*.

Anomalous Healers

458. Solfvin, "Mental Healing," 31.
459. Long, *Extrasensory Ecology*.
460. Puharich, "Psychic Research and the Healing Process."
461. Ibid.
462. Ibid.
463. Beloff, "Historical Overview."
464. Krippner and Welch, *Spiritual Dimensions of Healing*.
465. Ibid.
466. Turner, "Religious Specialists."
467. Lewis, "The Anthropologist's Encounter with the Supernatural."
468. Krippner and Welch, *Spiritual Dimensions of Healing*.
469. Ibid.
470. Ibid.
471. Turner, "Religious Specialists."
472. Krippner and Welch, *Spiritual Dimensions of Healing*.
473. Ibid.
474. Giesler, "Differential Micro-PK Effects Among Afro-Brazilian Cultists"; Giovetti, "Varieties of Healing Experience"; Heinze, "Healing in South and Southeast Asia"; Steffy, "Some Comparisons of Psychic Healing in the USSR, Eastern and Western Europe, North America, China and Brazil."
475. Schouten, "Psychic Healing and Complementary Medicine," 126.
476. Servadio, "Peasant-Healers and the Paranormal."
477. Bharati, "The Ontological Status of Psychic Phenomena in Hinduism and Buddhism."
478. Servadio, "Peasant-Healers and the Paranormal."
479. Ibid., 127.
480. Radin, *The Conscious Universe*.
481. Friel, *Dorland's Illustrated Medical Dictionary*.
482. Solfvin, "Mental Healing."
483. Irwin, "The Phenomenology of Parapsychological Experiences," 38.
484. Ibid., 39.
485. Murphy, *The Future of the Body*.
486. Ibid.
487. Irwin, *An Introduction to Parapsychology*.
488. Beloff, "Historical Overview."
489. Inglis, *Natural and Supernatural*, 142.
490. Ibid., 142.
491. Beloff, *Parapsychology*.
492. Irwin, *An Introduction to Parapsychology*.
493. Inglis, *Natural and Supernatural*, 142.
494. Beloff, "Historical Overview"; Inglis, *Natural and Supernatural*.
495. Inglis, *Natural and Supernatural*, 143.
496. Ibid., 143.
497. Ibid.
498. Ibid.
499. Ibid.
500. Beloff, *Parapsychology*, 177.
501. Inglis. *Natural and Supernatural*.
502. Ibid., 165.
503. Beloff, *Parapsychology*; Irwin, *An Introduction to Parapsychology*.
504. Zha and McConnell, "Parapsychology in the People's Republic of China: 1979–1989."
505. Murphy and White, *In the Zone*.
506. Hood, "Mystics, Ghosts and Faith Healers."
507. Ibid.
508. Hood, "Mystics, Ghosts and Faith Healers."
509. Neff, "They Fly through the Air with the Greatest of … Ki?"
510. Van de Castle, "Parapsychology and Anthropology."
511. McClenon, *Wondrous Events*.
512. Ibid.
513. Ehrenwald, "Parapsychology and the Healing Arts"; McClenon, *Wondrous Events*.
514. McClenon, *Wondrous Events*.
515. Ibid.
516. McClenon. *Wondrous Events*.
517. Greenfield, *Spirits with Scalpels*.
518. Puharich, "Psychic Research and the Healing Process."
519. Ibid.
520. Ibid.
521. Ibid.
522. Greenfield, *Spirits with Scalpels*.
523. Ibid.
524. McClenon, *Wondrous Events*.
525. Krippner and Welch, *Spiritual Dimensions of Healing*.
526. Ehrenwald, "Parapsychology and the Healing Arts."
527. Krippner, "Psychic Healing"; Krippner and Welch, *Spiritual Dimensions of Healing*; Van de Castle, "Parapsychology and Anthropology."

Martial Artists and Athletes

528. Wolf, "Various Fighting Systems all Stemmed from Kung Fu."
529. Dong and Raffill, *Empty Force*.
530. Murphy and White, *In the Zone*.
531. Ibid.
532. Dalton, "A Psi Experiment with the Martial Artist as Subject."
533. Barclay, *Mind over Matter*; Dong and Raffill, *Empty Force*.
534. Auerbach, *Mind over Matter*.
535. Alexander, Groller, and Morris, *The Warrior's Edge*; Auerbach, *Mind over Matter*.
536. Barclay, *Mind over Matter*.
537. Murphy and White, *In the Zone*.
538. Barclay, *Mind over Matter*.
539. Murphy and White, *In the Zone*.
540. Ibid.
541. Ibid.
542. Ibid.
543. Ibid.
544. Murphy, *The Future of the Body*.
545. Ibid., 429.
546. Ibid.
547. Murphy and White, *In the Zone*.
548. Taylor, "Enhancing Athletic and Psychic Performances through the Use of Imagery Based Mental Strategies."
549. Ibid., 99.
550. Ibid.
551. Herrigel, *Zen in the Art of Archery*; Murphy and White, *In the Zone*.
552. Murphy and White, *In the Zone*; Murphy and White, *The Psychic Side of Sports*.
553. Taylor, "Enhancing Athletic and Psychic Performances through the Use of Imagery Based Mental Strategies."
554. Murphy and White, *In the Zone*.

Poltergeists

555 William Roll, email communication to author, November 1, 2009.
556. Goss, *Poltergeists*.
557. Price, *Poltergeist*, 2.
558. Owen, *Can We Explain the Poltergeist?*, 1.
559. Price, *Poltergeist*.
560. Gauld and Cornell, *Poltergeists*; Goss, *Poltergeists*.
561. Goss, *Poltergeists*.
562. Rogo, *The Poltergeist Experience*.
563. Gauld and Cornell, *Poltergeists*; Goss, *Poltergeists*.
564. Gauld and Cornell, *Poltergeists*, 3.
565. Rogo, *On the Track of the Poltergeist*.
566. Rogo, *Miracles*.
567. Ibid., 158.
568. Gauld and Cornell, *Poltergeists*; Rogo, *The Poltergeist Experience*; Roll, "Poltergeists"; Thurston, *Ghosts and Poltergeists*.
569. Gauld and Cornell, *Poltergeists*.
570. Rogo, *The Poltergeist Experience*.
571. Gauld and Cornell, *Poltergeists*.
572. Price, *Poltergeist*, 9.
573. Ibid., 9.
574. *Literary Encyclopedia*, http://www.litencyc.com/php/stopics.php?rec=true&UID=1414 (April 15, 2007).

575. *Literary Encyclopedia,* http://www.litencyc.com/php/stopics.php?rec=true&UID=1414 (April 15, 2007); Price, *Poltergeist,* 9.
576. Price, *Poltergeist,* 9.
577. Ibid.
578. Ibid.
579. Gauld and Cornell, *Poltergeists;* Goss, *Poltergeists.*
580. Rogo, *The Poltergeist Experience.*

The Wild Card: Spontaneous Nonrecurrent MMI

581. Beloff, "Historical Overview."
582. Ibid., xi.
583. Murphy and White, *In the Zone.*
584. Stokes, "Spontaneous Psi Phenomena."
585. Rogo and Bayless, *Phone Calls From the Dead.*
586. Buchanan, *The Seventh Sense.*
587. Kelly, "Spontaneous Human Combustion."
588. Gaddis, *Mysterious Fires and Lights.*
589. Kelly, "Spontaneous Human Combustion"; Murphy, *The Future of the Body.*
590. Michell and Rickard, *Phenomena.*
591. Ibid.
592. Arnold, *Ablaze!.*
593. Murphy, "A Blaze of Glory."
594. Arnold, *Ablaze!,* 337.
595. Ibid., 337
596. Arnold, *Ablaze!.*
597. Michell and Rickard, *Phenomena.*
598. Gaddis, *Mysterious Fires and Lights;* Michell and Rickard, *Phenomena.*
599. Ibid.
600. Michell and Rickard, *Phenomena.*
601. Kelly, "Spontaneous Human Combustion."
602. Arnold, *Ablaze!;* Kelly, "Spontaneous Human Combustion"; Murphy, "A Blaze of Glory."
603. Arnold, *Ablaze!,* 419; Gaddis, *Mysterious Fires and Lights.*
604. Kelly, "Spontaneous Human Combustion."
605. Arnold, *Ablaze!,* 419.
606. Gaddis, *Mysterious Fires and Lights.*
607. Arnold, *Ablaze!,* 420.
608. Murphy, "A Blaze of Glory."
609. Kelly, "Spontaneous Human Combustion."
610. Michell and Rickard, *Phenomena.*
611. Gaddis, *Mysterious Fires and Lights.*
612. Carlson, *Mysteries of the Unexplained.*

613. Ibid.
614. Gaddis, *Mysterious Fires and Lights.*
615. Arnold, *Ablaze!,* 35–36.
616. Ibid.
617. Michell and Rickard, *Phenomena.*
618. Carlson, *Mysteries of the Unexplained.*
619. Arnold, *Ablaze!.*
620. Ibid., 460.
621. Ibid.
622. Cade and Davis, *The Taming of the Thunderbolts.*
623. Cade and Davis, *The Taming of the Thunderbolts;* Corliss, *Handbook of Unusual Natural Phenomena;* Turner, "The Missing Science of Ball Lightning."
624. Turner, "The Missing Science of Ball Lightning."
625. Corliss, *Handbook of Unusual Natural Phenomena.*
626. Ibid.
627. Cade and Davis, *The Taming of the Thunderbolts;* Michell and Rickard, *Phenomena.*
628. Gaddis, *Mysterious Fires and Lights.*
629. Rosenthal, *Winter Blues,* 4–5.
630. Ibid., 4–5.
631. Ibid.
632. Wetzel, *Clinical Handbook of Depression.*
633. Kunz and Kunz, "Depression and Suicide in the Dark Months."
634. Ibid.
635. Gaddis, *Mysterious Fires and Lights;* Jerry Solfvin, personal communication to author on April 24, 1998.

Summary

636. Rogo, *Miracles.*
637. Loewe and Blacker, *Oracles and Divination;* McClenon, *Wondrous Events.*
638. Barclay, *Mind over Matter;* Cavendish, *Man, Myth, and Magic.*
639. Rogo, *On the Track of the Poltergeist.*
640. Barclay, *Mind over Matter;* Murphy and White *In the Zone.*
641. Murphy and White *In the Zone;* Rogo, *Miracles.*
642. Murphy and White *In the Zone.*
643. Gauld and Cornell, *Poltergeists.*
644. Ibid.; Rhine, "Research Methods with Spontaneous Cases."
645. Stokes, "Spontaneous Psi Phenomena," 66.

PART II: RESEARCH AND THEORY

1. Stokes, "Spontaneous Psi Phenomena."
2. Ibid.
3. Ibid.

Spontaneous Case Collections

4. Beloff, "Historical Overview."
5. Ibid.; Beloff, *Parapsychology.*
6. Gurney, Myers, and Podmore, "Phantasms of the Living."
7. Rhine, "Research Methods with Spontaneous Cases."
8. Roll, "Recurrent and Nonrecurrent Psi Effects."
9. Stokes, "Spontaneous Psi Phenomena."
10. Rhine, *Hidden Channels of the Mind,* 216–217.
11. Stokes, "Spontaneous Psi Phenomena."
12. Roll, "Recurrent and Nonrecurrent Psi Effects."
13. Rao, "L. E. Rhine on Psi and its Place."
14. Rhine, "Research Methods with Spontaneous Cases."
15. Irwin, "The Phenomenology of Parapsychological Experiences," 30.

Poltergeist Research

16. Jahn, "The Persistent Paradox of Psychic Phenomena"; Gauld and Cornell, *Poltergeists.*
17. Jahn, "The Persistent Paradox of Psychic Phenomena."
18. Ebon, "A History of Parapsychology."
19. Nicol, "Historical Background."
20. Jahn, "The Persistent Paradox of Psychic Phenomena"; Rogo, *Miracles.*
21. Jahn, "The Persistent Paradox of Psychic Phenomena."
22. Gauld and Cornell, *Poltergeists.*
23. Ibid.
24. Ibid.
25. Ibid.
26. Ibid.
27. Ibid.
28. Ibid.
29. Ibid.
30. Rogo, "The Poltergeist and Family Dynamics."
31. Gauld and Cornell, *Poltergeists;* Goss, *Poltergeists.*
32. Irwin, "The Phenomenology of Parapsychological Experiences."
33. Roll, "Poltergeists, Electromagnetism, and Consciousness."
34. Rogo, *The Poltergeist Experience.*
35. Auerbach, *ESP, Hauntings, and Poltergeists;* Rogo, *The Poltergeist Experience;* Roll, "Poltergeists."
36. Gauld and Cornell, *Poltergeists;* Roll, *The Poltergeist.*
37. Rogo, *The Poltergeist Experience.*
38. Gauld and Cornell, *Poltergeists.*
39. Gauld and Cornell, *Poltergeists;* Goss, *Poltergeists.*
40. Gaddis, *Mysterious Fires and Lights.*
41. Ibid.

42. Ibid.

43. Ibid.

44. Ibid.

45. Ibid.

46. Ibid.

47. Cade and Davis, *The Taming of the Thunderbolts*.

48. Gaddis, *Mysterious Fires and Lights*, 203.

49. Roll, *The Poltergeist*.

50. Gauld and Cornell, *Poltergeists*.

51. Ibid.

52. Gauld and Cornell, *Poltergeists*; Roll, "Poltergeists"; Rogo, *The Poltergeist Experience*.

53. Auerbach, *Mind over Matter*.

54. Gauld and Cornell, *Poltergeists*.

55. Ibid., 336.

56. Owen, *Can We Explain the Poltergeist?*

57. Auerbach, *Mind over Matter*.

58. Gauld and Cornell, *Poltergeists*.

59. Ibid.

60. Ibid., 252.

61. Ibid.

62. Roll, "Poltergeists."

63. Martínez-Taboas, "An Appraisal of the Role of Aggression and the Central Nervous System in RSPK Agents."

64. Owen, *Can We Explain the Poltergeist?*

65. Ibid., 336

66. Rogo, *The Poltergeist Experience*, 85.

67. Fodor, *On the Trail of the Poltergeist*, 221.

68. Rogo, *The Poltergeist Experience*.

69. Martínez-Taboas, "An Appraisal of the Role of Aggression and the Central Nervous System in RSPK Agents."

70. Gauld and Cornell, *Poltergeists*.

71. Rogo, "The Poltergeist and Family Dynamics."

72. Lucadou and Zahradnik, "Predictions of the Model of Pragmatic Information About RSPK."

Early Research with Physical Mediums

73. Rogo, *Mind over Matter*.

74. Jolly, *Sir Oliver Lodge*.

75. Ibid., 106.

76. Gauld, *The Founders of Psychical Research*.

77. Ibid.

78. Beloff, *Parapsychology*; Rogo, *Mind over Matter*.

79. Beloff, *Parapsychology*; Podmore, *Mediums of the 19th Century*.

80. Beloff, *Parapsychology*, 47.

81. Braude, *The Limits of Influence*; Rogo, *Mind over Matter*.

82. Beloff, *Parapsychology*.

83. Ibid., 52.

84. Ibid.

85. Ibid., 55.

86. Gauld, *The Founders of Psychical Research*.

87. Ibid.

88. Randall, "Harry Price"; Rogo, *On the Track of the Poltergeist*.

89. *Archives in London and the M25 Area*, http://www.aim25.ac.uk/cgi bin/search2?coll_id=7397&inst_id=14 (April 17, 2007).

90. Ibid.; Randall, "Harry Price."

91. Beloff, *Parapsychology*.

92. Ibid., 94.

93. Rogo, *Mind over Matter*.

94. Randall, "Harry Price," 159.

95. Rogo, *Mind over Matter*.

96. Guiley, *Harper's Encyclopedia of Mystical and Paranormal Experience*, 254; Randall, "Harry Price."

97. *Harry Price*, http://www.harryprice.co.uk/index.html (April 17, 2007).

98. "Annual Report of the Council."

99. Randall, "Harry Price," 165.

100. *Harry Price*, http://www.harryprice.co.uk/Timeline/1946–1948.htm (April 17, 2007).

101. Rogo, *Mind over Matter*.

102. Gregory and Wilson, "London Experiences with Matthew Manning."

103. Rogo, *Mind over Matter*.

104. Gregory and Wilson, "London Experiences with Matthew Manning"; Rogo, *Mind over Matter*.

105. Ibid.

106. Rogo, *Mind over Matter*.

Dice and Sphere Experiments

107. Stanford, "Experimental Psychokinesis."

108. Murphy, *The Future of the Body*.

109. Stanford, "Experimental Psychokinesis."

110. Dalton, "A Psi Experiment with the Martial Artist as Subject."

111. Robinson, *To Stretch a Plank*.

112. Dalton, "A Psi Experiment with the Martial Artist as Subject"; Stanford, "Experimental Psychokinesis."

113. Stanford, "Experimental Psychokinesis."

114. Dale and White, "Glossary."

115. Stanford, "Experimental Psychokinesis."

116. Radin, *The Conscious Universe*.

117. Radin and Ferrari, "Effects of Consciousness on the Fall of Dice."

118. Radin, *The Conscious Universe*, 135–136.

119. Radin and Ferrari, "Effects of Consciousness on the Fall of Dice."

120. Jahn, "The Persistent Paradox of Psychic Phenomena"; Roger Nelson, email to author October 26, 2009.

121. Dunne, Nelson, and Jahn, "Operator-Related Anomalies in a Random Mechanical Cascade."

122. Ibid., 155.

Random Generator Research

123. Schmeidler, "Psychokinesis"; Stanford, "Experimental Psychokinesis."

124. Varvoglis, *Psychokinesis, Intentionality and the Attentional Object*.

125. Dalton, "A Psi Experiment with the Martial Artist as Subject."

126. Broughton and Perlstrom, "A Competitive Computer Game in PK Research"; Hansen, "A Cooperation-Competition PK Experiment with Computerized Horse Races"; Varvoglis, *Psi-explorer*.

127. Nelson, "2008 Presidential Address," 8–9.

128. Dalton, "A Psi Experiment with the Martial Artist as Subject."

129. Blasband, "The Ordering of Random Events by Emotional Expression."

130. Lumsden-Cook, "Mind, Matter and Emotion."

131. Radin, *The Conscious Universe*.

132. Ibid., 140–141.

133. Ibid.

134. Dunne and Jahn, "Consciousness and Anomalous Physical Phenomena"; Radin, *The Conscious Universe*.

135. Robinson, *To Stretch a Plank*.

136. Radin and Nelson, "Research on Mind-Matter Interactions (MMI)."

137. Ibid., 46

138. Ibid.

139. Ibid., 45.

140. Bosch, Steinkamp, and Boller. "Examining Psychokinesis"; Schub, "A Critique on the Parapsychological Random Number Generator Meta-Analyses of Radin and Nelson"; Wilson and Shadish, "On Blowing Trumpets to the Tulips."

141. Radin et al., "Reexamining Psychokinesis"; Scargle, "Comment on: 'A Critique of the Parapsychological Random Number Generator Meta-Analyses of Radin and Nelson' by Martin Schub."

142. Radin and Nelson, "Research on Mind-Matter Interactions (MMI)."

143. Nelson. "Correlation of Global Events with REG Data"; Radin, "Exploring Relationships Between Random Physical Events and Mass Human Attention," 534.

144. Nelson, "Coherent Consciousness and Reduced Randomness"; Nelson et al., "Correlations of Continuous Random Data with Major World Events"; Radin, "Exploring Relationships Between Random Physical Events and Mass Human Attention."

145. Radin and Nelson, "Research on Mind-Matter Interactions (MMI)," 50.

146. Roger Nelson, email to author October 26, 2009.

147. Nelson, "Coherent Consciousness and Reduced Randomness," 565.

148. Radin, *Entangled Minds*; Radin, "Science and the Taboo of Psi" lecture presented at Google Auditorium on January 16, 2008 (available at http://www.youtube.com).

149. Dean Radin, email to author, October 28, 2009.

150. Schmidt, "Human PK Effort on Pre-Recorded Targets, Previously Observed by Goldfish"; Schmidt, "PK Tests with and without Pre-Observation by Animals"; Schmidt, "Random Generators and Living systems as Targets in Retro-PK Experiments"; Schmidt and Stapp, "PK with Prerecorded Random Events and the Effects of Preobservation."

151. Schmidt and Stapp, "PK with Prerecorded Random Events and the Effects of Preobservation."

152. Ibid.

153. Radin, "Experiments Testing Models of Mind-Matter Interaction."

154. Ibid.

155. Etzold, "Solar-Periodic Full Moon Effect in the Fourmilab Retropsychokinesis Project Experiment Data."

156. Ibid., 245–246.

157. Morris, "Parapsychology, Biology, and ANPSI."

158. Bedford et al., "Chicks and Algae."

159. Schmidt and Stapp, "PK with Prerecorded Random Events and the Effects of Preobservation."

160. Walker, "A Comparison of the Intuitive Data Sorting and Quantum Mechanical Observer Theories."

161. Dean Radin, email to author, October 28, 2009.

162. Radin and Nelson, "Research on Mind-Matter Interactions (MMI)," 46.

Biological System Research

163. Houck, "Researching Remote Viewing and Psychokinesis," 18.

164. Ibid.

165. Ibid., 21.

166. Morris, "Parapsychology, Biology, and ANPSI."

167. Ibid., 710.

168. Braud, *Distant Mental Influence.*

169. Delanoy, "Anomalous Psychophysiological Responses to Remote Cognition," 30–31.

170. Ibid.

171. Delanoy and Morris, "A DMILS Training Study Utilising Two Shielded Environments," 53.

172. Ibid., 61.

173. Delanoy et al., "An EDA DMILS Study Exploring Agent-Receiver Pairing."

174. Delanoy, "Anomalous Psychophysiological Responses to Remote Cognition," 38.

175. Schneider, Binder, and Walach, "On the Role of the Agent in EDA-DMILS Experiments," 286.

176. Ibid., 62.

177. Schmidt and Walach, "Electrodermal Activity (EDA)— State-of-the-Art Measurement and Techniques for Parapsychological Purposes," 153.

178. Schmidt et al., "Investigating Methodological Issues in EDA-DMILS."

179. Schmidt and Walach, "Electrodermal Activity (EDA)–State-of-the-Art Measurement and Techniques for Parapsychological Purposes."

180. Ibid.

181. Ibid., 37.

182. Wiseman and Schlitz, "Examining the Remote Staring Effect."

183. Wiseman and Schlitz, "Experimenter Effects and the Remote Detection of Staring."

184. Schlitz et al., "Of Two Minds."

185. Braud, *Distant Mental Influence.*

186. Ibid.

187. Mulacz, "Deliberately Caused Bodily Damage (DCDB) Phenomena."

188. Ibid.

189. Dossey, "Deliberately Caused Bodily Damage."

190. Hall et al., "The Scientific Study of Unusual Rapid Wound Healing."

191. Ibid.

192. Solfvin, "Mental Healing."

193. Klimo, *Channeling*; Solfvin, "Mental Healing."

194. Beloff, "Historical Overview."

195. Solfvin, "Mental Healing."

196. Ibid.; Strauch, "Medical Aspects of 'Mental' Healing."

197. Solfvin, "Mental Healing."

198. Edwards, *The Healing Intelligence*, 110.

199. Ibid., 110.

200. Solfvin, "Mental Healing."

201. Ibid.

202. Schouten, "Psychic Healing and Complementary Medicine."

203. Ibid., 149.

204. Ibid.

205. Greenfield, "The Patients of Dr. Fritz."

206. Ibid.

207. Don and Moura, "Trance Surgery in Brazil."

208. Strauch, "Medical Aspects of 'Mental' Healing."

209. Ibid.

210. Ibid.

211. Ibid.

212. Ibid.

213. Haraldsson and Olafsson, "A Survey of Psychic Healing in Iceland"; Strauch, "Medical Aspects of 'Mental' Healing."

214. Strauch, "Medical Aspects of 'Mental' Healing," 160.

215. Solfvin, "Mental Healing."

216. Grad, Cadoret, and Paul, "The Influence of an Unorthodox Method of Treatment on Wound Healing in Mice"; Solfvin, "Mental Healing."

217. Solfvin, "Mental Healing."

218. Schmeidler, "Psychokinesis."

219. Solfvin, "Mental Healing."

220. Watkins and Watkins, "Possible PK Influence on the Resuscitation of Anesthetized Mice."

221. Ibid.

222. Ibid.

223. Solfvin, "Mental Healing."

224. Ibid.

225. Watkins and Watkins, "Possible PK Influence on the Resuscitation of Anesthetized Mice."

226. Solfvin, "Mental Healing."

227. Braud, "Distant Mental Influence of Rate of Hemolysis of Human Red Blood Cells."

228. Palmer, "A Statistical Artifact in William Braud's (1990) Experiment on Remote Mental Influence of Hemolysis."

229. Yount et al., "In Vitro Test of External Qigong."

230. Byrd, "Positive Therapeutic Effects of Intercessory Prayer in a Coronary Care Unit Population."

231. Schouten, "Psychic Healing and Complementary Medicine."

232. Wirth, "Unorthodox Healing."

233. Schouten, "Psychic Healing and Complementary Medicine."

234. Ibid., 142.

235. Sicher et al., "A Randomized Double-Blind Study of the Effect of Distant Healing in a Population With Advanced AIDS."

236. Lumsden-Cook, Edwards, and Thwala, "An Exploratory Study into Traditional Zulu Healing and REG Effects."

237. Schwartz and Boccuzzi, "Effects of Psychic Healing Intentions on Patterns of Cosmic Rays."

238. Schouten, "Psychic Healing and Complementary Medicine," 145.

239. Solfvin, "Mental Healing."

240. Schouten, "Psychic Healing and Complementary Medicine," 93.

241. Solfvin, "Mental Healing."

242. Schouten, "Psychic Healing and Complementary Medicine," 194–195.

243. Ibid., 195.

244. Solfvin, "Mental Healing."

245. Schouten, "Psychic Healing and Complementary Medicine."

246. Solfvin, "Mental Healing," 56.

247. Schouten, "Psychic Healing and Complementary Medicine."

248. Traut and Passarelli, "Placebos in the Treatment of Rheumatoid Arthritis and Other Rheumatic Conditions."

249. Schouten, "Psychic Healing and Complementary Medicine," 193.

250. Traut and Passarelli, "Placebos in the Treatment of Rheumatoid Arthritis and Other Rheumatic Conditions," 19.

251. Benor, "Fields and Energies Related to Healing."

252. Schwartz and Boccuzzi, "Effects of Psychic Healing Intentions on Patterns of Cosmic Rays."

253. Ibid.

254. Schouten, "Psychic Healing and Complementary Medicine," 139.

255. Ibid.

256. Ibid, 195–196.

257. Ibid., 192.

258. Ibid., 199–200.
259. Solfvin, "Mental Healing."
260. Ibid.
261. Ibid.

Macro-MMI Research

262. Robinson, *To Stretch a Plank.*
263. Honorton, "A Moving Experience."
264. Stanford, "Experimental Psychokinesis."
265. Dulnov et al., "Scientists Study Phenomena of Nina Kulagina"; Pratt, "Soviet Research in Parapsychology"; Rogo, *Mind over Matter.*
266. Pratt, "Soviet Research in Parapsychology."
267. Rogo, *Mind over Matter.*
268. Pratt, "Soviet Research in Parapsychology"; Rogo, *Mind over Matter.*
269. Auerbach, *Mind over Matter.*
270. Rogo, *Mind over Matter.*
271. Beloff, *Parapsychology.*
272. Dong and Raffill. *China's Super Psychics.*
273. Ibid.
274. Ibid.; Radin, *The Conscious Universe.*
275. Dong and Raffill. *China's Super Psychics.*
276. Zha and McConnell, "Parapsychology in the People's Republic of China: 1979–1989."
277. Dong and Raffill. *China's Super Psychics.*
278. Ibid.
279. Zha and McConnell, "Parapsychology in the People's Republic of China: 1979–1989."
280. Dong and Raffill. *China's Super Psychics.*
281. Zha and McConnell, "Parapsychology in the People's Republic of China: 1979–1989."
282. Pulos and Richman, *Miracles and Other Realities.*
283. Ibid.
284. Ibid.
285. Ibid.
286. Gregory, "London Experiences with Matthew Manning: Introduction."
287. Ibid.
288. Inglis, "London Experiences with Matthew Manning: Comments."
289. Manning, "London Experiences with Matthew Manning," http://www.matthewmanning.com (November 1, 2009).
290. Honorton, "A Moving Experience."
291. Ibid.
292. Honorton, "A Moving Experience"; Rogo, *Mind over Matter.*
293. Gissurarson, "Studies of Methods of Enhancing and Potentially Training Psychokinesis"; Rush, "Findings from Experimental PK Research."
294. Honorton "A Moving Experience."

295. Auerbach, *Mind over Matter.*
296. Caidin, "The Merlin Effect."
297. Auerbach, *Mind over Matter.*
298. William George Roll, personal communication to Dr. Michael Glancey, July 13, 1988.
299. Caidin, "The Merlin Effect."
300. Ibid.
301. Martin Caidin, personal communication to Phyllis Galde, October 18, 1993.
302. Caidin, "Fiction this Ain't."
303. Ibid., 218.
304. Caidin, "The Merlin Effect."
305. Stanford, "Experimental Psychokinesis."
306. Auerbach, *Mind over Matter.*
307. Ibid.
308. http://www.alextanous.org/news/newsletter.php?ID=7 (September 30, 2008).
309. Auerbach, *Mind over Matter.*
310. Ibid.
311. Vaughan, "Famous Western Sensitives."
312. Swann, "Remote Viewing: The Real Story."
313. Stanford, "Experimental Psychokinesis."
314. Tart, "Out-of-Body Experiences."
315. Vaughan, "Famous Western Sensitives."
316. Tart, "Out-of-Body Experiences."
317. Vaughan, "Famous Western Sensitives."
318. Rogo, *Mind over Matter.*
319. Targ and Harary, *The Mind Race.*
320. Palmer and Rush, "Experimental Methods in PK Research."
321. Batcheldor, "Contributions to the Theory of PK Induction from Sitter-Group Work."
322. Ibid.
323. Isaacs, "The Batcheldor Approach."
324. Batcheldor, "Contributions to the Theory of PK Induction from Sitter-Group Work."
325. Owen and Sparrow, *Conjuring Up Philip.*
326. Reinhart, "PK Induction."

Metal-Bending Research

327. Hasted, *The Metal-benders.*
328. Auerbach, *Mind over Matter.*
329. Hasted, *The Metal-benders.*
330. Ibid.
331. Ibid.
332. Houck, "Researching Remote Viewing and Psychokinesis."
333. Siegel, "PK Party Survey."
334. Hasted, *The Metal-benders.*
335. Beloff, *Parapsychology,* 197.
336. Hasted, *The Metal-benders.*
337. Gauld, *The Founders of Psychical Research.*
338. Hasted, *The Metal-benders.*
339. Ibid.

340. Hasted, *The Metal-benders*; Houck, "Researching Remote Viewing and Psychokinesis."
341. Auerbach, *Mind over Matter.*
342. Houck, "PK Party Format and Materials Required."
343. Houck, "PK Party Format and Materials Required"; Siegel, "PK Party Survey."
344. Houck, "Surface Change During Warm-Forming"; Houck, "Researching Remote Viewing and Psychokinesis."
345. Houck, "PK Party History."
346. Houck, "Surface Change During Warm-Forming."
347. Houck, "Researching Remote Viewing and Psychokinesis."
348. Auerbach, *Mind over Matter.*
349. Rauscher, "Psychokinetic Interaction with Laboratory Prepared Materials."
350. Randall and Davis, "Paranormal Deformation of Nitinol Wire."
351. Hasted, *The Metal-benders*; and Davis, "Paranormal Deformation of Nitinol Wire."
352. Houck, "PK Party Format and Materials Required."
353. Ibid., 1.
354. Caidin, "The Merlin Effect."
355. Houck, "Researching Remote Viewing and Psychokinesis."
356. Hasted, *The Metal-benders.*

Instrumental Transcommunication Research

357. Butler and Butler, *There is No Death and There Are No Dead,* 2.
358. Ibid.; Klimo, *Channeling.*
359. Bayless, "Correspondence."
360. Bayless, *Experiences of a Psychical Researcher.*
361. Butler and Butler, *There Is No Death and There Are No Dead.*
362. Raudive, *An Amazing Experiment,* 27–28.
363. Kubis and Macy, *Conversations Beyond the Light.*
364. From Tom and Lisa Butler at http://www.aaevp.com/examples/examples_voice.htm (January 18, 2006).
365. Devereux, "Letters."
366. Butler and Butler, *There is No Death and There Are No Dead*; MacRae, *EVP and New Dimensions*; Alexander MacRae, email communication to author, October 29, 2009.
367. Alexander MacRae, email communication to author, March 15, 2006.
368. Larry Flaxman, email communication forwarded to author, April 15, 2006.
369. Butler and Butler, *There is No Death and There Are No Dead,* 203.
370. Alexander MacRae, Personal communication to author, February 19, 2004.

371. Klimo, "Progress Report on a Grant-Supported Technological Survival Research Activities of Jon Klimo & Associates."

372. Jon Klimo, personal communication to author, March 1998.

373. Fontana and Cardoso, "*Instrumental Transcommunication Research Project.*"

374. Paranormal Research Organization meeting, August 2003.

375. Rogo and Bayless, *Phone Calls From the Dead.*

376. Klimo, *Channeling*; MacRae, *Mystery of the Voices*, 121–135.

377. Alexander MacRae, email to author January 29, 2008.

378. http://www.aaevp.com/articles/articles_about_evp2.htm (October 1, 2008); Fontana and Cardoso, "*Instrumental Transcommunication Research Project.*"

379. Klimo, *Channeling.*

380. Berger, Hovelmann, and von Lucadou, "Spirit Extras on Video Tape?"

381. Ibid., 163.

382. Personal communication to Jon Klimo on March 5, 1998.

383. Baruss, "Failure to Replicate Electronic Voice Phenomena."

384. Ibid., 358.

385. Bayless, "Correspondence."

386. Bander, *Voices from the Tapes.*

387. Berger, Hovelmann, and von Lucadou, "Spirit Extras on Video Tape?"

388. Ibid., 162.

389. Baruss, "Failure to Replicate Electronic Voice Phenomena," 358.

390. MacRae, "A Means of Producing the Electronic Voice Phenomenon Based on Electro-Dermal Activity."

391. Baruss, "An Experimental Test of Instrumental Transcommunication."

392. MacRae, "Report of an Electronic Voice Phenomenon Experiment."

393. Ibid.

394. MacRae, "Experiments to Determine if there is any Correlation Between Questions and Answers in EVP."

395. Ibid.

396. Butler and Butler, *There is No Death and There Are No Dead.*

397. MacRae, *EVP and New Dimensions.*

398. Butler and Butler, *There is No Death and There Are No Dead.*

399. Kubis and Macy, *Conversations Beyond the Light.*

400. Butler and Butler, *There is No Death and There Are No Dead.*

401. Personal communication to author, November 7, 2004.

402. Heath, "The Possible Role of Psychokinesis in Place Memory"; Williams and Roll, "Psi, Place Memory, & Laboratory Space."

403. Butler and Butler, *There is No Death and There Are No Dead,* 55.

404. Fontana, "Instrumental Transcommunication — The Gwen Tate Memorial Lecture by Dr. Anabela Cardoso," 16.

Anomalous Photography

405. Eisenbud, "Paranormal Photography."

406. Ibid.

407. Auerbach, *Mind over Matter.*

408. Krippner, "Parapsychological Methodology and Shamanistic Studies."

409. Haraldsson, *Modern Miracles.*

410. Ventola and Terhune, "Context, Individual Differences and Media Type in the Evaluation of Photographic Anomalies."

411. Terhune, Ventola, and Houran. "An Analysis of Contextual Variables and the Incidence of Photographic Anomalies at an Alleged Haunt and a Control Site."

412. Ibid.

Other Areas of Research

413. Rogo, *Mind over Matter.*

414. Hasted, *The Metal-benders.*

415. Murphy and White, *In the Zone.*

416. Haley, *Modern Loaves and Fishes And Other Studies in Psychic Phenomena.*

417. Ibid.

418. Ibid.

419. Ibid.

420. Radin, Wendland, and Rickenbach. "Does Consciousness Collapse the Quantum Wave-function?"

Performance Factors

421. Dalton, "A Psi Experiment with the Martial Artist as Subject."

422. Holt and Roe, "The Sender as PK Agent in ESP Studies."

423. Roe and Holt, "The Effect of Strategy ("Willing" versus Absorption) and Feedback (Intermediate versus Delayed) on Performance at a PK Task."

424. Batcheldor, "Contributions to the Theory of PK Induction from Sitter-Group Work"; Isaacs, "A Twelve Session Study of Micro PKMB Training"; Roll, "Poltergeists"; Rush, "Findings from Experimental PK Research."

425. Wilkinson and Gauld, "Geomagnetism and Anomalous Experiences, 1868–1980."

426. Marsha Adams, personal communication to author, August 13, 2005, at the 48th Annual Parapsychological Association Convention.

427. Ibid., 307.

428. May, "Toward the Physics of Psi"; Puhle, "Learning from Historical Cases."

429. Braud and Dennis, "Geophysical Variables and Behaviours."

430. "Nicola Tesla," http://en.wikipedia.org/wiki/Nikola_Tesla (October 5, 2008).

431. Roe, Davey and Stevens, "Are ESP and PK Aspects of a Unitary Phenomenon?"

432. Ibid., 349.

433. Chavin and Varjean. "Is it Possible to Strengthen the Psi Effect Using a Very Weak Magnetic Field?"

434. Gissurarson, "The Psychokinesis Effect: Geomagnetic Influence, Age and Sex Differences."

435. Schumacher, Heinen and Carter, "EVP and Geomagnetic Fields."

436. Wilkinson and Gauld, "Geomagnetism and Anomalous Experiences, 1868–1980," 308.

437. Spottiswoode, "Apparent Association Between Effect Size in Free Response Anomalous Cognition Experiments and Local Sidereal Time"; Spottiswoode, "Geomagnetic Fluctuations and Free Response Anomalous Cognition."

438. Ibid.; May, "Toward the Physics of Psi," 49–50.

439. Ibid.

440. Spottiswoode, "Apparent Association Between Effect Size in Free Response Anomalous Cognition Experiments and Local Sidereal Time."

441. Spottiswoode, "Geomagnetic Fluctuations and Free Response Anomalous Cognition: A New Understanding."

442. James Spoltiswoode, email to author November 30, 2010.

443. Wilkinson and Gauld, "Geomagnetism and Anomalous Experiences, 1868–1980."

444. Etzold, "Solar-Periodic Full Moon Effect in the Fourmilab Retropsychokinesis Project Experiment Data."

445. Gissurarson, "Studies of Methods of Enhancing and Potentially Training Psychokinesis"; Isaacs, "Clinical Issues in the Parapsychology Laboratory."

446. Schmeidler, *Parapsychology and Psychology.*

447. Ibid., 65.

448. Ibid.

449. Ibid., 77.

450. Ibid.

451. Palmer and Rush, "Experimental Methods in PK Research."

452. Tart, "Learning to Use Psychokinesis."

453. Bosch and Walach, "The Decline Phenomenon."

454. Lucadou, Röemer and Walach, "Synchronistic Phenomena as Entanglement Correlations in Generalized Quantum Theory," 52–53.

455. Radin, *The Conscious Universe.*

456. Schmeidler, "Methods for Controlled Research on ESP and PK."

457. Schmeidler, *Parapsychology and Psychology*.

458. Rosenthal, *Experimenter Effects in Behavioral Research*.

459. Schmeidler, *Parapsychology and Psychology*, 29.

460. Radin, *The Conscious Universe*; Rush, "Findings from Experimental PK Research."

461. Schlitz et al., "Of Two Minds"; Wiseman and Schlitz, "Examining the Remote Staring Effect"; Wiseman and Schlitz, "Experimenter Effects and the Remote Detection of Staring."

462. Ibid.

463. Schmeidler, "Psi-Conducive Experimenters and Psi-Permissive Ones."

464. Palmer and Rush, "Experimental Methods in PK Research."

465. Geschwind and Iacoboni. "Structural and Functional Asymmetries of the Human Frontal Lobes."

466. Edwards-Lee and Saul, "Neuropsychiatry of the Right Frontal Lobe"; Chow and Cummings, "Frontal-Subcortical Circuits."

467. Chow and Cummings, "Frontal-Subcortical Circuits."

468. Edwards-Lee and Saul, "Neuropsychiatry of the Right Frontal Lobe," 307.

469. Geschwind and Iacoboni. "Structural and Functional Asymmetries of the Human Frontal Lobes," 62.

470. Ibid., 53.

471. Ibid.

472. Heath, *Into the Psychokinetic Zone*.

473. Ibid.

474. Edwards-Lee and Saul, "Neuropsychiatry of the Right Frontal Lobe," 312.

475. Ibid., 312.

476. Heath, *Into the Psychokinetic Zone*.

477. Grady, "Neuroimaging and Activation of the Frontal Lobes," 207.

478. Ibid., 221–222.

479. Sadock and Sadock, *Kaplan and Sadock's Synopsis of Psychiatry*, 77.

480. Edwards-Lee and Saul, "Neuropsychiatry of the Right Frontal Lobe," 314.

481. Heath, *Into the Psychokinetic Zone*.

482. Freedman et al., "Effects of Frontal Lobe Lesions on Intentionality and Random Physical Phenomena."

483. Sadock and Sadock, *Kaplan and Sadock's Synopsis of Psychiatry*, 81–85.

MMI Facilitation and Training

484. Caidin, "Martin Caidin Faces the Mirror," 80.

485. Gissurarson, "Studies of Methods of Enhancing and Potentially Training Psychokinesis."

486. Gissurarson, "Methods of Enhancing PK Task Performance," 89.

487. Auerbach, *Mind over Matter*, 278.

488. Gissurarson and Morris, "Volition and Psychokinesis."

489. Ibid.

490. Gissurarson, "Methods of Enhancing PK Task Performance."

491. Ibid.

492. Beloff, "Historical Overview."

493. Rhine, "Hypnotic Suggestion in PK Tests."

494. Rush, "Findings from Experimental PK Research."

495. Gissurarson, "Methods of Enhancing PK Task Performance."

496. Stewart, Roll and Baumann, "Hypnotic Suggestion and RSPK."

497. Ibid.

498. Schmeidler, *Parapsychology and Psychology*.

499. Tart, "Learning to Use Psychokinesis."

500. Isaacs, "Clinical Issues in the Parapsychology Laboratory."

501. Radin, *The Conscious Universe*.

502. Varvoglis and McCarthy, "Conscious-Purposive Focus and PK."

503. Roe and Holt, "The Effect of Strategy ('Willing' versus Absorption) and Feedback (Intermediate versus Delayed) on Performance at a PK Task."

504. Dobyns et al., "The Yantra Experiment."

505. Ibid., 276.

506. Gissurarson, "Methods of Enhancing PK Task Performance."

507. Gissurarson, "Studies of Methods of Enhancing and Potentially Training Psychokinesis"; Honorton, "Psi and Internal Attention States."

508. Braud, "Meditation and Psychokinesis"; Braud and Hartgrove, "Clairvoyance and Psychokinesis in Transcendental Meditators and Matched Control Subjects."

509. Gissurarson, "Methods of Enhancing PK Task Performance," 95.

510. Schmeidler, *Parapsychology and Psychology*, 80.

511. Isaacs, "Clinical Issues in the Parapsychology Laboratory."

512. Gissurarson, "Studies of Methods of Enhancing and Potentially Training Psychokinesis."

513. Schmeidler, *Parapsychology and Psychology*.

514. Rogo, *The Poltergeist Experience*.

515. Schmeidler, *Parapsychology and Psychology*.

516. Ibid.

517. Obendorf, "The Effect of Attention on Psychokinesis."

518. Gissurarson, "Studies of Methods of Enhancing and Potentially Training Psychokinesis."

519. Gissurarson, "Methods of Enhancing PK Task Performance," 100.

520. Ibid., 100.

521. Rhine, J. B. "Hypnotic Suggestion in PK Tests."

522. Gissurarson, "Methods of Enhancing PK Task Performance," 101.

523. Palmer and Kramer, "Release of Effort in RNG PK."

524. Hasted, *The Metal-benders*.

525. Batcheldor, "Contributions to the Theory of PK Induction from Sitter-Group Work"; Isaacs, "Clinical Issues in the Parapsychology Laboratory"; Tart, "Learning to Use Psychokinesis."

526. Auerbach, *ESP, Hauntings, and Poltergeists*.

527. Ibid.

528. Auerbach, *Mind over Matter*; Honorton, "A Moving Experience."

529. Schmeidler, *Parapsychology and Psychology*, 80.

530. Gissurarson, "Methods of Enhancing PK Task Performance"; Isaacs, "Clinical Issues in the Parapsychology Laboratory."

531. Gissurarson, "Methods of Enhancing PK Task Performance."

532. Ibid.

533. Broughton, Millar and Johnson, "An Investigation into the use of Aversion Therapy Techniques for the Operant Control of PK Production in Humans."

534. Fadiman and Frager, *Personality and Personal Growth*; Williams, *Operant Learning*.

535. Morris, "The Airport Project."

536. Murphy and White, *In the Zone*; Taylor, "Enhancing Athletic and Psychic Performances through the Use of Imagery Based Mental Strategies."

537. Gissurarson, "Methods of Enhancing PK Task Performance," 107.

538. Ibid.; Taylor, "Enhancing Athletic and Psychic Performances through the Use of Imagery Based Mental Strategies."

539. Taylor, "Enhancing Athletic and Psychic Performances through the Use of Imagery Based Mental Strategies."

540. Gissurarson, "Methods of Enhancing PK Task Performance," 108.

541. Gissurarson and Morris, "Volition and Psychokinesis"; Taylor, "Enhancing Athletic and Psychic Performances through the Use of Imagery Based Mental Strategies."

542. Gissurarson, "Methods of Enhancing PK Task Performance"; Taylor, "Enhancing Athletic and Psychic Performances through the Use of Imagery Based Mental Strategies."

543. Gissurarson, "Methods of Enhancing PK Task Performance," 112.

544. Taylor, "Enhancing Athletic and Psychic Performances through the Use of Imagery Based Mental Strategies."

545. Lewis and Pucelik, *Magic Demystified*.

546. Cooperstein, "The Phenomenology of Paranormal Healing Practices," 190–191.

547. Taylor, "Enhancing Athletic and

Psychic Performances through the Use of Imagery Based Mental Strategies."

548. Karlis Osis, personal communication to Guy Savelli, August 10, 1982.

549. Isaacs, "A Twelve Session Study of Micro PKMB Training."

550. Gissurarson, "Studies of Methods of Enhancing and Potentially Training Psychokinesis"; Hasted, *The Metal-benders*.

551. Manning, "London Experiences with Matthew Manning."

552. Isaacs, "A Twelve Session Study of Micro PKMB Training"; Hasted, *The Metal-benders*.

553. Manning, "London Experiences with Matthew Manning."

554. Caidin, *The Merlin Effect*.

555. Dong and Raffill, *Empty Force*, 90.

556. Manning, "London Experiences with Matthew Manning."

557. Isaacs, "A Twelve Session Study of Micro PKMB Training."

558. Batcheldor, "Contributions to the Theory of PK Induction from Sitter-Group Work"; Caidin, *The Merlin Effect*; Debes and Morris, "Comparison of Striving and Non Striving Instructional Sets in a PK Study"; Rogo, *Mind over Matter*.

559. Manning, "London Experiences with Matthew Manning."

560. Ibid., 357

561. Gauld, *The Founders of Psychical Research*.

562. Caidin, *The Merlin Effect*.

563. Houck, "PK Party Format and Materials Required."

564. Gissurarson, "Methods of Enhancing PK Task Performance," 116.

565. Ibid.

566. Murphy, *The Future of the Body*.

What Learning Theories Suggest about MMI

567. Bharati, "The Ontological Status of Psychic Phenomena in Hinduism and Buddhism."

568. Schwartz, *Psychology of Learning and Behavior*.

569. Williams, *Operant Learning*.

570. Ibid.

571. Ibid.

572. *Encyclopedia Britannica CD98*.

573. Tart, "Learning to Use Psychokinesis."

574. Varvoglis and McCarthy, "Conscious-Purposive Focus and PK."

575. Tart, "Learning to Use Psychokinesis."

576. Fadiman and Frager, *Personality and Personal Growth*; Williams, *Operant Learning*.

577. Tart, "Learning to Use Psychokinesis."

578. Broughton, Millar and Johnson, "An Investigation into the Use of Aversion Therapy Techniques for the Operant Control of PK Production in Humans."

579. Bandura, *Social Learning Theory*.

580. Ibid.

581. Murphy, *The Future of the Body*.

582. Hasted, *The Metal-benders*.

583. Bandura, "Exercise of Personal and Collective Efficacy in Changing Societies."

584. Auerbach, *Mind over Matter*; Batcheldor, "Contributions to the Theory of PK Induction from Sitter-Group Work"; Broughton and Perlstrom, "PK Experiments with a Competitive Computer Game"; Varvoglis, *Psi-explorer*.

585. Stanford, "Experimental Psychokinesis."

586. Bandura, *Social Learning Theory*.

587. Tart, "Learning to Use Psychokinesis."

588. Caidin, *The Merlin Effect*.

589. Bandura, "Exercise of Personal and Collective Efficacy in Changing Societies."

590. Ibid.

591. Auerbach, *Mind over Matter*; Bandura, "Exercise of Personal and Collective Efficacy in Changing Societies."

592. Bandura, "Exercise of Personal and Collective Efficacy in Changing Societies."

593. Bandura, *Social Learning Theory*.

594. Bandura, "Exercise of Personal and Collective Efficacy in Changing Societies."

595. Ibid.

596. Heath, *Into the Psychokinetic Zone*.

597. Bandura, "Exercise of Personal and Collective Efficacy in Changing Societies."

598. Gissurarson, "Studies of Methods of Enhancing and Potentially Training Psychokinesis."

599. Bandura, "Exercise of Personal and Collective Efficacy in Changing Societies."

600. Ibid.

601. Owen and Sparrow, *Conjuring Up Philip*.

MMI Models and Theories

602. Varvoglis, "Goal-Directed and Observer-Dependent PK."

603. Fadiman and Frager, *Personality and Personal Growth*.

604. Zha and McConnell, "Parapsychology in the People's Republic of China: 1979–1989."

605. Dong and Raffill, *Empty Force*.

606. Rogo, "Theories about PK."

607. Reich, *Character Analysis*.

608. Klimo, *Channeling*; Reich, *Character Analysis*.

609. Fadiman and Frager, *Personality and Personal Growth*.

610. Reich, *Character Analysis*.

611. Beal, "The Emergence of a Paraphysics."

612. Beloff, *Parapsychology*.

613. Beal, "The Emergence of a Paraphysics."

614. Rogo, "Theories about PK."

615. Ibid.

616. Roll, "Some Physical and Psychological Aspects of a Series of Poltergeist Phenomena."

617. Gauld and Cornell, *Poltergeists*.

618. Roll, "The Rotating Beam Theory and the Olive Hill Poltergeist."

619. Ibid.

620. Gauld and Cornell, *Poltergeists*.

621. Rogo, *The Poltergeist Experience*.

622. Varvoglis and McCarthy, "Conscious-Purposive Focus and PK."

623. Gauld and Cornell, *Poltergeists*.

624. Ibid.; Ostrander and Schroeder, *Psychic Discoveries Behind the Iron Curtain*; Tart, "Out-of-Body Experiences."

625. Schmeidler, "Psychokinesis."

626. Stokes, "Spontaneous Psi Phenomena."

627. Radin, *The Conscious Universe*.

628. Schmeidler, "Psychokinesis."

629. Klimo, *Channeling*; Targ and Harary, *The Mind Race*.

630. Targ and Harary, *The Mind Race*.

631. Rao, "On the Nature of Psi."

632. May et al., "Psi Experiments with Random Number Generators"; May, Utts and Spottiswoode, "Decision Augmentation Theory."

633. May, Utts and Spottiswoode, "Decision Augmentation Theory."

634. Rogo, "Theories about PK."

635. Stanford, "An Experimentally Testable Model for Spontaneous Psi Events II."

636. Rao, "On the Nature of Psi."

637. Stanford, "An Experimentally Testable Model for Spontaneous Psi Events II."

638. Varvoglis, "Goal-Directed and Observer-Dependent PK."

639. Rao, "On the Nature of Psi."

640. Graham and Watkins, "Possible PK Influence on the Resuscitation of Anesthetized Mice"; Honorton, "A Moving Experience."

641. Rogo, *The Poltergeist Experience*.

642. Stanford, "Experimental Psychokinesis."

643. Palmer and Rush, "Experimental Methods in PK Research."

644. Carpenter, "First Sight."

645. James Carpenter, email to author October 5, 2009.

646. Schmeidler, "Psychokinesis."

647. Jean Burns, email to author September 28, 2009.

648. Atmanspacher, Röemer and Walach, "Weak Quantum Theory," 381.

649. Jean Burns, email to author September 28, 2009.

650. Ibid.

651. Schewe and Stein, "The Casimir Force."

652. Radin, "Experiments Testing Models of Mind-Matter Interaction"; Dean Radin, Presentation/Discussion at the 52nd Annual Parapsychological Association Meeting in Seattle, August 8, 2009.

653. Houtkooper, "Arguing for an Observational Theory of Paranormal Phenomena," 172.

654. Houtkooper, "A Study of Repeated Retroactive Psychokinesis in Relation to Direct and Random PK Effects," 2.

655. Radin, *Entangled Minds*, 252.

656. Houtkooper, "A Study of Repeated Retroactive Psychokinesis in Relation to Direct and Random PK Effects," 2.

657. Bohm, "A New Theory of the Relationship of Mind and Matter."

658. Rogo, "Theories about PK."

659. Houtkooper, "Arguing for an Observational Theory of Paranormal Phenomena."

660. Rao, "On the Nature of Psi."

661. Rogo, "Theories about PK."

662. Rao, "On the Nature of Psi"; Rogo, "Theories about PK."

663. Varvoglis, "Goal-Directed and Observer-Dependent PK."

664. Atmanspacher, Röemer and Walach, "Weak Quantum Theory."

665. Lucadou, "The Model of Pragmatic Information (MPI)"; Radin, *Entangled Minds*.

666. Lucadou, Röemer and Walach, "Synchronistic Phenomena as Entanglement Correlations in Generalized Quantum Theory"; Lucadou and Zahradnik, "Predictions of the Model of Pragmatic Information About RSPK."

667. Lucadou, Röemer and Walach, "Synchronistic Phenomena as Entanglement Correlations in Generalized Quantum Theory," 52–53.

668. Radin, *Entangled Minds*.

669. Roger Nelson, personal communication to author, August 6, 2009.

670. Burns, "What is Beyond the Edge of the Known World?"; Burns, "Quantum Fluctuations and the Action of the Mind."

671. Burns, "The Tumbling Cube and the Action of the Mind"; Burns, "The Effect of Ordered Air Molecules on a Tumbling Cube."

672. Rogo, "Theories about PK."

673. Targ and Harary, *The Mind Race*.

PART III: EXPERIENTIAL RESEARCH MATRIX: PHENOMENOLOGY

1. Heath, *Into the Psychokinetic Zone*; Heath, "The PK Zone."

2. Polkinghorne, "Phenomenological Research Methods."

3. Kuhn, *The Structure of Scientific Revolutions*.

4. Polkinghorne, "Phenomenological Research Methods."

5. Radin, *The Conscious Universe*.

6. Eckartsberg, "Existential-Phenomenological Research."

7. Polkinghorne, "Phenomenological Research Methods."

8. Alessi, "*Breakaway Into the Zone*."

9. Eckartsberg, "Introducing Existential-Phenomenological Psychology."

10. Valle, King and Halling, "An Introduction to Existential-Phenomenological Thought in Psychology."

11. Eckartsberg, "Introducing Existential-Phenomenological Psychology."

12. Ibid.

13. Ibid.

14. Polkinghorne, "Phenomenological Research Methods."

15. Eckartsberg, "Existential-Phenomenological Research."

16. Valle, King and Halling, "An Introduction to Existential-Phenomenological Thought in Psychology."

17. Giorgi, *Phenomenology and Psychological Research*.

18. Polkinghorne, "Phenomenological Research Methods."

19. Giorgi, *Phenomenology and Psychological Research*, 14.

20. Eckartsberg, "Introducing Existential-Phenomenological Psychology."

21. Barrett, *A Phenomenological Study of Channeling*; Hanson and Klimo, "Toward a Phenomenology of Synchronicity"; Murphy and White, *The Psychic Side of Sports*; Murphy and White, *In the Zone*; Reed, "Close Encounters in the Liminal Zone. Part I"; Reed, "Close Encounters in the Liminal Zone. Part II"; West, "On the Encounter with a Divine Presence During a Near-Death Experience: A Phenomenological Inquiry."

22. Heath, *Into the Psychokinetic Zone*.

23. Murphy and White, *In the Zone*.

Altered State of Consciousness

24. Alvarado, "ESP and Altered States of Consciousness," 27.

25. Auerbach, *Psychic Dreaming*; Loewe, and Blacker, *Oracles and Divination*.

26. Auerbach, *Psychic Dreaming*, 32.

27. Sidgwick, "On the Evidence for Premonitions."

28. Kruisinga, "Precognitive Dreams and the Dunne Experiment."

29. Rhine, "Frequency of Types of Experience in Spontaneous Precognition."

30. Van de Castle, "Parapsychology and Anthropology," 478–479.

31. Ibid.

32. Ibid., 494.

33. Stanford, "Experimental Psychokinesis."

34. Gissurarson, "Methods of Enhancing PK Task Performance."

35. Stewart, Roll, and Baumann, "Hypnotic Suggestion and RSPK."

36. Gissurarson, "Methods of Enhancing PK Task Performance."

37. Barclay, *Mind over Matter*.

38. Gissurarson, "Studies of Methods of Enhancing and Potentially Training Psychokinesis," Honorton, "Psi and Internal Attention States."

39. Honorton, "Psi and Internal Attention States."

40. Ibid., 73.

41. Rush, "Findings from Experimental PK Research," 266.

42. Isaacs, "A Twelve Session Study of Micro PKMB Training."

43. Irwin, "The Phenomenology of Parapsychological Experiences," 38–39.

44. Cooperstein, "The Phenomenology of Paranormal Healing Practices."

45. Stanford, "Experimental Psychokinesis."

46. Schmeidler, *Parapsychology and Psychology*, 96–97.

47. Murphy and White, *In the Zone*.

48. Herrigel, *Zen in the Art of Archery*; Murphy and White, *In the Zone*.

49. Murphy and White, *In the Zone*.

50. Ibid.

51. Taylor, "Enhancing Athletic and Psychic Performances through the Use of Imagery Based Mental Strategies."

52. Murphy and White, *In the Zone*.

Connection

53. Krippner, "Telepathy," 127.

54. LeShan, *The Medium, the Mystic, and the Physicist*.

55. Mintz, and Schmeidler, *The Psychic Thread*, 28.

56. Rhine, *Hidden Channels of the Mind*.

57. Ibid., 216.

58. Ibid., 225–226.

59. Houck, "Researching Remote Viewing and Psychokinesis," 6.

60. Caidin, "The Merlin Effect."

61. Gissurarson, "Studies of Methods of Enhancing and Potentially Training Psychokinesis," 331.

62. Hasted, *The Metal-benders*; Isaacs, "A Twelve Session Study of Micro PKMB Training."

63. Auerbach, *Mind over Matter*, 278.

64. Irwin, "The Phenomenology of Parapsychological Experiences."

65. Ibid., 39.

66. Cooperstein, "The Phenomenology of Paranormal Healing Practices," 191–192.

67. Murphy and White, *The Psychic Side of Sports*, 31–32.

68. White, "What are Exceptional Human Experiences?" 38.

69. Manning, "London Experiences with Matthew Manning: The Subject's Report."

Dissociation from the Individual Ego Identity

70. Krippner and Powers, *Broken Images, Broken Selves*.

71. Krippner, "Cross-Cultural Treatment Perspectives on Dissociative Disorders," 357.

72. Schmeidler, *Parapsychology and Psychology*, 110.

73. Ibid., 110.

74. Batcheldor, "Contributions to the Theory of PK Induction from Sitter-Group Work."

75. Braud, "On Varieties of Dissociation."

76. Schmeidler, *Parapsychology and Psychology*, 110.

77. Murphy and White, *In the Zone*.

78. White, "What are Exceptional Human Experiences?" 38.

79. Cooperstein, "The Phenomenology of Paranormal Healing Practices."

80. Ibid., 191.

Suspension of the Intellect

81. Houck, "PK Party Format and Materials Required."

82. Batcheldor, "Contributions to the Theory of PK Induction from Sitter-Group Work," 115.

83. Stanford, "Experimental Psychokinesis," 344.

84. Murphy and White, *In the Zone*.

85. Cooperstein, "The Phenomenology of Paranormal Healing Practices," 190.

Playfulness or Peak Emotion

86. Gauld and Cornell, *Poltergeists*; Rogo, *The Poltergeist Experience*; Roll, *The Poltergeist*.

87. Schmeidler, *Parapsychology and Psychology*.

88. Murphy and White, *The Psychic Side of Sports*.

89. Cooperstein, "The Phenomenology of Paranormal Healing Practices," 192.

90. Rhine et al., *Extrasensory Perception After Sixty Years*.

91. Thouless, "A Report on an Experiment on Psycho-kinesis with Dice, and a Discussion of Psychological Factors Favouring Success."

92. Ibid., 129.

93. Hasted, *The Metal-benders*.

94. Batcheldor, "Contributions to the Theory of PK Induction from Sitter-Group Work," 114–115.

95. Broughton and Perlstom, "PK Experiments with a Competitive Computer Game."

96. Broughton and Perlstom. "A Competitive Computer Game in PK Research," 390.

97. Broughton and Perlstom, "PK Experiments with a Competitive Computer Game," 209.

98. Murphy and White, *In the Zone*.

99. Manning, "London Experiences with Matthew Manning."

Sense of Energy

100. Barclay, *Mind over Matter*; Benor, "Believe It and You'll Be It."

101. Cooperstein, "The Phenomenology of Paranormal Healing Practices," 191; Irwin, "The Phenomenology of Parapsychological Experiences," 39.

102. Murphy and White, *In the Zone*, 76.

The Physical State

103. Irwin, "The Phenomenology of Parapsychological Experiences," 39.

104. Cooperstein, "The Phenomenology of Paranormal Healing Practices," 192.

105. Murphy and White, *In the Zone*.

106. Heath, *Into the Psychokinetic Zone*.

Focused Awareness (Attention)

107. Gissurarson, "Descriptive Analysis of Mentations on Volitional Tasks," 28.

108. Ibid., 32.

109. Murphy and White, *In the Zone*, 110.

110. Ibid., 107.

111. Cooperstein, "The Phenomenology of Paranormal Healing Practices," 190.

112. Herrigel, *Zen in the Art of Archery*.

113. Tart, *States of Consciousness*, 17.

Trust in the Process

114. Heath, *Into the Psychokinetic Zone*.

115. Caidin, "The Merlin Effect"; Gissurarson, "Studies of Methods of Enhancing and Potentially Training Psychokinesis"; Hasted, *The Metal-benders*; Houck, "PK Party Format and Materials Required"; Isaacs, "A Twelve Session Study of Micro PKMB Training."

116. Rush, "Findings from Experimental PK Research," 266.

117. Stanford, "Experimental Psychokinesis."

118. Houck, "Researching Remote Viewing and Psychokinesis."

119. Ibid., 6.

120. Gissurarson, "Studies of Methods of Enhancing and Potentially Training Psychokinesis," 101.

121. Murphy and White, *In the Zone*.

122. Stanford, "Experimental Psychokinesis," 333–334.

123. Ibid., 333.

124. Isaacs, "A Twelve Session Study of Micro PKMB Training."

125. Batcheldor, "Contributions to the Theory of PK Induction from Sitter-Group Work."; Caidin, "The Merlin Effect"; Debes and Morris, "Comparison of Striving and Non Striving Instructional Sets in a PK Study."

126. Debes and Morris, "Comparison of Striving and Non Striving Instructional Sets in a PK Study," 310.

127. Gissurarson, "Descriptive Analysis of Mentations on Volitional Tasks," 31.

128. Gissurarson, "Methods of Enhancing PK Task Performance," 115.

129. Heath, *Into the Psychokinetic Zone*.

130. Murphy and White, *In the Zone*, 26–27.

131. Musashi, *The Book of Five Rings*.

132. Ibid., 11.

133. Murphy and White, *The Psychic Side of Sports*; Murphy and White, *In the Zone*.

Investment

134. Heath, *Into the Psychokinetic Zone*.

135. Thouless, "A Report on an Experiment on Psycho-Kinesis with Dice, and a Discussion of Psychological Factors Favouring Success."

136. Ibid., 123.

137. Stanford, "Experimental Psychokinesis," 333.

138. Murphy and White, *In the Zone*, 110.

Openness to the Experience

139. Sadock and Sadock, *Kaplan and Sadock's Synopsis of Psychiatry*, 57.

140. Heath, *Into the Psychokinetic Zone.*

141. Gissurarson and Morris, "Examination of Six Questionnaires as Predictors of Psychokinesis Performance"; Schmeidler, *Parapsychology and Psychology.*

142. Zingrone, Alvarado, and Dalton, "Psi Experiences and the 'Big Five.'"

143. Murphy and White, *In the Zone.*

144. Ibid., 93.

145. Nelson, *Healing the Split*, 321.

146. Ibid., 321.

147. Mintz and Schmeidler, *The Psychic Thread*; Rhine, *Hidden Channels of the Mind.*

148. Heath, *Into the Psychokinetic Zone.*

"Knowing"

149. Murphy and White, *In the Zone.*

150. Ibid., 127.

151. Musashi, *The Book of Five Rings*, 11.

152. Gissurarson, "Descriptive Analysis of Mentations on Volitional Tasks."

153. Ibid., 31.

154. "Psychic Reward" was DOS-based psi-training software developed by Alan Vaughan. The computer generates random letters, which participants attempt to either guess (ESP) or try to force the computer to pick as the target (MMI). Because of this, successful results could be due to either (or both) precognition and MMI.

Guiding the Process

155. Gissurarson, "Descriptive Analysis of Mentations on Volitional Tasks."

156. Murphy and White, *In the Zone*, 87–89.

Impact

157. Heath, *Into the Psychokinetic Zone.*

158. Murphy and White, *In the Zone.*

159. Ibid.

ESP and MMI Overlap

160. Heath, *Into the Psychokinetic Zone.*

161. Heath, "The PK Zone," 70.

162. Ibid., 181.

163. Broughton and Perlstrom, "PK Experiments with a Competitive Computer Game," 208.

164. Stanford, "An Experimentally Testable Model for Spontaneous Psi Events II."

165. Storm and Thalbourne, "A Paradigm Shift Away from the ESP-PK Dichotomy," 280.

166. Thalbourne, "The Theory of Psychopraxia."

167. Murphy and White, *In the Zone.*

168. Hanson and Klimo, "Toward a Phenomenology of Synchronicity," 281.

169. Barrett, *A Phenomenological Study of Channeling.*

170. Ibid., 164.

171. Reed, "Close Encounters in the Liminal Zone. Part I"; Reed, "Close Encounters in the Liminal Zone. Part II."

172. West, "On the Encounter with a Divine Presence During a Near-Death Experience: A Phenomenological Inquiry."

173. Irwin, "The Disembodied Self: An Empirical Study of Dissociation and the Out-of-Body Experience."

174. Ibid., 261.

175. McMoneagle, *Remote Viewing Secrets.*

176. Ibid., 62.

177. Cooperstein, "The Phenomenology of Paranormal Healing Practices," 192–193.

MMI Facilitation and Inhibition

178. Gissurarson, "Methods of Enhancing PK Task Performance"; Morris, "The Airport Project"; Taylor, "Enhancing Athletic and Psychic Performances through the Use of Imagery Based Mental Strategies."

179. Gissurarson, "Descriptive Analysis of Mentations on Volitional Tasks."

180. Thouless, "A Report on an Experiment on Psycho-Kinesis with Dice, and a Discussion of Psychological Factors Favouring Success," 128.

181. Ibid., 128.

182. Manning, "London Experiences with Matthew Manning: The Subject's Report," 357.

183. Gauld, *The Founders of Psychical Research.*

184. Rhine, "Hypnotic Suggestion in PK Tests."

185. Gissurarson, "Studies of Methods of Enhancing and Potentially Training Psychokinesis"; Hasted, *The Metalbenders*; Isaacs, "A Twelve Session Study of Micro PKMB Training."

186. Batcheldor, "Contributions to the Theory of PK Induction from Sitter-Group Work."

187. Ibid.; Isaacs, "Clinical Issues in the Parapsychology Laboratory"; Tart, "Learning to Use Psychokinesis."

188. Auerbach, *ESP, Hauntings, and Poltergeists.*

189. Gissurarson, "Methods of Enhancing PK Task Performance."

190. Caidin, "The Merlin Effect"; Houck, "PK Party Format and Materials Required."

Bibliography

Albright, Matthew. "The Stigmata: The Psychological and Ethical Message of the Posttraumatic Sufferer." *Psychoanalysis and Contemporary Thought* 25 (2002):329–358.

Alessi, Lauren Elizabeth. *"Breakaway Into the Zone": A Phenomenological Investigation from the Athlete's Perspective.* Ann Arbor, MI: University Microfilms, 1994.

Alexander, Colonel John B., Major Richard Groller, and Janet Morris. *The Warrior's Edge: Front-Line Strategies for Victory on the Corporate Battlefield.* New York: Avon Books, 1990.

Alvarado, Carlos. "ESP and Altered States of Consciousness: An Overview of Conceptual and Research Trends." *The Journal of Parapsychology* 62 (1998): 28–63.

Anonymous. "Annual Report of the Council for 1930." *Journal of the Society for Psychical Research* 27, no. 472 (1931): 20–30.

Arnold, Larry E. *Ablaze! The Mysterious Fires of Spontaneous Human Combustion.* New York: M. Evans and Company, 1995.

Atmanspacher, Harald, Hartman Röemer, and Harald Walach. "Weak Quantum Theory: Complementarity and Entanglement in Physics and Beyond." *Foundations of Physics* 32, no. 3 (2002): 379–406.

Attar, Farid al-Din. *Muslim Saints and Mystics: Episodes from the Tadhkirat al-Auliya' ("Memorial of the Saints").* Translated and with an Introduction by A. J. Arberry, edited by Ehsan Yar-Shater. 1966. Reprint, Boston: Routledge & Kegan Paul, 1976.

Auerbach, Loyd. *ESP, Hauntings, and Poltergeists: A Parapsychologist's Handbook.* New York: Warner Books, 1986.

_____. *Mind over Matter.* New York: Kensington Books, 1996.

_____. *Psychic Dreaming: A Parapsychologist's Handbook.* New York: Warner Books, 1991.

Ball, Ann. *Modern Saints: Their Lives and Faces.* Rockford, IL: Tan Books and Publishers, Inc., 1983.

Bander, Peter. *Voices from the Tapes: Recordings from the Other World.* New York: Drake Publishers, 1973.

Bandura, Albert. "Exercise of Personal and Collective Efficacy in Changing Societies." In *Self-Efficacy in Changing Societies,* edited by Albert Bandura, 1–45. New York: Cambridge University Press, 1995.

_____. *Social Learning Theory.* Englewood Cliffs, NJ: Prentice Hall, 1977.

Barclay, Glen. *Mind over Matter: Beyond the Bounds of Nature.* Indianapolis/New York: The Bobbs-Merrill Company, 1973.

Barrett, Kathleen. *A Phenomenological Study of Channeling: The Experience of Transmitting Information from a Source Perceived as Paranormal.* Ann Arbor, MI: University Microfilms, 1996.

Bartlett, John. *Familiar Quotations: A Collection of Passages, Phrases and Proverbs Traced to Their Sources in Ancient and Modern Literature.* 15th ed., edited by Emily Morison Beck and the editorial staff of Little, Brown, and Company. Boston: Little, Brown and Company, 1980.

Baruss, Imants. "An Experimental Test of Instrumental Transcommunication." *Journal of Scientific Exploration* 21, no. 1 (2007): 89–98.

_____. "Failure to Replicate Electronic Voice Phenomena." *Journal of Scientific Exploration* 15, no. 3 (2001): 355–367.

Batcheldor, Kenneth J. "Contributions to the Theory of PK Induction from Sitter-Group Work." *Journal of the American Society for Psychical Research* 78, no. 2 (1984): 105–122.

_____. "Notes on the Elusiveness Problem in Relation to a Radical View of Paranormality," compiled, edited, and with a preface and notes by Patric V. Giesler. *Journal of the American Society for Psychical Research* 88, no. 2 (1994): 90–116.

Bayless, Raymond. "Correspondence." *Journal of the American Society for Psychical Research* 53, no. 1 (1959): 35–38.

_____. *Experiences of a Psychical Researcher.* New Hyde Park, NY: University Books, Inc., 1972.

Beal, James D. "The Emergence of a Paraphysics: Research and Applications." In Edgar D. Mitchell's *Psychic Exploration: A Challenge for Science,* edited by John White, 426–446. New York: G. P. Putnam's Sons, 1974.

Bedford, Donald, Herman Kruijsse, Will van der Leij, Anita Nel, and Mark Shuttleworth. "Chicks and Algae: The Remote Influence of Desire." In *Proceedings of the Parapsychological Association 48th Annual Convention,* 24–30. 2005.

Beloff, John. "Historical Overview." In *Handbook of Parapsychology,* edited by B. Wolman, L. Dale, G.

Schmeidler, and M. Ullman, 3–24. Jefferson, NC: McFarland & Company Inc., 1986. Original work published New York: Van Nostrand Reinhold, 1977.

Beloff, John. *Parapsychology: A Concise History*. New York: St. Martin's Press, 1993.

Benor, Daniel J. "Believe It and You'll Be It: Visualization in Psychic Healing." *Psi Research* 4, no. 1 (1985): 21–56.

______. "Fields and Energies Related to Healing: A Review of Soviet and Western Studies." *Psi Research* 3, no. 1 (1984): 21–35.

Benson, Herbert, John W. Lehmann, M.S. Malhotra, Ralph F. Goldman, Jeffrey Hopkins, and Mark D. Epstein. "Body Temperatures Changes During the Practice of G Tum-mo Yoga." *Nature* 295 (January 21, 1982): 234–236.

Berger, A., G. H. Hovelmann, and W. von Lucadou. "Spirit Extras on Video Tape? The First Field Investigation." *Journal of the Society for Psychical Research* 58, no. 826 (1992): 153–164.

Berger, Kathleen S. *The Developing Person Through the Life Span*. 3rd ed. New York: Worth Publishers, Inc., 1994.

Berkenbush, John. Interview by Garrett Husveth, *The Haunted New Jersey Podcast*, no. 15. http://haunted nj.libsyn.com/index.php?post_year=2006&post_month=02 (accessed February 13, 2006).

Bharati, Agehananda. "The Ontological Status of Psychic Phenomena in Hinduism and Buddhism." In *Parapsychology and Anthropology: Proceedings of an International Conference Held in London, England August 29–31, 1973*, edited by Allan Angoff and Diana Barth, 223–236. New York: Parapsychology Foundation, 1974.

Blasband, Richard A. "The Ordering of Random Events by Emotional Expression." *Journal of Scientific Exploration* 14, no. 2 (2000): 195–216.

Bohm, David J. "A New Theory of the Relationship of Mind and Matter." *Journal of the American Society for Psychical Research* 80 (1986): 113–135.

Bosch, Holger, Fiona Steinkamp, and Emil Boller. "Examining Psychokinesis: The Interaction of Human Intention with Random Number Generators — A Meta-Analysis." *Psychological Bulletin* 132, no. 4 (2006): 497–523.

Bosch, Holger, and Harald Walach. "The Decline Phenomenon: Effect or Artifact?" *Society for Scientific Exploration: Program and Abstracts* [database on-line], 1997: 2. Abstract from: http://www.igpp.de/sseengl3.htm (accessed May 1, 2003).

Braud, William. *Distant Mental Influence: Its Contributions to Science, Healing, and Human Interactions*. Charlottesville, VA: Hampton Roads, 2003.

______. "Distant Mental Influence of Rate of Hemolysis of Human Red Blood Cells." In *The Parapsychological Association's 31st Annual Convention Presented Papers*, 2–15. 1988.

______. "Meditation and Psychokinesis." *Parapsychology Review* 21, no. 1 (1990): 9–11.

______. "On Varieties of Dissociation: An Essay Review of Krippner and Powers' Broken Images, Broken Selves: Dissociative Narratives in Clinical Practice." *Journal of the American Society for Psychical Research* 93, no. 1 (1999): 116–140.

Braud, William G., and S. P. Dennis. "Geophysical Variables and Behaviours: LVIII. Autonomic Activity, Hemolysis, and Biological Psychokinesis: Possible Relationships with Geomagnetic Field Activity." *Perceptual and Motor Skills* 68 (1989): 1243–1254.

Braud, William G., and J. Hartgrove. "Clairvoyance and Psychokinesis in Transcendental Meditators and Matched Control Subjects: A Preliminary Study." *European Journal of Parapsychology* 1, no. 3 (1976): 6–16.

Braude, Stephen E. *The Limits of Influence: Psychokinesis and the Philosophy of Science*. London: Routledge and Kegan Paul, 1991.

Broughton, Richard S., Brian Millar, and Martin Johnson. "An Investigation into the Use of Aversion Therapy Techniques for the Operant Control of PK Production in Humans." *European Journal of Parapsychology* 3 (1981): 317–344.

Broughton, Richard S., and James R. Perlstrom. "A Competitive Computer Game in PK Research: Some Preliminary Findings." In *The Parapsychological Association 27th Annual Convention Presented Papers*, pp. 389–410. Dallas, TX: Parapsychological Association, 1984.

______, and ______. "PK Experiments with a Competitive Computer Game." *The Journal of Parapsychology* 50 (1986): 193–211.

Brown, Chip. "They Laughed at Galileo Too." *New York Times*, August 11, 1996. http://www.deanradin.com/nytimes._hires_f.html (accessed December 9, 2010).

Brown, Michael H. *PK: A Report on the Power of Psychokinesis, Mental Energy That Moves Matter*. Blauvelt, NY: Steinerbooks, 1976.

Brown, Raphael. *The Little Flowers of St. Francis: First Complete Edition An Entirely New Version with Twenty Additional Chapters*. Garden City, NY: Image Books, a division of Doubleday and Company, 1958.

Buchanan, Lyn. *The Seventh Sense: The Secrets of Remote Viewing as Told by a 'Psychic Spy' for the U.S. Military*. New York: Paraview Pocket Books, 2003.

Burns, Jean E. "The Arrow of Time and the Action of the Mind at the Molecular Level." In D. P. Sheehan's (ed.) *Frontiers of Time*, 75–88. Melville, NY: AIP Conference Proceedings, 2006.

______. "The Effect of Ordered Air Molecules on a Tumbling Cube." *Noetic Journal* 3, no. 4 (2002): 330–339.

______. "Quantum Fluctuations and the Action of the Mind." *Noetic Journal* 3, no. 4 (2002): 312–317.

______. "The Tumbling Cube and the Action of the Mind." *Noetic Journal* 3, no. 4 (2002): 318–329.

______. "What Is Beyond the Edge of the Known World?" In *Psi Wars*, edited by James Alcock, Jean Burns, and Anthony Freeman, 7–28. Charlottesville, VA: Imprint Academic, 2003.

Butler, Tom, and Lisa Butler. *There Is No Death and There Are No Dead*. Reno, NV: AA-EVP Publishing, 2004.

Byrd, R. C. "Positive Therapeutic Effects of Intercessory Prayer in a Coronary Care Unit Population." *Southern Medical Journal* 81 (1988): 826–829.

Cade, C. Maxwell, and Delphine Davis. *The Taming of the Thunderbolts*. New York: Abelard-Schuman, 1969.

Caidin, Martin. "Martin Caidin Faces the Mirror and Asks Himself, 'Would I Do It Again, If I Had It to Do All Over Again?'" *Writer's Digest* 68, no. 5 (1988): 80–84.

______. *The Merlin Effect*. Manuscript, 1986.

Caidin, Martin von Strasser. "Fiction This Ain't." In *New Destinies*, IV, Summer 1988, 211–222.

Carlson, H. G. *Mysteries of the Unexplained*. Chicago: Contemporary Books, 1994.

Carpenter, James C. "First Sight: Part Two, Elaboration

of a Model of Psi and the Mind." *Journal of Parapsychology* 69, no. 1 (2005): 63–112.

Cavendish, Richard, ed. *Man, Myth, and Magic: An Illustrated Encyclopedia of the Supernatural.* New York: Marshall Cavendish Corporation, BPC Publishing, 1970

Chauvin, Rémy, and Benjamin Vaijean. "Is It Possible to Strengthen the Psi Effect Using a Very Weak Magnetic Field?" *Journal of the Society for Psychical Research* 56, no. 818 (1990): 96–97.

Chow, Tiffany W., and Jeffrey Cummins. "Frontal-Subcortical Circuits." In *The Human Frontal Lobes: Functions and Disorders.* 2nd ed., edited by Bruce L. Miller and Jeffrey Cummings, 25–43. New York: The Guilford Press, 2007.

Cooperstein, Allan M. "The Phenomenology of Paranormal Healing Practices." In *Healing, Intention, and Energy Medicine: Science, Research Methods and Clinical Implications,* edited by Wayne B Jonas and Cindy C. Crawford, 187–209. New York: Churchill Livingstone, 2003.

Corliss, William R. *Handbook of Unusual Natural Phenomena: Eyewitness Accounts of Nature's Greatest Mysteries.* Garden City, NY: Anchor Press, 1983.

Crommie, William J. "Meditation Changes Temperatures: Mind Controls Body in Extreme Experiments." *Harvard University Gazette,* April 18, 2002. http://www.news.harvard.edu/gazette/2002/04.18/09tummo.html (accessed October 19, 2009).

Dakwar, Elias, and Ted Wissink. "Voodoo Therapy: History." http://altmed.creighton.edu/voodoo/history.htm (accessed April 20, 2010).

Dale, Laura A., and Rhea A. White. "Glossary." In *Handbook of Parapsychology,* edited by B. Wolman, L. Dale, G. Schmeidler, and M. Ullman, 921–936. Jefferson, NC: McFarland & Company, Inc., 1986. Original work published New York: Van Nostrand Reinhold, 1977.

Dalton, Kathy. "A Psi Experiment with the Martial Artist as Subject." Master's thesis, John F. Kennedy University, Orinda, California, 1992.

Debes, J., and R. L. Morris. "Comparison of Striving and Nonstriving Instructional Sets in a PK Study." *The Journal of Parapsychology* 46 (1982): 297–312.

Delanoy, Deborah L. "Anomalous Psychophysiological Responses to Remote Cognition: The DMILS Studies." *European Journal of Parapsychology* 16 (2001): 30–41.

_____, and Robert Morris. "A DMILS Training Study Utilising Two Shielded Environments." *European Journal of Parapsychology* 14 (1998–1999): 52–67.

_____, _____, Claire Brady, and Alison Roe. "An EDA DMILS Study Exploring Agent-Receiver Pairing." In *Proceedings of the Parapsychological Association 42nd Annual Convention,* 68–82. Palo Alto, CA: Parapsychological Association, 1999.

Devereux, P. "Letters." *Paranormal Review* 15 (2000): 28.

Dingwall, E. J. "The End of a Legend: A Note on the Magical Flight." In *Parapsychology and Anthropology: Proceedings of an International Conference Held in London, England August 29–31, 1973,* edited by Allan Angoff and Diana Barth, 243–256. New York: Parapsychology Foundation, 1974.

_____, ed. "A Report on a Series of Sittings with Mr. Willy Schneider." *Journal of the Society for Psychical Research* 36, no. 97 (1928): 1–33.

Dobyns, Y. H., J. C. Valentino, B. J. Dunne, and R. G. Jahn. "The Yantra Experiment." *Journal of Scientific Exploration* 21, no. 2 (2007): 261–279.

Don, Norman S., and Gilda Moura. "Trance Surgery in Brazil." *Alternative Therapies* 6, no. 4 (July 2000): 39–48.

Dong, Paul, and Thomas Raffill. *Empty Force: The Ultimate Martial Art.* Rockport, MA: Element Books, 1996.

_____, and _____. *China's Super Psychics.* New York: Marlowe and Company, 1997.

Dossey, Larry. "Deliberately Caused Bodily Damage." *Alternative Therapies in Health and Medicine* 4, no. 5 (1998): 11–111.

Dulnov, G. N., K. I. Krylov, V. V. Kulagin, I. K. Meshkovsky, N. V. Pilipenko, and A. G. Shvartsman. "Scientists Study Phenomena of Nina Kulagina." *Psi Research* 3, no. 3/4 (1984): 66–69.

Dunne, Brenda J., and Robert G. Jahn. "Consciousness and Anomalous Physical Phenomena," technical note PEAR 95004, May 1995 [database on-line]. http://www.princeton.edu/~rdnelson/abstracts.html (accessed October 19, 2009).

Dunne, Brenda J., R. D. Nelson, and Robert G. Jahn. "Operator-Related Anomalies in a Random Mechanical Cascade." *Journal of Scientific Exploration* 2, no. 2 (1988): 155–179.

Ebon, Martin. "A History of Parapsychology." In Edgar D. Mitchell's *Psychic Exploration: A Challenge for Science,* edited by John White, 53–72. New York: G. P. Putnam's Sons, 1974.

Eckartsberg, Rolf von. "Existential-Phenomenological Research." In *Phenomenological Inquiry in Psychology,* edited by Ronald S. Valle, 21–61. New York: Plenum Press, 1998.

_____. "Introducing Existential-Phenomenological Psychology." In *Phenomenological Inquiry in Psychology,* edited by Ronald S. Valle, 3–20. New York: Plenum Press, 1998.

Edwards, Harry. *The Healing Intelligence.* London: The Healer Publishing Company, 1965.

Edwards-Lee, Terri A., and Ronald E. Saul. "Neuropsychiatry of the Right Frontal Lobe." In *The Human Frontal Lobes: Functions and Disorders,* edited by Bruce L. Miller and Jeffrey Cummings, 304–320. New York: The Guilford Press, 1999.

Ehrenwald, Jan. "Parapsychology and the Healing Arts." In *Handbook of Parapsychology,* edited by B. Wolman, L. Dale, G. Schmeidler, and M. Ullman, 541–556. Jefferson, NC: McFarland & Company, Inc., 1986. Original work published New York: Van Nostrand Reinhold, 1977.

Eisenberg, Howard. *Inner Spaces: Parapsychological Explorations of the Mind.* Don Mills, Ontario: Musson Book Company, a division of General Publishing Co., 1977.

Eisenbud, Jule. "Paranormal Photography." In *Handbook of Parapsychology,* edited by B. Wolman, L. Dale, G. Schmeidler, and M. Ullman, 414–432. Jefferson, NC: McFarland & Company, Inc., 1986. Original work published New York: Van Nostrand Reinhold, 1977.

Ellis, D. J. "Listening to the 'Raudive Voices.'" *Journal of the Society for Psychical Research* 48, no. 763 (1975): 31–42.

Encyclopedia Britannica CD98: Knowledge for the Information Age [CD-ROM]. Encyclopedia Britannica, Chicago.

Etzold, Eckhard. "Solar-Periodic Full Moon Effect in the

Fourmilab Retropsychokinesis Project Experiment Data: An Exploratory Study." *Journal of Parapsychology* 69, no. 2 (2005): 233–261.

Fadiman, James, and Robert Frager. *Personality and Personal Growth*. 3rd ed. New York: Harper Collins College Publishers, 1994.

Finucane, R. C. *Ghosts: Appearances of the Dead and Cultural Transformation*. Amherst, NY: Prometheus Books, 1996.

Fodor, Nandor. *On the Trail of the Poltergeist*. New York: The Citadel Press, 1958.

Fontana, D. "Instrumental Transcommunication — The Gwen Tate Memorial Lecture by Dr. Anabela Cardoso." *The Paranormal Review* 32 (2004): 15–17.

Fontana, David, and Anabela Cardoso. "Instrumental Transcommunication Research Project." *The Paranormal Review* 35 (2005): 17–19.

Freedman, Morris, Stanley Jeffers, Karen Saeger, Malcolm Binns, and Sandra Black. "Effects of Frontal Lobe Lesions on Intentionality and Random Physical Phenomena." *Journal of Scientific Exploration* 17, no. 4 (2003): 651–668.

Friel, John P., ed. *Dorland's Illustrated Medical Dictionary*. 25th ed. Philadelphia: W. B. Saunders Company, 1974.

Gaddis, Vincent H. *Mysterious Fires and Lights*. New York: David McKay Company, 1967.

Gauld, Alan. *The Founders of Psychical Research*. New York: Schocken Books, 1968.

_____, and A. D. Cornell. *Poltergeists*. London, Boston, and Henley: Routledge and Kegan Paul, 1979.

Gershom, Rabbi Yonassan. *Beyond the Ashes: Cases of Reincarnation from the Holocaust*. Virginia Beach, VA: A. R. E. Press, 1992.

Gersi, Douchan. *Faces in the Smoke: An Eyewitness Experience of Voodoo, Shamanism, Psychic Healing, and Other Amazing Human Powers*. Los Angeles: Jeremy P. Tarcher, 1991.

Geschwind, Daniel H., and Marco Iacoboni. "Structural and Functional Asymmetries of the Human Frontal Lobes." In *The Human Frontal Lobes: Functions and Disorders*, edited by Bruce L. Miller and Jeffrey Cummings, 45–70. New York: The Guilford Press, 1999.

Giesler, Patric. "Differential Micro-PK Effects Among Afro-Brazilian Cultists." *The Journal of Parapsychology* 49 (1985): 329–366.

Giorgi, Amedeo, ed. *Phenomenology and Psychological Research: Edited and with an Introduction by Amedeo Giorgi*. Pittsburgh, Pennsylvania: Duquesne University Press, 1985.

Giovetti, Paola. "Varieties of Healing Experience: Folk Healers in Italy." *Psi Research* 3 (1984): 131–135.

Gissurarson, Loftur Reimar. "Descriptive Analysis of Mentations on Volitional Tasks." *Journal of the Society for Psychical Research* 62 (1997): 22–35.

_____. "Methods of Enhancing PK Task Performance." In *Advances in Parapsychological Research*, vol. 8, edited by Stanley Krippner, 88–125. Jefferson, NC: McFarland & Company, Inc., 1997.

_____. "The Psychokinesis Effect: Geomagnetic Influence, Age and Sex Differences." *Journal of Scientific Exploration* 6, no. 2 (1992): 157–165.

_____. "Studies of Methods of Enhancing and Potentially Training Psychokinesis: A Review." *Journal of the American Society for Psychical Research* 86 (1992): 303–346.

_____, and Robert L. Morris. "Examination of Six Questionnaires as Predictors of Psychokinesis Performance." *The Journal of Parapsychology* 55 (1991): 119–145.

_____, and _____. "Volition and Psychokinesis: Attempts to Enhance PK Performance Through the Practice of Imagery Strategies." *The Journal of Parapsychology* 54 (1990): 331–370.

Goss, Michael. *Poltergeists: An Annotated Bibliography of Works in English, Circa 1880–1975*. Metuchen, NJ and London: Scarecrow Press, 1979.

Grad, B., R. J. Cadoret, and G. I. Paul. "The Influence of an Unorthodox Method of Treatment on Wound Healing in Mice." *international Journal of Parapsychology* 3, no. 2, (1961): 5–24.

Grady, Cheryl L. "Neuroimaging and Activation of the Frontal Lobes." In *The Human Frontal Lobes: Functions and Disorders*, edited by Bruce L. Miller and Jeffrey Cummings, 196–230. New York: The Guilford Press, 1999.

Graham, K. and Anita M. Watkins. "Possible PK Influence on the Resuscitation of Anesthetized Mice." *The Journal of Parapsychology* 35 (1971): 257–272.

Greber, Johannes. *Communication with the Spirit World of God: Personal Experiences of a Catholic Priest*. 4th ed. Teaneck, N.J.: Johannes Greber Memorial Foundation, 1970.

Greenfield, Sidney M. "The Patients of Dr. Fritz: Assessments of Treatment by a Brazilian Spiritist Healer." *Journal of the Society for Psychical Research* 61, no. 847 (1997): 372–387.

_____. *Spirits with Scalpels: The Cultural Biology of Religious Healing in Brazil*. Walnut Creek, CA: Left Coast Press, 2008.

Gregory, Anita. "London Experiences with Matthew Manning: Introduction." *Proceedings of the Society for Psychical Research*, 56 (1982): 284–302.

_____. "London Experiences with Matthew Manning: Postscript." *Proceedings of the Society for Psychical Research*, 56 (1982): 363–365.

_____, and Kathleen Wilson. "London Experiences with Matthew Manning: Infrared Experiments." *Proceedings of the Society for Psychical Research*, 56 (1982): 311–348.

Grunebaum, G. E. von. "The Place of Parapsychological Phenomena in Islam." *International: The Journal of Parapsychology* 8, no. 2 (1966): 264–280.

Guiley, Rosemary Ellen. *Harper's Encyclopedia of Mystical and Paranormal Experience*. Edison, NJ: Castle Books, 1991.

Gurney, Edmond, Frederic W. H. Myers, and Frank Podmore. "Phantasms of the Living." In *Phantasms of the Living: Cases of Telepathy Printed in the Journal of the Society for Psychical Research During Thirty-five Years and Phantasms of the Living*, edited by Eleanor Mildred Sidgwick. New Hyde Park, NY: University Books, 1962. Original work published London, 1886.

Haley, Philip S. *Modern Loaves and Fishes and Other Studies in Psychic Phenomena*. 2nd ed. San Francisco, CA: Accommodation Letter Shop, 1960.

Hall, Howard. "Deliberately Caused Bodily Damage: Metahypnotic Phenomena?" *Journal of the Society for Psychical Research* 64, no. 861 (2000): 211–223.

_____, Norman S. Don, Jamal N. Hussein, Eugene White, and Robert Hostoffer. "The Scientific Study of Unusual Rapid Wound Healing: A Case Report." *Advances in Mind-Body Medicine* 17 (2001): 203–213.

Hansen, George P. "A Cooperation-Competition PK Experiment with Computerized Horse Races." *The Journal of Parapsychology* 54 (1990): 21–33.

Hanson, D., and Jon Klimo. "Toward a Phenomenology of Synchronicity." In *Phenomenological Inquiry in Psychology: Existential and Transpersonal Dimensions*, edited by Ron Valle, 281–307. New York: Plenum Press, 1998.

Haraldsson, Erlendur. *Modern Miracles: An Investigative Report on Psychic Phenomena Associated with Sathya Sai Baba*. Rev. and up. ed. Mamaroneck, NY: Hastings House, 1997.

_____, and O. Olafsson. "A Survey of Psychic Healing in Iceland." *The Christian Parapsychologist* 3, no. 8 (1980): 276–279.

Hasted, John. *The Metal-benders*. London: Routledge and Kegan Paul, 1981.

Hastings, Arthur. "A Comparison of Recent Research in Brain Stimulation and Virtual Reality with Psychological and Parapsychological Research on Out-of-Body Experiences." In *The Parapsychological Association 52nd Annual Convention Abstracts of Presented Papers, August 6–9, 2009*, 35–36. Seattle, WA: Parapsychological Association, 2009.

Heath, Pamela Rae. *Into the Psychokinetic Zone: A Phenomenological Study of the Experience of Performing Psychokinesis (PK)*. Ann Arbor, MI: University Microfilms, 1999.

_____. "A New Theory on Place Memory." *Australian Journal of Parapsychology* 5, no. 1 (2005): 40–58.

_____. "The PK Zone: A Phenomenological Study." *The Journal of Parapsychology* 64, no. 1 (2000): 53–72.

_____. "The Possible Role of Psychokinesis in Place Memory." *Australian Journal of Parapsychology* 4, no. 2 (2004): 69–80.

Heinze, Ruth-Inge. "Healing in South and Southeast Asia." *Psi Research* 3 (1984): 136–140.

Herrigel, Eugen. *Zen in the Art of Archery*. New York: Pantheon, 1953.

Holt, Nicola, and Chris A. Roe. "The Sender as PK Agent in ESP Studies: The Effects of Agent and Target System Lability Upon Performance at a Novel PK Task." *Journal of Parapsychology* 70, no. 1 (2006): 49–67.

Home, D. D. *Incidents in My Life*. 1864. Reprint of the 5th ed. with an introduction by Judge Edmonds. New York: Time-Life Books Inc., 1991.

Honorton, C. "Psi and Internal Attention States." In *Handbook of Parapsychology*, edited by B. Wolman, L. Dale, G. Schmeidler, and M. Ullman, 435–472. Jefferson, NC: McFarland & Company, Inc., 1986. Original work published New York: Van Nostrand Reinhold, 1977.

Honorton, Charles. "A Moving Experience." *Journal of the American Society for Psychical Research* 87 (1993): 329–340.

Hood, Marlowe. "Mystics, Ghosts and Faith Healers; Forces of China's Past Re-emerge in a New Occult Craze." *The Los Angeles Times*, magazine section. April 19, 1992: 20.

Houck, Jack. "PK Party Format and Materials Required." Private publication, March 16, 1982.

_____. "PK Party History." In *Proceedings: Symposium on Applications of Anomalous Phenomena*, 501–514. Kaman Tempo, 1994.

_____. "Researching Remote Viewing and Psychokinesis." In *TREAT V Conference Proceedings March 17–21 1993*, 1 22.

_____. "Surface Change During Warm-Forming: Metallurgical Analysis by Victor Kerlins." Private publication, February 5, 1982.

Houtkooper, Joop M. "Arguing for an Observational Theory of Paranormal Phenomena." *Journal of Scientific Exploration* 16, no. 2 (2002): 171–185.

_____. "A Study of Repeated Retroactive Psychokinesis in Relation to Direct and Random PK Effects." *European Journal of Parapsychology* 1, no. 4 (1977): 1–20.

Hussein, Jamal N., Louay J. Fatoohi, Howard Hall, and Shetha Al-Dargazelli. "Deliberately Caused Bodily Damage Phenomena." *Journal of the Society for Psychical Research* 62 (1997): 97–113.

Inglis, Brian. "London Experiences with Matthew Manning: Comments." *Proceedings of the Society for Psychical Research* 56 (1982): 361–362.

_____. *Natural and Supernatural: A History of the Paranormal from Earliest Times to 1914*. Rev. ed. Bridgeport, Dorset: Prism Press, 1992.

Irwin, H. J. *An Introduction to Parapsychology*. 2nd ed. Jefferson NC: McFarland & Company, Inc., 1994.

Irwin, Harvey J. "The Disembodied Self: An Empirical Study of Dissociation and the Out-of-Body Experience." *The Journal of Parapsychology* 64, no. 3 (2000): 261–277.

_____. "The Phenomenology of Parapsychological Experiences." In *Advances in Parapsychological Research*, vol. 7, edited by Stanley Krippner, 10–76. Jefferson, NC: McFarland & Company, Inc., 1994.

Isaacs, Julian. "The Batcheldor Approach: Some Strengths and Weaknesses." *Journal of the American Society for Psychical Research*, 78 (1984), 123–132.

_____. "Clinical Issues in the Parapsychology Laboratory." In *Spontaneous Psi, Depth Psychology, and Parapsychology*, edited by Betty Shapin and Lisette Coly, 28–60. New York: Parapsychology Foundation, 1992.

_____. "A Twelve Session Study of Micro PKMB Training." In *The Program of Presented Papers of the Society of Psychical Research and Parapsychological Association Centenary-Jubilee Conference*, vol. 1, 1–6. 1982.

Jahn, Robert G. "The Persistent Paradox of Psychic Phenomena: An Engineering Perspective." *Proceedings of the IEEE* 70, no. 2 (1982): 136–170.

_____, and Brenda Dunne. "The PEAR Proposition." *Journal of Scientific Exploration* 19, no. 2 (2005): 195–245.

Jolly, W. P. *Sir Oliver Lodge*. Rutherford, Madison, Teaneck: Fairleigh Dickinson University Press, 1975.

Keen, Montague, and David Fontana. "The Scole Report Five Years Later." *The Paranormal Review* 37 (January 2006): 19–24.

Kelly, Kevin. "Spontaneous Human Combustion." *Whole Earth Review*, vNON4, Autumn 1986, 52–53.

Kelly, Sean, and Rosemary Rogers. *Saints Preserve Us!* New York: Random House, 1993.

Klimo, Jon. *Channeling: Investigations on Receiving Information from Paranormal Sources*. Rev. and up. ed. Berkeley, CA: North Atlantic Books, 1998.

_____. "Progress Report on a Grant-Supported Technological Survival Research Activities of Jon Klimo & Associates" (unpublished paper). 2000. Available at http://www.jonklimo.com/Papers/EVParticle.pdf (accessed October 29, 2009).

Knox, E. L. Skip. "History of Western Civilization." Online course from Boise State University. http://www.boisestate.edu/courses/westciv/plague/02.shtml (accessed October 21, 2009).

Krippner, Stanley. "Cross-Cultural Treatment Perspectives on Dissociative Disorders." In *Dissociation: Clinical and Theoretical Perspectives*, edited by Steven Jay Lynn and Judith W. Rhue. New York: Guilford Press, 1994.

_____. "Parapsychological Methodology and Shamanistic Studies." *Psi Research* 3 no. 3/4 (1984): 4–16.

_____. "Psychic Healing: Past, Present, and Future." *Psi News: Bulletin of the Parapsychological Association* 5, no. 1 (1982): 1.

_____. "Telepathy." In Edgar D. Mitchell's *Psychic Exploration: A Challenge for Science*, edited by John White, 112–131. New York: G. P. Putnam's Sons, 1974.

_____, and Susan Marie Powers (eds). *Broken Images, Broken Selves: Dissociative Narratives in Clinical Practice*. Washington D.C.: Brunner/Mazel, 1997.

_____, and Jerry Solfvin. "Psychic Healing: A Research Survey." *Psi Research* 3, no. 2 (1984): 16–27.

_____, and Patrick Welch. *Spiritual Dimensions of Healing: From Native Shamanism to Contemporary Health Care*. New York: Irvington Publishers, 1992.

Kruisinga, J. C. M. "Precognitive Dreams and the Dunne Experiment." *Journal of the Society for Psychical Research* 34 (1948): 300–302.

Kubis, Pat and Mark Macy. *Conversations Beyond the Light: Communications with Departed Friends and Colleagues by Electronic Means*. Boulder, CO: Griffin Publishing in conjunction & Continuing Life Research, 1995.

Kuhn, Thomas S. *The Structure of Scientific Revolutions*. Chicago: University of Chicago Press, 1962.

Kunz, Phillip R., and Jenifer Kunz. "Depression and Suicide in the Dark Months." *Perceptual and Motor Skills* 84 (1993): 537–538.

Lapedes, Daniel N., ed. *McGraw-Hill Dictionary of Scientific and Technical Terms*. 2nd ed. New York: McGraw-Hill, 1978.

LeShan, Lawrence. *The Medium, the Mystic, and the Physicist: Toward a General Theory of the Paranormal*. New York: The Viking Press, 1974.

Lewis, Byron A., and R. Frank Pucelik. *Magic Demystified*. Lake Oswego, OR: Metamorphous Press, 1982.

Lewis, Ioan M. "The Anthropologist's Encounter with the Supernatural." In *Parapsychology and Anthropology: Proceedings of an International Conference Held in London, England August 29–31, 1973*, edited by Allan Angoff and Diana Barth, 22–31. New York: Parapsychology Foundation, 1974.

Lhalungpa, Lobsang P., trans. *The Life of Milarepa*. New York: Penguin Books, 1992.

Loewe, Michael, and Carmen Blacker, eds. *Oracles and Divination*. London: George Allen and Unwin, 1981.

Long, Joseph K. *Extrasensory Ecology: Parapsychology and Anthropology*. Metuchen, NJ: The Scarecrow Press, 1977.

Lucadou, Walter von. "The Model of Pragmatic Information (MPI)." *European Journal of Parapsychology* 11 (1995): 58–75.

_____, Hartmann Römer, and Harald Walach. "Synchronistic Phenomena as Entanglement Correlations in Generalized Quantum Theory." *Journal of Consciousness Studies* 14, no. 4 (2007): 50–74.

_____, and Frauke Zahradnik. "Predictions of the Model of Pragmatic Information About RSPK." In *The Parapsychological Association 47th Annual Convention Abstracts of Presented Papers, August 5–8, 2004*, 99–112. Vienna: Parapsychological Association, 2004.

Lumsden-Cook, J. J., Edwards, S. D., and J. Thwala. "An Exploratory Study into Traditional Zulu Healing and REG Effects." *Journal of Parapsychology* 69, no. 1 (2005): 129–138.

Lumsden-Cook, James. "Affect and Random Events: Examining the Effects of Induced Emotion Upon Mind-Matter Interaction." *Journal of the Society for Psychical Research* 69.3, no. 880 (2005): 128–142.

_____. "Mind, Matter and Emotion." *Journal of the Society for Psychical Research* 69.1, no. 878 (2005): 1–17.

Luke, David P., and Marios Kittenis. "A Preliminary Survey of Paranormal Experiences with Psychoactive Drugs." *Journal of Parapsychology* 69, no. 2 (2005): 305–327.

MacRae, Alexander. *EVP and New Dimensions*. 3rd ed. United States: Sanctuary Press, 2004.

_____. "Experiments to Determine if There Is Any Correlation Between Questions and Answers in EVP." Unpublished paper.

_____. "A Means of Producing the Electronic Voice Phenomenon Based on Electro-Dermal Activity." *Journal of the Society for Psychical Research* 68.1, no. 874 (2004), 35–50.

_____. *The Mystery of the Voices*, Raleigh, NC: Lulu, 2010.

_____. "Report of an Electronic Voice Phenomenon Experiment." *Journal of the Society for Psychical Research* 69.4, no. 881 (2005): 191–201.

Manning, Matthew. "London Experiences with Matthew Manning: The Subject's Report." *Proceedings of the Society for Psychical Research* 56 (1982): 353–361

Margnelli, Marco. "An Unusual Case of Stigmatization." *Journal of Scientific Exploration* 13, no. 3 (1999): 461–482.

Martin, Ron. *The Tarot Reader's Notebook*. Manassas, VA: Author, 1990.

Martínez-Taboas, Alfonso. "An Appraisal of the Role of Aggression and the Central Nervous System in RSPK Agents." *Journal of the American Society for Psychical Research* 78 (1984): 55–69.

May, Edwin C. "Toward the Physics of Psi: Correlation with Physical Variables." *European Journal of Parapsychology* 16 (2001): 42–52.

_____, Dean I. Radin, G. Scott Hubbard, Beverly S. Humphrey, and Jessica M. Utts. "Psi Experiments with Random Number Generators: An Informational Model." *Proceedings of the Parapsychological Association 28th Annual Convention*, vol. 1, 237–266. August 1985.

_____, Jessica M. Utts, and S. James P. Spottiswoode. "Decision Augmentation Theory: Toward a Model of Anomalous Mental Phenomena." May 16, 1995. http://www.jsasoc.com/docsDAI-1-JSE.pdf (accessed December 10, 2010).

McClenon, James. *Wondrous Events: Foundations of Religious Belief*. Philadelphia: University of Pennsylvania Press, 1994.

McMoneagle, Joseph. *Remote Viewing Secrets: A Handbook*. Charlottesville, VA: Hampton Roads, 2000.

Michell, John, and Robert J. M. Rickard. *Phenomena: A Book of Wonders*. New York: Pantheon Books, 1977.

Mintz, Elizabeth E. and Schmeidler, Gertrude. *The Psychic Thread: Paranormal and Transpersonal Aspects of Psychotherapy*. New York: Human Sciences Press, 1983.

Mishlove, Jeffrey. *The PK Man*. Charlottesville, VA: Hampton Roads, 2000.

Morris, R. L. "The Airport Project: A Survey of the Techniques for Psychical Development Advocated by Popular Books." In *Research in Parapsychology*, edited by J. D. Morris, W. G. Roll, and R. L. Morris, 54–56. Metuchen, NJ: Scarecrow Press, 1977.

Morris, Robert L. "Parapsychology, Biology, and ANPSI." In *Handbook of Parapsychology*, edited by B. Wolman, L. Dale, G. Schmeidler, and M. Ullman, 687–715. Jefferson, NC: McFarland & Company, Inc., 1986. Original work published New York: Van Nostrand Reinhold, 1977.

Mulacz, Peter. "Deliberately Caused Bodily Damage (DCDB) Phenomena: A Different Perspective." *Journal of the Society for Psychical Research* 62, no. 852 (1998): 434–444.

Murphy, Cullen. "A Blaze of Glory: Spontaneous Human Combustion Through History." *The Atlantic*, no. 259 (April 1987): 16 (2).

Murphy, Michael. *The Future of the Body: Explorations Into the Further Evolution of Human Nature*. Los Angeles: Jeremy P. Tarcher, 1992.

____, and Rhea White. *In the Zone: Transcendent Experience in Sports*. New York: Penguin Books, 1995.

____, and ____. *The Psychic Side of Sports*. Reading, MA: Addison-Wesley Publishing Company, 1978.

Musashi, Miyamoto. *The Book of Five Rings*. Translated by Thomas Cleary. Boston: Shambhala Publications, 1993. Original work published 1643.

Needles, William. "Stigmata Occurring in the Course of Psychoanalysis." *Psychoanalitic Quarterly* 12 (1943): 23–39.

Neff, Robert. "They Fly through the Air with the Greatest of ... Ki?" *Business Week* (International Edition), January 23, 1995, 21.

Nelson, John E. *Healing the Split: Integrating Spirit Into Our Understanding of the Mentally Ill*. Rev. ed. Albany, NY: State University of New York Press, 1994.

Nelson, R. D., Radin, D. I., Shoup, R and P. A. Bancel. "Correlations of Continuous Random Data with Major World Events." *Foundations of Physics Letters* 15, no. 6 (2003): 537–550.

Nelson, Roger. "Coherent Consciousness and Reduced Randomness: Correlations on September 11, 2001." *Journal of Scientific Exploration* 16, no. 4 (2002): 549–570.

____. "Correlation of Global Events with REG Data: An Internet-Based Nonlocal Anomalies Experiment." *Journal of Parapsychology* 65, no. 3 (2001): 247–267.

____. "2008 Presidential Address: Mind Matters: A New Scientific Era." *Journal of Parapsychology* 72 (2008): 3–18.

Neiman, Carol. *Miracles: The Extraordinary, the Impossible, and the Divine*. New York: Viking Studio Books, a division of Penguin Books USA, 1995.

Nickell, Joe. *Looking for a Miracle: Weeping Icons, Relics, Stigmata, Visions, and Healing Cures*. Amherst, NY: Prometheus Books, 1993.

Nicol, J. Fraser. "Historical Background." In *Handbook of Parapsychology*, edited by B. Wolman, L. Dale, G. Schmeidler, and M. Ullman, 305–323. Jefferson, NC: McFarland & Company, Inc., 1986. Original work published New York: Van Nostrand Reinhold, 1977.

Nigal, Gedalyah. *Magic, Mysticism, and Hasidism: The Supernatural in Jewish Thought*. Translated by Edward Levin. Northvale, NJ: Jason Aronson, 1994.

Noveck, Simon. *Great Jewish Personalities in Ancient and Medieval Times*. Clinton, MA: Colonial Press, 1959.

Obendorf, Margaret L. "The Effect of Attention on Psychokinesis." Master's thesis, John F. Kennedy University, Orinda, California, 1990.

Oman, John Campbell. *Mystics, Ascetics and Saints of India: A Study of Sadhuism, with an Account of the Yogis, Sanyasis, Bairagis, and Other Strange Hindu Sectarians*. Second impression. London: T. Fisher Unwin, 1905.

Ostrander, Sheila, and Lynn Schroeder. *Psychic Discoveries Behind the Iron Curtain*. New York: Bantam Books, 1971.

Owen, A. R. G. *Can We Explain the Poltergeist?* New York: Garrett Publications, 1964.

Owen, Iris, M., and Margaret Sparrow. *Conjuring Up Philip*. New York: Pocket Books, 1977.

Palmer, John. "ESP Research Findings: The Process Approach." In *Foundations of Parapsychology*, edited by Hoyt L Edge, Robert L. Morris, Joseph H. Rush, and John Palmer, 184–222. Boston: Routledge and Kegan Paul, 1986.

____. "A Statistical Artifact in William Braud's (1990) Experiment on Remote Mental Influence of Hemolysis." *Journal of Parapsychology* 71 (2007): 151–157.

____, and Wim Kramer. "Release of Effort in RNG PK: An Attempted Replication and Extension." *Journal of Parapsychology* 51 (1987): 125–136.

____, and Joseph Rush. "Experimental Methods in PK Research." In *Foundations of Parapsychology*, edited by Hoyt L Edge, Robert L. Morris, Joseph H. Rush, and John Palmer, 223–236. Boston: Routledge and Kegan Paul, 1986.

Parra, Alejandro. "PK Occurrences, Epilepsy, and Repressed Aggression: Analysis of Andrés Vernier's Case." *The Paranormal Review* 32 (October 2004): 23–27.

Podmore, Frank. *Mediums of the 19th Century*. 2 vols. New Hyde Park, NY: University Books, 1963. Original work published as *Modern Spiritualism* in 1902.

Polkinghorne, D. E. "Phenomenological Research Methods." In *Existential-Phenomenological Perspectives in Psychology*, edited by R. S. Valle and S. Halling. New York: Plenum Press, 1989.

Pratt, J. G. "Soviet Research in Parapsychology." In *Handbook of Parapsychology*, edited by B. Wolman, L. Dale, G. Schmeidler, and M. Ullman, 883–903. Jefferson, NC: McFarland & Company, Inc., 1986. Original work published New York: Van Nostrand Reinhold, 1977.

Price, Harry. *Fifty Years of Psychical Research: A Critical Survey*. Reprint. New York: Arno Press, 1975. Original work published in New York, 1939.

____. *Poltergeist: Tales of the Supernatural*. London: Bracken Books, 1993.

Puharich, Henry K. "Psychic Research and the Healing Process." In Edgar D. Mitchell's *Psychic Exploration:*

A Challenge for Science, edited by John White, 333–347. New York: G. P. Putnam's Sons, 1974.

Puhle, Annekatrin. "Learning from Historical Cases: Six Selected Poltergeist Cases from the 1700s in Germany." *European Journal of Parapsychology* 16 (2001): 61–72.

Pulos, Lee, and Gary Richman. *Miracles and Other Realities*. San Francisco: Omega Press, 1990.

Radin, D. I., and D. C. Ferrari. "Effects of Consciousness on the Fall of Dice: A Meta-Analysis." *Journal of Scientific Exploration* 5 (1991): 61–84.

Radin, Dean. *The Conscious Universe*. New York: Harper Collins Publishers, 1997.

______. *Entangled Minds: Extrasensory Experiences in a Quantum Reality*. New York: Paraview, 2006.

______. "Experiments Testing Models of Mind-Matter Interaction." *Journal of Scientific Exploration* 20, no. 3 (2006): 375–401.

______. "Exploring Relationships Between Random Physical Events and Mass Human Attention: Asking for Whom the Bell Tolls." *Journal of Scientific Exploration* 16, no. 4 (2002): 533–547.

______, and F. Holmes Atwater. "Exploratory Evidence for Correlations Between Entrained Mental Coherence and Random Physical Systems." *Journal of Scientific Exploration* 23, no. 3 (2009): 263–272.

______, and Roger Nelson. "Research on Mind-Matter Interactions (MMI): Individual Intention. In *Healing, Intention, and Energy Medicine: Science, Research Methods and Clinical Implications*, edited by Wayne B Jonas and Cindy C. Crawford, 39–48. New York: Churchill Livingstone, 2003.

______, and ______. "Research on Mind-Matter Interactions (MMI): Group Intention." In *Healing, Intention, and Energy Medicine: Science, Research Methods and Clinical Implications*, edited by Wayne B Jonas and Cindy C. Crawford, 49–57. New York: Churchill Livingstone, 2003.

______, ______, York Dobyns, and Joot Houtkooper. "Re-examining Psychokinesis: Comment on Bösch, Steinkamp, and Boller (2006)." *Psychological Bulletin* 132, no. 4 (2006): 529–532.

______, Paul Wendland, and Robert Rickenbach. "Does Consciousness Collapse the Quantum Wave-function? Experiments with an Optical Double-slit System." In *The Parapsychological Association 52nd Annual Convention Abstracts of Presented Papers, August 6–9, 2009*, 19. Seattle, WA: Parapsychological Association, 2009.

Randall, J. L., and C. P. Davis. "Paranormal Deformation of Nitinol Wire: A Confirmatory Experiment." *Journal of the Society for Psychical Research* 51 (1982): 368–373.

Randall, John L. "Harry Price: The Case for the Defence." *Journal of the Society for Psychical Research* 64, no. 860 (2000): 159–176.

Rao, K. Ramakrishna. "L. E. Rhine on Psi and Its Place." *The Journal of Parapsychology* 47 (1983): 347–359.

______. "On the Nature of Psi: An Examination of Some Attempts to Explain ESP and PK." *The Journal of Parapsychology* 41 (1977): 294–351.

Raudive, Konstantin. *An Amazing Experiment in Electronic Communication with the Dead*. Translated by Nadia Fowler, edited by Joyce Morton, with a preface by Peter Bander. New York: Lancer Books, 1971.

Rauscher, Elizabeth A. "Psychokinetic Interaction with Laboratory Prepared Materials: A Prototype Experimental Design." *Psi Research* 3, no. 3/4 (1984): 26–41.

Reed, Henry. "Close Encounters in the Liminal Zone: Experiments in Imaginal Communication. Part I." *Journal of Analytical Psychology* 41, no. 1 (1996): 81–116.

______. "Close Encounters in the Liminal Zone: Experiments in Imaginal Communication. Part II." *Journal of Analytical Psychology* 41, no. 2 (1996): 203–226.

Reich, Wilhelm. *Character Analysis*. 3rd ed. New York: Pocket Books, 1976.

Reinhart, Philip B. "PK Induction: An Extension to the Batcheldor Approach." *Journal of the American Society for Psychical Research*, 88 (1994), 137–145.

Rhine, J. B. "Hypnotic Suggestion in PK Tests." *Journal of Parapsychology* 10 (1946): 126–140.

______, J. G. Pratt, B. M. Smith, C. E. Stuart, and J. A. Greenwood. *Extrasensory Perception After Sixty Years*. New York: Henry Holt, 1940.

Rhine, Louisa E. "Frequency of Types of Experience in Spontaneous Precognition." *The Journal of Parapsychology* 18 (1954): 93–123.

______. *Hidden Channels of the Mind*. New York: William Morrow and Company, 1961.

______. "Research Methods with Spontaneous Cases." In *Handbook of Parapsychology*, edited by B. Wolman, L. Dale, G. Schmeidler, and M. Ullman, 324–381. New York: Jefferson, NC: McFarland & Company, Inc., 1986. Original work published New York: Van Nostrand Reinhold, 1977.

Robinson, Diana. *To Stretch a Plank*. Chicago: Nelson-Hall, 1981.

Roe, C. A., N. J. Holt, & C. Simmonds, "Considering the Sender as a PK Agent in Ganzfeld ESP Studies." *The Journal of Parapsychology* 67, no. 1 (2003): 129–145.

Roe, Chris A., Russell Davey, and Paul Stevens. "Are ESP and PK Aspects of a Unitary Phenomenon? A Preliminary Test of the Relationship Between ESP and PK." *Journal of Parapsychology* 67, no. 2 (2003): 343–366.

Roe, Chris A., and Nicola J. Holt. "The Effect of Strategy ("Willing" versus Absorption) and Feedback (Intermediate versus Delayed) on Performance at a PK Task." *Journal of Parapsychology* 70, no. 1 (2006): 69–90.

Rogo, D. Scott. *Mind Over Matter: Case for Psychokinesis*. Wellingborough, Northamptonshire: The Aquarian Press, 1986.

______. *Miracles: A Parascientific Inquiry Into Wondrous Phenomena*. New York: The Dial Press, 1982.

______. *On the Track of the Poltergeist*. Englewood Cliffs, NJ: Prentice-Hall, 1986.

______. *Parapsychology: A Century of Inquiry*. New York: Taplinger Publishing Company, 1975.

______. "The Poltergeist and Family Dynamics: A Report on a Recent Investigation." In *Proceedings of Presented Papers of the 22nd Annual Convention of the Parapsychological Association*, 1–10. 1979.

______. *The Poltergeist Experience: Investigations into Ghostly Phenomena*. New York: Penguin Books, 1979.

______. "Theories about PK: A Critical Evaluation." *Journal of the Society for Psychical Research* 50 (1980): 359–378.

Rogo, Scott, and Raymond Bayless. *Phone Calls from the Dead*. Englewood Cliffs, NJ: Prentice-Hall, 1979.

Roll, William G. *The Poltergeist*. Garden City, NY: Nelson Doubleday, 1972.

______. "Poltergeists." In *Handbook of Parapsychology*, edited by B. Wolman, L. Dale, G. Schmeidler, and M. Ullman, 382–413. Jefferson, NC: McFarland & Company, Inc., 1986. Original work published New York: Van Nostrand Reinhold, 1977.

_____. "Poltergeists, Electromagnetism, and Consciousness." *Journal of Scientific Exploration* 17, no. 1 (2003): 75–86.

_____. "Recurrent and Nonrecurrent Psi Effects." *The Journal of Parapsychology* 47 (1983): 341–346.

_____. "The Rotating Beam Theory and the Olive Hill Poltergeist." In *Research in Parapsychology*, edited by W.G. Roll, R. L. Morris, and J. Morris. Metuchen, NJ: Scarecrow Press, 1973.

_____. "Some Physical and Psychological Aspects of a Series of Poltergeist Phenomena." *Journal of the American Society for Psychical Research* 62 (1968): 263–308.

Rosenthal, Norman E. *Winter Blues.* New York: The Guilford Press, 1993.

Rosenthal, Robert. *Experimenter Effects in Behavioral Research.* New York: Appleton-Century-Crofts, 1966.

Rush, Joseph. "Findings from Experimental PK Research." In *Foundations of Parapsychology*, edited by Hoyt L Edge, Robert L. Morris, Joseph H. Rush, and John Palmer, 237–275. Boston: Routledge and Kegan Paul, 1986.

Rýzl, Milan. "Training the Psi Faculty by Hypnosis." *Journal of the Society for Psychical Research* 41 (1962): 234–252.

Sadock, Benjamin James and Virginia Alcott Sadock. *Kaplan and Sadock's Synopsis of Psychiatry.* 10th ed. Lippincott Williams and Wilkins: Philadelphia, 2007.

Scargle, Jeffrey. "Comment on: "A Critique of the Parapsychological Random Number Generator Meta-Analyses of Radin and Nelson" by Martin Schub." *Journal of Scientific Exploration* 20, no. 3 (2006): 420.

_____. "Publication Bias: The 'File-Drawer' Problem in Scientific Inference." *Journal of Scientific Exploration* 14, no. 1 (2000) 91–106.

Schewe, Phillip F. and Ben Stein. "The Casimir Force." *Inside Science Research—Physics News* no. 300 (December 20, 1996). American Institute of Physics. http://www.aip.org/pnu/1996/physnews.300.htm#3 (accessed September 24, 2009).

Schlitz, Marilyn, Richard Wiseman, Caroline Watt, and Dean Radin. "Of Two Minds: Sceptic-Proponent Collaboration Within Parapsychology." *British Journal of Psychology* 97 (2006): 313–322.

Schmeidler, Gertrude R. "Methods for Controlled Research on ESP and PK." In *Handbook of Parapsychology*, edited by B. Wolman, L. Dale, G. Schmeidler, and M. Ullman, 324–381. Jefferson, NC: McFarland, 1986. Original work published New York: Van Nostrand Reinhold, 1977.

_____. *Parapsychology and Psychology: Matches and Mismatches.* Jefferson, NC: McFarland, 1988.

_____. "Psi-Conducive Experimenters and Psi-Permissive Ones." *European Journal of Parapsychology* 13 (1997): 83–94.

_____. "Psychokinesis: Recent Studies and a Possible Paradigm Shift." In *Advances in Parapsychological Research*, edited by Stanley Krippner, 10–38. Jefferson, NC: McFarland, 1987.

Schmidt, Helmut. "Human PK Effort on Pre-Recorded Targets, Previously Observed by Goldfish." In *The Parapsychological Association 28th Annual Convention Presented papers*, 213–225. 1985.

_____. "PK Tests with and without Pre–Observation by Animals." *The Parapsychological Association 32nd Annual Convention Presented papers*, vol. 1, 61–81. 1989.

_____. "Random Generators and Living Systems as Targets in Retro-PK Experiments." *Journal of the American Society for Psychical Research* 91 (1997): 1–13.

_____, and Henry Stapp. "PK with Prerecorded Random Events and the Effects of Preobservation." *The Journal of Parapsychology* 57 (1993): 331–349.

Schmidt, Stefan, Rainer Schneider, Markus Binder, David Bürkle, and Harald Walach. "Investigating Methodological Issues in EDA-DMILS: Results from a Pilot Study." *The Journal of Parapsychology* 65, no. 1 (2001): 59–82.

Schmidt, Stefan, and Harald Walach. "Electrodermal Activity (EDA–State-of-the-Art Measurement and Techniques for Parapsychological Purposes." *The Journal of Parapsychology* 64, no. 2 (2000): 139–163.

Schneider, Rainer, Markus Binder, and Harald Walach. "Examining the Role of Neutral versus Personal Experimenter-Participant Interactions: An EDS-DMILS Experiment." *The Journal of Parapsychology* 64, no. 2 (2000): 181–194.

_____, _____, and _____. "On the Role of the Agent in EDA-DMILS Experiments." *The Journal of Parapsychology* 65, no. 3 (2001): 273–290.

_____, _____, and _____. "A Two-Person Effort: On the Role of the Agent in EDA-DMILS Experiments." *The Journal of Parapsychology* 65, no. 3 (2001): 273–290.

Schouten, Sybo A. "Psychic Healing and Complementary Medicine." In *Advances in Parapsychological Research*, vol. 8, edited by Stanley Krippner, 126–210. Jefferson, NC: McFarland, 1997.

Schub, M. H. "A Critique on the Parapsychological Random Number Generator Meta-Analyses of Radin and Nelson." *Journal of Scientific Exploration* 20, no. 3 (2006): 402–419.

Schumacher, Dave, Cindy Heinen, and Chris Carter. "EVP and Geomagnetic Fields: Is There a Correlation?" http://www.aaevp.com/research/research_geomagnetic_fields.htm (accessed October 5, 2008).

Schwartz, Barry. *Psychology of Learning and Behavior.* New York: W. W. Norton, 1984.

Schwartz, Gary, and Mark Boccuzzi. "Effects of Psychic Healing Intentions on Patterns of Cosmic Rays." In *The Parapsychological Association 52nd Annual Convention Abstracts of Presented Papers, August 6–9, 2009*, 20. Seattle, WA: Parapsychological Association, 2009.

Servadio, Emilio. "Peasant-Healers and the Paranormal." In *Parapsychology and Anthropology: Proceedings of an International Conference Held in London, England August 29–31, 1973*, edited by Allan Angoff and Diana Barth, 121–130. New York: Parapsychology Foundation, 1974.

Shah, Idries. *The Sufis.* New York: Doubleday, 1964.

Sicher, Fred, Elisabeth Targ, Dan Moore II, and Helene Smith. "A Randomized Double-Blind Study of the Effect of Distant Healing in a Population with Advanced AIDS: Report of a Small Scale Study." *Western Journal of Medicine* 169, no. 6 (1998): 356–363.

Sidgwick, Mrs. Henry. "On the Evidence for Premonitions." *Proceedings of the Journal for Psychical Research* 5 (1898–1889): 288–354.

Siegel, Cynthia E. "PK Party Survey." In *The Parapsychological Association 27th Annual Convention Presented Papers*, 38–74. 1984.

Skinner, Elliott P. "African Beliefs in the Psychic Manipulation of Material Phenomena: The Tengsoba in Mossi Society." In *Parapsychology and Anthropology: Proceedings of an International Conference Held in London, England August 29–31, 1973*, edited by Allan Angoff and Diana Barth, 22–31. New York: Parapsychology Foundation, 1974.

Solfvin, Jerry. "Mental Healing." In *Advances in Parapsychological Research*, vol. 4, edited by Stanley Krippner, 31–63. Jefferson, NC: McFarland, 1984.

Spottiswoode, S. James P. "Apparent Association Between Effect Size in Free Response Anomalous Cognition Experiments and Local Sidereal Time." *Journal of Scientific Exploration* 11, no. 2 (1997): 109–122.

_____. "Geomagnetic Fluctuations and Free Response Anomalous Cognition: A New Understanding." Journal of Parapsychology 61, no1 (1997): 3–12..

Stanford, Rex G. "Experimental Psychokinesis: A Review from Diverse Perspectives." In *Handbook of Parapsychology*, edited by B. Wolman, L. Dale, G. Schmeidler, and M. Ullman, 324–381. Jefferson, NC: McFarland & Company, Inc., 1986. Original work published New York: Van Nostrand Reinhold, 1977.

_____. "An Experimentally Testable Model for Spontaneous Psi Events II. Psychokinetic Events." *Journal of the American Society for Psychical Research* 68 (1974): 321–356.

Steffy, Joan. "Some Comparisons of Psychic Healing in the USSR, Eastern and Western Europe, North America, China and Brazil." *Psi Research* 3, no. 2 (1984): 29–52.

Stewart, Jeannie Lagle, William G. Roll, and Steve Baumann. "Hypnotic Suggestion and RSPK." In *The Parapsychological Association 29th Annual Convention Presented Papers*, 207–224. 1986.

Stokes, Douglas M. "Spontaneous Psi Phenomena." In *Advances in Parapsychological Research*, vol. 8, edited by Stanley Krippner, 6–87. Jefferson, NC: McFarland, 1997.

Storm, Lance, and Michael A. Thalbourne. "A Paradigm Shift Away from the ESP-PK Dichotomy: The Theory of Psychopraxia." *The Journal of Parapsychology* 64, no. 3 (2000): 279–300.

Strauch, Inge. "Medical Aspects of 'Mental' Healing." *International Journal of Parapsychology* 5, no. 2 (1963): 135–165.

Swann, Ingo. "Remote Viewing: The Real Story: An Autobiographical Memoir," 1996 http://www.biomind-superpowers.com/pages/realstorymain.html (accessed May 1, 2003).

Targ, Russell, and Keith Harary. *The Mind Race: Understanding and Using Psychic Abilities*. New York: Ballantine Books, 1984.

Tart, Charles T. "Learning to Use Psychokinesis: Theoretical and Methodological Notes." In *The Program of Presented Papers of the Society of Psychical Research and Parapsychological Association Centenary-Jubilee Conference*, vol. 1, 1–4. 1982.

_____. "Out-of-Body Experiences." In Edgar D. Mitchell's *Psychic Exploration: A Challenge for Science*, edited by John White, 349–373. New York: G. P. Putnam's Sons, 1974.

_____. *States of Consciousness*. New York: E. P. Dutton and Co., 1975.

Taylor, Robin. "Enhancing Athletic and Psychic Performances Through the Use of Imagery Based Mental Strategies." PhD diss., Edinburgh University, Scotland, 1992. Copy obtained from author.

Taylor, Robin K. "Training Imagery Skills for Enhanced Psychic Functioning." *European Journal of Parapsychology* 12 (1996): 1–19.

Terhune, Devin Blair, Ventola, Annalisa, and James Houran. "An Analysis of Contextual Variables and the Incidence of Photographic Anomalies at an Alleged Haunt and a Control Site." *Journal of Scientific Exploration* 21, no. 1 (2007): 99–120.

Thalbourne, Michael A. "The History of Miracles." *U.S. News and World Report* 114, no. 12, March 29 1993, 54.

_____. "The Theory of Psychopraxia: A Paradigm for the Future?" In *Parapsychology in the 21st Century: Essays on the Future of Psychical Research*, edited by Michael A. Thalbourne and Lance Storm, 189–204. Jefferson, NC: McFarland, 2005.

Thouless, Robert H. "A Report on an Experiment on Psycho-Kinesis with Dice, and a Discussion of Psychological Factors Favouring Success." *Proceedings of the Society for Psychical Research* 49 (1951): 107–130.

Thurston, Herbert. *Ghosts and Poltergeists*. Edited by J. H. Crehan. Reprint. London: Burns Oates, 1953.

_____. *The Physical Phenomena of Mysticism*. Chicago: Henry Regnery Company, 1952.

_____. *Surprising Mystics*. Chicago: Henry Regnery Company, 1955.

_____, and Donald Attwater. (Eds.) *Butler's Lives of the Saints* vol. 1–4. NY: P. J. Kenedy and Sons, 1963.

Trausch, Clarence P. *Psi Training through Meditation, and Self-Actualization as Related to Psi Performance*. Ann Arbor, MI: University Microfilms, 1981.

Traut, Eugene F. and Edwin W. Passarelli. "Placebos in the Treatment of Rheumatoid Arthritis and Other Rheumatic Conditions." *Annals of the Rheumatic Diseases* 16 (1957): 18–22.

Treece, Patricia. *The Sanctified Body*. New York: Doubleday, 1989.

Turner, David J. "The Missing Science of Ball Lightning." *Journal of Scientific Exploration* 17, no. 3 (2003): 435–496.

Turner, Victor W. "Religious Specialists." In *Magic, Witchcraft, and Religion: An Anthropological Study of the Supernatural*, 4th ed., edited by Arthur C. Lehmann and James E. Myers, 78–85. Mountain View, CA: Mayfield Publishing Company, 1977.

Valle, Ronald S., Mark King, and Steen Halling. "An Introduction to Existential-Phenomenological Thought in Psychology." In *Existential-Phenomenological Perspectives in Psychology: Exploring the Breadth of Human Experience*, edited by Ronald S. Valle and Steen Halling, 3–16. New York: Plenum Press, 1989.

Van de Castle, Robert L. "Parapsychology and Anthropology." In *Handbook of Parapsychology*, edited by B. Wolman, L. Dale, G. Schmeidler, and M. Ullman, 667–686. Jefferson, NC: McFarland, 1986. Original work published New York: Van Nostrand Reinhold, 1977.

Varvoglis, Mario P. "Goal-Directed and Observer-Dependent PK: An Evaluation of Conformance Theory and Observational Theory." *Parapsychological Association 27th Annual Convention Presented Papers* (1984): 327–354.

_____. *Psi-explorer* [CD-ROM]. Morsang/ Orge, France: Proxima Centauri, 1996.

_____. "A 'Psychic Contest' Using a Computer-RNG Task in a Non-laboratory Setting." In *The Parapsychological Association's 31st Annual Convention Presented Papers*, 36–52. 1988.

_____. *Psychokinesis, Intentionality and the Attentional Object: Specificity and Generality in Mind-Matter Interactions*. Ann Arbor, MI: University Microfilms, 1983.

_____, and Donald McCarthy. "Conscious-Purposive Focus and PK: RNG Activity in Relation to Awareness, Task-Orientation, and Feedback." *Journal of the American Society for Psychical Research* 80 (1986): 1–29.

Vaughan, Alan. "Famous Western Sensitives." In Edgar D. Mitchell's *Psychic Exploration: A Challenge for Science*, edited by John White, 74–92. New York: G. P. Putnam's Sons, 1974.

Ventola, Annalisa M., and Devin B. Terhune, "Context, Individual Differences and Media Type in the Evaluation of Photographic Anomalies." In *The Parapsychological Association 52nd Annual Convention Abstracts of Presented Papers, August 6–9, 2009*, 23. Seattle, WA: Parapsychological Association, 2009.

Vogl, Albert. *Life and Death of Therese Neumann, Mystic and Stigmatist*. New York: Vantage Press, 1978.

Walker, Evan Harris. "A Comparison of the Intuitive Data Sorting and Quantum Mechanical Observer Theories." *The Journal of Parapsychology* 51 (1987): 217–227.

Walsh, Michael, ed. *Butler's Lives of Patron Saints*. Rev. ed. San Francisco: Harper and Row, 1987.

Watkins, Graham K., and Anita M. Watkins. "Possible PK Influence on the Resuscitation of Anesthetized Mice." *The Journal of Parapsychology* 35 (1971): 257– 272.

Webster, Richard. *Miracles: Inviting the Extraordinary Into Your Life*. St. Paul, MN: Llewellyn Publications, 2004.

West, Timothy. "On the Encounter with a Divine Presence During a Near-Death Experience: A Phenomenological Inquiry." In *Phenomenological Inquiry in Psychology: Existential and Transpersonal Dimensions*, edited by Ron Valle, 387–405. New York: Plenum Press, 1998.

Wetzel, Janice Wood. *Clinical Handbook of Depression*. New York: Gardner Press, 1984.

White, Rhea. "The Influence of Experimenter Motivation, Attitudes, and Methods of Handling Subjects on Psi Test Results." In *Handbook of Parapsychology*, edited by B. Wolman, L. Dale, G. Schmeidler, and M. Ullman, 324–381. Jefferson, NC: McFarland & Company, Inc., 1986. Original work published New York: Van Nostrand Reinhold, 1977.

_____. "What Are Exceptional Human Experiences?" *Exceptional Human Experience* 15, no. 1 (1997): 37–39.

Wilkinson, H. P. and Alan Gauld. "Geomagnetism and Anomalous Experiences, 1868–1980." *Proceedings for the Society for Psychical Research* 57, part 217 (1993): 275–310.

Williams, B. J., & Roll, W. G. "Psi, Place Memory, & Laboratory Space." In *Proceedings of Presented Papers: The Parapsychological Association 49th Annual Convention*, 248–258. 2006.

Williams, Jon L. *Operant Learning: Procedures for Changing Behavior*. Monterey, CA: Brooks/Cole, 1973.

Wilson, David B. and William R. Shadish, "On Blowing Trumpets to the Tulips: To Prove or Not to Prove the Null Hypothesis–Comment on Bosch, Steinkamp, and Boller (2006)." *Psychological Bulletin* 132, no. 4 (July 2006): 524–528.

Wirth, Daniel P. "Unorthodox Healing: The Effect of Non Contact Therapeutic Touch on the Healing Rate of Full Thickness Dermal Wounds." In *The Parapsychological Association 32nd Annual Convention Presented Papers*, vol. 1, 251–268. 1989.

Wiseman, Richard, and Erlendur Haraldsson. "Investigating Macro-PK in India: Swami Premananda." *Journal of the Society for Psychical Research* 60, no. 839 (1995): 193–202.

_____, and _____. "Reactions to and an Assessment of a Videotape on Sathya Sai Baba." *Journal of the Society for Psychical Research* 60, no. 839 (1995): 203–213.

_____, and Marilyn Schlitz. "Examining the Remote Staring Effect." In *The Parapsychological Association 39th Annual Convention Presented Papers*, 149–155. San Diego, CA: Parapsychological Association, 1996.

_____, and _____. "Experimenter Effects and the Remote Detection of Staring: an Attempted Replication." *Proceedings of the 42nd Annual Convention of the Parapsychological Association*, 471–479.

_____, and Matthew Smith. "Can Pets Detect When Their Owners Are Returning Home?: An Experimental Test of the 'Psychic Pet' Phenomena." In *Proceedings of the Parapsychological Association 39th Annual Convention*, 35–43. San Diego, CA: Parapsychological Association, 1996.

Wolf, Robert. "Various Fighting Systems All Stemmed from Kung Fu." *Chicago Tribune*, Sports Final Edition, March 7 1986, 10.

Worrall, Abrose A., with Olga N. Worrall. *The Gift of Healing: A Personal Story of a Spiritual Therapy*. New York: Harper & Row, 1965.

Yogananda, Paramahansa. *Autobiography of a Yogi*. Los Angeles: Self-Realization Fellowship, 1990.

Yount, Garret, Jerry Solfvin, Dan Moore, Marilyn Schlitz, Melissa Reading, Ken Aldape, and Qian Yifang. "In Vitro Test of External Qigong." *BMC Complementary and Alternative Medicine* 4 (March 15, 2004): 5. at http://www.biomedcentral.com/1472-6882/4/5 (accessed October 29, 2009).

Zha, Leping, and Tron McConnell. "Parapsychology in the People's Republic of China: 1979–1989." *Journal of the American Society for Psychical Research* 85 (1991): 119–143.

Zingrone, Nancy L., Carlos S. Alvarado, and Kathy Dalton. "Psi Experiences and the 'Big Five': Relating the NEO PI-R to the Experience Claims of Experimental Subjects." *European Journal of Parapsychology* 14 (1998–1999): 31–35.

Index

www.ingramcontent.com/pod-product-compliance
Ingram Content Group UK Ltd.
Pitfield, Milton Keynes, MK11 3LW, UK
UKHW051853150726
7214IPUK00021B/396